Paul Kegan

The New Testament of Our Lord and Saviour Jesus Christ

Paul Kegan

The New Testament of Our Lord and Saviour Jesus Christ

ISBN/EAN: 9783744662710

Printed in Europe, USA, Canada, Australia, Japan

Cover: Foto ©Lupo / pixelio.de

More available books at **www.hansebooks.com**

THE
NEW TESTAMENT
OF
OUR LORD AND SAVIOUR

JESUS CHRIST

THE
NEW TESTAMENT

OF

OUR LORD AND SAVIOUR

JESUS CHRIST

TRANSLATED OUT OF THE GREEK

BEING THE VERSION SET FORTH A.D. 1611
COMPARED WITH THE MOST ANCIENT AUTHORITIES AND REVISED
A.D. 1881

NEW YORK
BAKER, PRATT, & CO., 19 BOND STREET
1881

PREFACE.

The English Version of the New Testament here presented to the reader is a Revision of the Translation published in the year of Our Lord 1611, and commonly known by the name of the Authorised Version.

That Translation was the work of many hands and of several generations. The foundation was laid by William Tyndale. His translation of the New Testament was the true primary Version. The Versions that followed were either substantially reproductions of Tyndale's translation in its final shape, or revisions of Versions that had been themselves almost entirely based on it. Three successive stages may be recognised in this continuous work of authoritative revision: first, the publication of the Great Bible of 1539–41 in the reign of Henry VIII.; next, the publication of the Bishops' Bible of 1568 and 1572 in the reign of Elizabeth; and lastly, the publication of the King's Bible of 1611 in the reign of James I. Besides these, the Genevan Version of 1560, itself founded on Tyndale's translation, must here be named; which, though not put forth by authority, was widely circulated in this country, and largely used by King James' Translators. Thus the form in which the English New Testament has now been read for 270 years was the result of various revisions made between 1525 and 1611; and the present Revision is an attempt, after a long interval, to follow the example set by a succession of honoured predecessors.

I. Of the many points of interest connected with the Translation of 1611, two require special notice: first, the Greek Text which it appears to have represented; and secondly, the character of the Translation itself.

1. With regard to the Greek Text, it would appear that, if to some extent the Translators exercised an independent judgement, it was mainly in choosing amongst readings contained in the principal editions of the Greek Text that had appeared in the sixteenth century. Wherever they seem to have followed a reading which is not found in any of those editions, their rendering may probably be traced to the Latin Vulgate. Their chief guides appear to have been the later editions of Stephanus and of Beza, and also, to a certain extent, the Complutensian Polyglott. All these were founded for the most part on manuscripts of late date, few in number, and used with little critical skill. But in those days it could hardly have been otherwise. Nearly all the more ancient of the documentary authorities have become known only within the last two centuries; some of the most important of them, indeed, within the last few years. Their publication has called forth not only improved editions of the Greek Text, but a succession of instructive discussions on the variations which have been brought to light, and on the best modes of distinguishing original readings from changes introduced in the course of transcription. While therefore it has long been the opinion of all scholars that the commonly received text needed thorough revision, it is but recently that materials have been acquired for executing such a work with even approximate completeness.

2. The character of the Translation itself will be best estimated by considering the leading rules under which it was made, and the extent to which these rules appear to have been observed.

The primary and fundamental rule was expressed in the following terms:—'The ordinary Bible read in the Church, commonly called the Bishops' Bible, to be followed, and as little altered as the truth of the Original will permit.' There was, however, this subsequent provision:—'These translations to be used, when they agree better with the text than the Bishops' Bible: Tindale's, Matthew's, Coverdale's, Whitchurch's, Geneva.' The first of these rules, which was substantially the same as that laid down at the revision of the Great Bible in the reign of Elizabeth, was strictly observed. The other rule was but partially followed. The Translators made much use of the Genevan Version. They do not, however, appear to have frequently returned to the renderings of the other Versions named in the rule, where those Versions differed from the Bishops' Bible. On the other hand, their work shews evident traces of the influence of a Version not specified in the rules, the Rhemish, made from the Latin Vulgate, but by scholars conversant with the Greek Original.

Another rule, on which it is stated that those in authority laid great stress, related to the rendering of words that admitted of different interpretations. It was as follows:—'When a word hath divers significations, that to be kept which hath been most commonly used by the most of the ancient fathers, being agreeable to the propriety of the place and the analogy of the faith.' With this rule was associated the following, on which equal stress appears to have been laid:—'The old ecclesiastical words to be kept, viz. the word *Church* not to be translated *Congregation*, &c.' This latter rule was for the most part carefully observed; but it may be doubted whether, in the case of words that admitted of different meanings, the instructions were at all closely followed. In dealing with the more difficult words of this class, the Translators appear to have paid much regard to traditional interpretations, and especially to the authority of the Vulgate; but, as to the large residue of words which might properly fall under the rule, they used considerable freedom. Moreover they profess in their Preface to have studiously adopted a variety of expression which would now be deemed hardly consistent with the requirements of faithful translation. They seem to have attempted its fulfilment, it will now be necessary for us to speak.

II. The present Revision had its origin in action taken by the Convocation of the Province of Canterbury in February, 1870, and it has been conducted throughout on the plan laid down in Resolutions of both Houses of the Province, and, more particularly, in accordance with Principles and Rules drawn up by a special Committee of Convocation in the following May. Two Companies, the one for the revision of the Authorised Version of the Old Testament, and the other for the revision of the same Version of the New Testament, were formed in the manner specified in the Resolutions, and the work was commenced on the twenty-second day of June, 1870. Shortly afterwards, steps were taken, under a resolution passed by both Houses of Convocation, for inviting the co-operation of American scholars; and eventually two Committees were formed in America, for the purpose of acting with the two English Companies, on the basis of the Principles and Rules drawn up by the Committee of Convocation.

The fundamental Resolutions adopted by the Convocation of Canterbury on the third and fifth days of May, 1870, were as follows:—

'1. That it is desirable that a revision of the Authorised Version of the Holy Scriptures be undertaken.

'2. That the revision be so conducted as to comprise both marginal renderings and such emendations as it may be found necessary to insert in the text of the Authorised Version.

'3. That in the above resolutions we do not contemplate any new translation of the Bible, or any alteration of the language, except where in the judgement of the most competent scholars such change is necessary.

'4. That in such necessary changes, the style of the language employed in the existing Version be closely followed.

'5. That it is desirable that Convocation should nominate a body of its own members to undertake the work of revision, who shall be at liberty to invite the co-operation of any eminent for scholarship, to whatever nation or religious body they may belong.'

The Principles and Rules agreed to by the Committee of Convocation on the twenty-fifth day of May, 1870, were as follows:—

'1. To introduce as few alterations as possible into the Text of the Authorised Version consistently with faithfulness.

'2. To limit, as far as possible, the expression of such alterations to the language of the Authorised and earlier English Versions.

'3. Each Company to go twice over the portion to be revised, once provisionally, the second time finally, and on principles of voting as hereinafter is provided.

'4. That the Text to be adopted be that for which the evidence is decidedly preponderating; and that when the Text so adopted differs from that from which the Authorised Version was made, the alteration be indicated in the margin.

'5. To make or retain no change in the Text on the second final revision by each Company, except *two thirds* of those present approve of the same, but on the first revision to decide by simple majorities.

'6. In every case of proposed alteration that may have given rise to discussion, to defer the voting thereupon till the next Meeting, whensoever the same shall be required by one third of those present at the Meeting, such intended vote to be announced in the notice for the next Meeting.

'7. To revise the headings of chapters and pages, paragraphs, italics, and punctuation.

'8. To refer, on the part of each Company, when considered desirable, to Divines, Scholars, and Literary Men, whether at home or abroad, for their opinions.'

These rules it has been our endeavour faithfully and consistently to follow. One only of them we found ourselves unable to observe in all particulars. In accordance with the seventh rule, we have carefully revised the paragraphs, italics, and punctuation. But the revision of the headings of chapters and pages would have involved so much of indirect, and indeed frequently of direct interpretation, that we judged it best to omit them altogether.

Our communications with the American Committee have been of the following nature. We transmitted to them from time to time each several portion of our First Revision, and received from them in return their criticisms and suggestions. These we considered with much care and attention during the time we were engaged on our Second Revision. We then sent over to them the various portions of the Second Revision as they were completed, and received further suggestions, which, like the former, were closely and carefully considered. Last of all, we forwarded to them the Revised Version in its final form; and a list of those passages in which they desire to place on record their preference of other readings and renderings will be found at the end of the volume.* We gratefully acknowledge their care, vigilance, and accuracy; and we humbly pray that their labours and our own, thus happily united, may be permitted to bear a blessing to both countries, and to all English-speaking people throughout the world.

The whole time devoted to the work has been ten years and a half. The First Revision occupied about six years; the Second, about two years and a half. The remaining time has been spent in the consideration of the suggestions from America on the Second Revision, and of many details and reserved questions arising out of our own labours. As a rule, a session of four days has been held every month (with the exception of August and September) in each year from the commencement of the work in June, 1870. The average attendance for the whole time has been sixteen each day: the whole Com-

---

* In this edition they are printed as foot-notes, excepting the readings and renderings of general passages, which are found on the page preceding the text.

pany consisting at first of twenty-seven, but for the greater part of the time of twenty-four members, many of them residing at great distances from London. Of the original number, four have been removed from us by death.

At an early stage in our labours, we entered into an agreement with the Universities of Oxford and Cambridge for the conveyance to them of our copyright in the work. This arrangement provided for the necessary expenses of the undertaking; and procured for the Revised Version the advantage of being published by Bodies long connected with the publication of the Authorised Version.

III. We now pass onward to give a brief account of the particulars of the present work. This we propose to do under the four heads of Text, Translation, Language, and Marginal Notes.

1. A revision of the Greek text was the necessary foundation of our work; but it did not fall within our province to construct a continuous and complete Greek text. In many cases the English rendering was considered to represent correctly either of two competing readings in the Greek, and then the question of the text was usually not raised. A sufficiently laborious task remained in deciding between the rival claims of various readings which might properly affect the translation. When these were adjusted, our deviations from the text presumed to underlie the Authorised Version had next to be indicated, in accordance with the fourth rule; but it proved inconvenient to record them in the margin. A better mode, however, of giving them publicity has been found, as the University Presses have undertaken to print them in connexion with complete Greek texts of the New Testament.

In regard of the readings thus approved, it may be observed that the fourth rule, by requiring that 'the text to be adopted' should be 'that for which the evidence is decidedly preponderating,' was in effect an instruction to follow the authority of documentary evidence without deference to any printed text of modern times, and therefore to employ the best resources of criticism for estimating the value of evidence. Textual criticism, as applied to the Greek New Testament, forms a special study of much intricacy and difficulty, and even now leaves room for considerable variety of opinion among competent critics. Different schools of criticism have been represented among us, and have together contributed to the final result. In the early part of the work every various reading requiring consideration was discussed and voted on by the Company. After a time the precedents thus established enabled the process to be safely shortened; but it was still at the option of every one to raise a full discussion on any particular reading, and the option was freely used. On the First Revision, in accordance with the fifth rule, the decisions were arrived at by simple majorities. On the Second Revision, at which a majority of two thirds was required to retain or introduce a reading at variance with the reading presumed to underlie the Authorised Version, many readings previously adopted were brought again into debate, and either reaffirmed or set aside.

Many places still remain in which, for the present, it would not be safe to accept one reading to the absolute exclusion of others. In these cases we have given alternative readings in the margin, wherever they seem to be of sufficient importance or interest to deserve notice. In the introductory formula, the phrases 'many ancient authorities,' 'some ancient authorities,' are used with some latitude to denote a greater or lesser proportion of those authorities which have a distinctive right to be called ancient. These ancient authorities comprise not only Greek manuscripts, some of which were written in the fourth and fifth centuries, but versions of a still earlier date in different languages, and also quotations by Christian writers of the second and following centuries.

2. We pass now from the Text to the Translation. The character of the Revision was determined for us from the outset by the first rule, 'to introduce as few alter-

ations as possible, consistently with faithfulness.' Our task was revision, not retranslation.

In the application however of this principle to the many and intricate details of our work, we have found ourselves constrained by faithfulness to introduce changes which might not at first sight appear to be included under the rule.

The alterations which we have made in the Authorised Version may be roughly grouped in five principal classes. First, alterations positively required by change of reading in the Greek Text. Secondly, alterations made where the Authorised Version appeared either to be incorrect, or to have chosen the less probable of two possible renderings. Thirdly, alterations of obscure or ambiguous renderings into such as are clear and express in their import. For it has been our principle not to leave any translation, or any arrangement of words, which could adapt itself to one or other of two interpretations, but rather to express as plainly as was possible that interpretation which seemed best to deserve a place in the text, and to put the other in the margin.

There remain yet two other classes of alterations which we have felt to be required by the same principle of faithfulness. These are,—Fourthly, alterations of the Authorised Version in cases where it was inconsistent with itself in the rendering of two or more passages confessedly alike or parallel. Fifthly, alterations rendered necessary *by consequence*, that is, arising out of changes already made, though not in themselves required by the general rule of faithfulness. Both these classes of alterations call for some further explanation.

The frequent inconsistencies in the Authorised Version have caused us much embarrassment from the fact already referred to, namely, that a studied variety of rendering, even in the same chapter and context, was a kind of principle with our predecessors, and was defended by them on grounds that have been mentioned above. The problem we had to solve was to discriminate between varieties of rendering which were compatible with fidelity to the true meaning of the text, and varieties which involved inconsistency, and were suggestive of differences that had no existence in the Greek. This problem we have solved to the best of our power, and for the most part in the following way.

Where there was a doubt as to the exact shade of meaning, we have looked to the context for guidance. If the meaning was fairly expressed by the word or phrase that was before us in the Authorised Version, we made no change, even where rigid adherence to the rule of translating, as far as possible, the same Greek word by the same English word might have prescribed some modification.

There are however numerous passages in the Authorised Version in which, whether regard be had to the recurrence (as in the first three Gospels) of identical clauses and sentences, to the repetition of the same word in the same passage, or to the characteristic use of particular words by the same writer, the studied variety adopted by the Translators of 1611 has produced a degree of inconsistency that cannot be reconciled with the principle of faithfulness. In such cases we have not hesitated to introduce alterations, even though the sense might not seem to the general reader to be materially affected.

The last class of alterations is that which we have described as rendered necessary *by consequence;* that is, by reason of some foregoing alteration. The cases in which these consequential changes have been found necessary are numerous and of very different kinds. Sometimes the change has been made to avoid tautology; sometimes to obviate an unpleasing alliteration or some other infelicity of sound; sometimes, in the case of smaller words, to preserve the familiar rhythm; sometimes for a convergence of reasons which, when explained, would at once be accepted, but until so explained might never be surmised even by intelligent readers.

This may be made plain by an example. When a particular word is found to recur with characteristic frequency in any one of the Sacred Writers, it is obviously desirable to adopt for it some uniform rendering. Again, where, as in the case of the first three Evangelists, precisely the same clauses or sentences are found in more than one of the Gospels, it is no less necessary to translate them in every place in the same way. These two principles may be illustrated by reference to a word that perpetually recurs in St. Mark's Gospel, and that may be translated either 'straightway,' 'forthwith,' or 'immediately.' Let it be supposed that the first rendering is chosen, and that the word, in accordance with the first of the above principles, is in that Gospel uniformly translated 'straightway.' Let it be further supposed that one of the passages of St. Mark in which it is so translated is found, word for word, in one of the other Gospels, but that there the rendering of the Authorised Version happens to be 'forthwith' or 'immediately.' That rendering must be changed on the second of the above principles; and yet such a change would not have been made but for this concurrence of two sound principles, and the consequent necessity of making a change on grounds extraneous to the passage itself.

This is but one of many instances of consequential alterations which might at first sight appear unnecessary, but which nevertheless have been deliberately made, and are not at variance with the rule of introducing as few changes in the Authorised Version as faithfulness would allow.

There are some other points of detail which it may be here convenient to notice. One of these, and perhaps the most important, is the rendering of the Greek aorist. There are numerous cases, especially in connexion with particles ordinarily expressive of present time, in which the use of the indefinite past tense in Greek and English is altogether different; and in such instances we have not attempted to violate the idiom of our language by forms of expression which it could not bear. But we have often ventured to represent the Greek aorist by the English preterite, even where the reader may find some passing difficulty in such a rendering, because we have felt convinced that the true meaning of the original was obscured by the presence of the familiar auxiliary. A remarkable illustration may be found in the seventeenth chapter of St. John's Gospel, where the combination of the aorist and the perfect shews, beyond all reasonable doubt, that different relations of time were intended to be expressed.

Changes of translation will also be found in connexion with the aorist participle, arising from the fact that the usual periphrasis of this participle in the Vulgate, which was rendered necessary by Latin idiom, has been largely reproduced in the Authorised Version by 'when' with the past tense (as for example in the second chapter of St. Matthew's Gospel), even where the ordinary participial rendering would have been easier and more natural in English.

In reference to the perfect and the imperfect tenses but little needs to be said. The correct translation of the former has been for the most part, though with some striking exceptions, maintained in the Authorised Version: while with regard to the imperfect, clear as its meaning may be in the Greek, the power of expressing it is so limited in English, that we have been frequently compelled to leave the force of the tense to be inferred from the context. In a few instances, where faithfulness imperatively required it, and especially where, in the Greek, the significance of the imperfect tense seemed to be additionally marked by the use of the participle with the auxiliary verb, we have introduced the corresponding form in English. Still, in the great majority of cases we have been obliged to retain the English preterite, and to rely either on slight changes in the order of the words, or on prominence given to the accompanying temporal particles, for the indication of the meaning which, in the Greek, the imperfect tense was designed to convey.

On other points of grammar it may be sufficient to speak more briefly.

Many changes, as might be anticipated, have been

made in the case of the definite article. Here again it was necessary to consider the peculiarities of English idiom, as well as the general tenor of each passage. Sometimes we have felt it enough to prefix the article to the first of a series of words to all of which it is prefixed in the Greek, and thus, as it were, to impart the idea of definiteness to the whole series, without running the risk of overloading the sentence. Sometimes, conversely, we have had to tolerate the presence of the definite article in our Version, when it is absent from the Greek, and perhaps not even grammatically latent; simply because English idiom would not allow the noun to stand alone, and because the introduction of the indefinite article might have introduced an idea of oneness or individuality, which was not in any degree traceable in the original. In a word, we have been careful to observe the use of the article wherever it seemed to be idiomatically possible: where it did not seem to be possible, we have yielded to necessity.

As to the pronouns and the place they occupy in the sentence, a subject often overlooked by our predecessors, we have been particularly careful; but here again we have frequently been baffled by structural or idiomatical peculiarities of the English language which precluded changes otherwise desirable.

In the case of the particles we have met with less difficulty, and have been able to maintain a reasonable amount of consistency. The particles in the Greek Testament are, as is well known, comparatively few, and they are commonly used with precision. It has therefore been the more necessary here to preserve a general uniformity of rendering, especially in the case of the particles of causality and inference, so far as English idiom would allow.

Lastly, many changes have been introduced in the rendering of the prepositions, especially where ideas of instrumentality or of mediate agency, distinctly marked in the original, had been confused or obscured in the translation. We have however borne in mind the comprehensive character of such prepositions as 'of' and 'by,' the one in reference to agency and the other in reference to means, especially in the English of the seventeenth century; and have rarely made any change where the true meaning of the original as expressed in the Authorised Version would be apparent to a reader of ordinary intelligence.

3. We now come to the subject of Language.

The second of the rules, by which the work has been governed, prescribed that the alterations to be introduced should be expressed, as far as possible, in the language of the Authorised Version or of the Versions that preceded it.

To this rule we have faithfully adhered. We have habitually consulted the earlier Versions; and in our sparing introduction of words not found in them or in the Authorised Version we have usually satisfied ourselves that such words were employed by standard writers of nearly the same date, and had also that general hue which justified their introduction into a Version which has held the highest place in the classical literature of our language. We have never removed any archaisms, whether in structure or in words, except where we were persuaded either that the meaning of the words was not generally understood, or that the nature of the expression led to some misconception of the true sense of the passage. The frequent inversions of the strict order of the words, which add much to the strength and variety of the Authorised Version, and give an archaic colour to many felicities of diction, have been seldom modified. Indeed, we have often adopted the same arrangement in our own alterations; and in this, as in other particulars, we have sought to assimilate the new work to the old.

In a few exceptional cases we have failed to find any word in the older stratum of our language that appeared to convey the precise meaning of the original. There, and there only, we have used words of a later date; but not without having first assured ourselves that they are to be found in the writings of the best authors of the period to which they belong.

In regard of Proper Names no rule was prescribed to us. In the case of names of frequent occurrence we have deemed it best to follow generally the rule laid down for our predecessors. That rule, it may be remembered, was to this effect, 'The names of the prophets and the holy writers, with the other names of the text, to be retained, as nigh as may be, accordingly as they were vulgarly used.' Some difficulty has been felt in dealing with names less familiarly known. Here our general practice has been to follow the Greek form of names, except in the case of persons and places mentioned in the Old Testament: in this case we have followed the Hebrew.

4. The subject of the Marginal Notes deserves special attention. They represent the results of a large amount of careful and elaborate discussion, and will, perhaps, by their very presence, indicate to some extent the intricacy of many of the questions that have almost daily come before us for decision. These Notes fall into four main groups: first, notes specifying such differences of reading as were judged to be of sufficient importance to require a particular notice; secondly, notes indicating the exact rendering of words to which, for the sake of English idiom, we were obliged to give a less exact rendering in the text; thirdly, notes, very few in number, affording some explanation which the original appeared to require; fourthly, alternative renderings in difficult or debateable passages. The notes of this last group are numerous, and largely in excess of those which were admitted by our predecessors. In the 270 years that have passed away since their labours were concluded, the Sacred Text has been minutely examined, discussed in every detail, and analysed with a grammatical precision unknown in the days of the last Revision. There has thus been accumulated a large amount of materials that have prepared the way for different renderings, which necessarily came under discussion. We have therefore placed

before the reader in the margin other renderings than those which were adopted in the text, wherever such renderings seemed to deserve consideration. The rendering in the text, where it agrees with the Authorised Version, was supported by at least one third, and, where it differs from the Authorised Version, by at least two thirds of those who were present at the second revision of the passage in question.

A few supplementary matters have yet to be mentioned. These may be thus enumerated,—the use of Italics, the arrangement in Paragraphs, the mode of printing Quotations from the Poetical Books of the Old Testament, the Punctuation, and, last of all, the Titles of the different Books that make up the New Testament,—all of them particulars on which it seems desirable to add a few explanatory remarks.

(a) The determination, in each place, of the words to be printed in italics has not been by any means easy; nor can we hope to be found in all cases perfectly consistent. In the earliest editions of the Authorised Version the use of a different type to indicate supplementary words not contained in the original was not very frequent, and cannot easily be reconciled with any settled principle. A review of the words so printed was made, after a lapse of some years, for the editions of the Authorised Version published at Cambridge in 1629 and 1638. Further, though slight, modifications were introduced at intervals between 1638 and the more systematic revisions undertaken respectively by Dr. Paris in the Cambridge Edition of 1762, and by Dr. Blayney in the Oxford Edition of 1769. None of them however rest on any higher authority than that of the persons who from time to time superintended the publication. The last attempt to bring the use of italics into uniformity and consistency was made by Dr. Scrivener in the Paragraph Bible published at Cambridge in 1870–73. In succeeding to these labours, we have acted on the general principle of printing in italics words which did not appear to be necessarily involved in the Greek. Our tendency has been to diminish rather than to increase the amount of italic printing; though, in the case of difference of readings, we have usually marked the absence of any words in the original which the sense might nevertheless require to be present in the Version; and again, in the case of inserted pronouns, where the reference did not appear to be perfectly certain, we have similarly had recourse to italics. Some of these cases, especially when there are slight differences of reading, are of singular intricacy, and make it impossible to maintain rigid uniformity.

(*b*) We have arranged the Sacred Text in paragraphs, after the precedent of the earliest English Versions, so as to assist the general reader in following the current of narrative or argument. The present arrangement will be found, we trust, to have preserved the due mean between a system of long portions which must often include several separate topics, and a system of frequent breaks which, though they may correctly indicate the separate movements of thought in the writer, often seriously impede a just perception of the true continuity of the passage. The traditional division into chapters, which the Authorised Version inherited from Latin Bibles of the later middle ages, is an illustration of the former method. These paragraphs, for such in fact they are, frequently include several distinct subjects. Moreover they sometimes, though rarely, end where there is no sufficient break in the sense. The division of chapters into verses, which was introduced into the New Testament for the first time in 1551, is an exaggeration of the latter method, with its accompanying inconveniences. The serious obstacles to the right understanding of Holy Scripture, which are interposed by minute subdivision, are often overlooked; but if any one will consider for a moment the injurious effect that would be produced by breaking up a portion of some great standard work into separate verses, he will at once perceive how necessary has been an alteration in this particular. The arrangement by chapters and verses undoubtedly affords facilities for reference: but this advantage we have been able to retain by placing the numerals on the inside margin of each page.

(c) A few words will suffice as to the mode of printing quotations from the Poetical Books of the Old Testament. Wherever the quotation extends to two or more lines, our practice has been to recognise the parallelism of their structure by arranging the lines in a manner that appears to agree with the metrical divisions of the Hebrew original. Such an arrangement will be found helpful to the reader; not only as directing his attention to the poetical character of the quotation, but as also tending to make its force and pertinence more fully felt. We have treated in the same way the hymns in the first two chapters of the Gospel according to St. Luke.

(d) Great care has been bestowed on the punctuation. Our practice has been to maintain what is sometimes called the heavier system of stopping, or, in other words, that system which, especially for convenience in reading aloud, suggests such pauses as will best ensure a clear and intelligent setting forth of the true meaning of the words. This course has rendered necessary, especially in the Epistles, a larger use of colons and semicolons than is customary in modern English printing.

(e) We may in the last place notice one particular to which we were not expressly directed to extend our revision, namely, the titles of the Books of the New Testament. These titles are no part of the original text; and the titles found in the most ancient manuscripts are of too short a form to be convenient for use. Under these circumstances, we have deemed it best to leave unchanged the titles which are given in the Authorised Version as printed in 1611.

We now conclude, humbly commending our labours to Almighty God, and praying that his favour and blessing may be vouchsafed to that which has been done in his name. We recognised from the first the responsibility of the undertaking; and through our manifold experience of its abounding difficulties we have felt more and more, as we went onward, that such a work can never be accomplished by organised efforts of scholarship and criticism, unless assisted by Divine help.

We know full well that defects must have their place in a work so long and so arduous as this which has now come to an end. Blemishes and imperfections there are in the noble Translation which we have been called upon to revise; blemishes and imperfections will assuredly be found in our own Revision. All endeavours to translate the Holy Scriptures into another tongue must fall short of their aim, when the obligation is imposed of producing a Version that shall be alike literal and idiomatic, faithful to each thought of the original, and yet, in the expression of it, harmonious and free. While we dare to hope that in places not a few of the New Testament the introduction of slight changes has cast a new light upon much that was difficult and obscure, we cannot forget how often we have failed in expressing some finer shade of meaning which we recognised in the original, how often idiom has stood in the way of a perfect rendering, and how often the attempt to preserve a familiar form of words, or even a familiar cadence, has only added another perplexity to those which already beset us.

Thus, in the review of the work which we have been permitted to complete, our closing words must be words of mingled thanksgiving, humility, and prayer. Of thanksgiving, for the many blessings vouchsafed to us throughout the unbroken progress of our corporate labours; of humility, for our failings and imperfections in the fulfilment of our task; and of prayer to Almighty God, that the Gospel of our Lord and Saviour Jesus Christ may be more clearly and more freshly shewn forth to all who shall be readers of this Book.

JERUSALEM CHAMBER,
  WESTMINSTER ABBEY.
    11*th November*, 1880.

THE NAMES AND ORDER

OF ALL THE

BOOKS OF THE NEW TESTAMENT.

	Page		Page
S. Matthew	1	I. Timothy	351
S. Mark	56	II. Timothy	357
S. Luke	91	To Titus	362
S. John	151	To Philemon	365
The Acts	195	To the Hebrews	367
To the Romans	253	James	386
I. Corinthians	277	I. Peter	392
II. Corinthians	300	II. Peter	399
To the Galatians	315	I. John	404
To the Ephesians	323	II. John	410
To the Philippians	331	III. John	411
To the Colossians	337	Jude	412
I. Thessalonians	343	Revelation	414
II. Thessalonians	348		

LIST OF READINGS AND RENDERINGS REFERRING TO GENERAL PASSAGES PREFERRED BY THE AMERICAN COMMITTEE, RECORDED AT THEIR DESIRE. (See Preface, page xii).

(The special readings and renderings are given in foot-notes.)

I. Strike out "S." (i. e. Saint) from the title of the Gospels and from the heading of the pages.

II. Strike out "the Apostle" from the title of the Pauline Epistles, and "of Paul the Apostle" from the title of the Epistle to the Hebrews; strike out the word "General" from the title of the Epistles of James, Peter, 1 John, and Jude; and let the title of the Revelation run "The Revelation of John."

III. For "Holy Ghost" adopt uniformly the rendering "Holy Spirit."

IV. At the word "worship" in Matt. ii. 2, etc., add the marginal note "The Greek word denotes an act of reverence, whether paid to man (see chap. xviii. 26) or to God (see chap. iv. 10)."

V. Put into the text uniformly the marginal rendering "through" in place of "by" when it relates to prophecy, viz. in Matt. ii. 5, 17, 23; iii. 3; iv. 14; viii. 17; xii. 17; xiii. 35; xxi. 4; xxiv. 15; xxvii. 9; Luke xviii. 31; Acts ii. 16; xxviii. 25.

VI. For "tempt" ("temptation") substitute "try" or "make trial of" ("trial") wherever enticement to what is wrong is not evidently spoken of; viz. in the following instances: Matt. iv. 7; xvi. 1; xix. 3; xxii. 18, 35; Mark viii. 11; x. 2; xii. 15; Luke iv. 12; x. 25; xi. 16; xxii. 28; John viii. 6; Acts v. 9; xv. 10; 1 Cor. x. 9; Heb. iii. 8, 9; 1 Pet. i. 6.

VII. Substitute modern forms of speech for the following archaisms, viz. "who" or "that" for "which" when used of persons; "are" for "be" in the present indicative; "know" "knew" for "wot" "wist"; "drag" or "drag away" for "hale."

VIII. Substitute for "devil" ("devils") the word "demon" ("demons") wherever the latter word is given in the margin (or represents the Greek words δαίμων δαιμόνιον); and for "possessed with a devil" (or "devils") substitute either "demoniac" or "possessed with a demon" (or "demons").

IX. After "baptize" let the marg. "Or, *in*" and the text "with" exchange places.

X. Let the word "testament" be everywhere changed to "covenant" (without an alternate in the margin), except in Heb. ix. 15-17.

XI. Wherever "patience" occurs as the rendering of ὑπομονή add "stedfastness" as an alternate in the margin, except in 2 Cor. i. 6; James v. 11; Luke viii. 15; Heb. xii. 1.

XII. Let ἀσσάριον (Matt. x. 29; Luke xii. 6) be translated "penny," and δηνάριον "shilling," except in Matt. xxii. 29; Mark xii. 15; Luke xx. 24, where the name of the coin, "a denarius," should be given.

XIII. Against the expression "the God and Father of our Lord Jesus Christ" add the marginal rendering "Or, *God and the Father*" etc.; viz. in Rom. xv. 6; 2 Cor. i. 3; xi. 31; Eph. i. 3; Col. i. 3; 1 Pet. i. 3. And against the expression "our God and Father" add the marg. "Or, *God and our Father*"; viz. in Gal. i. 4; Phil. iv. 20; 1 Thess. i. 3; iii. 11, 13; James i. 27. And against the expression "his God and Father" add the marg. "Or, *God and his Father*," viz. in Rev. i. 6.

XIV. Let the use of "fulfil" be confined to those cases in which it denotes "accomplish," "bring to pass," or the like.

THE GOSPEL ACCORDING TO
S. MATTHEW.

1 ¹The book of the ²generation of Jesus Christ, the son of David, the son of Abraham.
2 Abraham begat Isaac; and Isaac begat Jacob; and
3 Jacob begat Judah and his brethren; and Judah begat Perez and Zerah of Tamar; and Perez begat
4 Hezron; and Hezron begat ³Ram; and ³Ram begat Amminadab; and Amminadab begat Nahshon; and
5 Nahshon begat Salmon; and Salmon begat Boaz of Rahab; and Boaz begat Obed of Ruth; and Obed
6 begat Jesse; and Jesse begat David the king.
 And David begat Solomon of her *that had been the*
7 *wife* of Uriah; and Solomon begat Rehoboam; and Rehoboam begat Abijah; and Abijah begat ⁴Asa;
8 and ⁴Asa begat Jehoshaphat; and Jehoshaphat begat
9 Joram; and Joram begat Uzziah; and Uzziah begat Jotham; and Jotham begat Ahaz; and Ahaz begat
10 Hezekiah; and Hezekiah begat Manasseh; and Ma-
11 nasseh begat ⁵Amon; and ⁵Amon begat Josiah; and Josiah begat Jechoniah and his brethren, at the time of the ⁶carrying away to Babylon.
12 And after the ⁶carrying away to Babylon, Jechoniah begat ⁷Shealtiel; and ⁷Shealtiel begat Zerubba-
13 bel; and Zerubbabel begat Abiud; and Abiud begat
14 Eliakim; and Eliakim begat Azor; and Azor begat Sadoc; and Sadoc begat Achim; and Achim begat
15 Eliud; and Eliud begat Eleazar; and Eleazar begat
16 Matthan; and Matthan begat Jacob; and Jacob begat Joseph the husband of Mary, of whom was born Jesus, who is called Christ.
17 So all the generations from Abraham unto David are fourteen generations; and from David unto the ⁶carrying away to Babylon fourteen generations;

1 Or, *The genealogy of Jesus Christ*
2 Or, *birth*: as in ver. 18.
3 Gr. *Aram.*
4 Gr. *Asaph.*
5 Gr. *Amos.*
6 Or, *removal to Babylon*
7 Gr. *Salathiel.*

S. MATTHEW.

and from the ¹carrying away to Babylon unto the Christ fourteen generations.

Now the ²birth ³of Jesus Christ was on this wise: When his mother Mary had been betrothed to Joseph, before they came together she was found with child of the ⁴Holy Ghost. And Joseph her husband, being a righteous man, and not willing to make her a public example, was minded to put her away privily. But when he thought on these things, behold, an angel of the Lord appeared unto him in a dream, saying, Joseph, thou son of David, fear not to take unto thee Mary thy wife: for that which is ⁵conceived in her is of the Holy Ghost. And she shall bring forth a son; and thou shalt call his name JESUS; for it is he that shall save his people from their sins. Now all this is come to pass, that it might be fulfilled which was spoken by the Lord through the prophet, saying,

Behold, the virgin shall be with child, and shall bring forth a son,

And they shall call his name ⁶Immanuel;

which is, being interpreted, God with us. And Joseph arose from his sleep, and did as the angel of the Lord commanded him, and took unto him his wife; and knew her not till she had brought forth a son: and he called his name JESUS.

Now when Jesus was born in Bethlehem of Judæa in the days of Herod the king, behold, ⁷wise men from the east came to Jerusalem, saying, ⁸Where is he that is born King of the Jews? for we saw his star in the east, and are come to worship him. And when Herod the king heard it, he was troubled, and all Jerusalem with him. And gathering together all the chief priests and scribes of the people, he inquired of them where the Christ should be born. And they said unto him, In Bethlehem of Judæa: for thus it is written ⁹by the prophet,

And thou Bethlehem, land of Judah,

Art in no wise least among the princes of Judah:

For out of thee shall come forth a governor,

Which shall be shepherd of my people Israel.

Then Herod privily called the ⁷wise men, and learned of them carefully ¹⁰what time the star appeared. And he sent them to Bethlehem, and said, Go and search out carefully concerning the young child; and when ye have found *him*, bring me word, that I also may come and worship him. And they, having heard the king, went their way; and lo, the star,

---

1 Or, *removal to Babylon*
2 Or, *generation: as in ver. 1.*
3 Some ancient authorities read *of the Christ*.
4 Or, *Holy Spirit*; and so throughout this book.
5 Gr. *begotten*.
6 Gr. *Emmanuel*.
7 Gr. *Magi*. Compare Esther i. 13; Dan. ii. 12.
8 Or, *Where is the King of the Jews that is born?*
9 Or, *through*
10 Or, *the time of the star that appeared*

which they saw in the east, went before them, till it came and stood over where the young child was.
10 And when they saw the star, they rejoiced with ex-
11 ceeding great joy. And they came into the house and saw the young child with Mary his mother; and they fell down and worshipped him; and opening their treasures they offered unto him gifts, gold and
12 frankincense and myrrh. And being warned *of God* in a dream that they should not return to Herod, they departed into their own country another way.
13 Now when they were departed, behold, an angel of the Lord appeareth to Joseph in a dream, saying, Arise and take the young child and his mother, and flee into Egypt, and be thou there until I tell thee: for Herod will seek the young child to destroy him.
14 And he arose and took the young child and his
15 mother by night, and departed into Egypt; and was there until the death of Herod: that it might be fulfilled which was spoken by the Lord through the prophet, saying, Out of Egypt did I call my son.
16 Then Herod, when he saw that he was mocked of the [1] wise men, was exceeding wroth, and sent forth, and slew all the male children that were in Bethlehem, and in all the borders thereof, from two years old and under, according to the time which he had
17 carefully learned of the [1] wise men. Then was fulfilled that which was spoken [2] by Jeremiah the prophet, saying,
18   A voice was heard in Ramah,
    Weeping and great mourning,
    Rachel weeping for her children;
    And she would not be comforted, because they are not.
19 But when Herod was dead, behold, an angel of the
20 Lord appeareth in a dream to Joseph in Egypt, saying, Arise and take the young child and his mother, and go into the land of Israel: for they are dead
21 that sought the young child's life. And he arose and took the young child and his mother, and came
22 into the land of Israel. But when he heard that Archelaus was reigning over Judæa in the room of his father Herod, he was afraid to go thither; and being warned *of God* in a dream, he withdrew into
23 the parts of Galilee, and came and dwelt in a city called Nazareth: that it might be fulfilled which was spoken [2] by the prophets, that he should be called a Nazarene.

1 Gr. *Magi*.

2 Or, *through*

3 And in those days cometh John the Baptist,
2 preaching in the wilderness of Judæa, saying, Re-
3 pent ye; for the kingdom of heaven is at hand. For
this is he that was spoken of ¹by Isaiah the prophet,
saying,
 The voice of one crying in the wilderness,
 Make ye ready the way of the Lord,
 Make his paths straight.
4 Now John himself had his raiment of camel's hair,
and a leathern girdle about his loins; and his food
5 was locusts and wild honey. Then went out unto
him Jerusalem, and all Judæa, and all the region
6 round about Jordan; and they were baptized of him
7 in the river Jordan, confessing their sins. But when
he saw many of the Pharisees and Sadducees coming
to his baptism*, he said unto them, Ye offspring of
vipers, who warned you to flee from the wrath to
8 come? Bring forth therefore fruit worthy of ²re-
9 pentance: and think not to say within yourselves,
We have Abraham to our father: for I say unto you,
that God is able of these stones to raise up children
unto Abraham. And even now is the axe laid unto † 10
the root of the trees: every tree therefore that bringeth not forth good fruit is hewn down, and cast into
11 the fire. I indeed baptize you ³with water unto repentance: but he that cometh after me is mightier
than I, whose shoes I am not ⁴worthy to bear: he
shall baptize you ³with the Holy Ghost and *with* fire:
12 whose fan is in his hand, and he will throughly
cleanse his threshing-floor; and he will gather his
wheat into the garner, but the chaff he will burn up
with unquenchable fire.
13 Then cometh Jesus from Galilee to the Jordan
14 unto John, to be baptized of him. But John would
have hindered him, saying, I have need to be bap-
15 tized of thee, and comest thou to me? But Jesus
answering said unto him, Suffer ⁵*it* now: for thus it
becometh us to fulfil all righteousness. Then he
16 suffereth him. And Jesus, when he was baptized,
went up straightway from the water: and lo, the
heavens were opened ⁶unto him, and he saw the
Spirit of God descending as a dove, and coming
17 upon him; and lo, a voice out of the heavens, saying, ⁷This is my beloved Son, in whom I am well
pleased.

1 Or, *through*

2 Or, *your repentance*

3 Or, *in*

4 Gr. *sufficient.*

5 Or, *me*

6 Some ancient authorities omit *unto him.*

7 Or, *This is my Son; my beloved in whom I am well pleased.* See ch. xii. 18.

---
* Against "to his baptism" add marg. Or, *for baptism—Am. Com.*
† For "is the axe laid unto" read "the axe lieth at" So in Luke iii. 9.—*Am. Com.*

4 Then was Jesus led up of the Spirit into the wil-
2 derness to be tempted of the devil. And when he
had fasted forty days and forty nights, he afterward
3 hungered. And the tempter came and said unto
him, If thou art the Son of God, command that these
4 stones become ¹bread. But he answered and said, [1 Gr. *loaves.*]
It is written, Man shall not live by bread alone, but
by every word that proceedeth out of the mouth of
5 God. Then the devil taketh him into the holy city;
6 and he set him on the ²pinnacle of the temple, and [2 Gr. *wing.*]
saith unto him, If thou art the Son of God, cast thyself down: for it is written,
> He shall give his angels charge concerning thee:
> And on their hands they shall bear thee up,
> Lest haply thou dash thy foot against a stone.
7 Jesus said unto him, Again it is written, Thou shalt
8 not tempt the Lord thy God. Again, the devil taketh him unto an exceeding high mountain, and sheweth him all the kingdoms of the world, and the glory
9 of them; and he said unto him, All these things will
I give thee, if thou wilt fall down and worship me.
10 Then saith Jesus unto him, Get thee hence, Satan:
for it is written, Thou shalt worship the Lord thy
11 God, and him only shalt thou serve. Then the devil
leaveth him; and behold, angels came and ministered unto him.
12 Now when he heard that John was delivered up, he
13 withdrew into Galilee; and leaving Nazareth, he
came and dwelt in Capernaum, which is by the sea,
14 in the borders of Zebulun and Naphtali: that it
might be fulfilled which was spoken ³by Isaiah the [3 Or, *through*]
prophet, saying,
15 > The land of Zebulun and the land of Naphtali, [4 Gr. *The way of the sea.*]
> ⁴Toward the sea, beyond Jordan,
> Galilee of the ⁵Gentiles, [5 Gr. *nations*: and so elsewhere.]
16 > The people which sat in darkness
> Saw a great light,
> And to them which sat in the region and shad-
> ow of death,
> To them did light spring up.
17 From that time began Jesus to preach, and to say,
Repent ye; for the kingdom of heaven is at hand.
18 And walking by the sea of Galilee, he saw two
brethren, Simon who is called Peter, and Andrew
his brother, casting a net into the sea; for they were
19 fishers. And he saith unto them, Come ye after me,
20 and I will make you fishers of men. And they
21 straightway left the nets, and followed him. And

going on from thence he saw other two brethren, ¹James the *son* of Zebedee, and John his brother, in the boat with Zebedee their father, mending their nets; and he called them. And they straightway left the boat and their father, and followed him. 22

And ²Jesus went about in all Galilee, teaching in their synagogues, and preaching the ³gospel of the kingdom, and healing all manner of disease and all manner of sickness among the people. And the report of him went forth into all Syria: and they brought unto him all that were sick, holden with divers diseases and torments, ⁴possessed with devils, and epileptic, and palsied; and he healed them. And there followed him great multitudes from Galilee and Decapolis and Jerusalem and Judæa and *from* beyond Jordan. 23 24 25

And seeing the multitudes, he went up into the mountain: and when he had sat down, his disciples came unto him: and he opened his mouth and taught them, saying, 5 2

Blessed are the poor in spirit: for theirs is the kingdom of heaven. 3

⁵Blessed are they that mourn: for they shall be comforted. 4

Blessed are the meek: for they shall inherit the earth. 5

Blessed are they that hunger and thirst after righteousness: for they shall be filled. 6

Blessed are the merciful: for they shall obtain mercy. 7

Blessed are the pure in heart: for they shall see God. 8

Blessed are the peacemakers: for they shall be called sons of God. 9

Blessed are they that have been persecuted for righteousness' sake: for theirs is the kingdom of heaven. Blessed are ye when *men* shall reproach you, and persecute you, and say all manner of evil against you falsely, for my sake. Rejoice, and be exceeding glad: for great is your reward in heaven: for so persecuted they the prophets which were before you. 10 11 12

Ye are the salt of the earth: but if the salt have lost its savour, wherewith shall it be salted? it is thenceforth good for nothing, but to be cast out and trodden under foot of men. Ye are the light of the world. A city set on a hill cannot be hid. Neither do *men* light a lamp, and put it under the bushel, but on the stand; and it shineth unto all that 13 14 15

---

1 Or, *Jacob:* and so elsewhere.

2 Some ancient authorities read *he.*

3 Or, *good tidings:* and so elsewhere.

4 Or, *demoniacs*

5 Some ancient authorities transpose ver. 4 and 5.

16 are in the house. Even so let your light shine before men, that they may see your good works, and glorify your Father which is in heaven.
17 Think not that I came to destroy the law or the
18 prophets: I came not to destroy, but to fulfil. For verily I say unto you, Till heaven and earth pass away, one jot or one tittle shall in no wise pass away
19 from the law, till all things be accomplished. Whosoever therefore shall break one of these least commandments, and shall teach men so, shall be called least in the kingdom of heaven: but whosoever shall do and teach them, he shall be called great in the
20 kingdom of heaven. For I say unto you, that except your righteousness shall exceed *the righteousness* of the scribes and Pharisees, ye shall in no wise enter into the kingdom of heaven.
21 Ye have heard that it was said to them of old time, Thou shalt not kill; and whosoever shall kill
22 shall be in danger of the judgement: but I say unto you, that every one who is angry with his brother[1] shall be in danger of the judgement; and whosoever shall say to his brother, [2]Raca, shall be in danger of the council; and whosoever shall say, [3]Thou fool,
23 shall be in danger [4]of the [5]hell of fire. If therefore thou art offering thy gift at the altar, and there rememberest that thy brother hath aught against thee,
24 leave there thy gift before the altar, and go thy way, first be reconciled to thy brother, and then come and
25 offer thy gift. Agree with thine adversary quickly, whiles thou art with him in the way; lest haply the adversary deliver thee to the judge, and the judge [6]deliver thee to the officer, and thou be cast
26 into prison. Verily I say unto thee, Thou shalt by no means come out thence, till thou have paid the last farthing.
27 Ye have heard that it was said, Thou shalt not
28 commit adultery: but I say unto you, that every one that looketh on a woman to lust after her hath com-
29 mitted adultery with her already in his heart. And if thy right eye causeth thee to stumble, pluck it out, and cast it from thee: for it is profitable for thee that one of thy members should perish, and not thy
30 whole body be cast into [7]hell. And if thy right hand causeth thee to stumble, cut it off, and cast it from thee: for it is profitable for thee that one of thy members should perish, and not thy whole body
31 go into [7]hell. It was said also, Whosoever shall put away his wife, let him give her a writing of divorce-

[1] Many ancient authorities insert *without cause*.
[2] An expression of contempt.
[3] Or, *Moreh*, a Hebrew expression of condemnation.
[4] Gr. *unto* or *into*.
[5] Gr. *Gehenna of fire*.
[6] Some ancient authorities omit *deliver thee*.
[7] Gr. *Gehenna*.

ment: but I say unto you, that every one that put- 32
teth away his wife, saving for the cause of fornication, maketh her an adulteress: and whosoever shall
marry her when she is put away committeth adultery.

Again, ye have heard that it was said to them of 33
old time, Thou shalt not forswear thyself, but shalt
perform unto the Lord thine oaths: but I say unto 34
you, Swear not at all; neither by the heaven, for it
is the throne of God; nor by the earth, for it is 35
the footstool of his feet; nor [1]by Jerusalem, for it
is the city of the great King. Neither shalt thou 36
swear by thy head, for thou canst not make one
hair white or black. [2]But let your speech be, Yea, 37
yea; Nay, nay: and whatsoever is more than these
is of [3]the evil *one*.

Ye have heard that it was said, An eye for an eye, 38
and a tooth for a tooth: but I say unto you, Resist 39
not [4]him that is evil: but whosoever smiteth thee
on thy right cheek, turn to him the other also. And 40
if any man would go to law with thee, and take
away thy coat, let him have thy cloke also. And 41
whosoever shall [5]compel thee to go one mile, go
with him twain. Give to him that asketh thee, and 42
from him that would borrow of thee turn not thou
away.

Ye have heard that it was said, Thou shalt love 43
thy neighbour, and hate thine enemy: but I say unto 44
you, Love your enemies, and pray for them that
persecute you; that ye may be sons of your Father 45
which is in heaven: for he maketh his sun to rise
on the evil and the good, and sendeth rain on the
just and the unjust. For if ye love them that love 46
you, what reward have ye? do not even the [6]publi-
cans the same? And if ye salute your brethren only, 47
what do ye more *than others*? do not even the Gentiles the same? Ye therefore shall be perfect, as 48
your heavenly Father is perfect.

Take heed that ye do not your righteousness be- 6
fore men, to be seen of them: else ye have no reward with your Father which is in heaven.

When therefore thou doest alms, sound not a 2
trumpet before thee, as the hypocrites do in the synagogues and in the streets, that they may have glory
of men. Verily I say unto you, They have received
their reward. But when thou doest alms, let not 3
thy left hand know what thy right hand doeth: that 4
thine alms may be in secret; and thy Father which
seeth in secret shall recompense thee.

---

[1] Or, *toward*
[2] Some ancient authorities read *But your speech shall be.*
[3] Or, *evil*: as in ver. 39; vi. 13.
[4] Or, *evil*
[5] Gr. *impress.*
[6] That is, *collectors or renters of Roman taxes*: and so elsewhere.

5 And when ye pray, ye shall not be as the hypocrites: for they love to stand and pray in the synagogues and in the corners of the streets, that they may be seen of men. Verily I say unto you, They
6 have received their reward. But thou, when thou prayest, enter into thine inner chamber, and having shut thy door, pray to thy Father which is in secret, and thy Father which seeth in secret shall recom-
7 pense thee. And in praying use not vain repetitions, as the Gentiles do: for they think that they shall be
8 heard for their much speaking. Be not therefore like unto them: for ¹your Father knoweth what
9 things ye have need of, before ye ask him. After this manner therefore pray ye: Our Father which
10 art in heaven, Hallowed be thy name. Thy kingdom come. Thy will be done, as in heaven, so on
11 earth. Give us this day ²our daily bread*. And
12 forgive us our debts, as we also have forgiven our
13 debtors. And bring us not into temptation, but de-
14 liver us from ³the evil one.⁴ For if ye forgive men their trespasses, your heavenly Father will also for-
15 give you. But if ye forgive not men their trespasses, neither will your Father forgive your trespasses.
16 Moreover when ye fast, be not, as the hypocrites, of a sad countenance: for they disfigure their faces, that they may be seen of men to fast. Verily I say
17 unto you, They have received their reward. But thou, when thou fastest, anoint thy head, and wash
18 thy face; that thou be not seen of men to fast, but of thy Father which is in secret: and thy Father, which seeth in secret, shall recompense thee.
19 Lay not up for yourselves treasures upon the earth, where moth and rust doth consume, and where
20 thieves ⁵break through and steal: but lay up for yourselves treasures in heaven, where neither moth nor rust doth consume, and where thieves do not
21 ⁵break through nor steal: for where thy treasure is,
22 there will thy heart be also. The lamp of the body is the eye: if therefore thine eye be single, thy whole
23 body shall be full of light. But if thine eye be evil, thy whole body shall be full of darkness. If therefore the light that is in thee be darkness, how great
24 is the darkness! No man can serve two masters: for either he will hate the one, and love the other; or else he will hold to one, and despise the other.

1 Some ancient authorities read *God your Father*.

2 Gr. *our bread for the coming day*.

3 Or, *evil*

4 Many authorities, some ancient, but with variations, add *For thine is the kingdom, and the power, and the glory, for ever. Amen.*

5 Gr. *dig through.*

---

* Let the marg. read Gr. *our bread for the coming day*, or *our needful bread*. So in Luke xi. 3.—*Am. Com.*

Ye cannot serve God and mammon. Therefore I 25 say unto you, Be not anxious for your life, what ye shall eat, or what ye shall drink; nor yet for your body, what ye shall put on. Is not the life more than the food, and the body than the raiment? Be- 26 hold the birds of the heaven, that they sow not, neither do they reap, nor gather into barns; and your heavenly Father feedeth them. Are not ye of much more value than they? And which of you by 27 being anxious can add one cubit unto his ¹stature*? And why are ye anxious concerning raiment? Con- 28 sider the lilies of the field, how they grow; they toil not, neither do they spin: yet I say unto you, that 29 even Solomon in all his glory was not arrayed like one of these. But if God doth so clothe the grass of 30 the field, which to-day is, and to-morrow is cast into the oven, *shall he* not much more *clothe* you, O ye of little faith? Be not therefore anxious, saying, What 31 shall we eat? or, What shall we drink? or, Wherewithal shall we be clothed? For after all these 32 things do the Gentiles seek; for your heavenly Father knoweth that ye have need of all these things. But seek ye first his kingdom, and his righteousness; 33 and all these things shall be added unto you. Be 34 not therefore anxious for the morrow: for the morrow will be anxious for itself. Sufficient unto the day is the evil thereof.

Judge not, that ye be not judged. For with 7 what judgement ye judge, ye shall be judged: and 2 with what measure ye mete, it shall be measured unto you. And why beholdest thou the mote that 3 is in thy brother's eye, but considerest not the beam that is in thine own eye? Or how wilt thou say to 4 thy brother, Let me cast out the mote out of thine eye; and lo, the beam is in thine own eye? Thou 5 hypocrite, cast out first the beam out of thine own eye; and then shalt thou see clearly to cast out the mote out of thy brother's eye.

Give not that which is holy unto the dogs, neither 6 cast your pearls before the swine, lest haply they trample them under their feet, and turn and rend you.

Ask, and it shall be given you; seek, and ye shall 7 find; knock, and it shall be opened unto you: for 8 every one that asketh receiveth; and he that seeketh findeth; and to him that knocketh it shall be opened.

¹ Or, *age*

---

* For "his stature" read "the measure of his life" (with marg. Or, *his stature*) So in Luke xii. 25.—*Am. Com.*

9 Or what man is there of you, who, if his son shall
10 ask him for a loaf will give him a stone; or if he shall
11 ask for a fish, will give him a serpent? If ye then, being evil, know how to give good gifts unto your children, how much more shall your Father which is in heaven give good things to them that ask him?
12 All things therefore whatsoever ye would that men should do unto you, even so do ye also unto them: for this is the law and the prophets.
13 Enter ye in by the narrow gate: for wide ¹is the gate, and broad is the way, that leadeth to destruc-
14 tion, and many be they that enter in thereby. ²For narrow is the gate, and straitened the way, that leadeth unto life, and few be they that find it.
15 Beware of false prophets, which come to you in sheep's clothing, but inwardly are ravening wolves.
16 By their fruits ye shall know them. Do *men* gather
17 grapes of thorns, or figs of thistles? Even so every good tree bringeth forth good fruit; but the corrupt
18 tree bringeth forth evil fruit. A good tree cannot bring forth evil fruit, neither can a corrupt tree bring
19 forth good fruit. Every tree that bringeth not forth
20 good fruit is hewn down, and cast into the fire.
21 Therefore by their fruits ye shall know them. Not every one that saith unto me, Lord, Lord, shall enter into the kingdom of heaven; but he that doeth the
22 will of my Father which is in heaven. Many will say to me in that day, Lord, Lord, did we not prophesy by thy name, and by thy name cast out ³devils,
23 and by thy name do many ⁴mighty works? And then will I profess unto them, I never knew you:
24 depart from me, ye that work iniquity. Every one therefore which heareth these words of mine, and doeth them, shall be likened unto a wise man, which
25 built his house upon the rock: and the rain descended, and the floods came, and the winds blew, and beat upon that house; and it fell not: for it was
26 founded upon the rock. And every one that heareth these words of mine, and doeth them not, shall be likened unto a foolish man, which built his house
27 upon the sand: and the rain descended, and the floods came, and the winds blew, and smote upon that house; and it fell: and great was the fall thereof.
28 And it came to pass, when Jesus ended these words, the multitudes were astonished at his teach-
29 ing: for he taught them as *one* having authority, and not as their scribes.

8 And when he was come down from the moun-

---

1 Some ancient authorities omit *is the gate.*
2 Many ancient authorities read *How narrow is the gate &c.*
3 Gr. *demons.*
4 Gr. *powers.*

tain, great multitudes followed him. And behold, 2
there came to him a leper and worshipped him, saying, Lord, if thou wilt, thou canst make me clean.
And he stretched forth his hand, and touched him, 3
saying, I will; be thou made clean. And straightway his leprosy was cleansed. And Jesus saith 4
unto him, See thou tell no man; but go thy way*,
shew thyself to the priest, and offer the gift that
Moses commanded, for a testimony unto them.

And when he was entered into Capernaum, there 5
came unto him a centurion, beseeching him, and 6
saying, Lord, my ¹servant lieth in the house sick of
the palsy, grievously tormented. And he saith unto 7
him, I will come and heal him. And the centurion 8
answered and said, Lord, I am not ²worthy that thou
shouldest come under my roof: but only say ³the
word, and my ¹servant shall be healed. For I also 9
am a man ⁴under authority, having under myself
soldiers: and I say to this one, Go, and he goeth;
and to another, Come, and he cometh; and to my
⁵servant, Do this, and he doeth it. And when Jesus 10
heard it, he marvelled, and said to them that followed, Verily I say unto you, ⁶I have not found so
great faith, no, not in Israel. And I say unto you, 11
that many shall come from the east and the west,
and shall ⁷sit down with Abraham, and Isaac, and
Jacob, in the kingdom of heaven: but the sons of 12
the kingdom shall be cast forth into the outer darkness: there shall be the weeping and gnashing of
teeth. And Jesus said unto the centurion, Go thy 13
way; as thou hast believed, *so* be it done unto thee.
And the ¹servant was healed in that hour.

And when Jesus was come into Peter's house, he 14
saw his wife's mother lying sick of a fever. And 15
he touched her hand, and the fever left her; and she
arose, and ministered unto him. And when even 16
was come, they brought unto him many ⁸possessed
with devils: and he cast out the spirits with a word,
and healed all that were sick: that it might be ful- 17
filled which was spoken ⁹by Isaiah the prophet,
saying, Himself took our infirmities, and bare our
diseases.

Now when Jesus saw great multitudes about him, 18
he gave commandment to depart unto the other side.
And there came ¹⁰a scribe, and said unto him, ¹¹Mas- 19

1 Or, *boy*
2 Gr. *sufficient.*
3 Gr. *with a word.*
4 Some ancient authorities insert *set: as in Luke vii. 8.*
5 Gr. *bondservant.*
6 Many ancient authorities read *With no man in Israel have I found so great faith.*
7 Gr. *recline.*
8 Or, *demoniacs*
9 Or, *through*
10 Gr. *one scribe.*
11 Or, *Teacher*

---

* Here and in Matt. xxvii. 65; Mark i. 44, for "go thy [your] way" read simply "go"—*Am. Com.*

ter, I will follow thee whithersoever thou goest.
20 And Jesus saith unto him, The foxes have holes, and the birds of the heaven *have* ¹nests; but the Son
21 of man hath not where to lay his head. And another of the disciples said unto him, Lord, suffer
22 me first to go and bury my father. But Jesus saith unto him, Follow me; and leave the dead to bury their own dead.
23 And when he was entered into a boat, his disci-
24 ples followed him. And behold, there arose a great tempest in the sea, insomuch that the boat was cov-
25 ered with the waves: but he was asleep. And they came to him, and awoke him, saying, Save, Lord;
26 we perish. And he saith unto them, Why are ye fearful, O ye of little faith? Then he arose, and rebuked the winds and the sea; and there was a great
27 calm. And the men marvelled, saying, What manner of man is this, that even the winds and the sea obey him?
28 And when he was come to the other side into the country of the Gadarenes, there met him two ²possessed with devils, coming forth out of the tombs, exceeding fierce, so that no man could pass by that
29 way. And behold, they cried out, saying, What have we to do with thee, thou Son of God? art thou
30 come hither to torment us before the time? Now there was afar off from them a herd of many swine
31 feeding. And the ³devils besought him, saying, If thou cast us out, send us away into the herd of
32 swine. And he said unto them, Go. And they came out, and went into the swine: and behold, the whole herd rushed down the steep into the sea, and
33 perished in the waters. And they that fed them fled, and went away into the city, and told every thing, and what was befallen to them that were ²pos-
34 sessed with devils. And behold, all the city came out to meet Jesus: and when they saw him, they besought *him* that he would depart from their borders.

9 And he entered into a boat, and crossed over, and
2 came into his own city. And behold, they brought to him a man sick of the palsy, lying on a bed: and Jesus seeing their faith said unto the sick of the palsy, ⁴Son, be of good cheer; thy sins are forgiven.
3 And behold, certain of the scribes said within them-
4 selves, This man blasphemeth. And Jesus ⁵knowing their thoughts said, Wherefore think ye evil in
5 your hearts? For whether is easier, to say, Thy sins

¹ Gr. *lodging-places.*

² Or, *demoniacs*

³ Gr. *demons.*

⁴ Gr. *Child.*

⁵ Many ancient authorities read *seeing.*

are forgiven; or to say, Arise, and walk? But that 6
ye may know that the Son of man hath ¹power* on
earth to forgive sins (then saith he to the sick of the
palsy), Arise, and take up thy bed, and go unto thy
house. And he arose, and departed to his house. 7
But when the multitudes saw it, they were afraid, 8
and glorified God, which had given such ¹power*
unto men.

And as Jesus passed by from thence, he saw a 9
man, called Matthew, sitting at the place of toll:
and he saith unto him, Follow me. And he arose,
and followed him.

And it came to pass, as he ²sat at meat in the 10
house, behold, many publicans and sinners came and
sat down with Jesus and his disciples. And when 11
the Pharisees saw it, they said unto his disciples,
Why eateth your ³Master with the publicans and
sinners? But when he heard it, he said, They that 12
are ⁴whole have no need of a physician, but they
that are sick. But go ye and learn what *this* mean- 13
eth, I desire mercy, and not sacrifice: for I came not
to call the righteous, but sinners.

Then come to him the disciples of John, saying, 14
Why do we and the Pharisees fast ⁵oft, but thy
disciples fast not? And Jesus said unto them, Can 15
the sons of the bride-chamber mourn, as long as the
bridegroom is with them? but the days will come,
when the bridegroom shall be taken away from
them, and then will they fast. And no man put- 16
teth a piece of undressed cloth upon an old garment;
for that which should fill it up taketh from the garment, and a worse rent is made. Neither do *men* 17
put new wine into old ⁶wine-skins: else the skins
burst, and the wine is spilled, and the skins perish:
but they put new wine into fresh wine-skins, and
both are preserved.

While he spake these things unto them, behold, 18
there came ⁷a ruler, and worshipped him, saying,
My daughter is even now dead: but come and lay
thy hand upon her, and she shall live. And Jesus 19
arose, and followed him, and *so did* his disciples.
And behold, a woman, who had an issue of blood 20
twelve years, came behind him, and touched the
border of his garment: for she said within herself, If 21
I do but touch his garment, I shall be ⁸made whole.

1 Or, *authority*
2 Gr. *reclined: and so always.*
3 Or, *Teacher*
4 Gr. *strong.*
5 Some ancient authorities omit *oft.*
6 That is, *skins used as bottles.*
7 Gr. *one ruler.*
8 Or, *saved*

---

* For "power" read "authority" (see marg. 15) So in Mark ii.
10; Luke v. 24.—*Am. Com.*

22 But Jesus turning and seeing her said, Daughter, be of good cheer; thy faith hath ¹made thee whole. And the woman was ²made whole from that hour.
23 And when Jesus came into the ruler's house, and saw the flute-players, and the crowd making a
24 tumult, he said, Give place: for the damsel is not dead, but sleepeth. And they laughed him to scorn.
25 But when the crowd was put forth, he entered in, and took her by the hand; and the damsel arose.
26 And ³the fame hereof went forth into all that land.

27 And as Jesus passed by from thence, two blind men followed him, crying out, and saying, Have
28 mercy on us, thou son of David. And when he was come into the house, the blind men came to him: and Jesus saith unto them, Believe ye that I am able
29 to do this? They say unto him, Yea, Lord. Then touched he their eyes, saying, According to your
30 faith be it done unto you. And their eyes were opened. And Jesus ⁴strictly charged them, saying,
31 See that no man know it. But they went forth, and spread abroad his fame in all that land.

32 And as they went forth, behold, there was brought
33 to him a dumb man possessed with a ⁵devil. And when the ⁵devil was cast out, the dumb man spake: and the multitudes marvelled, saying, It was never
34 so seen in Israel. But the Pharisees said, ⁶By the prince of the ⁷devils casteth he out ⁷devils.

35 And Jesus went about all the cities and the villages, teaching in their synagogues, and preaching the gospel of the kingdom, and healing all manner
36 of disease and all manner of sickness. But when he saw the multitudes, he was moved with compassion for them, because they were distressed and
37 scattered, as sheep not having a shepherd. Then saith he unto his disciples, The harvest truly is plen-
38 teous, but the labourers are few. Pray ye therefore the Lord of the harvest, that he send forth labourers
10 into his harvest. And he called unto him his twelve disciples, and gave them authority over unclean spirits, to cast them out, and to heal all manner of disease and all manner of sickness.
2 Now the names of the twelve apostles are these: The first, Simon, who is called Peter, and Andrew his brother; James the *son* of Zebedee, and John his
3 brother; Philip, and Bartholomew; Thomas, and Matthew the publican; James the *son* of Alphæus,
4 and Thaddæus; Simon the ⁸Canaanæan, and Judas

1 Or, *saved thee*
2 Or, *saved*

3 Gr. *this fame.*

4 Or, *sternly*

5 Gr. *demon.*

6 Or, *In*
7 Gr. *demons.*

8 Or, *Zealot* See Luke vi. 15; Acts i. 13.

Iscariot, who also ¹betrayed him. These twelve 5
Jesus sent forth, and charged them, saying,

Go not into *any* way of the Gentiles, and enter not
into any city of the Samaritans: but go rather to the 6
lost sheep of the house of Israel. And as ye go, 7
preach, saying, The kingdom of heaven is at hand.
Heal the sick, raise the dead, cleanse the lepers, cast 8
out ²devils: freely ye received, freely give. Get you 9
no gold, nor silver, nor brass in your ³purses; no 10
wallet for *your* journey, neither two coats, nor shoes,
nor staff: for the labourer is worthy of his food.
And into whatsoever city or village ye shall enter, 11
search out who in it is worthy; and there abide till
ye go forth. And as ye enter into the house, salute 12
it. And if the house be worthy, let your peace come 13
upon it: but if it be not worthy, let your peace return to you. And whosoever shall not receive you, 14
nor hear your words, as ye go forth out of that house
or that city, shake off the dust of your feet. Verily 15
I say unto you, It shall be more tolerable for the
land of Sodom and Gomorrah in the day of judgement, than for that city.

Behold, I send you forth as sheep in the midst of 16
wolves: be ye therefore wise as serpents, and ⁴harmless as doves. But beware of men: for they will 17
deliver you up to councils, and in their synagogues
they will scourge you; yea and before governors and 18
kings shall ye be brought for my sake, for a testimony to them and to the Gentiles. But when they 19
deliver you up, be not anxious how or what ye shall
speak: for it shall be given you in that hour what
ye shall speak. For it is not ye that speak, but the 20
Spirit of your Father that speaketh in you. And 21
brother shall deliver up brother to death, and the
father his child: and children shall rise up against
parents, and ⁵cause them to be put to death. And 22
ye shall be hated of all men for my name's sake:
but he that endureth to the end, the same shall be
saved. But when they persecute you in this city, 23
flee into the next: for verily I say unto you, Ye shall
not have gone through the cities of Israel, till the
Son of man be come.

A disciple is not above his ⁶master, nor a ⁷servant 24
above his lord. It is enough for the disciple that he 25
be as his ⁶master, and the ⁷servant as his lord. If
they have called the master of the house ⁸Beelzebub,
how much more *shall they call* them of his household! Fear them not therefore: for there is nothing 26

---

¹ Or, *delivered him up: and so always.*
² Gr. *demons.*
³ Gr. *girdles.*
⁴ Or, *simple*
⁵ Or, *put them to death*
⁶ Or, *teacher*
⁷ Gr. *bondservant.*
⁸ Gr. *Beelzebul:* and so elsewhere.

S. MATTHEW.

covered, that shall not be revealed; and hid, that
27 shall not be known. What I tell you in the darkness, speak ye in the light: and what ye hear in the
28 ear, proclaim upon the housetops. And be not afraid of them which kill the body, but are not able to kill the soul: but rather fear him which is able to destroy
29 both soul and body in ¹hell. Are not two sparrows sold for a farthing? and not one of them shall fall
30 on the ground without your Father: but the very
31 hairs of your head are all numbered. Fear not therefore; ye are of more value than many sparrows.
32 Every one therefore who shall confess ²me before men, ³him will I also confess before my Father which
33 is in heaven. But whosoever shall deny me before men, him will I also deny before my Father which is in heaven.
34 Think not that I came to ⁴send peace on the earth:
35 I came not to ⁴send peace, but a sword. For I came to set a man at variance against his father, and the daughter against her mother, and the daughter in
36 law against her mother in law: and a man's foes
37 *shall be* they of his own household. He that loveth father or mother more than me is not worthy of me: and he that loveth son or daughter more than me is
38 not worthy of me. And he that doth not take his
39 cross and follow after me, is not worthy of me. He that ⁵findeth his ⁶life* shall lose it; and he that ⁷loseth his ⁶life for my sake shall find it.
40 He that receiveth you receiveth me, and he that
41 receiveth me receiveth him that sent me. He that receiveth a prophet in the name of a prophet shall receive a prophet's reward; and he that receiveth a righteous man in the name of a righteous man shall
42 receive a righteous man's reward. And whosoever shall give to drink unto one of these little ones a cup of cold water only, in the name of a disciple, verily I say unto you, he shall in no wise lose his reward.

11 And it came to pass, when Jesus had made an end of commanding his twelve disciples, he departed thence to teach and preach in their cities.
2 Now when John heard in the prison the works of
3 the Christ, he sent by his disciples, and said unto him, Art thou he that cometh, or look we for an-
4 other? And Jesus answered and said unto them, Go your way and tell John the things which ye do

1 Gr. *Gehenna.*

2 Gr. *in me.*
3 Gr. *in him.*

4 Gr. *cast.*

5 Or, *found*
6 Or, *soul*
7 Or, *lost*

---

* "life" strike out the marg. So in xvi. 25; Mark viii. 35; Luke ix. 24; xvii. 33; John xii. 25.—*Am. Com.*

hear and see: the blind receive their sight, and the 5
lame walk, the lepers are cleansed, and the deaf
hear, and the dead are raised up, and the poor have
¹good tidings preached to them. And blessed is he, 6
whosoever shall find none occasion of stumbling in
me. And as these went their way, Jesus began to 7
say unto the multitudes concerning John, What
went ye out into the wilderness to behold? a reed
shaken with the wind? But what went ye out for 8
to see? a man clothed in soft *raiment*? Behold,
they that wear soft *raiment* are in kings' houses.
²But wherefore went ye out? to see a prophet? Yea, 9
I say unto you, and much more than a prophet. This 10
is he, of whom it is written,

    Behold, I send my messenger before thy face,
    Who shall prepare thy way before thee.

Verily I say unto you, Among them that are born 11
of women there hath not arisen a greater than John
the Baptist: yet he that is ³but little in the kingdom
of heaven is greater than he. And from the days 12
of John the Baptist until now the kingdom of heaven suffereth violence, and men of violence take it
by force. For all the prophets and the law proph- 13
esied until John. And if ye are willing to receive 14
⁴*it*, this is Elijah, which is to come. He that hath 15
ears ⁵to hear, let him hear. But whereunto shall I 16
liken this generation? It is like unto children sitting
in the marketplaces, which call unto their fellows, and 17
say, We piped unto you, and ye did not dance; we
wailed, and ye did not ⁶mourn. For John came 18
neither eating nor drinking, and they say, He hath
a ⁷devil. The Son of man came eating and drink- 19
ing, and they say, Behold, a gluttonous man, and a
winebibber, a friend of publicans and sinners! And
wisdom ⁸is justified by her ⁹works.

Then began he to upbraid the cities wherein most 20
of his ¹⁰mighty works were done, because they repented not. Woe unto thee, Chorazin! woe unto 21
thee, Bethsaida! for if the ¹⁰mighty works had been
done in Tyre and Sidon which were done in you,
they would have repented long ago in sackcloth and
ashes. Howbeit I say unto you, it shall be more tol- 22
erable for Tyre and Sidon in the day of judgement,
than for you. And thou, Capernaum, shalt thou 23
be exalted unto heaven? thou shalt ¹¹go down unto
Hades: for if the ¹⁰mighty works had been done in
Sodom which were done in thee, it would have remained until this day. Howbeit I say unto you, 24

---

1 Or, *the gospel*

2 Many ancient authorities read *But what went ye out to see? a prophet?*

3 Gr. *lesser.*

4 Or, *him*
5 Some ancient authorities omit *to hear.*

6 Gr. *beat the breast.*

7 Gr. *demon.*

8 Or, *was*
9 Many ancient authorities read *children: as in* Luke vii. 35.
10 Gr. *powers.*

11 Many ancient authorities read *be brought down.*

that it shall be more tolerable for the land of Sodom in the day of judgement, than for thee.

25 At that season Jesus answered and said, I ¹thank thee, O Father, Lord of heaven and earth, that thou didst hide these things from the wise and under-
26 standing, and didst reveal them unto babes: yea, Father, ²for so it was well-pleasing in thy sight.
27 All things have been delivered unto me of my Father: and no one knoweth the Son, save the Father; neither doth any know the Father, save the Son, and he to whomsoever the Son willeth to reveal *him*.
28 Come unto me, all ye that labour and are heavy
29 laden, and I will give you rest. Take my yoke upon you, and learn of me: for I am meek and lowly in heart: and ye shall find rest unto your souls.
30 For my yoke is easy, and my burden is light.

12 At that season Jesus went on the sabbath day through the cornfields; and his disciples were an hungred, and began to pluck ears of corn, and to
2 eat. But the Pharisees, when they saw it, said unto him, Behold, thy disciples do that which it is not
3 lawful to do upon the sabbath. But he said unto them, Have ye not read what David did, when he was
4 an hungred, and they that were with him; how he entered into the house of God, and ³did eat the shewbread, which it was not lawful for him to eat, neither for them that were with him, but only for the priests?
5 Or have ye not read in the law, how that on the sabbath day the priests in the temple profane the sab-
6 bath, and are guiltless? But I say unto you, that
7 ⁴one greater than the temple is here. But if ye had known what this meaneth, I desire mercy, and not sacrifice, ye would not have condemned the guilt-
8 less. For the Son of man is lord of the sabbath.
9 And he departed thence, and went into their syna-
10 gogue: and behold, a man having a withered hand. And they asked him, saying, Is it lawful to heal on
11 the sabbath day? that they might accuse him. And he said unto them, What man shall there be of you, that shall have one sheep, and if this fall into a pit on the sabbath day, will he not lay hold on it, and
12 lift it out? How much then is a man of more value than a sheep! Wherefore it is lawful to do good
13 on the sabbath day. Then saith he to the man, Stretch forth thy hand. And he stretched it forth;
14 and it was restored whole, as the other. But the Pharisees went out, and took counsel against him,
15 how they might destroy him. And Jesus perceiving

---

1 Or, *praise*

2 Or, *that*

3 Some ancient authorities read *they did eat.*

4 Gr. *a greater thing.*

it withdrew from thence: and many followed him; and he healed them all, and charged them that they should not make him known: that it might be fulfilled which was spoken ¹by Isaiah the prophet, saying,

> Behold, my servant whom I have chosen;
> My beloved in whom my soul is well pleased:
> I will put my Spirit upon him,
> And he shall declare judgement to the Gentiles.
> He shall not strive, nor cry aloud;
> Neither shall any one hear his voice in the streets.
> A bruised reed shall he not break,
> And smoking flax shall he not quench,
> Till he send forth judgement unto victory.
> And in his name shall the Gentiles hope.

Then was brought unto him ²one possessed with a devil, blind and dumb: and he healed him, insomuch that the dumb man spake and saw. And all the multitudes were amazed, and said, Is this the son of David*? But when the Pharisees heard it, they said, This man doth not cast out ³devils, but ⁴by Beelzebub the prince of the ³devils. And knowing their thoughts he said unto them, Every kingdom divided against itself is brought to desolation; and every city or house divided against itself shall not stand: and if Satan casteth out Satan, he is divided against himself; how then shall his kingdom stand? And if I ⁴by Beelzebub cast out ³devils, ⁴by whom do your sons cast them out? therefore shall they be your judges. But if I ⁴by the Spirit of God cast out ³devils, then is the kingdom of God come upon you. Or how can one enter into the house of the strong *man*, and spoil his goods, except he first bind the strong *man*? and then he will spoil his house. He that is not with me is against me; and he that gathereth not with me scattereth. Therefore I say unto you, Every sin and blasphemy shall be forgiven ⁵unto men†; but the blasphemy against the Spirit shall not be forgiven. And whosoever shall speak a word against the Son of man, it shall be forgiven him; but whosoever shall speak against the Holy Spirit, it shall not be forgiven him, neither in this ⁶world, nor in that which is to come. Either make the tree good, and its fruit good; or

---

Margin notes:
1 Or, *through*
2 Or, *a demoniac*
3 Gr. *demons*.
4 Or, *in*
5 Some ancient authorities read *unto you men*.
6 Or, *age*

---

* For "Is this the son of David?" read "Can this be the son of David?" [comp. John iv. 29].—*Am. Com.*
† "unto men" strike out the marg.—*Am. Com.*

make the tree corrupt, and its fruit corrupt: for
34 the tree is known by its fruit. Ye offspring of vipers, how can ye, being evil, speak good things? for out of the abundance of the heart the mouth speak-
35 eth. The good man out of his good treasure bringeth forth good things: and the evil man out of his
36 evil treasure bringeth forth evil things. And I say unto you, that every idle word that men shall speak, they shall give account thereof in the day of judge-
37 ment. For by thy words thou shalt be justified, and by thy words thou shalt be condemned.
38 Then certain of the scribes and Pharisees answered him, saying, ¹Master, we would see a sign from
39 thee. But he answered and said unto them, An evil and adulterous generation seeketh after a sign; and there shall no sign be given to it but the sign
40 of Jonah the prophet: for as Jonah was three days and three nights in the belly of the ²whale; so shall the Son of man be three days and three nights in
41 the heart of the earth. The men of Nineveh shall stand up in the judgement with this generation, and shall condemn it: for they repented at the preaching of Jonah; and behold, ³a greater than Jonah is
42 here. The queen of the south shall rise up in the judgement with this generation, and shall condemn it: for she came from the ends of the earth to hear the wisdom of Solomon; and behold, ³a greater than
43 Solomon is here. But the unclean spirit, when ⁴he is gone out of the man, passeth through waterless
44 places, seeking rest, and findeth it not. Then ⁴he saith, I will return into my house whence I came out; and when ⁴he is come, ⁴he findeth it empty,
45 swept, and garnished. Then goeth ⁴he, and taketh with ⁵himself seven other spirits more evil than ⁵himself, and they enter in and dwell there: and the last state of that man becometh worse than the first. Even so shall it be also unto this evil generation.
46 While he was yet speaking to the multitudes, behold, his mother and his brethren stood without,
47 seeking to speak to him. ⁶And one said unto him, Behold, thy mother and thy brethren stand without,
48 seeking to speak to thee. But he answered and said unto him that told him, Who is my mother?
49 and who are my brethren? And he stretched forth his hand toward his disciples, and said, Behold,
50 my mother and my brethren! For whosoever shall do the will of my Father which is in heaven, he is my brother, and sister, and mother.

1 Or, *Teacher*
2 Gr. *sea-monster.*
3 Gr. *more than.*
4 Or, *it*
5 Or, *itself*
6 Some ancient authorities omit ver. 47.

S. MATTHEW. 13. 1—

13 On that day went Jesus out of the house, and sat by the sea side. And there were gathered unto him great multitudes, so that he entered into a boat, and sat; and all the multitude stood on the beach. And he spake to them many things in parables, saying, Behold, the sower went forth to sow; and as he sowed, some *seeds* fell by the way side, and the birds came and devoured them: and others fell upon the rocky places, where they had not much earth: and straightway they sprang up, because they had no deepness of earth: and when the sun was risen, they were scorched; and because they had no root, they withered away. And others fell upon the thorns; and the thorns grew up, and choked them: and others fell upon the good ground, and yielded fruit, some a hundredfold, some sixty, some thirty. He that hath ears[1], let him hear.

And the disciples came, and said unto him, Why speakest thou unto them in parables? And he answered and said unto them, Unto you it is given to know the mysteries of the kingdom of heaven, but to them it is not given. For whosoever hath, to him shall be given, and he shall have abundance: but whosoever hath not, from him shall be taken away even that which he hath. Therefore speak I to them in parables; because seeing they see not, and hearing they hear not, neither do they understand. And unto them is fulfilled the prophecy of Isaiah, which saith,

> By hearing ye shall hear, and shall in no wise understand;
> And seeing ye shall see, and shall in no wise perceive:
> For this people's heart is waxed gross,
> And their ears are dull of hearing,
> And their eyes they have closed;
> Lest haply they should perceive with their eyes,
> And hear with their ears,
> And understand with their heart,
> And should turn again,
> And I should heal them.

But blessed are your eyes, for they see; and your ears, for they hear. For verily I say unto you, that many prophets and righteous men desired to see the things which ye see, and saw them not; and to hear the things which ye hear, and heard them not. Hear then ye the parable of the sower. When any one heareth the word of the kingdom, and understandeth

---

[1] Some ancient authorities add here, and in ver. 43, *to hear:* as in Mark iv. 9; Luke viii. 8.

it not, *then* cometh the evil *one*, and snatcheth away that which hath been sown in his heart. This is he 20 that was sown by the way side. And he that was sown upon the rocky places, this is he that heareth 21 the word, and straightway with joy receiveth it; yet hath he not root in himself, but endureth for a while; and when tribulation or persecution ariseth because 22 of the word, straightway he stumbleth. And he that was sown among the thorns, this is he that heareth the word; and the care of the ¹world, and the de- ceitfulness of riches, choke the word, and he be- 23 cometh unfruitful. And he that was sown upon the good ground, this is he that heareth the word, and understandeth it; who verily beareth fruit, and bringeth forth, some a hundredfold, some sixty, some thirty.

24 Another parable set he before them, saying, The kingdom of heaven is likened unto a man that sowed 25 good seed in his field: but while men slept, his ene- my came and sowed ²tares also among the wheat, 26 and went away. But when the blade sprang up, and brought forth fruit, then appeared the tares also. 27 And the ³servants of the householder came and said unto him, Sir, didst thou not sow good seed in thy 28 field? whence then hath it tares? And he said unto them, ⁴An enemy hath done this. And the ³servants say unto him, Wilt thou then that we go and gather 29 them up? But he saith, Nay; lest haply while ye gather up the tares, ye root up the wheat with them. 30 Let both grow together until the harvest: and in the time of the harvest I will say to the reapers, Gather up first the tares, and bind them in bundles to burn them: but gather the wheat into my barn.

31 Another parable set he before them, saying, The kingdom of heaven is like unto a grain of mustard seed, which a man took, and sowed in his field: 32 which indeed is less than all seeds; but when it is grown, it is greater than the herbs, and becometh a tree, so that the birds of the heaven come and lodge in the branches thereof.

33 Another parable spake he unto them; The king- dom of heaven is like unto leaven, which a woman took, and hid in three ⁵measures of meal, till it was all leavened.

34 All these things spake Jesus in parables unto the multitudes; and without a parable spake he noth- 35 ing unto them: that it might be fulfilled which was spoken ⁶by the prophet, saying,

1 Or, *age*

2 Or, *darnel*

3 Gr. *bondservants.*

4 Gr. *A man that is an enemy.*

5 The word in the Greek denotes the Hebrew *seah*, a measure con- taining nearly a peck and a half.

6 Or, *through*

I will open my mouth in parables;
I will utter things hidden from the foundation ¹of the world.

Then he left the multitudes, and went into the 36 house: and his disciples came unto him, saying, Explain unto us the parable of the tares of the field. And he answered and said, He that soweth the good 37 seed is the Son of man; and the field is the world; 38 and the good seed, these are the sons of the kingdom; and the tares are the sons of the evil *one*; and the 39 enemy that sowed them is the devil: and the harvest is ²the end of the world; and the reapers are angels. As therefore the tares are gathered up and burned 40 with fire; so shall it be in ²the end of the world. The Son of man shall send forth his angels, and they 41 shall gather out of his kingdom all things that cause stumbling, and them that do iniquity, and shall cast 42 them into the furnace of fire: there shall be the weeping and gnashing of teeth. Then shall the 43 righteous shine forth as the sun in the kingdom of their Father. He that hath ears, let him hear.

The kingdom of heaven is like unto a treasure 44 hidden in the field; which a man found, and hid; and ³in his joy he goeth and selleth all that he hath, and buyeth that field.

Again, the kingdom of heaven is like unto a man 45 that is a merchant seeking goodly pearls: and hav- 46 ing found one pearl of great price, he went and sold all that he had, and bought it.

Again, the kingdom of heaven is like unto a ⁴net, 47 that was cast into the sea, and gathered of every kind: which, when it was filled, they drew up on 48 the beach; and they sat down, and gathered the good into vessels, but the bad they cast away. So 49 shall it be in ²the end of the world: the angels shall come forth, and sever the wicked from among the righteous, and shall cast them into the furnace of 50 fire: there shall be the weeping and gnashing of teeth.

Have ye understood all these things? They say 51 unto him, Yea. And he said unto them, Therefore 52 every scribe who hath been made a disciple to the kingdom of heaven is like unto a man that is a householder, which bringeth forth out of his treasure things new and old.

And it came to pass, when Jesus had finished 53 these parables, he departed thence. And coming 54 into his own country he taught them in their syn-

---

¹ Many ancient authorities omit *of the world*.

² Or, *the consummation of the age*

³ Or, *for joy thereof*

⁴ Gr. *drag-net*.

agogue, insomuch that they were astonished, and
said, Whence hath this man this wisdom, and these
55 ¹mighty works? Is not this the carpenter's son? is
not his mother called Mary? and his brethren,
56 James, and Joseph, and Simon, and Judas? And
his sisters, are they not all with us? Whence then
57 hath this man all these things? And they were
²offended in him. But Jesus said unto them, A
prophet is not without honour, save in his own
58 country, and in his own house. And he did not
many ¹mighty works there because of their unbelief.

14 At that season Herod the tetrarch heard the re-
2 port concerning Jesus, and said unto his servants,
This is John the Baptist; he is risen from the dead;
3 and therefore do these powers work in him. For
Herod had laid hold on John, and bound him, and
put him in prison for the sake of Herodias, his
4 brother Philip's wife. For John said unto him, It
5 is not lawful for thee to have her. And when he
would have put him to death, he feared the multi-
6 tude, because they counted him as a prophet. But
when Herod's birthday came, the daughter of Herodias
danced in the midst, and pleased Herod.
7 Whereupon he promised with an oath to give her
8 whatsoever she should ask. And she, being put
forward by her mother, saith, Give me here in a
9 charger the head of John the Baptist. And the
king was grieved; but for the sake of his oaths, and
of them which sat at meat with him, he commanded
10 it to be given; and he sent, and beheaded John in
11 the prison. And his head was brought in a charger,
and given to the damsel: and she brought it to her
12 mother. And his disciples came, and took up the
corpse, and buried him; and they went and told
Jesus.
13 Now when Jesus heard *it*, he withdrew from
thence in a boat, to a desert place apart: and when
the multitudes heard *thereof*, they followed him ³on
14 foot from the cities. And he came forth, and saw
a great multitude, and he had compassion on them,
15 and healed their sick. And when even was come,
the disciples came to him, saying, The place is desert,
and the time is already past; send the multitudes
away, that they may go into the villages, and
16 buy themselves food. But Jesus said unto them,
They have no need to go away; give ye them to
17 eat. And they say unto him, We have here but

1 Gr. *powers*.

2 Gr. *caused to stumble*.

3 Or, *by land*

five loaves, and two fishes. And he said, Bring 18
them hither to me. And he commanded the multi- 19
tudes to ¹sit down on the grass; and he took the
five loaves, and the two fishes, and looking up to
heaven, he blessed, and brake and gave the loaves
to the disciples, and the disciples to the multitudes.
And they did all eat, and were filled: and they took 20
up that which remained over of the broken pieces,
twelve baskets full. And they that did eat were 21
about five thousand men, beside women and children.

And straightway he constrained the disciples to 22
enter into the boat, and to go before him unto the
other side, till he should send the multitudes away.
And after he had sent the multitudes away, he went 23
up into the mountain apart to pray: and when even
was come, he was there alone. But the boat ²was 24
now in the midst of the sea, distressed by the waves;
for the wind was contrary. And in the fourth 25
watch of the night he came unto them, walking
upon the sea. And when the disciples saw him 26
walking on the sea, they were troubled, saying, It
is an apparition; and they cried out for fear. But 27
straightway Jesus spake unto them, saying, Be of
good cheer; it is I; be not afraid. And Peter an- 28
swered him and said, Lord, if it be thou, bid me
come unto thee upon the waters. And he said, 29
Come. And Peter went down from the boat, and
walked upon the waters, ³to come to Jesus. But 30
when he saw the wind⁴, he was afraid; and beginning
to sink, he cried out, saying, Lord, save me.
And immediately Jesus stretched forth his hand, 31
and took hold of him, and saith unto him, O thou
of little faith, wherefore didst thou doubt? And 32
when they were gone up into the boat, the wind
ceased. And they that were in the boat worshipped 33
him, saying, Of a truth thou art the Son of God.

And when they had crossed over, they came to 34
the land, unto Gennesaret. And when the men of 35
that place knew him, they sent into all that region
round about, and brought unto him all that were
sick; and they besought him that they might only 36
touch the border of his garment: and as many as
touched were made whole.

Then there come to Jesus from Jerusalem Phari- **15**
sees and scribes, saying, Why do thy disciples trans- 2
gress the tradition of the elders? for they wash not
their hands when they eat bread. And he answered 3

---

¹ Gr. *recline.*

² Some ancient authorities read *was many furlongs distant from the land.*

³ Some ancient authorities read *and came.*

⁴ Many ancient authorities add *strong.*

and said unto them, Why do ye also transgress the commandment of God because of your tradition? 4 For God said, Honour thy father and thy mother: and, He that speaketh evil of father or mother, let 5 him ¹die the death. But ye say, Whosoever shall say to his father or his mother, That wherewith thou mightest have been profited by me is given *to God*; 6 he shall not honour his father². And ye have made void the ³word of God because of your tradition. 7 Ye hypocrites, well did Isaiah prophesy of you, saying,

8   This people honoureth me with their lips;
    But their heart is far from me.
9   But in vain do they worship me,
    Teaching *as their* doctrines the precepts of men.

10 And he called to him the multitude, and said unto 11 them, Hear, and understand: Not that which entereth into the mouth defileth the man; but that which proceedeth out of the mouth, this defileth the man. 12 Then came the disciples, and said unto him, Knowest thou that the Pharisees were ⁴offended, when they 13 heard this saying? But he answered and said, Every ⁵plant which my heavenly Father planted not, shall 14 be rooted up. Let them alone: they are blind guides. And if the blind guide the blind, both shall fall into 15 a pit. And Peter answered and said unto him, 16 Declare unto us the parable. And he said, Are ye 17 also even yet without understanding? Perceive ye not, that whatsoever goeth into the mouth passeth 18 into the belly, and is cast out into the draught? But the things which proceed out of the mouth come 19 forth out of the heart; and they defile the man. For out of the heart come forth evil thoughts, murders, adulteries, fornications, thefts, false witness, rail- 20 ings: these are the things which defile the man: but to eat with unwashen hands defileth not the man.
21 And Jesus went out thence, and withdrew into the 22 parts of Tyre and Sidon. And behold, a Canaan- itish woman came out from those borders, and cried, saying, Have mercy on me, O Lord, thou son of Da- vid; my daughter is grievously vexed with a ⁶devil. 23 But he answered her not a word. And his disciples came and besought him, saying, Send her away; for 24 she crieth after us. But he answered and said, I was not sent but unto the lost sheep of the house 25 of Israel. But she came and worshipped him, say- 26 ing, Lord, help me. And he answered and said, It is not meet to take the children's ⁷bread and cast it

1 Or, *surely die*
2 Some ancient authorities add *or his mother.*
3 Some ancient authorities read *law.*
4 Gr. *caused to stumble.*
5 Gr. *planting.*
6 Gr. *demon.*
7 Or, *loaf*

to the dogs. But she said, Yea, Lord: for even the 27 dogs eat of the crumbs which fall from their masters' table. Then Jesus answered and said unto her, O 28 woman, great is thy faith: be it done unto thee even as thou wilt. And her daughter was healed from that hour.

And Jesus departed thence, and came nigh unto 29 the sea of Galilee; and he went up into the mountain, and sat there. And there came unto him great 30 multitudes, having with them the lame, blind, dumb, maimed, and many others, and they cast them down at his feet; and he healed them: insomuch that the 31 multitude wondered, when they saw the dumb speaking, the maimed whole, and the lame walking, and the blind seeing: and they glorified the God of Israel.

And Jesus called unto him his disciples, and said, 32 I have compassion on the multitude, because they continue with me now three days and have nothing to eat: and I would not send them away fasting, lest haply they faint in the way. And the disciples 33 say unto him, Whence should we have so many loaves in a desert place, as to fill so great a multitude? And Jesus saith unto them, How many loaves 34 have ye? And they said, Seven, and a few small fishes. And he commanded the multitude to sit 35 down on the ground; and he took the seven loaves 36 and the fishes; and he gave thanks and brake, and gave to the disciples, and the disciples to the multitudes. And they did all eat, and were filled: and 37 they took up that which remained over of the broken pieces, seven baskets full. And they that did eat 38 were four thousand men, beside women and children. And he sent away the multitudes, and en- 39 tered into the boat, and came into the borders of Magadan.

And the Pharisees and Sadducees came, and **16** tempting him asked him to shew them a sign from heaven. But he answered and said unto them, 2 [1]When it is evening, ye say, *It will be* fair weather: for the heaven is red. And in the morning, *It will be* 3 foul weather to-day: for the heaven is red and lowring. Ye know how to discern the face of the heaven; but ye cannot *discern* the signs of the times. An 4 evil and adulterous generation seeketh after a sign; and there shall no sign be given unto it, but the sign of Jonah. And he left them, and departed.

And the disciples came to the other side and for- 5

---

[1] The following words, to the end of ver. 3, are omitted by some of the most ancient and other important authorities.

6 got to take ¹bread. And Jesus said unto them, Take
7 heed and beware of the leaven of the Pharisees and
Sadducees. And they reasoned among themselves,
8 saying, ²We took no ¹bread. And Jesus perceiving
it said, O ye of little faith, why reason ye among
9 yourselves, because ye have no ¹bread? Do ye not
yet perceive, neither remember the five loaves of the
five thousand, and how many ³baskets ye took up?
10 Neither the seven loaves of the four thousand, and
11 how many ³baskets ye took up? How is it that ye
do not perceive that I spake not to you concerning
¹bread? But beware of the leaven of the Pharisees
12 and Sadducees. Then understood they how that he
bade them not beware of the leaven of ¹bread, but of
the teaching of the Pharisees and Sadducees.

13 Now when Jesus came into the parts of Cæsarea
Philippi, he asked his disciples, saying, Who do men
14 say ⁴that the Son of man is? And they said, Some
say John the Baptist; some, Elijah: and others, Jer-
15 emiah, or one of the prophets. He saith unto them,
16 But who say ye that I am? And Simon Peter answered and said, Thou art the Christ, the Son of the
17 living God. And Jesus answered and said unto
him, Blessed art thou, Simon Bar-Jonah: for flesh
and blood hath not revealed it unto thee, but my
18 Father which is in heaven. And I also say unto
thee, that thou art ⁵Peter, and upon this ⁶rock I will
build my church; and the gates of Hades shall not
19 prevail against it. I will give unto thee the keys of
the kingdom of heaven: and whatsoever thou shalt
bind on earth shall be bound in heaven: and whatsoever thou shalt loose on earth shall be loosed in
20 heaven. Then charged he the disciples that they
should tell no man that he was the Christ.

21 From that time began ⁷Jesus to shew unto his disciples, how that he must go unto Jerusalem, and suffer many things of the elders and chief priests and
scribes, and be killed, and the third day be raised up.
22 And Peter took him, and began to rebuke him, saying,
⁸Be it far from thee, Lord: this shall never be unto
23 thee. But he turned, and said unto Peter, Get thee
behind me, Satan: thou art a stumblingblock unto
me: for thou mindest not the things of God, but the
24 things of men. Then said Jesus unto his disciples,
If any man would come after me, let him deny him-
25 self, and take up his cross, and follow me. For
whosoever would save his ⁹life shall lose it: and
whosoever shall lose his ⁹life for my sake shall find

1 Gr. *loaves.*

2 Or, It is *because we took no bread.*

3 *Basket* in ver. 9 and 10 represents different Greek words.

4 Many ancient authorities read *that I the Son of man am.* See Mark viii. 27; Luke ix. 18.

5 Gr. *Petros.*
6 Gr. *petra.*

7 Some ancient authorities read *Jesus Christ.*

8 Or, God have mercy on thee

9 Or, *soul*

it. For what shall a man be profited, if he shall 26 gain the whole world, and forfeit his ¹life? or what shall a man give in exchange for his ¹life? For the 27 Son of man shall come in the glory of his Father with his angels; and then shall he render unto every man according to his ²deeds. Verily I say unto 28 you, There be some of them that stand here, which shall in no wise taste of death, till they see the Son of man coming in his kingdom.

And after six days Jesus taketh with him Peter, **17** and James, and John his brother, and bringeth them up into a high mountain apart: and he was trans- 2 figured before them: and his face did shine as the sun, and his garments became white as the light. And behold, there appeared unto them Moses and 3 Elijah talking with him. And Peter answered, and 4 said unto Jesus, Lord, it is good for us to be here: if thou wilt, I will make here three ³tabernacles; one for thee, and one for Moses, and one for Elijah. While he was yet speaking, behold, a bright cloud 5 overshadowed them: and behold, a voice out of the cloud, saying, This is my beloved Son, in whom I am well pleased; hear ye him. And when the dis- 6 ciples heard it, they fell on their face, and were sore afraid. And Jesus came and touched them and said, 7 Arise, and be not afraid. And lifting up their eyes, 8 they saw no one, save Jesus only.

And as they were coming down from the moun- 9 tain, Jesus commanded them, saying, Tell the vision to no man, until the Son of man be risen from the dead. And his disciples asked him, saying, Why 10 then say the scribes that Elijah must first come? And he answered and said, Elijah indeed cometh, 11 and shall restore all things: but I say unto you, that 12 Elijah is come already, and they knew him not, but did unto him whatsoever they listed. Even so shall the Son of man also suffer of them. Then under- 13 stood the disciples that he spake unto them of John the Baptist.

And when they were come to the multitude, there 14 came to him a man, kneeling to him, and saying, Lord, have mercy on my son: for he is epileptic, 15 and suffereth grievously: for oft-times he falleth into the fire, and oft-times into the water. And I 16 brought him to thy disciples, and they could not cure him. And Jesus answered and said, O faithless 17 and perverse generation, how long shall I be with you? how long shall I bear with you? bring him

---

1 Or, *soul*

2 Gr. *doing*.

3 Or, *booths*

18 hither to me. And Jesus rebuked him; and the ¹devil went out from him: and the boy was cured
19 from that hour. Then came the disciples to Jesus
20 apart, and said, Why could not we cast it out? And he saith unto them, Because of your little faith: for verily I say unto you, If ye have faith as a grain of mustard seed, ye shall say unto this mountain, Remove hence to yonder place; and it shall remove; and nothing shall be impossible unto you.²
22 And while they ³abode in Galilee, Jesus said unto them, The Son of man shall be delivered up into the
23 hands of men; and they shall kill him, and the third day he shall be raised up. And they were exceeding sorry.
24 And when they were come to Capernaum, they that received the ⁴half-shekel came to Peter, and said,
25 Doth not your ⁵master pay the ⁴half-shekel? He saith, Yea. And when he came into the house, Jesus spake first to him, saying, What thinkest thou, Simon? the kings of the earth, from whom do they receive toll or tribute? from their sons, or from
26 strangers? And when he said, From strangers, Jesus said unto him, Therefore the sons are free.
27 But, lest we cause them to stumble, go thou to the sea, and cast a hook, and take up the fish that first cometh up; and when thou hast opened his mouth, thou shalt find a ⁶shekel: that take, and give unto them for me and thee.

¹ Gr. *demon*.

² Many authorities, some ancient, insert ver. 21 *But this kind goeth not out save by prayer and fasting.* See Mark ix. 29.

³ Some ancient authorities read *were gathering themselves together.*

⁴ Gr. *didrachma*.

⁵ Or, *teacher*

⁶ Gr. *stater*.

18 In that hour came the disciples unto Jesus, saying, Who then is ⁷greatest in the kingdom of heaven?
2 And he called to him a little child, and set him in
3 the midst of them, and said, Verily I say unto you, Except ye turn, and become as little children, ye shall in no wise enter into the kingdom of heaven.
4 Whosoever therefore shall humble himself as this little child, the same is the ⁷greatest in the kingdom
5 of heaven. And whoso shall receive one such little
6 child in my name receiveth me: but whoso shall cause one of these little ones which believe on me to stumble, it is profitable for him that ⁸a great millstone should be hanged about his neck, and *that* he
7 should be sunk in the depth of the sea. Woe unto the world because of occasions of stumbling! for it must needs be that the occasions come; but woe to
8 that man through whom the occasion cometh! And if thy hand or thy foot causeth thee to stumble, cut it off, and cast it from thee: it is good for thee to enter into life maimed or halt, rather than having

⁷ Gr. *greater*.

⁸ Gr. *a millstone turned by an ass*.

two hands or two feet to be cast into the eternal fire.
And if thine eye causeth thee to stumble, pluck it 9
out, and cast it from thee: it is good for thee to
enter into life with one eye, rather than having two
eyes to be cast into the ¹hell of fire. See that ye 10
despise not one of these little ones; for I say unto
you, that in heaven their angels do always behold
the face of my Father which is in heaven.² How 12
think ye? if any man have a hundred sheep, and
one of them be gone astray, doth he not leave the
ninety and nine, and go unto the mountains, and
seek that which goeth astray? And if so be that 13
he find it, verily I say unto you, he rejoiceth over it
more than over the ninety and nine which have not
gone astray. Even so it is not ³the will of ⁴your 14
Father which is in heaven, that one of these little
ones should perish.
And if thy brother sin ⁵against thee, go, shew him 15
his fault between thee and him alone: if he hear
thee, thou hast gained thy brother. But if he hear 16
thee not, take with thee one or two more, that at the
mouth of two witnesses or three every word may be
established. And if he refuse to hear them, tell it 17
unto the ⁶church; and if he refuse to hear the ⁶church
also, let him be unto thee as the Gentile and the publican.
Verily I say unto you, What things soever ye 18
shall bind on earth shall be bound in heaven: and
what things soever ye shall loose on earth shall be
loosed in heaven. Again I say unto you, that if two 19
of you shall agree on earth as touching anything that
they shall ask, it shall be done for them of my Father
which is in heaven. For where two or three 20
are gathered together in my name, there am I in the
midst of them.

Then came Peter, and said to him, Lord, how oft 21
shall my brother sin against me, and I forgive him?
until seven times? Jesus saith unto him, I say not 22
unto thee, Until seven times; but, Until ⁷seventy
times seven. Therefore is the kingdom of heaven 23
likened unto a certain king, which would make a
reckoning with his ⁸servants. And when he had 24
begun to reckon, one was brought unto him, which
owed him ten thousand ⁹talents. But forasmuch as 25
he had not *wherewith* to pay, his lord commanded
him to be sold, and his wife, and children, and all
that he had, and payment to be made. The ¹⁰servant 26
therefore fell down and worshipped him, saying,
Lord, have patience with me, and I will pay

---

1 Gr. *Gehenna of fire.*

2 Many authorities, some ancient, insert ver. 11 *For the Son of man came to save that which was lost.* See Luke xix. 10.

3 Gr. *a thing willed before your Father.*

4 Some ancient authorities read *my.*

5 Some ancient authorities omit *against thee.*

6 Or, *congregation*

7 Or, *seventy times and seven*

8 Gr. *bondservants.*

9 This talent was probably worth about £240.

10 Gr. *bondservant.*

27 thee all. And the lord of that ¹servant, being moved with compassion, released him, and forgave him the
28 ²debt. But that ¹servant went out, and found one of his fellow-servants, which owed him a hundred ³pence: and he laid hold on him, and took *him* by the
29 throat, saying, Pay what thou owest. So his fellow-servant fell down and besought him, saying, Have
30 patience with me, and I will pay thee. And he would not: but went and cast him into prison, till
31 he should pay that which was due. So when his fellow-servants saw what was done, they were exceeding sorry, and came and told unto their lord all
32 that was done. Then his lord called him unto him, and saith to him, Thou wicked ¹servant, I forgave thee all that debt, because thou besoughtest me:
33 shouldest not thou also have had mercy on thy fel-
34 low-servant, even as I had mercy on thee? And his lord was wroth, and delivered him to the tormentors,
35 till he should pay all that was due. So shall also my heavenly Father do unto you, if ye forgive not every one his brother from your hearts.

1 Gr. *bondservant.*
2 Gr. *loan.*
3 The word in the Greek denotes a coin worth about eight pence halfpenny.

19 And it came to pass when Jesus had finished these words, he departed from Galilee, and came into the
2 borders of Judæa beyond Jordan; and great multitudes followed him; and he healed them there.
3 And there came unto him ⁴Pharisees, tempting him, and saying, Is it lawful *for a man* to put away
4 his wife for every cause? And he answered and said, Have ye not read, that he which ⁵made *them* from the beginning made them male and female,
5 and said, For this cause shall a man leave his father and mother, and shall cleave to his wife; and the
6 twain shall become one flesh? So that they are no more twain, but one flesh. What therefore God
7 hath joined together, let not man put asunder. They say unto him, Why then did Moses command to give
8 a bill of divorcement, and to put *her* away? He saith unto them, Moses for your hardness of heart suffered you to put away your wives: but from the begin-
9 ning it hath not been so. And I say unto you, Whosoever shall put away his wife, ⁶except for fornication, and shall marry another, committeth adultery: ⁷and he that marrieth her when she is put away
10 committeth adultery. The disciples say unto him, If the case of the man is so with his wife, it is not
11 expedient to marry. But he said unto them, All men cannot receive this saying, but they to whom it
12 is given. For there are eunuchs, which were so

4 Many authorities, some ancient, insert *the.*

5 Some ancient authorities read *created.*

6 Some ancient authorities read *saving for the cause of fornication, maketh her an adulteress:* as in ch. v. 32.

7 The following words, to the end of the verse, are omitted by some ancient authorities.

born from their mother's womb: and there are
eunuchs, which were made eunuchs by men: and
there are eunuchs, which made themselves eunuchs
for the kingdom of heaven's sake. He that is able
to receive it, let him receive it.

Then were there brought unto him little children, 13
that he should lay his hands on them, and pray: and
the disciples rebuked them. But Jesus said, Suffer 14
the little children, and forbid them not, to come unto
me: for of such is* the kingdom of heaven. And he 15
laid his hands on them, and departed thence.

> 1 Or, *Teacher*
> 2 Some ancient authorities read *Good Master.* See Mark x. 17; Luke xviii. 18.
> 3 Some ancient authorities read *Why callest thou me good? None is good save one, even God.* See Mark x. 18; Luke xviii. 19.

And behold, one came to him and said, [1,2]Master, 16
what good thing shall I do, that I may have eternal
life? And he said unto him, [3]Why askest thou me 17
concerning that which is good? One there is who
is good: but if thou wouldest enter into life, keep
the commandments. He saith unto him, Which? 18
And Jesus said, Thou shalt not kill, Thou shalt not
commit adultery, Thou shalt not steal, Thou shalt
not bear false witness, Honour thy father and thy 19
mother: and, Thou shalt love thy neighbour as thyself.
The young man saith unto him, All these 20
things have I observed: what lack I yet? Jesus 21
said unto him, If thou wouldest be perfect, go, sell
that thou hast, and give to the poor, and thou shalt
have treasure in heaven: and come, follow me. But 22
when the young man heard the saying, he went away
sorrowful: for he was one that had great possessions.

And Jesus said unto his disciples, Verily I say 23
unto you, It is hard for a rich man to enter into the
kingdom of heaven. And again I say unto you, It 24
is easier for a camel to go through a needle's eye,
than for a rich man to enter into the kingdom of
God. And when the disciples heard it, they were 25
astonished exceedingly, saying, Who then can be
saved? And Jesus looking upon *them* said to them, 26
With men this is impossible; but with God all things
are possible. Then answered Peter and said unto 27
him, Lo, we have left all, and followed thee; what
then shall we have? And Jesus said unto them, 28
Verily I say unto you, that ye which have followed
me, in the regeneration when the Son of man shall
sit on the throne of his glory, ye also shall sit upon
twelve thrones, judging the twelve tribes of Israel.

---

* For "of such is" read "to such belongeth" with marg. Or, *of such is* So in Mark x. 14; Luke xviii. 16.—*Am. Com.*

29 And every one that hath left houses, or brethren, or sisters, or father, or mother,[1] or children, or lands, for my name's sake, shall receive [2]a hundredfold, 30 and shall inherit eternal life. But many shall be last *that are* first; and first *that are* last. **20** For the kingdom of heaven is like unto a man that is* a householder, which went out early in the morning 2 to hire labourers into his vineyard. And when he had agreed with the labourers for a [3]penny a day, 3 he sent them into his vineyard. And he went out about the third hour, and saw others standing in the 4 marketplace idle; and to them he said, Go ye also into the vineyard, and whatsoever is right I will 5 give you. And they went their way. Again he went out about the sixth and the ninth hour, and 6 did likewise. And about the eleventh *hour* he went out, and found others standing; and he saith unto 7 them, Why stand ye here all the day idle? They say unto him, Because no man hath hired us. He 8 saith unto them, Go ye also into the vineyard. And when even was come, the lord of the vineyard saith unto his steward, Call the labourers, and pay them their hire, beginning from the last unto the first. 9 And when they came that *were hired* about the eleventh hour, they received every man a [3]penny. 10 And when the first came, they supposed that they would receive more; and they likewise received 11 every man a [3]penny. And when they received it, they murmured against the householder, saying, 12 These last have spent *but* one hour, and thou hast made them equal unto us, which have borne the 13 burden of the day and the [4]scorching heat. But he answered and said to one of them, Friend, I do thee no wrong: didst not thou agree with me for a 14 [3]penny? Take up that which is thine, and go thy way; it is my will to give unto this last, even as 15 unto thee. Is it not lawful for me to do what I will with mine own? or is thine eye evil, because I am 16 good? So the last shall be first, and the first last.

17 And as Jesus was going up to Jerusalem, he took the twelve disciples apart, and in the way he said 18 unto them, Behold, we go up to Jerusalem; and the Son of man shall be delivered unto the chief priests and scribes; and they shall condemn him to death, 19 and shall deliver him unto the Gentiles to mock,

[1] Many ancient authorities add *or wife*: as in Luke xviii. 29.
[2] Some ancient authorities read *manifold*.
[3] See marginal note on ch. xviii. 28.
[4] Or, *hot wind*

---

* For "that is" read "that was"—*Am. Com.*

and to scourge, and to crucify: and the third day he shall be raised up.

20 Then came to him the mother of the sons of Zebedee with her sons, worshipping *him*, and asking a certain thing of him. 21 And he said unto her, What wouldest thou? She saith unto him, Command that these my two sons may sit, one on thy right hand, and one on thy left hand, in thy kingdom. 22 But Jesus answered and said, Ye know not what ye ask. Are ye able to drink the cup that I am about to drink? They say unto him, We are able. 23 He saith unto them, My cup indeed ye shall drink: but to sit on my right hand, and on *my* left hand, is not mine to give, but *it is for them* for whom it hath been prepared of my Father. 24 And when the ten heard it, they were moved with indignation concerning the two brethren. 25 But Jesus called them unto him, and said, Ye know that the rulers of the Gentiles lord it over them, and their great ones exercise authority over them. 26 Not so shall it be among you: but whosoever would become great among you shall be your ¹minister; 27 and whosoever would be first among you shall be your ²servant: 28 even as the Son of man came not to be ministered unto, but to minister, and to give his life a ransom for many.

29 And as they went out from Jericho, a great multitude followed him. 30 And behold, two blind men sitting by the way side, when they heard that Jesus was passing by, cried out, saying, Lord, have mercy on us, thou son of David. 31 And the multitude rebuked them, that they should hold their peace: but they cried out the more, saying, Lord, have mercy on us, thou son of David. 32 And Jesus stood still, and called them, and said, What will ye that I should do unto you? 33 They say unto him, Lord, that our eyes may be opened. 34 And Jesus, being moved with compassion, touched their eyes: and straightway they received their sight, and followed him.

21 And when they drew nigh unto Jerusalem, and came unto Bethphage, unto the mount of Olives, then Jesus sent two disciples, 2 saying unto them, Go into the village that is over against you, and straightway ye shall find an ass tied, and a colt with her: loose *them*, and bring *them* unto me. 3 And if any one say aught unto you, ye shall say, The Lord hath need of them; and straightway he will send

---

¹ Or, *servant*
² Gr. *bondservant*.

4 them. Now this is come to pass, that it might be
fulfilled which was spoken ¹by the prophet, saying,   1 Or, *through*
5   Tell ye the daughter of Zion,
   Behold, thy King cometh unto thee,
   Meek, and riding upon an ass,
   And upon a colt the foal of an ass.
6 And the disciples went, and did even as Jesus ap-
7 pointed them, and brought the ass, and the colt, and
put on them their garments; and he sat thereon.
8 And the most part of the multitude spread their
garments in the way; and others cut branches from
9 the trees, and spread them in the way. And the
multitudes that went before him, and that followed,
cried, saying, Hosanna to the son of David: Blessed
is he that cometh in the name of the Lord; Hosanna
10 in the highest. And when he was come into Jerusalem, all the city was stirred, saying, Who is this?
11 And the multitudes said, This is the prophet, Jesus,
from Nazareth of Galilee.
12 And Jesus entered into the temple ²of God, and   2 Many ancient authorities omit *of God*.
cast out all them that sold and bought in the tem-
ple, and overthrew the tables of the money-changers,
13 and the seats of them that sold the doves; and he
saith unto them, It is written, My house shall be
called a house of prayer: but ye make it a den of
14 robbers. And the blind and the lame came to him
15 in the temple: and he healed them. But when the
chief priests and the scribes saw the wonderful
things that he did, and the children that were crying in the temple and saying, Hosanna to the son
16 of David; they were moved with indignation, and
said unto him, Hearest thou what these are saying?
And Jesus saith unto them, Yea: did ye never read,
   Out of the mouth of babes and sucklings thou hast
17   perfected praise? And he left them, and went forth
out of the city to Bethany, and lodged there.
18 Now in the morning as he returned to the city, he
19 hungered. And seeing ³a fig tree by the way side,   3 Or, *a single*
he came to it, and found nothing thereon, but leaves
only; and he saith unto it, Let there be no fruit from
thee henceforward for ever. And immediately the
20 fig tree withered away. And when the disciples
saw it, they marvelled, saying, How did the fig tree
21 immediately wither away? And Jesus answered
and said unto them, Verily I say unto you, If ye
have faith, and doubt not, ye shall not only do what
is done to the fig tree, but even if ye shall say unto
this mountain, Be thou taken up and cast into the

sea, it shall be done. And all things, whatsoever 22
ye shall ask in prayer, believing, ye shall receive.

And when he was come into the temple, the chief 23
priests and the elders of the people came unto him
as he was teaching, and said, By what authority
doest thou these things? and who gave thee this authority? And Jesus answered and said unto them, I 24
¹ Gr. *word*.   also will ask you one ¹question, which if ye tell me, I
likewise will tell you by what authority I do these
things. The baptism of John, whence was it? from 25
heaven or from men? And they reasoned with
themselves, saying, If we shall say, From heaven;
he will say unto us, Why then did ye not believe
him? But if we shall say, From men; we fear the 26
multitude; for all hold John as a prophet. And 27
they answered Jesus, and said, We know not. He
also said unto them, Neither tell I you by what
authority I do these things. But what think ye? A 28
man had two sons; and he came to the first, and
² Gr. *Child*.   said, ²Son, go work to-day in the vineyard. And 29
he answered and said, I will not: but afterward he
repented himself, and went. And he came to the 30
second, and said likewise. And he answered and
said, I *go*, sir: and went not. Whether of the 31
twain did the will of his father? They say, The
first. Jesus saith unto them, Verily I say unto you,
that the publicans and the harlots go into the kingdom of God before you. For John came unto you 32
in the way of righteousness, and ye believed him
not: but the publicans and the harlots believed him:
and ye, when ye saw it, did not even repent yourselves afterward, that ye might believe him.

Hear another parable: There was a man that was 33
a householder, which planted a vineyard, and set a
hedge about it, and digged a winepress in it, and
built a tower, and let it out to husbandmen, and
went into another country. And when the season 34
³ Gr. *bondservants*.   of the fruits drew near, he sent his ³servants to the
⁴ Or, *the fruits of it*   husbandmen, to receive ⁴his fruits. And the hus- 35
bandmen took his ³servants, and beat one, and killed
another, and stoned another. Again, he sent other 36
³servants more than the first: and they did unto
them in like manner. But afterward he sent unto 37
them his son, saying, They will reverence my son.
But the husbandmen, when they saw the son, said 38
among themselves, This is the heir; come, let us kill
him, and take his inheritance. And they took him, 39
and cast him forth out of the vineyard, and killed

40 him. When therefore the lord of the vineyard shall come, what will he do unto those husband-
41 men? They say unto him, He will miserably destroy those miserable men, and will let out the vineyard unto other husbandmen, which shall render
42 him the fruits in their seasons. Jesus saith unto them, Did ye never read in the scriptures,

The stone which the builders rejected,
The same was made the head of the corner:
This was from the Lord,
And it is marvellous in our eyes?

43 Therefore say I unto you, The kingdom of God shall be taken away from you, and shall be given
44 to a nation bringing forth the fruits thereof. [1]And he that falleth on this stone shall be broken to pieces: but on whomsoever it shall fall, it will scat-
45 ter him as dust. And when the chief priests and the Pharisees heard his parables, they perceived that
46 he spake of them. And when they sought to lay hold on him, they feared the multitudes, because they took him for a prophet.

22 And Jesus answered and spake again in parables
2 unto them, saying, The kingdom of heaven is likened unto a certain king, which made a marriage feast
3 for his son, and sent forth his [2]servants to call them that were bidden to the marriage feast: and they
4 would not come. Again he sent forth other [2]servants, saying, Tell them that are bidden, Behold, I have made ready my dinner: my oxen and my fatlings are killed, and all things are ready: come to
5 the marriage feast. But they made light of it, and went their ways, one to his own farm, another to his
6 merchandise: and the rest laid hold on his [2]servants, and entreated them shamefully, and killed them.
7 But the king was wroth; and he sent his armies, and destroyed those murderers, and burned their
8 city. Then saith he to his [2]servants, The wedding is ready, but they that were bidden were not worthy.
9 Go ye therefore unto the partings of the highways, and as many as ye shall find, bid to the marriage
10 feast. And those [2]servants went out into the highways, and gathered together all as many as they found, both bad and good: and the wedding was
11 filled with guests. But when the king came in to behold the guests, he saw there a man which had
12 not on a wedding-garment: and he saith unto him, Friend, how camest thou in hither not having a
13 wedding-garment? And he was speechless. Then

[1] Some ancient authorities omit ver. 44.

[2] Gr. *bondservants*.

the king said to the ¹servants, Bind him hand and foot, and cast him out into the outer darkness; there shall be the weeping and gnashing of teeth. For many are called, but few chosen.

Then went the Pharisees, and took counsel how they might ensnare him in *his* talk. And they send to him their disciples, with the Herodians, saying, ²Master, we know that thou art true, and teachest the way of God in truth, and carest not for any one: for thou regardest not the person of men. Tell us therefore, What thinkest thou? Is it lawful to give tribute unto Cæsar, or not? But Jesus perceived their wickedness, and said, Why tempt ye me, ye hypocrites? Shew me the tribute money. And they brought unto him a ³penny. And he saith unto them, Whose is this image and superscription? They say unto him, Cæsar's. Then saith he unto them, Render therefore unto Cæsar the things that are Cæsar's; and unto God the things that are God's. And when they heard it, they marvelled, and left him, and went their way.

On that day there came to him Sadducees, ⁴which say that there is no resurrection: and they asked him, saying, ²Master, Moses said, If a man die, having no children, his brother ⁵shall marry his wife, and raise up seed unto his brother. Now there were with us seven brethren: and the first married and deceased, and having no seed left his wife unto his brother; in like manner the second also, and the third, unto the ⁶seventh. And after them all the woman died. In the resurrection therefore whose wife shall she be of the seven? for they all had her. But Jesus answered and said unto them, Ye do err, not knowing the scriptures, nor the power of God. For in the resurrection they neither marry, nor are given in marriage, but are as angels⁷ in heaven. But as touching the resurrection of the dead, have ye not read that which was spoken unto you by God, saying, I am the God of Abraham, and the God of Isaac, and the God of Jacob? God is not *the God* of the dead, but of the living. And when the multitudes heard it, they were astonished at his teaching.

But the Pharisees, when they heard that he had put the Sadducees to silence, gathered themselves together. And one of them, a lawyer, asked him a

---

Marginal notes:
1 Or, *ministers*
2 Or, *Teacher*
3 See marginal note on ch. xviii. 28.
4 Gr. *saying.**
5 Gr. *shall perform the duty of a husband's brother to his wife.* Compare Deut. xxv. 5.
6 Gr. *seven.*
7 Many ancient authorities add *of God.*

* For marg. ⁴ read "Many ancient authorities read *saying.*"—*Am. Com.*

36 question, tempting him, ¹Master, which is the great
37 commandment in the law? And he said unto him,
Thou shalt love the Lord thy God with all thy
38 heart, and with all thy soul, and with all thy mind.
39 This is the great and first commandment. ²And a
second like *unto it* is this, Thou shalt love thy
40 neighbour as thyself. On these two commandments hangeth the whole law, and the prophets.
41 Now while the Pharisees were gathered together,
42 Jesus asked them a question, saying, What think ye
of the Christ? whose son is he? They say unto
43 him, *The son* of David. He saith unto them, How
then doth David in the Spirit call him Lord, saying,
44 The Lord said unto my Lord,
Sit thou on my right hand,
Till I put thine enemies underneath thy feet?
45 If David then calleth him Lord, how is he his son?
46 And no one was able to answer him a word, neither durst any man from that day forth ask him any more questions.

¹ Or, *Teacher*
² Or, *And a second is like unto it, Thou shalt love &c.*

23

Then spake Jesus to the multitudes and to his
2 disciples, saying, The scribes and the Pharisees sit
3 on Moses' seat: all things therefore whatsoever they
bid you, *these* do and observe: but do not ye after
4 their works; for they say, and do not. Yea, they
bind heavy burdens ³and grievous to be borne, and
lay them on men's shoulders; but they themselves
5 will not move them with their finger. But all their
works they do for to be seen of men: for they make
broad their phylacteries, and enlarge the borders *of*
6 *their garments*, and love the chief place at feasts,
7 and the chief seats in the synagogues, and the salutations in the marketplaces, and to be called of men,
8 Rabbi. But be not ye called Rabbi: for one is your
9 teacher, and all ye are brethren. And call no man
your father on the earth: for one is your Father,
10 ⁴which is in heaven.* Neither be ye called masters:
11 for one is your master, *even* the Christ. But he that
12 is ⁵greatest among you shall be your ⁶servant. And
whosoever shall exalt himself shall be humbled;
and whosoever shall humble himself shall be exalted.
13 But woe unto you, scribes and Pharisees, hypocrites! because ye shut the kingdom of heaven

³ Many ancient authorities omit *and grievous to be borne*.

⁴ Gr. *the heavenly*.
⁵ Gr. *greater*.
⁶ Or, *minister*

---

* For "Father, which is in heaven" read "Father, *even* he who is in heaven"—*Am. Com.*

¹against men: for ye enter not in yourselves, neither suffer ye them that are entering in to enter.²

Woe unto you, scribes and Pharisees, hypocrites! 15 for ye compass sea and land to make one proselyte; and when he is become so, ye make him twofold more a son of ³hell than yourselves.

Woe unto you, ye blind guides, which say, Who- 16 soever shall swear by the ⁴temple, it is nothing; but whosoever shall swear by the gold of the ⁴temple, he is ⁵a debtor. Ye fools and blind: for whether is 17 greater, the gold, or the ⁴temple that hath sanctified the gold? And, Whosoever shall swear by the al- 18 tar, it is nothing; but whosoever shall swear by the gift that is upon it, he is ⁵a debtor. Ye blind: for 19 whether is greater, the gift, or the altar that sanctifieth the gift? He therefore that sweareth by the 20 altar, sweareth by it, and by all things thereon. And 21 he that sweareth by the ⁴temple, sweareth by it, and by him that dwelleth therein. And he that swear- 22 eth by the heaven, sweareth by the throne of God, and by him that sitteth thereon.

Woe unto you, scribes and Pharisees, hypocrites! 23 for ye tithe mint and ⁶anise and cummin, and have left undone the weightier matters of the law, judgement*, and mercy, and faith: but these ye ought to have done, and not to have left the other undone. Ye blind guides, which strain out the gnat, and swal- 24 low the camel.

Woe unto you, scribes and Pharisees, hypocrites! 25 for ye cleanse the outside of the cup and of the platter, but within they are full from extortion and excess. Thou blind Pharisee, cleanse first the inside 26 of the cup and of the platter, that the outside thereof may become clean also.

Woe unto you, scribes and Pharisees, hypocrites! 27 for ye are like unto whited sepulchres, which outwardly appear beautiful, but inwardly are full of dead men's bones, and of all uncleanness. Even so 28 ye also outwardly appear righteous unto men, but inwardly ye are full of hypocrisy and iniquity.

Woe unto you, scribes and Pharisees, hypocrites! 29 for ye build the sepulchres of the prophets, and garnish the tombs of the righteous, and say, If we had 30 been in the days of our fathers, we should not have been partakers with them in the blood of the prophets. Wherefore ye witness to yourselves, that ye are 31

Marginal notes:
1 Gr. *before*.
2 Some authorities insert here, or after ver. 12, ver. 14 *Woe unto you, scribes and Pharisees, hypocrites! for ye devour widows' houses, even while for a pretence ye make long prayers: therefore ye shall receive greater condemnation.* See Mark xii. 40; Luke xx. 47.
3 Gr. *Gehenna*.
4 Or, *sanctuary*: as in ver. 35.
5 Or, *bound by his oath*
6 Or, *dill*

---

* For "judgement" read "justice" So in Luke xi. 42.—*Am. Com.*

32 sons of them that slew the prophets. Fill ye up then
33 the measure of your fathers. Ye serpents, ye offspring of vipers, how shall ye escape the judgement
34 of ¹hell? Therefore, behold, I send unto you prophets, and wise men, and scribes: some of them shall ye kill and crucify; and some of them shall ye scourge in your synagogues, and persecute from city to city:
35 that upon you may come all the righteous blood shed on the earth, from the blood of Abel the righteous unto the blood of Zachariah son of Barachiah, whom
36 ye slew between the sanctuary and the altar. Verily I say unto you, All these things shall come upon this generation.
37 O Jerusalem, Jerusalem, which killeth the prophets, and stoneth them that are sent unto her! how often would I have gathered thy children together, even as a hen gathereth her chickens under her
38 wings, and ye would not! Behold, your house is
39 left unto you ²desolate. For I say unto you, Ye shall not see me henceforth, till ye shall say, Blessed *is* he that cometh in the name of the Lord.

1 Gr. *Gehenna*.

2 Some ancient authorities omit *desolate*.

24 And Jesus went out from the temple, and was going on his way; and his disciples came to him to
2 shew him the buildings of the temple. But he answered and said unto them, See ye not all these things? verily I say unto you, There shall not be left here one stone upon another, that shall not be thrown down.
3 And as he sat on the mount of Olives, the disciples came unto him privately, saying, Tell us, when shall these things be? and what *shall be* the sign of
4 thy ³coming, and of ⁴the end of the world? And Jesus answered and said unto them, Take heed that
5 no man lead you astray. For many shall come in my name, saying, I am the Christ; and shall lead
6 many astray. And ye shall hear of wars and rumours of wars: see that ye be not troubled: for *these things* must needs come to pass; but the end is not
7 yet. For nation shall rise against nation, and kingdom against kingdom: and there shall be famines
8 and earthquakes in divers places. But all these
9 things are the beginning of travail. Then shall they deliver you up unto tribulation, and shall kill you: and ye shall be hated of all the nations for my name's
10 sake. And then shall many stumble, and shall deliver up one another, and shall hate one another.
11 And many false prophets shall arise, and shall lead
12 many astray. And because iniquity shall be multi-

3 Gr. *presence*.

4 Or, *the consummation of the age*

plied, the love of the many shall wax cold. But he 13
that endureth to the end, the same shall be saved.
And ¹this gospel of the kingdom shall be preached 14
in the whole ²world for a testimony unto all the nations; and then shall the end come.

When therefore ye see the abomination of desola- 15
tion, which was spoken of ³by Daniel the prophet,
standing in ⁴the holy place (let him that readeth understand), then let them that are in Judæa flee unto 16
the mountains: let him that is on the housetop not 17
go down to take out the things that are in his house:
and let him that is in the field not return back to 18
take his cloke. But woe unto them that are with 19
child and to them that give suck in those days! And 20
pray ye that your flight be not in the winter, neither
on a sabbath: for then shall be great tribulation, 21
such as hath not been from the beginning of the
world until now, no, nor ever shall be. And except 22
those days had been shortened, no flesh would have
been saved: but for the elect's sake those days shall
be shortened. Then if any man shall say unto you, 23
Lo, here is the Christ, or, Here; believe ⁵*it* not. For 24
there shall arise false Christs, and false prophets,
and shall shew great signs and wonders; so as to
lead astray, if possible, even the elect. Behold, I 25
have told you beforehand. If therefore they shall 26
say unto you, Behold, he is in the wilderness; go not
forth: Behold, he is in the inner chambers; believe
⁶*it* not. For as the lightning cometh forth from the 27
east, and is seen even unto the west; so shall be the
⁷coming of the Son of man. Wheresoever the car- 28
case is, there will the ⁸eagles be gathered together.

But immediately, after the tribulation of those 29
days, the sun shall be darkened, and the moon shall
not give her light, and the stars shall fall from heaven, and the powers of the heavens shall be shaken:
and then shall appear the sign of the Son of man in 30
heaven: and then shall all the tribes of the earth
mourn, and they shall see the Son of man coming on
the clouds of heaven with power and great glory.
And he shall send forth his angels ⁹with ¹⁰a great 31
sound of a trumpet, and they shall gather together
his elect from the four winds, from one end of
heaven to the other.

Now from the fig tree learn her parable: when her 32
branch is now become tender, and putteth forth its
leaves, ye know that the summer is nigh; even so 33
ye also, when ye see all these things, know ye that

---

1 Or, *these good tidings*
2 Gr. *inhabited earth.*
3 Or, *through*
4 Or, *a holy place*
5 Or, *him*
6 Or, *them*
7 Gr. *presence.*
8 Or, *vultures*
9 Many ancient authorities read *with a great trumpet, and they shall gather &c.*
10 Or, *a trumpet of great sound*

34 he is nigh, *even* at the doors. Verily I say unto
35 you, This generation shall not pass away, till all these things be accomplished. Heaven and earth shall pass away, but my words shall not pass away.
36 But of that day and hour knoweth no one, not even
37 the angels of heaven, ²neither the Son, but the Father only. And as *were* the days of Noah, so shall
38 be the ³coming of the Son of man. For as in those days which were before the flood they were eating and drinking, marrying and giving in marriage, un-
39 til the day that Noah entered into the ark, and they knew not until the flood came, and took them all away; so shall be the ³coming of the Son of man.
40 Then shall two men be in the field; one is taken,
41 and one is left: two women *shall be* grinding at the
42 mill; one is taken, and one is left. Watch therefore: for ye know not on what day your Lord com-
43 eth. ⁴But know this, that if the master of the house had known in what watch the thief was coming, he would have watched, and would not have suffered
44 his house to be ⁵broken through. Therefore be ye also ready: for in an hour that ye think not the Son
45 of man cometh. Who then is the faithful and wise ⁶servant, whom his lord hath set over his household,
46 to give them their food in due season? Blessed is that ⁶servant, whom his lord when he cometh shall
47 find so doing. Verily I say unto you, that he will
48 set him over all that he hath. But if that evil ⁶ser-
49 vant shall say in his heart, My lord tarrieth; and shall begin to beat his fellow-servants, and shall eat
50 and drink with the drunken; the lord of that ⁶servant shall come in a day when he expecteth not, and
51 in an hour when he knoweth not, and shall ⁷cut him asunder, and appoint his portion with the hypocrites: there shall be the weeping and gnashing of teeth.

25 Then shall the kingdom of heaven be likened unto ten virgins, which took their ⁸lamps, and went
2 forth to meet the bridegroom. And five of them
3 were foolish, and five were wise. For the foolish, when they took their ⁸lamps, took no oil with them:
4 but the wise took oil in their vessels with their
5 ⁸lamps. Now while the bridegroom tarried, they all
6 slumbered and slept. But at midnight there is a cry, Behold, the bridegroom! Come ye forth to
7 meet him. Then all those virgins arose, and trimmed
8 their ⁸lamps. And the foolish said unto the wise, Give us of your oil; for our ⁸lamps are going out.

¹ Or, *it*
² Many authorities, some ancient, omit *neither the Son.*
³ Gr. *presence.*
⁴ Or, *But this ye know*
⁵ Gr. *digged through.*
⁶ Gr. *bondservant.*
⁷ Or, *severely scourge him*
⁸ Or, *torches*

But the wise answered, saying, Peradventure there 9
will not be enough for us and you: go ye rather to
them that sell, and buy for yourselves. And while 10
they went away to buy, the bridegroom came; and
they that were ready went in with him to the marriage feast: and the door was shut. Afterward 11
come also the other virgins, saying, Lord, Lord, open
to us. But he answered and said, Verily I say unto 12
you, I know you not. Watch therefore, for ye know 13
not the day nor the hour.

 For *it is* as *when* a man, going into another coun- 14
try, called his own ¹servants, and delivered unto
them his goods. And unto one he gave five talents, 15
to another two, to another one; to each according
to his several ability; and he went on his journey.
Straightway he that received the five talents went 16
and traded with them, and made other five talents.
In like manner he also that *received* the two gained 17
other two. But he that received the one went away 18
and digged in the earth, and hid his lord's money.
Now after a long time the lord of those ¹servants 19
cometh, and maketh a reckoning with them. And 20
he that received the five talents came and brought
other five talents, saying, Lord, thou deliveredst
unto me five talents: lo, I have gained other five
talents. His lord said unto him, Well done, good 21
and faithful ²servant: thou hast been faithful over
a few things, I will set thee over many things: enter
thou into the joy of thy lord. And he also that 22
received the two talents came and said, Lord, thou
deliveredst unto me two talents: lo, I have gained
other two talents. His lord said unto him, Well 23
done, good and faithful ²servant; thou hast been
faithful over a few things, I will set thee over many
things: enter thou into the joy of thy lord. And 24
he also that had received the one talent came and
said, Lord, I knew thee that thou art a hard man,
reaping where thou didst not sow, and gathering
where thou didst not scatter: and I was afraid, and 25
went away and hid thy talent in the earth: lo, thou
hast thine own. But his lord answered and said 26
unto him, Thou wicked and slothful ²servant, thou
knewest that I reap where I sowed not, and gather
where I did not scatter; thou oughtest therefore to 27
have put my money to the bankers, and at my coming I should have received back mine own with interest. Take ye away therefore the talent from him, 28
and give it unto him that hath the ten talents. For 29

1 Gr. *bondservants.*

2 Gr. *bondservant.*

unto every one that hath shall be given, and he shall have abundance: but from him that hath not, even
30 that which he hath shall be taken away. And cast ye out the unprofitable ¹servant into the outer darkness: there shall be the weeping and gnashing of teeth.

¹ Gr. *bondservant.*

31 But when the Son of man shall come in his glory, and all the angels with him, then shall he sit on the
32 throne of his glory: and before him shall be gathered all the nations: and he shall separate them one from another, as the shepherd separateth the sheep
33 from the ²goats: and he shall set the sheep on his
34 right hand, but the ²goats on the left. Then shall the King say unto them on his right hand, Come, ye blessed of my Father, inherit the kingdom prepared for you from the foundation of the world:
35 for I was an hungred, and ye gave me meat: I was thirsty, and ye gave me drink: I was a stranger,
36 and ye took me in; naked, and ye clothed me: I was sick, and ye visited me: I was in prison, and
37 ye came unto me. Then shall the righteous answer him, saying, Lord, when saw we thee an hungred,
38 and fed thee? or athirst, and gave thee drink? And when saw we thee a stranger, and took thee in? or
39 naked, and clothed thee? And when saw we thee
40 sick, or in prison, and came unto thee? And the King shall answer and say unto them, Verily I say unto you, Inasmuch as ye did it unto one of these my brethren, *even* these least, ye did it unto me.
41 Then shall he say also unto them on the left hand, ³Depart from me, ye cursed, into the eternal fire
42 which is prepared for the devil and his angels: for I was an hungred, and ye gave me no meat: I was
43 thirsty, and ye gave me no drink: I was a stranger, and ye took me not in; naked, and ye clothed me not; sick, and in prison, and ye visited me not.
44 Then shall they also answer, saying, Lord, when saw we thee an hungred, or athirst, or a stranger, or naked, or sick, or in prison, and did not minister
45 unto thee? Then shall he answer them, saying, Verily I say unto you, Inasmuch as ye did it not
46 unto one of these least, ye did it not unto me. And these shall go away into eternal punishment: but the righteous into eternal life.

² Gr. *kids.*

³ Or, *Depart from me under a curse*

26 And it came to pass, when Jesus had finished all
2 these words, he said unto his disciples, Ye know that after two days the passover cometh, and the
3 Son of man is delivered up to be crucified. Then

were gathered together the chief priests, and the elders of the people, unto the court of the high priest, who was called Caiaphas; and they took counsel together that they might take Jesus by subtilty, and kill him. But they said, Not during the feast, lest a tumult arise among the people.

Now when Jesus was in Bethany, in the house of Simon the leper, there came unto him a woman having ¹an alabaster cruse of exceeding precious ointment, and she poured it upon his head, as he sat at meat. But when the disciples saw it, they had indignation, saying, To what purpose is this waste? For this *ointment* might have been sold for much, and given to the poor. But Jesus perceiving it said unto them, Why trouble ye the woman? for she hath wrought a good work upon me. For ye have the poor always with you; but me ye have not always. For in that she ²poured this ointment upon my body, she did it to prepare me for burial. Verily I say unto you, Wheresoever ³this gospel shall be preached in the whole world, that also which this woman hath done shall be spoken of for a memorial of her.

Then one of the twelve, who was called Judas Iscariot, went unto the chief priests, and said, What are ye willing to give me, and I will deliver him unto you? And they weighed unto him thirty pieces of silver. And from that time he sought opportunity to deliver him *unto them*.

Now on the first *day* of unleavened bread the disciples came to Jesus, saying, Where wilt thou that we make ready for thee to eat the passover? And he said, Go into the city to such a man, and say unto him, The ⁴Master saith, My time is at hand; I keep the passover at thy house with my disciples. And the disciples did as Jesus appointed them; and they made ready the passover. Now when even was come, he was sitting at meat with the twelve ⁵disciples; and as they were eating, he said, Verily I say unto you, that one of you shall betray me. And they were exceeding sorrowful, and began to say unto him every one, Is it I, Lord? And he answered and said, He that dipped his hand with me in the dish, the same shall betray me. The Son of man goeth, even as it is written of him: but woe unto that man through whom the Son of man is betrayed! good were it ⁶for that man if he had not been born. And Judas, which betrayed him, an-

---

1 Or, *a flask*

2 Gr. *cast*.

3 Or, *these good tidings*

4 Or, *Teacher*

5 Many authorities, some ancient, omit *disciples*.

6 Gr. *for him if that man*.

swered and said, Is it I, Rabbi? He saith unto him,
26 Thou hast said. And as they were eating, Jesus took ¹bread, and blessed, and brake it; and he gave to the disciples, and said, Take, eat; this is my
27 body. And he took ²a cup, and gave thanks, and
28 gave to them, saying, Drink ye all of it; for this is my blood of ³the⁴ covenant, which is shed for many
29 unto remission of sins. But I say unto you, I will not drink* henceforth of this fruit of the vine, until that day when I drink it new with you in my Father's kingdom.
30 And when they had sung a hymn, they went out unto the mount of Olives.
31 Then saith Jesus unto them, All ye shall be ⁵offended in me this night: for it is written, I will smite the shepherd, and the sheep of the flock shall
32 be scattered abroad. But after I am raised up, I
33 will go before you into Galilee. But Peter answered and said unto him, If all shall be ⁵offended in
34 thee, I will never be ⁵offended. Jesus said unto him, Verily I say unto thee, that this night, before
35 the cock crow, thou shalt deny me thrice. Peter saith unto him, Even if I must die with thee, *yet* will I not deny thee. Likewise also said all the disciples.
36 Then cometh Jesus with them unto ⁶a place called Gethsemane, and saith unto his disciples, Sit ye here,
37 while I go yonder and pray. And he took with him Peter and the two sons of Zebedee, and began to be
38 sorrowful and sore troubled. Then saith he unto them, My soul is exceeding sorrowful, even unto
39 death: abide ye here, and watch with me. And he went forward a little, and fell on his face, and prayed, saying, O my Father, if it be possible, let this cup pass away from me: nevertheless, not as I will, but
40 as thou wilt. And he cometh unto the disciples, and findeth them sleeping, and saith unto Peter, What, could ye not watch with me one hour?
41 ⁷Watch and pray, that ye enter not into temptation: the spirit indeed is willing, but the flesh is weak.
42 Again a second time he went away, and prayed, saying, O my Father, if this cannot pass away, ex-
43 cept I drink it, thy will be done. And he came again and found them sleeping, for their eyes were heavy.
44 And he left them again, and went away, and prayed

1 Or, *a loaf*
2 Some ancient authorities read *the cup.*
3 Or, *the testament*
4 Many ancient authorities insert *new.*

5 Gr. *caused to stumble.*

6 Gr. *an enclosed piece of ground.*

7 Or, *Watch ye, and pray that ye enter not*

---

* For "I will not drink" read "I shall not drink" Similarly in Mark xiv. 25; Luke xxii. 16, 18.—*Am. Com.*

a third time, saying again the same words. Then 45
cometh he to the disciples, and saith unto them,
Sleep on now, and take your rest: behold, the hour
is at hand, and the Son of man is betrayed unto the
hands of sinners. Arise, let us be going: behold, he 46
is at hand that betrayeth me.

And while he yet spake, lo, Judas, one of the 47
twelve, came, and with him a great multitude with
swords and staves, from the chief priests and elders
of the people. Now he that betrayed him gave them 48
a sign, saying, Whomsoever I shall kiss, that is he:
take him. And straightway he came to Jesus, and 49
said, Hail, Rabbi; and ¹kissed him. And Jesus said 50
unto him, Friend, *do* that for which thou art come.
Then they came and laid hands on Jesus, and took
him. And behold, one of them that were with Jesus 51
stretched out his hand, and drew his sword, and
smote the ²servant of the high priest, and struck off
his ear. Then saith Jesus unto him, Put up again 52
thy sword into its place: for all they that take the
sword shall perish with the sword. Or thinkest thou 53
that I cannot beseech my Father, and he shall even
now send me more than twelve legions of angels?
How then should the scriptures be fulfilled, that thus 54
it must be? In that hour said Jesus to the multi- 55
tudes, Are ye come out as against a robber with
swords and staves to seize me? I sat daily in the
temple teaching, and ye took me not. But all this 56
is come to pass, that the scriptures of the prophets
might be fulfilled. Then all the disciples left him,
and fled.

And they that had taken Jesus led him away to 57
the house of Caiaphas the high priest, where the
scribes and the elders were gathered together. But 58
Peter followed him afar off, unto the court of the
high priest, and entered in, and sat with the officers,
to see the end. Now the chief priests and the whole 59
council sought false witness against Jesus, that they
might put him to death; and they found it not, 60
though many false witnesses came. But afterward
came two, and said, This man said, I am able to de- 61
stroy the ³temple of God, and to build it in three
days. And the high priest stood up, and said unto 62
him, Answerest thou nothing? what is it which these
witness against thee? But Jesus held his peace. 63
And the high priest said unto him, I adjure thee by
the living God, that thou tell us whether thou be the
Christ, the Son of God. Jesus saith unto him, Thou 64

---

¹ Gr. *kissed him much.*

² Gr. *bondservant.*

³ Or, *sanctuary*: as in ch. xxiii. 25; xxvii. 5.

hast said: nevertheless I say unto you, Henceforth ye shall see the Son of man sitting at the right hand of power, and coming on the clouds of heaven.
65 Then the high priest rent his garments, saying, He hath spoken blasphemy: what further need have we of witnesses? behold, now ye have heard the blas-
66 phemy: what think ye? They answered and said,
67 He is ¹worthy of death. Then did they spit in his face and buffet him: and some smote him ²with the
68 palms of their hands, saying, Prophesy unto us, thou Christ: who is he that struck thee?

1 Gr. *liable to.*
2 Or, *with rods*

69 Now Peter was sitting without in the court: and a maid came unto him, saying, Thou also wast with
70 Jesus the Galilæan. But he denied before them all,
71 saying, I know not what thou sayest. And when he was gone out into the porch, another *maid* saw him, and saith unto them that were there, This man also
72 was with Jesus the Nazarene. And again he denied
73 with an oath, I know not the man. And after a little while they that stood by came and said to Peter, Of a truth thou also art *one* of them; for thy speech
74 bewrayeth thee. Then began he to curse and to swear, I know not the man. And straightway the
75 cock crew. And Peter remembered the word which Jesus had said, Before the cock crow, thou shalt deny me thrice. And he went out, and wept bitterly.

27 Now when morning was come, all the chief priests and the elders of the people took counsel against
2 Jesus to put him to death: and they bound him, and led him away, and delivered him up to Pilate the governor.
3 Then Judas, which betrayed him, when he saw that he was condemned, repented himself, and brought back the thirty pieces of silver to the chief
4 priests and elders, saying, I have sinned in that I betrayed ³innocent blood. But they said, What is that
5 to us? see thou *to it.* And he cast down the pieces of silver into the sanctuary, and departed; and he
6 went away and hanged himself. And the chief priests took the pieces of silver, and said, It is not lawful to put them into the ⁴treasury, since it is the
7 price of blood. And they took counsel, and bought with them the potter's field, to bury strangers in.
8 Wherefore that field was called, The field of blood,
9 unto this day. Then was fulfilled that which was spoken ⁵by Jeremiah the prophet, saying, And ⁶they took the thirty pieces of silver, the price of him that

3 Many ancient authorities read *righteous.*

4 Gr. *corbanas, that is, sacred treasury.* Compare Mark vii. 11.

5 Or, *through*
6 Or, *I took*

was priced, ¹whom *certain* of the children of Israel did price; and ²they gave them for the potter's field, as the Lord appointed me.

Now Jesus stood before the governor: and the governor asked him, saying, Art thou the King of the Jews? And Jesus said unto him, Thou sayest. And when he was accused by the chief priests and elders, he answered nothing. Then saith Pilate unto him, Hearest thou not how many things they witness against thee? And he gave him no answer, not even to one word: insomuch that the governor marvelled greatly. Now at ³the feast the governor was wont to release unto the multitude one prisoner, whom they would. And they had then a notable prisoner, called Barabbas. When therefore they were gathered together, Pilate said unto them, Whom will ye that I release unto you? Barabbas, or Jesus which is called Christ? For he knew that for envy they had delivered him up. And while he was sitting on the judgement-seat, his wife sent unto him, saying, Have thou nothing to do with that righteous man: for I have suffered many things this day in a dream because of him. Now the chief priests and the elders persuaded the multitudes that they should ask for Barabbas, and destroy Jesus. But the governor answered and said unto them, Whether of the twain will ye that I release unto you? And they said, Barabbas. Pilate saith unto them, What then shall I do unto Jesus which is called Christ? They all say, Let him be crucified. And he said, Why, what evil hath he done? But they cried out exceedingly, saying, Let him be crucified. So when Pilate saw that he prevailed nothing, but rather that a tumult was arising, he took water, and washed his hands before the multitude, saying, I am innocent ⁴of the blood of this righteous man: see ye *to it*. And all the people answered and said, His blood *be* on us, and on our children. Then released he unto them Barabbas: but Jesus he scourged and delivered to be crucified.

Then the soldiers of the governor took Jesus into the ⁵palace*, and gathered unto him the whole ⁶band. And they ⁷stripped him, and put on him a scarlet robe. And they plaited a crown of thorns and put it upon his head, and a reed in his right hand; and

---

¹ Or, *whom they priced on the part of the sons of Israel*
² Some ancient authorities read *I gave*.
³ Or, *a feast*
⁴ Some ancient authorities read *of this blood: see ye &c.*
⁵ Gr. *Prætorium.* See Mark xv. 16.
⁶ Or, *cohort*
⁷ Some ancient authorities read *clothed.*

* For "palace" read "Prætorium" with marg. Or, *palace* [as in Mark xv. 16] So in John xviii. 28, 33; xix. 9.—*Am. Com.*

they kneeled down before him, and mocked him,
30 saying, Hail, King of the Jews! And they spat upon him, and took the reed and smote him on the head.
31 And when they had mocked him, they took off from him the robe, and put on him his garments, and led him away to crucify him.
32 And as they came out, they found a man of Cyrene, Simon by name: him they ¹compelled to go [1 Gr. *impressed.*]
33 with them, that he might bear his cross. And when they were come unto a place called Golgotha, that is
34 to say, The place of a skull, they gave him wine to drink mingled with gall: and when he had tasted it,
35 he would not drink. And when they had crucified
36 him, they parted his garments among them, casting lots: and they sat and watched him there. And
37 they set up over his head his accusation written,
38 THIS IS JESUS THE KING OF THE JEWS. Then are there crucified with him two robbers, one on the
39 right hand, and one on the left. And they that passed by railed on him, wagging their heads, and
40 saying, Thou that destroyest the ²temple, and buildest it in three days, save thyself: if thou art the Son [2 Or, *sanctuary*]
41 of God, come down from the cross. In like manner also the chief priests mocking *him*, with the scribes
42 and elders, said, He saved others; ³himself he cannot save. He is the King of Israel; let him now come down from the cross, and we will believe on him. [3 Or, *can he not save himself?*]
43 He trusteth on God; let him deliver him now, if he desireth him: for he said, I am the Son of God.
44 And the robbers also that were crucified with him cast upon him the same reproach.
45 Now from the sixth hour there was darkness over
46 all the ⁴land until the ninth hour. And about the ninth hour Jesus cried with a loud voice, saying, Eli, Eli, lama sabachthani? that is, My God, my God, [4 Or, *earth*]
47 ⁵why hast thou forsaken me? And some of them that stood there, when they heard it, said, This man [5 Or, *why didst thou forsake me?*]
48 calleth Elijah. And straightway one of them ran, and took a sponge, and filled it with vinegar, and
49 put it on a reed, and gave him to drink. And the rest said, Let be; let us see whether Elijah cometh
50 to save him.⁶ And Jesus cried again with a loud
51 voice, and yielded up his spirit. And behold, the veil of the ²temple was rent in twain from the top to the bottom; and the earth did quake; and the [6 Many ancient authorities add *And another took a spear and pierced his side, and there came out water and blood.* See John xix. 34.]
52 rocks were rent; and the tombs were opened; and many bodies of the saints that had fallen asleep
53 were raised; and coming forth out of the tombs

after his resurrection they entered into the holy city and appeared unto many. Now the centurion, and 54 they that were with him watching Jesus, when they saw the earthquake, and the things that were done, feared exceedingly, saying, Truly this was ¹the Son of God. And many women were 55 there beholding from afar, which had followed Jesus from Galilee, ministering unto him: among 56 whom was Mary Magdalene, and Mary the mother of James and Joses, and the mother of the sons of Zebedee.

And when even was come, there came a rich man 57 from Arimathæa, named Joseph, who also himself was Jesus' disciple: this man went to Pilate, and 58 asked for the body of Jesus. Then Pilate commanded it to be given up. And Joseph took the body 59 and wrapped it in a clean linen cloth, and laid it in 60 his own new tomb, which he had hewn out in the rock: and he rolled a great stone to the door of the tomb, and departed. And Mary Magdalene was 61 there, and the other Mary, sitting over against the sepulchre.

Now on the morrow, which is *the day* after the 62 Preparation, the chief priests and the Pharisees were gathered together unto Pilate, saying, Sir, we remem- 63 ber that that deceiver said, while he was yet alive, After three days I rise again. Command therefore 64 that the sepulchre be made sure until the third day, lest haply his disciples come and steal him away, and say unto the people, He is risen from the dead: and the last error will be worse than the first. Pilate 65 said unto them, ²Ye have a guard: go your way, ³make it *as* sure as ye can. So they went, and made 66 the sepulchre sure, sealing the stone, the guard being with them.

Now late on the sabbath day, as it began to dawn 28 toward the first *day* of the week, came Mary Magdalene and the other Mary to see the sepulchre. And 2 behold, there was a great earthquake; for an angel of the Lord descended from heaven, and came and rolled away the stone, and sat upon it. His appear- 3 ance was as lightning, and his raiment white as snow: and for fear of him the watchers did quake, 4 and became as dead men. And the angel answered and said unto the women, Fear not ye: for I know 5 that ye seek Jesus, which hath been crucified. He 6 is not here; for he is risen, even as he said. Come, see the place ⁴where the Lord lay. And go quickly, 7

---

¹ Or, *a son of God*

² Or, *Take a guard*
³ Gr. *make it sure, as ye know.*

⁴ Many ancient authorities read *where he lay.*

and tell his disciples, He is risen from the dead; and lo, he goeth before you into Galilee; there shall ye 8 see him: lo, I have told you. And they departed quickly from the tomb with fear and great joy, and 9 ran to bring his disciples word. And behold, Jesus met them, saying, All hail. And they came and 10 took hold of his feet, and worshipped him. Then saith Jesus unto them, Fear not: go tell my brethren that they depart into Galilee, and there shall they see me.

11 Now while they were going, behold, some of the guard came into the city, and told unto the chief 12 priests all the things that were come to pass. And when they were assembled with the elders, and had taken counsel, they gave large money unto the sol- 13 diers, saying, Say ye, His disciples came by night, 14 and stole him away while we slept. And if this ¹come to the governor's ears, we will persuade him, 15 and rid you of care. So they took the money, and did as they were taught: and this saying was spread abroad among the Jews, *and continueth* until this day.

16 But the eleven disciples went into Galilee, unto 17 the mountain where Jesus had appointed them. And when they saw him, they worshipped *him*: but some 18 doubted. And Jesus came to them and spake unto them, saying, All authority hath been given unto 19 me in heaven and on earth. Go ye therefore, and make disciples of all the nations, baptizing them into the name of the Father and of the Son and of 20 the Holy Ghost: teaching them to observe all things whatsoever I commanded you: and lo, I am with you ²alway, even unto ³the end of the world.

---

1 Or, *come to a hearing before the governor*

2 Gr. *all the days.*

3 Or, *the consummation of the age.*

THE GOSPEL

ACCORDING TO

S. MARK.

---

1 The beginning of the gospel of Jesus Christ, [1]the Son of God. 2 Even as it is written [2]in Isaiah the prophet,

Behold, I send my messenger before thy face,
Who shall prepare thy way;
3 The voice of one crying in the wilderness,
Make ye ready the way of the Lord,
Make his paths straight;

4 John came, who baptized in the wilderness and preached the baptism of repentance unto remission of sins. 5 And there went out unto him all the country of Judæa, and all they of Jerusalem; and they were baptized of him in the river Jordan, confessing their sins. 6 And John was clothed with camel's hair, and *had* a leathern girdle about his loins, and did eat locusts and wild honey. 7 And he preached, saying, There cometh after me he that is mightier than I, the latchet of whose shoes I am not [3]worthy to stoop down and unloose. 8 I baptized you [4]with water; but he shall baptize you [4]with the [5]Holy Ghost.

9 And it came to pass in those days, that Jesus came from Nazareth of Galilee, and was baptized of John [6]in the Jordan. 10 And straightway coming up out of the water, he saw the heavens rent asunder, and the Spirit as a dove descending upon him: 11 and a voice came out of the heavens, Thou art my beloved Son, in thee I am well pleased.

12 And straightway the Spirit driveth him forth into the wilderness. 13 And he was in the wilderness forty days tempted of Satan; and he was with the wild beasts; and the angels ministered unto him.

14 Now after that John was delivered up, Jesus came into Galilee, preaching the gospel of God, 15 and say-

---

[1] Some ancient authorities omit *the Son of God.*
[2] Some ancient authorities read *in the prophets.*
[3] Gr. *sufficient.*
[4] Or, *in*
[5] Or, *Holy Spirit*: and so throughout this book.
[6] Gr. *into.*

ing, The time is fulfilled, and the kingdom of God is at hand: repent ye, and believe in the gospel.

16 And passing along by the sea of Galilee, he saw Simon and Andrew the brother of Simon casting a
17 net in the sea: for they were fishers. And Jesus said unto them, Come ye after me, and I will make
18 you to become fishers of men. And straightway
19 they left the nets, and followed him. And going on a little further, he saw James the *son* of Zebedee, and John his brother, who also were in the boat mend-
20 ing the nets. And straightway he called them: and they left their father Zebedee in the boat with the hired servants, and went after him.
21 And they go into Capernaum; and straightway on the sabbath day he entered into the synagogue
22 and taught. And they were astonished at his teaching: for he taught them as having authority, and
23 not as the scribes. And straightway there was in their synagogue a man with an unclean spirit; and
24 he cried out, saying, What have we to do with thee, thou Jesus of Nazareth? art thou come to destroy us? I know thee who thou art, the Holy One of
25 God. And Jesus rebuked [1]him, saying, Hold thy
26 peace, and come out of him. And the unclean spirit, [2]tearing him and crying with a loud voice, came
27 out of him. And they were all amazed, insomuch that they questioned among themselves, saying, What is this? a new teaching! with authority he commandeth even the unclean spirits, and they obey
28 him. And the report of him went out straightway everywhere into all the region of Galilee round about.
29 And straightway, [3]when they were come out of the synagogue, they came into the house of Simon
30 and Andrew, with James and John. Now Simon's wife's mother lay sick of a fever; and straightway
31 they tell him of her: and he came and took her by the hand, and raised her up; and the fever left her, and she ministered unto them.
32 And at even, when the sun did set, they brought unto him all that were sick, and them that were [4]pos-
33 sessed with devils. And all the city was gathered
34 together at the door. And he healed many that were sick with divers diseases, and cast out many [5]devils; and he suffered not the [5]devils to speak, because they knew him[6].
35 And in the morning, a great while before day, he rose up and went out, and departed into a desert
36 place, and there prayed. And Simon and they that

[1] Or, *it*
[2] Or, *convulsing*
[3] Some ancient authorities read *when he was come out of the synagogue, he came, &c.*
[4] Or, *demoniacs*
[5] Gr. *demons.*
[6] Many ancient authorities add *to be Christ.* See Luke iv. 41.

were with him followed after him; and they found 37
him, and say unto him, All are seeking thee. And 38
he saith unto them, Let us go elsewhere into the
next towns, that I may preach there also; for to this
end came I forth. And he went into their syna- 39
gogues throughout all Galilee, preaching and casting out ¹devils.

¹ Gr. *demons.*
² Some ancient authorities omit *and kneeling down to him.*

And there cometh to him a leper, beseeching him, 40
²and kneeling down to him, and saying unto him,
If thou wilt, thou canst make me clean. And be- 41
ing moved with compassion, he stretched forth his
hand, and touched him, and saith unto him, I will;
be thou made clean. And straightway the leprosy 42
departed from him, and he was made clean. And 43

³ Or, *sternly*

he ³strictly charged him, and straightway sent him
out, and saith unto him, See thou say nothing to any 44
man: but go thy way, shew thyself to the priest, and
offer for thy cleansing the things which Moses commanded, for a testimony unto them. But he went 45

⁴ Gr. *word.*
⁵ Gr. *he.*
⁶ Or, *the city*

out, and began to publish it much, and to spread
abroad the ⁴matter, insomuch that ⁵Jesus could no
more openly enter into ⁶a city, but was without in desert places: and they came to him from every quarter.

And when he entered again into Capernaum after 2

⁷ Or, *at home*

some days, it was noised that he was ⁷in the house.
And many were gathered together, so that there 2
was no longer room *for them,* no, not even about
the door: and he spake the word unto them. And 3
they come, bringing unto him a man sick of the

⁸ Many ancient authorities read *bring him unto him.*

palsy, borne of four. And when they could not 4
⁸come nigh unto him for the crowd, they uncovered
the roof where he was: and when they had broken
it up, they let down the bed* whereon the sick of the
palsy lay. And Jesus seeing their faith saith unto 5

⁹ Gr. *Child.*

the sick of the palsy, ⁹Son, thy sins are forgiven.
But there were certain of the scribes sitting there, 6
and reasoning in their hearts, Why doth this man 7
thus speak? he blasphemeth: who can forgive sins
but one, *even* God? And straightway Jesus, per- 8
ceiving in his spirit that they so reasoned within
themselves, saith unto them, Why reason ye these
things in your hearts? Whether is easier, to say to 9
the sick of the palsy, Thy sins are forgiven; or to
say, Arise, and take up thy bed*, and walk? But 10

¹⁰ Or, *authority*

that ye may know that the Son of man hath ¹⁰power

---

* "Bed" add marg. Or, *pallet.* So in vi. 55; John v. 8, 9, 10, 11, 12; Acts v. 15; ix. 33.—*Am. Com.*

on earth to forgive sins (he saith to the sick of the
11 palsy), I say unto thee, Arise, take up thy bed*, and
12 go unto thy house. And he arose, and straightway
took up the bed*, and went forth before them all;
insomuch that they were all amazed, and glorified
God, saying, We never saw it on this fashion.
13 And he went forth again by the sea side; and all
the multitude resorted unto him, and he taught them.
14 And as he passed by, he saw Levi the *son* of Alphæus
sitting at the place of toll, and he saith unto him,
15 Follow me. And he arose and followed him. And
it came to pass, that he was sitting at meat in his
house, and many ¹publicans and sinners sat down
with Jesus and his disciples: for there were many,
16 and they followed him. And the scribes ²of the
Pharisees, when they saw that he was eating with
the sinners and publicans, said unto his disciples,
³He eateth ⁴and drinketh with publicans and sin-
17 ners. And when Jesus heard it, he saith unto them,
They that are ⁵whole have no need of a physician,
but they that are sick: I came not to call the righteous, but sinners.
18 And John's disciples and the Pharisees were fasting: and they come and say unto him, Why do
John's disciples and the disciples of the Pharisees
19 fast, but thy disciples fast not? And Jesus said
unto them, Can the sons of the bride-chamber fast,
while the bridegroom is with them? as long as they
have the bridegroom with them, they cannot fast.
20 But the days will come, when the bridegroom shall
be taken away from them, and then will they fast
21 in that day. No man seweth a piece of undressed
cloth on an old garment: else that which should fill
it up taketh from it, the new from the old, and a
22 worse rent is made. And no man putteth new wine
into old ⁶wine-skins: else the wine will burst the
skins, and the wine perisheth, and the skins: but
they put new wine into fresh wine-skins.
23 And it came to pass, that he was going on the
sabbath day through the cornfields; and his disciples ⁷began, as they went, to pluck the ears of corn.
24 And the Pharisees said unto him, Behold, why do
they on the sabbath day that which is not lawful?
25 And he said unto them, Did ye never read what David did, when he had need, and was an hungred,

1 See marginal note on Matt. v. 46.
2 Some ancient authorities read *and the Pharisees.*
3 Or, How is it *that he eateth . . . sinners?*
4 Some ancient authorities omit *and drinketh.*
5 Gr. *strong.*
6 That is, *skins used as bottles.*
7 Gr. *began to make their way plucking.*

---

* "Bed" add marg. Or, *pallet.* So in vi. 55; John v. 8, 9, 10, 11, 12; Acts v. 15; ix. 33.—*Am. Com.*

he, and they that were with him? How he entered into the house of God ¹when Abiathar was high priest, and did eat the shewbread, which it is not lawful to eat save for the priests, and gave also to them that were with him? And he said unto them, The sabbath was made for man, and not man for the sabbath: so that the Son of man is lord even of the sabbath.

And he entered again into the synagogue; and there was a man there which had his hand withered. And they watched him, whether he would heal him on the sabbath day; that they might accuse him. And he saith unto the man that had his hand withered, ²Stand forth. And he saith unto them, Is it lawful on the sabbath day to do good, or to do harm? to save a life, or to kill? But they held their peace. And when he had looked round about on them with anger, being grieved at the hardening of their heart, he saith unto the man, Stretch forth thy hand. And he stretched it forth: and his hand was restored. And the Pharisees went out, and straightway with the Herodians took counsel against him, how they might destroy him.

And Jesus with his disciples withdrew to the sea: and a great multitude from Galilee followed: and from Judæa, and from Jerusalem, and from Idumæa, and beyond Jordan, and about Tyre and Sidon, a great multitude, hearing ³what great things he did, came unto him. And he spake to his disciples, that a little boat should wait on him because of the crowd, lest they should throng him: for he had healed many; insomuch that as many as had ⁴plagues ⁵pressed upon him that they might touch him. And the unclean spirits, whensoever they beheld him, fell down before him, and cried, saying, Thou art the Son of God. And he charged them much that they should not make him known.

And he goeth up into the mountain, and calleth unto him whom he himself would: and they went unto him. And he appointed twelve,⁶ that they might be with him, and that he might send them forth to preach, and to have authority to cast out ⁷devils: ⁸and Simon he surnamed Peter; and James the *son* of Zebedee, and John the brother of James; and them he surnamed Boanerges, which is, Sons of thunder: and Andrew, and Philip, and Bartholomew, and Matthew, and Thomas, and James the *son* of Alphæus, and Thaddæus, and Simon the ⁹Cana-

---

¹ Some ancient authorities read *in the days of Abiathar the high priest.*
² Gr. *Arise into the midst.*
³ Or, *all the things that he did*
⁴ Gr. *scourges.*
⁵ Gr. *fell.*
⁶ Some ancient authorities add *whom also he named apostles.* See Luke vi. 13.
⁷ Gr. *demons.*
⁸ Some ancient authorities insert *and he appointed twelve.*
⁹ Or, *Zealot.* See Luke vi. 15; Acts i. 13.

19 man, and Judas Iscariot, which also betrayed him.
20 And he cometh ¹into a house. And the multitude cometh together again, so that they could not so
21 much as eat bread. And when his friends heard it, they went out to lay hold on him: for they said, He
22 is beside himself. And the scribes which came down from Jerusalem said, He hath Beelzebub, and, ²By the prince of the ³devils casteth he out the ³devils.
23 And he called them unto him, and said unto them
24 in parables, How can Satan cast out Satan? And if a kingdom be divided against itself, that kingdom
25 cannot stand. And if a house be divided against
26 itself, that house will not be able to stand. And if Satan hath risen up against himself, and is divided,
27 he cannot stand, but hath an end. But no one can enter into the house of the strong *man*, and spoil his goods, except he first bind the strong *man*; and
28 then he will spoil his house. Verily I say unto you, All their sins shall be forgiven unto the sons of men, and their blasphemies wherewith soever they shall
29 blaspheme: but whosoever shall blaspheme against the Holy Spirit hath never forgiveness, but is guilty
30 of an eternal sin: because they said, He hath an unclean spirit.
31 And there come his mother and his brethren; and, standing without, they sent unto him, calling him.
32 And a multitude was sitting about him; and they say unto him, Behold, thy mother and thy brethren
33 without seek for thee. And he answereth them, and
34 saith, Who is my mother and my brethren? And looking round on them which sat round about him,
35 he saith, Behold, my mother and my brethren! For whosoever shall do the will of God, the same is my brother, and sister, and mother.

4 And again he began to teach by the sea side. And there is gathered unto him a very great multitude, so that he entered into a boat, and sat in the sea; and all the multitude were by the sea on the land.
2 And he taught them many things in parables, and
3 said unto them in his teaching, Hearken: Behold,
4 the sower went forth to sow: and it came to pass, as he sowed, some *seed* fell by the way side, and the
5 birds came and devoured it. And other fell on the rocky *ground*, where it had not much earth; and straightway it sprang up, because it had no deep-
6 ness of earth: and when the sun was risen, it was scorched; and because it had no root, it withered

1 Or, *home*
2 Or, *In*
3 Gr. *demons*.

away. And other fell among the thorns, and the 7
thorns grew up, and choked it, and it yielded no
fruit. And others fell into the good ground, and 8
yielded fruit, growing up and increasing; and
brought forth, thirtyfold, and sixtyfold, and a hundredfold.
And he said, Who hath ears to hear, let 9
him hear.

And when he was alone, they that were about 10
him with the twelve asked of him the parables.
And he said unto them, Unto you is given the mys- 11
tery of the kingdom of God: but unto them that
are without, all things are done in parables: that 12
seeing they may see, and not perceive; and hearing
they may hear, and not understand; lest haply they
should turn again, and it should be forgiven them.
And he saith unto them, Know ye not this parable? 13
and how shall ye know all the parables? The sow- 14
er soweth the word. And these are they by the way 15
side, where the word is sown; and when they have
heard, straightway cometh Satan, and taketh away
the word which hath been sown in them. And 16
these in like manner are they that are sown upon
the rocky *places*, who, when they have heard the
word, straightway receive it with joy; and they 17
have no root in themselves, but endure for a while;
then, when tribulation or persecution ariseth because
of the word, straightway they stumble. And others 18
are they that are sown among the thorns; these are
they that have heard the word, and the cares of the 19
[1] ¹world, and the deceitfulness of riches, and the lusts
of other things entering in, choke the word, and it
becometh unfruitful. And those are they that were 20
sown upon the good ground; such as hear the word,
and accept it, and bear fruit, thirtyfold, and sixtyfold,
and a hundredfold.

And he said unto them, Is the lamp brought to be 21
put under the bushel, or under the bed, *and* not to
be put on the stand? For there is nothing hid, save 22
that it should be manifested; neither was *anything*
made secret, but that it should come to light. If 23
any man hath ears to hear, let him hear. And he 24
said unto them, Take heed what ye hear: with what
measure ye mete it shall be measured unto you: and
more shall be given unto you. For he that hath, to 25
him shall be given: and he that hath not, from him
shall be taken away even that which he hath.

And he said, So is the kingdom of God, as if a 26
man should cast seed upon the earth; and should 27

---
[1] ¹ Or, *age*

sleep and rise night and day, and the seed should
28 spring up and grow, he knoweth not how. The
earth ¹beareth fruit of herself; first the blade, then
29 the ear, then the full corn in the ear. But when the
fruit ²is ripe, straightway he ³putteth forth the sickle,
because the harvest is come.

30 And he said, How shall we liken the kingdom of
31 God? or in what parable shall we set it forth? ⁴It
is like a grain of mustard seed, which, when it is
sown upon the earth, though it be less than all the
32 seeds that are upon the earth, yet when it is sown,
groweth up, and becometh greater than all the
herbs, and putteth out great branches; so that the
birds of the heaven can lodge under the shadow
thereof.

33 And with many such parables spake he the word
34 unto them, as they were able to hear it: and without
a parable spake he not unto them: but privately to
his own disciples he expounded all things.

35 And on that day, when even was come, he saith
36 unto them, Let us go over unto the other side. And
leaving the multitude, they take him with them,
even as he was, in the boat. And other boats were
37 with him. And there ariseth a great storm of wind,
and the waves beat into the boat, insomuch that the
38 boat was now filling. And he himself was in the
stern, asleep on the cushion: and they awake him,
and say unto him, ⁵Master, carest thou not that we
39 perish? And he awoke, and rebuked the wind, and
said unto the sea, Peace, be still. And the wind
40 ceased, and there was a great calm. And he said
unto them, Why are ye fearful? have ye not yet
41 faith? And they feared exceedingly, and said one
to another, Who then is this, that even the wind and
the sea obey him?

5 And they came to the other side of the sea, into the
2 country of the Gerasenes. And when he was come
out of the boat, straightway there met him out of
3 the tombs a man with an unclean spirit, who had his
dwelling in the tombs: and no man could any more
4 bind him, no, not with a chain; because that he had
been often bound with fetters and chains, and the
chains had been rent asunder by him, and the fetters broken in pieces: and no man had strength to
5 tame him. And always, night and day, in the tombs
and in the mountains, he was crying out, and cut-
6 ting himself with stones. And when he saw Jesus
7 from afar, he ran and worshipped him; and crying

1 Or, *yieldeth*
2 Or, *alloweth*
3 Or, *sendeth forth*
4 Gr. *As unto*.
5 Or, *Teacher*

out with a loud voice, he saith, What have I to do with thee, Jesus, thou Son of the Most High God? I adjure thee by God, torment me not. For he said 8 unto him, Come forth, thou unclean spirit, out of the man. And he asked him, What is thy name? 9 And he saith unto him, My name is Legion; for we are many. And he besought him much that he 10 would not send them away out of the country. Now 11 there was there on the mountain side a great herd of swine feeding. And they besought him, saying, 12 Send us into the swine, that we may enter into them. And he gave them leave. And the unclean 13 spirits came out, and entered into the swine: and the herd rushed down the steep into the sea, *in number* about two thousand; and they were choked in the sea. And they that fed them fled, and told it in 14 the city, and in the country. And they came to see what it was that had come to pass. And they 15 come to Jesus, and behold ¹him that was possessed with devils sitting, clothed and in his right mind, *even* him that had the legion: and they were afraid. And they that saw it declared unto them how it be- 16 fell ¹him that was possessed with devils, and concerning the swine. And they began to beseech him 17 to depart from their borders. And as he was entering 18 into the boat, he that had been possessed with ²devils besought him that he might be with him. And 19 he suffered him not, but saith unto him, Go to thy house unto thy friends, and tell them how great things the Lord hath done for thee, and *how* he had mercy on thee. And he went his way, and began 20 to publish in Decapolis how great things Jesus had done for him: and all men did marvel.

And when Jesus had crossed over again in the 21 boat unto the other side, a great multitude was gathered unto him: and he was by the sea. And there 22 cometh one of the rulers of the synagogue, Jaïrus by name; and seeing him, he falleth at his feet, and 23 beseecheth him much, saying, My little daughter is at the point of death: *I pray thee*, that thou come and lay thy hands on her, that she may be ³made whole, and live. And he went with him; and a 24 great multitude followed him, and they thronged him.

And a woman, which had an issue of blood twelve 25 years, and had suffered many things of many phy- 26 sicians, and had spent all that she had, and was nothing bettered, but rather grew worse, having 27

1 Or, *the demoniac*

2 Gr. *demons.*

3 Or, *saved*

heard the things concerning Jesus, came in the
28 crowd behind, and touched his garment. For she
said, If I touch but his garments, I shall be ¹made   1 Or, *saved*
29 whole. And straightway the fountain of her blood
was dried up; and she felt in her body that she was
30 healed of her ²plague. And straightway Jesus, per-   2 Gr. *scourge*.
ceiving in himself that the power *proceeding* from
him had gone forth, turned him about in the crowd,
31 and said, Who touched my garments? And his
disciples said unto him, Thou seest the multitude
thronging thee, and sayest thou, Who touched me?
32 And he looked round about to see her that had done
33 this thing. But the woman fearing and trembling,
knowing what had been done to her, came and fell
34 down before him, and told him all the truth. And
he said unto her, Daughter, thy faith hath ³made   3 Or, *saved thee*
thee whole; go in peace, and be whole of thy
²plague.
35   While he yet spake, they come from the ruler of
the synagogue's *house*, saying, Thy daughter is dead:
36 why troublest thou the ⁴Master any further? But   4 Or, *Teacher*
Jesus, ⁵not heeding the word spoken, saith unto the   5 Or, *overhearing*
37 ruler of the synagogue, Fear not, only believe. And
he suffered no man to follow with him, save Peter,
38 and James, and John the brother of James. And
they come to the house of the ruler of the synagogue;
and he beholdeth a tumult, and *many* weeping and
39 wailing greatly. And when he was entered in, he
saith unto them, Why make ye a tumult, and weep?
40 the child is not dead, but sleepeth. And they laughed him to scorn. But he, having put them all forth,
taketh the father of the child and her mother and
them that were with him, and goeth in where the
41 child was. And taking the child by the hand, he
saith unto her, Talitha cumi; which is, being in-
42 terpreted, Damsel, I say unto thee, Arise. And
straightway the damsel rose up, and walked; for
she was twelve years old. And they were amazed
43 straightway with a great amazement. And he
charged them much that no man should know
this: and he commanded that *something* should be
given her to eat.

6   And he went out from thence; and he cometh
into his own country; and his disciples follow him.
2 And when the sabbath was come, he began to teach   6 Some ancient au-
in the synagogue: and ⁶many hearing him were as-   thorities insert *the*.
tonished, saying, Whence hath this man these things?
and, What is the wisdom that is given unto this

man, and *what mean* such ¹mighty works wrought by his hands? Is not this the carpenter, the son of 3 Mary, and brother of James, and Joses, and Judas, and Simon? and are not his sisters here with us? And they were ²offended in him. And Jesus said 4 unto them, A prophet is not without honour, save in his own country, and among his own kin, and in his own house. And he could there do no ³mighty 5 work, save that he laid his hands upon a few sick folk, and healed them. And he marvelled because 6 of their unbelief.

And he went round about the villages teaching.

And he called unto him the twelve, and began to 7 send them forth by two and two; and he gave them authority over the unclean spirits; and he charged 8 them that they should take nothing for *their* journey, save a staff only; no bread, no wallet, no ⁴money in their ⁵purse; but *to go* shod with sandals: and, *said* 9 *he,* put not on two coats. And he said unto them, 10 Wheresoever ye enter into a house, there abide till ye depart thence. And whatsoever place shall not 11 receive you, and they hear you not, as ye go forth thence, shake off the dust that is under your feet for a testimony unto them. And they went out, and 12 preached that *men* should repent. And they cast 13 out many ⁶devils, and anointed with oil many that were sick, and healed them.

And king Herod heard *thereof*; for his name had 14 become known: and ⁷he said, John ⁸the Baptist is risen from the dead, and therefore do these powers work in him. But others said, It is Elijah. And 15 others said, *It is* a prophet, *even* as one of the prophets. But Herod, when he heard *thereof*, said, John, 16 whom I beheaded, he is risen. For Herod himself 17 had sent forth and laid hold upon John, and bound him in prison for the sake of Herodias, his brother Philip's wife: for he had married her. For John 18 said unto Herod, It is not lawful for thee to have thy brother's wife. And Herodias set herself against 19 him, and desired to kill him; and she could not; for Herod feared John, knowing that he was a 20 righteous man and a holy, and kept him safe. And when he heard him, he ⁹was much perplexed; and he heard him gladly. And when a convenient day 21 was come, that Herod on his birthday made a supper to his lords, and the ¹⁰high captains, and the chief men of Galilee; and when ¹¹the daughter of 22 Herodias herself came in and danced, ¹²she pleased

---

1 Gr. *powers.*
2 Gr. *caused to stumble.*
3 Gr. *power.*
4 Gr. *brass.*
5 Gr. *girdle.*
6 Gr. *demons.*
7 Some ancient authorities read *they.*
8 Gr. *the Baptizer.*
9 Many ancient authorities read *did many things.*
10 Or, *military tribunes* Gr. *chiliarchs.*
11 Some ancient authorities read *his daughter Herodias.*
12 Or, *it*

Herod and them that sat at meat with him ; and
the king said unto the damsel, Ask of me whatso-
23 ever thou wilt, and I will give it thee. And he
sware unto her, Whatsoever thou shalt ask of me,
I will give it thee, unto the half of my kingdom.
24 And she went out, and said unto her mother, What
shall I ask ? And she said, The head of John ¹the   1 Gr. *the Baptizer*.
25 Baptist. And she came in straightway with haste
unto the king, and asked, saying, I will that thou
forthwith give me in a charger the head of John
26 ¹the Baptist. And the king was exceeding sorry;
but for the sake of his oaths, and of them that sat
27 at meat, he would not reject her. And straightway
the king sent forth a soldier of his guard, and commanded to bring his head: and he went and be-
28 headed him in the prison, and brought his head in
a charger, and gave it to the damsel; and the dam-
29 sel gave it to her mother. And when his disciples
heard *thereof*, they came and took up his corpse,
and laid it in a tomb.
30   And the apostles gather themselves together unto
Jesus; and they told him all things, whatsoever they
31 had done, and whatsoever they had taught. And
he saith unto them, Come ye yourselves apart into
a desert place, and rest a while. For there were
many coming and going, and they had no leisure so
32 much as to eat. And they went away in the boat to
33 a desert place apart. And *the people* saw them going,
and many knew *them*, and they ran there together
²on foot from all the cities, and outwent them.   2 Or, *by land*
34 And he came forth and saw a great multitude, and
he had compassion on them, because they were as
sheep not having a shepherd: and he began to teach
35 them many things. And when the day was now
far spent, his disciples came unto him, and said,
The place is desert, and the day is now far spent:
36 send them away, that they may go into the country
and villages round about, and buy themselves some-
37 what to eat. But he answered and said unto them,
Give ye them to eat. And they say unto him, Shall   3 See marginal note
we go and buy two hundred ³pennyworth of bread,   on Matt. xviii.
38 and give them to eat? And he saith unto them, How   28.
many loaves have ye? go *and* see. And when they
39 knew, they say, Five, and two fishes. And he commanded them that all should ⁴sit down by compa-   4 Gr. *recline*.
40 nies upon the green grass. And they sat down in
41 ranks, by hundreds, and by fifties. And he took
the five loaves and the two fishes, and looking up

to heaven, he blessed, and brake the loaves; and he gave to the disciples to set before them; and the two fishes divided he among them all. And they 42 did all eat, and were filled. And they took up 43 broken pieces, twelve basketfuls, and also of the fishes. And they that ate the loaves were five 44 thousand men.

And straightway he constrained his disciples to 45 enter into the boat, and to go before *him* unto the other side to Bethsaida, while he himself sendeth the multitude away. And after he had taken leave 46 of them, he departed into the mountain to pray. And when even was come, the boat was in the 47 midst of the sea, and he alone on the land. And 48 seeing them distressed in rowing, for the wind was contrary unto them, about the fourth watch of the night he cometh unto them, walking on the sea; and he would have passed by them: but they, 49 when they saw him walking on the sea, supposed that it was an apparition, and cried out: for they 50 all saw him, and were troubled. But he straightway spake with them, and saith unto them, Be of good cheer: it is I; be not afraid. And he went 51 up unto them into the boat; and the wind ceased: and they were sore amazed in themselves; for they 52 understood not concerning the loaves, but their heart was hardened.

¹ Or, *crossed over to the land, they came unto Gennesaret*

And when they had ¹crossed over, they came to 53 the land unto Gennesaret, and moored to the shore. And when they were come out of the boat, straight- 54 way *the people* knew him, and ran round about that 55 whole region, and began to carry about on their beds those that were sick, where they heard he was. And wheresoever he entered, into villages, or into 56 cities, or into the country, they laid the sick in the marketplaces, and besought him that they might touch if it were but the border of his garment: and

² Or, *it*

as many as touched ²him were made whole.

And there are gathered together unto him the Pha- **7** risees, and certain of the scribes, which had come from Jerusalem, and had seen that some of his disci- 2

³ Or, *common*
⁴ Or, *up to the elbow* Gr. *with the fist.*
⁵ Gr. *baptize.* Some ancient authorities read *sprinkle themselves.*

ples ate their bread with ³defiled, that is, unwashen, hands. For the Pharisees, and all the Jews, except 3 they wash their hands ⁴diligently, eat not, holding the tradition of the elders: and *when they come* from 4 the marketplace, except they ⁵wash* themselves,

---

* For "wash" read "bathe" [comp. Luke xi. 38].—*Am. Com.*

they eat not: and many other things there be, which they have received to hold, ¹washings of cups, and
5 pots, and brasen vessels². And the Pharisees and the scribes ask him, Why walk not thy disciples according to the tradition of the elders, but eat their
6 bread with ³defiled hands? And he said unto them, Well did Isaiah prophesy of you hypocrites, as it is written,

This people honoureth me with their lips,
But their heart is far from me.
7 But in vain do they worship me,
Teaching *as their* doctrines the precepts of men.
8 Ye leave the commandment of God, and hold fast the
9 tradition of men. And he said unto them, Full well do ye reject the commandment of God, that ye may
10 keep your tradition. For Moses said, Honour thy father and thy mother; and, He that speaketh evil of
11 father or mother, let him ⁴die the death: but ye say, If a man shall say to his father or his mother, That wherewith thou mightest have been profited by me is
12 Corban, that is to say, Given *to God*; ye no longer suffer him to do aught for his father or his mother;
13 making void the word of God by your tradition, which ye have delivered: and many such like things
14 ye do. And he called to him the multitude again, and said unto them, Hear me all of you, and under-
15 stand: there is nothing from without the man, that going into him can defile him: but the things which proceed out of the man are those that defile the man.⁵
17 And when he was entered into the house from the multitude, his disciples asked of him the parable.
18 And he saith unto them, Are ye so without understanding also? Perceive ye not, that whatsoever from without goeth into the man, *it* cannot defile
19 him; because it goeth not into his heart, but into his belly, and goeth out into the draught? *This he said,*
20 making all meats clean. And he said, That which proceedeth out of the man, that defileth the man.
21 For from within, out of the heart of men, ⁶evil
22 thoughts proceed, fornications, thefts, murders, adulteries, covetings, wickednesses, deceit, lascivious-
23 ness, an evil eye, railing, pride, foolishness: all these evil things proceed from within, and defile the man.
24 And from thence he arose, and went away into the borders of Tyre ⁷and Sidon. And he entered into a house, and would have no man know it: and he could
25 not be hid. But straightway a woman, whose little daughter had an unclean spirit, having heard of him,

¹ Gr. *baptizings.*
² Many ancient authorities add *and couches.*
³ Or, *common*
⁴ Or, *surely die*
⁵ Many ancient authorities insert ver. 16 *If any man hath ears to hear, let him hear.*
⁶ Gr. *thoughts that are evil.*
⁷ Some ancient authorities omit *and Sidon.*

S. MARK. 7. 25—

¹ Or, *Gentile*
² Gr. *demon.*

³ Or, *loaf*

came and fell down at his feet. Now the woman was 26 a ¹Greek, a Syrophœnician by race. And she besought him that he would cast forth the ²devil out of her daughter. And he said unto her, Let the chil- 27 dren first be filled: for it is not meet to take the children's ³bread and cast it to the dogs. But she an- 28 swered and saith unto him, Yea, Lord: even the dogs under the table eat of the children's crumbs. And he said unto her, For this saying go thy way; 29 the ²devil is gone out of thy daughter. And she 30 went away unto her house, and found the child laid upon the bed, and the ²devil gone out.

And again he went out from the borders of Tyre, 31 and came through Sidon unto the sea of Galilee, through the midst of the borders of Decapolis. And 32 they bring unto him one that was deaf, and had an impediment in his speech; and they beseech him to lay his hand upon him. And he took him aside from 33 the multitude privately, and put his fingers into his ears, and he spat, and touched his tongue; and look- 34 ing up to heaven, he sighed, and saith unto him, Ephphatha, that is, Be opened. And his ears were open- 35 ed, and the bond of his tongue was loosed, and he spake plain. And he charged them that they should 36 tell no man: but the more he charged them, so much the more a great deal they published it. And they 37 were beyond measure astonished, saying, He hath done all things well: he maketh even the deaf to hear, and the dumb to speak.

⁴ Gr. *loaves.*

In those days, when there was again a great multi- **8** tude, and they had nothing to eat, he called unto him his disciples, and saith unto them, I have compassion 2 on the multitude, because they continue with me now three days, and have nothing to eat: and if I send 3 them away fasting to their home, they will faint in the way; and some of them are come from far. And 4 his disciples answered him, Whence shall one be able to fill these men with ⁴bread here in a desert place? And he asked them, How many loaves have ye? And 5 they said, Seven. And he commandeth the multi- 6 tude to sit down on the ground: and he took the seven loaves, and having given thanks, he brake, and gave to his disciples, to set before them; and they set them before the multitude. And they had a few 7 small fishes: and having blessed them, he commanded to set these also before them. And they did eat, 8 and were filled: and they took up, of broken pieces that remained over, seven baskets. And they were 9

10 about four thousand: and he sent them away. And straightway he entered into the boat with his disciples, and came into the parts of Dalmanutha.
11 And the Pharisees came forth, and began to question with him, seeking of him a sign from heaven,
12 tempting him. And he sighed deeply in his spirit, and saith, Why doth this generation seek a sign? verily I say unto you, There shall no sign be given
13 unto this generation. And he left them, and again entering into *the boat* departed to the other side.
14 And they forgot to take bread; and they had not
15 in the boat with them more than one loaf. And he charged them, saying, Take heed, beware of the leaven of the Pharisees and the leaven of Herod.
16 And they reasoned one with another, ¹saying, ²We
17 have no bread. And Jesus perceiving it saith unto them, Why reason ye, because ye have no bread? do ye not yet perceive, neither understand? have
18 ye your heart hardened? Having eyes, see ye not? and having ears, hear ye not? and do ye not remem-
19 ber? When I brake the five loaves among the five thousand, how many ³baskets full of broken pieces
20 took ye up? They say unto him, Twelve. And when the seven among the four thousand, how many
21 ³basketfuls of broken pieces took ye up? And they say unto him, Seven. And he said unto them, Do ye not yet understand?
22 And they come unto Bethsaida. And they bring to him a blind man, and beseech him to touch him.
23 And he took hold of the blind man by the hand, and brought him out of the village; and when he had spit on his eyes, and laid his hands upon him,
24 he asked him, Seest thou aught? And he looked up, and said, I see men; for I behold *them* as trees,
25 walking. Then again he laid his hands upon his eyes; and he looked stedfastly, and was restored,
26 and saw all things clearly. And he sent him away to his home, saying, Do not even enter into the village.
27 And Jesus went forth, and his disciples, into the villages of Cæsarea Philippi: and in the way he asked his disciples, saying unto them, Who do men
28 say that I am? And they told him, saying, John the Baptist: and others, Elijah; but others, One of the
29 prophets. And he asked them, But who say ye that I am? Peter answereth and saith unto him, Thou
30 art the Christ. And he charged them that they
31 should tell no man of him. And he began to teach them, that the Son of man must suffer many things,

¹ Some ancient authorities read *because they had no bread*.

² Or, *It is because we have no bread*.

³ *Basket* in ver. 19 and 20 represents different Greek words.

and be rejected by the elders, and the chief priests, and the scribes, and be killed, and after three days rise again. And he spake the saying openly. And 32 Peter took him, and began to rebuke him. But he 33 turning about, and seeing his disciples, rebuked Peter, and saith, Get thee behind me, Satan: for thou mindest not the things of God, but the things of men. And he called unto him the multitude with 34 his disciples, and said unto them, If any man would come after me, let him deny himself, and take up his cross, and follow me. For whosoever would save 35 his ¹life shall lose it; and whosoever shall lose his ¹life for my sake and the gospel's shall save it. For 36 what doth it profit a man, to gain the whole world, and forfeit his ¹life? For what should a man give 37 in exchange for his ¹life? For whosoever shall be 38 ashamed of me and of my words in this adulterous and sinful generation, the Son of man also shall be ashamed of him, when he cometh in the glory of his Father with the holy angels. And he said unto 9 them, Verily I say unto you, There be some here of them that stand *by*, which shall in no wise taste of death, till they see the kingdom of God come with power.

And after six days Jesus taketh with him Peter, 2 and James, and John, and bringeth them up into a high mountain apart by themselves: and he was transfigured before them: and his garments became 3 glistering, exceeding white; so as no fuller on earth can whiten them. And there appeared unto them 4 Elijah with Moses: and they were talking with Jesus. And Peter answereth and saith to Jesus, Rabbi, it 5 is good for us to be here: and let us make three ²tabernacles; one for thee, and one for Moses, and one for Elijah. For he wist not what to answer; 6 for they became sore afraid. And there came a 7 cloud overshadowing them: and there came a voice out of the cloud, This is my beloved Son: hear ye him. And suddenly looking round about, they saw 8 no one any more, save Jesus only with themselves.

And as they were coming down from the moun- 9 tain, he charged them that they should tell no man what things they had seen, save when the Son of man should have risen again from the dead. And 10 they kept the saying, questioning among themselves what the rising again from the dead should mean. And they asked him, saying, ³The scribes say that 11 Elijah must first come. And he said unto them, 12

¹ Or, *soul*

² Or, *booths*

³ Or, *How is it that the scribes say ... come?*

Elijah indeed cometh first, and restoreth all things: and how is it written of the Son of man, that he should suffer many things and be set at nought? 13 But I say unto you, that Elijah is come, and they have also done unto him whatsoever they listed, even as it is written of him.

14 And when they came to the disciples, they saw a great multitude about them, and scribes question-15 ing with them. And straightway all the multitude, when they saw him, were greatly amazed, and run-16 ning to him saluted him. And he asked them, 17 What question ye with them? And one of the multitude answered him, ¹Master, I brought unto 18 thee my son, which hath a dumb spirit; and wheresoever it taketh him, it ²dasheth him down: and he foameth, and grindeth his teeth, and pineth away: and I spake to thy disciples that they should cast 19 it out; and they were not able. And he answereth them and saith, O faithless generation, how long shall I be with you? how long shall I bear 20 with you? bring him unto me. And they brought him unto him: and when he saw him, straightway the spirit ³tare him grievously; and he fell on the 21 ground, and wallowed foaming. And he asked his father, How long time is it since this hath come 22 unto him? And he said, From a child. And ofttimes it hath cast him both into the fire and into the waters, to destroy him: but if thou canst do any-23 thing, have compassion on us, and help us. And Jesus said unto him, If thou canst! All things are 24 possible to him that believeth. Straightway the father of the child cried out, and said⁴, I believe; help 25 thou mine unbelief. And when Jesus saw that a multitude came running together, he rebuked the unclean spirit, saying unto him, Thou dumb and deaf spirit, I command thee, come out of him, and 26 enter no more into him. And having cried out, and ³torn him much, he came out: and *the child* became as one dead; insomuch that the more part 27 said, He is dead. But Jesus took him by the hand, 28 and raised him up; and he arose. And when he was come into the house, his disciples asked him 29 privately, ⁵*saying*, We could not cast it out. And he said unto them, This kind can come out by nothing, save by prayer⁶.

30 And they went forth from thence, and passed through Galilee; and he would not that any man 31 should know it. For he taught his disciples, and

1 Or, *Teacher*

2 Or, *rendeth him*

3 Or, *convulsed*

4 Many ancient authorities add *with tears*.

5 Or, How is it *that we could not cast it out?*

6 Many ancient authorities add *and fasting*.

said unto them, The Son of man is delivered up into the hands of men, and they shall kill him; and when he is killed, after three days he shall rise again. But they understood not the saying, and 32 were afraid to ask him.

And they came to Capernaum: and when he was 33 in the house he asked them, What were ye reasoning in the way? But they held their peace: for 34 they had disputed one with another in the way, who *was* the ¹greatest. And he sat down, and call-35 ed the twelve; and he saith unto them, If any man would be first, he shall be last of all, and minister of all. And he took a little child, and set him in the 36 midst of them: and taking him in his arms, he said unto them, Whosoever shall receive one of such lit-37 tle children in my name, receiveth me: and whosoever receiveth me, receiveth not me, but him that sent me.

John said unto him, ²Master, we saw one casting 38 out ³devils in thy name: and we forbade him, because he followed not us. But Jesus said, Forbid 39 him not: for there is no man which shall do a ⁴mighty work in my name, and be able quickly to speak evil of me. For he that is not against us is 40 for us. For whosoever shall give you a cup of wa-41 ter to drink, ⁵because ye are Christ's, verily I say unto you, he shall in no wise lose his reward. And 42 whosoever shall cause one of these little ones that believe ⁶on me to stumble, it were better for him if ⁷a great millstone were hanged about his neck, and he were cast into the sea. And if thy hand cause 43 thee to stumble, cut it off: it is good for thee to enter into life maimed, rather than having thy two hands to go into ⁸hell, into the unquenchable fire.⁹ And if thy foot cause thee to stumble, cut it off: it is 45 good for thee to enter into life halt, rather than having thy two feet to be cast into ⁸hell. And if thine 47 eye cause thee to stumble, cast it out: it is good for thee to enter into the kingdom of God with one eye, rather than having two eyes to be cast into ⁸hell; 48 where their worm dieth not, and the fire is not quench-49 ed. For every one shall be salted with fire¹⁰. Salt is 50 good: but if the salt have lost its saltness, wherewith will ye season it? Have salt in yourselves, and be at peace one with another.

And he arose from thence, and cometh into the **10** borders of Judæa and beyond Jordan: and multitudes come together unto him again; and, as he was

---

1 Gr. *greater.*

2 Or, *Teacher*
3 Gr. *demons.*

4 Gr. *power.*

5 Gr. *in name that ye are.*

6 Many ancient authorities omit *on me.*

7 Gr. *a millstone turned by an ass.*

8 Gr. *Gehenna.*

9 Ver. 44 and 46 (which are identical with ver. 48) are omitted by the best ancient authorities.

10 Many ancient authorities add *and every sacrifice shall be salted with salt.* See Lev. ii. 13.

2 wont, he taught them again. And there came unto him Pharisees, and asked him, Is it lawful for a man
3 to put away *his* wife? tempting him. And he answered and said unto them, What did Moses com-
4 mand you? And they said, Moses suffered to write
5 a bill of divorcement, and to put her away. But Jesus said unto them, For your hardness of heart he
6 wrote you this commandment. But from the beginning of the creation, Male and female made he
7 them. For this cause shall a man leave his father
8 and mother, ¹and shall cleave to his wife; and the twain shall become one flesh: so that they are no
9 more twain, but one flesh. What therefore God
10 hath joined together, let not man put asunder. And in the house the disciples asked him again of this
11 matter. And he saith unto them, Whosoever shall put away his wife, and marry another, committeth
12 adultery against her: and if she herself shall put away her husband, and marry another, she committeth adultery.
13 And they brought* unto him little children, that he should touch them: and the disciples rebuked
14 them. But when Jesus saw it, he was moved with indignation, and said unto them, Suffer the little children to come unto me; forbid them not: for of
15 such is the kingdom of God. Verily I say unto you, Whosoever shall not receive the kingdom of God as a little child, he shall in no wise enter there-
16 in. And he took them in his arms, and blessed them, laying his hands upon them.
17 And as he was going forth ²into the way, there ran one to him, and kneeled to him, and asked him, Good ³Master, what shall I do that I may inherit eternal
18 life? And Jesus said unto him, Why callest thou
19 me good? none is good save one, *even* God. Thou knowest the commandments, Do not kill, Do not commit adultery, Do not steal, Do not bear false witness, Do not defraud, Honor thy father and mother.
20 And he said unto him, ³Master, all these things have
21 I observed from my youth. And Jesus looking upon him loved him, and said unto him, One thing thou lackest: go, sell whatsoever thou hast, and give to the poor, and thou shalt have treasure in heaven:
22 and come, follow me. But his countenance fell at the saying, and he went away sorrowful: for he was one that had great possessions.

1 Some ancient authorities omit *and shall cleave to his wife.*

2 Or, *on his way*

3 Or, *Teacher*

---

* For "brought" read "were bringing." So in Luke xviii. 15.— *Am. Com.*

And Jesus looked round about, and saith unto his 23
disciples, How hardly shall they that have riches enter into the kingdom of God! And the disciples were 24
amazed at his words. But Jesus answereth again,
and saith unto them, Children, how hard is it ¹for
them that trust in riches to enter into the kingdom
of God! It is easier for a camel to go through a nee- 25
dle's eye, than for a rich man to enter into the kingdom of God. And they were astonished exceeding- 26
ly, saying ²unto him, Then who can be saved? Jesus 27
looking upon them saith, With men it is impossible,
but not with God: for all things are possible with
God. Peter began to say unto him, Lo, we have left 28
all, and have followed thee. Jesus said, Verily I say 29
unto you, There is no man that hath left house, or
brethren, or sisters, or mother, or father, or children,
or lands, for my sake, and for the gospel's sake, but 30
he shall receive a hundredfold now in this time,
houses, and brethren, and sisters, and mothers, and
children, and lands, with persecutions; and in the
³world to come eternal life. But many *that are* first 31
shall be last; and the last first.

And they were in the way, going up to Jerusalem; 32
and Jesus was going before them: and they were
amazed; ⁴and they that followed* were afraid. And
he took again the twelve, and began to tell them the
things that were to happen unto him, *saying*, Behold, 33
we go up to Jerusalem; and the Son of man shall be
delivered unto the chief priests and the scribes; and
they shall condemn him to death, and shall deliver
him unto the Gentiles: and they shall mock him, and 34
shall spit upon him, and shall scourge him, and shall
kill him; and after three days he shall rise again.

And there come near unto him James and John, 35
the sons of Zebedee, saying unto him, ⁵Master, we
would that thou shouldest do for us whatsoever we
shall ask of thee. And he said unto them, What 36
would ye that I should do for you? And they said 37
unto him, Grant unto us that we may sit, one on thy
right hand, and one on *thy* left hand, in thy glory.
But Jesus said unto them, Ye know not what ye ask. 38
Are ye able to drink the cup that I drink? or to be
baptized with the baptism that I am baptized with?
And they said unto him, We are able. And Jesus 39
said unto them, The cup that I drink ye shall drink;
and with the baptism that I am baptized withal shall

Marginal notes:
1 Some ancient authorities omit *for them that trust in riches.*
2 Many ancient authorities read *among themselves.*
3 Or, *age*
4 Or, *but some as they followed were afraid*
5 Or, *Teacher*

* "and they that followed" etc. omit the marg.—*Am. Com.*

40 ye be baptized: but to sit on my right hand or on *my* left hand is not mine to give: but *it is for them* for
41 whom it hath been prepared. And when the ten heard it, they began to be moved with indignation
42 concerning James and John. And Jesus called them to him, and saith unto them, Ye know that they which are accounted to rule over the Gentiles lord it over them; and their great ones exercise authority
43 over them. But it is not so among you: but whosoever would become great among you, shall be your
44 ¹minister: and whosoever would be first among you,
45 shall be ²servant of all. For verily* the Son of man came not to be ministered unto, but to minister, and to give his life a ransom for many.

1 Or, *servant*
2 Gr. *bondservant.*

46 And they come to Jericho: and as he went out from Jericho, with his disciples and a great multitude, the son of Timæus, Bartimæus, a blind beggar,
47 was sitting by the way side. And when he heard that it was Jesus of Nazareth, he began to cry out, and say, Jesus, thou son of David, have mercy on
48 me. And many rebuked him, that he should hold his peace: but he cried out the more a great deal,
49 Thou son of David, have mercy on me. And Jesus stood still, and said, Call ye him. And they call the blind man, saying unto him, Be of good cheer: rise,
50 he calleth thee. And he, casting away his garment,
51 sprang up, and came to Jesus. And Jesus answered him, and said, What wilt thou that I should do unto thee? And the blind man said unto him, ³Rabboni,
52 that I may receive my sight. And Jesus said unto him, Go thy way; thy faith hath ⁴made thee whole. And straightway he received his sight, and followed him in the way.

3 See John xx. 16.
4 Or, *saved thee*

11 And when they draw nigh unto Jerusalem, unto Bethphage and Bethany, at the mount of Olives, he
2 sendeth two of his disciples, and saith unto them, Go your way into the village that is over against you: and straightway as ye enter into it, ye shall find a colt tied, whereon no man ever yet sat; loose him,
3 and bring him. And if any one say unto you, Why do ye this? say ye, The Lord hath need of him; and
4 straightway he ⁵will send him ⁶back hither. And they went away, and found a colt tied at the door
5 without in the open street; and they loose him. And certain of them that stood there said unto them, What

5 Gr. *sendeth.*
6 Or, *again*

---

* For "For verily" etc. read "For the Son of man also" etc.—*Am. Com.*

do ye, loosing the colt? And they said unto them **6**
even as Jesus had said: and they let them go. And **7**
they bring the colt unto Jesus, and cast on him their
garments; and he sat upon him. And many spread **8**
their garments upon the way; and others ¹branches,
which they had cut from the fields. And they that **9**
went before, and they that followed, cried, Hosanna;
Blessed *is* he that cometh in the name of the Lord:
Blessed *is* the kingdom that cometh, *the kingdom* of **10**
our father David: Hosanna in the highest.

And he entered into Jerusalem, into the temple; **11**
and when he had looked round about upon all things,
it being now eventide, he went out unto Bethany
with the twelve.

And on the morrow, when they were come out **12**
from Bethany, he hungered. And seeing a fig tree **13**
afar off having leaves, he came, if haply he might
find anything thereon: and when he came to it, he
found nothing but leaves; for it was not the season
of figs. And he answered and said unto it, No man **14**
eat fruit from thee henceforward for ever. And his
disciples heard it.

And they come to Jerusalem: and he entered into **15**
the temple, and began to cast out them that sold and
them that bought in the temple, and overthrew the
tables of the money-changers, and the seats of them
that sold the doves; and he would not suffer that **16**
any man should carry a vessel through the temple.
And he taught, and said unto them, Is it not written, **17**
My house shall be called a house of prayer for all
the nations? but ye have made it a den of robbers.
And the chief priests and the scribes heard it, and **18**
sought how they might destroy him: for they feared him, for all the multitude was astonished at his
teaching.

And ²every evening ³he went forth out of the **19**
city.

And as they passed by in the morning, they saw **20**
the fig tree withered away from the roots. And **21**
Peter calling to remembrance saith unto him, Rabbi, behold, the fig tree which thou cursedst is withered away. And Jesus answering saith unto them, **22**
Have faith in God. Verily I say unto you, Whoso- **23**
ever shall say unto this mountain, Be thou taken up
and cast into the sea; and shall not doubt in his
heart, but shall believe that what he saith cometh
to pass; he shall have it. Therefore I say unto you, **24**
All things whatsoever ye pray and ask for, believe

---

¹ Gr. *layers of leaves.*

² Gr. *whenever evening came.*

³ Some ancient authorities read *they.*

that ye have received* them, and ye shall have them.
25 And whensoever ye stand praying, forgive, if ye
have aught against any one; that your Father also
which is in heaven may forgive you your trespasses.¹
27 And they come again to Jerusalem: and as he
was walking in the temple, there come to him the
28 chief priests, and the scribes, and the elders; and
they said unto him, By what authority doest thou
these things? or who gave thee this authority to do
29 these things? And Jesus said unto them, I will ask
of you one ²question, and answer me, and I will tell
30 you by what authority I do these things. The baptism of John, was it from heaven, or from men? an-
31 swer me. And they reasoned with themselves, saying, If we shall say, From heaven; he will say, Why
32 then did ye not believe him? ³But should we say,
From men—they feared the people: ⁴for all verily
33 held John to be a prophet. And they answered
Jesus and say, We know not. And Jesus saith unto
them, Neither tell I you by what authority I do these
things.

12 And he began to speak unto them in parables. A
man planted a vineyard, and set a hedge about it,
and digged a pit for the winepress, and built a tower, and let it out to husbandmen, and went into an-
2 other country. And at the season he sent to the
husbandmen a ⁵servant, that he might receive from
3 the husbandmen of the fruits of the vineyard. And
they took him, and beat him, and sent him away
4 empty. And again he sent unto them another ⁵servant; and him they wounded in the head, and han-
5 dled shamefully. And he sent another; and him
they killed: and many others; beating some, and
6 killing some. He had yet one, a beloved son: he
sent him last unto them, saying, They will rever-
7 ence my son. But those husbandmen said among
themselves, This is the heir; come, let us kill him,
8 and the inheritance shall be ours. And they took
him, and killed him, and cast him forth out of the
9 vineyard. What therefore will the lord of the vineyard do? he will come and destroy the husbandmen,
10 and will give the vineyard unto others. Have ye
not read even this scripture;

The stone which the builders rejected,
The same was made the head of the corner:

¹ Many ancient authorities add ver. 26 *But if ye do not forgive, neither will your Father which is in heaven forgive your trespasses.*

² Gr. *word.*

³ Or, *But shall we say, From men?*
⁴ Or, *for all held John to be a prophet indeed.*

⁵ Gr. *bondservant.*

---

* For "have received" read "receive" with marg. Gr. *received.*—
Am. Com.

This was from the Lord, 11
And it is marvellous in our eyes?

And they sought to lay hold on him; and they fear- 12
ed the multitude; for they perceived that he spake
the parable against them: and they left him, and
went away.

And they send unto him certain of the Pharisees 13
and of the Herodians, that they might catch him in
talk. And when they were come, they say unto 14
[1] Or, *Teacher* him, ¹Master, we know that thou art true, and carest
not for any one: for thou regardest not the person
of men, but of a truth teachest the way of God: Is
it lawful to give tribute unto Cæsar, or not? Shall 15
we give, or shall we not give? But he, knowing
their hypocrisy, said unto them, Why tempt ye me?
[2] See marginal note on Matt.xviii.28. bring me a ²penny, that I may see it. And they 16
brought it. And he saith unto them, Whose is this
image and superscription? And they said unto him,
Cæsar's. And Jesus said unto them, Render unto 17
Cæsar the things that are Cæsar's, and unto God the
things that are God's. And they marvelled greatly
at him.

And there come unto him Sadducees, which say 18
that there is no resurrection; and they asked him,
saying, ¹Master, Moses wrote unto us, If a man's 19
brother die, and leave a wife behind him, and leave
no child, that his brother should take his wife, and
raise up seed unto his brother. There were seven 20
brethren: and the first took a wife, and dying left
no seed; and the second took her, and died, leaving 21
no seed behind him; and the third likewise: and 22
the seven left no seed. Last of all the woman also
died. In the resurrection whose wife shall she be 23
of them? for the seven had her to wife. Jesus said 24
unto them, Is it not for this cause that ye err, that
ye know not the scriptures, nor the power of God?
For when they shall rise from the dead, they neither 25
marry, nor are given in marriage; but are as angels
in heaven. But as touching the dead, that they are 26
raised; have ye not read in the book of Moses, in *the
place concerning* the Bush, how God spake unto him,
saying I *am* the God of Abraham, and the God of
Isaac, and the God of Jacob? He is not the God of 27
the dead, but of the living: ye do greatly err.

And one of the scribes came, and heard them 28
questioning together, and knowing that he had answered them well, asked him, What commandment
is the first of all? Jesus answered, The first is, 29

Hear, O Israel; ¹The Lord our God, the Lord is
30 one: and thou shalt love the Lord thy God ²with
all thy heart, and ²with all thy soul, and ²with all
31 thy mind, and ²with all thy strength. The second
is this, Thou shalt love thy neighbour as thyself.
There is none other commandment greater than these.
32 And the scribe said unto him, Of a truth, ³Master,
thou hast well said that he is one; and there is none
33 other but he: and to love him with all the heart, and
with all the understanding, and with all the strength,
and to love his neighbour as himself, is much more
34 than all whole burnt offerings and sacrifices. And
when Jesus saw that he answered discreetly, he said
unto him, Thou art not far from the kingdom of
God. And no man after that durst ask him any
question.

35 And Jesus answered and said, as he taught in the
temple, How say the scribes that the Christ is the son
36 of David? David himself said in the Holy Spirit,

> The Lord said unto my Lord,
> Sit thou on my right hand,
> Till I make thine enemies ⁴the footstool of thy
> feet.

37 David himself calleth him Lord; and whence is he
his son? And ⁵the common people heard him gladly.
38 And in his teaching he said, Beware of the scribes,
which desire to walk in long robes, and *to have* salu-
39 tations in the marketplaces, and chief seats in the
40 synagogues, and chief places at feasts: they which
devour widows' houses, ⁶and for a pretence make
long prayers; these shall receive greater condemnation.

41 And he sat down over against the treasury, and
beheld how the multitude cast ⁷money into the treas-
42 ury: and many that were rich cast in much. And
there came ⁸a poor widow, and she cast in two mites,
43 which make a farthing. And he called unto him
his disciples, and said unto them, Verily I say unto
you, This poor widow cast in more than all they
44 which are casting into the treasury: for they all did
cast in of their superfluity; but she of her want did
cast in all that she had, *even* all her living.

13 And as he went forth out of the temple, one of
his disciples saith unto him, ³Master, behold, what
manner of stones and what manner of buildings!
2 And Jesus said unto him, Seest thou these great
buildings? there shall not be left here one stone
upon another, which shall not be thrown down.

¹ Or, *The Lord is our God; the Lord is one*
² Gr. *from.*
³ Or, *Teacher*
⁴ Some ancient authorities read *underneath thy feet.*
⁵ Or, *the great multitude*
⁶ Or, *even while for a pretence they make*
⁷ Gr. *brass.*
⁸ Gr. *one.*

And as he sat on the mount of Olives over against 3 the temple, Peter and James and John and Andrew asked him privately, Tell us, when shall these things 4 be? and what *shall be* the sign when these things are all about to be accomplished? And Jesus began to 5 say unto them, Take heed that no man lead you astray. Many shall come in my name, saying, I am 6 *he*; and shall lead many astray. And when ye shall 7 hear of wars and rumours of wars, be not troubled: *these things* must needs come to pass; but the end is not yet. For nation shall rise against nation, and 8 kingdom against kingdom: there shall be earthquakes in divers places; there shall be famines: these things are the beginning of travail.

But take ye heed to yourselves: for they shall 9 deliver you up to councils; and in synagogues shall ye be beaten; and before governors and kings shall ye stand for my sake, for a testimony unto them. And the gospel must first be preached unto all the 10 nations. And when they lead you *to judgement*, and 11 deliver you up, be not anxious beforehand what ye shall speak: but whatsoever shall be given you in that hour, that speak ye: for it is not ye that speak, but the Holy Ghost. And brother shall deliver up 12 brother to death, and the father his child; and children shall rise up against parents, and [1]cause them to be put to death. And ye shall be hated of all 13 men for my name's sake: but he that endureth to the end, the same shall be saved.

But when ye see the abomination of desolation 14 standing where he ought not (let him that readeth understand), then let them that are in Judæa flee unto the mountains: and let him that is on the 15 housetop not go down, nor enter in, to take anything out of his house: and let him that is in the field not 16 return back to take his cloke. But woe unto them 17 that are with child and to them that give suck in those days! And pray ye that it be not in the win- 18 ter. For those days shall be tribulation, such as there 19 hath not been the like from the beginning of the creation which God created until now, and never shall be. And except the Lord had shortened the 20 days, no flesh would have been saved: but for the elect's sake, whom he chose, he shortened the days. And then if any man shall say unto you, Lo, here 21 is the Christ; or, Lo, there; believe [2]*it* not: for there 22 shall arise false Christs and false prophets, and shall shew signs and wonders, that they may lead astray,

---

[1] Or, *put them to death*

[2] Or, him

23 if possible, the elect. But take ye heed: behold, I have told you all things beforehand.
24 But in those days, after that tribulation, the sun shall be darkened, and the moon shall not give her
25 light, and the stars shall be falling from heaven, and the powers that are in the heavens shall be shaken.
26 And then shall they see the Son of man coming in
27 clouds with great power and glory. And then shall he send forth the angels, and shall gather together his elect from the four winds, from the uttermost part of the earth to the uttermost part of heaven.
28 Now from the fig tree learn her parable: when her branch is now become tender, and putteth forth
29 its leaves, ye know that the summer is nigh; even so ye also, when ye see these things coming to pass,
30 know ye that ¹he is nigh, *even* at the doors. Verily I say unto you, This generation shall not pass away,
31 until all these things be accomplished. Heaven and earth shall pass away: but my words shall not pass
32 away. But of that day or that hour knoweth no one, not even the angels in heaven, neither the Son,
33 but the Father. Take ye heed, watch ²and pray:
34 for ye know not when the time is. *It is as when* a man, sojourning in another country, having left his house, and given authority to his ³servants, to each one his work, commanded also the porter to watch.
35 Watch therefore: for ye know not when the lord of the house cometh, whether at even, or at midnight,
36 or at cockcrowing, or in the morning; lest coming
37 suddenly he find you sleeping. And what I say unto you I say unto all, Watch.

14 Now after two days was *the feast of* the passover and the unleavened bread: and the chief priests and the scribes sought how they might take him
2 with subtilty, and kill him: for they said, Not during the feast, lest haply there shall be a tumult of the people.
3 And while he was in Bethany in the house of Simon the leper, as he sat at meat, there came a woman having ⁴an alabaster cruse of ointment of ⁵spikenard* very costly; *and* she brake the cruse, and pour-
4 ed it over his head. But there were some that had indignation among themselves, *saying*, To what purpose hath this waste of the ointment been made?
5 For this ointment might have been sold for above

¹ Or, *it*

² Some ancient authorities omit *and pray*.

³ Gr. *bondservants*.

⁴ Or, *a flask*

⁵ Gr. *pistic nard*, pistic being perhaps a local name. Others take it to mean *genuine*; others, *liquid*.

---

* For "spikenard" read "pure nard" (with marg. Or, *liquid nard*), and omit marg. ⁵. So in John xii. 3.—*Am. Com.*

three hundred ¹pence, and given to the poor. And they murmured against her. But Jesus said, Let her alone; why trouble ye her? she hath wrought a good work on me. For ye have the poor always with you, and whensoever ye will ye can do them good: but me ye have not always. She hath done what she could: she hath anointed my body aforehand for the burying. And verily I say unto you, Wheresoever the gospel shall be preached throughout the whole world, that also which this woman hath done shall be spoken of for a memorial of her.

And Judas Iscariot, ²he that was one of the twelve, went away unto the chief priests, that he might deliver him unto them. And they, when they heard it, were glad, and promised to give him money. And he sought how he might conveniently deliver him *unto them*.

And on the first day of unleavened bread, when they sacrificed the passover, his disciples say unto him, Where wilt thou that we go and make ready that thou mayest eat the passover? And he sendeth two of his disciples, and saith unto them, Go into the city, and there shall meet you a man bearing a pitcher of water: follow him; and wheresoever he shall enter in, say to the goodman of the house, The ³Master saith, Where is my guest-chamber, where I shall eat the passover with my disciples? And he will himself shew you a large upper room furnished *and* ready: and there make ready for us. And the disciples went forth, and came into the city, and found as he had said unto them: and they made ready the passover.

And when it was evening he cometh with the twelve. And as they ⁴sat and were eating, Jesus said, Verily I say unto you, One of you shall betray me, *even* he that eateth with me. They began to be sorrowful, and to say unto him one by one, Is it I? And he said unto them, *It is* one of the twelve, he that dippeth with me in the dish. For the Son of man goeth, even as it is written of him: but woe unto that man through whom the Son of man is betrayed! good were it ⁵for that man if he had not been born.

And as they were eating, he took ⁶bread, and when he had blessed, he brake it, and gave to them, and said, Take ye: this is my body. And he took a cup, and when he had given thanks, he gave to them: and they all drank of it. And he said unto

Marginal notes:
1 See marginal note on Matt. xviii. 28.
2 Gr. *the one of the twelve*.
3 Or, *Teacher*
4 Gr. *reclined*.
5 Gr. *for him if that man*.
6 Or, *a loaf*

them, This is my blood of ¹the ²covenant, which is
25 shed for many. Verily I say unto you, I will no
more drink of the fruit of the vine, until that day
when I drink it new in the kingdom of God.
26 And when they had sung a hymn, they went out
unto the mount of Olives.
27 And Jesus saith unto them, All ye shall be ³offended: for it is written, I will smite the shepherd,
28 and the sheep shall be scattered abroad. Howbeit,
after I am raised up, I will go before you into Gali-
29 lee. But Peter said unto him, Although all shall be
30 ³offended, yet will not I. And Jesus saith unto him,
Verily I say unto thee, that thou to-day, *even* this
night, before the cock crow twice, shalt deny me
31 thrice. But he spake exceeding vehemently, If I
must die with thee, I will not deny thee. And in
like manner also said they all.
32 And they come unto ⁴a place which was named
Gethsemane: and he saith unto his disciples, Sit ye
33 here, while I pray. And he taketh with him Peter
and James and John, and began to be greatly
34 amazed, and sore troubled. And he saith unto
them, My soul is exceeding sorrowful even unto
35 death: abide ye here, and watch. And he went
forward a little, and fell on the ground, and prayed
that, if it were possible, the hour might pass away
36 from him. And he said, Abba, Father, all things
are possible unto thee; remove this cup from me:
37 howbeit not what I will, but what thou wilt. And
he cometh, and findeth them sleeping, and saith unto
Peter, Simon, sleepest thou? couldest thou not
38 watch one hour? ⁵Watch and pray, that ye enter
not into temptation: the spirit indeed is willing, but
39 the flesh is weak. And again he went away, and
40 prayed, saying the same words. And again he came,
and found them sleeping, for their eyes were very
41 heavy; and they wist not what to answer him. And
he cometh the third time, and saith unto them, Sleep
on now, and take your rest: it is enough; the hour
is come; behold, the Son of man is betrayed into the
42 hands of sinners. Arise, let us be going: behold, he
that betrayeth me is at hand.
43 And straightway, while he yet spake, cometh Judas, one of the twelve, and with him a multitude
with swords and staves, from the chief priests and
44 the scribes and the elders. Now he that betrayed
him had given them a token, saying, Whomsoever
I shall kiss, that is he; take him, and lead him away

1 Or, *the testament*
2 Some ancient authorities insert *new*.
3 Gr. *caused to stumble*.
4 Gr. *an enclosed piece of ground*.
5 Or, *Watch ye, and pray that ye enter not*

safely. And when he was come, straightway he came to him, and saith, Rabbi; and ¹kissed him. And they laid hands on him, and took him. But a certain one of them that stood by drew his sword, and smote the ²servant of the high priest, and struck off his ear. And Jesus answered and said unto them, Are ye come out, as against a robber, with swords and staves to seize me? I was daily with you in the temple teaching, and ye took me not: but *this is done* that the scriptures might be fulfilled. And they all left him, and fled.

And a certain young man followed with him, having a linen cloth cast about him, over *his* naked *body*: and they lay hold on him; but he left the linen cloth, and fled naked.

And they led Jesus away to the high priest: and there come together with him all the chief priests and the elders and the scribes. And Peter had followed him afar off, even within, into the court of the high priest; and he was sitting with the officers, and warming himself in the light *of the fire*. Now the chief priests and the whole council sought witness against Jesus to put him to death; and found it not. For many bare false witness against him, and their witness agreed not together. And there stood up certain, and bare false witness against him, saying, We heard him say, I will destroy this ³temple that is made with hands, and in three days I will build another made without hands. And not even so did their witness agree together. And the high priest stood up in the midst, and asked Jesus, saying, Answerest thou nothing? what is it which these witness against thee? But he held his peace, and answered nothing. Again the high priest asked him, and saith unto him, Art thou the Christ, the Son of the Blessed? And Jesus said, I am: and ye shall see the Son of man sitting at the right hand of power, and coming with the clouds of heaven. And the high priest rent his clothes, and saith, What further need have we of witnesses? Ye have heard the blasphemy: what think ye? And they all condemned him to be ⁴worthy of death. And, some began to spit on him, and to cover his face, and to buffet him, and to say unto him, Prophesy: and the officers received him with ⁵blows of their hands.

And as Peter was beneath in the court, there cometh one of the maids of the high priest; and seeing Peter warming himself, she looked upon him, and

---

1 Gr. *kissed him much.*

2 Gr. *bondservant.*

3 Or, *sanctuary*

4 Gr. *liable to.*

5 Or, *strokes of rods*

saith, Thou also wast with the Nazarene, *even* Jesus.
68 But he denied, saying, ¹I neither know, nor understand what thou sayest: and he went out into the
69 ²porch; ³and the cock crew. And the maid saw him, and began again to say to them that stood by,
70 This is *one* of them. But he again denied it. And after a little while again they that stood by said to Peter, Of a truth thou art *one* of them; for thou art
71 a Galilæan. But he began to curse, and to swear, I
72 know not this man of whom ye speak. And straightway the second time the cock crew. And Peter called to mind the word, how that Jesus said unto him, Before the cock crow twice, thou shalt deny me thrice. ⁴And when he thought thereon, he wept.

15 And straightway in the morning the chief priests with the elders and scribes, and the whole council, held a consultation, and bound Jesus, and carried
2 him away, and delivered him up to Pilate. And Pilate asked him, Art thou the King of the Jews? And he answering saith unto him, Thou sayest.
3 And the chief priests accused him of many things.
4 And Pilate again asked him, saying, Answerest thou nothing? behold how many things they accuse thee
5 of. But Jesus no more answered anything; insomuch that Pilate marvelled.
6 Now at ⁵the feast he used to release unto them one
7 prisoner, whom they asked of him. And there was one called Barabbas, *lying* bound with them that had made insurrection, men who in the insurrection had
8 committed murder. And the multitude went up and began to ask him *to do* as he was wont to do unto
9 them. And Pilate answered them, saying, Will ye
10 that I release unto you the King of the Jews? For he perceived that for envy the chief priests had de-
11 livered him up. But the chief priests stirred up the multitude, that he should rather release Barabbas
12 unto them. And Pilate again answered and said unto them, What then shall I do unto him whom ye
13 call the King of the Jews? And they cried out
14 again, Crucify him. And Pilate said unto them, Why, what evil hath he done? But they cried out
15 exceedingly, Crucify him. And Pilate, wishing to content the multitude, released unto them Barabbas, and delivered Jesus, when he had scourged him, to be crucified.
16 And the soldiers led him away within the court, which is the ⁶Prætorium; and they call together the
17 whole ⁷band. And they clothe him with purple, and

1 Or, *I neither know, nor understand: thou, what sayest thou?*
2 Gr. *forecourt.*
3 Many ancient authorities omit *and the cock crew.*
4 Or, *And he began to weep.*
5 Or, *a feast*
6 Or, *palace*
7 Or, *cohort*

plaiting a crown of thorns, they put it on him; and 18 they began to salute him, Hail, King of the Jews! And they smote his head with a reed, and did spit 19 upon him, and bowing their knees worshipped him. And when they had mocked him, they took off from 20 him the purple, and put on him his garments. And they lead him out to crucify him.

¹ Gr. *impress.*

And they ¹compel one passing by, Simon of Cy- 21 rene, coming from the country, the father of Alexander and Rufus, to go *with them*, that he might bear his cross. And they bring him unto the place Gol- 22 gotha, which is, being interpreted, The place of a skull. And they offered him wine mingled with 23 myrrh: but he received it not. And they crucify 24 him, and part his garments among them, casting lots upon them, what each should take. And it was the 25 third hour, and they crucified him. And the super- 26 scription of his accusation was written over, THE KING OF THE JEWS. And with him they crucify two 27 robbers; one on his right hand, and one on his left. ² And they that passed by railed on him, wagging their 29 heads, and saying, Ha! thou that destroyest the ³temple, and buildest it in three days, save thyself, and 30 come down from the cross. In like manner also the 31 chief priests mocking *him* among themselves with the scribes said, He saved others; ⁴himself he cannot save. Let the Christ, the King of Israel, now come 32 down from the cross, that we may see and believe. And they that were crucified with him reproached him.

² Many ancient authorities insert ver. 28 *And the scripture was fulfilled, which saith, And he was reckoned with transgressors.* See Luke xxii. 37.

³ Or, *sanctuary*

⁴ Or, *can he not save himself?*

And when the sixth hour was come, there was 33 darkness over the whole ⁵land until the ninth hour. And at the ninth hour Jesus cried with a loud voice, 34 Eloi, Eloi, lama sabachthani? which is, being interpreted, My God, my God, ⁶why hast thou forsaken me? And some of them that stood by, when they 35 heard it, said, Behold, he calleth Elijah. And one 36 ran, and filling a sponge full of vinegar, put it on a reed, and gave him to drink, saying, Let be; let us see whether Elijah cometh to take him down. And 37 Jesus uttered a loud voice, and gave up the ghost. And the veil of the ³temple was rent in twain from 38 the top to the bottom. And when the centurion, 39 which stood by over against him, saw that he ⁷so gave up the ghost, he said, Truly this man was ⁸the Son of God. And there were also women beholding from 40 afar: among whom *were* both Mary Magdalene, and Mary the mother of James the ⁹less and of Joses,

⁵ Or, *earth*

⁶ Or, *why didst thou forsake me?*

⁷ Many ancient authorities read *so cried out, and gave up the ghost.*

⁸ Or, *a son of God*

⁹ Gr. *little.*

41 and Salome; who, when he was in Galilee, followed him, and ministered unto him; and many other women which came up with him unto Jerusalem.
42 And when even was now come, because it was the
43 Preparation, that is, the day before the sabbath, there came Joseph of Arimathæa, a councillor of honourable estate, who also himself was looking for the kingdom of God; and he boldly went in unto Pi-
44 late, and asked for the body of Jesus. And Pilate marvelled if he were already dead: and calling unto him the centurion, he asked him whether he ¹had
45 been any while dead. And when he learned it of the centurion, he granted the corpse to Joseph.
46 And he bought a linen cloth, and taking him down, wound him in the linen cloth, and laid him in a tomb which had been hewn out of a rock; and he rolled
47 a stone against the door of the tomb. And Mary Magdalene and Mary the *mother* of Joses beheld where he was laid.

16 And when the sabbath was past, Mary Magdalene, and Mary the *mother* of James, and Salome, bought spices, that they might come and anoint
2 him. And very early on the first day of the week, they come to the tomb when the sun was risen.
3 And they were saying among themselves, Who shall roll us away the stone from the door of the tomb?
4 and looking up, they see that the stone is rolled
5 back: for it was exceeding great. And entering into the tomb, they saw a young man sitting on the right side, arrayed in a white robe; and they were amazed.
6 And he saith unto them, Be not amazed: ye seek Jesus, the Nazarene, which hath been crucified: he is risen; he is not here: behold, the place where they
7 laid him! But go, tell his disciples and Peter, He goeth before you into Galilee: there shall ye see him,
8 as he said unto you. And they went out, and fled from the tomb; for trembling and astonishment had come upon them: and they said nothing to any one; for they were afraid.

9 ²Now when he was risen early on the first day of the week, he appeared first to Mary Magdalene, from
10 whom he had cast out seven ³devils. She went and told them that had been with him, as they mourned
11 and wept. And they, when they heard that he was alive, and had been seen of her, disbelieved.
12 And after these things he was manifested in an-

¹ Many ancient authorities read *were already dead.*

² The two oldest Greek manuscripts, and some other authorities, omit from ver. 9 to the end. Some other authorities have a different ending to the Gospel.

³ Gr. *demons.*

other form unto two of them, as they walked, on their way into the country. And they went away and told it unto the rest: neither believed they them. 13

And afterward he was manifested unto the eleven themselves as they sat at meat; and he upbraided them with their unbelief and hardness of heart, because they believed not them which had seen him after he was risen. And he said unto them, Go ye into all the world, and preach the gospel to the whole creation. He that believeth and is baptized shall be saved; but he that disbelieveth shall be condemned. And these signs shall follow them that believe: in my name shall they cast out [1]devils; they shall speak with [2]new tongues; they shall take up serpents, and if they drink any deadly thing, it shall in no wise hurt them; they shall lay hands on the sick, and they shall recover. 14 15 16 17 18

So then the Lord Jesus, after he had spoken unto them, was received up into heaven, and sat down at the right hand of God. And they went forth, and preached everywhere, the Lord working with them, and confirming the word by the signs that followed. Amen. 19 20

[1] Gr. *demons*.
[2] Some ancient authorities omit *new*.

THE GOSPEL

ACCORDING TO

S. LUKE.

1 Forasmuch as many have taken in hand to draw up a narrative concerning those matters which have
2 been ¹fulfilled among us, even as they delivered them unto us, which from the beginning were eyewitness-
3 es and ministers of the word, it seemed good to me also, having traced the course of all things accurate- ly from the first, to write unto thee in order, most
4 excellent Theophilus; that thou mightest know the certainty concerning the ²things ³wherein thou wast instructed.

¹ Or, *fully established*

² Gr. *words.*

³ Or, *which thou wast taught by word of mouth*

5 There was in the days of Herod, king of Judæa, a certain priest named Zacharias, of the course of Abi- jah: and he had a wife of the daughters of Aaron,
6 and her name was Elisabeth. And they were both righteous before God, walking in all the command-
7 ments and ordinances of the Lord blameless. And they had no child, because that Elisabeth was bar- ren, and they both were *now* ⁴well stricken in years.
8 Now it came to pass, while he executed the priest's
9 office before God in the order of his course, accord- ing to the custom of the priest's office, his lot was to enter into the ⁵temple of the Lord and burn in-
10 cense. And the whole multitude of the people were
11 praying without at the hour of incense. And there appeared unto him an angel of the Lord standing on
12 the right side of the altar of incense. And Zacharias was troubled when he saw *him*, and fear fell upon him.
13 But the angel said unto him, Fear not, Zacharias: be- cause thy supplication is heard, and thy wife Elisabeth shall bear thee a son, and thou shalt call his name
14 John. And thou shalt have joy and gladness; and

⁴ Gr. *advanced in their days.*

⁵ Or, *sanctuary*

many shall rejoice at his birth. For he shall be great 15
in the sight of the Lord, and he shall drink no wine
nor ¹strong drink; and he shall be filled with the ²Holy
Ghost, even from his mother's womb. And many 16
of the children of Israel shall he turn unto the Lord
their God. And he shall ³go before his face in the 17
spirit and power of Elijah, to turn the hearts of the
fathers to the children, and the disobedient *to walk*
in the wisdom of the just; to make ready for the
Lord a people prepared *for him*. And Zacharias 18
said unto the angel, Whereby shall I know this? for
I am an old man, and my wife ⁴well stricken in
years. And the angel answering said unto him, I 19
am Gabriel, that stand in the presence of God; and
I was sent to speak unto thee, and to bring thee these
good tidings. And behold, thou shalt be silent and 20
not able to speak, until the day that these things
shall come to pass, because thou believedst not my
words, which shall be fulfilled in their season. And 21
the people were waiting for Zacharias, and they marvelled ⁵while he tarried in the ⁶temple. And when 22
he came out, he could not speak unto them: and
they perceived that he had seen a vision in the ⁶temple: and he continued making signs unto them, and
remained dumb. And it came to pass, when the 23
days of his ministration were fulfilled, he departed
unto his house.

And after these days Elisabeth his wife conceived; 24
and she hid herself five months, saying, Thus hath 25
the Lord done unto me in the days wherein he looked upon *me*, to take away my reproach among men.

Now in the sixth month the angel Gabriel was sent 26
from God unto a city of Galilee, named Nazareth, to 27
a virgin betrothed to a man whose name was Joseph,
of the house of David; and the virgin's name was
Mary. And he came in unto her, and said, Hail, 28
thou that art highly.⁷favoured, the Lord *is* with thee⁸.
But she was greatly troubled at the saying, and cast 29
in her mind what manner of salutation this might
be. And the angel said unto her, Fear not, Mary: 30
for thou hast found ⁹favour with God. And behold, 31
thou shalt conceive in thy womb, and bring forth a
son, and shalt call his name JESUS. He shall be 32
great, and shall be called the Son of the Most High:
and the Lord God shall give unto him the throne of
his father David: and he shall reign over the house 33
of Jacob ¹⁰for ever; and of his kingdom there shall
be no end. And Mary said unto the angel, How 34

---

1 Gr. *sikera*.
2 Or, *Holy Spirit*: and so throughout this book.
3 Some ancient authorities read *come nigh before his face*.
4 Gr. *advanced in her days*.
5 Or, *at his tarrying*
6 Or, *sanctuary*
7 Or, *endued with grace*
8 Many ancient authorities add *blessed art thou among women*. See ver. 42.
9 Or, *grace*
10 Gr. *unto the ages*.

35 shall this be, seeing I know not a man? And the angel answered and said unto her, The Holy Ghost shall come upon thee, and the power of the Most High shall overshadow thee: wherefore* also ¹that which ²is to be born ³shall be called holy, the Son
36 of God. And behold, Elisabeth thy kinswoman, she also hath conceived a son in her old age: and this is the sixth month with her that ⁴was called barren.
37 For no word from God shall be void of power. And
38 Mary said, Behold, the ⁵handmaid of the Lord; be it unto me according to thy word. And the angel departed from her.

39 And Mary arose in these days and went into the
40 hill country with haste, into a city of Judah; and entered into the house of Zacharias and saluted Eli-
41 sabeth. And it came to pass, when Elisabeth heard the salutation of Mary, the babe leaped in her womb;
42 and Elisabeth was filled with the Holy Ghost; and she lifted up her voice with a loud cry, and said, Blessed *art* thou among women, and blessed *is* the
43 fruit of thy womb. And whence is this to me, that
44 the mother of my Lord should come unto me? For behold, when the voice of thy salutation came into
45 mine ears, the babe leaped in my womb for joy. And blessed *is* she that ⁶believed; for there shall be a ful-filment of the things which have been spoken to her
46 from the Lord. And Mary said,

My soul doth magnify the Lord,
47 And my spirit hath rejoiced in God my Saviour.
48 For he hath looked upon the low estate of his ⁷handmaiden:
For behold, from henceforth all generations shall call me blessed.
49 For he that is mighty hath done to me great things;
And holy is his name.
50 And his mercy is unto generations and generations
On them that fear him.
51 He hath shewed strength with his arm;
He hath scattered the proud ⁸in the imagination of their heart.
52 He hath put down princes from *their* thrones,
And hath exalted them of low degree.
53 The hungry he hath filled with good things;

---

¹ Or, *the holy thing which is to be born shall be called the Son of God.*
² Or, *is begotten*
³ Some ancient authorities insert *of thee.*
⁴ Or, *is*
⁵ Gr. *bondmaid.*
⁶ Or, *believed that there shall be*
⁷ Gr. *bondmaiden.*
⁸ Or, *by*

* Let the text run "wherefore also the holy thing which is begotten shall be called the Son of God" with the present text in the margin.—*Am. Com.*

And the rich he hath sent empty away.
He hath holpen Israel his servant, 54
That he might remember mercy
(As he spake unto our fathers) 55
Toward Abraham and his seed for ever.

And Mary abode with her about three months, 56
and returned unto her house.

Now Elisabeth's time was fulfilled that she should 57
be delivered; and she brought forth a son. And 58
her neighbours and her kinsfolk heard that the Lord
had magnified his mercy toward her; and they rejoiced with her. And it came to pass on the eighth 59
day, that they came to circumcise the child; and
they would have called him Zacharias, after the
name of his father. And his mother answered and 60
said, Not so; but he shall be called John. And 61
they said unto her, There is none of thy kindred
that is called by this name. And they made signs 62
to his father, what he would have him called. And 63
he asked for a writing tablet, and wrote, saying, His
name is John. And they marvelled all. And his 64
mouth was opened immediately, and his tongue
loosed, and he spake, blessing God. And fear came 65
on all that dwelt round about them: and all these
sayings were noised abroad throughout all the hill
country of Judæa. And all that heard them laid 66
them up in their heart, saying, What then shall this
child be? For the hand of the Lord was with him.

And his father Zacharias was filled with the Holy 67
Ghost, and prophesied, saying,

Blessed *be* the Lord, the God of Israel; 68
For he hath visited and wrought redemption for
his people,
And hath raised up a horn of salvation for us 69
In the house of his servant David
(As he spake by the mouth of his holy prophets 70
which have been since the world began*),
Salvation from our enemies, and from the hand 71
of all that hate us;
To shew mercy towards our fathers, 72
And to remember his holy covenant;
The oath which he sware unto Abraham our 73
father,
To grant unto us that we being delivered out of 74
the hand of our enemies

---

* For "since the world began" read "of old" Similarly Acts iii. 21; xv. 18.—*Am. Com.*

	Should serve him without fear,
75	In holiness and righteousness before him all our days.
76	Yea and thou, child, shalt be called the prophet of the Most High:
	For thou shalt go before the face of the Lord to make ready his ways;
77	To give knowledge of salvation unto his people In the remission of their sins,
78	Because of the ¹tender mercy of our God, ²Whereby the dayspring from on high ³shall visit us,
79	To shine upon them that sit in darkness and the shadow of death;
	To guide our feet into the way of peace.
80	And the child grew, and waxed strong in spirit, and was in the deserts till the day of his shewing unto Israel.

¹ Or, *heart of mercy*
² Or, *Wherein*
³ Many ancient authorities read *hath visited us*.

2 Now it came to pass in those days, there went out a decree from Cæsar Augustus, that all ⁴the world 2 should be enrolled. This was the first enrolment 3 made when Quirinius was governor of Syria. And all went to enrol themselves, every one to his own 4 city. And Joseph also went up from Galilee, out of the city of Nazareth, into Judæa, to the city of David, which is called Bethlehem, because he was 5 of the house and family of David; to enrol himself with Mary, who was betrothed to him, being great 6 with child. And it came to pass, while they were there, the days were fulfilled that she should be de-7 livered. And she brought forth her firstborn son; and she wrapped him in swaddling clothes, and laid him in a manger, because there was no room for them in the inn.

⁴ Gr. *the inhabited earth*.

8 And there were shepherds in the same country abiding in the field, and keeping ⁵watch by night 9 over their flock. And an angel of the Lord stood by them, and the glory of the Lord shone round 10 about them: and they were sore afraid. And the angel said unto them, Be not afraid; for behold, I bring you good tidings of great joy which shall be 11 to all the people: for there is born to you this day in the city of David a Saviour, which is ⁶Christ the 12 Lord. And this is the sign unto you: Ye shall find a babe wrapped in swaddling clothes, and lying in a 13 manger. And suddenly there was with the angel a multitude of the heavenly host praising God, and saying,

⁵ Or, *nightwatches*
⁶ Or, *Anointed Lord*

> Glory to God in the highest, 14
> And on earth ¹peace among ²men in whom he is well pleased.

And it came to pass, when the angels went away 15 from them into heaven, the shepherds said one to another, Let us now go even unto Bethlehem, and see this ³thing that is come to pass, which the Lord hath made known unto us. And they came with 16 haste, and found both Mary and Joseph, and the babe lying in the manger. And when they saw it, 17 they made known concerning the saying which was spoken to them about this child. And all that heard 18 it wondered at the things which were spoken unto them by the shepherds. But Mary kept all these 19 ⁴sayings, pondering them in her heart. And the 20 shepherds returned, glorifying and praising God for all the things that they had heard and seen, even as it was spoken unto them.

And when eight days were fulfilled for circum- 21 cising him, his name was called JESUS, which was so called by the angel before he was conceived in the womb.

And when the days of their purification according 22 to the law of Moses were fulfilled, they brought him up to Jerusalem, to present him to the Lord (as it 23 is written in the law of the Lord, Every male that openeth the womb shall be called holy to the Lord), and to offer a sacrifice according to that which is 24 said in the law of the Lord, A pair of turtledoves, or two young pigeons. And behold, there was a 25 man in Jerusalem, whose name was Simeon; and this man was righteous and devout, looking for the consolation of Israel: and the Holy Spirit was upon him. And it had been revealed unto him by the 26 Holy Spirit, that he should not see death, before he had seen the Lord's Christ. And he came in 27 the Spirit into the temple: and when the parents brought in the child Jesus, that they might do concerning him after the custom of the law, then he re- 28 ceived him into his arms, and blessed God, and said,

> Now lettest thou thy ⁵servant depart, O ⁶Lord, 29
> According to thy word, in peace;
> For mine eyes have seen thy salvation, 30
> Which thou hast prepared before the face of all 31 peoples;
> A light for ⁷revelation to the Gentiles, 32
> And the glory of thy people Israel.

And his father and his mother were marvelling at 33

---

¹ Many ancient authorities read peace, good pleasure among men.
² Gr. men of good pleasure.
³ Or, saying
⁴ Or, things
⁵ Gr. bondservant.
⁶ Gr. Master.
⁷ Or, the unveiling of the Gentiles

the things which were spoken concerning him;
34 and Simeon blessed them, and said unto Mary his mother, Behold, this *child* is set for the falling and rising up* of many in Israel; and for a sign which
35 is spoken against; yea and a sword shall pierce through thine own soul; that thoughts out of many
36 hearts may be revealed. And there was one Anna, a prophetess, the daughter of Phanuel, of the tribe of Asher (she was ¹of a great age, having lived with
37 a husband seven years from her virginity, and she had been a widow even for† fourscore and four years), which departed not from the temple, worshipping with fastings and supplications night and
38 day. And coming up at that very hour she gave thanks unto God, and spake of him to all them that
39 were looking for the redemption of Jerusalem. And when they had accomplished all things that were according to the law of the Lord, they returned into Galilee, to their own city Nazareth.
40 And the child grew, and waxed strong, ²filled with wisdom: and the grace of God was upon him.
41 And his parents went every year to Jerusalem at
42 the feast of the passover. And when he was twelve years old, they went up after the custom of the
43 feast; and when they had fulfilled the days, as they were returning, the boy Jesus tarried behind in Je-
44 rusalem; and his parents knew it not; but supposing him to be in the company, they went a day's journey; and they sought for him among their kins-
45 folk and acquaintance: and when they found him not, they returned to Jerusalem, seeking for him.
46 And it came to pass, after three days they found him in the temple, sitting in the midst of the ³doctors, both hearing them, and asking them questions:
47 and all that heard him were amazed at his under-
48 standing and his answers. And when they saw him, they were astonished: and his mother said unto him, ⁴Son, why hast thou thus dealt with us? behold, thy
49 father and I sought thee sorrowing. And he said unto them, How is it that ye sought me? wist ye
50 not that I must be ⁵in my Father's house? And they understood not the saying which he spake
51 unto them. And he went down with them, and came to Nazareth; and he was subject unto them: and his mother kept all *these* ⁶sayings in her heart.

¹ Gr. *advanced in many days.*

² Gr. *becoming full of wisdom.*

³ Or, *teachers*

⁴ Gr. *Child.*

⁵ Or, *about my Father's business.* Gr. *in the things of my Father.*

⁶ Or, *things*

---

* For "and rising up" read "and the rising."—*Am. Com.*
† For "even for" read "even unto"—*Am. Com.*

And Jesus advanced in wisdom and ¹stature, and 52
in ²favour with God and men.

Now in the fifteenth year of the reign of Tiberius 3
Cæsar, Pontius Pilate being governor of Judæa, and
Herod being tetrarch of Galilee, and his brother
Philip tetrarch of the region of Ituræa and Tracho‑
nitis, and Lysanias tetrarch of Abilene, in the high‑ 2
priesthood of Annas and Caiaphas, the word of God
came unto John the son of Zacharias in the wilder‑
ness. And he came into all the region round about 3
Jordan, preaching the baptism of repentance unto
remission of sins; as it is written in the book of the 4
words of Isaiah the prophet,

> The voice of one crying in the wilderness,
> Make ye ready the way of the Lord,
> Make his paths straight.
> Every valley shall be filled, 5
> And every mountain and hill shall be brought
>   low;
> And the crooked shall become straight,
> And the rough ways smooth;
> And all flesh shall see the salvation of God. 6

He said therefore to the multitudes that went out 7
to be baptized of him, Ye offspring of vipers, who
warned you to flee from the wrath to come? Bring 8
forth therefore fruits worthy of ³repentance, and be‑
gin not to say within yourselves, We have Abraham
to our father: for I say unto you, that God is able
of these stones to raise up children unto Abraham.
And even now is the axe also laid unto the root of 9
the trees: every tree therefore that bringeth not forth
good fruit is hewn down, and cast into the fire.
And the multitudes asked him, saying, What then 10
must we do? And he answered and said unto them, 11
He that hath two coats, let him impart to him that
hath none; and he that hath food, let him do like‑
wise. And there came also ⁴publicans to be bap‑ 12
tized, and they said unto him, ⁵Master, what must
we do? And he said unto them, Extort no more 13
than that which is appointed you. And ⁶soldiers 14
also asked him, saying, And we, what must we do?
And he said unto them, Do violence to no man*,
neither ⁷exact *anything* wrongfully; and be content
with your wages.

And as the people were in expectation, and all 15

Marginal notes:
1 Or, *age*
2 Or, *grace*
3 Or, *your repentance*
4 See marginal note on Matt. v. 46.
5 Or, *Teacher*
6 Gr. *soldiers on service.*
7 Or, *accuse* any one

* For "Do violence to no man" etc. read "Extort from no man by violence, neither accuse *any one* wrongfully" and omit marg.⁷—Am. Com.

men reasoned in their hearts concerning John,
16 whether haply he were the Christ; John answered, saying unto them all, I indeed baptize you with water; but there cometh he that is mightier than I, the latchet of whose shoes I am not ¹worthy to unloose: he shall baptize you ²with the Holy Ghost and *with*
17 fire: whose fan is in his hand, throughly to cleanse his threshing-floor, and to gather the wheat into his garner; but the chaff he will burn up with unquenchable fire.
18 With many other exhortations therefore preached
19 he ³good tidings unto the people; but Herod the tetrarch, being reproved by him for Herodias his brother's wife, and for all the evil things which
20 Herod had done, added yet this above all*, that he shut up John in prison.
21 Now it came to pass, when all the people were baptized, that, Jesus also having been baptized, and
22 praying, the heaven was opened, and the Holy Ghost descended in a bodily form, as a dove, upon him, and a voice came out of heaven, Thou art my beloved Son; in thee I am well pleased.
23 And Jesus himself, when he began *to teach*, was about thirty years of age, being the son (as was sup-
24 posed) of Joseph, the *son* of Heli, the *son* of Matthat, the *son* of Levi, the *son* of Melchi, the *son* of Jannai,
25 the *son* of Joseph, the *son* of Mattathias, the *son* of Amos, the *son* of Nahum, the *son* of Esli, the *son* of
26 Naggai, the *son* of Maath, the *son* of Mattathias, the
27 *son* of Semein, the *son* of Josech, the *son* of Joda, the *son* of Joanan, the *son* of Rhesa, the *son* of Zerubba-
28 bel, the *son* of ⁴Shealtiel, the *son* of Neri, the *son* of Melchi, the *son* of Addi, the *son* of Cosam, the *son* of
29 Elmadam, the *son* of Er, the *son* of Jesus, the *son* of Eliezer, the *son* of Jorim, the *son* of Matthat, the *son*
30 of Levi, the *son* of Symeon, the *son* of Judas, the *son*
31 of Joseph, the *son* of Jonam, the *son* of Eliakim, the *son* of Melea, the *son* of Menna, the *son* of Mattatha,
32 the *son* of Nathan, the *son* of David, the *son* of Jesse, the *son* of Obed, the *son* of Boaz, the *son* of ⁵Salmon,
33 the *son* of Nahshon, the *son* of Amminadab, ⁶the *son* of ⁷Arni, the *son* of Hezron, the *son* of Perez, the *son*
34 of Judah, the *son* of Jacob, the *son* of Isaac, the *son* of
35 Abraham, the *son* of Terah, the *son* of Nahor, the *son* of Serug, the *son* of Reu, the *son* of Peleg, the *son* of

1 Gr. *sufficient.*
2 Or, *in*
3 Or, *the gospel*
4 Gr. *Salathiel.*
5 Some ancient authorities write *Sala.*
6 Many ancient authorities insert *the son of Admin:* and one writes *Admin* for *Amminadab.*
7 Some ancient authorities write *Aram.*

---

* For "added yet this above all" read "added this also to them all"—*Am. Com.*

Eber, the *son* of Shelah, the *son* of Cainan, the *son* of 36 Arphaxad, the *son* of Shem, the *son* of Noah, the *son* of Lamech, the *son* of Methuselah, the *son* of Enoch, 37 the *son* of Jared, the *son* of Mahalaleel, the *son* of Cainan, the *son* of Enos, the *son* of Seth, the *son* of 38 Adam, the *son* of God.

And Jesus, full of the Holy Spirit, returned from 4 the Jordan, and was led ¹by the Spirit* in the wilderness during forty days, being tempted of the 2 devil. And he did eat nothing in those days: and when they were completed, he hungered. And the 3 devil said unto him, If thou art the Son of God, command this stone that it become ²bread. And Jesus 4 answered unto him, It is written, Man shall not live by bread alone. And he led him up, and shewed 5 him all the kingdoms of ³the world in a moment of time. And the devil said unto him, To thee will I 6 give all this authority, and the glory of them: for it hath been delivered unto me; and to whomsoever I will I give it. If thou therefore wilt worship before 7 me, it shall all be thine. And Jesus answered and 8 said unto him, It is written, Thou shalt worship the Lord thy God, and him only shalt thou serve. And 9 he led him to Jerusalem, and set him on the ⁴pinnacle of the temple, and said unto him, If thou art the Son of God, cast thyself down from hence: for it is 10 written,

> He shall give his angels charge concerning thee,
>> to guard thee:

and, 11

> On their hands they shall bear thee up,
> Lest haply thou dash thy foot against a stone.

And Jesus answering said unto him, It is said, Thou 12 shalt not tempt the Lord thy God.

And when the devil had completed every tempta- 13 tion, he departed from him ⁵for a season.

And Jesus returned in the power of the Spirit into 14 Galilee: and a fame went out concerning him through all the region round about. And he taught in their 15 synagogues, being glorified of all.

And he came to Nazareth, where he had been 16 brought up: and he entered, as his custom was, into the synagogue on the sabbath day, and stood up to read. And there was delivered unto him ⁶the book 17 of the prophet Isaiah. And he opened the ⁷book, and found the place where it was written,

1 Or, *in*
2 Or, *a loaf*
3 Gr. *the inhabited earth.*
4 Gr. *wing.*
5 Or, *until*
6 Or, *a roll*
7 Or, *roll*

---

* For "by the Spirit" read "in the Spirit" and omit the marg.—*Am. Com.*

S. LUKE.

18 The Spirit of the Lord is upon me,
   ¹Because he anointed me to preach ²good tidings to the poor:
   He hath sent me to proclaim release to the captives,
   And recovering of sight to the blind,
   To set at liberty them that are bruised,
19 To proclaim the acceptable year of the Lord.
20 And he closed the ³book, and gave it back to the attendant, and sat down: and the eyes of all in the
21 synagogue were fastened on him. And he began to say unto them, To-day hath this scripture been ful-
22 filled in your ears. And all bare him witness, and wondered at the words of grace which proceeded out of his mouth: and they said, Is not this Joseph's
23 son? And he said unto them, Doubtless ye will say unto me this parable, Physician, heal thyself: whatsoever we have heard done at Capernaum, do also
24 here in thine own country. And he said, Verily I say unto you, No prophet is acceptable in his own
25 country. But of a truth I say unto you, There were many widows in Israel in the days of Elijah, when the heaven was shut up three years and six months, when there came a great famine over all the land;
26 and unto none of them was Elijah sent, but only to ⁴Zarephath, in the land of Sidon, unto a woman that
27 was a widow. And there were many lepers in Israel in the time of Elisha the prophet; and none of them
28 was cleansed, but only Naaman the Syrian. And they were all filled with wrath in the synagogue, as
29 they heard these things; and they rose up, and cast him forth out of the city, and led him unto the brow of the hill whereon their city was built, that they
30 might throw him down headlong. But he passing through the midst of them went his way.
31 And he came down to Capernaum, a city of Galilee. And he was teaching them on the sabbath day:
32 and they were astonished at his teaching; for his
33 word was with authority. And in the synagogue there was a man, which had a spirit of an unclean
34 ⁵devil; and he cried out with a loud voice, ⁶Ah! what have we to do with thee, thou Jesus of Nazareth? art thou come to destroy us? I know thee
35 who thou art, the Holy One of God. And Jesus rebuked him, saying, Hold thy peace, and come out of him. And when the ⁵devil had thrown him down in the midst, he came out of him, having done him
36 no hurt. And amazement came upon all, and they

1 Or, *Wherefore*
2 Or, *the gospel*
3 Or, *roll*
4 Gr. *Sarepta*.
5 Gr. *demon*.
6 Or, *Let alone*

spake together, one with another, saying, What is ¹this word? for with authority and power he commandeth the unclean spirits, and they come out. And there went forth a rumour concerning him 37 into every place of the region round about.

And he rose up from the synagogue, and entered 38 into the house of Simon. And Simon's wife's mother was holden with a great fever; and they besought him for her. And he stood over her, and rebuked 39 the fever; and it left her: and immediately she rose up and ministered unto them.

And when the sun was setting, all they that had 40 any sick with divers diseases brought them unto him; and he laid his hands on every one of them, and healed them. And ²devils also came out from 41 many, crying out, and saying, Thou art the Son of God. And rebuking them, he suffered them not to speak, because they knew that he was the Christ.

And when it was day, he came out and went into 42 a desert place: and the multitudes sought after him, and came unto him, and would have stayed him, that he should not go from them. But he said unto 43 them, I must preach the ³good tidings of the kingdom of God to the other cities also: for therefore was I sent.

And he was preaching in the synagogues of ⁴Galilee. 44

Now it came to pass, while the multitude pressed 5 upon him and heard the word of God, that he was standing by the lake of Gennesaret; and he saw two 2 boats standing by the lake: but the fishermen had gone out of them, and were washing their nets. And 3 he entered into one of the boats, which was Simon's, and asked him to put out a little from the land. And he sat down and taught the multitudes out of the boat. And when he had left speaking, he said unto 4 Simon, Put out into the deep, and let down your nets for a draught. And Simon answered and said, 5 Master, we toiled all night, and took nothing: but at thy word I will let down the nets. And when they 6 had this done, they inclosed a great multitude of fishes; and their nets were breaking; and they beckoned 7 unto their partners in the other boat, that they should come and help them. And they came, and filled both the boats, so that they began to sink. But 8 Simon Peter, when he saw it, fell down at Jesus' knees, saying, Depart from me; for I am a sinful man, O Lord. For he was amazed, and all that 9 were with him, at the draught of the fishes which

---

1 Or, *this word, that with authority ... comes out?*

2 Gr. *demons.*

3 Or, *gospel*

4 Very many ancient authorities read *Judæa.*

10 they had taken; and so were also James and John, sons of Zebedee, which were partners with Simon. And Jesus said unto Simon, Fear not; from hence-
11 forth thou shalt ¹catch men. And when they had brought their boats to land, they left all, and followed him.

¹ Gr. *take alive.*

12 And it came to pass, while he was in one of the cities, behold, a man full of leprosy: and when he saw Jesus, he fell on his face, and besought him, saying, Lord, if thou wilt, thou canst make me clean.
13 And he stretched forth his hand, and touched him, saying, I will; be thou made clean. And straightway
14 the leprosy departed from him. And he charged him to tell no man: but go thy way, and shew thyself to the priest, and offer for thy cleansing, according as Moses commanded, for a testimony unto them.
15 But so much the more went abroad the report concerning him: and great multitudes came together to
16 hear, and to be healed of their infirmities. But he withdrew himself in the deserts, and prayed.
17 And it came to pass on one of those days, that he was teaching; and there were Pharisees and doctors of the law sitting by, which were come out of every village of Galilee and Judæa and Jerusalem: and
18 the power of the Lord was with him ²to heal. And behold, men bring on a bed a man that was palsied: and they sought to bring him in, and to lay him be-
19 fore him. And not finding by what *way* they might bring him in because of the multitude, they went up to the housetop, and let him down through the tiles
20 with his couch into the midst before Jesus. And seeing their faith, he said, Man, thy sins are forgiven
21 thee. And the scribes and the Pharisees began to reason, saying, Who is this that speaketh blasphe-
22 mies? Who can forgive sins, but God alone? But Jesus perceiving their reasonings, answered and said
23 unto them, ³What reason ye in your hearts? Whether is easier, to say, Thy sins are forgiven thee; or to
24 say, Arise and walk? But that ye may know that the Son of man hath ⁴power on earth to forgive sins (he said unto him that was palsied), I say unto thee, Arise, and take up thy couch, and go unto thy house.
25 And immediately he rose up before them, and took up that whereon he lay, and departed to his house,
26 glorifying God. And amazement took hold on all, and they glorified God; and they were filled with fear, saying, We have seen strange things to-day.
27 And after these things he went forth, and beheld a

² Gr. *that he should heal.* Many ancient authorities read *that* he *should heal them.*

³ Or, *Why*

⁴ Or, *authority*

publican, named Levi, sitting at the place of toll, and said unto him, Follow me. And he forsook all, and 28 rose up and followed him. And Levi made him a 29 great feast in his house: and there was a great multitude of publicans and of others that were sitting at meat with them. And ¹the Pharisees and their scribes 30 murmured against his disciples, saying, Why do ye eat and drink with the publicans and sinners? And Jesus 31 answering said unto them, They that are whole have no need of a physician; but they that are sick. I am 32 not come to call the righteous but sinners to repentance. And they said unto him, The disciples of John 33 fast often, and make supplications; likewise also the *disciples* of the Pharisees; but thine eat and drink. And Jesus said unto them, Can ye make the sons of 34 the bride-chamber fast, while the bridegroom is with them? But the days will come; and when the bride- 35 groom shall be taken away from them, then will they fast in those days. And he spake also a parable unto 36 them; No man rendeth a piece from a new garment and putteth it upon an old garment; else he will rend the new, and also the piece from the new will not agree with the old. And no man putteth new wine into 37 old ²wine-skins; else the new wine will burst the skins, and itself will be spilled, and the skins will perish. But new wine must be put into fresh wine-skins. 38 And no man having drunk old *wine* desireth new: 39 for he saith, The old is ³good.

Now it came to pass on a ⁴sabbath, that he was **6** going through the cornfields; and his disciples plucked the ears of corn, and did eat, rubbing them in their hands. But certain of the Pharisees said, 2 Why do ye that which it is not lawful to do on the sabbath day? And Jesus answering them said, Have 3 ye not read even this, what David did, when he was an hungred, he, and they that were with him; how 4 he entered into the house of God, and did take and eat the shewbread, and gave also to them that were with him; which it is not lawful to eat save for the priests alone? And he said unto them, The Son of 5 man is lord of the sabbath.

And it came to pass on another sabbath, that he 6 entered into the synagogue and taught: and there was a man there, and his right hand was withered. And 7 the scribes and the Pharisees watched him, whether he would heal on the sabbath; that they might find how to accuse him. But he knew their thoughts; and he 8 said to the man that had his hand withered, Rise up,

---

1 Or, *the Pharisees and the scribes among them*

2 That is, *skins used as bottles.*

3 Many ancient authorities read *better.*

4 Many ancient authorities insert *second-first.*

and stand forth in the midst. And he arose and stood
9 forth. And Jesus said unto them, I ask you, Is it
lawful on the sabbath to do good, or to do harm? to
10 save a life, or to destroy it? And he looked round
about on them all, and said unto him, Stretch forth
thy hand. And he did *so*: and his hand was restored.
11 But they were filled with ¹madness; and communed   1 Or, *foolishness*
one with another what they might do to Jesus.
12   And it came to pass in these days, that he went out
into the mountain to pray; and he continued all night
13 in prayer to God. And when it was day, he called his
disciples: and he chose from them twelve, whom also
14 he named apostles; Simon, whom he also named
Peter, and Andrew his brother, and James and John,
15 and Philip and Bartholomew, and Matthew and
Thomas, and James *the son* of Alphæus, and Simon
16 which was called the Zealot, and Judas *the* ²*son* of   2 Or, brother. See Jude 1.
James, and Judas Iscariot, which was the traitor*;
17 and he came down with them, and stood on a level
place, and a great multitude of his disciples, and a
great number of the people from all Judæa and Jerusalem, and the sea coast of Tyre and Sidon, which
came to hear him, and to be healed of their diseases;
18 and they that were troubled with unclean spirits
19 were healed. And all the multitude sought to touch
him: for power came forth from him, and healed
them all.
20   And he lifted up his eyes on his disciples, and
said, Blessed *are* ye poor: for yours is the kingdom
21 of God. Blessed *are* ye that hunger now: for ye
shall be filled. Blessed *are* ye that weep now: for
22 ye shall laugh. Blessed are ye, when men shall hate
you, and when they shall separate you *from their company*, and reproach you, and cast out your name as
23 evil, for the Son of man's sake. Rejoice in that day,
and leap *for joy*: for behold, your reward is great
in heaven: for in the same manner did their fathers
24 unto the prophets. But woe unto you that are rich!
25 for ye have received your consolation. Woe unto
you, ye that are full now! for ye shall hunger. Woe
unto you, ye that laugh now! for ye shall mourn and
26 weep. Woe *unto you*, when all men shall speak well
of you! for in the same manner did their fathers to
the false prophets.
27   But I say unto you which hear, Love your ene-
28 mies, do good to them that hate you, bless them that

---

* For "was the traitor" read "became a traitor"—*Am. Com.*

curse you, pray for them that despitefully use you.
To him that smiteth thee on the *one* cheek offer also 29
the other; and from him that taketh away thy cloke
withhold not thy coat also. Give to every one that 30
asketh thee; and of him that taketh away thy goods
ask them not again. And as ye would that men 31
should do to you, do ye also to them likewise. And 32
if ye love them that love you, what thank have ye?
for even sinners love those that love them. And if 33
ye do good to them that do good to you, what thank
have ye? for even sinners do the same. And if ye 34
lend to them of whom ye hope to receive, what thank
have ye? even sinners lend to sinners, to receive
again as much. But love your enemies, and do *them* 35
good, and lend, [1]never despairing; and your reward
shall be great, and ye shall be sons of the Most
High: for he is kind toward the unthankful and
evil. Be ye merciful, even as your Father is mer- 36
ciful. And judge not, and ye shall not be judged: 37
and condemn not, and ye shall not be condemned:
release, and ye shall be released: give, and it shall 38
be given unto you; good measure, pressed down,
shaken together, running over, shall they give into
your bosom. For with what measure ye mete it
shall be measured to you again.

And he spake also a parable unto them, Can the 39
blind guide the blind? shall they not both fall into a
pit? The disciple is not above his [2]master: but ev- 40
ery one when he is perfected shall be as his [2]master.
And why beholdest thou the mote that is in thy 41
brother's eye, but considerest not the beam that is
in thine own eye? Or how canst thou say to thy 42
brother, Brother, let me cast out the mote that is in
thine eye, when thou thyself beholdest not the beam
that is in thine own eye? Thou hypocrite, cast out
first the beam out of thine own eye, and then shalt
thou see clearly to cast out the mote that is in thy
brother's eye. For there is no good tree that bring- 43
eth forth corrupt fruit; nor again a corrupt tree that
bringeth forth good fruit. For each tree is known 44
by its own fruit. For of thorns men do not gather
figs, nor of a bramble bush gather they grapes. The 45
good man out of the good treasure of his heart bringeth forth that which is good; and the evil *man* out
of the evil *treasure* bringeth forth that which is evil:
for out of the abundance of the heart his mouth
speaketh.

And why call ye me, Lord, Lord, and do not the 46

---

[1] Some ancient authorities rend despairing of no man.

[2] Or, *teacher*

47 things which I say? Every one that cometh unto me, and heareth my words, and doeth them, I will
48 shew you to whom he is like: he is like a man building a house, who digged and went deep, and laid a foundation upon the rock: and when a flood arose, the stream brake against that house, and could not shake it: ¹because it had been well builded.
49 But he that heareth, and doeth not, is like a man that built a house upon the earth without a foundation; against which the stream brake, and straightway it fell in; and the ruin of that house was great.

¹ Many ancient authorities read *for it had been founded upon the rock*: as in Matt. vii. 25.

7 After he had ended all his sayings in the ears of the people, he entered into Capernaum.
2 And a certain centurion's ²servant, who was ³dear
3 unto him, was sick and at the point of death. And when he heard concerning Jesus, he sent unto him elders of the Jews, asking him that he would come
4 and save his ⁴servant. And they, when they came to Jesus, besought him earnestly, saying, He is worthy
5 that thou shouldest do this for him: for he loveth our
6 nation, and himself built us our synagogue. And Jesus went with them. And when he was now not far from the house, the centurion sent friends to him, saying unto him, Lord, trouble not thyself: for I am not ⁴worthy that thou shouldest come under my roof:
7 wherefore neither thought I myself worthy to come unto thee: but ⁵say the word, and my ⁶servant shall
8 be healed. For I also am a man set under authority, having under myself soldiers: and I say to this one, Go, and he goeth; and to another, Come, and he cometh; and to my ²servant, Do this, and he doeth
9 it. And when Jesus heard these things, he marvelled at him, and turned and said unto the multitude that followed him, I say unto you, I have not
10 found so great faith, no, not in Israel. And they that were sent, returning to the house, found the ²servant whole.
11 And it came to pass ⁷soon afterwards, that he went to a city called Nain; and his disciples went with
12 him, and a great multitude. Now when he drew near to the gate of the city, behold, there was carried out one that was dead, the only son of his mother, and she was a widow: and much people of the city
13 was with her. And when the Lord saw her, he had compassion on her, and said unto her, Weep not.
14 And he came nigh and touched the bier: and the bearers stood still. And he said, Young man, I say

² Gr. *bondservant*.
³ Or, *precious to him* Or, *honourable with him*
⁴ Gr. *sufficient*.
⁵ Gr. *say with a word*.
⁶ Or, *boy*
⁷ Many ancient authorities read *on the next day*.

unto thee, Arise. And he that was dead sat up, and 15
began to speak. And he gave him to his mother.
And fear took hold on all: and they glorified God, 16
saying, A great prophet is arisen among us: and,
God hath visited his people. And this report went 17
forth concerning him in the whole of Judæa, and all
the region round about.

And the disciples of John told him of all these 18
things. And John calling unto him ¹two of his 19
disciples sent them to the Lord, saying, Art thou he
that cometh, or look we for another? And when 20
the men were come unto him, they said, John the
Baptist hath sent us unto thee, saying, Art thou he
that cometh, or look we for another? In that hour 21
he cured many of diseases and ²plagues and evil
spirits; and on many that were blind he bestowed
sight. And he answered and said unto them, Go 22
your way, and tell John what things ye have seen
and heard; the blind receive their sight, the lame
walk, the lepers are cleansed, and the deaf hear, the
dead are raised up, the poor have ³good tidings
preached to them. And blessed is he, whosoever 23
shall find none occasion of stumbling in me.

And when the messengers of John were departed, 24
he began to say unto the multitudes concerning
John, What went ye out into the wilderness to behold?
a reed shaken with the wind? But what 25
went ye out to see? a man clothed in soft raiment?
Behold, they which are gorgeously apparelled, and
live delicately, are in kings' courts. But what went 26
ye out to see? a prophet? Yea, I say unto you, and
much more than a prophet. This is he of whom it 27
is written,

Behold, I send my messenger before thy face,
Who shall prepare thy way before thee.

I say unto you, Among them that are born of wom- 28
en there is none greater than John: yet he that is
⁴but little in the kingdom of God is greater than he.
And all the people when they heard, and the publi- 29
cans, justified God, ⁵being baptized with the baptism
of John. But the Pharisees and the lawyers re- 30
jected for themselves the counsel of God, ⁶being
not baptized of him. Whereunto then shall I liken 31
the men of this generation, and to what are they
like? They are like unto children that sit in the 32
marketplace, and call one to another; which say, We
piped unto you, and ye did not dance; we wailed,
and ye did not weep. For John the Baptist is come 33

Margin:
1 Gr. *certain two.*
2 Gr. *scourges.*
3 Or, *the gospel*
4 Gr. *lesser.*
5 Or, *having been*
6 Or, *not having been*

eating no bread nor drinking wine; and ye say,
34 He hath a ¹devil. The Son of man is come eating
and drinking; and ye say, Behold, a gluttonous man,
and a winebibber, a friend of publicans and sinners!
35 And wisdom ²is justified of all her children.
36 And one of the Pharisees desired him that he
would eat with him. And he entered into the
37 Pharisee's house, and sat down to meat. And behold, a woman which was in the city, a sinner; and
when she knew that he was sitting at meat in the
Pharisee's house, she brought ³an alabaster cruse of
38 ointment, and standing behind at his feet, weeping,
she began to wet his feet with her tears, and wiped
them with the hair of her head, and ⁴kissed his feet,
39 and anointed them with the ointment. Now when
the Pharisee which had bidden him saw it, he spake
within himself, saying, This man, if he were ⁵a
prophet, would have perceived who and what manner of woman this is which toucheth him, that she
40 is a sinner. And Jesus answering said unto him,
Simon, I have somewhat to say unto thee. And he
41 saith, ⁶Master, say on. A certain lender had two
debtors: the one owed five hundred ⁷pence, and the
42 other fifty. When they had not *wherewith* to pay,
he forgave them both. Which of them therefore
43 will love him most? Simon answered and said, He,
I suppose, to whom he forgave the most. And he
44 said unto him, Thou hast rightly judged. And
turning to the woman, he said unto Simon, Seest
thou this woman? I entered into thine house, thou
gavest me no water for my feet: but she hath wetted my feet with her tears, and wiped them with
45 her hair. Thou gavest me no kiss: but she, since
the time I came in, hath not ceased to ⁸kiss my feet.
46 My head with oil thou didst not anoint: but she
47 hath anointed my feet with ointment. Wherefore
I say unto thee, Her sins, which are many, are forgiven; for she loved much: but to whom little is
48 forgiven, *the same* loveth little. And he said unto
49 her, Thy sins are forgiven. And they that sat at
meat with him began to say ⁹within themselves,
50 Who is this that even forgiveth sins? And he said
unto the woman, Thy faith hath saved thee; go in
peace.

8 And it came to pass soon afterwards, that he went
about through cities and villages, preaching and
bringing the ¹⁰good tidings of the kingdom of God,
2 and with him the twelve, and certain women which

1 Gr. *demon.*

2 Or, *was*

3 Or, *a flask*

4 Gr. *kissed much.*

5 Some ancient authorities read *the prophet.* See John i. 21, 25.

6 Or, *Teacher*

7 See marginal note on Matt. xviii. 28.

8 Gr. *kiss much.*

9 Or, *among*

10 Or, *gospel*

had been healed of evil spirits and infirmities, Mary that was called Magdalene, from whom seven ¹devils had gone out, and Joanna the wife of Chuza* 3 Herod's steward, and Susanna, and many others, which ministered unto ²them of their substance.

And when a great multitude came together, and 4 they of every city resorted unto him, he spake by a parable: The sower went forth to sow his seed: and 5 as he sowed, some fell by the way side; and it was trodden under foot, and the birds of the heaven devoured it. And other fell on the rock; and as soon 6 as it grew, it withered away, because it had no moisture. And other fell amidst the thorns; and the 7 thorns grew with it, and choked it. And other fell 8 into the good ground, and grew, and brought forth fruit a hundredfold. As he said these things, he cried, He that hath ears to hear, let him hear.

And his disciples asked him what this parable 9 might be. And he said, Unto you it is given to 10 know the mysteries of the kingdom of God: but to the rest in parables; that seeing they may not see, and hearing they may not understand. Now the 11 parable is this: The seed is the word of God. And 12 those by the way side are they that have heard; then cometh the devil, and taketh away the word from their heart, that they may not believe and be saved. And those on the rock *are* they which, when they 13 have heard, receive the word with joy; and these have no root, which for a while believe, and in time of temptation fall away. And that which fell 14 among the thorns, these are they that have heard, and as they go on their way they are choked with cares and riches and pleasures of *this* life, and bring no fruit to perfection. And that in the good ground, 15 these are such as in an honest and good heart, having heard the word, hold it fast, and bring forth fruit with patience.

And no man, when he hath lighted a lamp, cover- 16 eth it with a vessel, or putteth it under a bed; but putteth it on a stand, that they which enter in may see the light. For nothing is hid, that shall not be 17 made manifest; nor *anything* secret, that shall not be known and come to light. Take heed therefore 18 how ye hear: for whosoever hath, to him shall be given; and whosoever hath not, from him shall be taken away even that which he ³thinketh he hath.

¹ Gr. *demons.*

² Many ancient authorities read *him.*

³ Or, *seemeth to have*

---

* For "Chuza" read "Chuzas"—*Am. Com.*

19 And there came to him his mother and brethren,
20 and they could not come at him for the crowd. And it was told him, Thy mother and thy brethren stand
21 without, desiring to see thee. But he answered and said unto them, My mother and my brethren are these which hear the word of God, and do it.
22 Now it came to pass on one of those days, that he entered into a boat, himself and his disciples; and he said unto them, Let us go over unto the other
23 side of the lake: and they launched forth. But as they sailed he fell asleep: and there came down a storm of wind on the lake; and they were filling
24 *with water*, and were in jeopardy. And they came to him, and awoke him, saying, Master, master, we perish. And he awoke, and rebuked the wind and the raging of the water: and they ceased, and there
25 was a calm. And he said unto them, Where is your faith? And being afraid they marvelled, saying one to another, Who then is this, that he commandeth even the winds and the water, and they obey him?
26 And they arrived at the country of the ¹Gera-
27 senes, which is over against Galilee. And when he was come forth upon the land, there met him a certain man out of the city, who had ²devils; and for a long time he had worn no clothes, and abode not in
28 *any* house, but in the tombs. And when he saw Jesus, he cried out, and fell down before him, and with a loud voice said, What have I to do with thee, Jesus, thou Son of the Most High God? I beseech
29 thee, torment me not. For he commanded* the unclean spirit to come out from the man. For ³oftentimes it had seized him: and he was kept under guard, and bound with chains and fetters; and breaking the bands asunder, he was driven of the
30 ⁴devil into the deserts. And Jesus asked him, What is thy name? And he said, Legion; for many ²dev-
31 ils were entered into him. And they intreated him that he would not command them to depart into the
32 abyss. Now there was there a herd of many swine feeding on the mountain: and they intreated him that he would give them leave to enter into them.
33 And he gave them leave. And the ²devils came out from the man, and entered into the swine: and the herd rushed down the steep into the lake, and were
34 choked†. And when they that fed them saw what

¹ Many ancient authorities read *Gergesenes*; others, *Gadarenes*: and so in ver. 37.

² Gr. *demons.*

³ Or, *of a long time*

⁴ Gr. *demon.*

---

* For "commanded" read "was commanding."—*Am. Com.*
† For "were choked" read "were drowned"—*Am. Com.*

had come to pass, they fled, and told it in the city and in the country. And they went out to see what 35 had come to pass; and they came to Jesus, and found the man, from whom the ¹devils were gone out, sitting, clothed and in his right mind, at the feet of Jesus: and they were afraid. And they that saw it 36 told them how he that was possessed with ¹devils was ²made whole. And all the people of the coun- 37 try of the Gerasenes round about asked him to depart from them; for they were holden with great fear: and he entered into a boat, and returned. But 38 the man from whom the ¹devils were gone out prayed him that he might be with him: but he sent him away, saying, Return to thy house, and declare how 39 great things God hath done for thee. And he went his way, publishing throughout the whole city how great things Jesus had done for him.

And as Jesus returned, the multitude welcomed 40 him; for they were all waiting for him. And 41 behold, there came a man named Jaïrus, and he was a ruler of the synagogue: and he fell down at Jesus' feet, and besought him to come into his house; for he had an only daughter, about twelve 42 years of age, and she lay a dying. But as he went the multitudes thronged him.

And a woman having an issue of blood twelve 43 years, which ³had spent all her living upon physicians, and could not be healed of any, came behind 44 him, and touched the border of his garment: and immediately the issue of her blood stanched. And 45 Jesus said, Who is it that touched me? And when all denied, Peter said, ⁴and they that were with him, Master, the multitudes press thee and crush *thee*. But Jesus said, Some one did touch me: for I per- 46 ceived that power had gone forth from me. And 47 when the woman saw that she was not hid, she came trembling, and falling down before him declared in the presence of all the people for what cause she touched him, and how she was healed immediately. And he said unto her, Daughter, thy 48 faith hath ⁵made thee whole; go in peace.

While he yet spake, there cometh one from the 49 ruler of the synagogue's *house*, saying, Thy daughter is dead; trouble not the ⁶Master. But Jesus hearing 50 it, answered him, Fear not: only believe, and she shall be ²made whole. And when he came to the 51 house, he suffered not any man to enter in with him, save Peter, and John, and James, and the father of

---

1 Gr. *demons*.

2 Or, *saved*

3 Some ancient authorities omit *had spent all her living upon physicians, and*.

4 Some ancient authorities omit *and they that were with him*.

5 Or, *saved thee*

6 Or, *Teacher*

52 the maiden and her mother. And all were weeping, and bewailing her: but he said, Weep not; for
53 she is not dead, but sleepeth. And they laughed
54 him to scorn, knowing that she was dead. But he, taking her by the hand, called, saying, Maiden, arise.
55 And her spirit returned, and she rose up immediately: and he commanded that *something* be given her
56 to eat. And her parents were amazed: but he charged them to tell no man what had been done.

9 And he called the twelve together, and gave them power and authority over all ¹devils, and to cure
2 diseases. And he sent them forth to preach the
3 kingdom of God, and to heal ²the sick. And he said unto them, Take nothing for your journey, neither staff, nor wallet, nor bread, nor money; nei-
4 ther have two coats. And into whatsoever house
5 ye enter, there abide, and thence depart. And as many as receive you not, when ye depart from that city, shake off the dust from your feet for a testi-
6 mony against them. And they departed, and went throughout the villages, preaching the gospel, and healing everywhere.

7 Now Herod the tetrarch heard of all that was done: and he was much perplexed, because that it was said by some, that John was risen from the
8 dead; and by some, that Elijah had appeared; and by others, that one of the old prophets was risen
9 again. And Herod said, John I beheaded: but who is this, about whom I hear such things? And he sought to see him.

10 And the apostles, when they were returned, declared unto him what things they had done. And he took them, and withdrew apart to a city called
11 Bethsaida. But the multitudes perceiving it followed him: and he welcomed them, and spake to them of the kingdom of God, and them that had
12 need of healing he healed. And the day began to wear away; and the twelve came, and said unto him, Send the multitude away, that they may go into the villages and country round about, and lodge, and get victuals*: for we are here in a desert
13 place. But he said unto them, Give ye them to eat. And they said, We have no more than five loaves and two fishes; except we should go and buy food
14 for all this people. For they were about five thousand men. And he said unto his disciples, Make

¹ Gr. *demons*.
² Some ancient authorities omit *the sick*.

---

* For "victuals" read "provisions"—*Am. Com.*

them ¹sit down in companies, about fifty each. And they did so, and made them all ¹sit down. And he took the five loaves and the two fishes, and looking up to heaven, he blessed them, and brake; and gave to the disciples to set before the multitude. And they did eat, and were all filled: and there was taken up that which remained over to them of broken pieces, twelve baskets.

And it came to pass, as he was praying alone*, the disciples were with him: and he asked them, saying, Who do the multitudes say that I am? And they answering said, John the Baptist; but others *say*, Elijah; and others, that one of the old prophets is risen again. And he said unto them, But who say ye that I am? And Peter answering said, The Christ of God. But he charged them, and commanded *them* to tell this to no man; saying, The Son of man must suffer many things, and be rejected of the elders and chief priests and scribes, and be killed, and the third day be raised up. And he said unto all, If any man would come after me, let him deny himself, and take up his cross daily, and follow me. For whosoever would save his ²life shall lose it; but whosoever shall lose his ²life for my sake, the same shall save it. For what is a man profited, if he gain the whole world, and lose or forfeit his own self? For whosoever shall be ashamed of me and of my words, of him shall the Son of man be ashamed, when he cometh in his own glory, and *the glory* of the Father, and of the holy angels. But I tell you of a truth, There be some of them that stand here, which shall in no wise taste of death, till they see the kingdom of God.

And it came to pass about eight days after these sayings, he took with him Peter and John and James, and went up into the mountain to pray. And as he was praying, the fashion of his countenance was altered, and his raiment *became* white *and* dazzling. And behold, there talked with him two men, which were Moses and Elijah; who appeared in glory, and spake of his ³decease which he was about to accomplish at Jerusalem. Now Peter and they that were with him were heavy with sleep: but ⁴when they were fully awake, they saw his glory, and the two men that stood with him. And it came to pass, as they were parting from him,

---

¹ Gr. *recline*.

² Or, *soul*

³ Or, *departure*

⁴ Or, *having remained awake*

* For "alone" read "apart"—*Am. Com.*

Peter said unto Jesus, Master, it is good for us to be here: and let us make three ¹tabernacles; one for thee, and one for Moses, and one for Elijah: not 34 knowing what he said. And while he said these things, there came a cloud, and overshadowed them: and they feared as they entered into the cloud. 35 And a voice came out of the cloud, saying, This is 36 ²my Son, my chosen: hear ye him. And when the voice ³came, Jesus was found alone. And they held their peace, and told no man in those days any of the things which they had seen.

37 And it came to pass, on the next day, when they were come down from the mountain, a great multi- 38 tude met him. And behold, a man from the multitude cried, saying, ⁴Master, I beseech thee to look 39 upon my son; for he is mine only child: and behold, a spirit taketh him, and he suddenly crieth out; and it ⁵teareth him that he foameth, and it hardly departeth from him, bruising him sorely. 40 And I besought thy disciples to cast it out; and 41 they could not. And Jesus answered and said, O faithless and perverse generation, how long shall I be with you, and bear with you? bring hither thy 42 son. And as he was yet a coming, the ⁶devil ⁷dashed him down, and ⁸tare *him* grievously. But Jesus rebuked the unclean spirit, and healed the boy, and 43 gave him back to his father. And they were all astonished at the majesty of God.

But while all were marvelling at all the things 44 which he did, he said unto his disciples, Let these words sink into your ears: for the Son of man shall 45 be delivered up into the hands of men. But they understood not this saying, and it was concealed from them, that they should not perceive it: and they were afraid to ask him about this saying.

46 And there arose a reasoning among them, which 47 of them should be ⁹greatest*. But when Jesus saw the reasoning of their heart, he took a little child, 48 and set him by his side, and said unto them, Whosoever shall receive this little child in my name receiveth me: and whosoever shall receive me receiveth him that sent me: for he that is ¹⁰least among you all, the same is great.

49 And John answered and said, Master, we saw one casting out ¹¹devils in thy name; and we forbade 50 him, because he followeth not with us. But Jesus

---

1 Or, *booths*

2 Many ancient authorities read *my beloved Son.* See Matt. xvii. 5; Mark ix. 7,

3 Or, *was past*

4 Or, *Teacher*

5 Or, *convulseth*

6 Gr. *demon.*
7 Or, *rent him*
8 Or, *convulsed*

9 Gr. *greater.*

10 Gr. *lesser.*

11 Gr. *demons.*

---

* For "should be greatest" read "was the greatest"—*Am. Com.*

said unto him, Forbid *him* not: for he that is not against you is for you.

¹ Gr. *were being fulfilled.*

51 And it came to pass, when the days ¹were wellnigh come that he should be received up, he stedfastly set his face to go to Jerusalem, 52 and sent messengers before his face: and they went, and entered into a village of the Samaritans, to make ready for him. 53 And they did not receive him, because his face was *as though he were* going to Jerusalem. 54 And when his disciples James and John saw *this*, they said, Lord, wilt thou that we bid fire to come down from heaven, and consume them²? 55 But he turned, and rebuked them³. 56 And they went to another village.

² Many ancient authorities add *even as Elijah did.*

³ Some ancient authorities add *and said, Ye know not what manner of spirit ye are of.* Some, but fewer, add also *For the Son of man came not to destroy men's lives, but to save them.*

57 And as they went in the way, a certain man said unto him, I will follow thee whithersoever thou goest. 58 And Jesus said unto him, The foxes have holes, and the birds of the heaven have ⁴nests; but the Son of man hath not where to lay his head. 59 And he said unto another, Follow me. But he said, Lord, suffer me first to go and bury my father. 60 But he said unto him, Leave the dead to bury their own dead; but go thou and publish abroad the kingdom of God. 61 And another also said, I will follow thee, Lord; but first suffer me to bid farewell to them that are at my house. 62 But Jesus said unto him, No man, having put his hand to the plough, and looking back, is fit for the kingdom of God.

⁴ Gr. *lodging-places.*

10

⁵ Many ancient authorities add *and two:* and so in ver. 17.

Now after these things the Lord appointed seventy⁵ others, and sent them two and two before his face into every city and place, whither he himself was about to come. 2 And he said unto them, The harvest is plenteous, but the labourers are few: pray ye therefore the Lord of the harvest, that he send forth labourers into his harvest. 3 Go your ways: behold, I send you forth as lambs in the midst of wolves. 4 Carry no purse, no wallet, no shoes: and salute no man on the way. 5 And into whatsoever house ye shall ⁶enter, first say, Peace *be* to this house. 6 And if a son of peace be there, your peace shall rest upon ⁷him: but if not, it shall turn to you again. 7 And in that same house remain, eating and drinking such things as they give: for the labourer is worthy of his hire. Go not from house to house. 8 And into whatsoever city ye enter, and they receive you, eat such things as are set before you: 9 and heal the sick that are therein, and say unto them, The kingdom of God is come nigh unto you. 10 But into

⁶ Or, *enter first, say*

⁷ Or, *it*

whatsoever city ye shall enter, and they receive you
11 not, go out into the streets thereof and say, Even the
dust from your city, that cleaveth to our feet, we do
wipe off against you: howbeit know this, that the
12 kingdom of God is come nigh. I say unto you, It
shall be more tolerable in that day for Sodom, than
13 for that city. Woe unto thee, Chorazin! woe unto
thee, Bethsaida! for if the ¹mighty works had been 1 Gr. *powers*.
done in Tyre and Sidon, which were done in you,
they would have repented long ago, sitting in sack-
14 cloth and ashes. Howbeit it shall be more tolerable
for Tyre and Sidon in the judgement, than for you.
15 And thou, Capernaum, shalt thou be exalted unto
heaven? thou shalt be brought down unto Hades.
16 He that heareth you heareth me; and he that rejecteth you rejecteth me; and he that rejecteth me rejecteth him that sent me.
17 And the seventy returned with joy, saying, Lord,
even the ²devils are subject unto us in thy name. 2 Gr. *demons*.
18 And he said unto them, I beheld Satan fallen as
19 lightning from heaven. Behold, I have given you
authority to tread upon serpents and scorpions, and
over all the power of the enemy: and nothing shall
20 in any wise hurt you. Howbeit in this rejoice not,
that the spirits are subject unto you; but rejoice
that your names are written in heaven.
21 In that same hour he rejoiced ³in the Holy Spirit, 3 Or, *by*
and said, I ⁴thank thee, O Father, Lord of heaven 4 Or, *praise*
and earth, that thou didst hide these things from the
wise and understanding, and didst reveal them unto
babes: yea, Father; ⁵for so it was well-pleasing in 5 Or, *that*
22 thy sight. All things have been delivered unto me
of my Father: and no one knoweth who the Son is,
save the Father; and who the Father is, save the
Son, and he to whomsoever the Son willeth to re-
23 veal *him*. And turning to the disciples, he said privately, Blessed *are* the eyes which see the things
24 that ye see: for I say unto you, that many prophets
and kings desired to see the things which ye see,
and saw them not; and to hear the things which ye
hear, and heard them not.
25 And behold, a certain lawyer stood up and tempt-
ed him, saying, ⁶Master, what shall I do to inherit 6 Or, *Teacher*
26 eternal life? And he said unto him, What is written
27 in the law? how readest thou? And he answering
said, Thou shalt love the Lord thy God ⁷with all 7 Gr. *from*.
thy heart, and with all thy soul, and with all thy
strength, and with all thy mind; and thy neighbour

as thyself. And he said unto him, Thou hast an-28
swered right: this do, and thou shalt live. But he 29
desiring to justify himself, said unto Jesus, And
who is my neighbour? Jesus made answer and 30
said, A certain man was going down from Jerusalem
to Jericho; and he fell among robbers, which both
stripped him and beat him, and departed, leaving
him half dead. And by chance a certain priest was 31
going down that way: and when he saw him, he
passed by on the other side. And in like manner a 32
Levite also, when he came to the place, and saw him,
passed by on the other side. But a certain Samari- 33
tan, as he journeyed, came where he was: and when
he saw him, he was moved with compassion, and 34
came to him, and bound up his wounds, pouring
on *them* oil and wine: and he set him on his own
beast, and brought him to an inn, and took care of
him. And on the morrow he took out two ¹pence, 35
and gave them to the host, and said, Take care of
him; and whatsoever thou spendest more, I, when
I come back again, will repay thee. Which of these 36
three, thinkest thou, proved neighbour unto him
that fell among the robbers? And he said, He that 37
shewed mercy on him. And Jesus said unto him,
Go, and do thou likewise.

Now as they went on their way, he entered into 38
a certain village: and a certain woman named Martha received him into her house. And she had a 39
sister called Mary, which also sat at the Lord's feet,
and heard his word. But Martha was ²cumbered 40
about much serving; and she came up to him, and
said, Lord, dost thou not care that my sister did
leave me to serve alone? bid her therefore that she
help me. But the Lord answered and said unto 41
her, ³Martha, Martha, thou art anxious and troubled
about many things: ⁴but one thing is needful: for 42
Mary hath chosen the good part, which shall not be
taken away from her.

And it came to pass, as he was praying in a cer- 11
tain place, that when he ceased, one of his disciples
said unto him, Lord, teach us to pray, even as John
also taught his disciples. And he said unto them, 2
When ye pray, say, ⁵Father, Hallowed be thy name.
Thy kingdom come.⁶ Give us day by day ⁷our daily 3
bread. And forgive us our sins; for we ourselves 4
also forgive every one that is indebted to us. And
bring us not into temptation⁸.

And he said unto them, Which of you shall have 5

---

¹ See marginal note on Matt. xviii. 28.

² Gr. *distracted*.

³ A few ancient authorities read *Martha, Martha, thou art troubled: Mary hath chosen*, &c.

⁴ Many ancient authorities read *but few things are needful, or one*.

⁵ Many ancient authorities read *Our Father, which art in heaven*. See Matt. vi. 9.

⁶ Many ancient authorities add *Thy will be done, as in heaven, so on earth*. See Matt. vi. 10.

⁷ Gr. *our bread for the coming day*.

⁸ Many ancient authorities add *but deliver us from the evil one* (or, *from evil*). See Matt. vi. 13.

a friend, and shall go unto him at midnight, and say
to him, Friend, lend me three loaves; for a friend
of mine is come to me from a journey, and I have
nothing to set before him; and he from within shall
answer and say, Trouble me not: the door is now
shut, and my children are with me in bed: I cannot
rise and give thee? I say unto you, Though he will
not rise and give him, because he is his friend, yet
because of his importunity he will arise and give
him ¹as many as he needeth. And I say unto you,
Ask, and it shall be given you; seek, and ye shall
find; knock, and it shall be opened unto you. For
every one that asketh receiveth: and he that seeketh findeth; and to him that knocketh it shall be
opened. And of which of you that is a father shall
his son ask ²a loaf, and he give him a stone? or a
fish, and he for a fish give him a serpent? Or *if* he
shall ask an egg, will he give him a scorpion? If
ye then, being evil, know how to give good gifts
unto your children, how much more shall *your*
heavenly Father give the Holy Spirit to them that
ask him?

14 And he was casting out a ³devil *which was* dumb.
And it came to pass, when the ³devil was gone out,
the dumb man spake; and the multitudes marvelled.
15 But some of them said, ⁴By Beelzebub the prince of
16 the ⁵devils casteth he out ⁵devils. And others, tempt-
17 ing *him*, sought of him a sign from heaven. But he,
knowing their thoughts, said unto them, Every kingdom divided against itself is brought to desolation;
18 ⁶and a house *divided* against a house falleth. And
if Satan also is divided against himself, how shall
his kingdom stand? because ye say that I cast out
19 ⁵devils ⁴by Beelzebub. And if I ⁴by Beelzebub cast
out ⁵devils, by whom do your sons cast them out?
20 therefore shall they be your judges. But if I by
the finger of God cast out ⁵devils, then is the king-
21 dom of God come upon you. When the strong *man*
fully armed guardeth his own court, his goods are
22 in peace: but when a stronger than he shall come
upon him, and overcome him, he taketh from him
his whole armour wherein he trusted, and divideth
23 his spoils. He that is not with me is against me;
24 and he that gathereth not with me scattereth. The
unclean spirit when ⁷he is gone out of the man,
passeth through waterless places, seeking rest; and
finding none, ⁷he saith, I will turn back unto my
25 house whence I came out. And when he is come,

¹ Or, *whatsoever things*

² Some ancient authorities omit *a loaf, and he give him a stone? or.*

³ Gr. *demon.*

⁴ Or, *In*

⁵ Gr. *demons.*

⁶ Or, *and house falleth upon house.*

⁷ Or, *it*

¹he findeth it swept and garnished. Then goeth ¹he, 26
and taketh *to him* seven other spirits more evil than
²himself; and they enter in and dwell there: and the
last state of that man becometh worse than the first.

And it came to pass, as he said these things, a cer- 27
tain woman out of the multitude lifted up her voice,
and said unto him, Blessed is the womb that bare
thee, and the breasts which thou didst suck. But 28
he said, Yea rather, blessed are they that hear the
word of God, and keep it.

And when the multitudes were gathering together 29
unto him, he began to say, This generation is an evil
generation: it seeketh after a sign; and there shall
no sign be given to it but the sign of Jonah. For 30
even as Jonah became a sign unto the Ninevites, so
shall also the Son of man be to this generation. The 31
queen of the south shall rise up in the judgement
with the men of this generation, and shall condemn
them: for she came from the ends of the earth to
hear the wisdom of Solomon; and behold, ³a greater
than Solomon is here. The men of Nineveh shall 32
stand up in the judgement with this generation, and
shall condemn it: for they repented at the preaching
of Jonah; and behold, ³a greater than Jonah is here.

No man, when he hath lighted a lamp, putteth 33
it in a cellar, neither under the bushel, but on the
stand, that they which enter in may see the light.
The lamp of thy body is thine eye: when thine eye is 34
single, thy whole body also is full of light; but when
it is evil, thy body also is full of darkness. Look 35
therefore whether the light that is in thee be not
darkness. If therefore thy whole body be full of 36
light, having no part dark, it shall be wholly full of
light, as when the lamp with its bright shining doth
give thee light.

Now as he spake, a Pharisee asketh him to ⁴dine 37
with him: and he went in, and sat down to meat.
And when the Pharisee saw it, he marvelled that he 38
had not first washed* before ⁴dinner. And the Lord 39
said unto him, Now do ye Pharisees cleanse the outside of the cup and of the platter; but your inward
part is full of extortion and wickedness. Ye fool- 40
ish ones, did not he that made the outside make the
inside also? Howbeit give for alms those things 41
which ⁵are within; and behold, all things are clean
unto you.

---

1 Or, *it*

2 Or, *itself*

3 Gr. *more than*.

4 Gr. *breakfast*.

5 Or, *ye can*

* For "washed" read "bathed himself" [comp. Mark vii. 4].—*Am. Com.*

42 But woe unto you Pharisees! for ye tithe mint and rue and every herb, and pass over judgement and the love of God: but these ought ye to have
43 done, and not to leave the other undone. Woe unto you Pharisees! for ye love the chief seats in the synagogues, and the salutations in the market-
44 places. Woe unto you! for ye are as the tombs which appear not, and the men that walk over *them* know it not.
45 And one of the lawyers answering saith unto him,
46 ¹Master, in saying this thou reproachest us also. And he said, Woe unto you lawyers also! for ye lade men with burdens grievous to be borne, and ye yourselves
47 touch not the burdens with one of your fingers. Woe unto you! for ye build the tombs of the prophets,
48 and your fathers killed them. So ye are witnesses and consent unto the works of your fathers: for
49 they killed them, and ye build *their tombs*. Therefore also said the wisdom of God, I will send unto them prophets and apostles; and *some* of them they
50 shall kill and persecute; that the blood of all the prophets, which was shed from the foundation of
51 the world, may be required of this generation; from the blood of Abel unto the blood of Zachariah, who perished between the altar and the ²sanctuary: yea, I say unto you, it shall be required of this genera-
52 tion. Woe unto you lawyers! for ye took away the key of knowledge: ye entered not in yourselves, and them that were entering in ye hindered.
53 And when he was come out from thence, the scribes and the Pharisees began to ³press upon *him* vehemently, and to provoke him to speak of ⁴many
54 things; laying wait for him, to catch something out of his mouth.

12 In the mean time, when ⁵the many thousands of the multitude were gathered together, insomuch that they trode one upon another, he began to ⁶say unto his disciples first of all, Beware ye of the leaven of
2 the Pharisees, which is hypocrisy. But there is nothing covered up, that shall not be revealed: and hid,
3 that shall not be known. Wherefore whatsoever ye have said in the darkness shall be heard in the light; and what ye have spoken in the ear in the inner chambers shall be proclaimed upon the housetops.
4 And I say unto you my friends, Be not afraid of them which kill the body, and after that have no
5 more that they can do. But I will warn you whom ye shall fear: Fear him, which after he hath killed

1 Or, *Teacher*

2 Gr. *house.*

3 Or, *set themselves vehemently against* him
4 Or, *more*

5 Gr. *the myriads of.*
6 Or, *say unto his disciples, First of all beware ye*

hath ¹power to cast into ²hell; yea, I say unto you, Fear him. Are not five sparrows sold for two farthings? and not one of them is forgotten in the sight of God. But the very hairs of your head are all numbered. Fear not: ye are of more value than many sparrows. And I say unto you, Every one who shall confess ³me before men, ⁴him shall the Son of man also confess before the angels of God: but he that denieth me in the presence of men shall be denied in the presence of the angels of God. And every one who shall speak a word against the Son of man, it shall be forgiven him: but unto him that blasphemeth against the Holy Spirit it shall not be forgiven. And when they bring you before the synagogues, and the rulers, and the authorities, be not anxious how or what ye shall answer, or what ye shall say: for the Holy Spirit shall teach you in that very hour what ye ought to say.

And one out of the multitude said unto him, ⁵Master, bid my brother divide the inheritance with me. But he said unto him, Man, who made me a judge or a divider over you? And he said unto them, Take heed, and keep yourselves from all covetousness: ⁶for a man's life consisteth not in the abundance of the things which he possesseth. And he spake a parable unto them, saying, The ground of a certain rich man brought forth plentifully: and he reasoned within himself, saying, What shall I do, because I have not where to bestow my fruits? And he said, This will I do: I will pull down my barns, and build greater; and there will I bestow all my corn and my goods. And I will say to my ⁷soul, ⁷Soul, thou hast much goods laid up for many years; take thine ease, eat, drink, be merry. But God said unto him, Thou foolish one, this night ⁸is thy ⁷soul required of thee; and the things which thou hast prepared, whose shall they be? So is he that layeth up treasure for himself, and is not rich toward God.

And he said unto his disciples, Therefore I say unto you, Be not anxious for *your* ⁹life, what ye shall eat; nor yet for your body, what ye shall put on. For the ⁹life is more than the food, and the body than the raiment. Consider the ravens, that they sow not, neither reap; which have no storechamber nor barn; and God feedeth them: of how much more value are ye than the birds! And which of you by being anxious can add a cubit unto his ¹⁰stature? If then ye are not able to do even that

---

1 Or, *authority*
2 Gr. *Gehenna.*

3 Gr. *in me.*
4 Gr. *in him.*

5 Or, *Teacher*

6 Gr. *for not in a man's abundance consisteth his life, from the things which he possesseth.*

7 Or, *life*

8 Gr. *they require thy soul.*

9 Or, *soul*

10 Or, *age*

which is least, why are ye anxious concerning the
27 rest? Consider the lilies, how they grow: they toil
not, neither do they spin; yet I say unto you, Even
Solomon in all his glory was not arrayed like one
28 of these. But if God doth so clothe the grass in the
field, which to-day is, and to-morrow is cast into the
oven; how much more *shall he clothe* you, O ye of
29 little faith? And seek not ye what ye shall eat, and
what ye shall drink, neither be ye of doubtful mind.
30 For all these things do the nations of the world seek
after: but your Father knoweth that ye have need
31 of these things. Howbeit seek ye ¹his kingdom, and
32 these things shall be added unto you. Fear not, little flock; for it is your Father's good pleasure to give
33 you the kingdom. Sell that ye have, and give alms;
make for yourselves purses which wax not old, a
treasure in the heavens that faileth not, where no
34 thief draweth near, neither moth destroyeth. For
where your treasure is, there will your heart be also.
35 Let your loins be girded about, and your lamps
36 burning; and be ye yourselves like unto men looking for their lord, when he shall return from the
marriage feast; that, when he cometh and knock-
37 eth, they may straightway open unto him. Blessed
are those ²servants, whom the lord when he cometh
shall find watching: verily I say unto you, that he
shall gird himself, and make them sit down to meat,
38 and shall come and serve them. And if he shall
come in the second watch, and if in the third, and
39 find *them* so, blessed are those *servants*. ³But know
this, that if the master of the house had known in
what hour the thief was coming, he would have
watched, and not have left his house to be ⁴broken
40 through. Be ye also ready: for in an hour that ye
think not the Son of man cometh.
41 And Peter said, Lord, speakest thou this parable
42 unto us, or even unto all? And the Lord said, Who
then is ⁵the faithful and wise steward, whom his lord
shall set over his household, to give them their por-
43 tion of food in due season? Blessed is that ⁶servant, whom his lord when he cometh shall find so
44 doing. Of a truth I say unto you, that he will set
45 him over all that he hath. But if that ⁶servant shall
say in his heart, My lord delayeth his coming; and
shall begin to beat the menservants and the maid-
servants, and to eat and drink, and to be drunken;
46 the lord of that ⁶servant shall come in a day when
he expecteth not, and in an hour when he knoweth

1 Many ancient authorities read *the kingdom of God*.

2 Gr. *bondservants*.

3 Or, *But this ye know*

4 Gr. *digged through*.

5 Or, *the faithful steward, the wise man whom, &c.*

6 Gr. *bondservant*.

¹ Or, *severely scourge him*
² Gr. *bondservant*.

not, and shall ¹cut him asunder, and appoint his portion with the unfaithful. And that ²servant, which knew his lord's will, and made not ready, nor did according to his will, shall be beaten with many *stripes*; but he that knew not, and did things worthy of stripes, shall be beaten with few *stripes*. And to whomsoever much is given, of him shall much be required: and to whom they commit much, of him will they ask the more.

I came to cast fire upon the earth; and what will I*, if it is already kindled? But I have a baptism to be baptized with; and how am I straitened till it be accomplished! Think ye that I am come to give peace in the earth? I tell you, Nay; but rather division: for there shall be from henceforth five in one house divided, three against two, and two against three. They shall be divided, father against son, and son against father; mother against daughter, and daughter against her mother; mother in law against her daughter in law, and daughter in law against her mother in law.

And he said to the multitudes also, When ye see a cloud rising in the west, straightway ye say, There cometh a shower; and so it cometh to pass. And when *ye see* a south wind blowing, ye say, There

³ Or, *hot wind*
⁴ Gr. *prove*.

will be a ³scorching heat; and it cometh to pass. Ye hypocrites, ye know how to ⁴interpret the face of the earth and the heaven; but how is it that ye know not how to ⁴interpret this time? And why even of yourselves judge ye not what is right? For as thou art going with thine adversary before the magistrate, on the way give diligence to be quit of him; lest haply he hale thee unto the judge, and the judge

⁵ Gr. *exactor*.

shall deliver thee to the ⁵officer, and the ⁵officer shall cast thee into prison. I say unto thee, Thou shalt by no means come out thence, till thou have paid the very last mite.

Now there were some present at that very season **13** which told him of the Galilæans, whose blood Pilate had mingled with their sacrifices. And he answered and said unto them, Think ye that these Galilæans were sinners above all the Galilæans, because they have suffered these things? I tell you, Nay: but, except ye repent, ye shall all in like manner perish. Or those eighteen, upon whom the tower in

---

* For "what will I" etc. read "what do I desire" (with the marg. Or, *how I would that it were already kindled!*) —*Am. Com.*

Siloam fell, and killed them, think ye that they were ¹offenders above all the men that dwell in Jerusa- 5 lem? I tell you, Nay: but, except ye repent, ye shall all likewise perish.

^{1 Gr. *debtors*.}

6 And he spake this parable; A certain man had a fig tree planted in his vineyard; and he came seek- 7 ing fruit thereon, and found none. And he said unto the vinedresser, Behold, these three years I come seeking fruit on this fig tree, and find none: cut it 8 down; why doth it also cumber the ground? And he answering saith unto him, Lord, let it alone this 9 year also, till I shall dig about it, and dung it: and if it bear fruit thenceforth, *well*; but if not, thou shalt cut it down.

10 And he was teaching in one of the synagogues on 11 the sabbath day. And behold, a woman which had a spirit of infirmity eighteen years; and she was bowed together, and could in no wise lift herself up. 12 And when Jesus saw her, he called her, and said to her, Woman, thou art loosed from thine infirmity. 13 And he laid his hands upon her: and immediately 14 she was made straight, and glorified God. And the ruler of the synagogue, being moved with indignation because Jesus had healed on the sabbath, answered and said to the multitude, There are six days in which men ought to work: in them therefore come and be healed, and not on the day of the sab- 15 bath. But the Lord answered him, and said, Ye hypocrites, doth not each one of you on the sabbath loose his ox or his ass from the ²stall, and lead him 16 away to watering? And ought not this woman, being a daughter of Abraham, whom Satan had bound, lo, *these* eighteen years, to have been loosed from 17 this bond on the day of the sabbath? And as he said these things, all his adversaries were put to shame: and all the multitude rejoiced for all the glorious things that were done by him.

^{2 Gr. *manger*.}

18 He said therefore, Unto what is the kingdom of 19 God like? and whereunto shall I liken it? It is like unto a grain of mustard seed, which a man took, and cast into his own garden; and it grew, and became a tree; and the birds of the heaven lodged in the 20 branches thereof. And again he said, Whereunto 21 shall I liken the kingdom of God? It is like unto leaven, which a woman took and hid in three ³measures of meal, till it was all leavened.

^{3 See marginal note on Matt. xiii. 33.}

22 And he went on his way through cities and villages, teaching, and journeying on unto Jerusalem.

And one said unto him, Lord, are they few that be 23
saved? And he said unto them, Strive to enter in 24
by the narrow door: for many, I say unto you,
shall seek to enter in, and shall not be ¹able. When 25
once the master of the house is risen up, and hath
shut to the door, and ye begin to stand without, and
to knock at the door, saying, Lord, open to us; and
he shall answer and say to you, I know you not
whence ye are; then shall ye begin to say, We did 26
eat and drink in thy presence, and thou didst teach
in our streets; and he shall say, I tell you, I know 27
not whence ye are; depart from me, all ye workers
of iniquity. There shall be the weeping and gnash- 28
ing of teeth, when ye shall see Abraham, and Isaac,
and Jacob, and all the prophets, in the kingdom of
God, and yourselves cast forth without. And they 29
shall come from the east and west, and from the
north and south, and shall ²sit down in the kingdom
of God. And behold, there are last which shall be 30
first, and there are first which shall be last.

In that very hour there came certain Pharisees, 31
saying to him, Get thee out, and go hence: for Herod
would fain kill thee. And he said unto them, Go 32
and say to that fox, Behold, I cast out ³devils and
perform cures to-day and to-morrow, and the third
day I am perfected*. Howbeit I must go on my 33
way to-day and to-morrow and the *day* following:
for it cannot be that a prophet perish out of Jerusalem. O Jerusalem, Jerusalem, which killeth the 34
prophets, and stoneth them that are sent unto her!
how often would I have gathered thy children together, even as a hen *gathereth* her own brood under
her wings, and ye would not! Behold, your house 35
is left unto you *desolate*: and I say unto you, Ye
shall not see me, until ye shall say, Blessed *is* he that
cometh in the name of the Lord.

And it came to pass, when he went into the house **14**
of one of the rulers of the Pharisees on a sabbath
to eat bread, that they were watching him. And 2
behold, there was before him a certain man which
had the dropsy. And Jesus answering spake unto 3
the lawyers and Pharisees, saying, Is it lawful to heal
on the sabbath, or not? But they held their peace. 4
And he took him, and healed him, and let him go.
And he said unto them, Which of you shall have 5
⁴an ass or an ox fallen into a well, and will not

---

¹ Or, *able, when once*
² Gr. *recline.*
³ Gr. *demons.*
⁴ Many ancient authorities read *a son.* See ch. xiii. 15.

* "I am perfected" add marg. Or, *I end my course* —*Am. Com.*

6 straightway draw him up on a sabbath day? And they could not answer again unto these things.

7 And he spake a parable unto those which were bidden, when he marked how they chose out the
8 chief seats; saying unto them, When thou art bidden of any man to a marriage feast, ¹sit not down in the chief seat; lest haply a more honourable man
9 than thou be bidden of him, and he that bade thee and him shall come and say to thee, Give this man place; and then thou shalt begin with shame to take
10 the lowest place. But when thou art bidden, go and sit down in the lowest place; that when he that hath bidden thee cometh, he may say to thee, Friend, go up higher: then shalt thou have glory in the pres-
11 ence of all that sit at meat with thee. For every one that exalteth himself shall be humbled; and he that humbleth himself shall be exalted.

12 And he said to him also that had bidden him, When thou makest a dinner or a supper, call not thy friends, nor thy brethren, nor thy kinsmen, nor rich neighbours; lest haply they also bid thee again, and
13 a recompense be made thee. But when thou makest a feast, bid the poor, the maimed, the lame, the
14 blind: and thou shalt be blessed; because they have not *wherewith* to recompense thee: for thou shalt be recompensed in the resurrection of the just.

15 And when one of them that sat at meat with him heard these things, he said unto him, Blessed is he
16 that shall eat bread in the kingdom of God. But he said unto him, A certain man made a great supper;
17 and he bade many: and he sent forth his ²servant at supper time to say to them that were bidden, Come;
18 for *all* things are now ready. And they all with one *consent* began to make excuse. The first said unto him, I have bought a field, and I must needs go out
19 and see it: I pray thee have me excused. And another said, I have bought five yoke of oxen, and I go
20 to prove them: I pray thee have me excused. And another said, I have married a wife, and therefore I
21 cannot come. And the ²servant came, and told his lord these things. Then the master of the house being angry said to his ²servant, Go out quickly into the streets and lanes of the city, and bring in hither
22 the poor and maimed and blind and lame. And the ²servant said, Lord, what thou didst command
23 is done, and yet there is room. And the lord said unto the ²servant, Go out into the highways and hedges, and constrain *them* to come in, that my house

1 Gr. *recline not.*

2 Gr. *bondservant.*

may be filled. For I say unto you, that none of those 24 men which were bidden shall taste of my supper.

Now there went with him great multitudes: and he 25 turned, and said unto them, If any man cometh unto 26 me, and hateth not his own father, and mother, and wife, and children, and brethren, and sisters, yea, and his own life also, he cannot be my disciple. Whoso- 27 ever doth not bear his own cross, and come after me, cannot be my disciple. For which of you, desiring 28 to build a tower, doth not first sit down and count the cost, whether he have *wherewith* to complete it? Lest haply, when he hath laid a foundation, and 29 is not able to finish, all that behold begin to mock him, saying, This man began to build, and was not 30 able to finish. Or what king, as he goeth to encoun- 31 ter another king in war, will not sit down first and take counsel whether he is able with ten thousand to meet him that cometh against him with twenty thousand? Or else, while the other is yet a great way off, 32 he sendeth an ambassage, and asketh conditions of peace. So therefore whosoever he be of you that 33 renounceth not all that he hath, he cannot be my disciple. Salt therefore is good: but if even the salt 34 have lost its savour, wherewith shall it be seasoned? It is fit neither for the land nor for the dunghill: *men* 35 cast it out. He that hath ears to hear, let him hear.

Now all the publicans and sinners were drawing **15** near unto him for to hear him. And both the Phar- 2 isees and the scribes murmured, saying, This man receiveth sinners, and eateth with them.

And he spake unto them this parable, saying, What 3
man of you, having a hundred sheep, and having lost 4
one of them, doth not leave the ninety and nine in the wilderness, and go after that which is lost, until he find it? And when he hath found it, he layeth 5 it on his shoulders, rejoicing. And when he cometh 6 home, he calleth together his friends and his neighbours, saying unto them, Rejoice with me, for I have found my sheep which was lost. I say unto you, 7 that even so there shall be joy in heaven over one sinner that repenteth, *more* than over ninety and nine righteous persons, which need no repentance.

1 Gr. *drachma*, a coin worth about eight pence.

Or what woman having ten ¹pieces of silver, if she 8 lose one piece, doth not light a lamp, and sweep the house, and seek diligently until she find it? And 9 when she hath found it, she calleth together her friends and neighbours, saying, Rejoice with me, for I have found the piece which I had lost. Even so, 10

I say unto you, there is joy in the presence of the angels of God over one sinner that repenteth.

11 And he said, A certain man had two sons: and
12 the younger of them said to his father, Father, give me the portion of ¹*thy* substance that falleth to me. 1 Gr. *the*.
13 And he divided unto them his living. And not many days after the younger son gathered all together, and took his journey into a far country; and there he
14 wasted his substance with riotous living. And when he had spent all, there arose a mighty famine in that
15 country; and he began to be in want. And he went and joined himself to one of the citizens of that country; and he sent him into his fields to feed swine. 2 Gr. *the pods of the carob tree*.
16 And he would fain have been filled* with ²the husks that the swine did eat: and no man gave unto him.
17 But when he came to himself he said, How many hired servants of my father's have bread enough and
18 to spare, and I perish here with hunger! I will arise and go to my father, and will say unto him, Father, I
19 have sinned against heaven, and in thy sight: I am no more worthy to be called thy son: make me as one
20 of thy hired servants. And he arose, and came to his father. But while he was yet afar off, his father saw him, and was moved with compassion, and ran,
21 and fell on his neck, and ³kissed him. And the son 3 Gr. *kissed him much*.
said unto him, Father, I have sinned against heaven, 4 Some ancient authorities add *make me as one*
and in thy sight: I am no more worthy to be called *of thy hired servants*. See ver.
22 thy son⁴. But the father said to his ⁵servants, Bring 19.
forth quickly the best robe, and put it on him; and
23 put a ring on his hand, and shoes on his feet: and 5 Gr. *bondservants*.
bring the fatted calf, *and* kill it, and let us eat, and
24 make merry: for this my son was dead, and is alive again; he was lost, and is found. And they began to
25 be merry. Now his elder son was in the field: and as he came and drew nigh to the house, he heard
26 music and dancing. And he called to him one of the ⁵servants, and inquired what these things might be.
27 And he said unto him, Thy brother is come; and thy father hath killed the fatted calf, because he hath re-
28 ceived him safe and sound. But he was angry, and would not go in: and his father came out, and in-
29 treated him. But he answered and said to his father, Lo, these many years do I serve thee, and I never transgressed a commandment of thine: and *yet* thou never gavest me a kid, that I might make merry with

---

* For "have been filled" read "have filled his belly" (with the marg. Many ancient authorities read *have been filled*).—*Am. Com.*

my friends: but when this thy son came, which hath 30 devoured thy living with harlots, thou killedst for him the fatted calf. And he said unto him, ¹Son, 31 thou art ever with me, and all that is mine is thine. But it was meet to make merry and be glad: for this 32 thy brother was dead, and is alive *again*; and *was* lost, and is found.

And he said also unto the disciples, There was a **16** certain rich man, which had a steward; and the same was accused unto him that he was wasting his goods. And he called him, and said unto him, What is this 2 that I hear of thee? render the account of thy stewardship; for thou canst be no longer steward. And 3 the steward said within himself, What shall I do, seeing that my lord taketh away the stewardship from me? I have not strength to dig; to beg I am ashamed. I am resolved what to do, that, when I am put out of the 4 stewardship, they may receive me into their houses. And calling to him each one of his lord's debtors, he 5 said to the first, How much owest thou unto my lord? And he said, A hundred ²measures of oil. And he 6 said unto him, Take thy ³bond, and sit down quickly and write fifty. Then said he to another, And how 7 much owest thou? And he said, A hundred ⁴measures of wheat. He saith unto him, Take thy ³bond, and write fourscore. And his lord commended ⁵the 8 unrighteous steward because he had done wisely: for the sons of this ⁶world are for their own generation wiser than the sons of the light. And I say unto 9 you, Make to yourselves friends ⁷by means of the mammon of unrighteousness; that, when it shall fail, they may receive you into the eternal tabernacles. He that is faithful in a very little is faithful also in 10 much: and he that is unrighteous in a very little is unrighteous also in much. If therefore ye have not 11 been faithful in the unrighteous mammon, who will commit to your trust the true *riches*? And if ye 12 have not been faithful in that which is another's, who will give you that which is your ⁸own? No 13 ⁹servant can serve two masters: for either he will hate the one, and love the other; or else he will hold to one, and despise the other. Ye cannot serve God and mammon.

And the Pharisees, who were lovers of money, 14 heard all these things; and they scoffed at him. And 15 he said unto them, Ye are they that justify yourselves in the sight of men; but God knoweth your hearts: for that which is exalted among men is an abomina-

---

1 Gr. *Child*.

2 Gr. *baths*, the bath being a Hebrew measure. See Ezek. xlv. 10, 11, 14.

3 Gr. *writings*.

4 Gr. *cors*, the cor being a Hebrew measure. See Ezek. xlv. 14.

5 Gr. *the steward of unrighteousness*.

6 Or, *age*

7 Gr. *out of*.

8 Some ancient authorities read *our own*.

9 Gr. *household-servant*.

16 tion in the sight of God. The law and the prophets *were* until John: from that time the gospel of the kingdom of God is preached, and every man entereth
17 violently into it. But it is easier for heaven and earth to pass away, than for one tittle of the law to
18 fall. Every one that putteth away his wife, and marrieth another, committeth adultery: and he that marrieth one that is put away from a husband committeth adultery.
19 Now there was a certain rich man, and he was clothed in purple and fine linen, ¹faring sumptuously
20 every day: and a certain beggar named Lazarus was
21 laid at his gate, full of sores, and desiring to be fed with the *crumbs* that fell from the rich man's table;
22 yea, even the dogs came and licked his sores. And it came to pass, that the beggar died, and that he was carried away by the angels into Abraham's bosom:
23 and the rich man also died, and was buried. And in Hades he lifted up his eyes, being in torments, and seeth Abraham afar off, and Lazarus in his bosom.
24 And he cried and said, Father Abraham, have mercy on me, and send Lazarus, that he may dip the tip of his finger in water, and cool my tongue; for I am
25 in anguish in this flame. But Abraham said, ²Son, remember that thou in thy lifetime receivedst thy good things, and Lazarus in like manner evil things: but now here he is comforted, and thou art in an-
26 guish. And ³beside all this, between us and you there is a great gulf fixed, that they which would pass from hence to you may not be able, and that
27 none may cross over from thence to us. And he said, I pray thee therefore, father, that thou wouldest send
28 him to my father's house; for I have five brethren; that he may testify unto them, lest they also come
29 into this place of torment. But Abraham saith, They have Moses and the prophets; let them hear
30 them. And he said, Nay, father Abraham: but if
31 one go to them from the dead, they will repent. And he said unto him, If they hear not Moses and the prophets, neither will they be persuaded, if one rise from the dead.

17 And he said unto his disciples, It is impossible but that occasions of stumbling should come: but
2 woe unto him, through whom they come! It were well for him if a millstone were hanged about his neck, and he were thrown into the sea, rather than that he should cause one of these little ones to stum-
3 ble. Take heed to yourselves: if thy brother sin, re-

1 Or, *living in mirth and splendour every day*

2 Gr. *Child.*

3 Or, *in all these things*

buke him; and if he repent, forgive him. And if he sin against thee seven times in the day, and seven times turn again to thee, saying, I repent; thou shalt forgive him.

And the apostles said unto the Lord, Increase our faith. And the Lord said, If ye have faith* as a grain of mustard seed, ye would say unto this sycamine tree, Be thou rooted up, and be thou planted in the sea; and it would have obeyed you. But who is there of you, having a ¹servant plowing or keeping sheep, that will say unto him, when he is come in from the field, Come straightway and sit down to meat; and will not rather say unto him, Make ready wherewith I may sup, and gird thyself, and serve me, till I have eaten and drunken; and afterward thou shalt eat and drink? Doth he thank the ¹servant because he did the things that were commanded? Even so ye also, when ye shall have done all the things that are commanded you, say, We are unprofitable ²servants; we have done that which it was our duty to do.

And it came to pass, ³as they were on the way to Jerusalem, that he was passing ⁴through the midst of† Samaria and Galilee. And as he entered into a certain village, there met him ten men that were lepers, which stood afar off: and they lifted up their voices, saying, Jesus, Master, have mercy on us. And when he saw them, he said unto them, Go and shew yourselves unto the priests. And it came to pass, as they went, they were cleansed. And one of them, when he saw that he was healed, turned back, with a loud voice glorifying God; and he fell upon his face at his feet, giving him thanks: and he was a Samaritan. And Jesus answering said, Were not the ten cleansed? but where are the nine? ⁵Were there none found that returned to give glory to God, save this ⁶stranger? And he said unto him, Arise, and go thy way: thy faith hath ⁷made thee whole.

And being asked by the Pharisees, when the kingdom of God cometh, he answered them and said, The kingdom of God cometh not with observation: neither shall they say, Lo, here! or, There! for lo, the kingdom of God is ⁸within you.

---

1 Gr. *bondservant.*
2 Gr. *bondservants.*
3 Or, *as he was*
4 Or, *between*
5 Or, *There were none found … save this stranger.*
6 Or, *alien*
7 Or, *saved thee*
8 Or, *in the midst of you*

---

* Read "If ye had faith" etc. and "it would obey you."—*Am. Com.*

† For "through the midst of" read "along the borders of" and substitute the present text for marg.⁴—*Am. Com.*

22 And he said unto the disciples, The days will come, when ye shall desire to see one of the days of the Son
23 of man, and ye shall not see it. And they shall say to you, Lo, there! Lo, here! go not away, nor follow
24 after *them*: for as the lightning, when it lighteneth out of the one part under the heaven, shineth unto the other part under heaven; so shall the Son of man
25 be ¹in his day. But first must he suffer many things
26 and be rejected of this generation. And as it came to pass in the days of Noah, even so shall it be also
27 in the days of the Son of man. They ate, they drank, they married, they were given in marriage, until the day that Noah entered into the ark, and the flood
28 came, and destroyed them all. Likewise even as it came to pass in the days of Lot; they ate, they drank, they bought, they sold, they planted, they builded;
29 but in the day that Lot went out from Sodom it rained fire and brimstone from heaven, and destroyed
30 them all: after the same manner shall it be in the day
31 that the Son of man is revealed. In that day, he which shall be on the housetop, and his goods in the house, let him not go down to take them away: and let him that is in the field likewise not return back.
32 Remember Lot's wife. Whosoever shall seek to gain
33 his ²life shall lose it: but whosoever shall lose *his* ²*life*
34 shall ³preserve it. I say unto you, In that night there shall be two men on one bed; the one shall be taken,
35 and the other shall be left. There shall be two wom-
36 en grinding together; the one shall be taken, and
37 the other shall be left.⁴ And they answering say unto him, Where, Lord? And he said unto them, Where the body *is*, thither will the ⁵eagles also be gathered together.

1 Some ancient authorities omit *in his day.*

2 Or, *soul*

3 Gr. *save it alive.*

4 Some ancient authorities add ver. 36 *There shall be two men in the field; the one shall be taken, and the other shall be left.*

5 Or, *vultures*

18 And he spake a parable unto them to the end that
2 they ought always to pray, and not to faint; saying, There was in a city a judge, which feared not God,
3 and regarded not man: and there was a widow in that city; and she came oft unto him, saying, ⁶Avenge
4 me of mine adversary. And he would not for a while: but afterward he said within himself, Though
5 I fear not God, nor regard man; yet because this widow troubleth me, I will avenge her, lest she
6 ⁷wear me* out by her continual coming. And the Lord said, Hear what ⁸the unrighteous judge saith.
7 And shall not God avenge his elect, which cry to

6 Or, *Do me justice of*: and so in ver. 5, 7, 8.

7 Gr. *bruise.*

8 Gr. *the judge of unrighteousness.*

---

* "lest she wear me" etc. add marg. Or, *lest at last by her coming she wear me out* —Am. Com.

him day and night, and he* is longsuffering over
them? I say unto you, that he will avenge them 8
speedily. Howbeit when the Son of man cometh,
shall he find ¹faith on the earth?

> ¹ Or, *the faith*

And he spake also this parable unto certain which 9
trusted in themselves that they were righteous, and
set ²all others at nought: Two men went up into 10
the temple to 'pray; the one a Pharisee, and the other
a publican. The Pharisee stood and prayed thus 11
with himself, God, I thank thee, that I am not as the
rest of men, extortioners, unjust, adulterers, or even
as this publican. I fast twice in the week; I give 12
tithes of all that I get. But the publican, stand- 13
ing afar off, would not lift up so much as his eyes
unto heaven, but smote his breast, saying, God, ³be
merciful to me ⁴a sinner. I say unto you, This man 14
went down to his house justified rather than the
other: for every one that exalteth himself shall be
humbled; but he that humbleth himself shall be
exalted.

> ² Gr. *the rest.*
> ³ Or, *be propitiated*
> ⁴ Or, *the sinner*

And they brought unto him also their babes, that 15
he should touch them: but when the disciples saw
it, they rebuked them. But Jesus called them unto 16
him, saying, Suffer the little children to come unto
me, and forbid them not; for of such is the kingdom
of God. Verily I say unto you, Whosoever shall 17
not receive the kingdom of God as a little child, he
shall in no wise enter therein.

And a certain ruler asked him, saying, Good ⁵Mas- 18
ter, what shall I do to inherit eternal life? And 19
Jesus said unto him, Why callest thou me good?
none is good, save one, *even* God. Thou knowest 20
the commandments, Do not commit adultery, Do not
kill, Do not steal, Do not bear false witness, Honour
thy father and mother. And he said, All these 21
things have I observed from my youth up. And 22
when Jesus heard it, he said unto him, One thing
thou lackest yet: sell all that thou hast, and distribute unto the poor, and thou shalt have treasure in
heaven: and come, follow me. But when he heard 23
these things, he became exceeding sorrowful; for
he was very rich. And Jesus seeing him said, How 24
hardly shall they that have riches enter into the
kingdom of God! For it is easier for a camel to 25
enter in through a needle's eye, than for a rich man

> ⁵ Or, *Teacher*

---

* For "and he" etc. read "and *yet* he" etc. with the marg. Or, *and is he slow to punish on their behalf?*—*Am. Com.*

26 to enter into the kingdom of God. And they that
27 heard it said, Then who can be saved? But he
said, The things which are impossible with men are
28 possible with God. And Peter said, Lo, we have
29 left ¹our own, and followed thee. And he said unto   ¹ Or, *our own homes*
them, Verily I say unto you, There is no man that
hath left house, or wife, or brethren, or parents, or
30 children, for the kingdom of God's sake, who shall
not receive manifold more in this time, and in the
²world to come eternal life.   ² Or, *age*
31 And he took unto him the twelve, and said unto
them, Behold, we go up to Jerusalem, and all the
things that are written ³by the prophets shall be ac- ³ Or, *through*
32 complished unto the Son of man. For he shall be
delivered up unto the Gentiles, and shall be mocked,
33 and shamefully entreated, and spit upon: and they
shall scourge and kill him: and the third day he
34 shall rise again. And they understood none of
these things; and this saying was hid from them,
and they perceived not the things that were said.
35 And it came to pass, as he drew nigh unto Jericho, a certain blind man sat by the way side beg-
36 ging: and hearing a multitude going by, he inquired
37 what this meant. And they told him, that Jesus of
38 Nazareth passeth by. And he cried, saying, Jesus,
39 thou son of David, have mercy on me. And they
that went before rebuked him, that he should hold
his peace: but he cried out the more a great deal,
40 Thou son of David, have mercy on me. And Jesus
stood, and commanded him to be brought unto him:
41 and when he was come near, he asked him, What
wilt thou that I should do unto thee? And he said,
42 Lord, that I may receive my sight. And Jesus said
unto him, Receive thy sight: thy faith hath ⁴made ⁴ Or, *saved thee*
43 thee whole. And immediately he received his sight,
and followed him, glorifying God: and all the people, when they saw it, gave praise unto God.

19 And he entered and was passing through Jeri-
2 cho. And behold, a man called by name Zacchæus; and he was a chief publican, and he was rich.
3 And he sought to see Jesus who he was; and could
not for the crowd, because he was little of stature.
4 And he ran on before, and climbed up into a syco-
more tree to see him: for he was to pass that way.
5 And when Jesus came to the place, he looked up,
and said unto him, Zacchæus, make haste, and come
6 down; for to-day I must abide at thy house. And
he made haste, and came down, and received him

joyfully. And when they saw it, they all murmur- 7
ed, saying, He is gone in to lodge with a man that is
a sinner. And Zacchæus stood, and said unto the 8
Lord, Behold, Lord, the half of my goods I give to
the poor; and if I have wrongfully exacted aught
of any man, I restore fourfold. And Jesus said 9
unto him, To-day is salvation come to this house,
forasmuch as he also is a son of Abraham. For the 10
Son of man came to seek and to save that which
was lost.

And as they heard these things, he added and 11
spake a parable, because he was nigh to Jerusalem,
and *because* they supposed that the kingdom of God
was immediately to appear. He said therefore, A 12
certain nobleman went into a far country, to receive
for himself a kingdom, and to return. And he call- 13
ed ten [1]servants of his, and gave them ten [2]pounds,
and said unto them, Trade ye *herewith* till I come.
But his citizens hated him, and sent an ambassage 14
after him, saying, We will not that this man reign
over us. And it came to pass, when he was come 15
back again, having received the kingdom, that he
commanded these [1]servants, unto whom he had
given the money, to be called to him, that he might
know what they had gained by trading. And the 16
first came before him, saying, Lord, thy pound hath
made ten pounds more. And he said unto him, 17
Well done, thou good [3]servant: because thou wast
found faithful in a very little, have thou authority
over ten cities. And the second came, saying, Thy 18
pound, Lord, hath made five pounds. And he said 19
unto him also, Be thou also over five cities. And 20
[4]another came, saying, Lord, behold, *here is* thy
pound, which I kept laid up in a napkin: for I fear- 21
ed thee, because thou art an austere man: thou
takest up that thou layedst not down, and reapest
that thou didst not sow. He saith unto him, Out of 22
thine own mouth will I judge thee, thou wicked
[3]servant. Thou knewest that I am an austere man,
taking up that I laid not down, and reaping that
I did not sow; then wherefore gavest thou not 23
my money into the bank, and [5]I at my coming
should have required it with interest? And he said 24
unto them that stood by, Take away from him the
pound, and give it unto him that hath the ten
pounds. And they said unto him, Lord, he hath ten 25
pounds. I say unto you, that unto every one that 26
hath shall be given; but from him that hath not,

---

[1] Gr. *bondservants*.
[2] *Mina*, here translated a pound, is equal to one hundred drachmas. See ch. xv. 8.
[3] Gr. *bondservant*.
[4] Gr. *the other*.
[5] Or, *I should have gone and required*

even that which he hath shall be taken away from
27 him. Howbeit these mine enemies, which would
not that I should reign over them, bring hither, and
slay them before me.
28 And when he had thus spoken, he went on before,
going up to Jerusalem.
29 And it came to pass, when he drew nigh unto
Bethphage and Bethany, at the mount that is called
the mount of Olives*, he sent two of the disciples,
30 saying, Go your way into the village over against
you; in the which as ye enter ye shall find a colt tied,
whereon no man ever yet sat: loose him, and bring
31 him. And if any one ask you, Why do ye loose
him? thus shall ye say, The Lord hath need of him.
32 And they that were sent went away, and found even
33 as he had said unto them. And as they were loosing
the colt, the owners thereof said unto them, Why
34 loose ye the colt? And they said, The Lord hath
35 need of him. And they brought him to Jesus: and
they threw their garments upon the colt, and set
36 Jesus thereon. And as he went, they spread their
37 garments in the way. And as he was now drawing
nigh, *even* at the descent of the mount of Olives, the
whole multitude of the disciples began to rejoice
and praise God with a loud voice for all the ¹mighty
38 works which they had seen; saying, Blessed *is* the
King that cometh in the name of the Lord: peace
39 in heaven, and glory in the highest. And some of
the Pharisees from the multitude said unto him,
40 ²Master, rebuke thy disciples. And he answered
and said, I tell you that, if these shall hold their
peace, the stones will cry out.
41 And when he drew nigh, he saw the city and wept
42 over it, saying, ³If thou hadst known in this day†,
even thou, the things which belong unto peace‡! but
43 now they are hid from thine eyes. For the days
shall come upon thee, when thine enemies shall cast
up a ⁴bank about thee, and compass thee round, and
44 keep thee in on every side, and shall dash thee to
the ground, and thy children within thee; and they
shall not leave in thee one stone upon another; because thou knewest not the time of thy visitation.

1 Gr. *powers*.

2 Or, *Teacher*

3 Or, *O that thou hadst known*

4 Gr. *palisade*.

---

* For "*the mount* of Olives" read "Olivet." So in xxi. 37; see Acts i. 12.—*Am. Com.*

† "day" add marg. Some ancient authorities read *thy day*.—*Am. Com.*

‡ "peace" add marg. Some ancient authorities read *thy peace*.—*Am. Com.*

And he entered into the temple, and began to cast 45 out them that sold, saying unto them, It is written, 46 And my house shall be a house of prayer: but ye have made it a den of robbers.

And he was teaching daily in the temple. But 47 the chief priests and the scribes and the principal men of the people sought to destroy him: and they 48 could not find what they might do; for the people all hung upon him, listening.

And it came to pass, on one of the days, as he **20** was teaching the people in the temple, and preaching the gospel, there came upon him the chief priests and the scribes with the elders; and they spake, say- 2 ing unto him, Tell us: By what authority doest thou these things? or who is he that gave thee this authority? And he answered and said unto them, I 3 also will ask you a ¹question; and tell me: The 4 baptism of John, was it from heaven, or from men? And they reasoned with themselves, saying, If we 5 shall say, From heaven; he will say, Why did ye not believe him? But if we shall say, From men; all 6 the people will stone us: for they be persuaded that John was a prophet. And they answered, that they 7 knew not whence *it was*. And Jesus said unto 8 them, Neither tell I' you by what authority I do these things.

And he began to speak unto the people this par- 9 able: A man planted a vineyard, and let it out to husbandmen, and went into another country for a long time. And at the season he sent unto the 10 husbandmen a ²servant, that they should give him of the fruit of the vineyard: but the husbandmen beat him, and sent him away empty. And he sent 11 yet another ²servant: and him also they beat, and handled him shamefully, and sent him away empty. And he sent yet a third: and him also they wound- 12 ed, and cast him forth. And the lord of the vine- 13 yard said, What shall I do? I will send my beloved son: it may be they will reverence him. But when 14 the husbandmen saw him, they reasoned one with another, saying, This is the heir: let us kill him, that the inheritance may be ours. And they cast 15 him forth out of the vineyard, and killed him. What therefore will the lord of the vineyard do 16 unto them? He will come and destroy these husbandmen, and will give the vineyard unto others. And when they heard it, they said, ³God forbid. But he looked upon them, and said, What then is 17 this that is written,

---

1 Gr. *word*.

2 Gr. *bondservant*.

3 Gr. *Be it not so.*

> The stone which the builders rejected,
> The same was made the head of the corner?

18 Every one that falleth on that stone shall be broken to pieces; but on whomsoever it shall fall, it will scatter him as dust.

19 And the scribes and the chief priests sought to lay hands on him in that very hour; and they feared the people: for they perceived that he spake this

20 parable against them. And they watched him, and sent forth spies, which feigned themselves to be righteous, that they might take hold of his speech, so as to deliver him up to the rule* and to the au-

21 thority of the governor. And they asked him, saying, ¹Master, we know that thou sayest and teachest rightly, and acceptest not the person *of any*, but

22 of a truth teachest the way of God: Is it lawful for

23 us to give tribute unto Cæsar, or not? But he per-

24 ceived their craftiness, and said unto them, Shew me a ²penny. Whose image and superscription

25 hath it? And they said, Cæsar's. And he said unto them, Then render unto Cæsar the things that are Cæsar's, and unto God the things that are God's.

26 And they were not able to take hold of the saying before the people: and they marvelled at his answer, and held their peace.

27 And there came to him certain of the Sadducees, they which say that there is no resurrection; and

28 they asked him, saying, ¹Master, Moses wrote unto us, that if a man's brother die, having a wife, and he be childless, his brother should take the wife,

29 and raise up seed unto his brother. There were

30 therefore seven brethren : and the first took a wife,

31 and died childless; and the second; and the third took her; and likewise the seven also left no chil-

32 dren, and died. Afterward the woman also died.

33 In the resurrection therefore whose wife of them

34 shall she be? for the seven had her to wife. And Jesus said unto them, The sons of this ³world mar-

35 ry, and are given in marriage: but they that are accounted worthy to attain to that ³world, and the resurrection from the dead, neither marry, nor are

36 given in marriage: for neither can they die any more: for they are equal unto the angels; and are

37 sons of God, being sons of the resurrection. But that the dead are raised, even Moses shewed, in *the place concerning* the Bush, when he calleth the Lord

1 Or, *Teacher*

2 See marginal note on Matt. xviii. 28.

3 Or, *age*

---

* "rule" add marg. Or, *ruling power* —Am. Com.

the God of Abraham, and the God of Isaac, and the
God of Jacob. Now he is not the God of the dead, 38
but of the living: for all live unto him. And cer- 39
tain of the scribes answering said, ¹Master, thou
hast well said. For they durst not any more ask 40
him any question.

And he said unto them, How say they that the 41
Christ is David's son? For David himself saith in 42
the book of Psalms,

> The Lord said unto my Lord,
> Sit thou on my right hand,
> Till I make thine enemies the footstool of thy 43
> feet.

David therefore calleth him Lord, and how is he his 44
son?

And in the hearing of all the people he said unto 45
his disciples, Beware of the scribes, which desire to 46
walk in long robes, and love salutations in the marketplaces, and chief seats in the synagogues, and
chief places at feasts; which devour widows' houses, 47
and for a pretence make long prayers: these shall
receive greater condemnation.

And he looked up, ²and saw the rich men that **21**
were casting their gifts into the treasury. And he 2
saw a certain poor widow casting in thither two
mites. And he said, Of a truth I say unto you, 3
This poor widow cast in more than they all: for all 4
these did of their superfluity cast in unto the gifts:
but she of her want did cast in all the living that
she had.

And as some spake of the temple, how it was 5
adorned with goodly stones and offerings, he said,
As for these things which ye behold, the days will 6
come, in which there shall not be left here one stone
upon another, that shall not be thrown down. And 7
they asked him, saying, ¹Master, when therefore shall
these things be? and what *shall be* the sign when
these things are about to come to pass? And he 8
said, Take heed that ye be not led astray: for many
shall come in my name, saying, I am *he*; and, The
time is at hand: go ye not after them. And when 9
ye shall hear of wars and tumults, be not terrified:
for these things must needs come to pass first; but
the end is not immediately.

Then said he unto them, Nation shall rise against 10
nation, and kingdom against kingdom: and there 11
shall be great earthquakes, and in divers places famines and pestilences; and there shall be terrors

---

1 Or, *Teacher*

2 Or, *and saw them that ... treasury, and they were rich.*

12 and great signs from heaven. But before all these things, they shall lay their hands on you, and shall persecute you, delivering you up to the synagogues and prisons, ¹bringing you before kings and govern- 13 ors for my name's sake. It shall turn unto you for 14 a testimony. Settle it therefore in your hearts, not 15 to meditate beforehand how to answer: for I will give you a mouth and wisdom, which all your adversaries shall not be able to withstand or to gainsay. 16 But ye shall be delivered up even by parents, and brethren, and kinsfolk, and friends; and *some* of you 17 ²shall they cause to be put to death. And ye shall 18 be hated of all men for my name's sake. And not 19 a hair of your head shall perish. In your patience ye shall win your ³souls.

20   But when ye see Jerusalem compassed with armies, 21 then know that her desolation is at hand. Then let them that are in Judæa flee unto the mountains; and let them that are in the midst of her depart out; and let not them that are in the country enter there- 22 in. For these are days of vengeance, that all things 23 which are written may be fulfilled. Woe unto them that are with child and to them that give suck in those days! for there shall be great distress upon 24 the ⁴land, and wrath unto this people. And they shall fall by the edge of the sword, and shall be led captive into all the nations: and Jerusalem shall be trodden down of the Gentiles, until the times of the 25 Gentiles be fulfilled. And there shall be signs in sun and moon and stars; and upon the earth distress of nations, in perplexity for the roaring of the 26 sea and the billows; men ⁵fainting for fear, and for expectation of the things which are coming on ⁶the world: for the powers of the heavens shall be sha- 27 ken. And then shall they see the Son of man com- 28 ing in a cloud with power and great glory. But when these things begin to come to pass, look up, and lift up your heads; because your redemption draweth nigh.

29   And he spake to them a parable: Behold the fig 30 tree, and all the trees: when they now shoot forth, ye see it and know of your own selves that the sum- 31 mer is now nigh. Even so ye also, when ye see these things coming to pass, know ye that the king- 32 dom of God is nigh. Verily I say unto you, This generation shall not pass away, till all things be ac- 33 complished. Heaven and earth shall pass away: but my words shall not pass away.

1 Gr. *you being brought.*

2 Or, *shall they put to death*

3 Or, *lives*

4 Or, *earth*

5 Or, *expiring*
6 Gr. *the inhabited earth.*

But take heed to yourselves, lest haply your hearts 34
be overcharged with surfeiting, and drunkenness,
and cares of this life, and that day come on you
suddenly as a snare: for *so* shall it come upon all 35
them that dwell on the face of all the earth. But 36
watch ye at every season, making supplication, that
ye may prevail to escape all these things that shall
come to pass, and to stand before the Son of man.

And every day he was teaching in the temple; and 37
every night he went out, and lodged in the mount
that is called *the mount* of Olives. And all the peo- 38
ple came early in the morning to him in the temple,
to hear him.

Now the feast of unleavened bread drew nigh, **22**
which is called the Passover. And the chief priests 2
and the scribes sought how they might put him to
death; for they feared the people.

And Satan entered into Judas who was called 3
Iscariot, being of the number of the twelve. And 4
he went away, and communed with the chief priests
and captains, how he might deliver him unto them.
And they were glad, and covenanted to give him 5
money. And he consented, and sought opportunity 6
to deliver him unto them [1]in the absence of the multitude.

[1] Or, *without tumult*

And the day of unleavened bread came, on which 7
the passover must be sacrificed. And he sent Peter 8
and John, saying, Go and make ready for us the
passover, that we may eat. And they said unto him, 9
Where wilt thou that we make ready? And he said 10
unto them, Behold, when ye are entered into the
city, there shall meet you a man bearing a pitcher of
water; follow him into the house whereinto he goeth. And ye shall say unto the goodman of the 11
house, The [2]Master saith unto thee, Where is the
guest-chamber, where I shall eat the passover with
my disciples? And he will shew you a large upper 12
room furnished: there make ready. And they went, 13
and found as he had said unto them: and they made
ready the passover.

[2] Or, *Teacher*

And when the hour was come, he sat down, and 14
the apostles with him. And he said unto them, With 15
desire I have desired to eat this passover with you
before I suffer: for I say unto you, I will not eat it, 16
until it be fulfilled in the kingdom of God. And he 17
received a cup, and when he had given thanks, he
said, Take this, and divide it among yourselves: for 18
I say unto you, I will not drink from henceforth of

the fruit of the vine, until the kingdom of God shall
19 come. And he took ¹bread, and when he had given
thanks, he brake it, and gave to them, saying, This is
my body ²which is given for you: this do in remem-
20 brance of me. And the cup in like manner after
supper, saying, This cup is the new ³covenant in my
21 blood, *even* that which is poured out for you. But
behold, the hand of him that betrayeth me is with
22 me on the table. For the Son of man indeed goeth,
as it hath been determined: but woe unto that man
23 through whom he is betrayed! And they began to
question among themselves, which of them it was
that should do this thing.
24 And there arose also a contention among them,
25 which of them is accounted* to be ⁴greatest. And
he said unto them, The kings of the Gentiles have
lordship over them; and they that have authority
26 over them are called Benefactors. But ye *shall* not *be*
so: but he that is the greater among you, let him
become as the younger; and he that is chief, as he
27 that doth serve. For whether is greater, he that
⁵sitteth at meat, or he that serveth? is not he that
⁵sitteth at meat? but I am in the midst of you as he
28 that serveth. But ye are they which have continued
29 with me in my temptations; and ⁶I appoint unto you a
30 kingdom, even as my Father appointed unto me, that
ye may eat and drink at my table in my kingdom;
and ye shall sit on thrones judging the twelve tribes
31 of Israel. Simon, Simon, behold, Satan ⁷asked to
32 have you, that he might sift you as wheat: but I made
supplication for thee, that thy faith fail not: and do
thou, when once thou hast turned again, stablish thy
33 brethren. And he said unto him, Lord, with thee I
34 am ready to go both to prison and to death. And he
said, I tell thee, Peter, the cock shall not crow this
day, until thou shalt thrice deny that thou knowest
me.
35 And he said unto them, When I sent you forth
without purse, and wallet, and shoes, lacked ye any
36 thing? And they said, Nothing. And he said unto
them, But now, he that hath a purse, let him take it,
and likewise a wallet: ⁸and he that hath none, let
37 him sell his cloke, and buy a sword. For I say unto
you, that this which is written must be fulfilled in
me, And he was reckoned with transgressors: for
38 that which concerneth me hath ⁹fulfilment. And

¹ Or, *a loaf*
² Some ancient authorities omit *which is given for you . . . which is poured out for you.*
³ Or, *testament*
⁴ Gr. *greater.*
⁵ Gr. *reclineth.*
⁶ Or, *I appoint unto you, even as my Father appointed unto me a kingdom, that ye may eat and drink,* &c.
⁷ Or, *obtained you by asking*
⁸ Or, *and he that hath no sword, let him sell his cloke, and buy one.*
⁹ Gr. *end.*

---

* For "is accounted" read "was accounted"—*Am. Com.*

they said, Lord, behold, here are two swords. And he said unto them, It is enough.

And he came out, and went, as his custom was, 39 unto the mount of Olives; and the disciples also followed him. And when he was at the place, he 40 said unto them, Pray that ye enter not into temptation. And he was parted from them about a stone's 41 cast; and he kneeled down and prayed, saying, Fa- 42 ther, if thou be willing, remove this cup from me: nevertheless not my will, but thine, be done. [1]And 43 there appeared unto him an angel from heaven, strengthening him. And being in an agony he 44 prayed more earnestly: and his sweat became as it were great drops of blood falling down upon the ground. And when he rose up from his prayer, he 45 came unto the disciples, and found them sleeping for sorrow, and said unto them, Why sleep ye? rise 46 and pray, that ye enter not into temptation.

While he yet spake, behold, a multitude, and he 47 that was called Judas, one of the twelve, went before them ; and he drew near unto Jesus to kiss him. But Jesus said unto him, Judas, betrayest thou the 48 Son of man with a kiss? And when they that were 49 about him saw what would follow, they said, Lord, shall we smite with the sword? And a certain one 50 of them smote the [2]servant of the high priest, and struck off his right ear. But Jesus answered and 51 said, Suffer ye thus far. And he touched his ear, and healed him. And Jesus said unto the chief 52 priests, and captains of the temple, and elders, which were come against him, Are ye come out, as against a robber, with swords and staves? When I was daily 53 with you in the temple, ye stretched not forth your hands against me: but this is your hour, and the power of darkness.

And they seized him, and led him *away*, and 54 brought him into the high priest's house. But Peter followed afar off. And when they had kindled 55 a fire in the midst of the court, and had sat down together, Peter sat in the midst of them. And 56 a certain maid seeing him as he sat in the light *of the fire*, and looking stedfastly upon him, said, This man also was with him. But he denied, saying, 57 Woman, I know him not. And after a little while 58 another saw him, and said, Thou also art *one* of them. But Peter said, Man, I am not. And after 59 the space of about one hour another confidently affirmed, saying, Of a truth this man also was with

[1] Many ancient authorities omit ver. 43, 44.

[2] Gr. *bondservant*.

60 him: for he is a Galilæan. But Peter said, Man, I know not what thou sayest. And immediately,
61 while he yet spake, the cock crew. And the Lord turned, and looked upon Peter. And Peter remembered the word of the Lord, how that he said unto him, Before the cock crow this day, thou shalt deny
62 me thrice. And he went out, and wept bitterly.
63 And the men that held ¹*Jesus* mocked him, and ¹ Gr. *him.*
64 beat him. And they blindfolded him, and asked him, saying, Prophesy: who is he that struck thee?
65 And many other things spake they against him, reviling him.
66 And as soon as it was day, the assembly of the elders of the people was gathered together, both chief priests and scribes; and they led him away into their
67 council, saying, If thou art the Christ, tell us. But
68 he said unto them, If I tell you, ye will not believe:
69 and if I ask *you*, ye will not answer. But from henceforth shall the Son of man be seated at the
70 right hand of the power of God. And they all said, Art thou then the Son of God? And he said unto
71 them, ²Ye say that I am*. And they said, What further need have we of witness? for we ourselves have heard from his own mouth.

² Or, *Ye say it, because I am.*

23 And the whole company of them rose up, and
2 brought him before Pilate. And they began to accuse him, saying, We found this man perverting our nation, and forbidding to give tribute to Cæsar, and
3 saying that he himself is ³Christ a king†. And Pilate asked him, saying, Art thou the King of the Jews? And he answered him and said, Thou say-
4 est. And Pilate said unto the chief priests and the
5 multitudes, I find no fault in this man. But they were the more urgent, saying, He stirreth up the people, teaching throughout all Judæa, and begin-
6 ning from Galilee even unto this place. But when Pilate heard it, he asked whether the man were a
7 Galilæan. And when he knew that he was of Herod's jurisdiction, he sent him unto Herod, who himself also was at Jerusalem in these days.
8 Now when Herod saw Jesus, he was exceeding glad: for he was of a long time desirous to see him, because he had heard concerning him; and he hoped
9 to see some ⁴miracle done by him. And he questioned him in many words; but he answered him

³ Or, *an anointed king*

⁴ Gr. *sign.*

* For "Ye say that I am" read "Ye say *it*, for I am" and substitute the text for the marg.—*Am. Com.*
† "Christ a king" omit the marg.—*Am. Com.*

nothing. And the chief priests and the scribes 10 stood, vehemently accusing him. And Herod with 11 his soldiers set him at nought, and mocked him, and arraying him in gorgeous apparel sent him back to Pilate. And Herod and Pilate became friends with 12 each other that very day: for before they were at enmity between themselves.

And Pilate called together the chief priests and 13 the rulers and the people, and said unto them, Ye 14 brought unto me this man, as one that perverteth the people: and behold, I, having examined him before you, found no fault in this man touching those things whereof ye accuse him; no, nor yet Herod: 15 for he sent him* back unto us; and behold, nothing worthy of death hath been done by him. I will therefore chastise him, and release him.[1] But they cried 16 out all together, saying, Away with this man, and release unto us Barabbas: one who for a certain insurrection made in the city, and for murder, was cast 18 into prison. And Pilate spake unto them again, desiring to release Jesus; but they shouted, saying, 20 Crucify, crucify him. And he said unto them the 21 third time, Why, what evil hath this man done? I 22 have found no cause of death in him: I will therefore chastise him and release him. But they were 23 instant† with loud voices, asking that he might be crucified. And their voices prevailed. And Pilate 24 gave sentence that what they asked for should be done. And he released him that for insurrection 25 and murder had been cast into prison, whom they asked for; but Jesus he delivered up to their will.

And when they led him away, they laid hold upon 26 one Simon of Cyrene, coming from the country, and laid on him the cross, to bear it after Jesus.

And there followed him a great multitude of the 27 people, and of women who bewailed and lamented him. But Jesus turning unto them said, Daughters 28 of Jerusalem, weep not for me, but weep for yourselves, and for your children. For behold, the days 29 are coming, in which they shall say, Blessed are the barren, and the wombs that never bare, and the breasts that never gave suck. Then shall they begin to say to the mountains, Fall on us; and to the 30 hills, Cover us. For if they do these things in the 31 green tree, what shall be done in the dry?

[1] Many ancient authorities insert ver. 17 *Now he must needs release unto them at the feast one prisoner.* Others add the same words after ver. 19.

---

* "he sent him" etc. add marg. Many ancient authorities read *I sent you to him.*—*Am. Com.*

† For "instant" read "urgent"—*Am. Com.*

S. LUKE.

32 And there were also two others, malefactors, led with him to be put to death.
33 And when they came unto the place which is called ¹The skull, there they crucified him, and the malefactors, one on the right hand and the other on the
34 left. ²And Jesus said, Father, forgive them; for they know not what they do. And parting his gar-
35 ments among them, they cast lots. And the people stood beholding. And the rulers also scoffed at him, saying, He saved others; let him save himself,
36 if this is the Christ of God, his chosen. And the soldiers also mocked him, coming to him, offering
37 him vinegar, and saying, If thou art the King of
38 the Jews, save thyself. And there was also a superscription over him, THIS IS THE KING OF THE JEWS.
39 And one of the malefactors which were hanged railed on him, saying, Art not thou the Christ? save
40 thyself and us. But the other answered, and rebuking him said, Dost thou not even fear God, see-
41 ing thou art in the same condemnation? And we indeed justly; for we receive the due reward of our
42 deeds: but this man hath done nothing amiss. And he said, Jesus, remember me when thou comest ³in
43 thy kingdom. And he said unto him, Verily I say unto thee, To-day shalt thou be with me in Paradise.
44 And it was now about the sixth hour, and a darkness came over the whole ⁴land until the ninth hour,
45 ⁵the sun's light failing: and the veil of the ⁶temple
46 was rent in the midst. ⁷And* when Jesus had cried with a loud voice, he said, Father, into thy hands I commend my spirit: and having said this, he gave up
47 the ghost. And when the centurion saw what was done, he glorified God, saying, Certainly this was a
48 righteous man. And all the multitudes that came together to this sight, when they beheld the things
49 that were done, returned smiting their breasts. And all his acquaintance, and the women that followed with him from Galilee, stood afar off, seeing these things.
50 And behold, a man named Joseph, who was a
51 councillor, a good man and a righteous (he had not consented to their counsel and deed), *a man* of Arimathæa, a city of the Jews, who was looking for
52 the kingdom of God: this man went to Pilate, and
53 asked for the body of Jesus. And he took it down,

---

1 According to the Latin, *Calvary*, which has the same meaning.

2 Some ancient authorities omit *And Jesus said, Father, forgive them; for they know not what they do.*

3 Some ancient authorities read *in to thy kingdom.*

4 Or, *earth*

5 Gr. *the sun failing.*

6 Or, *sanctuary*

7 Or, *And Jesus, crying with a loud voice, said*

* Let margin and text exchange places.—*Am. Com.*

and wrapped it in a linen cloth, and laid him in a tomb that was hewn in stone, where never man had yet lain. And it was the day of the Preparation, and 54 the sabbath ¹drew on. And the women, which had 55 come with him out of Galilee, followed after, and beheld the tomb, and how his body was laid. And 56 they returned, and prepared spices and ointments.

And on the sabbath they rested according to the **24** commandment. But on the first day of the week, at early dawn, they came unto the tomb, bringing the spices which they had prepared. And they 2 found the stone rolled away from the tomb. And 3 they entered in, and found not the body ²of the Lord Jesus. And it came to pass, while they were perplexed thereabout, behold, two men stood by them 4 in dazzling apparel: and as they were affrighted, 5 and bowed down their faces to the earth, they said unto them, Why seek ye ³the living among the dead? ⁴He is not here, but is risen: remember how 6 he spake unto you when he was yet in Galilee, say- 7 ing that the Son of man must be delivered up into the hands of sinful men, and be crucified, and the third day rise again. And they remembered his 8 words, and returned ⁵from the tomb, and told all these 9 things to the eleven, and to all the rest. Now they 10 were Mary Magdalene, and Joanna, and Mary the *mother* of James: and the other women with them told these things unto the apostles. And these 11 words appeared in their sight as idle talk; and they disbelieved them. ⁶But Peter arose, and ran unto 12 the tomb; and stooping and looking in, he seeth the linen cloths by themselves; and he ⁷departed to his home, wondering at that which was come to pass.

And behold, two of them were going that very 13 day to a village named Emmaus, which was threescore furlongs from Jerusalem. And they com- 14 muned with each other of all these things which had happened. And it came to pass, while they 15 communed and questioned together, that Jesus himself drew near, and went with them. But their eyes 16 were holden that they should not know him. And 17 he said unto them, ⁸What communications are these that ye have one with another, as ye walk? And they stood still, looking sad. And one of them, named 18 Cleopas, answering said unto him, ⁹Dost thou alone sojourn in Jerusalem and not know the things which are come to pass there in these days? And he said 19 unto them, What things? And they said unto him,

---

¹ Gr. *began to dawn.*

² Some ancient authorities omit *of the Lord Jesus.*

³ Gr. *him that liveth.*

⁴ Some ancient authorities omit *He is not here, but is risen.*

⁵ Some ancient authorities omit *from the tomb.*

⁶ Some ancient authorities omit ver. 12.

⁷ Or, *departed, wondering with himself*

⁸ Gr. *What words are these that ye exchange one with another.*

⁹ Or, *Dost thou sojourn alone in Jerusalem, and knowest thou not the things*

The things concerning Jesus of Nazareth, which was a prophet mighty in deed and word before God and 20 all the people: and how the chief priests and our rulers delivered him up to be condemned to death, 21 and crucified him. But we hoped that it was he which should redeem Israel. Yea and beside all this, it is now the third day since these things came 22 to pass. Moreover certain women of our company 23 amazed us, having been early at the tomb; and when they found not his body, they came, saying, that they had also seen a vision of angels, which said 24 that he was alive. And certain of them that were with us went to the tomb, and found it even so as 25 the women had said: but him they saw not. And he said unto them, O foolish men, and slow of heart 26 to believe ¹in all that the prophets have spoken! Be- 1 Or, *after* hoved it not the Christ to suffer these things, and to 27 enter into his glory? And beginning from Moses and from all the prophets, he interpreted to them in all the scriptures the things concerning himself. 28 And they drew nigh unto the village, whither they were going: and he made as though he would go 29 further. And they constrained him, saying, Abide with us: for it is toward evening, and the day is now 30 far spent. And he went in to abide with them. And it came to pass, when he had sat down with them to meat, he took the ²bread, and blessed it, and brake, 2 Or, *loaf* 31 and gave to them*. And their eyes were opened, and they knew him; and he vanished out of their 32 sight. And they said one to another, Was not our heart burning within us, while he spake to us in the 33 way, while he opened to us the scriptures? And they rose up that very hour, and returned to Jerusalem, and found the eleven gathered together, and 34 them that were with them, saying, The Lord is risen 35 indeed, and hath appeared to Simon. And they rehearsed the things *that happened* in the way, and how he was known of them in the breaking of the bread. 36 And as they spake these things, he himself stood ³ Some ancient authorities omit in the midst of them, ³and saith unto them, Peace *be* *and saith unto* *them, Peace be* 37 unto you. But they were terrified and affrighted, *unto you.* 38 and supposed that they beheld a spirit. And he said unto them, Why are ye troubled? and wherefore 39 do reasonings† arise in your heart? See my hands and my feet, that it is I myself: handle me,

---

* Read "he took the bread and blessed; and breaking *it* he gave to them"—*Am. Com.*
† For "reasonings" read "questionings"—*Am. Com.*

and see; for a spirit hath not flesh and bones, as ye behold me having. ¹And when he had said this, he shewed them his hands and his feet. And while they still disbelieved for joy, and wondered, he said unto them, Have ye here anything to eat? And they gave him a piece of a broiled fish². And he took it, and did eat before them.

And he said unto them, These are my words which I spake unto you, while I was yet with you, how that all things must needs be fulfilled, which are written in the law of Moses, and the prophets, and the psalms, concerning me. Then opened he their mind, that they might understand the scriptures; and he said unto them, Thus it is written, that the Christ should suffer, and rise again from the dead the third day; and that repentance ³and remission of sins should be preached in his name unto all the ⁴nations, beginning from Jerusalem. Ye are witnesses of these things. And behold, I send forth the promise of my Father upon you: but tarry ye in the city, until ye be clothed with power from on high.

And he led them out until *they were* over against Bethany: and he lifted up his hands, and blessed them. And it came to pass, while he blessed them, he parted from them, ⁵and was carried up into heaven. And they ⁶worshipped him, and returned to Jerusalem with great joy: and were continually in the temple, blessing God.

---

1 Some ancient authorities omit ver. 40.
2 Many ancient authorities add *and a honeycomb*.
3 Some ancient authorities read *unto*.
4 Or, *nations. Beginning from Jerusalem, ye are witnesses*
5 Some ancient authorities omit *and was carried up into heaven*.
6 Some ancient authorities omit *worshipped him, and*.

THE GOSPEL
ACCORDING TO
S. JOHN.

1 In the beginning was the Word, and the Word was
2 with God, and the Word was God. The same was
3 in the beginning with God. All things were made
   ¹by* him; and without him ²was not anything made
4 that hath been made. In him was life; and the life
5 was the light of men. And the light shineth in the
   darkness; and the darkness ³apprehended it not.
6 There came a man, sent from God, whose name was
7 John. The same came for witness, that he might
   bear witness of the light, that all might believe
8 through him. He was not the light, but *came* that
9 he might bear witness of the light. ⁴There was the
   true light, *even the light* which lighteth ⁵every man,
10 coming into the world. He was in the world, and
   the world was made ¹by* him, and the world knew
11 him not. He came unto ⁶his own, and they that
12 were his own received him not. But as many as
   received him, to them gave he the right to become
   children of God, *even* to them that believe on his
13 name: which were ⁷born, not of ⁸blood, nor of the
   will of the flesh, nor of the will of man, but of God.
14 And the Word became flesh, and ⁹dwelt among us
   (and we beheld his glory, glory as of ¹⁰the only begotten from the Father), full of grace and truth.
15 John beareth witness of him, and crieth, saying,
   ¹¹This was he of whom I said, He that cometh after
   me is become before me: for he was ¹²before me.
16 For of his fulness we all received, and grace for
17 grace. For the law was given ¹by* Moses; grace and
18 truth came ¹by Jesus Christ. No man hath seen

1 Or, *through*
2 Or, *was not anything made. That which hath been made was life in him; and the life &c.*
3 Or, *overcame* See ch. xii. 35 (Gr.).
4 Or, *The true light, which lighteth every man, was coming*
5 Or, *every man as he cometh*
6 Gr. *his own things*.
7 Or, *begotten*
8 Gr. *bloods*.
9 Gr. *tabernacled*.
10 Or, *an only begotten from a father*
11 Some ancient authorities read (*this was he that said*).
12 Gr. *first in regard of me.*

---
* Substitute the marginal rendering for the text. —*Am. Com.*

God at any time; ¹the only begotten Son, which is in the bosom of the Father, he hath declared *him*.

¹ Many very ancient authorities read *God only begotten*.

And this is the witness of John, when the Jews sent unto him from Jerusalem priests and Levites to ask him, Who art thou? And he confessed, and denied not; and he confessed, I am not the Christ. And they asked him, What then? Art thou Elijah? And he saith, I am not. Art thou the prophet? And he answered, No. They said therefore unto him, Who art thou? that we may give an answer to them that sent us. What sayest thou of thyself? He said, I am the voice of one crying in the wilderness, Make straight the way of the Lord, as said Isaiah the prophet. ²And they had been sent from the Pharisees. And they asked him, and said unto him, Why then baptizest thou, if thou art not the Christ, neither Elijah, neither the prophet? John answered them, saying, I baptize ³with water: in the midst of you standeth one whom ye know not, *even* he that cometh after me, the latchet of whose shoe I am not worthy to unloose. These things were done in ⁴Bethany beyond Jordan, where John was baptizing.

² Or, *And certain had been sent from among the Pharisees.*

³ Or, *in*

⁴ Many ancient authorities read *Bethabarah*, some *Betharabah*.

On the morrow he seeth Jesus coming unto him, and saith, Behold, the Lamb of God, which ⁵taketh away the sin of the world! This is he of whom I said, After me cometh a man which is become before me: for he was ⁶before me. And I knew him not; but that he should be made manifest to Israel, for this cause came I baptizing ³with water. And John bare witness, saying, I have beheld the Spirit descending as a dove out of heaven; and it abode upon him. And I knew him not: but he that sent me to baptize ³with water, he said unto me, Upon whomsoever thou shalt see the Spirit descending, and abiding upon him, the same is he that baptizeth ³with the Holy Spirit. And I have seen, and have borne witness that this is the Son of God.

⁵ Or, *beareth the sin.*

⁶ Gr. *first in regard of me.*

Again on the morrow John was standing, and two of his disciples; and he looked upon Jesus as he walked, and saith, Behold, the Lamb of God! And the two disciples heard him speak, and they followed Jesus. And Jesus turned, and beheld them following, and saith unto them, What seek ye? And they said unto him, Rabbi (which is to say, being interpreted, ⁷Master), where abidest thou? He saith unto them, Come, and ye shall see. They came therefore and saw where he abode; and they abode with him that day: it was about the tenth hour.

⁷ Or, *Teacher*

40 One of the two that heard John *speak*, and followed
41 him, was Andrew, Simon Peter's brother. He findeth first his own brother Simon, and saith unto him, We have found the Messiah (which is, being inter-
42 preted, ¹Christ). He brought him unto Jesus. Jesus looked upon him, and said, Thou art Simon the son of ²John: thou shalt be called Cephas (which is by interpretation, ³Peter).
43 On the morrow he was minded to go forth into Galilee, and he findeth Philip: and Jesus saith unto
44 him, Follow me. Now Philip was from Bethsaida,
45 of the city of Andrew and Peter. Philip findeth Nathanael, and saith unto him, We have found him, of whom Moses in the law, and the prophets, did
46 write, Jesus of Nazareth, the son of Joseph. And Nathanael said unto him, Can any good thing come out of Nazareth? Philip saith unto him, Come and
47 see. Jesus saw Nathanael coming to him, and saith of him, Behold, an Israelite indeed, in whom is no
48 guile! Nathanael saith unto him, Whence knowest thou me? Jesus answered and said unto him, Before Philip called thee, when thou wast under the
49 fig tree, I saw thee. Nathanael answered him, Rabbi, thou art the Son of God; thou art King of Israel.
50 Jesus answered and said unto him, Because I said unto thee, I saw thee underneath the fig tree, believest thou? thou shalt see greater things than these.
51 And he saith unto him, Verily, verily, I say unto you, Ye shall see the heaven opened, and the angels of God ascending and descending upon the Son of man.

2 And the third day there was a marriage in Cana
2 of Galilee; and the mother of Jesus was there: and Jesus also was bidden, and his disciples, to the mar-
3 riage. And when the wine failed, the mother of Je-
4 sus saith unto him, They have no wine. And Jesus saith unto her, Woman, what have I to do with
5 thee? mine hour is not yet come. His mother saith unto the servants, Whatsoever he saith unto you, do
6 it. Now there were six waterpots of stone set there after the Jews' manner of purifying, containing two
7 or three firkins apiece. Jesus saith unto them, Fill the waterpots with water. And they filled them up
8 to the brim. And he saith unto them, Draw out now, and bear unto the ⁴ruler of the feast. And
9 they bare it. And when the ruler of the feast tasted the water ⁵now become wine, and knew not whence it was (but the servants which had drawn the water

1 That is, *Anointed*.
2 Gr. *Joanes*: called in Matt. xvi. 17, *Jonah*.
3 That is, *Rock* or *Stone*.
4 Or, *steward*
5 Or, *that it had become*

knew), the ruler of the feast calleth the bridegroom, and saith unto him, Every man setteth on first the good wine; and when *men* have drunk freely, *then* that which is worse: thou hast kept the good wine until now. This beginning of his signs did Jesus in Cana of Galilee, and manifested his glory; and his disciples believed on him.

After this he went down to Capernaum, he, and his mother, and *his* brethren, and his disciples: and there they abode not many days.

And the passover of the Jews was at hand, and Jesus went up to Jerusalem. And he found in the temple those that sold oxen and sheep and doves, and the changers of money sitting: and he made a scourge of cords, and cast all out of the temple, both the sheep and the oxen; and he poured out the changers' money, and overthrew their tables; and to them that sold the doves he said, Take these things hence; make not my Father's house a house of merchandise. His disciples remembered that it was written, The zeal of thine house* shall eat me up. The Jews therefore answered and said unto him, What sign shewest thou unto us, seeing that thou doest these things? Jesus answered and said unto them, Destroy this ¹temple, and in three days I will raise it up. The Jews therefore said, Forty and six years was this ¹temple in building, and wilt thou raise it up in three days? But he spake of the ¹temple of his body. When therefore he was raised from the dead, his disciples remembered that he spake this; and they believed the scripture, and the word which Jesus had said.

Now when he was in Jerusalem at the passover, during the feast, many believed on his name, beholding his signs which he did. But Jesus did not trust himself unto them, for that he knew all men, and because he needed not that any one should bear witness concerning ²man; for he himself knew what was in man.

Now there was a man of the Pharisees, named Nicodemus, a ruler of the Jews: the same came unto him by night, and said to him, Rabbi, we know that thou art a teacher come from God: for no man can do these signs that thou doest, except God be with him. Jesus answered and said unto him, Ver-

1 Or, *sanctuary*

2 Or, *a man; for . . . the man*

---

* For "The zeal of thine house" read "Zeal for thy house"—*Am. Com.*

ily, verily, I say unto thee, Except a man be born
4 ¹anew, he cannot see the kingdom of God. Nico- demus saith unto him, How can a man be born when he is old? can he enter a second time into his mother's
5 womb, and be born? Jesus answered, Verily, verily, I say unto thee, Except a man be born of water and the Spirit, he cannot enter into the kingdom of God.
6 That which is born of the flesh is flesh; and that
7 which is born of the Spirit is spirit. Marvel not
8 that I said unto thee, Ye must be born ¹anew. ²The wind bloweth where it listeth, and thou hearest the voice thereof, but knowest not whence it cometh, and whither it goeth: so is every one that is born of
9 the Spirit. Nicodemus answered and said unto him,
10 How can these things be? Jesus answered and said unto him, Art thou the teacher of Israel, and under-
11 standest not these things? Verily, verily, I say unto thee, We speak that we do know, and bear witness of that we have seen; and ye receive not our wit-
12 ness. If I told you earthly things, and ye believe not, how shall ye believe, if I tell you heavenly
13 things? And no man hath ascended into heaven, but he that descended out of heaven, *even* the Son
14 of man, ³which is in heaven. And as Moses lifted up the serpent in the wilderness, even so must the
15 Son of man be lifted up: that whosoever ⁴believ- eth may in him have eternal life.
16 For God so loved the world, that he gave his only begotten Son, that whosoever believeth on him
17 should not perish, but have eternal life. For God sent not the Son into the world to judge the world; but that the world should be saved through him.
18 He that believeth on him is not judged: he that be- lieveth not hath been judged already, because he hath not believed on the name of the only begotten
19 Son of God. And this is the judgement, that the light is come into the world, and men loved the darkness rather than the light; for their works were
20 evil. For every one that ⁵doeth ill* hateth the light, and cometh not to the light, lest his works should
21 be ⁶reproved. But he that doeth the truth cometh to the light, that his works may be made manifest,
⁷that they have been wrought in God.
22 After these things came Jesus and his disciples into the land of Judæa; and there he tarried with
23 them, and baptized. And John also was baptizing in

1 Or, *from above*

2 Or, *The Spirit breatheth*

3 Many ancient authorities omit *which is in heaven*.

4 Or, *believeth in him may have*

5 Or, *practiseth*

6 Or, *convicted*

7 Or, *because*

---

* For "ill" read "evil" So in v. 29.—*Am. Com.*

¹ Gr. *were many waters*.

Ænon near to Salim, because there ¹was much water there: and they came, and were baptized. For John was not yet cast into prison. There arose therefore a questioning on the part of John's disciples with a Jew about purifying. And they came unto John, and said to him, Rabbi, he that was with thee beyond Jordan, to whom thou hast borne witness, behold, the same baptizeth, and all men come to him. John answered and said, A man can receive nothing, except it have been given him from heaven. Ye yourselves bear me witness, that I said, I am not the Christ, but, that I am sent before him. He that hath the bride is the bridegroom: but the friend of the bridegroom, which standeth and heareth him, rejoiceth greatly because of the bridegroom's voice: this my joy therefore is fulfilled.* He must increase, but I must decrease. 24 25 26 27 28 29 30

² Some ancient authorities read *he that cometh from heaven beareth witness of what he hath seen and heard*.

He that cometh from above is above all: he that is of the earth is of the earth, and of the earth he speaketh: ²he that cometh from heaven is above all. What he hath seen and heard, of that he beareth witness; and no man receiveth his witness. He that hath received his witness hath set his seal to *this*, that God is true. For he whom God hath sent speaketh the words of God: for he giveth not the Spirit by measure. The Father loveth the Son, and hath given all things into his hand. He that believeth on the 31 32 33 34 35 36

³ Or, *believeth not*

Son hath eternal life; but he that ³obeyeth not the Son shall not see life, but the wrath of God abideth on him.

⁴ Gr. *spring*: and so in ver. 14; but not in ver. 11, 12.
⁵ Or, *as he was*

When therefore the Lord knew how that the Pharisees had heard that Jesus was making and baptizing more disciples than John (although Jesus himself baptized not, but his disciples), he left Judæa, and departed again into Galilee. And he must needs pass through Samaria. So he cometh to a city of Samaria, called Sychar, near to the parcel of ground that Jacob gave to his son Joseph: and Jacob's ⁴well was there. Jesus therefore, being wearied with his journey, sat ⁵thus by the ⁴well. It was about the sixth hour. There cometh a woman of Samaria to draw water: Jesus saith unto her, Give me to drink. For his disciples were gone away into the city to buy food. The Samaritan woman therefore saith unto him, How is it that 4 2 3 4 5 6 7 8 9

---

* For "fulfilled" read "made full" [and so xv. 11; xvi. 24; xvii. 13. See "Classes of Passages," xiv.]—*Am. Com.*

thou, being a Jew, askest drink of me, which am a [1] Some ancient authorities omit *For Jews have no dealings with Samaritans.*
Samaritan woman? ('For Jews have no dealings
10 with Samaritans.) Jesus answered and said unto
her, If thou knewest the gift of God, and who it is
that saith to thee, Give me to drink; thou wouldest
have asked of him, and he would have given thee
11 living water. The woman saith unto him, [2]Sir, [2] Or, *Lord*
thou hast nothing to draw with, and the well is
deep: from whence then hast thou that living water?
12 Art thou greater than our father Jacob, which gave
us the well, and drank thereof himself, and his sons,
13 and his cattle? Jesus answered and said unto her,
Every one that drinketh of this water shall thirst
14 again: but whosoever drinketh of the water that I
shall give him shall never thirst; but the water that
I shall give him shall become in him a well of water
15 springing up unto eternal life. The woman saith
unto him, [2]Sir, give me this water, that I thirst not,
16 neither come all the way hither to draw. Jesus
saith unto her, Go, call thy husband, and come hith-
17 er. The woman answered and said unto him, I
have no husband. Jesus saith unto her, Thou saidst
18 well, I have no husband: for thou hast had five husbands; and he whom thou now hast is not thy hus-
19 band: this hast thou said truly. The woman saith
unto him, [2]Sir, I perceive that thou art a prophet.
20 Our fathers worshipped in this mountain; and ye
say, that in Jerusalem is the place where men ought
21 to worship. Jesus saith unto her,. Woman, believe
me, the hour cometh, when neither in this mountain,
22 nor in Jerusalem, shall ye worship the Father. Ye
worship that which ye know not: we worship that
which we know: for salvation is from the Jews.
23 But the hour cometh, and now is, when the true
worshippers shall worship the Father in spirit and [3] Or, *for such the Father also seeketh.*
truth: [3]for such doth the Father seek to be his wor-
24 shippers. [4]God is a Spirit: and they that worship [4] Or, *God is spirit*
25 him must worship in spirit and truth. The woman
saith unto him, I know that Messiah cometh (which
is called Christ): when he is come, he will declare
26 unto us all things. Jesus saith unto her, I that
speak unto thee am *he*.
27 And upon this came his disciples; and they marvelled that he was speaking with a woman; yet no
man said, What seekest thou? or, Why speakest
28 thou with her? So the woman left her waterpot,
and went away into the city, and saith to the men,
29 Come, see a man, which told me all things that

ever I did: can this be the Christ? They went out of the city, and were coming to him. In the mean while the disciples prayed him, saying, Rabbi, eat. But he said unto them, I have meat to eat that ye know not. The disciples therefore said one to another, Hath any man brought him *aught* to eat? Jesus saith unto them, My meat is to do the will of him that sent me, and to accomplish his work. Say not ye, There are yet four months, and *then* cometh the harvest? behold, I say unto you, Lift up your eyes, and look on the fields, that they are ¹white already unto harvest. He that reapeth receiveth wages, and gathereth fruit unto life eternal; that he that soweth and he that reapeth may rejoice together. For herein is the saying true, One soweth, and another reapeth. I sent you to reap that whereon ye have not laboured: others have laboured, and ye are entered into their labour. 30 31 32 33 34 35 36 37 38

And from that city many of the Samaritans believed on him because of the word of the woman, who testified, He told me all things that *ever* I did. So when the Samaritans came unto him, they besought him to abide with them: and he abode there two days. And many more believed because of his word; and they said to the woman, Now we believe, not because of thy speaking: for we have heard for ourselves, and know that this is indeed the Saviour of the world. 39 40 41 42

And after the two days he went forth from thence into Galilee. For Jesus himself testified, that a prophet hath no honour in his own country. So when he came into Galilee, the Galilæans received him, having seen all the things that he did in Jerusalem at the feast: for they also went unto the feast. 43 44 45

He came therefore again unto Cana of Galilee, where he made the water wine. And there was a certain ²nobleman, whose son was sick at Capernaum. When he heard that Jesus was come out of Judæa into Galilee, he went unto him, and besought *him* that he would come down, and heal his son; for he was at the point of death. Jesus therefore said unto him, Except ye see signs and wonders, ye will in no wise believe. The ²nobleman saith unto him, ³Sir, come down ere my child die. Jesus saith unto him, Go thy way; thy son liveth. The man believed the word that Jesus spake unto him, and he went his way. And as he was now going down, his ⁴ser- 46 47 48 49 50 51

1 Or, *white unto harvest. Already he that reapeth &c.*

2 Or, *king's officer*

3 Or, *Lord*

4 Gr. *bondservants.*

52 vants met him, saying, that his son lived. So he inquired of them the hour when he began to amend. They said therefore unto him, Yesterday at the sev-
53 enth hour the fever left him. So the father knew that *it was* at that hour in which Jesus said unto him, Thy son liveth: and himself believed, and his
54 whole house. This is again the second sign that Jesus did, having come out of Judæa into Galilee.

5 After these things there was ¹a feast of the Jews; and Jesus went up to Jerusalem.
2 Now there is in Jerusalem by the sheep *gate* a pool, which is called in Hebrew ²Bethesda, having
3 five porches. In these lay a multitude of them that
5 were sick, blind, halt, withered³. And a certain man was there, which had been thirty and eight
6 years in his infirmity. When Jesus saw him lying, and knew that he had been now a long time *in that case*, he saith unto him, Wouldest thou be made
7 whole? The sick man answered him, ⁴Sir, I have no man, when the water is troubled, to put me into the pool: but while I am coming, another steppeth
8 down before me. Jesus saith unto him, Arise, take
9 up thy bed, and walk. And straightway the man was made whole, and took up his bed and walked.
10 Now it was the sabbath on that day. So the Jews said unto him that was cured, It is the sabbath, and
11 it is not lawful for thee to take up thy bed. But he answered them, He that made me whole, the same
12 said unto me, Take up thy bed, and walk. They asked him, Who is the man that said unto thee, Take
13 up *thy bed*, and walk? But he that was healed wist not who it was: for Jesus had conveyed himself
14 away, a multitude being in the place. Afterward Jesus findeth him in the temple, and said unto him, Behold, thou art made whole: sin no more, lest a
15 worse thing befall thee. The man went away, and told the Jews that it was Jesus which had made
16 him whole. And for this cause did the Jews per-
17 secute Jesus, because he did these things on the sabbath. But Jesus answered them, My Father
18 worketh even until now, and I work. For this cause therefore the Jews sought the more to kill him, because he not only brake the sabbath, but also called God his own Father, making himself equal with God.
19 Jesus therefore answered and said unto them,
Verily, verily, I say unto you, The Son can do nothing of himself, but what he seeth the Father

1 Many ancient authorities read *the feast*.
2 Some ancient authorities read *Bethsaida*, others, *Bethzatha*.
3 Many ancient authorities insert, wholly or in part, *waiting for the moving of the water:*
4 *for an angel of the Lord went down at certain seasons into the pool, and troubled the water: whosoever then first after the troubling of the water stepped in was made whole, with whatsoever disease he was holden.*
4 Or, *Lord*

doing: for what things soever he doeth, these the Son also doeth in like manner. For the Father loveth the Son, and sheweth him all things that himself doeth: and greater works than these will he shew him, that ye may marvel. For as the Father raiseth the dead and quickeneth them, even so the Son also quickeneth whom he will. For neither doth the Father judge any man, but he hath given all judgement unto the Son; that all may honour the Son, even as they honour the Father. He that honoureth not the Son honoureth not the Father which sent him. Verily, verily, I say unto you, He that heareth my word, and believeth him that sent me, hath eternal life, and cometh not into judgement, but hath passed out of death into life. Verily, verily, I say unto you, The hour cometh, and now is, when the dead shall hear the voice of the Son of God; and they that hear shall live. For as the Father hath life in himself, even so gave he to the Son also to have life in himself: and he gave him authority to execute judgement, because he is ¹the Son of man*. Marvel not at this: for the hour cometh, in which all that are in the tombs shall hear his voice, and shall come forth; they that have done good, unto the resurrection of life; and they that have ²done ill, unto the resurrection of judgement.

I can of myself do nothing: as I hear, I judge: and my judgement is righteous; because I seek not mine own will, but the will of him that sent me. If I bear witness of myself, my witness is not true. It is another that beareth witness of me; and I know that the witness which he witnesseth of me is true. Ye have sent unto John, and he hath borne witness unto the truth. But the witness which I receive is not from man: howbeit I say these things, that ye may be saved. He was the lamp that burneth and shineth: and ye were willing to rejoice for a season in his light. But the witness which I have is greater than *that of* John: for the works which the Father hath given me to accomplish, the very works that I do, bear witness of me, that the Father hath sent me. And the Father which sent me, he hath borne witness of me. Ye have neither heard his voice at any time, nor seen his form. And ye have not his word abiding in you: for whom he sent, him ye be-

---

¹ Or, *a son of man*

² Or, *practised*

* Substitute the marginal rendering for the text.—*Am. Com.*

39 lieve not. ¹Ye search the scriptures, because ye think that in them ye have eternal life; and these
40 are they which bear witness of me; and ye will not
41 come to me, that ye may have life. I receive not
42 glory from men. But I know you, that ye have not
43 the love of God in yourselves. I am come in my Father's name, and ye receive me not: if another shall come in his own name, him ye will receive.
44 How can ye believe, which receive glory one of another, and the glory that *cometh* from ²the only God
45 ye seek not? Think not that I will accuse you to the Father: there is one that accuseth you, *even*
46 Moses, on whom ye have set your hope. For if ye believed Moses, ye would believe me; for he wrote
47 of me. But if ye believe not his writings, how shall ye believe my words?

¹ Or, *Search the scriptures*
² Some ancient authorities read *the only one.*

6 After these things Jesus went away to the other side of the sea of Galilee, which is *the sea* of Tibe-
2 rias. And a great multitude followed him, because they beheld the signs which he did on them that
3 were sick. And Jesus went up into the mountain,
4 and there he sat with his disciples. Now the pass-
5 over, the feast of the Jews, was at hand. Jesus therefore lifting up his eyes, and seeing that a great multitude cometh unto him, saith unto Philip, Whence are we to buy ³bread, that these may eat?
6 And this he said to prove him: for he himself knew
7 what he would do. Philip answered him, Two hundred ⁴pennyworth of ³bread is not sufficient for
8 them, that every one may take a little. One of his disciples, Andrew, Simon Peter's brother, saith unto
9 him, There is a lad here, which hath five barley loaves, and two fishes: but what are these among
10 so many? Jesus said, Make the people sit down. Now there was much grass in the place. So the men sat down, in number about five thousand.
11 Jesus therefore took the loaves; and having given thanks, he distributed to them that were set down; likewise also of the fishes as much as they would.
12 And when they were filled, he saith unto his disciples, Gather up the broken pieces which remain
13 over, that nothing be lost. So they gathered them up, and filled twelve baskets with broken pieces from the five barley loaves, which remained over
14 unto them that had eaten. When therefore the people saw the ⁵sign which he did, they said, This is of a truth the prophet that cometh into the world.
15 Jesus therefore perceiving that they were about

³ Gr. *loaves.*
⁴ See marginal note on Matt. xviii. 28.
⁵ Some ancient authorities read *signs.*

to come and take him by force, to make him king, withdrew again into the mountain himself alone.

And when evening came, his disciples went down 16 unto the sea; and they entered into a boat, and 17 were going over the sea unto Capernaum. And it was now dark, and Jesus had not yet come to them. And the sea was rising by reason of a great wind 18 that blew. When therefore they had rowed about 19 five and twenty or thirty furlongs, they behold Jesus walking on the sea, and drawing nigh unto the boat: and they were afraid. But he saith unto 20 them, It is I; be not afraid. They were willing 21 therefore to receive him into the boat: and straightway the boat was at the land whither they were going.

On the morrow the multitude which stood on the 22 other side of the sea saw that there was none other ¹boat there, save one, and that Jesus entered not with his disciples into the boat, but *that* his disciples went away alone (howbeit there came ²boats from 23 Tiberias nigh unto the place where they ate the bread after the Lord had given thanks): when the 24 multitude therefore saw that Jesus was not there, neither his disciples, they themselves got into the ²boats, and came to Capernaum, seeking Jesus. And when they found him on the other side of the 25 sea, they said unto him, Rabbi, when camest thou hither? Jesus answered them and said, Verily, 26 verily, I say unto you, Ye seek me, not because ye saw signs, but because ye ate of the loaves, and were filled. Work not for the meat which perisheth, but 27 for the meat which abideth unto eternal life, which the Son of man shall give unto you: for him the Father, *even* God, hath sealed. They said therefore 28 unto him, What must we do, that we may work the works of God? Jesus answered and said unto them, 29 This is the work of God, that ye believe on him whom ³he hath sent. They said therefore unto him, 30 What then doest thou for a sign, that we may see, and believe thee? what workest thou? Our fathers 31 ate the manna in the wilderness; as it is written, He gave them bread out of heaven to eat. Jesus there- 32 fore said unto them, Verily, verily, I say unto you, It was not Moses that gave you the bread out of heaven; but my Father giveth you the true bread out of heaven. For the bread of God is that which 33 cometh down out of heaven, and giveth life unto the world. They said therefore unto him, Lord, 34

---

1 Gr. *little boat.*

2 Gr. *little boats.*

3 Or, *he sent*

35 evermore give us this bread. Jesus said unto them, I am the bread of life: he that cometh to me shall not hunger, and he that believeth on me shall never
36 thirst. But I said unto you, that ye have seen me,
37 and yet believe not. All that which the Father giveth me shall come unto me; and him that cometh
38 to me I will in no wise cast out. For I am come down from heaven, not to do mine own will, but the
39 will of him that sent me. And this is the will of him that sent me, that of all that which he hath given me I should lose nothing, but should raise it up at the
40 last day. For this is the will of my Father, that every one that beholdeth the Son, and believeth on him, should have eternal life; and ¹I will raise him up at the last day.

¹ Or, *that I should raise him up*

41 The Jews therefore murmured concerning him, because he said, I am the bread which came down
42 out of heaven. And they said, Is not this Jesus, the son of Joseph, whose father and mother we know? how doth he now say, I am come down out of
43 heaven? Jesus answered and said unto them, Mur-
44 mur not among yourselves. No man can come to me, except the Father which sent me draw him:
45 and I will raise him up in the last day. It is written in the prophets, And they shall all be taught of God. Every one that hath heard from the Father, and hath
46 learned, cometh unto me. Not that any man hath seen the Father, save he which is from God, he hath
47 seen the Father. Verily, verily, I say unto you, He
48 that believeth hath eternal life. I am the bread of
49 life. Your fathers did eat the manna in the wilder-
50 ness, and they died. This is the bread which cometh down out of heaven, that a man may eat thereof,
51 and not die. I am the living bread which came down out of heaven: if any man eat of this bread, he shall live for ever: yea and the bread which I will give is my flesh, for the life of the world.
52 The Jews therefore strove one with another, saying, How can this man give us his flesh to eat?
53 Jesus therefore said unto them, Verily, verily, I say unto you, Except ye eat the flesh of the Son of man and drink his blood, ye have not life in yourselves.
54 He that eateth my flesh and drinketh my blood hath eternal life; and I will raise him up at the last day.
55 For my flesh is ²meat indeed, and my blood is ³drink
56 indeed. He that eateth my flesh and drinketh my
57 blood abideth in me, and I in him. As the living

² Gr. *true meat.*
³ Gr. *true drink.*

Father sent me, and I live because of the Father; so
he that eateth me, he also shall live because of me.
This is the bread which came down out of heaven: 58
not as the fathers did eat, and died: he that eateth
this bread shall live for ever. These things said he 59
in ¹the synagogue, as he taught in Capernaum.

Many therefore of his disciples, when they heard 60
this, said, This is a hard saying; who can hear ²it?
But Jesus knowing in himself that his disciples mur- 61
mured at this, said unto them, Doth this cause you
to stumble? *What* then if ye should behold the Son 62
of man ascending where he was before? It is the 63
spirit that quickeneth; the flesh profiteth nothing:
the words that I have spoken unto you are spirit,
and are life. But there are some of you that believe 64
not. For Jesus knew from the beginning who they
were that believed not, and who it was that should
betray him. And he said, For this cause have I 65
said unto you, that no man can come unto me, except it be given unto him of the Father.

Upon this many of his disciples went back, and 66
walked no more with him. Jesus said therefore 67
unto the twelve, Would ye also go away? Simon 68
Peter answered him, Lord, to whom shall we go?
thou ³hast the words of eternal life. And we have 69
believed and know that thou art the Holy One of
God. Jesus answered them, Did not I choose you 70
the twelve, and one of you is a devil? Now he spake 71
of Judas *the son* of Simon Iscariot, for he it was that
should betray him, *being* one of the twelve.

And after these things Jesus walked in Galilee: **7**
for he would not walk in Judæa, because the Jews
sought to kill him. Now the feast of the Jews, the 2
feast of tabernacles, was at hand. His brethren 3
therefore said unto him, Depart hence, and go into
Judæa, that thy disciples also may behold thy works
which thou doest. For no man doeth anything in 4
secret, ⁴and himself seeketh to be known openly.
If thou doest these things, manifest thyself to the
world. For even his brethren did not believe on 5
him. Jesus therefore saith unto them, My time is 6
not yet come; but your time is alway ready. The 7
world cannot hate you; but me it hateth, because
I testify of it, that its works are evil. Go ye up 8
unto the feast: I go not up ⁵yet* unto this feast; be-

1 Or, *a synagogue*

2 Or, *him*

3 Or, *hast words*

4 Some ancient authorities read *and seeketh it to be known openly*.

5 Many ancient authorities omit *yet*.

---

* For "I go not up yet" read "I go not up" and change the marg. to Many ancient authorities add *yet*.—*Am. Com.*

9 cause my time is not yet fulfilled. And having said these things unto them, he abode *still* in Galilee.
10 But when his brethren were gone up unto the feast, then went he also up, not publicly, but as it
11 were in secret. The Jews therefore sought him at
12 the feast, and said, Where is he? And there was much murmuring among the multitudes concerning him: some said, He is a good man; others said,
13 Not so, but he leadeth the multitude astray. Howbeit no man spake openly of him for fear of the Jews.
14 But when it was now the midst of the feast Jesus
15 went up into the temple, and taught. The Jews therefore marvelled, saying, How knoweth this man
16 letters, having never learned? Jesus therefore answered them, and said, My teaching is not mine,
17 but his that sent me. If any man willeth to do his will, he shall know of the teaching, whether it be
18 of God, or *whether* I speak from myself. He that speaketh from himself seeketh his own glory: but he that seeketh the glory of him that sent him, the same
19 is true, and no unrighteousness is in him. Did not Moses give you the law, and *yet* none of you doeth
20 the law? Why seek ye to kill me? The multitude answered, Thou hast a ¹devil: who seeketh to kill
21 thee? Jesus answered and said unto them, I did one
22 work, and ye all ²marvel. For this cause hath Moses* given you circumcision (not that it is of Moses, but of the fathers); and on the sabbath ye circumcise a
23 man. If a man receiveth circumcision on the sabbath, that the law of Moses may not be broken; are ye wroth with me, because I made a man every whit
24 whole† on the sabbath? Judge not according to appearance, but judge righteous judgement.
25 Some therefore of them of Jerusalem said, Is not
26 this he whom they seek to kill? And lo, he speaketh openly, and they say nothing unto him. Can it be that the rulers indeed know that this is the Christ?
27 Howbeit we know this man whence he is: but when the Christ cometh, no one knoweth whence he is.
28 Jesus therefore cried in the temple, teaching and saying, Ye both know me, and know whence I am; and I am not come of myself, but he that sent me
29 is true, whom ye know not. I know him; because

1 Gr. *demon.*
2 Or, *marvel because of this. Moses hath given you circumcision.*

---

* For "marvel. For this cause hath Moses" etc. read "marvel because thereof. Moses hath" etc. and omit the marg.—*Am. Com.*
† "a man every whit whole" add marg. Gr. *a whole man sound.*—*Am. Com.*

I am from him, and he sent me. They sought there-30 fore to take him: and no man laid his hand on him, because his hour was not yet come. But of the 31 multitude many believed on him; and they said, When the Christ shall come, will he do more signs than those which this man hath done? The Phari-32 sees heard the multitude murmuring these things concerning him; and the chief priests and the Pharisees sent officers to take him. Jesus therefore said, 33 Yet a little while am I with you, and I go unto him that sent me. Ye shall seek me, and shall not find 34 me: and where I am, ye cannot come. The Jews 35 therefore said among themselves, Whither will this man go that we shall not find him? will he go unto the Dispersion ¹among the Greeks, and teach the Greeks? What is this word that he said, Ye shall 36 seek me, and shall not find me: and where I am, ye cannot come?

Now on the last day, the great *day* of the feast, 37 Jesus stood and cried, saying, If any man thirst, let him come unto me, and drink. He that believeth 38 on me, as the Scripture hath said, out of his belly* shall flow rivers of living water. But this spake 39 he of the Spirit, which they that believed on him were to receive: ²for the Spirit was not yet *given*; because Jesus was not yet glorified. *Some* of the 40 multitude therefore, when they heard these words, said, This is of a truth the prophet. Others said, 41 This is the Christ. But some said, What, doth the Christ come out of Galilee? Hath not the scripture 42 said that the Christ cometh of the seed of David, and from Bethlehem, the village where David was? So there arose a division in the multitude because 43 of him. And some of them would have taken him; 44 but no man laid hands on him.

The officers therefore came to the chief priests 45 and Pharisees; and they said unto them, Why did ye not bring him? The officers answered, Never 46 man so spake. The Pharisees therefore answered 47 them, Are ye also led astray? Hath any of the 48 rulers believed on him, or of the Pharisees? But 49 this multitude which knoweth not the law are accursed. Nicodemus saith unto them (he that came 50 to him before, being one of them), Doth our law 51 judge a man, except it first hear from himself and

1 Gr. *of.*

2 Some ancient authorities read *for the Holy Spirit was not yet given.*

---

* For "out of his belly" read "from within him" (with marg. Gr. *out of his belly*)—*Am. Com.*

52 know what he doeth? They answered and said unto him, Art thou also of Galilee? Search, and ¹see that out of Galilee ariseth no prophet.

¹ Or, see: for out of Galilee &c.

² Most of the ancient authorities omit John vii. 53 — viii. 11. Those which contain it vary much from each other.

53 ²[And they went every man unto his own house:
8 but Jesus went unto the mount of Olives. And early in the morning he came again into the temple, and all the people came unto him; and he sat down,
3 and taught them. And the scribes and the Pharisees bring a woman taken in adultery; and having set her
4 in the midst, they say unto him, ³Master, this woman
5 hath been taken in adultery, in the very act. Now in the law Moses commanded us to stone such: what
6 then sayest thou of her? And this they said, ⁴tempting him, that they might have *whereof* to accuse him. But Jesus stooped down, and with his finger wrote
7 on the ground. But when they continued asking him, he lifted up himself, and said unto them, He that is without sin among you, let him first cast a
8 stone at her. And again he stooped down, and with
9 his finger wrote on the ground. And they, when they heard it, went out one by one, beginning from the eldest, *even* unto the last: and Jesus was left alone, and the woman, where she was, in the midst.
10 And Jesus lifted up himself, and said unto her, Woman, where are they? did no man condemn
11 thee? And she said, No man, Lord. And Jesus said, Neither do I condemn thee: go thy way; from henceforth sin no more.]

³ Or, *Teacher*

⁴ Or, *trying*

12 Again therefore Jesus spake unto them, saying, I am the light of the world: he that followeth me shall not walk in the darkness, but shall have the light of
13 life. The Pharisees therefore said unto him, Thou bearest witness of thyself; thy witness is not true.
14 Jesus answered and said unto them, Even if I bear witness of myself, my witness is true; for I know whence I came, and whither I go; but ye know
15 not whence I come, or whither I go. Ye judge after
16 the flesh; I judge no man. Yea and if I judge, my judgement is true; for I am not alone, but I and the
17 Father that sent me. Yea and in your law it is writ-
18 ten, that the witness of two men is true. I am he that beareth witness of myself, and the Father that
19 sent me beareth witness of me. They said therefore unto him, Where is thy Father? Jesus an-

swered, Ye know neither me, nor my Father: if ye
knew me, ye would know my Father also. These 20
words spake he in the treasury, as he taught in the
temple: and no man took him; because his hour
was not yet come.

He said therefore again unto them, I go away, and 21
ye shall seek me, and shall die in your sin: whither
I go, ye cannot come. The Jews therefore said, 22
Will he kill himself, that he saith, Whither I go, ye
cannot come? And he said unto them, Ye are from 23
beneath; I am from above: ye are of this world; I
am not of this world. I said therefore unto you, 24
that ye shall die in your sins: for except ye believe
that ¹I am he*, ye shall die in your sins. They said 25
therefore unto him, Who art thou? Jesus said unto
them, ²Even that which I have also spoken unto you
from the beginning†. I have many things to speak 26
and to judge concerning you: howbeit he that sent
me is true; and the things which I heard from him,
these speak I ³unto the world‡. They perceived not 27
that he spake to them of the Father. Jesus there- 28
fore said, When ye have lifted up the Son of man,
then shall ye know that ⁴I am he*, and *that* I do nothing of myself, but as the Father taught me, I speak
these things. And he that sent me is with me; he 29
hath not left me alone; for I do always the things
that are pleasing to him. As he spake these things, 30
many believed on him.

Jesus therefore said to those Jews which had be- 31
lieved him, If ye abide in my word, *then* are ye truly
my disciples; and ye shall know the truth, and the 32
truth shall make you free. They answered unto 33
him, We be Abraham's seed, and have never yet
been in bondage to any man: how sayest thou, Ye
shall be made free? Jesus answered them, Verily, 34
verily, I say unto you, Every one that committeth
sin is the bondservant of sin. And the bondservant 35
abideth not in the house for ever: the son abideth
for ever. If therefore the Son shall make you free, 36
ye shall be free indeed. I know that ye are Abra- 37
ham's seed; yet ye seek to kill me, because my word
⁵hath not free course in you. I speak the things 38
which I have seen with ⁶*my* Father: and ye also do

1 Or, *I am*
2 Or, *How is it that I even speak to you at all?*
3 Gr. *into.*
4 Or, *I am*
  Or, *I am* he: *and I do*
5 Or, *hath no place in you*
6 Or, *the Father: do ye also therefore the things which ye heard from the Father.*

---

* "I am he" omit marg. ¹ (and the corresponding portion of marg. ⁴) So in xiii. 19.—*Am. Com.*

† Substitute for the present marg. ² Or, *Altogether that which I also speak unto you.*—*Am. Com.*

‡ "unto the world" omit marg. ³ "Gr. *into.*"—*Am. Com.*

39 the things which ye heard from *your* father. They answered and said unto him, Our father is Abraham. Jesus saith unto them, If ye ¹were Abraham's chil-
40 dren, ²ye would do the works of Abraham. But now ye seek to kill me, a man that hath told you the truth, which I heard from God: this did not Abra-
41 ham. Ye do the works of your father. They said unto him, We were not born of fornication; we have
42 one Father, *even* God. Jesus said unto them, If God were your Father, ye would love me: for I came forth and am come from God; for neither have I
43 come of myself, but he sent me. Why do ye not ³understand my speech? *Even* because ye cannot
44 hear my word. Ye are of *your* father the devil, and the lusts of your father it is your will to do. He was a murderer from the beginning, and ⁴stood* not in the truth, because there is no truth in him. ⁵When he speaketh a lie, he speaketh of his own:
45 for he is a liar, and the father thereof. But because
46 I say the truth, ye believe me not. Which of you convicteth me of sin? If I say truth, why do ye not
47 believe me? He that is of God heareth the words of God: for this cause ye hear *them* not, because ye are
48 not of God. The Jews answered and said unto him, Say we not well that thou art a Samaritan, and
49 hast a ⁶devil? Jesus answered, I have not a ⁶devil;
50 but I honour my Father, and ye dishonour me. But I seek not mine own glory: there is one that seeketh
51 and judgeth. Verily, verily, I say unto you, If a
52 man keep my word, he shall never see death. The Jews said unto him, Now we know that thou hast a ⁶devil. Abraham is dead†, and the prophets; and thou sayest, If a man keep my word, he shall never
53 taste of death. Art thou greater than our father Abraham, which is dead†? and the prophets are dead†:
54 whom makest thou thyself? Jesus answered, If I glorify myself, my glory is nothing: it is my Father that glorifieth me; of whom ye say, that he is your
55 God; and ye have not known him: but I know him; and if I should say, I know him not, I shall be like unto you, a liar: but I know him, and keep his word.
56 Your father Abraham rejoiced ⁷to see my day; and
57 he saw it, and was glad. The Jews therefore said unto him, Thou art not yet fifty years old, and hast
58 thou seen Abraham? Jesus said unto them, Verily,

1 Gr. *are.*
2 Some ancient authorities read *ye do the works of Abraham.*
3 Or, *know*
4 Some ancient authorities read *standeth.*
5 Or, *When one speaketh a lie, he speaketh of his own: for his father also is a liar.*
6 Gr. *demon.*
7 Or, *that he should see*

---

* For "stood" read "standeth" and omit marg. ⁴.—*Am. Com.*
† For "is dead" and "are dead" read "died" [Compare vi. 49, 58]—*Am. Com.*

S. JOHN.

¹ Gr. *was born.*
² Or, *was hidden, and went &c.*
³ Many ancient authorities add *and going through the midst of them went his way, and so passed by.*

verily, I say unto you, Before Abraham ¹was*, I am. They took up stones therefore to cast at him: but Jesus ²hid himself, and went out of the temple³.

And as he passed by, he saw a man blind from his birth. And his disciples asked him, saying, Rabbi, who did sin, this man, or his parents, that he should be born blind? Jesus answered, Neither did this man sin, nor his parents: but that the works of God should be made manifest in him. We must work the works of him that sent me, while it is day: the night cometh, when no man can work. When I am in the world, I am the light of the world. When

⁴ Or, *and with the clay thereof anointed his eyes*

he had thus spoken, he spat on the ground, and made clay of the spittle, ⁴and anointed his eyes with the clay, and said unto him, Go, wash in the pool of Siloam (which is by interpretation, Sent). He went away therefore, and washed, and came seeing. The neighbours therefore, and they which saw him aforetime, that he was a beggar, said, Is not this he that sat and begged? Others said, It is he: others said, No, but he is like him. He said, I am *he*. They said therefore unto him, How then were thine eyes opened? He answered, The man that is called Jesus made clay, and anointed mine eyes, and said unto me, Go to Siloam, and wash: so I went away and washed, and I received sight. And they said unto him, Where is he? He saith, I know not.

They bring to the Pharisees him that aforetime was blind. Now it was the sabbath on the day when Jesus made the clay, and opened his eyes. Again therefore the Pharisees also asked him how he received his sight. And he said unto them, He put clay upon mine eyes, and I washed, and do see. Some therefore of the Pharisees said, This man is not from God, because he keepeth not the sabbath. But others said, How can a man that is a sinner do such signs? And there was a division among them. They say therefore unto the blind man again, What sayest thou of him, in that he opened thine eyes? And he said, He is a prophet. The Jews therefore did not believe concerning him, that he had been blind, and had received his sight, until they called the parents of him that had received his sight, and asked them, saying, Is this your son, who ye say was born blind? how then doth he now see? His parents answered and said, We know that this is our

---

* For "was" read "was born" and omit marg. ¹.—*Am. Com.*

21 son, and that he was born blind: but how he now seeth, we know not; or who opened his eyes, we know not: ask him; he is of age; he shall speak for
22 himself. These things said his parents, because they feared the Jews: for the Jews had agreed already, that if any man should confess him *to be* Christ, he
23 should be put out of the synagogue. Therefore said
24 his parents, He is of age; ask him. So they called a second time the man that was blind, and said unto him, Give glory to God: we know that this
25 man is a sinner. He therefore answered, Whether he be a sinner, I know not: one thing I know, that,
26 whereas I was blind, now I see. They said therefore unto him, What did he to thee? how opened
27 he thine eyes? He answered them, I told you even now, and ye did not hear: wherefore would ye hear
28 it again? would ye also become his disciples? And they reviled him, and said, Thou art his disciple;
29 but we are disciples of Moses. We know that God hath spoken unto Moses: but as for this man, we
30 know not whence he is. The man answered and said unto them, Why, herein is the marvel, that ye know not whence he is, and *yet* he opened mine
31 eyes. We know that God heareth not sinners: but if any man be a worshipper of God, and do his will,
32 him he heareth. Since the world began it was never heard that any one opened the eyes of a man born
33 blind. If this man were not from God, he could do
34 nothing. They answered and said unto him, Thou wast altogether born in sins, and dost thou teach us? And they cast him out.
35 Jesus heard that they had cast him out; and finding him, he said, Dost thou believe on [1]the Son of
36 God? He answered and said, And who is he, Lord,
37 that I may believe on him? Jesus said unto him, Thou hast both seen him, and he it is that speaketh
38 with thee. And he said, Lord, I believe. And he
39 worshipped him. And Jesus said, For judgement came I into this world, that they which see not may see; and that they which see may become blind.
40 Those of the Pharisees which were with him heard these things, and said unto him, Are we also blind?
41 Jesus said unto them, If ye were blind, ye would have no sin: but now ye say, We see: your sin remaineth.

10 Verily, verily, I say unto you, He that entereth not by the door into the fold of the sheep, but climbeth up some other way, the same is a thief and

[1] Many ancient authorities read *the Son of man.*

a robber. But he that entereth in by the door is 2 ¹the shepherd of the sheep. To him the porter 3 openeth; and the sheep hear his voice: and he calleth his own sheep by name, and leadeth them out. When he hath put forth all his own, he goeth before 4 them, and the sheep follow him: for they know his voice. And a stranger will they not follow, but will 5 flee from him: for they know not the voice of strangers. This ²parable spake Jesus unto them: but 6 they understood not what things they were which he spake unto them.

Jesus therefore said unto them again, Verily, 7 verily, I say unto you, I am the door of the sheep. All that came before me* are thieves and robbers: 8 but the sheep did not hear them. I am the door: 9 by me if any man enter in, he shall be saved, and shall go in and go out, and shall find pasture. The 10 thief cometh not, but that he may steal, and kill, and destroy: I came that they may have life, and may ³have it abundantly. I am the good shepherd: the 11 good shepherd layeth down his life for the sheep. He that is a hireling, and not a shepherd, whose 12 own the sheep are not, beholdeth the wolf coming, and leaveth the sheep, and fleeth, and the wolf snatcheth them, and scattereth *them*: *he fleeth* be- 13 cause he is a hireling, and careth not for the sheep. I am the good shepherd; and I know mine own, 14 and mine own know me, even as the Father know- 15 eth me, and I know the Father; and I lay down my life for the sheep. And other sheep I have, which 16 are not of this fold: them also I must ⁴bring, and they shall hear my voice; and ⁵they shall become one flock, one shepherd. Therefore doth the Father 17 love me, because I lay down my life, that I may take it again. No one ⁶taketh it away from me, but 18 I lay it down of myself. I have ⁷power to lay it down, and I have ⁷power to take it again. This commandment received I from my Father.

There arose a division again among the Jews be- 19 cause of these words. And many of them said, 20 He hath a ⁸devil, and is mad; why hear ye him? Others said, These are not the sayings of one pos- 21 sessed with a ⁸devil. Can a ⁸devil open the eyes of the blind?

⁹And it was the feast of the dedication at Jeru- 22

---

1 Or, *a shepherd*
2 Or, *proverb*
3 Or, *have abundance*
4 Or, *lead*
5 Or, *there shall be one flock*
6 Some ancient authorities read *took it away.*
7 Or, *right*
8 Gr. *demon.*
9 Some ancient authorities read *At that time was the feast.*

* "before me" add marg. Some ancient authorities omit *before me.—Am. Com.*

23 salem: it was winter; and Jesus was walking in the
24 temple in Solomon's porch. The Jews therefore came round about him, and said unto him, How long dost thou hold us in suspense? If thou art
25 the Christ, tell us plainly. Jesus answered them, I told you, and ye believe not: the works that I do
26 in my Father's name, these bear witness of me. But
27 ye believe not, because ye are not of my sheep. My sheep hear my voice, and I know them, and they
28 follow me: and I give unto them eternal life; and they shall never perish, and no one shall snatch
29 them out of my hand. ¹My Father, which hath given *them* unto me, is greater than all; and no one
30 is able to snatch ²*them* out of the Father's hand. I
31 and the Father are one. The Jews took up stones
32 again to stone him. Jesus answered them, Many good works have I shewed you from the Father;
33 for which of those works do ye stone me? The Jews answered him, For a good work we stone thee not, but for blasphemy; and because that thou, be-
34 ing a man, makest thyself God. Jesus answered them, Is it not written in your law, I said, Ye are
35 gods? If he called them gods, unto whom the word of God came (and the scripture cannot be broken),
36 say ye of him, whom the Father ³sanctified and sent into the world, Thou blasphemest; because I said,
37 I am *the* Son of God? If I do not the works of my
38 Father, believe me not. But if I do them, though ye believe not me, believe the works: that ye may
39 know and understand that the Father is in me, and I in the Father. They sought again to take him: and he went forth out of their hand.
40 And he went away again beyond Jordan into the place where John was at the first baptizing; and
41 there he abode. And many came unto him; and they said, John indeed did no sign: but all things
42 whatsoever John spake of this man were true. And many believed on him there.

¹ Some ancient authorities read *That which my Father hath given unto me.*

² Or, aught

³ Or, *consecrated*

11 Now a certain man was sick, Lazarus of Bethany, of the village of Mary and her sister Martha.
2 And it was that Mary which anointed the Lord with ointment, and wiped his feet with her hair, whose
3 brother Lazarus was sick. The sisters therefore sent unto him, saying, Lord, behold, he whom thou
4 lovest is sick. But when Jesus heard it, he said, This sickness is not unto death, but for the glory of God, that the Son of God may be glorified thereby.
5 Now Jesus loved Martha, and her sister, and Laza-

rus. When therefore he heard that he was sick, he 6
abode at that time two days in the place where he
was. Then after this he saith to the disciples, Let 7
us go into Judæa again. The disciples say unto 8
him, Rabbi, the Jews were but now seeking to stone
thee; and goest thou thither again? Jesus answered, 9
Are there not twelve hours in the day? If a man
walk in the day, he stumbleth not, because he seeth
the light of this world. But if a man walk in the 10
night, he stumbleth, because the light is not in him.
These things spake he: and after this he saith unto 11
them, Our friend Lazarus is fallen asleep; but I go,
that I may awake him out of sleep. The disciples 12

¹ Gr. *be saved*. therefore said unto him, Lord, if he is fallen asleep,
he will ¹recover. Now Jesus had spoken of his 13
death: but they thought that he spake of taking
rest in sleep. Then Jesus therefore said unto them 14
plainly, Lazarus is dead. And I am glad for your 15
sakes that I was not there, to the intent ye may believe; nevertheless let us go unto him. Thomas 16

² That is, *Twin*. therefore, who is called ²Didymus, said unto his
fellow-disciples, Let us also go, that we may die
with him.

So when Jesus came, he found that he had been 17
in the tomb four days already. Now Bethany was 18
nigh unto Jerusalem, about fifteen furlongs off; and 19
many of the Jews had come to Martha and Mary,
to console them concerning their brother. Martha 20
therefore, when she heard that Jesus was coming,
went and met him: but Mary still sat in the house.
Martha therefore said unto Jesus, Lord, if thou 21
hadst been here, my brother had not died. And 22
even now I know that, whatsoever thou shalt ask of
God, God will give thee. Jesus saith unto her, Thy 23
brother shall rise again. Martha saith unto him, I 24
know that he shall rise again in the resurrection at
the last day. Jesus said unto her, I am the resur- 25
rection and the life: he that believeth on me, though
he die, yet shall he live: and whosoever liveth and 26
believeth on me shall never die. Believest thou this?
She saith unto him, Yea, Lord: I have believed that 27
thou art the Christ, the Son of God, *even* he that
cometh into the world. And when she had said 28

³ Or, *her sister, saying secretly*
⁴ Or, *Teacher*
this, she went away, and called Mary ³her sister secretly, saying, The ⁴Master is here, and calleth thee.
And she, when she heard it, arose quickly, and went 29
unto him. (Now Jesus was not yet come into the 30
village, but was still in the place where Martha met

31 him.) The Jews then which were with her in the house, and were comforting her, when they saw Mary, that she rose up quickly and went out, followed her, supposing that she was going unto the tomb
32 to ¹weep there. Mary therefore, when she came
where Jesus was, and saw him, fell down at his feet, saying unto him, Lord, if thou hadst been here,
33 my brother had not died. When Jesus therefore saw her ²weeping, and the Jews *also* ²weeping which came with her, he ³groaned in the spirit, and ⁴was
34 troubled, and said, Where have ye laid him? They
35 say unto him, Lord, come and see. Jesus wept.
36 The Jews therefore said, Behold how he loved him!
37 But some of them said, Could not this man, which opened the eyes of him that was blind, have caused
38 that this man also should not die? Jesus therefore again ⁵groaning in himself cometh to the tomb.
39 Now it was a cave, and a stone lay ⁶against it. Je-
sus saith, Take ye away the stone. Martha, the sister of him that was dead, saith unto him, Lord, by this time he stinketh: for he hath been *dead* four
40 days. Jesus saith unto her, Said I not unto thee, that, if thou believedst, thou shouldest see the glory
41 of God? So they took away the stone. And Jesus lifted up his eyes, and said, Father, I thank thee
42 that thou heardest me. And I knew that thou hear-
est me always: but because of the multitude which standeth around I said it, that they may believe
43 that thou didst send me. And when he had thus spoken, he cried with a loud voice, Lazarus, come
44 forth. He that was dead came forth, bound hand and foot with ⁷grave-clothes; and his face was bound about with a napkin. Jesus saith unto them, Loose him, and let him go.

Many therefore of the Jews, which came to Mary
45 and beheld ⁸that which he did, believed on him.
46 But some of them went away to the Pharisees, and told them the things which Jesus had done.
47 The chief priests therefore and the Pharisees gathered a council, and said, What do we? for this
48 man doeth many signs. If we let him thus alone, all men will believe on him: and the Romans will come and take away both our place and our nation.
49 But a certain one of them, Caiaphas, being high priest that year, said unto them, Ye know nothing
50 at all, nor do ye take account that it is expedient for you that one man should die for the people, and
51 that the whole nation perish not. Now this he said

1 Gr. *wail.*

2 Gr. *wailing.*
3 Or, *was moved with indignation in the spirit*
4 Gr. *troubled himself.*

5 Or, *being moved with indignation in himself*
6 Or, *upon*

7 Or, *grave-bands*

8 Many ancient authorities read *the things which he did.*

not of himself: but being high priest that year, he prophesied that Jesus should die for the nation; and not for the nation only, but that he might also 52 gather together into one the children of God that are scattered abroad. So from that day forth they 53 took counsel that they might put him to death.

Jesus therefore walked no more openly among 54 the Jews, but departed thence into the country near to the wilderness, into a city called Ephraim; and there he tarried with the disciples. Now the pass- 55 over of the Jews was at hand: and many went up to Jerusalem out of the country before the passover, to purify themselves. They sought therefore 56 for Jesus, and spake one with another, as they stood in the temple, What think ye? That he will not come to the feast? Now the chief priests and the 57 Pharisees had given commandment, that, if any man knew where he was, he should shew it, that they might take him.

Jesus therefore six days before the passover came 12 to Bethany, where Lazarus was, whom Jesus raised from the dead. So they made him a supper there: 2 and Martha served; but Lazarus was one of them that sat at meat with him. Mary therefore took a 3 pound of ointment of [1]spikenard, very precious, and anointed the feet of Jesus, and wiped his feet with her hair: and the house was filled with the odour of the ointment. But Judas Iscariot, one of his disci- 4 ples, which should betray him, saith, Why was not 5 this ointment sold for three hundred [2]pence, and given to the poor? Now this he said, not because 6 he cared for the poor; but because he was a thief, and having the [3]bag [4]took away what was put therein. Jesus therefore said, [5]Suffer her to keep it against 7 the day of my burying. For the poor ye have al- 8 ways with you; but me ye have not always.

The common people therefore of the Jews learned 9 that he was there: and they came, not for Jesus' sake only, but that they might see Lazarus also, whom he had raised from the dead. But the chief 10 priests took counsel that they might put Lazarus also to death; because that by reason of him many 11 of the Jews went away, and believed on Jesus.

On the morrow [6]a great multitude that had come 12 to the feast, when they heard that Jesus was coming to Jerusalem, took the branches of the palm 13 trees, and went forth to meet him, and cried out, Hosanna: Blessed *is* he that cometh in the name of

---

1 See marginal note on Mark xiv. 3.

2 See marginal note on Matt. xviii. 28.

3 Or, *box*

4 Or, *carried what was put therein*

5 Or, *Let her alone: it was that she might keep it*

6 Some ancient authorities read *the common people*.

14 the Lord, even the King of Israel. And Jesus, having found a young ass, sat thereon; as it is written,
15 Fear not, daughter of Zion: behold, thy King com-
16 eth, sitting on an ass's colt. These things understood not his disciples at the first: but when Jesus was glorified, then remembered they that these things were written of him, and that they had done these
17 things unto him. The multitude therefore that was with him when he called Lazarus out of the tomb,
18 and raised him from the dead, bare witness. For this cause also the multitude went and met him, for
19 that they heard that he had done this sign. The Pharisees therefore said among themselves, [1]Behold how ye prevail nothing: lo, the world is gone after him.

[1] Or, *Ye behold*

20 Now there were certain Greeks among those that
21 went up to worship at the feast: these therefore came to Philip, which was of Bethsaida of Galilee, and asked him, saying, Sir, we would see Jesus.
22 Philip cometh and telleth Andrew: Andrew cometh,
23 and Philip, and they tell Jesus. And Jesus answereth them, saying, The hour is come, that the
24 Son of man should be glorified. Verily, verily, I say unto you, Except a grain of wheat fall into the earth and die, it abideth by itself alone; but if it die,
25 it beareth much fruit. He that loveth his [2]life loseth it; and he that hateth his [2]life in this world shall
26 keep it unto life eternal. If any man serve me, let him follow me; and where I am, there shall also my servant be: if any man serve me, him will the Father
27 honour. Now is my soul troubled; and what shall I say? Father, save me from this [3]hour. But for
28 this cause came I unto this hour. Father, glorify thy name. There came therefore a voice out of heaven, *saying*, I have both glorified it, and will glo-
29 rify it again. The multitude therefore, that stood by, and heard it, said that it had thundered: others
30 said, An angel hath spoken to him. Jesus answered and said, This voice hath not come for my sake, but
31 for your sakes. Now is [4]the judgement of this world: now shall the prince of this world be cast
32 out. And I, if I be lifted up [5]from the earth, will
33 draw all men unto myself. But this he said, signi-
34 fying by what manner of death he should die. The multitude therefore answered him, We have heard out of the law that the Christ abideth for ever: and how sayest thou, The Son of man must be lifted up?
35 who is this Son of man? Jesus therefore said unto

[2] Or, *soul*
[3] Or, *hour?*
[4] Or, *a judgement*
[5] Or, *out of*

them, Yet a little while is the light ¹among you.
Walk while ye have the light, that darkness overtake you not: and he that walketh in the darkness knoweth not whither he goeth. While ye have the light, believe on the light, that ye may become sons of light. 36

These things spake Jesus, and he departed and ²hid himself from them. But though he had done so many signs before them, yet they believed not on him: that the word of Isaiah the prophet might be fulfilled, which he spake, 37 38

> Lord, who hath believed our report?
> And to whom hath the arm of the Lord been revealed?

For this cause they could not believe, for that Isaiah said again, 39

> He hath blinded their eyes, and he hardened their heart; 40
> Lest they should see with their eyes, and perceive with their heart,
> And should turn,
> And I should heal them.

These things said Isaiah, because he saw his glory; and he spake of him. Nevertheless even of the rulers many believed on him; but because of the Pharisees they did not confess ³it, lest they should be put out of the synagogue: for they loved the glory of men more than the glory of God*. 41 42 43

And Jesus cried and said, He that believeth on me, believeth not on me, but on him that sent me. And he that beholdeth me beholdeth him that sent me. I am come a light into the world, that whosoever believeth on me may not abide in the darkness. And if any man hear my sayings, and keep them not, I judge him not: for I came not to judge the world, but to save the world. He that rejecteth me, and receiveth not my sayings, hath one that judgeth him: the word that I spake, the same shall judge him in the last day. For I spake not from myself; but the Father which sent me, he hath given me a commandment, what I should say, and what I should speak. And I know that his commandment is life eternal: the things therefore which I speak, even as the Father hath said unto me, so I speak. 44 45 46 47 48 49 50

Now before the feast of the passover, Jesus know- 13

¹ Or, in
² Or, was hidden from them.
³ Or, him

---

* For "the glory of men ... the glory of God" read "the glory *that is* of men ... the glory *that is* of God."—*Am. Com.*

ing that his hour was come that he should depart out of this world unto the Father, having loved his own which were in the world, he loved them ¹unto 2 the end. And during supper, the devil having already put into the heart of Judas Iscariot, Simon's 3 *son*, to betray him, *Jesus*, knowing that the Father had given all things into his hands, and that he came 4 forth from God, and goeth unto God, riseth from supper, and layeth aside his garments; and he took 5 a towel, and girded himself. Then he poureth water into the bason, and began to wash the disciples' feet, and to wipe them with the towel wherewith he was 6 girded. So he cometh to Simon Peter. He saith 7 unto him, Lord, dost thou wash my feet? Jesus answered and said unto him, What I do thou knowest 8 not now; but thou shalt understand hereafter. Peter saith unto him, Thou shalt never wash my feet. Jesus answered him, If I wash thee not, thou hast 9 no part with me. Simon Peter saith unto him, Lord, not my feet only, but also my hands and my head. 10 Jesus saith to him, He that is bathed needeth not ²save to wash his feet, but is clean every whit: and 11 ye are clean, but not all. For he knew him that should betray him; therefore said he, Ye are not all clean.

12 So when he had washed their feet, and taken his garments, and ³sat down again, he said unto them, 13 Know ye what I have done to you? Ye call me, ⁴Master, and, Lord: and ye say well; for so I am. 14 If I then, the Lord and the ⁴Master, have washed your feet, ye also ought to wash one another's feet. 15 For I have given you an example, that ye also should 16 do as I have done to you. Verily, verily, I say unto you, A ⁵servant is not greater than his lord; neither 17 ⁶one that is sent greater than he that sent him. If ye know these things, blessed are ye if ye do them. 18 I speak not of you all: I know whom I ⁷have chosen: but that the scripture may be fulfilled, He that eat- 19 eth ⁸my bread lifted up his heel against me. From henceforth I tell you before it come to pass, that, when it is come to pass, ye may believe that ⁹I am 20 *he*. Verily, verily, I say unto you, He that receiveth whomsoever I send receiveth me; and he that receiveth me receiveth him that sent me.

21 When Jesus had thus said, he was troubled in the spirit, and testified, and said, Verily, verily, I say 22 unto you, that one of you shall betray me. The disciples looked one on another, doubting of whom he

---

1 Or, *to the uttermost.*

2 Some ancient authorities omit *save,* and *his feet.*

3 Gr. *reclined.*

4 Or, *Teacher*

5 Gr. *bondservant.*

6 Gr. *an apostle.*

7 Or, *chose*

8 Many ancient authorities read *his bread with me.*

9 Or, *I am.*

spake. There was at the table reclining in Jesus' 23
bosom one of his disciples, whom Jesus loved. Si- 24
mon Peter therefore beckoneth to him, and saith
unto him, Tell *us* who it is of whom he speaketh.
He leaning back, as he was, on Jesus' breast saith 25
unto him, Lord, who is it? Jesus therefore answer- 26
eth, He it is, for whom I shall dip the sop, and give
it him. So when he had dipped the sop, he taketh
and giveth it to Judas, *the son* of Simon Iscariot.
And after the sop, then entered Satan into him. 27
Jesus therefore saith unto him, That thou doest, do
quickly. Now no man at the table knew for what 28
intent he spake this unto him. For some thought, 29
because Judas had the ¹bag, that Jesus said unto
him, Buy what things we have need of for the feast;
or, that he should give something to the poor. He 30
then having received the sop went out straightway:
and it was night.

When therefore he was gone out, Jesus saith, Now 31
²is the Son of man glorified, and God ²is glorified
in him; and God shall glorify him in himself, and 32
straightway shall he glorify him. Little children, 33
yet a little while I am with you. Ye shall seek me:
and as I said unto the Jews, Whither I go, ye cannot come; so now I say unto you. A new com- 34
mandment I give unto you, that ye love one another; ³even as I have loved you, that ye also love
one another. By this shall all men know that 35
ye are my disciples, if ye have love one to another.

Simon Peter saith unto him, Lord, whither goest 36
thou? Jesus answered, Whither I go, thou canst not
follow me now; but thou shalt follow afterward.
Peter saith unto him, Lord, why cannot I follow 37
thee even now? I will lay down my life for thee.
Jesus answereth, Wilt thou lay down thy life for 38
me? Verily, verily, I say unto thee, The cock shall
not crow, till thou hast denied me thrice.

Let not your heart be troubled: ⁴ye believe in **14**
God, believe also in me. In my Father's house are 2
many ⁵mansions; if it were not so, I would have told
you; for I go to prepare a place for you. And if I go 3
and prepare a place for you, I come again, and will
receive you unto myself; that where I am, *there* ye
may be also. ⁶And whither I go, ye know the way. 4
Thomas saith unto him, Lord, we know not whither 5

¹ Or, *box*

² Or, *was*

³ Or, *even as I loved you, that ye also may love one another.*

⁴ Or, *believe in God*ª

⁵ Or, *abiding-places*

⁶ Many ancient authorities read *And whither I go ye know, and the way ye know.*

ª Let marg. ⁴ and the text exchange places.—*Am. Com.*

6 thou goest; how know we the way? Jesus saith unto him, I am the way, and the truth, and the life:
7 no one cometh unto the Father, but ¹by me. If ye had known me, ye would have known my Father also: from henceforth ye know him, and have seen
8 him. Philip saith unto him, Lord, shew us the Fa-
9 ther, and it sufficeth us. Jesus saith unto him, Have I been so long time with you, and dost thou not know me, Philip? he that hath seen me hath seen the Father; how sayest thou, Shew us the Father?
10 Believest thou not that I am in the Father, and the Father in me? the words that I say unto you I speak not from myself: but the Father abiding in me
11 doeth his works. Believe me that I am in the Father, and the Father in me: or else believe me for
12 the very works' sake. Verily, verily, I say unto you, He that believeth on me, the works that I do shall he do also; and greater *works* than these shall he
13 do; because I go unto the Father. And whatsoever ye shall ask in my name, that will I do, that the Fa-
14 ther may be glorified in the Son. If ye shall ask
15 ²me anything* in my name, that will I do. If ye
16 love me, ye will keep my commandments. And I will ³pray the Father, and he shall give you another
17 ⁴Comforter, that he may be with you for ever, *even* the Spirit of truth: whom the world cannot receive; for it beholdeth him not, neither knoweth him: ye know him; for he abideth with you, and shall be in
18 you. I will not leave you ⁵desolate: I come unto
19 you. Yet a little while, and the world beholdeth me no more; but ye behold me: because I live, ⁶ye
20 shall live also. In that day ye shall know that I am
21 in my Father, and ye in me, and I in you. He that hath my commandments, and keepeth them, he it is that loveth me: and he that loveth me shall be loved of my Father, and I will love him, and will mani-
22 fest myself unto him. Judas (not Iscariot) saith unto him, Lord, what is come to pass that thou wilt manifest thyself unto us, and not unto the world?
23 Jesus answered and said unto him, If a man love me, he will keep my word: and my Father will love him, and we will come unto him, and make our
24 abode with him. He that loveth me not keepeth not my words: and the word which ye hear is not mine, but the Father's who sent me.

1 Or, *through*

2 Many ancient authorities omit *me.*

3 Gr. *make request of.*

4 Or, *Advocate*
Or, *Helper*
Gr. *Paraclete.*

5 Or, *orphans*

6 Or, *and ye shall live*

---

* For "shall ask me anything" read "shall ask anything" and let marg. ² read Many ancient authorities add *me.—Am. Com.*

25 These things have I spoken unto you, while *yet*
26 abiding with you. But the ¹Comforter, *even* the
Holy Spirit, whom the Father will send in my name,
he shall teach you all things, and bring to your remembrance all that I said unto you.
27 Peace I leave with you; my peace I give unto you: not as the world giveth, give I unto you. Let not your heart be troubled, neither let it be fearful.
28 Ye heard how I said to you, I go away, and I come unto you. If ye loved me, ye would have rejoiced, because I go unto the Father: for the Father is greater than I.
29 And now I have told you before it come to pass, that, when it is come to pass, ye may believe.
30 I will no more speak much with you, for the prince of the world cometh: and he hath nothing in me;
31 but that the world may know that I love the Father, and as the Father gave me commandment, even so I do. Arise, let us go hence.

15 I am the true vine, and my Father is the husbandman.
2 Every branch in me that beareth not fruit, he taketh it away: and every *branch* that beareth fruit, he cleanseth it, that it may bear more fruit.
3 Already ye are clean because of the word which I have spoken unto you.
4 Abide in me, and I in you. As the branch cannot bear fruit of itself, except it abide in the vine; so neither can ye, except ye abide in me.
5 I am the vine, ye are the branches: He that abideth in me, and I in him, the same beareth much fruit: for apart from me ye can do nothing.
6 If a man abide not in me, he is cast forth as a branch, and is withered; and they gather them, and cast them into the fire, and they are burned.
7 If ye abide in me, and my words abide in you, ask whatsoever ye will, and it shall be done unto you.
8 Herein ²is my Father glorified, ³that ye bear much fruit; and *so* shall ye be my disciples.
9 Even as the Father hath loved me, I also have loved you: abide ye in my love.
10 If ye keep my commandments, ye shall abide in my love; even as I have kept my Father's commandments, and abide in his love.
11 These things have I spoken unto you, that my joy may be in you, and *that* your joy may be fulfilled.
12 This is my commandment, that ye love one another, even as I have loved you.
13 Greater love hath no man than this, that a man lay down his life for his friends.
14 Ye are my friends, if ye do the things which I command you.
15 No longer do I call you ⁴servants; for the ⁵servant knoweth not what his lord doeth: but I have called

---

¹ Or, *Advocate* Or, *Helper* Gr. *Paraclete*.
² Or, *was*
³ Many ancient authorities read *that ye bear much fruit, and be my disciples.*
⁴ Gr. *bondservants*.
⁵ Gr. *bondservant*.

you friends; for all things that I heard from my Fa-
16 ther I have made known unto you. Ye did not
choose me, but I chose you, and appointed you, that
ye should go and bear fruit, and *that* your fruit
should abide: that whatsoever ye shall ask of the
17 Father in my name, he may give it you. These
things I command you, that ye may love one an-
18 other. If the world hateth you, ¹ye know that it
19 hath hated me before *it hated* you. If ye were of the
world, the world would love its own: but because
ye are not of the world, but I chose you out of the
20 world, therefore the world hateth you. Remember
the word that I said unto you, A ²servant is not
greater than his lord. If they persecuted me, they
will also persecute you; if they kept my word, they
21 will keep yours also. But all these things will they
do unto you for my name's sake, because they know
22 not him that sent me. If I had not come and spoken
unto them, they had not had sin: but now they have
23 no excuse for their sin. He that hateth me hateth
24 my Father also. If I had not done among them the
works which none other did, they had not had sin:
but now have they both seen and hated both me and
25 my Father. But *this cometh to pass*, that the word
may be fulfilled that is written in their law, They
26 hated me without a cause. But when the ³Comforter
is come, whom I will send unto you from the Father,
even the Spirit of truth, which ⁴proceedeth from the
27 Father, he shall bear witness of me: ⁵and ye also bear
witness, because ye have been with me from the beginning.

16 These things have I spoken unto you, that ye should
2 not be made to stumble. They shall put you out of
the synagogues: yea, the hour cometh, that whosoever killeth you shall think that he offereth service
3 unto God. And these things will they do, because
4 they have not known the Father, nor me. But these
things have I spoken unto you, that when their hour
is come, ye may remember them, how that I told you.
And these things I said not unto you from the be-
5 ginning, because I was with you. But now I go
unto him that sent me; and none of you asketh me,
6 Whither goest thou? But because I have spoken
these things unto you, sorrow hath filled your heart.
7 Nevertheless I tell you the truth; It is expedient for
you that I go away: for if I go not away, the ³Comforter will not come unto you; but if I go, I will
8 send him unto you. And he, when he is come, will

1 Or, *know ye*

2 Gr. *bondservant.*

3 Or, *Advocate*
Or, *Helper*
Gr. *Paraclete.*

4 Or, *goeth forth from*

5 Or, *and bear ye also witness*

convict the world in respect of sin, and of righteousness, and of judgement: of sin, because they believe 9 not on me; of righteousness, because I go to the Fa- 10 ther, and ye behold me no more; of judgement, be- 11 cause the prince of this world hath been judged. I 12 have yet many things to say unto you, but ye cannot bear them now. Howbeit when he, the Spirit of 13 truth, is come, he shall guide you into all the truth: for he shall not speak from himself; but what things soever he shall hear, *these* shall he speak: and he shall declare unto you the things that are to come. He 14 shall glorify me: for he shall take of mine, and shall declare *it* unto you. All things whatsoever the Fa- 15 ther hath are mine: therefore said I, that he taketh of mine, and shall declare *it* unto you. A little while, 16 and ye behold me no more; and again a little while, and ye shall see me. *Some* of his disciples therefore 17 said one to another, What is this that he saith unto us, A little while, and ye behold me not; and again a little while, and ye shall see me: and, Because I go to the Father? They said therefore, What is this that 18 he saith, A little while? We know not what he saith. Jesus perceived that they were desirous to ask him, 19 and he said unto them, Do ye inquire among yourselves concerning this, that I said, A little while, and ye behold me not, and again a little while, and ye shall see me? Verily, verily, I say unto you, that ye 20 shall weep and lament, but the world shall rejoice: ye shall be sorrowful, but your sorrow shall be turned into joy. A woman when she is in travail hath 21 sorrow, because her hour is come: but when she is delivered of the child, she remembereth no more the anguish, for the joy that a man is born into the world. And ye therefore now have sorrow: but I 22 will see you again, and your heart shall rejoice, and your joy no one taketh away from you. And in that 23 day ye shall [1]ask me nothing. Verily, verily, I say unto you, If ye shall ask anything of the Father, he will give it you in my name. Hitherto have ye ask- 24 ed nothing in my name: ask, and ye shall receive, that your joy may be fulfilled.

These things have I spoken unto you in [2]prov- 25 erbs*: the hour cometh, when I shall no more speak unto you in [2]proverbs, but shall tell you plainly of the Father. In that day ye shall ask in my 26 name: and I say not unto you, that I will [3]pray the Father for you; for the Father himself loveth you, 27

[1] Or, *ask me no question*

[2] Or, *parables*

[3] Gr. *make request of.*

* For "proverbs" read "dark sayings"—*Am. Com.*

because ye have loved me, and have believed that I
28 came forth from the Father. I came out from the
Father, and am come into the world: again, I leave
29 the world, and go unto the Father. His disciples
say, Lo, now speakest thou plainly, and speakest no
30 ¹proverb*. Now know we that thou knowest all   1 Or, *parable.*
things, and needest not that any man should ask
thee: by this we believe that thou camest forth from
31 God. Jesus answered them, Do ye now believe?
32 Behold, the hour cometh, yea, is come, that ye shall
be scattered, every man to his own, and shall leave
me alone: and *yet* I am not alone, because the Fa-
33 ther is with me. These things have I spoken unto
you, that in me ye may have peace. In the world
ye have tribulation: but be of good cheer; I have
overcome the world.

17 These things spake Jesus; and lifting up his eyes
to heaven, he said, Father, the hour is come; glori-
2 fy thy Son, that the Son may glorify thee: even as
thou gavest him authority over all flesh, that whatsoever thou hast given him, to them he should give
3 eternal life. And this is life eternal, that they should
know thee the only true God, and him whom thou
4 didst send, *even* Jesus Christ. I glorified thee on
the earth, having accomplished the work which thou
5 hast given me to do. And now, O Father, glorify
thou me with thine own self with the glory which I
6 had with thee before the world was. I manifested
thy name unto the men whom thou gavest me out
of the world: thine they were, and thou gavest them
7 to me; and they have kept thy word. Now they
know that all things whatsoever thou hast given me
8 are from thee: for the words which thou gavest me
I have given unto them; and they received *them*,
and knew of a truth that I came forth from thee,   2 Gr. *make request.*
9 and they believed that thou didst send me. I ²pray
for them: I ²pray not for the world, but for those
10 whom thou hast given me; for they are thine: and
all things that are mine are thine, and thine are
11 mine: and I am glorified in them. And I am no
more in the world, and these are in the world, and I
come to thee. Holy Father, keep them in thy name
which thou hast given me, that they may be one,
12 even as we *are*. While I was with them, I kept
them in thy name which thou hast given me: and I
guarded them, and not one of them perished, but the
son of perdition; that the scripture might be ful-

---

* For "proverb" read "dark saying."—*Am. Com.*

filled. But now I come to thee; and these things I 13
speak in the world, that they may have my joy fulfilled in themselves. I have given them thy word; 14
and the world hated them, because they are not of
the world, even as I am not of the world. I ¹pray 15
not that thou shouldest take them ²from the world,
but that thou shouldest keep them ²from ³the evil
one. They are not of the world, even as I am not 16
of the world. ⁴Sanctify them in the truth: thy 17
word is truth. As thou didst send me into the 18
world, even so sent I them into the world. And for 19
their sakes I ⁴sanctify myself, that they themselves
also may be sanctified in truth. Neither for these 20
only do I ¹pray, but for them also that believe on me
through their word; that they may all be one; even 21
as thou, Father, *art* in me, and I in thee, that they
also may be in us: that the world may believe that
thou didst send me. And the glory which thou hast 22
given me I have given unto them; that they may be
one, even as we *are* one; I in them, and thou in me, 23
that they may be perfected into one; that the world
may know that thou didst send me, and lovedst
them, even as thou lovedst me. Father, ⁵that which 24
thou hast given me, I will* that, where I am, they
also may be with me; that they may behold my
glory, which thou hast given me: for thou lovedst
me before the foundation of the world. O righteous 25
Father, the world knew thee not, but I knew thee;
and these knew that thou didst send me; and I 26
made known unto them thy name, and will make it
known; that the love wherewith thou lovedst me
may be in them, and I in them.

When Jesus had spoken these words, he went **18**
forth with his disciples over the ⁶brook ⁷Kidron,
where was a garden, into the which he entered,
himself and his disciples. Now Judas also, which 2
betrayed him, knew the place: for Jesus oft-times
resorted thither with his disciples. Judas then, 3
having received the ⁸band *of soldiers*, and officers
from the chief priests and the Pharisees, cometh
thither with lanterns and torches and weapons.
Jesus therefore, knowing all the things that were 4
coming upon him, went forth, and saith unto them,
Whom seek ye? They answered him, Jesus of 5
Nazareth. Jesus saith unto them, I am *he*. And
Judas also, which betrayed him, was standing with

---

1 Gr. *make request*.
2 Gr. *out of*.
3 Or, *evil*
4 Or, *Consecrate*
5 Many ancient authorities read *those whom*.
6 Or, *ravine* Gr. *winter-torrent*.
7 Or, *of the Cedars*
8 Or, *cohort*

* For "I will" read "I desire"—*Am. Com.*

6 them. When therefore he said unto them, I am *he*,
7 they went backward, and fell to the ground. Again therefore he asked them, Whom seek ye? And they
8 said, Jesus of Nazareth. Jesus answered, I told you that I am *he*: if therefore ye seek me, let these go
9 their way: that the word might be fulfilled which he spake, Of those whom thou hast given me I lost
10 not one. Simon Peter therefore having a sword drew it, and struck the high priest's ¹servant, and cut off his right ear. Now the ¹servant's name was
11 Malchus. Jesus therefore said unto Peter, Put up the sword into the sheath: the cup which the Father hath given me, shall I not drink it?
12 So the ²band and the ³chief captain, and the offi-
13 cers of the Jews, seized Jesus and bound him, and led him to Annas first; for he was father in law to
14 Caiaphas, which was high priest that year. Now Caiaphas was he which gave counsel to the Jews, that it was expedient that one man should die for the people.
15 And Simon Peter followed Jesus, and *so did* another disciple. Now that disciple was known unto the high priest, and entered in with Jesus into the
16 court of the high priest; but Peter was standing at the door without. So the other disciple, which was known unto the high priest, went out and spake unto her that kept the door, and brought in Peter.
17 The maid therefore that kept the door saith unto Peter, Art thou also *one* of this man's disciples? He
18 saith, I am not. Now the ⁴servants and the officers were standing *there*, having made ⁵a fire of coals; for it was cold; and they were warming themselves: and Peter also was with them, standing and warming himself.
19 The high priest therefore asked Jesus of his dis-
20 ciples, and of his teaching. Jesus answered him, I have spoken openly to the world; I ever taught in ⁶synagogues, and in the temple, where all the Jews
21 come together; and in secret spake I nothing. Why askest thou me? ask them that have heard *me*, what I spake unto them: behold, these know the things
22 which I said. And when he had said this, one of the officers standing by struck Jesus ⁷with his hand,
23 saying, Answerest thou the high priest so? Jesus answered him, If I have spoken evil, bear witness
24 of the evil: but if well, why smitest thou me? Annas therefore sent him bound unto Caiaphas the high priest.

1 Gr. *bondservant.*

2 Or, *cohort*
3 Or, *military tribune*
Gr. *chiliarch.*

4 Gr. *bondservants.*
5 Gr. *a fire of charcoal.*

6 Gr. *synagogue.*

7 Or, *with a rod*

Now Simon Peter was standing and warming 25
himself. They said therefore unto him, Art thou
also *one* of his disciples? He denied, and said, I am
not. One of the ¹servants of the high priest, being 26
a kinsman of him whose ear Peter cut off, saith, Did
not I see thee in the garden with him? Peter there- 27
fore denied again: and straightway the cock crew.

They lead Jesus therefore from Caiaphas into the 28
²palace: and it was early; and they themselves entered not into the ²palace, that they might not be
defiled, but might eat the passover. Pilate there- 29
fore went out unto them, and saith, What accusation bring ye against this man? They answered 30
and said unto him, If this man were not an evil-
doer, we should not have delivered him up unto
thee. Pilate therefore said unto them, Take him 31
yourselves, and judge him according to your law.
The Jews said unto him, It is not lawful for us to
put any man to death: that the word of Jesus 32
might be fulfilled, which he spake, signifying by
what manner of death he should die.

Pilate therefore entered again into the ²palace, 33
and called Jesus, and said unto him, Art thou the
King of the Jews? Jesus answered, Sayest thou 34
this of thyself, or did others tell it thee concerning
me? Pilate answered, Am I a Jew? Thine own 35
nation and the chief priests delivered thee unto me:
what hast thou done? Jesus answered, My king- 36
dom is not of this world: if my kingdom were of
this world, then would my ³servants fight, that I
should not be delivered to the Jews: but now is
my kingdom not from hence. Pilate therefore said 37
unto him, Art thou a king then? Jesus answered,
⁴Thou sayest that I am a king*. To this end have
I been born, and to this end am I come into the
world, that I should bear witness unto the truth.
Every one that is of the truth heareth my voice.
Pilate saith unto him, What is truth? 38

And when he had said this, he went out again
unto the Jews, and saith unto them, I find no crime
in him. But ye have a custom, that I should re- 39
lease unto you one at the passover: will ye therefore that I release unto you the King of the Jews?
They cried out therefore again, saying, Not this man, 40
but Barabbas. Now Barabbas was a robber.

¹ Or, *bondservants*.

² Gr. *Prætorium*.

³ Or, *officers*: as in ver. 3, 12, 18, 22.

⁴ Or, *Thou sayest it, because I am a king.*

* For "Thou sayest that" etc. read "Thou sayest *it*, for I am a king" and substitute the present text for the marg. [comp. Luke xxii. 70]. —*Am. Com.*

19 Then Pilate therefore took Jesus, and scourged
2 him. And the soldiers plaited a crown of thorns,
and put it on his head, and arrayed him in a purple
3 garment; and they came unto him, and said, Hail,
King of the Jews! and they struck him ¹with their
4 hands. And Pilate went out again, and saith unto
them, Behold, I bring him out to you, that ye may
5 know that I find no crime in him. Jesus therefore
came out, wearing the crown of thorns and the purple garment. And *Pilate* saith unto them, Behold,
6 the man! When therefore the chief priests and
the officers saw him, they cried out, saying, Crucify
him, crucify *him*. Pilate saith unto them, Take him
yourselves, and crucify him: for I find no crime in
7 him. The Jews answered him, We have a law, and
by that law he ought to die, because he made him-
8 self the Son of God. When Pilate therefore heard
9 this saying, he was the more afraid; and he entered
into the ²palace again, and saith unto Jesus, Whence
10 art thou? But Jesus gave him no answer. Pilate
therefore saith unto him, Speakest thou not unto
me? knowest thou not that I have ³power to re-
11 lease thee, and have ³power to crucify thee? Jesus
answered him, Thou wouldest have no ³power
against me, except it were given thee from above:
therefore he that delivered me unto thee hath great-
12 er sin. Upon this Pilate sought to release him:
but the Jews cried out, saying, If thou release this
man, thou art not Cæsar's friend: every one that
maketh himself a king ⁴speaketh against Cæsar.
13 When Pilate therefore heard these words, he
brought Jesus out, and sat down on the judgement-
seat at a place called The Pavement, but in He-
14 brew, Gabbatha. Now it was the Preparation of
the passover: it was about the sixth hour. And he
15 saith unto the Jews, Behold, your King! They therefore cried out, Away with *him*, away with *him*, crucify him. Pilate saith unto them, Shall I crucify
your King? The chief priests answered, We have
16 no king but Cæsar. Then therefore he delivered
him unto them to be crucified.
17   They took Jesus therefore: and he went out,
bearing the cross for himself, unto the place called
The place of a skull, which is called in Hebrew
18 Golgotha: where they crucified him, and with him
two others, on either side one, and Jesus in the midst.
19 And Pilate wrote a title also, and put it on the cross.
And there was written, JESUS OF NAZARETH, THE

1 Or, *with rods*.

2 Gr. *Prætorium*.

3 Or, *authority*

4 Or, *opposeth Cæsar*.

¹ Or, *for the place of the city where Jesus was crucified was nigh at hand*

² Or, *tunic*

KING OF THE JEWS. This title therefore read many 20 of the Jews: ¹for the place where Jesus was crucified was nigh to the city: and it was written in Hebrew, *and* in Latin, *and* in Greek. The chief 21 priests of the Jews therefore said to Pilate, Write not, The King of the Jews; but, that he said, I am King of the Jews. Pilate answered, What I have 22 written I have written.

The soldiers therefore, when they had crucified 23 Jesus, took his garments, and made four parts, to every soldier a part; and also the ²coat: now the ²coat was without seam, woven from the top throughout. They said therefore one to another, Let us not 24 rend it, but cast lots for it, whose it shall be: that the scripture might be fulfilled, which saith,

They parted my garments among them,
And upon my vesture did they cast lots.

These things therefore the soldiers did. But there 25 were standing by the cross of Jesus his mother, and his mother's sister, Mary the *wife* of Clopas, and Mary Magdalene. When Jesus therefore saw his 26 mother, and the disciple standing by, whom he loved, he saith unto his mother, Woman, behold, thy son! Then saith he to the disciple, Behold, thy 27 mother! And from that hour the disciple took her unto his own *home*.

After this Jesus, knowing that all things are now 28 finished, that the scripture might be accomplished, saith, I thirst. There was set there a vessel full of 29 vinegar: so they put a sponge full of the vinegar upon hyssop, and brought it to his mouth. When 30 Jesus therefore had received the vinegar, he said, It is finished: and he bowed his head, and gave up his spirit.

The Jews therefore, because it was the Preparation, 31 that the bodies should not remain on the cross upon the sabbath (for the day of that sabbath was a high *day*), asked of Pilate that their legs might be broken, and *that* they might be taken away. The 32 soldiers therefore came, and brake the legs of the first, and of the other which was crucified with him: but when they came to Jesus, and saw that 33 he was dead already, they brake not his legs: howbeit 34 one of the soldiers with a spear pierced his side, and straightway there came out blood and water. And he that hath seen hath borne witness, 35 and his witness is true: and he knoweth that he saith true, that ye also may believe. For these 36

things came to pass, that the scripture might be
37 fulfilled, A bone of him shall not be ¹broken. And
again another scripture saith, They shall look on
him whom they pierced.

¹ Or, *crushed*.

38 And after these things Joseph of Arimathæa, being a disciple of Jesus, but secretly for fear of the Jews, asked of Pilate that he might take away the body of Jesus: and Pilate gave *him* leave. He
39 came therefore, and took away his body. And there came also Nicodemus, he who at the first came to him by night, bringing a ²mixture of myrrh and
40 aloes, about a hundred pound *weight*. So they took the body of Jesus, and bound it in linen cloths with the spices, as the custom of the Jews is to bury.

² Some ancient authorities read *roll*.

41 Now in the place where he was crucified there was a garden; and in the garden a new tomb wherein
42 was never man yet laid. There then because of the Jews' Preparation (for the tomb was nigh at hand) they laid Jesus.

20 Now on the first *day* of the week cometh Mary Magdalene early, while it was yet dark, unto the tomb, and seeth the stone taken away from the
2 tomb. She runneth therefore, and cometh to Simon Peter, and to the other disciple, whom Jesus loved, and saith unto them, They have taken away the Lord out of the tomb, and we know not where
3 they have laid him. Peter therefore went forth, and the other disciple, and they went toward the
4 tomb. And they ran both together: and the other disciple outran Peter, and came first to the tomb;
5 and stooping and looking in, he seeth the linen
6 cloths lying; yet entered he not in. Simon Peter therefore also cometh, following him, and entered into the tomb; and he beholdeth the linen cloths
7 lying, and the napkin, that was upon his head, not lying with the linen cloths, but rolled up in a place
8 by itself. Then entered in therefore the other disciple also, which came first to the tomb, and he
9 saw, and believed. For as yet they knew not the scripture, that he must rise again from the dead.
10 So the disciples went away again unto their own home.
11 But Mary was standing without at the tomb weeping: so, as she wept, she stooped and looked into the
12 tomb; and she beholdeth two angels in white sitting, one at the head, and one at the feet, where the body
13 of Jesus had lain. And they say unto her, Woman, why weepest thou? She saith unto them, Because

they have taken away my Lord, and I know not where they have laid him. When she had thus said, she turned herself back, and beholdeth Jesus standing, and knew not that it was Jesus. Jesus saith unto her, Woman, why weepest thou? whom seekest thou? She, supposing him to be the gardener, saith unto him, Sir, if thou hast borne him hence, tell me where thou hast laid him, and I will take him away. Jesus saith unto her, Mary. She turneth herself, and saith unto him in Hebrew, Rabboni; which is to say, ¹Master. Jesus saith to her, ²Touch me not; for I am not yet ascended unto the Father: but go unto my brethren, and say to them, I ascend unto my Father and your Father, and my God and your God. Mary Magdalene cometh and telleth the disciples, I have seen the Lord; and *how that* he had said these things unto her.

When therefore it was evening, on that day, the first *day* of the week, and when the doors were shut where the disciples were, for fear of the Jews, Jesus came and stood in the midst, and saith unto them, Peace *be* unto you. And when he had said this, he shewed unto them his hands and his side. The disciples therefore were glad, when they saw the Lord. Jesus therefore said to them again, Peace *be* unto you: as the Father hath sent me, even so send I you. And when he had said this, he breathed on them, and saith unto them, Receive ye the ³Holy Ghost: whose soever sins ye forgive, they are forgiven unto them; whose soever *sins* ye retain, they are retained. But Thomas, one of the twelve, called ⁴Didymus, was not with them when Jesus came. The other disciples therefore said unto him, We have seen the Lord. But he said unto them, Except I shall see in his hands the print of the nails, and put my finger into the print of the nails, and put my hand into his side, I will not believe.

And after eight days again his disciples were within, and Thomas with them. Jesus cometh, the doors being shut, and stood in the midst, and said, Peace *be* unto you. Then saith he to Thomas, Reach hither thy finger, and see my hands; and reach *hither* thy hand, and put it into my side: and be not faithless, but believing. Thomas answered and said unto him, My Lord and my God. Jesus saith unto him, Because thou hast seen me, ⁵thou hast believed: blessed *are* they that have not seen, and *yet* have believed.

Many other signs therefore did Jesus in the pres-

---

1 Or, *Teacher.*
2 Or, *Take not hold on me*
3 Or, *Holy Spirit*
4 That is, *Twin.*
5 Or, *hast thou believed?*

ence of the disciples, which are not written in this
31 book: but these are written, that ye may believe that Jesus is the Christ, the Son of God; and that believing ye may have life in his name.

21 After these things Jesus manifested himself again to the disciples at the sea of Tiberias; and he mani-
2 fested *himself* on this wise. There were together Simon Peter, and Thomas called ¹Didymus, and Nathanael of Cana in Galilee, and the *sons* of Zebe-
3 dee, and two other of his disciples. Simon Peter saith unto them, I go a fishing. They say unto him, We also come with thee. They went forth, and entered into the boat; and that night they took noth-
4 ing. But when day was now breaking, Jesus stood on the beach: howbeit the disciples knew not that
5 it was Jesus. Jesus therefore saith unto them, Children, have ye aught to eat? They answered
6 him, No. And he said unto them, Cast the net on the right side of the boat, and ye shall find. They cast therefore, and now they were not able to draw
7 it for the multitude of fishes. That disciple therefore whom Jesus loved saith unto Peter, It is the Lord. So when Simon Peter heard that it was the Lord, he girt his coat about him (for he was naked*),
8 and cast himself into the sea. But the other disciples came in the little boat (for they were not far from the land, but about two hundred cubits off),
9 dragging the net *full* of fishes. So when they got out upon the land, they see ²a fire of coals there, and
10 ³fish laid thereon, and ⁴bread. Jesus saith unto them, Bring of the fish which ye have now taken.
11 Simon Peter therefore went ⁵up, and drew the net to land, full of great fishes, a hundred and fifty and three: and for all there were so many, the net was
12 not rent. Jesus saith unto them, Come *and* break your fast. And none of the disciples durst inquire of him, Who art thou? knowing that it was the
13 Lord. Jesus cometh, and taketh the ⁶bread, and
14 giveth them, and the fish likewise. This is now the third time that Jesus was manifested to the disciples, after that he was risen from the dead.
15 So when they had broken their fast, Jesus saith to Simon Peter, Simon, *son* of ⁷John, ⁸lovest thou me more than these? He saith unto him, Yea, Lord; thou knowest that I ⁹love thee. He saith unto him,

1 That is, *Twin*.

2 Gr. *a fire of charcoal*.
3 Or, *a fish*.
4 Or, *a loaf*.
5 Or, *aboard*

6 Or, *loaf*

7 Gr. *Joanes*. See ch. I. 42, margin.
8, 9 *Love* in these places represents two different Greek words.

---

* "was naked" add marg. Or, *had on his under garment only*—Am. Com.

S. JOHN. 21. 15.

Feed my lambs. He saith to him again a second 16 time, Simon, *son* of ¹John, ²lovest thou me? He saith unto him, Yea, Lord; thou knowest that I ³love thee. He saith unto him, Tend my sheep. He saith 17 unto him the third time, Simon, *son* of ¹John, ²lovest thou me? Peter was grieved because he said unto him the third time, ²Lovest thou me? And he said unto him, Lord, thou knowest all things; thou ⁴knowest that I ³love thee. Jesus saith unto him, Feed my sheep. Verily, verily, I say unto thee, When thou 18 wast young, thou girdedst thyself, and walkedst whither thou wouldest: but when thou shalt be old, thou shalt stretch forth thy hands, and another shall gird thee, and carry thee whither thou wouldest not. Now this he spake, signifying by what man- 19 ner of death he should glorify God. And when he had spoken this, he saith unto him, Follow me. Peter, turning about, seeth the disciple whom Jesus 20 loved following; which also leaned back on his breast at the supper, and said, Lord, who is he that betrayeth thee? Peter therefore seeing him saith to 21 Jesus, Lord, ⁵and what shall this man do? Jesus 22 saith unto him, If I will that he tarry till I come, what *is that* to thee? follow thou me. This saying 23 therefore went forth among the brethren, that that disciple should not die: yet Jesus said not unto him, that he should not die; but, If I will that he tarry till I come, what *is that* to thee?

This is the disciple which beareth witness of these 24 things, and wrote these things: and we know that his witness is true.

And there are also many other things which Jesus 25 did, the which if they should be written every one, I suppose that even the world itself would not contain the books that should be written.

---

¹ Gr. *Joanes*. See ch. 1. 42, margin.
², ³ *Love* in these places represents two different Greek words.
⁴ Or, *perceivest*
⁵ Gr. *and this man, what?*

THE
ACTS OF THE APOSTLES.

1 THE ¹former treatise I made, O Theophilus, concerning all that Jesus began both to do and to teach, 2 until the day in which he was received up, after that he had given commandment through the ²Holy 3 Ghost unto the apostles whom he had chosen: to whom he also ³shewed himself alive after his passion by many proofs, appearing unto them by the space of forty days, and speaking the things con-4 cerning the kingdom of God: and, ⁴being assembled together with them, he charged them not to depart from Jerusalem, but to wait for the promise of the 5 Father, which, *said he*, ye heard from me: for John indeed baptized with water; but ye shall be baptized ⁵with the Holy Ghost not many days hence. 6 They therefore, when they were come together, asked him, saying, Lord, dost thou at this time re-7 store the kingdom to Israel? And he said unto them, It is not for you to know times or seasons, which the Father hath ⁶set within his own authori-8 ty. But ye shall receive power, when the Holy Ghost is come upon you: and ye shall be my witnesses both in Jerusalem, and in all Judæa and Samaria, and unto the uttermost part of the earth. 9 And when he had said these things, as they were looking, he was taken up; and a cloud received him 10 out of their sight. And while they were looking stedfastly into heaven as he went, behold, two men 11 stood by them in white apparel; which also said, Ye men of Galilee, why stand ye looking into heaven? this Jesus, which was received up from you into heaven, shall so come in like manner as ye beheld him going into heaven.

1 Gr. *first.*

2 Or, *Holy Spirit*: and so throughout this book.

3 Gr. *presented.*

4 Or, *eating with them*

5 Or, *in*

6 Or, *appointed by*

Then returned they unto Jerusalem from the mount called Olivet, which is nigh unto Jerusalem, a sabbath day's journey off. And when they were come in, they went up into the upper chamber, where they were abiding; both Peter and John and James and Andrew, Philip and Thomas, Bartholomew and Matthew, James *the son* of Alphæus, and Simon the Zealot, and Judas *the* [1]*son* of James. These all with one accord continued stedfastly in prayer, [2]with the women, and Mary the mother of Jesus, and with his brethren.

And in these days Peter stood up in the midst of the brethren, and said (and there was a multitude of [3]persons *gathered* together, about a hundred and twenty), Brethren, it was needful that the scripture should be fulfilled, which the Holy Ghost spake before by the mouth of David concerning Judas, who was guide to them that took Jesus. For he was numbered among us, and received his [4]portion in this ministry. (Now this man obtained a field with the reward of his iniquity; and falling headlong, he burst asunder in the midst, and all his bowels gushed out. And it became known to all the dwellers at Jerusalem; insomuch that in their language that field was called Akeldama, that is, The field of blood.) For it is written in the book of Psalms,

Let his habitation be made desolate,
And let no man dwell therein:

and,

His [5]office let another take.

Of the men therefore which have companied with us all the time that the Lord Jesus went in and went out [6]among us, beginning from the baptism of John, unto the day that he was received up from us, of these must one become a witness with us of his resurrection. And they put forward two, Joseph called Barsabbas, who was surnamed Justus, and Matthias. And they prayed, and said, Thou, Lord, which knowest the hearts of all men, shew of these two the one whom thou hast chosen, to take the place in this ministry and apostleship, from which Judas fell away, that he might go to his own place. And they gave lots [7]for them; and the lot fell upon Matthias; and he was numbered with the eleven apostles.

And when the day of Pentecost [8]was now come, they were all together in one place. And suddenly there came from heaven a sound as of the rushing

---

[1] Or, brother. See Jude 1.
[2] Or, *with* certain *women*.
[3] Gr. *names*.
[4] Or, *lot*
[5] Gr. *overseership*.
[6] Or, *over*
[7] Or, *unto*
[8] Gr. *was being fulfilled*.

of a mighty wind, and it filled all the house where
3 they were sitting. And there appeared unto them
tongues ¹parting asunder, like as of fire; and it sat
4 upon each one of them. And they were all filled
with the Holy Spirit, and began to speak with other
tongues, as the Spirit gave them utterance.
5 Now there were dwelling at Jerusalem Jews, de-
6 vout men, from every nation under heaven. And
when this sound was heard, the multitude came together, and were confounded, because that every
man heard them speaking in his own language.
7 And they were all amazed and marvelled, saying,
Behold, are not all these which speak Galilæans?
8 And how hear we, every man in our own language,
9 wherein we were born? Parthians and Medes and
Elamites, and the dwellers in Mesopotamia, in Judæa
10 and Cappadocia, in Pontus and Asia, in Phrygia and
Pamphylia, in Egypt and the parts of Libya about
Cyrene, and sojourners from Rome, both Jews and
11 proselytes, Cretans and Arabians, we do hear them
speaking in our tongues the mighty works of God.
12 And they were all amazed, and were perplexed, say-
13 ing one to another, What meaneth this? But others
mocking said, They are filled with new wine.
14 But Peter, standing up with the eleven, lifted up
his voice, and spake forth unto them, *saying*, Ye
men of Judæa, and all ye that dwell at Jerusalem,
be this known unto you, and give ear unto my
15 words. For these are not drunken, as ye suppose;
16 seeing it is *but* the third hour of the day; but this is
that which hath been spoken ²by the prophet Joel;
17   And it shall be in the last days, saith God,
    I will pour forth of my Spirit upon all flesh:
    And your sons and your daughters shall proph-
      esy,
    And your young men shall see visions,
    And your old men shall dream dreams:
18   Yea and on my ³servants and on my ⁴hand-
      maidens in those days
    Will I pour forth of my Spirit; and they shall
      prophesy.
19   And I will shew wonders in the heaven above,
    And signs on the earth beneath;
    Blood, and fire, and vapour of smoke:
20   The sun shall be turned into darkness,
    And the moon into blood,
    Before the day of the Lord come,
    That great and notable *day*:

---

1 Or, *parting among them*
Or, *distributing themselves*

2 Or, *through*

3 Gr. *bondmen.*
4 Gr. *bondmaidens.*

And it shall be, that whosoever shall call on the 21
name of the Lord shall be saved.

Ye men of Israel, hear these words: Jesus of Naza- 22
reth, a man approved of God unto you by ¹mighty
works and wonders and signs, which God did by
him in the midst of you, even as ye yourselves
know; him, being delivered up by the determinate 23
counsel and foreknowledge of God, ye by the hand
of ²lawless men did crucify and slay: whom God 24
raised up, having loosed the pangs of death: because
it was not possible that he should be holden of it.
For David saith concerning him, 25

  I beheld the Lord always before my face;
  For he is on my right hand, that I should not
    be moved:
  Therefore my heart was glad, and my tongue 26
    rejoiced;
  Moreover my flesh also shall ³dwell in hope:
  Because thou wilt not leave my soul in Hades, 27
  Neither wilt thou give thy Holy One to see
    corruption.
  Thou madest known unto me the ways of life; 28
  Thou shalt make me full of gladness ⁴with thy
    countenance.

Brethren, I may say unto you freely of the patriarch 29
David, that he both died and was buried, and his
tomb is with us unto this day. Being therefore 30
a prophet, and knowing that God had sworn with
an oath to him, that of the fruit of his loins ⁵he
would set *one* upon his throne; he foreseeing *this* 31
spake of the resurrection of the Christ, that neither
was he left in Hades, nor did his flesh see corruption. This Jesus did God raise up, ⁶whereof we 32
all are witnesses. Being therefore ⁷by the right 33
hand of God exalted, and having received of the
Father the promise of the Holy Ghost, he hath
poured forth this, which ye see and hear. For 34
David ascended not into the heavens: but he saith
himself,

  The Lord said unto my Lord, Sit thou on my
    right hand,
  Till I make thine enemies the footstool of thy 35
    feet.

Let ⁸all the house of Israel therefore know assured- 36
ly, that God hath made him both Lord and Christ,
this Jesus whom ye crucified.

Now when they heard *this*, they were pricked in 37
their heart, and said unto Peter and the rest of the

---

¹ Gr. *powers*.

² Or, *men without the law*.

³ Or, *tabernacle*.

⁴ Or, *in thy presence*.

⁵ Or, *one should sit*.

⁶ Or, *of whom*.

⁷ Or, *at*.

⁸ Or, *every house*.

38 apostles, Brethren, what shall we do? And Peter *said* unto them, Repent ye, and be baptized every one of you in the name of Jesus Christ unto the remission of your sins; and ye shall receive the gift
39 of the Holy Ghost. For to you is the promise, and to your children, and to all that are afar off, *even* as
40 many as the Lord our God shall call unto him. And with many other words he testified, and exhorted them, saying, Save yourselves from this crooked
41 generation. They then ¹that received his word were baptized: and there were added *unto them* in
42 that day about three thousand souls. And they continued stedfastly in the apostles' teaching and ²fellowship, in the breaking of bread and the prayers.
43 And fear came upon every soul: and many won-
44 ders and signs were done ³by the apostles.⁴ And all that believed were together, and had all things com-
45 mon; and they sold their possessions and goods, and parted them to all, according as any man had need.
46 And day by day, continuing stedfastly with one accord in the temple, and breaking bread at home, they did take their food with gladness and singleness
47 of heart, praising God, and having favour with all the people. And the Lord added ⁵to them day by day those that were being saved*.

3 Now Peter and John were going up into the tem-
2 ple at the hour of prayer, *being* the ninth *hour*. And a certain man that was lame from his mother's womb was carried, whom they laid daily at the door of the temple which is called Beautiful, to ask alms of them
3 that entered into the temple; who seeing Peter and John about to go into the temple, asked to receive
4 an alms. And Peter, fastening his eyes upon him,
5 with John, said, Look on us. And he gave heed unto them, expecting to receive something from
6 them. But Peter said, Silver and gold have I none; but what I have, that give I thee. In the name of
7 Jesus Christ of Nazareth, walk. And he took him by the right hand, and raised him up: and immediately his feet and his ankle-bones received strength.
8 And leaping up, he stood, and began to walk; and he entered with them into the temple, walking, and
9 leaping, and praising God. And all the people saw
10 him walking and praising God: and they took knowledge of him, that it was he which sat for alms at the Beautiful Gate of the temple: and they were filled

1 Or, *having received*
2 Or, *in fellowship*
3 Or, *through*
4 Many ancient authorities add *in Jerusalem; and great fear was upon all.*
5 Gr. *together.*

---
* For "those that were being saved" read "those that were saved" with the text in the marg.—*Am. Com.*

with wonder and amazement at that which had happened unto him.

And as he held Peter and John, all the people ran together unto them in the ¹porch that is called Solomon's, greatly wondering. And when Peter saw it, he answered unto the people, Ye men of Israel, why marvel ye at this ²man? or why fasten ye your eyes on us, as though by our own power or godliness we had made him to walk? The God of Abraham, and of Isaac, and of Jacob, the God of our fathers, hath glorified his ³Servant Jesus; whom ye delivered up, and denied before the face of Pilate, when he had determined to release him. But ye denied the Holy and Righteous One, and asked for a murderer to be granted unto you, and killed the ⁴Prince of life; whom God raised from the dead; ⁵whereof we are witnesses. And ⁶by faith in his name hath his name made this man strong, whom ye behold and know: yea, the faith which is through him hath given him this perfect soundness in the presence of you all. And now, brethren, I wot that in ignorance ye did it, as did also your rulers. But the things which God foreshewed by the mouth of all the prophets, that his Christ should suffer, he thus fulfilled. Repent ye therefore, and turn again, that your sins may be blotted out, that so there may come seasons of refreshing from the presence of the Lord; and that he may send the Christ who hath been appointed for you, *even* Jesus: whom the heaven must receive until the times of restoration of all things, whereof God spake by the mouth of his holy prophets which have been since the world began*. Moses indeed said, A prophet shall the Lord God raise up unto you from among your brethren, ⁷like unto me; to him shall ye hearken in all things whatsoever he shall speak unto you. And it shall be, that every soul, which shall not hearken to that prophet, shall be utterly destroyed from among the people. Yea and all the prophets from Samuel and them that followed after, as many as have spoken, they also told of these days. Ye are the sons of the prophets, and of the covenant which God ⁸made with your fathers, saying unto Abraham, And in thy seed shall all the families of the earth be blessed. Unto you first God, having raised up his Servant, sent him to bless you, in turning away every one of you from your iniquities.

---

* For "since the world began" read "from of old."—*Am. Com.*

Margin notes:
1 Or, *portico*
2 Or, *thing*
3 Or, *Child*: and so in ver. 26; iv. 27, 30. See Matt. xii. 18; Isa. xlii. 1; lii. 13; liii. 11.
4 Or, *Author*
5 Or, *of whom*
6 Or, *on the ground of*
7 Or, *as he raised up me*
8 Gr. *covenanted.*

THE ACTS.

4 And as they spake unto the people, [1]the priests and the captain of the temple and the Sadducees
2 came upon them, being sore troubled because they taught the people, and proclaimed in Jesus the res-
3 urrection from the dead. And they laid hands on them, and put them in ward unto the morrow: for
4 it was now eventide. But many of them that heard the word believed; and the number of the men came to be about five thousand.
5 And it came to pass on the morrow, that their rulers and elders and scribes were gathered together
6 in Jerusalem; and Annas the high priest *was there*, and Caiaphas, and John, and Alexander, and as many as were of the kindred of the high priest.
7 And when they had set them in the midst, they inquired, By what power, or in what name, have ye
8 done this? Then Peter, filled with the Holy Ghost, said unto them, Ye rulers of the people, and elders,
9 if we this day are examined concerning a good deed done to an impotent man, [2]by what means this man
10 is [3]made whole; be it known unto you all, and to all the people of Israel, that in the name of Jesus Christ of Nazareth, whom ye crucified, whom God raised from the dead, *even* in [4]him doth this man stand here
11 before you whole. He is the stone which was set at nought of you the builders, which was made the
12 head of the corner. And in none other is there salvation: for neither is there any other name under heaven, that is given among men, wherein we must be saved.
13 Now when they beheld the boldness of Peter and John, and had perceived that they were unlearned and ignorant men, they marvelled; and they took knowledge of them, that they had been with Jesus.
14 And seeing the man which was healed standing with
15 them, they could say nothing against it. But when they had commanded them to go aside out of the
16 council, they conferred among themselves, saying, What shall we do to these men? for that indeed a notable [5]miracle hath been wrought through them, is manifest to all that dwell in Jerusalem; and we can-
17 not deny it. But that it spread no further among the people, let us threaten them, that they speak
18 henceforth to no man in this name. And they called them, and charged them not to speak at all nor
19 teach in the name of Jesus. But Peter and John answered and said unto them, Whether it be right in the sight of God to hearken unto you rather than

[1] Some ancient authorities read *the chief priests*.

[2] Or, *in whom*

[3] Or, *saved*

[4] Or, *this* name

[5] Gr. *sign*.

unto God, judge ye: for we cannot but speak the things which we saw and heard. And they, when they had further threatened them, let them go, finding nothing how they might punish them, because of the people; for all men glorified God for that which was done. For the man was more than forty years old, on whom this ¹miracle of healing was wrought.

And being let go, they came to their own company, and reported all that the chief priests and the elders had said unto them. And they, when they heard it, lifted up their voice to God with one accord, and said, O ²Lord, ³thou that didst make the heaven and the earth and the sea, and all that in them is: ⁴who by the Holy Ghost, *by* the mouth of our father David thy servant, didst say,

Why did the Gentiles rage,
And the peoples ⁵imagine vain things?
The kings of the earth set themselves in array,
And the rulers were gathered together,
Against the Lord, and against his ⁶Anointed:

for of a truth in this city against thy holy Servant Jesus, whom thou didst anoint, both Herod and Pontius Pilate, with the Gentiles and the peoples of Israel, were gathered together, to do whatsoever thy hand and thy counsel foreordained to come to pass. And now, Lord, look upon their threatenings: and grant unto thy ⁷servants to speak thy word with all boldness, while thou stretchest forth thy hand to heal; and that signs and wonders may be done through the name of thy holy Servant Jesus. And when they had prayed, the place was shaken wherein they were gathered together; and they were all filled with the Holy Ghost, and they spake the word of God with boldness.

And the multitude of them that believed were of one heart and soul: and not one *of them* said that aught of the things which he possessed was his own; but they had all things common. And with great power gave the apostles their witness of the resurrection of the Lord Jesus⁸: and great grace was upon them all. For neither was there among them any that lacked: for as many as were possessors of lands or houses sold them, and brought the prices of the things that were sold, and laid them at the apostles' feet: and distribution was made unto each, according as any one had need.

And Joseph, who by the apostles was surnamed

---

¹ Gr. *sign.*

² Or, *Master*
³ Or, *thou art he that did make*
⁴ The Greek text in this clause is somewhat uncertain.

⁵ Or, *meditate*

⁶ Gr. *Christ.*

⁷ Gr. *bondservants.*

⁸ Some ancient authorities add *Christ.*

Barnabas (which is, being interpreted, Son of ¹exhor- [1 Or, *consolation*]
37 tation), a Levite, a man of Cyprus by race, having a field, sold it, and brought the money, and laid it at the apostles' feet.

5 But a certain man named Ananias, with Sapphira
2 his wife, sold a possession, and kept back *part* of the price, his wife also being privy to it, and brought
3 a certain part, and laid it at the apostles' feet. But Peter said, Ananias, why hath Satan filled thy heart to ²lie to the Holy Ghost, and to keep back *part* of [2 Or, *deceive*]
4 the price of the land? Whiles it remained, did it not remain thine own? and after it was sold, was it not in thy power? How is it that thou hast conceived this thing in thy heart? thou hast not lied unto men,
5 but unto God. And Ananias hearing these words fell down and gave up the ghost: and great fear
6 came upon all that heard it. And the ³young men [3 Gr. *younger*.] arose and wrapped him round, and they carried him out and buried him.
7 And it was about the space of three hours after, when his wife, not knowing what was done, came
8 in. And Peter answered unto her, Tell me whether ye sold the land for so much. And she said, Yea,
9 for so much. But Peter *said* unto her, How is it that ye have agreed together to tempt the Spirit of the Lord? behold, the feet of them which have buried thy husband are at the door, and they shall
10 carry thee out. And she fell down immediately at his feet, and gave up the ghost: and the young men came in and found her dead, and they carried her
11 out and buried her by her husband. And great fear came upon the whole church, and upon all that heard these things.
12 And by the hands of the apostles were many signs and wonders wrought among the people; and they
13 were all with one accord in Solomon's porch. But of the rest durst no man join himself to them: how- [4 Or, *and there were the more added to them, believing on the Lord*.]
14 beit the people magnified them; ⁴and believers were the more added to the Lord, multitudes both of
15 men and women; insomuch that they even carried out the sick into the streets, and laid them on beds and couches, that, as Peter came by, at the least his
16 shadow might overshadow some one of them. And there also came together the multitude from the cities round about Jerusalem, bringing sick folk, and them that were vexed with unclean spirits: and they were healed every one.
17 But the high priest rose up, and all they that were

with him (which is the sect of the Sadducees), and they were filled with jealousy, and laid hands on the apostles, and put them in public ward. But an angel of the Lord by night opened the prison doors, and brought them out, and said, Go ye, and stand and speak in the temple to the people all the words of this Life. And when they heard *this*, they entered into the temple about daybreak, and taught. But the high priest came, and they that were with him, and called the council together, and all the senate of the children of Israel, and sent to the prisonhouse to have them brought. But the officers that came found them not in the prison; and they returned, and told, saying, The prison-house we found shut in all safety, and the keepers standing at the doors: but when we had opened, we found no man within. Now when the captain of the temple and the chief priests heard these words, they were much perplexed concerning them whereunto this would grow. And there came one and told them, Behold, the men whom ye put in the prison are in the temple standing and teaching the people. Then went the captain with the officers, and brought them, *but* without violence; for they feared the people, lest they should be stoned. And when they had brought them, they set them before the council. And the high priest asked them, saying, We straitly charged you not to teach in this name: and behold, ye have filled Jerusalem with your teaching, and intend to bring this man's blood upon us. But Peter and the apostles answered and said, We must obey God rather than men. The God of our fathers raised up Jesus, whom ye slew, hanging him on a tree. Him did God exalt [1]with his right hand *to be* a Prince and a Saviour, for to give repentance to Israel, and remission of sins. And we are witnesses[2] of these [3]things; [4]and *so is* the Holy Ghost, whom God hath given to them that obey him.

But they, when they heard this, were cut to the heart, and were minded to slay them. But there stood up one in the council, a Pharisee, named Gamaliel, a doctor of the law, had in honour of all the people, and commanded to put the men forth a little while. And he said unto them, Ye men of Israel, take heed to yourselves as touching these men, what ye are about to do. For before these days rose up Theudas, giving himself out to be somebody; to whom a number of men, about four

[1] Or, *at*
[2] Some ancient authorities add *in him.*
[3] Gr. *sayings.*
[4] Some ancient authorities read *and God hath given the Holy Ghost to them that obey him.*

hundred, joined themselves: who was slain; and all, as many as obeyed him, were dispersed, and
37 came to nought. After this man rose up Judas of Galilee in the days of the enrolment, and drew away *some of the* people after him: he also perished; and all, as many as obeyed him, were scattered abroad.
38 And now I say unto you, Refrain from these men, and let them alone: for if this counsel or this work
39 be of men, it will be overthrown: but if it is of God, ye will not be able to overthrow them; lest haply
40 ye be found even to be fighting against God. And to him they agreed: and when they had called the apostles unto them, they beat them and charged them not to speak in the name of Jesus, and let
41 them go. They therefore departed from the presence of the council, rejoicing that they were count-
42 ed worthy to suffer dishonour for the Name. And every day, in the temple and at home, they ceased not to teach and to preach Jesus *as* the Christ.

6 Now in these days, when the number of the disciples was multiplying, there arose a murmuring of the ¹Grecian Jews against the Hebrews, because
2 their widows were neglected in the daily ministration. And the twelve called the multitude of the disciples unto them, and said, It is not ²fit that we should forsake the word of God, and ³serve tables.
3 ⁴Look ye out therefore, brethren, from among you seven men of good report, full of the Spirit and of wisdom, whom we may appoint over this business.
4 But we will continue stedfastly in prayer, and in
5 the ministry of the word. And the saying pleased the whole multitude: and they chose Stephen, a man full of faith and of the Holy Spirit, and Philip, and Prochorus, and Nicanor, and Timon, and Par-
6 menas, and Nicolas a proselyte of Antioch: whom they set before the apostles: and when they had prayed, they laid their hands on them.
7 And the word of God increased; and the number of the disciples multiplied in Jerusalem exceedingly; and a great company of the priests were obedient to the faith.
8 And Stephen, full of grace and power, wrought
9 great wonders and signs among the people. But there arose certain of them that were of the synagogue called *the synagogue* of the Libertines, and of the Cyrenians, and of the Alexandrians, and of them
10 of Cilicia and Asia, disputing with Stephen. And they were not able to withstand the wisdom and the

1 Gr. *Hellenists*.
2 Gr. *pleasing*.
3 Or, *minister to tables*.
4 Some ancient authorities read *But, brethren, look ye out from among you*.

Spirit by which he spake. Then they suborned men, 11 which said, We have heard him speak blasphemous words against Moses, and *against* God. And they 12 stirred up the people, and the elders, and the scribes, and came upon him, and seized him, and brought him into the council, and set up false witnesses, 13 which said, This man ceaseth not to speak words against this holy place, and the law: for we have 14 heard him say, that this Jesus of Nazareth shall destroy this place, and shall change the customs which Moses delivered unto us. And all that sat in the 15 council, fastening their eyes on him, saw his face as it had been the face of an angel.

And the high priest said, Are these things so? 7 And he said, 2

Brethren and fathers, hearken. The God of glory appeared unto our father Abraham, when he was in Mesopotamia, before he dwelt in Haran, and said 3 unto him, Get thee out of thy land, and from thy kindred, and come into the land which I shall shew thee. Then came he out of the land of the Chaldæ- 4 ans, and dwelt in Haran: and from thence, when his father was dead, *God* removed him into this land, wherein ye now dwell: and he gave him none in- 5 heritance in it, no, not so much as to set his foot on: and he promised that he would give it to him in possession, and to his seed after him, when *as yet* he had no child. And God spake on this wise, that his 6 seed should sojourn in a strange land, and that they should bring them into bondage, and entreat them evil, four hundred years. And the nation to which 7 they shall be in bondage will I judge, said God: and after that shall they come forth, and serve me in this place. And he gave him the covenant of cir- 8 cumcision: and so *Abraham* begat Isaac, and circumcised him the eighth day; and Isaac *begat* Jacob, and Jacob the twelve patriarchs. And the patri- 9 archs, moved with jealousy against Joseph, sold him into Egypt: and God was with him, and delivered 10 him out of all his afflictions, and gave him favour and wisdom before Pharaoh king of Egypt; and he made him governor over Egypt and all his house. Now there came a famine over all Egypt and Canaan, 11 and great affliction: and our fathers found no sustenance. But when Jacob heard that there was 12 corn in Egypt, he sent forth our fathers the first time. And at the second time Joseph was made 13 known to his brethren; and Joseph's race became

14 manifest unto Pharaoh. And Joseph sent, and called to him Jacob his father, and all his kindred, three-
15 score and fifteen souls. And Jacob went down into
16 Egypt; and he died, himself, and our fathers; and they were carried over unto Shechem, and laid in the tomb that Abraham bought for a price in silver
17 of the sons of ¹Hamor in Shechem. But as the time of the promise drew nigh, which God vouchsafed unto Abraham, the people grew and multiplied in
18 Egypt, till there arose another king over Egypt,
19 which knew not Joseph. The same dealt subtilly with our race, and evil entreated our fathers, that ²they should cast out their babes to the end they
20 might not ³live. At which season Moses was born, and was ⁴exceeding fair; and he was nourished three
21 months in his father's house: and when he was cast out, Pharaoh's daughter took him up, and nourished
22 him for her own son. And Moses was instructed in all the wisdom of the Egyptians; and he was mighty
23 in his words and works. But when he was well-nigh forty years old, it came into his heart to visit
24 his brethren the children of Israel. And seeing one *of them* suffer wrong, he defended him, and avenged
25 him that was oppressed, smiting the Egyptian: and he supposed that his brethren understood how that God by his hand was giving them ⁵deliverance; but
26 they understood not. And the day following he appeared unto them as they strove, and would have set them at one again, saying, Sirs, ye are brethren;
27 why do ye wrong one to another? But he that did his neighbour wrong thrust him away, saying, Who
28 made thee a ruler and a judge over us? Wouldest thou kill me, as thou killedst the Egyptian yester-
29 day? And Moses fled at this saying, and became a sojourner in the land of Midian, where he begat two
30 sons. And when forty years were fulfilled, an angel appeared to him in the wilderness of mount Sinai,
31 in a flame of fire in a bush. And when Moses saw it, he wondered at the sight: and as he drew near to
32 behold, there came a voice of the Lord, I am the God of thy fathers, the God of Abraham, and of Isaac, and of Jacob. And Moses trembled, and
33 durst not behold. And the Lord said unto him, Loose the shoes from thy feet: for the place whereon
34 thou standest is holy ground. I have surely seen the affliction of my people which is in Egypt, and have heard their groaning, and I am come down to deliver them: and now come, I will send thee into

1 Gr. *Emmor.*

2 Or, *he*
3 Gr. *be preserved alive.*
4 Or, *fair unto God*

5 Or, *salvation*

Egypt. This Moses whom they refused, saying, 35
Who made thee a ruler and a judge? him hath God
sent *to be* both a ruler and a ¹deliverer with the hand
of the angel which appeared to him in the bush.
This man led them forth, having wrought wonders 36
and signs in Egypt, and in the Red Sea, and in the
wilderness forty years. This is that Moses, which 37
said unto the children of Israel, A prophet shall God
raise up unto you from among your brethren, ²like
unto me. This is he that was in the ³church in 38
the wilderness with the angel which spake to him
in the mount Sinai, and with our fathers: who received living oracles to give unto us: to whom our 39
fathers would not be obedient, but thrust him from
them, and turned back in their hearts unto Egypt,
saying unto Aaron, Make us gods which shall go 40
before us: for as for this Moses, which led us forth
out of the land of Egypt, we wot not what is become
of him. And they made a calf in those days, and 41
brought a sacrifice unto the idol, and rejoiced in the
works of their hands. But God turned, and gave 42
them up to serve the host of heaven; as it is written
in the book of the prophets,

> Did ye offer unto me slain beasts and sacrifices
> Forty years in the wilderness, O house of Israel?
> And ye took up the tabernacle of Moloch, 43
> And the star of the god Rephan,
> The figures which ye made to worship them:
> And I will carry you away beyond Babylon.

Our fathers had the tabernacle of the testimony in 44
the wilderness, even as he appointed who spake unto
Moses, that he should make it according to the figure
that he had seen. Which also our fathers, in their 45
turn, brought in with ⁴Joshua when they entered
on the possession of the nations, which God thrust
out before the face of our fathers, unto the days of
David; who found favour in the sight of God, and 46
asked to find a habitation for the God of Jacob. 47
But Solomon built him a house. Howbeit the Most 48
High dwelleth not in *houses* made with hands; as
saith the prophet,

> The heaven is my throne, 49
> And the earth the footstool of my feet:
> What manner of house will ye build me? saith
>   the Lord:
> Or what is the place of my rest?
> Did not my hand make all these things? 50

Ye stiffnecked and uncircumcised in heart and 51

---

1 Gr. *redeemer*.

2 Or, *as he raised up me*.

3 Or, *congregation*

4 Gr. *Jesus*.

ears, ye do always resist the Holy Ghost: as your fa-
52 thers did, so do ye. Which of the prophets did not your fathers persecute? and they killed them which shewed before of the coming of the Righteous One; of whom ye have now become betrayers and mur-
53 derers; ye who received the law ¹as it was ordained by angels, and kept it not.
54 Now when they heard these things, they were cut to the heart, and they gnashed on him with their
55 teeth. But he, being full of the Holy Ghost, looked up stedfastly into heaven, and saw the glory of God, and Jesus standing on the right hand of God,
56 and said, Behold, I see the heavens opened, and the Son of man standing on the right hand of God.
57 But they cried out with a loud voice, and stopped their ears, and rushed upon him with one accord;
58 and they cast him out of the city, and stoned him: and the witnesses laid down their garments at the
59 feet of a young man named Saul. And they stoned Stephen, calling upon *the Lord*, and saying, Lord
60 Jesus, receive my spirit. And he kneeled down, and cried with a loud voice, Lord, lay not this sin to their charge. And when he had said this, he fell
8 asleep. And Saul was consenting unto his death.

And there arose on that day a great persecution against the church which was in Jerusalem; and they were all scattered abroad throughout the regions of Judæa and Samaria, except the apostles.
2 And devout men buried Stephen, and made great
3 lamentation over him. But Saul laid waste the church, entering into every house, and haling men and women committed them to prison.
4 They therefore that were scattered abroad went
5 about preaching the word. And Philip went down to the city of Samaria, and proclaimed unto them
6 the Christ. And the multitudes gave heed with one accord unto the things that were spoken by Philip, when they heard, and saw the signs which
7 he did. ²For *from* many of those which had unclean spirits, they came out, crying with a loud voice: and many that were palsied, and that were
8 lame, were healed. And there was much joy in that city.
9 But there was a certain man, Simon by name, which beforetime in the city used sorcery, and amazed the ³people of Samaria, giving out that him-
10 self was some great one: to whom they all gave heed, from the least to the greatest, saying, This

¹ Or, *as the ordinance of angels* Gr. *unto ordinances of angels.*

² Or, *For many of those which had unclean spirits that cried with a loud voice came forth*

³ Gr. *nation.*

man is that power of God which is called Great. And they gave heed to him, because that of long time he had amazed them with his sorceries. But when they believed Philip preaching good tidings concerning the kingdom of God and the name of Jesus Christ, they were baptized, both men and women. And Simon also himself believed: and being baptized, he continued with Philip; and beholding signs and great ¹miracles wrought, he was amazed.

Now when the apostles which were at Jerusalem heard that Samaria had received the word of God, they sent unto them Peter and John: who, when they were come down, prayed for them, that they might receive the Holy Ghost: for as yet he was fallen* upon none of them: only they had been baptized into the name of the Lord Jesus. Then laid they their hands on them, and they received the Holy Ghost. Now when Simon saw that through the laying on of the apostles' hands the ²Holy Ghost was given, he offered them money, saying, Give me also this power, that on whomsoever I lay my hands, he may receive the Holy Ghost. But Peter said unto him, Thy silver perish with thee, because thou hast thought to obtain the gift of God with money. Thou hast neither part nor lot in this ³matter: for thy heart is not right before God. Repent therefore of this thy wickedness, and pray the Lord, if perhaps the thought of thy heart shall be forgiven thee. For I see that thou ⁴art in the gall of bitterness and in the bond of iniquity. And Simon answered and said, Pray ye for me to the Lord, that none of the things which ye have spoken come upon me.

They therefore, when they had testified and spoken the word of the Lord, returned to Jerusalem, and preached the gospel to many villages of the Samaritans.

But an angel of the Lord spake unto Philip, saying, Arise, and go ⁵toward the south unto the way that goeth down from Jerusalem unto Gaza: the same is desert. And he arose and went: and behold, a man of Ethiopia, a eunuch of great authority under Candace, queen of the Ethiopians, who was over all her treasure, who had come to Jerusalem for to worship; and he was returning and sitting in

---

1 Gr. *powers*.

2 Some ancient authorities omit *Holy*.

3 Gr. *word*.

4 Or, *wilt become gall* (or, *a gall root*) *of bitterness and a bond of iniquity*.

5 Or, *at noon*.

* For "he was fallen" read "it was fallen"—*Am. Com.*

his chariot, and was reading the prophet Isaiah. 29 And the Spirit said unto Philip, Go near, and join 30 thyself to this chariot. And Philip ran to him, and heard him reading Isaiah the prophet, and said, Un-31 derstandest thou what thou readest? And he said, How can I, except some one shall guide me? And he besought Philip to come up and sit with him. 32 Now the place of the scripture which he was reading was this,

> He was led as a sheep to the slaughter;
> And as a lamb before his shearer is dumb,
> So he openeth not his mouth:

33 In his humiliation his judgement was taken away:
> His generation who shall declare?
> For his life is taken from the earth.

34 And the eunuch answered Philip, and said, I pray thee, of whom speaketh the prophet this? of him-35 self, or of some other? And Philip opened his mouth, and beginning from this scripture, preached 36 unto him Jesus. And as they went on the way, they came unto a certain water; and the eunuch saith, Behold, *here is* water; what doth hinder me to 38 be baptized?[1] And he commanded the chariot to stand still: and they both went down into the water, both Philip and the eunuch; and he baptized him. 39 And when they came up out of the water, the Spirit of the Lord caught away Philip; and the eunuch saw him no more, for he went on his way rejoicing. 40 But Philip was found at Azotus: and passing through he preached the gospel to all the cities, till he came to Cæsarea.

9 But Saul, yet breathing threatening and slaughter against the disciples of the Lord, went unto the 2 high priest, and asked of him letters to Damascus unto the synagogues, that if he found any that were of the Way, whether men or women, he might bring 3 them bound to Jerusalem. And as he journeyed, it came to pass that he drew nigh unto Damascus: and suddenly there shone round about him a light 4 out of heaven: and he fell upon the earth, and heard a voice saying unto him, Saul, Saul, why persecutest 5 thou me? And he said, Who art thou, Lord? And 6 he *said*, I am Jesus whom thou persecutest: but rise, and enter into the city, and it shall be told thee 7 what thou must do. And the men that journeyed with him stood speechless, hearing the [2]voice, but 8 beholding no man. And Saul arose from the earth;

[1] Some ancient authorities insert, wholly or in part, ver. 37 *And Philip said, If thou believest with all thy heart, thou mayest. And he answered and said, I believe that Jesus Christ is the Son of God.*

[2] Or, *sound*

and when his eyes were opened, he saw nothing; and they led him by the hand, and brought him into Damascus. And he was three days without 9 sight, and did neither eat nor drink.

Now there was a certain disciple at Damascus, 10 named Ananias; and the Lord said unto him in a vision, Ananias. And he said, Behold, I *am here*, Lord. And the Lord *said* unto him, Arise, and go 11 to the street which is called Straight, and inquire in the house of Judas for one named Saul, a man of Tarsus: for behold, he prayeth; and he hath seen a 12 man named Ananias coming in, and laying his hands on him, that he might receive his sight. But Ana- 13 nias answered, Lord, I have heard from many of this man, how much evil he did to thy saints at Jerusalem: and here he hath authority from the chief 14 priests to bind all that call upon thy name. But 15 the Lord said unto him, Go thy way: for he is a [1]chosen vessel unto me, to bear my name before the Gentiles and kings, and the children of Israel: for I 16 will shew him how many things he must suffer for my name's sake. And Ananias departed, and en- 17 tered into the house; and laying his hands on him said, Brother Saul, the Lord, *even* Jesus, who appeared unto thee in the way which thou camest, hath sent me, that thou mayest receive thy sight, and be filled with the Holy Ghost. And straight- 18 way there fell from his eyes as it were scales, and he received his sight; and he arose and was baptized; and he took food and was strengthened. 19

And he was certain days with the disciples which were at Damascus. And straightway in the syna- 20 gogues he proclaimed Jesus, that he is the Son of God. And all that heard him were amazed, and 21 said, Is not this he that in Jerusalem made havock of them which called on this name? and he had come hither for this intent, that he might bring them bound before the chief priests. But Saul increased 22 the more in strength, and confounded the Jews which dwelt at Damascus, proving that this is the Christ.

And when many days were fulfilled, the Jews 23 took counsel together to kill him: but their plot be- 24 came known to Saul. And they watched the gates also day and night that they might kill him: but 25 his disciples took him by night, and let him down through the wall, lowering him in a basket.

And when he was come to Jerusalem, he assayed 26

---

[1] Gr. *vessel of election*.

to join himself to the disciples: and they were all afraid of him, not believing that he was a disciple. 27 But Barnabas took him, and brought him to the apostles, and declared unto them how he had seen the Lord in the way, and that he had spoken to him, and how at Damascus he had preached boldly 28 in the name of Jesus. And he was with them go-29 ing in and going out at Jerusalem, preaching boldly in the name of the Lord: and he spake and disputed against the ¹Grecian Jews; but they went 30 about to kill him. And when the brethren knew it, they brought him down to Cæsarea, and sent him forth to Tarsus.

31 So the church throughout all Judæa and Galilee and Samaria had peace, being ²edified; and, walking ³in the fear of the Lord and ³in the comfort of the Holy Ghost, was multiplied.

32 And it came to pass, as Peter went throughout all parts, he came down also to the saints which dwelt 33 at Lydda. And there he found a certain man named Æneas, which had kept his bed eight years; 34 for he was palsied. And Peter said unto him, Æneas, Jesus Christ healeth thee: arise, and make 35 thy bed. And straightway he arose. And all that dwelt at Lydda and in Sharon saw him, and they turned to the Lord.

36 Now there was at Joppa a certain disciple named Tabitha, which by interpretation is called ⁴Dorcas: this woman was full of good works and almsdeeds 37 which she did. And it came to pass in those days, that she fell sick, and died: and when they had washed her, they laid her in an upper chamber. 38 And as Lydda was nigh unto Joppa, the disciples, hearing that Peter was there, sent two men unto him, intreating him, Delay not to come on unto us. 39 And Peter arose and went with them. And when he was come, they brought him into the upper chamber: and all the widows stood by him weeping, and shewing the coats and garments which 40 Dorcas made, while she was with them. But Peter put them all forth, and kneeled down, and prayed; and turning to the body, he said, Tabitha, arise. And she opened her eyes; and when she saw Peter, 41 she sat up. And he gave her his hand, and raised her up; and calling the saints and widows, he pre-42 sented her alive. And it became known through-43 out all Joppa: and many believed on the Lord. And it came to pass, that he abode many days in Joppa with one Simon a tanner.

1 Gr. *Hellenists*.

2 Gr. *builded up*.
3 Or, *by*

4 That is, *Gazelle*.

Now *there was* a certain man in Cæsarea, Cornelius by name, a centurion of the band called the Italian ¹band, a devout man, and one that feared God with all his house, who gave much alms to the people, and prayed to God alway. He saw in a vision openly, as it were about the ninth hour of the day, an angel of God coming in unto him, and saying to him, Cornelius. And he, fastening his eyes upon him, and being affrighted, said, What is it, Lord? And he said unto him, Thy prayers and thine alms are gone up for a memorial before God. And now send men to Joppa, and fetch one Simon, who is surnamed Peter: he lodgeth with one Simon a tanner, whose house is by the sea side. And when the angel that spake unto him was departed, he called two of his household-servants, and a devout soldier of them that waited on him continually; and having rehearsed all things unto them, he sent them to Joppa.

Now on the morrow, as they were on their journey, and drew nigh unto the city, Peter went up upon the housetop to pray, about the sixth hour: and he became hungry, and desired to eat: but while they made ready, he fell into a trance; and he beholdeth the heaven opened, and a certain vessel descending, as it were a great sheet, let down by four corners upon the earth: wherein were all manner of fourfooted beasts and creeping things of the earth and fowls of the heaven. And there came a voice to him, Rise, Peter; kill and eat. But Peter said, Not so, Lord; for I have never eaten any thing that is common and unclean. And a voice *came* unto him again the second time, What God hath cleansed, make not thou common. And this was done thrice: and straightway the vessel was received up into heaven.

Now while Peter was much perplexed in himself what the vision which he had seen might mean, behold, the men that were sent by Cornelius, having made inquiry for Simon's house, stood before the gate, and called and asked whether Simon, which was surnamed Peter, were lodging there. And while Peter thought on the vision, the Spirit said unto him, Behold, three men seek thee. But arise, and get thee down, and go with them, nothing doubting: for I have sent them. And Peter went down to the men, and said, Behold, I am he whom ye seek: what is the cause wherefore ye are come? And

¹ Or, *cohort*

they said, Cornelius a centurion, a righteous man and one that feareth God, and well reported of by all the nation of the Jews, was warned *of God* by a holy angel to send for thee into his house, and to 23 hear words from thee. So he called them in and lodged them.

And on the morrow he arose and went forth with them, and certain of the brethren from Joppa ac-24 companied him. And on the morrow ¹they entered into Cæsarea. And Cornelius was waiting for them, having called together his kinsmen and his near 25 friends. And when it came to pass that Peter entered, Cornelius met him, and fell down at his feet, 26 and worshipped him. But Peter raised him up, 27 saying, Stand up; I myself also am a man. And as he talked with him, he went in, and findeth 28 many come together: and he said unto them, Ye yourselves know ²how that it is an unlawful thing for a man that is a Jew to join himself or come unto one of another nation; and *yet* unto me hath God shewed that I should not call any man com-29 mon or unclean: wherefore also I came without gainsaying, when I was sent for. I ask therefore 30 with what intent ye sent for me. And Cornelius said, Four days ago, until this hour, I was keeping the ninth hour of prayer in my house; and behold, 31 a man stood before me in bright apparel, and saith, Cornelius, thy prayer is heard, and thine alms are 32 had in remembrance in the sight of God. Send therefore to Joppa, and call unto thee Simon, who is surnamed Peter; he lodgeth in the house of Si-33 mon a tanner, by the sea side. Forthwith therefore I sent to thee; and thou hast well done that thou art come. Now therefore we are all here present in the sight of God, to hear all things that have been 34 commanded thee of the Lord. And Peter opened his mouth, and said,

Of a truth I perceive that God is no respecter of 35 persons: but in every nation he that feareth him, and worketh righteousness, is acceptable to him. 36 ³The word which he sent unto the children of Israel, preaching ⁴good tidings of peace by Jesus Christ 37 (he is Lord of all)—that saying ye yourselves know, which was published throughout all Judæa, beginning from Galilee, after the baptism which John 38 preached; *even* Jesus of Nazareth, how that God anointed him with the Holy Ghost and with power: who went about doing good, and healing all that

¹ Some ancient authorities read *he.*

² Or, *how unlawful it is for a man &c.*

³ Many ancient authorities read *He sent the word unto.*
⁴ Or, *the gospel*

were oppressed of the devil; for God was with him. And we are witnesses of all things which he did both in the country of the Jews, and in Jerusalem; whom also they slew, hanging him on a tree. Him God raised up the third day, and gave him to be made manifest, not to all the people, but unto witnesses that were chosen before of God, *even* to us, who did eat and drink with him after he rose from the dead. And he charged us to preach unto the people, and to testify that this is he which is ordained of God *to be* the Judge of quick and dead. To him bear all the prophets witness, that through his name every one that believeth on him shall receive remission of sins.

While Peter yet spake these words, the Holy Ghost fell on all them which heard the word. And they of the circumcision which believed were amazed, as many as came with Peter, because that on the Gentiles also was poured out the gift of the Holy Ghost. For they heard them speak with tongues, and magnify God. Then answered Peter, Can any man forbid the water, that these should not be baptized, which have received the Holy Ghost as well as we? And he commanded them to be baptized in the name of Jesus Christ. Then prayed they him to tarry certain days.

Now the apostles and the brethren that were in Judæa heard that the Gentiles also had received the word of God. And when Peter was come up to Jerusalem, they that were of the circumcision contended with him, saying, Thou wentest in to men uncircumcised, and didst eat with them. But Peter began, and expounded *the matter* unto them in order, saying, I was in the city of Joppa praying: and in a trance I saw a vision, a certain vessel descending, as it were a great sheet let down from heaven by four corners; and it came even unto me: upon the which when I had fastened mine eyes, I considered, and saw the fourfooted beasts of the earth and wild beasts and creeping things and fowls of the heaven. And I heard also a voice saying unto me, Rise, Peter; kill and eat. But I said, Not so, Lord: for nothing common or unclean hath ever entered into my mouth. But a voice answered the second time out of heaven, What God hath cleansed, make not thou common. And this was done thrice: and all were drawn up again into heaven. And behold, forthwith three men stood before

the house in which we were, having been sent from
12 Cæsarea unto me. And the Spirit bade me go with
them, making no distinction. And these six brethren also accompanied me; and we entered into the
13 man's house: and he told us how he had seen the
angel standing in his house, and saying, Send to
Joppa, and fetch Simon, whose surname is Peter;
14 who shall speak unto thee words, whereby thou
15 shalt be saved, thou and all thy house. And as I
began to speak, the Holy Ghost fell on them, even
16 as on us at the beginning. And I remembered the
word of the Lord, how that he said, John indeed
baptized with water; but ye shall be baptized [1]with
17 the Holy Ghost. If then God gave unto them the
like gift as *he did* also unto us, when we believed
on the Lord Jesus Christ, who was I, that I could
18 withstand God? And when they heard these things,
they held their peace, and glorified God, saying,
Then to the Gentiles also hath God granted repentance unto life.
19 They therefore that were scattered abroad upon
the tribulation that arose about Stephen travelled as
far as Phœnicia, and Cyprus, and Antioch, speaking
20 the word to none save only to Jews. But there were
some of them, men of Cyprus and Cyrene, who,
when they were come to Antioch, spake unto the
21 [2]Greeks also, preaching the Lord Jesus. And the
hand of the Lord was with them: and a great num-
22 ber that believed turned unto the Lord. And the
report concerning them came to the ears of the
church which was in Jerusalem: and they sent forth
23 Barnabas as far as Antioch: who, when he was
come, and had seen the grace of God, was glad; and
he exhorted them all, [3]that with purpose of heart
24 they would cleave unto the Lord: for he was a good
man, and full of the Holy Ghost and of faith: and
25 much people was added unto the Lord. And he
26 went forth to Tarsus to seek for Saul: and when he
had found him, he brought him unto Antioch. And
it came to pass, that even for a whole year they were
gathered together [4]with the church, and taught
much people; and that the disciples were called
Christians first in Antioch.
27 Now in these days there came down prophets
28 from Jerusalem unto Antioch. And there stood up
one of them named Agabus, and signified by the
Spirit that there should be a great famine over all
[5]the world: which came to pass in the days of

[1] Or, *in*
[2] Many ancient authorities read *Grecian Jews.*
[3] Some ancient authorities read *that they would cleave unto the purpose of their heart in the Lord.*
[4] Gr. *in.*
[5] Gr. *the inhabited earth.*

Claudius. And the disciples, every man according 29 to his ability, determined to send ¹relief unto the brethren that dwelt in Judæa: which also they did, 30 sending it to the elders by the hand of Barnabas and Saul.

Now about that time Herod the king put forth 12 his hands to afflict certain of the church. And he killed James the brother of John with the sword. 2 And when he saw that it pleased the Jews, he proceeded to seize Peter also. And *those* were the days 3 of unleavened bread. And when he had taken him, he put him in prison, and delivered him to four 4 quaternions of soldiers to guard him; intending after the passover to bring him forth to the people. Peter therefore was kept in the prison: but prayer was made earnestly of the church unto God for 5 him. And when Herod was about to bring him forth, the same night Peter was sleeping between 6 two soldiers, bound with two chains: and guards before the door kept the prison. And behold, an 7 angel of the Lord stood by him, and a light shined in the cell: and he smote Peter on the side, and awoke him, saying, Rise up quickly. And his chains fell off from his hands. And the angel said 8 unto him, Gird thyself, and bind on thy sandals. And he did so. And he saith unto him, Cast thy garment about thee, and follow me. And he went 9 out, and followed; and he wist not that it was true which was done ²by the angel, but thought he saw a vision. And when they were past the first and the 10 second ward, they came unto the iron gate that leadeth into the city; which opened to them of its own accord: and they went out, and passed on through one street; and straightway the angel departed from him. And when Peter was come to himself, he said, 11 Now I know of a truth, that the Lord hath sent forth his angel and delivered me out of the hand of Herod, and from all the expectation of the people of the Jews. And when he had considered *the thing*, he 12 came to the house of Mary the mother of John whose surname was Mark; where many were gathered together and were praying. And when he 13 knocked at the door of the gate, a maid came to answer, named Rhoda. And when she knew Peter's 14 voice, she opened not the gate for joy, but ran in, and told that Peter stood before the gate. And 15 they said unto her, Thou art mad. But she confidently affirmed that it was even so. And they said, 16

¹ Gr. *for ministry.*

² Or, *through*

It is his angel. But Peter continued knocking: and when they had opened, they saw him, and were
17 amazed. But he, beckoning unto them with the hand to hold their peace, declared unto them how the Lord had brought him forth out of the prison. And he said, Tell these things unto James, and to the brethren. And he departed, and went to an-
18 other place. Now as soon as it was day, there was no small stir among the soldiers, what was become
19 of Peter. And when Herod had sought for him, and found him not, he examined the guards, and commanded that they should be ¹put to death. And he went down from Judæa to Cæsarea, and tarried there.

¹ Gr. *led away to death.*

20 Now he was highly displeased with them of Tyre and Sidon: and they came with one accord to him, and, having made Blastus the king's chamberlain their friend, they asked for peace, because their
21 country was fed from the king's country. And upon a set day Herod arrayed himself in royal apparel, and sat on the ²throne, and made an oration
22 unto them. And the people shouted, *saying*, The
23 voice of a god, and not of a man. And immediately an angel of the Lord smote him, because he gave not God the glory: and he was eaten of worms, and gave up the ghost.

² Or, *judgement-seat*

24 But the word of God grew and multiplied.
25 And Barnabas and Saul returned ³from Jerusalem, when they had fulfilled their ministration, taking with them John whose surname was Mark.

³ Many ancient authorities read *to Jerusalem.*

13 Now there were at Antioch, in the church that was *there*, prophets and teachers, Barnabas, and Symeon that was called Niger, and Lucius of Cyrene, and Manaen the foster-brother of Herod the
2 tetrarch, and Saul. And as they ministered to the Lord, and fasted, the Holy Ghost said, Separate me Barnabas and Saul for the work whereunto I have
3 called them. Then, when they had fasted and prayed and laid their hands on them, they sent them away.
4 So they, being sent forth by the Holy Ghost, went down to Seleucia; and from thence they sail-
5 ed to Cyprus. And when they were at Salamis, they proclaimed the word of God in the synagogues of the Jews: and they had also John as their at-
6 tendant. And when they had gone through the whole island unto Paphos, they found a certain ⁴sorcerer, a false prophet, a Jew, whose name was

⁴ Gr. *Magus:* as in Matt. ii. 1, 7, 16.

Bar-Jesus; which was with the proconsul, Sergius 7
Paulus, a man of understanding. The same called
unto him Barnabas and Saul, and sought to hear
the word of God. But Elymas the ¹sorcerer (for 8.
so is his name by interpretation) withstood them,
seeking to turn aside the proconsul from the faith.
But Saul, who is also *called* Paul, filled with the 9
Holy Ghost, fastened his eyes on him, and said, O 10
full of all guile and all villany, thou son of the
devil, thou enemy of all righteousness, wilt thou
not cease to pervert the right ways of the Lord?
And now, behold, the hand of the Lord is upon 11
thee, and thou shalt be blind, not seeing the sun
²for a season. And immediately there fell on him
a mist and a darkness; and he went about seeking
some to lead him by the hand. Then the procon- 12
sul, when he saw what was done, believed, being
astonished at the teaching of the Lord.

Now Paul and his company set sail from Paphos, 13
and came to Perga in Pamphylia: and John departed from them and returned to Jerusalem. But they, 14
passing through from Perga, came to Antioch of
Pisidia; and they went into the synagogue on the
sabbath day, and sat down. And after the reading 15
of the law and the prophets the rulers of the synagogue sent unto them, saying, Brethren, if ye have
any word of exhortation for the people, say on.
And Paul stood up, and beckoning with the hand 16
said,

Men of Israel, and ye that fear God, hearken.
The God of this people Israel chose our fathers, and 17
exalted the people when they sojourned in the land
of Egypt, and with a high arm led he them forth
out of it. And for about the time of forty years 18
³suffered he their manners* in the wilderness. And 19
when he had destroyed seven nations in the land of
Canaan, he gave *them* their land for an inheritance,
for about four hundred and fifty years: and after 20
these things he gave *them* judges until Samuel the
prophet. And afterward they asked for a king: 21
and God gave unto them Saul the son of Kish, a man
of the tribe of Benjamin, for the space of forty years.
And when he had removed him, he raised up David 22
to be their king; to whom also he bare witness, and
said, I have found David the son of Jesse, a man

---

1 Gr. *Magus*: as in Matt. ii. 1, 7, 16.

2 Or, *until*

3 Many ancient authorities read *bare he them as a nursing-father in the wilderness.* See Deut. i. 31.

* For "suffered he their manners" read "as a nursing-father bare he them", and in the marg. read "Many ancient authorities read *suffered he their manners*"—*Am. Com.*

23 after my heart, who shall do all my ¹will. Of this
man's seed hath God according to promise brought
24 unto Israel a Saviour, Jesus; when John had first
preached ²before his coming the baptism of repent-
25 ance to all the people of Israel. And as John was
fulfilling his course, he said, What suppose ye that
I am? I am not *he*. But behold, there cometh one
after me, the shoes of whose feet I am not worthy
26 to unloose. Brethren, children of the stock of
Abraham, and those among you that fear God, to us
27 is the word of this salvation sent forth. For they
that dwell in Jerusalem, and their rulers, because
they knew him not, nor the voices of the prophets
which are read every sabbath, fulfilled *them* by con-
28 demning *him*. And though they found no cause of
death *in him*, yet asked they of Pilate that he should
29 be slain. And when they had fulfilled all things
that were written of him, they took him down from
30 the tree, and laid him in a tomb. But God raised
31 him from the dead: and he was seen for many days
of them that came up with him from Galilee to Jerusalem, who are now his witnesses unto the people.
32 And we bring you good tidings of the promise
33 made unto the fathers, how that God hath fulfilled
the same unto our children, in that he raised up
Jesus; as also it is written in the second psalm,
Thou art my Son, this day have I begotten thee.
34 And as concerning that he raised him up from the
dead, now no more to return to corruption, he hath
spoken on this wise, I will give you the holy and
35 sure *blessings* of David. Because he saith also in
another *psalm*, Thou wilt not give thy Holy One to
36 see corruption. For David, after he had ³in his
own generation served the counsel of God, fell on
sleep, and was laid unto his fathers, and saw cor-
37 ruption: but he whom God raised up saw no cor-
38 ruption. Be it known unto you therefore, brethren,
that through this man is proclaimed unto you re-
39 mission of sins: and by him every one that believeth is justified from all things, from which ye
40 could not be justified by the law of Moses. Beware
therefore, lest that come upon *you*, which is spoken
in the prophets;
41 Behold, ye despisers, and wonder, and ⁴perish;
 For I work a work in your days,
 A work which ye shall in no wise believe, if
  one declare it unto you.
42 And as they went out, they besought that these

¹ Gr. *wills*.

² Gr. *before the face of his entering in.*

³ Or, *served his own generation by the counsel of God, fell on sleep.*
Or, *served his own generation, fell on sleep by the counsel of God*

⁴ Or, *vanish away*

words might be spoken to them the next sabbath. Now when the synagogue broke up, many of the 43 Jews and of the devout proselytes followed Paul and Barnabas: who, speaking to them, urged them to continue in the grace of God.

And the next sabbath almost the whole city was 44 gathered together to hear the word of ¹God. But 45 when the Jews saw the multitudes, they were filled with jealousy, and contradicted the things which were spoken by Paul, and ²blasphemed. And Paul 46 and Barnabas spake out boldly, and said, It was necessary that the word of God should first be spoken to you. Seeing ye thrust it from you, and judge yourselves unworthy of eternal life, lo, we turn to the Gentiles. For so hath the Lord com- 47 manded us, *saying*,

I have set thee for a light of the Gentiles,
That thou shouldest be for salvation unto the uttermost part of the earth.

And as the Gentiles heard this, they were glad, and 48 glorified the word of ¹God: and as many as were ordained to eternal life believed. And the word of 49 the Lord was spread abroad throughout all the region. But the Jews urged on the devout women of 50 honourable estate, and the chief men of the city, and stirred up a persecution against Paul and Barnabas, and cast them out of their borders. But 51 they shook off the dust of their feet against them, and came unto Iconium. And the disciples were 52 filled with joy and with the Holy Ghost.

And it came to pass in Iconium, that they en- **14** tered together into the synagogue of the Jews, and so spake, that a great multitude both of Jews and of Greeks believed. But the Jews that were diso- 2 bedient stirred up the souls of the Gentiles, and made them evil affected against the brethren. Long 3 time therefore they tarried *there* speaking boldly in the Lord, which bare witness unto the word of his grace, granting signs and wonders to be done by their hands. But the multitude of the city was di- 4 vided; and part held with the Jews, and part with the apostles. And when there was made an onset 5 both of the Gentiles and of the Jews with their rulers, to entreat them shamefully, and to stone them, they became aware of it, and fled unto the 6 cities of Lycaonia, Lystra and Derbe, and the region round about: and there they preached the 7 gospel.

¹ Many ancient authorities read *the Lord*.

² Or, *railed*.

8 And at Lystra there sat a certain man, impotent in his feet, a cripple from his mother's womb, who
9 never had walked. The same heard Paul speaking: who, fastening his eyes upon him, and seeing
10 that he had faith to be ¹made whole*, said with a loud voice, Stand upright on thy feet. And he
11 leaped up and walked. And when the multitudes saw what Paul had done, they lifted up their voice, saying in the speech of Lycaonia, The gods are
12 come down to us in the likeness of men. And they called Barnabas, ²Jupiter; and Paul, ³Mercury, be-
13 cause he was the chief speaker. And the priest of ²Jupiter whose *temple* was before the city, brought oxen and garlands unto the gates, and would have
14 done sacrifice with the multitudes. But when the apostles, Barnabas and Paul, heard of it, they rent their garments, and sprang forth among the multi-
15 tude, crying out and saying, Sirs, why do ye these things? We also are men of like ⁴passions with you, and bring you good tidings, that ye should turn from these vain things unto the living God, who made the heaven and the earth and the sea, and
16 all that in them is: who in the generations gone by suffered all the nations to walk in their own ways.
17 And yet he left not himself without witness, in that he did good, and gave you from heaven rains and fruitful seasons, filling your hearts with food and
18 gladness. And with these sayings scarce restrained they the multitudes from doing sacrifice unto them.
19 But there came Jews thither from Antioch and Iconium: and having persuaded the multitudes, they stoned Paul, and dragged him out of the city, sup-
20 posing that he was dead. But as the disciples stood round about him, he rose up, and entered into the city: and on the morrow he went forth with Barnabas
21 to Derbe. And when they had preached the gospel to that city, and had made many disciples, they returned to Lystra, and to Iconium, and to Antioch,
22 confirming the souls of the disciples, exhorting them to continue in the faith, and that through many tribulations we must enter into the kingdom of God.
23 And when they had appointed for them elders in every church, and had prayed with fasting, they commended them to the Lord, on whom they had
24 believed. And they passed through Pisidia, and
25 came to Pamphylia. And when they had spoken

1 Or, *saved*
2 Gr. *Zeus.*
3 Gr. *Hermes.*
4 Or, *nature*

---

* "made whole" omit marg. ¹—*Am. Com.*

the word in Perga, they went down to Attalia; and 26
thence they sailed to Antioch, from whence they
had been committed to the grace of God for the
work which they had fulfilled. And when they 27
were come, and had gathered the church together,
they rehearsed all things that God had done with
them, and how that he had opened a door of faith
unto the Gentiles. And they tarried no little time 28
with the disciples.

And certain men came down from Judæa and **15**
taught the brethren, *saying*, Except ye be circumcised after the custom of Moses, ye cannot be saved.
And when Paul and Barnabas had no small dissension 2
and questioning with them, *the brethren* appointed
that Paul and Barnabas, and certain other of them,
should go up to Jerusalem unto the apostles and elders
about this question. They therefore, being 3
brought on their way by the church, passed through
both Phœnicia and Samaria, declaring the conversion
of the Gentiles: and they caused great joy unto
all the brethren. And when they were come to Jerusalem, 4
they were received of the church and the
apostles and the elders, and they rehearsed all things
that God had done with them. But there rose up 5
certain of the sect of the Pharisees who believed,
saying, It is needful to circumcise them, and to charge
them to keep the law of Moses.

And the apostles and the elders were gathered together 6
to consider of this matter. And when there 7
had been much questioning, Peter rose up, and said
unto them,

¹ Gr. *from early days*.

Brethren, ye know how that ¹a good while ago
God made choice among you, that by my mouth the
Gentiles should hear the word of the gospel, and believe.
And God, which knoweth the heart, bare 8
them witness, giving them the Holy Ghost, even as
he did unto us; and he made no distinction between 9
us and them, cleansing their hearts by faith. Now 10
therefore why tempt ye God, that ye should put a
yoke upon the neck of the disciples, which neither
our fathers nor we were able to bear? But we believe 11
that we shall be saved through the grace of the
Lord Jesus, in like manner as they.

And all the multitude kept silence; and they 12
hearkened unto Barnabas and Paul rehearsing what
signs and wonders God had wrought among the Gentiles
by them. And after they had held their peace, 13
James answered, saying,

14 Brethren, hearken unto me: Symeon hath rehearsed how first God did visit the Gentiles, to take
15 out of them a people for his name. And to this agree the words of the prophets; as it is written,
16 After these things I will return,
And I will build again the tabernacle of David, which is fallen;
And I will build again the ruins thereof,
And I will set it up:
17 That the residue of men may seek after the Lord,
And all the Gentiles, upon whom my name is called,
18 Saith the Lord,[1] who maketh these things known from the beginning of the world*.
19 Wherefore my judgement is, that we trouble not them which from among the Gentiles turn to God;
20 but that we [2] write unto them, that they abstain from the pollutions of idols, and from fornication, and
21 from what is strangled, and from blood. For Moses from generations of old hath in every city them that preach him, being read in the synagogues every sabbath.
22 Then it seemed good to the apostles and the elders, with the whole church, to choose men out of their company, and send them to Antioch with Paul and Barnabas; *namely*, Judas called Barsabbas, and
23 Silas, chief men among the brethren: and they wrote *thus* by them, The apostles and the elder brethren† unto the brethren which are of the Gentiles in An-
24 tioch and Syria and Cilicia, greeting: Forasmuch as we have heard that certain [3] which went out from us have troubled you with words, subverting your
25 souls; to whom we gave no commandment; it seemed good unto us, having come to one accord, to choose out men and send them unto you with
26 our beloved Barnabas and Paul, men that have hazarded their lives for the name of our Lord Jesus
27 Christ. We have sent therefore Judas and Silas, who themselves also shall tell you the same things
28 by word of mouth. For it seemed good to the Holy Ghost, and to us, to lay upon you no greater burden
29 than these necessary things; that ye abstain from

[1] Or, *who doeth these things* which were *known*

[2] Or, *enjoin them*

[3] Some ancient authorities omit *which went out.*

---

* For "from the beginning of the world" read "from of old"—*Am. Com.*
† For "The apostles and the elder brethren" read "The apostles and the elders, brethren," and put the present text into the marg.—*Am. Com.*

things sacrificed to idols, and from blood, and from things strangled, and from fornication; from which if ye keep yourselves, it shall be well with you. Fare ye well.

30 So they, when they were dismissed, came down to Antioch; and having gathered the multitude together, they delivered the epistle. 31 And when they had read it, they rejoiced for the [1]consolation. 32 And Judas and Silas, being themselves also prophets, [2]exhorted the brethren with many words, and confirmed them. 33 And after they had spent some time *there*, they were dismissed in peace from the brethren unto those that had sent them forth[3]. 35 But Paul and Barnabas tarried in Antioch, teaching and preaching the word of the Lord, with many others also.

36 And after some days Paul said unto Barnabas, Let us return now and visit the brethren in every city wherein we proclaimed the word of the Lord, *and see* how they fare. 37 And Barnabas was minded to take with them John also, who was called Mark. 38 But Paul thought not good to take with them him who withdrew from them from Pamphylia, and went not with them to the work. 39 And there arose a sharp contention, so that they parted asunder one from the other, and Barnabas took Mark with him, and sailed away unto Cyprus; 40 but Paul chose Silas, and went forth, being commended by the brethren to the grace of the Lord. 41 And he went through Syria and Cilicia, confirming the churches.

16 And he came also to Derbe and to Lystra: and behold, a certain disciple was there, named Timothy, the son of a Jewess which believed; but his father was a Greek. 2 The same was well reported of by the brethren that were at Lystra and Iconium. 3 Him would Paul have to go forth with him; and he took and circumcised him because of the Jews that were in those parts: for they all knew that his father was a Greek. 4 And as they went on their way through the cities, they delivered them the decrees for to keep, which had been ordained of the apostles and elders that were at Jerusalem. 5 So the churches were strengthened in the faith, and increased in number daily.

6 And they went through the region of Phrygia and Galatia, having been forbidden of the Holy Ghost to speak the word in Asia; 7 and when they were come over against Mysia, they assayed to go into Bithynia; and the Spirit of Jesus suffered them

---

[1] Or, *exhortation*.
[2] Or, *comforted*.
[3] Some ancient authorities insert, with variations, ver. 34 *But it seemed good unto Silas to abide there*.

8 not; and passing by Mysia, they came down to Troas.
9 And a vision appeared to Paul in the night; There was a man of Macedonia standing, beseeching him, and saying, Come over into Macedonia, and help us.
10 And when he had seen the vision, straightway we sought to go forth into Macedonia, concluding that God had called us for to preach the gospel unto them.
11 Setting sail therefore from Troas, we made a straight course to Samothrace, and the day follow-
12 ing to Neapolis; and from thence to Philippi, which is a city of Macedonia, the first of the district, a *Roman* colony: and we were in this city tarrying
13 certain days. And on the sabbath day we went forth without the gate by a river side, where we supposed there was a place of prayer; and we sat down, and spake unto the women which were come
14 together. And a certain woman named Lydia, a seller of purple, of the city of Thyatira, one that worshipped God, heard us: whose heart the Lord opened, to give heed unto the things which were
15 spoken by Paul. And when she was baptized, and her household, she besought us, saying, If ye have judged me to be faithful to the Lord, come into my house, and abide *there*. And she constrained us.
16 And it came to pass, as we were going to the place of prayer, that a certain maid having ¹a spirit of divination met us, which brought her masters much
17 gain by soothsaying. The same following after Paul and us cried out, saying, These men are ²servants of the Most High God, which proclaim unto you ³the
18 way of salvation. And this she did for many days. But Paul, being sore troubled, turned and said to the spirit, I charge thee in the name of Jesus Christ to come out of her. And it came out that very hour.
19 But when her masters saw that the hope of their gain was ⁴gone, they laid hold on Paul and Silas, and dragged them into the marketplace before the rulers,
20 and when they had brought them unto the ⁵magistrates, they said, These men, being Jews, do exceed-
21 ingly trouble our city, and set forth customs which it is not lawful for us to receive, or to observe, being
22 Romans. And the multitude rose up together against them: and the ⁵magistrates rent their garments off
23 them, and commanded to beat them with rods. And when they had laid many stripes upon them, they cast them into prison, charging the jailor to keep
24 them safely: who, having received such a charge,

---

1 Gr. *a spirit, a Python.*

2 Gr. *bondservants.*

3 Or, *a way*

4 Gr. *come out.*

5 Gr. *prætors.*

cast them into the inner prison, and made their feet fast in the stocks. But about midnight Paul and Silas were praying and singing hymns unto God, and the prisoners were listening to them; and suddenly there was a great earthquake, so that the foundations of the prison-house were shaken: and immediately all the doors were opened; and every one's bands were loosed. And the jailor being roused out of sleep, and seeing the prison doors open, drew his sword, and was about to kill himself, supposing that the prisoners had escaped. But Paul cried with a loud voice, saying, Do thyself no harm: for we are all here. And he called for lights, and sprang in, and, trembling for fear, fell down before Paul and Silas, and brought them out, and said, Sirs, what must I do to be saved? And they said, Believe on the Lord Jesus, and thou shalt be saved, thou and thy house. And they spake the word of ¹the Lord unto him, with all that were in his house. And he took them the same hour of the night, and washed their stripes; and was baptized, he and all his, immediately. And he brought them up into his house, and set ²meat before them, and rejoiced greatly, with all his house, ³having believed in God.

But when it was day, the ⁴magistrates sent the ⁵serjeants, saying, Let those men go. And the jailor reported the words to Paul, *saying*, The ⁴magistrates have sent to let you go: now therefore come forth, and go in peace. But Paul said unto them, They have beaten us publicly, uncondemned, men that are Romans, and have cast us into prison; and do they now cast us out privily? nay verily; but let them come themselves and bring us out. And the ⁵serjeants reported these words unto the ⁴magistrates: and they feared, when they heard that they were Romans; and they came and besought them; and when they had brought them out, they asked them to go away from the city. And they went out of the prison, and entered into *the house of* Lydia: and when they had seen the brethren, they ⁶comforted them, and departed.

Now when they had passed through Amphipolis and Apollonia, they came to Thessalonica, where was a synagogue of the Jews: and Paul, as his custom was, went in unto them, and for three ⁷sabbath days reasoned with them from the scriptures, opening and alleging, that it behoved the Christ to suffer, and to rise again from the dead; and that this Jesus,

---

1 Some ancient authorities read *God*.

2 Gr. *a table.*
3 Or, *having believed God.*
4 Gr. *prætors.*
5 Gr. *lictors.*

6 Or, *exhorted*

7 Or, *weeks*

whom, *said he*, I proclaim unto you, is the Christ.
4 And some of them were persuaded, and consorted with Paul and Silas; and of the devout Greeks a great multitude, and of the chief women not a few.
5 But the Jews, being moved with jealousy, took unto them certain vile fellows of the rabble, and gathering a crowd, set the city on an uproar; and assaulting the house of Jason, they sought to bring them
6 forth to the people. And when they found them not, they dragged Jason and certain brethren before the rulers of the city, crying, These that have turned
7 ¹the world upside down are come hither also; whom Jason hath received: and these all act contrary to the decrees of Cæsar, saying that there is another
8 king, *one* Jesus. And they troubled the multitude and the rulers of the city, when they heard these
9 things. And when they had taken security from Jason and the rest, they let them go.
10 And the brethren immediately sent away Paul and Silas by night unto Berœa: who when they were come thither went into the synagogue of the
11 Jews. Now these were more noble than those in Thessalonica, in that they received the word with all readiness of mind, examining the scriptures daily,
12 whether these things were so. Many of them therefore believed; also of the Greek women of honour-
13 able estate, and of men, not a few. But when the Jews of Thessalonica had knowledge that the word of God was proclaimed of Paul at Berœa also, they came thither likewise, stirring up and troubling the
14 multitudes. And then immediately the brethren sent forth Paul to go as far as to the sea: and Silas
15 and Timothy abode there still. But they that conducted Paul brought him as far as Athens: and receiving a commandment unto Silas and Timothy that they should come to him with all speed, they departed.
16 Now while Paul waited for them at Athens, his spirit was provoked within him, as he beheld the
17 city full of idols. So he reasoned in the synagogue with the Jews and the devout persons, and in the
18 marketplace every day with them that met him. And certain also of the Epicurean and Stoic philosophers encountered him. And some said, What would this babbler say? other some, He seemeth to be a setter forth of strange ²gods: because he preached Jesus
19 and the resurrection. And they took hold of him, and brought him ³unto the ⁴Areopagus, saying, May

¹ Gr. *the inhabited earth.*

² Gr. *demons.*

³ Or, *before*

⁴ Or, *the hill of Mars*

we know what this new teaching is, which is spoken by thee? For thou bringest certain strange things to our ears: we would know therefore what these things mean. (Now all the Athenians and the strangers sojourning there ¹spent their time in nothing else, but either to tell or to hear some new thing.) And Paul stood in the midst of the Areopagus, and said,

Ye men of Athens, in all things I perceive that ye are somewhat ²superstitious*. For as I passed along, and observed the objects of your worship, I found also an altar with this inscription, ³TO AN UNKNOWN GOD. What therefore ye worship in ignorance, this set I forth unto you. The God that made the world and all things therein, he, being Lord of heaven and earth, dwelleth not in ⁴temples made with hands; neither is he served by men's hands, as though he needed anything, seeing he himself giveth to all life, and breath, and all things; and he made of one every nation of men for to dwell on all the face of the earth, having determined *their* appointed seasons, and the bounds of their habitation; that they should seek God, if haply they might feel after him, and find him, though he is not far from each one of us: for in him we live, and move, and have our being; as certain even of your own poets have said, For we are also his offspring. Being then the offspring of God, we ought not to think that ⁵the Godhead is like unto gold, or silver, or stone, graven by art and device of man. The times of ignorance therefore God overlooked; but now he ⁶commandeth men that they should all everywhere repent: inasmuch as he hath appointed a day, in the which he will judge ⁷the world in righteousness ⁸by ⁹the man whom he hath ordained; whereof he hath given assurance unto all men, in that he hath raised him from the dead.

Now when they heard of the resurrection of the dead, some mocked; but others said, We will hear thee concerning this yet again. Thus Paul went out from among them. But certain men clave unto him, and believed: among whom also was Dionysius the Areopagite, and a woman named Damaris, and others with them.

After these things he departed from Athens, and

---

1 Or, *had leisure for nothing else*
2 Or, *religious*.
3 Or, TO THE UNKNOWN GOD.
4 Or, *sanctuaries*
5 Or, *that which is divine*
6 Some ancient authorities read *declareth to men*.
7 Gr *the inhabited earth*.
8 Gr. *in*.
9 Or, *a man*

---

* For "somewhat superstitious" read "very religious' and put the present text in the marg.—*Am. Com.*

2 came to Corinth. And he found a certain Jew named Aquila, a man of Pontus by race, lately come from Italy, with his wife Priscilla, because Claudius had commanded all the Jews to depart from Rome: and
3 he came unto them; and because he was of the same trade, he abode with them, and they wrought; for
4 by their trade they were tentmakers. And he reasoned in the synagogue every sabbath, and ¹persuaded Jews and Greeks.

¹ Gr. *sought to persuade*.

5 But when Silas and Timothy came down from Macedonia, Paul was constrained by the word, testi-
6 fying to the Jews that Jesus was the Christ. And when they opposed themselves, and ²blasphemed, he shook out his raiment, and said unto them, Your blood *be* upon your own heads; I am clean: from
7 henceforth I will go unto the Gentiles. And he departed thence, and went into the house of a certain man named Titus Justus, one that worshipped God,
8 whose house joined hard to the synagogue. And Crispus, the ruler of the synagogue, ³believed in the Lord with all his house; and many of the Corin-
9 thians hearing believed, and were baptized. And the Lord said unto Paul in the night by a vision, Be not
10 afraid, but speak, and hold not thy peace: for I am with thee, and no man shall set on thee to harm
11 thee: for I have much people in this city. And he dwelt *there* a year and six months, teaching the word of God among them.

² Or, *railed*

³ Gr. *believed the Lord*.

12 But when Gallio was proconsul of Achaia, the Jews with one accord rose up against Paul, and
13 brought him before the judgement-seat, saying, This man persuadeth men to worship God contrary
14 to the law. But when Paul was about to open his mouth, Gallio said unto the Jews, If indeed it were a matter of wrong or of wicked villany, O ye Jews,
15 reason would that I should bear with you: but if they are questions about words and names and your own law, look to it yourselves; I am not minded to
16 be a judge of these matters. And he drave them
17 from the judgement-seat. And they all laid hold on Sosthenes, the ruler of the synagogue, and beat him before the judgement-seat. And Gallio cared for none of these things.
18 And Paul, having tarried after this yet many days, took his leave of the brethren, and sailed thence for Syria, and with him Priscilla and Aquila; having shorn his head in Cenchreæ: for he had a
19 vow. And they came to Ephesus, and he left them

there: but he himself entered into the synagogue, and reasoned with the Jews. And when they asked him to abide a longer time, he consented not; but taking his leave of them, and saying, I will return again unto you, if God will, he set sail from Ephesus. And when he had landed at Cæsarea, he went up and saluted the church, and went down to Antioch. And having spent some time *there*, he departed, and went through the region of Galatia and Phrygia in order, stablishing all the disciples.

Now a certain Jew named Apollos, an Alexandrian by race, ¹a learned man, came to Ephesus; and he was mighty in the scriptures. This man had been ²instructed in the way of the Lord; and being fervent in spirit, he spake and taught carefully the things concerning Jesus, knowing only the baptism of John: and he began to speak boldly in the synagogue. But when Priscilla and Aquila heard him, they took him unto them, and expounded unto him the way of God more carefully. And when he was minded to pass over into Achaia, the brethren encouraged him, and wrote to the disciples to receive him: and when he was come, he ³helped them much which had believed through grace: for he powerfully confuted the Jews, ⁴*and that* publicly, shewing by the scriptures that Jesus was the Christ.

And it came to pass, that, while Apollos was at Corinth, Paul having passed through the upper country came to Ephesus, and found certain disciples: and he said unto them, Did ye receive the Holy Ghost when ye believed? And they *said* unto him, Nay, we did not so much as hear whether ⁵the Holy Ghost was *given*. And he said, Into what then were ye baptized? And they said, Into John's baptism. And Paul said, John baptized with the baptism of repentance, saying unto the people, that they should believe on him which should come after him, that is, on Jesus. And when they heard this, they were baptized into the name of the Lord Jesus. And when Paul had laid his hands upon them, the Holy Ghost came on them; and they spake with tongues, and prophesied. And they were in all about twelve men.

And he entered into the synagogue, and spake boldly for the space of three months, reasoning and persuading *as to* the things concerning the kingdom of God. But when some were hardened and disobe-

---

Marginal notes:

1 Or, *an eloquent man*
2 Gr. *taught by word of mouth.*
3 Or, *helped much through grace them which had believed*
4 Or, *shewing publicly*
5 Or, *there is a Holy Ghost.*

dient, speaking evil of the Way before the multitude, he departed from them, and separated the disciples, reasoning daily in the school of Tyrannus.
10 And this continued for the space of two years; so that all they which dwelt in Asia heard the word
11 of the Lord, both Jews and Greeks. And God wrought special ¹miracles by the hands of Paul: 1 Gr. *powers.*
12 insomuch that unto the sick were carried away from his body handkerchiefs or aprons, and the diseases departed from them, and the evil spirits
13 went out. But certain also of the strolling Jews, exorcists, took upon them to name over them which had the evil spirits the name of the Lord Jesus, saying, I adjure you by Jesus whom Paul preach-
14 eth. And there were seven sons of one Sceva, a
15 Jew, a chief priest, which did this. And the evil spirit answered and said unto them, Jesus I ²know, 2 Or, *recognise*
16 and Paul I know; but who are ye? And the man in whom the evil spirit was leaped on them, and mastered both of them, and prevailed against them, so that they fled out of that house naked and
17 wounded. And this became known to all, both Jews and Greeks, that dwelt at Ephesus; and fear fell upon them all, and the name of the Lord Jesus
18 was magnified. Many also of them that had believed came, confessing, and declaring their deeds.
19 And not a few of them that practised ³curious arts 3 Or, *magical* brought their books together, and burned them in the sight of all: and they counted the price of them,
20 and found it fifty thousand pieces of silver. So mightily grew the word of the Lord and prevailed.
21 Now after these things were ended, Paul purposed in the spirit, when he had passed through Macedonia and Achaia, to go to Jerusalem, saying, After I have been there, I must also see Rome.
22 And having sent into Macedonia two of them that ministered unto him, Timothy and Erastus, he himself stayed in Asia for a while.
23 And about that time there arose no small stir con-
24 cerning the Way. For a certain man named Demetrius, a silversmith, which made silver shrines of ⁴Diana, brought no little business unto the crafts- 4 Gr. *Artemis.*
25 men; whom he gathered together, with the workmen of like occupation, and said, Sirs, ye know that
26 by this business we have our wealth. And ye see and hear, that not alone at Ephesus, but almost throughout all Asia, this Paul hath persuaded and turned away much people, saying that they be no

gods, which are made with hands: and not only is 27
there danger that this our trade come into disrepute; but also that the temple of the great goddess ¹Diana be made of no account, and that she should even be deposed from her magnificence, whom all Asia and ²the world worshippeth. And 28 when they heard this, they were filled with wrath, and cried out, saying, Great is ¹Diana of the Ephesians. And the city was filled with the confusion: 29 and they rushed with one accord into the theatre, having seized Gaius and Aristarchus, men of Macedonia, Paul's companions in travel. And when Paul 30 was minded to enter in unto the people, the disciples suffered him not. And certain also of the ³chief 31 officers of Asia*, being his friends, sent unto him, and besought him not to adventure himself into the theatre. Some therefore cried one thing, and some 32 another: for the assembly was in confusion; and the more part knew not wherefore they were come together. ⁴And they brought Alexander out of the 33 multitude, the Jews putting him forward. And Alexander beckoned with the hand, and would have made a defence unto the people. But when they 34 perceived that he was a Jew, all with one voice about the space of two hours cried out, Great is ¹Diana of the Ephesians. And when the townclerk 35 had quieted the multitude, he saith, Ye men of Ephesus, what man is there who knoweth not how that the city of the Ephesians is temple-keeper of the great ¹Diana, and of the *image* which fell down from ⁵Jupiter? Seeing then that these things can- 36 not be gainsaid, ye ought to be quiet, and to do nothing rash. For ye have brought *hither* these 37 men, which are neither robbers of temples nor blasphemers of our goddess. If therefore Demetrius, 38 and the craftsmen that are with him, have a matter against any man, ⁶the courts are open, and there are proconsuls: let them accuse one another. But if 39 ye seek anything about other matters, it shall be settled in the regular assembly. For indeed we are 40 in danger to be ⁷accused concerning this day's riot, there being no cause *for it*: and as touching it we shall not be able to give account of this concourse. And when he had thus spoken, he dismissed the as- 41 sembly.

1 Gr. *Artemis.*
2 Gr. *the inhabited earth.*
3 Gr. *Asiarchs.*
4 Or, *And some of the multitude instructed Alexander*
5 Or, *heaven.*
6 Or, *court days are kept*
7 Or, *accused of riot concerning this day*

---

* For "chief officers of Asia" read "Asiarchs" (with marg. i. e. officers having charge of festivals in the Roman province of Asia).—*Am. Com.*

20 And after the uproar was ceased, Paul having sent for the disciples and exhorted them, took leave of them, and departed for to go into Macedonia. 2 And when he had gone through those parts, and had given them much exhortation, he came into 3 Greece. And when he had spent three months *there*, and a plot was laid against him by the Jews, as he was about to set sail for Syria, he determined 4 to return through Macedonia. And there accompanied him ¹as far as Asia Sopater of Beroea, *the son* of Pyrrhus; and of the Thessalonians, Aristarchus and Secundus; and Gaius of Derbe, and Timothy; 5 and of Asia, Tychicus and Trophimus. But these ²had gone before, and were waiting for us at Troas. 6 And we sailed away from Philippi after the days of unleavened bread, and came unto them to Troas in five days; where we tarried seven days. 7 And upon the first day of the week, when we were gathered together to break bread, Paul discoursed with them, intending to depart on the morrow; and prolonged his speech until midnight. 8 And there were many lights in the upper chamber, 9 where we were gathered together. And there sat in the window a certain young man named Eutychus, borne down with deep sleep; and as Paul discoursed yet longer, being borne down by his sleep he fell down from the third story, and was taken up 10 dead. And Paul went down, and fell on him, and embracing him said, Make ye no ado; for his life is 11 in him. And when he was gone up, and had broken the bread, and eaten, and had talked with them a long while, even till break of day, so he departed. 12 And they brought the lad alive, and were not a little comforted.

13 But we, going before to the ship, set sail for Assos, there intending to take in Paul: for so had he 14 appointed, intending himself to go ³by land. And when he met us at Assos, we took him in, and came 15 to Mitylene. And sailing from thence, we came the following day over against Chios; and the next day we touched at Samos; and ⁴the day after we 16 came to Miletus. For Paul had determined to sail past Ephesus, that he might not have to spend time in Asia; for he was hastening, if it were possible for him, to be at Jerusalem the day of Pentecost.

17 And from Miletus he sent to Ephesus, and called 18 to him the ⁵elders of the church. And when they were come to him, he said unto them,

---

1 Many ancient authorities omit *as far as Asia*.

2 Many ancient authorities read *came, and were waiting*.

3 Or, *on foot*.

4 Many ancient authorities insert *having tarried at Trogyllium*.

5 Or, *presbyters*.

Ye yourselves know, from the first day that I set foot in Asia, after what manner I was with you all the time, serving the Lord with all lowliness of mind, and with tears, and with trials which befell me by the plots of the Jews: how that I shrank not from declaring unto you anything that was profitable, and teaching you publicly, and from house to house, testifying both to Jews and to Greeks repentance toward God, and faith toward our Lord Jesus ¹Christ. And now, behold, I go bound in the spirit unto Jerusalem, not knowing the things that shall befall me there: save that the Holy Ghost testifieth unto me in every city, saying that bonds and afflictions abide me. But I hold not my life of any account, as dear unto myself, ²so that I may accomplish my course, and the ministry which I received from the Lord Jesus, to testify the gospel of the grace of God. And now, behold, I know that ye all, among whom I went about preaching the kingdom, shall see my face no more. Wherefore I testify unto you this day, that I am pure from the blood of all men. For I shrank not from declaring unto you the whole counsel of God. Take heed unto yourselves, and to all the flock, in the which the Holy Ghost hath made you ³bishops, to feed the church of ⁴God*, which he ⁵purchased with his own blood. I know that after my departing grievous wolves shall enter in among you, not sparing the flock; and from among your own selves shall men arise, speaking perverse things, to draw away the disciples after them. Wherefore watch ye, remembering that by the space of three years I ceased not to admonish every one night and day with tears. And now I commend you to ⁶God, and to the word of his grace, which is able to build *you* up, and to give *you* the inheritance among all them that are sanctified. I coveted no man's silver, or gold, or apparel. Ye yourselves know that these hands ministered unto my necessities, and to them that were with me. In all things I gave you an example, how that so labouring ye ought to help the weak, and to remember the words of the Lord Jesus, how he himself said, It is more blessed to give than to receive.

And when he had thus spoken, he kneeled down, and prayed with them all. And they all wept sore,

---

¹ Many ancient authorities omit *Christ*.
² Or, *in comparison of accomplishing my course*.
³ Or, *overseers*
⁴ Many ancient authorities read *the Lord*.
⁵ Gr. *acquired*.
⁶ Some ancient authorities read *the Lord*.

* For "God" read "the Lord" (with marg. Some ancient authorities, including the two oldest MSS., read *God*)—*Am. Com.*

38 and fell on Paul's neck, and kissed him, sorrowing most of all for the word which he had spoken, that they should behold his face no more. And they brought him on his way unto the ship.

21 And when it came to pass that we were parted from them, and had set sail, we came with a straight course unto Cos, and the next day unto Rhodes, and 2 from thence unto Patara: and having found a ship crossing over unto Phœnicia, we went aboard, and 3 set sail. And when we had come in sight of Cyprus, leaving it on the left hand, we sailed unto Syria, and landed at Tyre: for there the ship was to 4 unlade her burden. And having found the disciples, we tarried there seven days: and these said to Paul through the Spirit, that he should not set foot 5 in Jerusalem. And when it came to pass that we had accomplished the days, we departed and went on our journey; and they all, with wives and children, brought us on our way, till we were out of the city: 6 and kneeling down on the beach, we prayed, and bade each other farewell; and we went on board the ship, but they returned home again.

7 And when we had finished the voyage from Tyre, we arrived at Ptolemais; and we saluted the breth-8 ren, and abode with them one day. And on the morrow we departed, and came unto Cæsarea: and entering into the house of Philip the evangelist, who was one of the seven, we abode with him. 9 Now this man had four daughters, virgins, which 10 did prophesy. And as we tarried there ¹many days*, ¹ Or, *some* there came down from Judæa a certain prophet, 11 named Agabus. And coming to us, and taking Paul's girdle, he bound his own feet and hands, and said, Thus saith the Holy Ghost, So shall the Jews at Jerusalem bind the man that owneth this girdle, and shall deliver him into the hands of the 12 Gentiles. And when we heard these things, both we and they of that place besought him not to go 13 up to Jerusalem. Then Paul answered, What do ye, weeping and breaking my heart? for I am ready not to be bound only, but also to die at Jerusalem 14 for the name of the Lord Jesus. And when he would not be persuaded, we ceased, saying, The will of the Lord be done.

15 And after these days we ²took up our baggage, ² Or, *made ready* 16 and went up to Jerusalem. And there went with

---

* For "many days" read "some days"—*Am. Com.*

us also *certain* of the disciples from Cæsarea, bringing *with them* one Mnason of Cyprus, an early disciple, with whom we should lodge.

And when we were come to Jerusalem, the brethren received us gladly. And the day following Paul went in with us unto James; and all the elders were present. And when he had saluted them, he rehearsed one by one the things which God had wrought among the Gentiles by his ministry. And they, when they heard it, glorified God; and they said unto him, Thou seest, brother, how many [1]thousands there are among the Jews of them which have believed; and they are all zealous for the law: and they have been informed concerning thee, that thou teachest all the Jews which are among the Gentiles to forsake Moses, telling them not to circumcise their children, neither to walk after the customs. What is it therefore? they will certainly hear that thou art come. Do therefore this that we say to thee: We have four men which have a vow on them; these take, and purify thyself with them, and be at charges for them, that they may shave their heads: and all shall know that there is no truth in the things whereof they have been informed concerning thee; but that thou thyself also walkest orderly, keeping the law. But as touching the Gentiles which have believed, we [2]wrote, giving judgement that they should keep themselves from things sacrificed to idols, and from blood, and from what is strangled, and from fornication. Then Paul [3]took the men, and the next day purifying himself with them went into the temple, declaring the fulfilment of the days of purification, until the offering was offered for every one of them.

And when the seven days were almost completed, the Jews from Asia, when they saw him in the temple, stirred up all the multitude, and laid hands on him, crying out, Men of Israel, help: This is the man, that teacheth all men everywhere against the people, and the law, and this place: and moreover he brought Greeks also into the temple, and hath defiled this holy place. For they had before seen with him in the city Trophimus the Ephesian, whom they supposed that Paul had brought into the temple. And all the city was moved, and the people ran together: and they laid hold on Paul, and dragged him out of the temple: and straightway the doors were shut. And as they were seeking to kill him,

---

1 Gr. *myriads*.

2 Or, *enjoined*
Many ancient authorities read *sent*.

3 Or, *took the men the next day, and purifying himself &c.*

tidings came up to the ¹chief captain of the ²band, that all Jerusalem was in confusion. 32 And forthwith he took soldiers and centurions, and ran down upon them: and they, when they saw the chief captain and the soldiers, left off beating Paul. 33 Then the chief captain came near, and laid hold on him, and commanded him to be bound with two chains; and inquired who he was, and what he had done. 34 And some shouted one thing, some another, among the crowd: and when he could not know the certainty for the uproar, he commanded him to be brought 35 into the castle. And when he came upon the stairs, so it was, that he was borne of the soldiers for the 36 violence of the crowd; for the multitude of the people followed after, crying out, Away with him. 37 And as Paul was about to be brought into the castle, he saith unto the chief captain, May I say something unto thee? And he said, Dost thou know 38 Greek? Art thou not then the Egyptian, which before these days stirred up to sedition and led out into the wilderness the four thousand men of the Assas- 39 sins? But Paul said, I am a Jew, of Tarsus in Cilicia, a citizen of no mean city: and I beseech thee, give 40 me leave to speak unto the people. And when he had given him leave, Paul, standing on the stairs, beckoned with the hand unto the people; and when there was made a great silence, he spake unto them in the Hebrew language, saying,

¹ Or, *military tribune*
Gr. *chiliarch:* and so throughout this book.
² Or, *cohort*

22 Brethren and fathers, hear ye the defence which I now make unto you.

2 And when they heard that he spake unto them in the Hebrew language, they were the more quiet: and he saith,

3 I am a Jew, born in Tarsus of Cilicia, but brought up in this city, at the feet of Gamaliel, instructed according to the strict manner of the law of our fathers, being zealous for God, even as ye all are 4 this day: and I persecuted this Way unto the death, binding and delivering into prisons both men and 5 women. As also the high priest doth bear me witness, and all the estate of the elders: from whom also I received letters unto the brethren, and journeyed to Damascus, to bring them also which were there unto Jerusalem in bonds, for to be punished.

6 And it came to pass, that, as I made my journey, and drew nigh unto Damascus, about noon, suddenly there shone from heaven a great light round 7 about me. And I fell unto the ground, and heard

a voice saying unto me, Saul, Saul, why persecutest
thou me? And I answered, Who art thou, Lord?
And he said unto me, I am Jesus of Nazareth, whom
thou persecutest. And they that were with me beheld indeed the light, but they heard not the voice
of him that spake to me. And I said, What shall
I do, Lord? And the Lord said unto me, Arise,
and go into Damascus; and there it shall be told
thee of all things which are appointed for thee to do.
And when I could not see for the glory of that
light, being led by the hand of them that were with
me, I came into Damascus. And one Ananias, a
devout man according to the law, well reported of
by all the Jews that dwelt there, came unto me, and
standing by me said unto me, Brother Saul, receive
thy sight. And in that very hour I [1]looked up on
him. And he said, The God of our fathers hath appointed thee to know his will, and to see the Righteous One, and to hear a voice from his mouth. For
thou shalt be a witness for him unto all men of what
thou hast seen and heard. And now why tarriest
thou? arise, and be baptized, and wash away thy
sins, calling on his name. And it came to pass,
that, when I had returned to Jerusalem, and while
I prayed in the temple, I fell into a trance, and saw
him saying unto me, Make haste, and get thee quickly out of Jerusalem: because they will not receive
of thee testimony concerning me. And I said,
Lord, they themselves know that I imprisoned and
beat in every synagogue them that believed on thee:
and when the blood of Stephen thy witness was
shed, I also was standing by, and consenting, and
keeping the garments of them that slew him. And
he said unto me, Depart: for I will send thee forth
far hence unto the Gentiles.

And they gave him audience unto this word; and
they lifted up their voice, and said, Away with such
a fellow from the earth: for it is not fit that he
should live. And as they cried out, and threw off
their garments, and cast dust into the air, the chief
captain commanded him to be brought into the castle, bidding that he should be examined by scourging, that he might know for what cause they so shouted against him. And when they had tied him up
[2]with the thongs, Paul said unto the centurion that
stood by, Is it lawful for you to scourge a man that
is a Roman, and uncondemned? And when the centurion heard it, he went to the chief captain, and

[1] Or, *received my sight* and *looked upon him*.

[2] Or, *for*

told him, saying, What art thou about to do? for
27 this man is a Roman. And the chief captain came,
and said unto him, Tell me, art thou a Roman? And
28 he said, Yea. And the chief captain answered,
With a great sum obtained I this citizenship. And
29 Paul said, But I am *a Roman* born. They then
which were about to examine him straightway departed from him: and the chief captain also was
afraid, when he knew that he was a Roman, and
because he had bound him.
30 But on the morrow, desiring to know the certainty, wherefore he was accused of the Jews, he loosed
him, and commanded the chief priests and all the
council to come together, and brought Paul down,
and set him before them.

23 And Paul, looking stedfastly on the council,
said, Brethren, I have lived before God in all good
2 conscience until this day. And the high priest Ananias commanded them that stood by him to smite
3 him on the mouth. Then said Paul unto him, God
shall smite thee, thou whited wall: and sittest thou
to judge me according to the law, and commandest
4 me to be smitten contrary to the law? And they
that stood by said, Revilest thou God's high priest?
5 And Paul said, I wist not, brethren, that he was
high priest: for it is written, Thou shalt not speak
6 evil of a ruler of thy people. But when Paul perceived that the one part were Sadducees, and the
other Pharisees, he cried out in the council, Brethren, I am a Pharisee, a son of Pharisees: touching
the hope and resurrection of the dead I am called
7 in question. And when he had so said, there arose
a dissension between the Pharisees and Sadducees:
8 and the assembly was divided. For the Sadducees
say that there is no resurrection, neither angel, nor
9 spirit: but the Pharisees confess both. And there
arose a great clamour: and some of the scribes of
the Pharisees' part stood up, and strove, saying, We
find no evil in this man: and what if a spirit hath
10 spoken to him, or an angel? And when there arose
a great dissension, the chief captain, fearing lest
Paul should be torn in pieces by them, commanded
the soldiers to go down and take him by force from
among them, and bring him into the castle.
11 And the night following the Lord stood by him,
and said, Be of good cheer: for as thou hast testified
concerning me at Jerusalem, so must thou bear witness also at Rome.

16

And when it was day, the Jews banded together, 12 and bound themselves under a curse, saying that they would neither eat nor drink till they had killed Paul. And they were more than forty which 13 made this conspiracy. And they came to the chief 14 priests and the elders, and said, We have bound ourselves under a great curse, to taste nothing until we have killed Paul. Now therefore do ye with the 15 council signify to the chief captain that he bring him down unto you, as though ye would judge of his case more exactly: and we, or ever he come near, are ready to slay him. But Paul's sister's son heard 16 of their lying in wait, ¹and he came and entered into the castle, and told Paul. And Paul called unto him 17 one of the centurions, and said, Bring this young man unto the chief captain: for he hath something to tell him. So he took him, and brought him to 18 the chief captain, and saith, Paul the prisoner called me unto him, and asked me to bring this young man unto thee, who hath something to say to thee. And the chief captain took him by the hand, and 19 going aside asked him privately, What is that thou hast to tell me? And he said, The Jews have agreed 20 to ask thee to bring down Paul to-morrow unto the council, as though thou wouldest inquire somewhat more exactly concerning him. Do not thou there- 21 fore yield unto them: for there lie in wait for him of them more than forty men, which have bound themselves under a curse, neither to eat nor to drink till they have slain him: and now are they ready, looking for the promise from thee. So the chief cap- 22 tain let the young man go, charging him, Tell no man that thou hast signified these things to me. And he called unto him two of the centurions, and 23 said, Make ready two hundred soldiers to go as far as Cæsarea, and horsemen threescore and ten, and spearmen two hundred, at the third hour of the night: and *he bade them* provide beasts, that they 24 might set Paul thereon, and bring him safe unto Felix the governor. And he wrote a letter after this 25 form:

Claudius Lysias unto the most excellent governor 26 Felix, greeting. This man was seized by the Jews, 27 and was about to be slain of them, when I came upon them with the soldiers, and rescued him, having learned that he was a Roman. And desiring 28 to know the cause wherefore they accused him, ²I brought him down unto their council: whom I 29

---

1 Or, *having come in upon them, and he entered &c.*

2 Some ancient authorities omit *I brought him down unto their council.*

found to be accused about questions of their law, but to have nothing laid to his charge worthy of 30 death or of bonds. And when it was shewn to me that there would be a plot against the man*, I sent him to thee forthwith, charging his accusers also to speak against him before thee.¹
31 So the soldiers, as it was commanded them, took Paul, and brought him by night to Antipatris.
32 But on the morrow they left the horsemen to go 33 with him, and returned to the castle: and they, when they came to Cæsarea, and delivered the letter to the governor, presented Paul also before him.
34 And when he had read it, he asked of what province he was; and when he understood that he was of Cilicia,
35 I will hear thy cause†, said he, when thine accusers also are come: and he commanded him to be kept in Herod's ²palace.

¹ Many ancient authorities add *Farewell.*

² Gr. *Prætorium*

24

And after five days the high priest Ananias came down with certain elders, and *with* an orator, one Tertullus; and they informed the governor against 2 Paul. And when he was called, Tertullus began to accuse him, saying,

Seeing that by thee we enjoy much peace, and that by thy providence evils are corrected for this na- 3 tion, we accept it in all ways and in all places, most 4 excellent Felix, with all thankfulness. But, that I be not further tedious unto thee, I intreat thee to 5 hear us of thy clemency a few words. For we have found this man a pestilent fellow, and a mover of insurrections among all the Jews throughout ³the world, and a ringleader of the sect of the Naza- 6 renes: who moreover assayed to profane the tem- 8 ple: on whom also we laid hold:⁴ from whom thou wilt be âble, by examining him thyself, to take knowledge of all these things, whereof we accuse 9 him. And the Jews also joined in the charge, affirming that these things were so.

10 And when the governor had beckoned unto him to speak, Paul answered,

Forasmuch as I know that thou hast been of many years a judge unto this nation, I do cheerfully make 11 my defence: seeing that thou canst take knowledge, that it is not more than twelve days since I went up 12 to worship at Jerusalem: and neither in the temple

³ Gr. *the inhabited earth.*

⁴ Some ancient authorities insert *and we would have judged him according to our law.* 7 *But the chief captain Lysias came, and with great violence took him away out of our hands,* 8 *commanding his accusers to come before thee.*

---

* "against the man" etc. add marg. Many ancient authorities read *against the man on their part, I sent him to thee, charging* etc. —*Am. Com.*

† For "hear thy cause" read "hear thee fully"—*Am. Com.*

did they find me disputing with any man or stirring up a crowd, nor in the synagogues, nor in the city. Neither can they prove to thee the things whereof they now accuse me. But this I confess unto thee, that after the Way which they call ¹a sect, so serve I the God of our fathers, believing all things which are according to the law, and which are written in the prophets: having hope toward God, which these also themselves ²look for, that there shall be a resurrection both of the just and unjust. Herein do I also exercise myself to have a conscience void of offence toward God and men alway. Now after ³many years* I came to bring alms to my nation, and offerings: ⁴amidst which they found me purified in the temple, with no crowd, nor yet with tumult: but *there were* certain Jews from Asia—who ought to have been here before thee, and to make accusation, if they had aught against me. Or else let these men themselves say what wrong-doing they found, when I stood before the council, except it be for this one voice, that I cried standing among them, Touching the resurrection of the dead I am called in question before you this day.

But Felix, having more exact knowledge concerning the Way, deferred them, saying, When Lysias the chief captain shall come down, I will determine your matter. And he gave order to the centurion that he should be kept in charge, and should have indulgence; and not to forbid any of his friends to minister unto him.

But after certain days, Felix came with Drusilla, ⁵his wife, which was a Jewess, and sent for Paul, and heard him concerning the faith in Christ Jesus. And as he reasoned of righteousness, and ⁶temperance, and the judgement to come, Felix was terrified, and answered, Go thy way for this time; and when I have a convenient season, I will call thee unto me. He hoped withal that money would be given him of Paul: wherefore also he sent for him the oftener, and communed with him. But when two years were fulfilled, Felix was succeeded by Porcius Festus, and desiring to gain favour with the Jews, Felix left Paul in bonds.

Festus therefore, ⁷having come into the province, after three days went up to Jerusalem from Cæsarea. And the chief priests and the principal men

---

1 Or, *heresy*
2 Or, *accept*
3 Or, *some*
4 Or, *in presenting which*
5 Gr. *his own wife.*
6 Or, *self-control*
7 Or, *having entered upon his province*

* For "many years" read "some years"—*Am. Com.*

of the Jews informed him against Paul; and they
3 besought him, asking favour against him, that he
would send for him to Jerusalem; laying wait* to kill
4 him on the way. Howbeit Festus answered, that
Paul was kept in charge at Cæsarea, and that he
5 himself was about to depart *thither* shortly. Let them
therefore, saith he, which are of power among you,
go down with me, and if there is anything amiss in
the man, let them accuse him.
6 And when he had tarried among them not more
than eight or ten days, he went down unto Cæsarea;
and on the morrow he sat on the judgement-seat, and
7 commanded Paul to be brought. And when he was
come, the Jews which had come down from Jerusalem stood round about him, bringing against him
many and grievous charges, which they could not
8 prove; while Paul said in his defence, Neither
against the law of the Jews, nor against the temple,
9 nor against Cæsar, have I sinned at all. But Festus,
desiring to gain favour with the Jews, answered
Paul, and said, Wilt thou go up to Jerusalem, and
10 there be judged of these things before me? But
Paul said, I am standing before Cæsar's judgement-
seat, where I ought to be judged: to the Jews have
I done no wrong, as thou also very well knowest.
11 If then I am a wrong-doer, and have committed any
thing worthy of death, I refuse not to die: but if
none of those things is *true*, whereof these accuse
me, no man can ¹give me up unto them. I appeal
12 unto Cæsar. Then Festus, when he had conferred
with the council, answered, Thou hast appealed unto
Cæsar: unto Cæsar shalt thou go.
13 Now when certain days were passed, Agrippa the
king and Bernice arrived at Cæsarea, ²and saluted
14 Festus. And as they tarried there many days, Festus laid Paul's case before the king, saying, There is
15 a certain man left a prisoner by Felix: about whom,
when I was at Jerusalem, the chief priests and the
elders of the Jews informed *me*, asking for sentence
16 against him. To whom I answered, that it is not
the custom of the Romans to give up any man, before that the accused have the accusers face to face,
and have had opportunity to make his defence con-
17 cerning the matter laid against him. When therefore they were come together here, I made no delay,
but on the next day sat down on the judgement-seat,

1 Gr. *grant me by favour*: and so in ver. 16.

2 Or, *having saluted*

---

* For "laying wait" read "laying a plot"—*Am. Com.*

and commanded the man to be brought. Concerning whom, when the accusers stood up, they brought no charge of such evil things as I supposed; but had certain questions against him of their own ¹religion, and of one Jesus, who was dead, whom Paul affirmed to be alive. And I, being perplexed how to inquire concerning these things, asked whether he would go to Jerusalem, and there be judged of these matters. But when Paul had appealed to be kept for the decision of ²the emperor, I commanded him to be kept till I should send him to Cæsar. And Agrippa *said* unto Festus, I also ³could wish to hear the man myself. To-morrow, saith he, thou shalt hear him.

So on the morrow, when Agrippa was come, and Bernice, with great pomp, and they were entered into the place of hearing, with the chief captains, and the principal men of the city, at the command of Festus Paul was brought in. And Festus saith, King Agrippa, and all men which are here present with us, ye behold this man, about whom all the multitude of the Jews made suit to me, both at Jerusalem and here, crying that he ought not to live any longer. But I found that he had committed nothing worthy of death: and as he himself appealed to ²the emperor I determined to send him. Of whom I have no certain thing to write unto my lord. Wherefore I have brought him forth before you, and specially before thee, king Agrippa, that, after examination had, I may have somewhat to write. For it seemeth to me unreasonable, in sending a prisoner, not withal to signify the charges against him.

And Agrippa said unto Paul, Thou art permitted to speak for thyself. Then Paul stretched forth his hand, and made his defence:

I think myself happy, king Agrippa, that I am to make my defence before thee this day touching all the things whereof I am accused by the Jews: ⁴especially because thou art expert in all customs and questions which are among the Jews: wherefore I beseech thee to hear me patiently. My manner of life then from my youth up, which was from the beginning among mine own nation, and at Jerusalem, know all the Jews; having knowledge of me from the first, if they be willing to testify, how that after the straitest sect of our religion I lived a Pharisee. And now I stand *here* to be judged for the

---

1 Or, *superstition*

2 Gr. *the Augustus*.

3 Or, *was wishing*

4 Or, *because thou art especially expert.*

hope of the promise made of God unto our fathers;
7 unto which *promise* our twelve tribes, earnestly serving *God* night and day, hope to attain. And concerning this hope I am accused by the Jews, O king!
8 Why is it judged incredible with you, if God doth
9 raise the dead? I verily thought with myself, that I ought to do many things contrary to the name of
10 Jesus of Nazareth. And this I also did in Jerusalem: and I both shut up many of the saints in prisons, having received authority from the chief priests, and when they were put to death, I gave my vote
11 against them. And punishing them oftentimes in all the synagogues, I strove to make them blaspheme; and being exceedingly mad against them, I perse-
12 cuted them even unto foreign cities. ¹Whereupon as I journeyed to Damascus with the authority and
13 commission of the chief priests, at midday, O king, I saw on the way a light from heaven, above the brightness of the sun, shining round about me and
14 them that journeyed with me. And when we were all fallen to the earth, I heard a voice saying unto me in the Hebrew language, Saul, Saul, why persecutest thou me? it is hard for thee to kick against
15 ²the goad. And I said, Who art thou, Lord? And the Lord said, I am Jesus whom thou persecutest.
16 But arise, and stand upon thy feet: for to this end have I appeared unto thee, to appoint thee a minister and a witness both of the things ³wherein thou hast seen me, and of the things wherein I will ap-
17 pear unto thee; delivering thee from the people, and from the Gentiles, unto whom I send thee, to open
18 their eyes, ⁴that they may turn from darkness to light, and from the power of Satan unto God, that they may receive remission of sins and an inheritance among them that are sanctified by faith in me.
19 Wherefore, O king Agrippa, I was not disobedient
20 unto the heavenly vision: but declared both to them of Damascus first, and at Jerusalem, and throughout all the country of Judæa, and also to the Gentiles, that they should repent and turn to God, doing
21 works worthy of ⁵repentance. For this cause the Jews seized me in the temple, and assayed to kill
22 me. Having therefore obtained the help that is from God, I stand unto this day testifying both to small and great, saying nothing but what the proph-
23 ets and Moses did say should come; ⁶how that the Christ ⁷must suffer, *and* ⁶how that he first by the resurrection of the dead should proclaim light both to the people and to the Gentiles.

1 Or, *On which errand*

2 Gr. *goads*.

3 Many ancient authorities read *which thou hast seen*.

4 Or, *to turn them*

5 Or, *their repentance*.

6 Or, *if* Or, *whether*

7 Or, *is subject to suffering*

And as he thus made his defence, Festus saith 24 with a loud voice, Paul, thou art mad; thy much learning doth turn thee to madness. But Paul saith, 25 I am not mad, most excellent Festus; but speak forth words of truth and soberness. For the king 26 knoweth of these things, unto whom also I speak freely: for I am persuaded that none of these things is hidden from him; for this hath not been done in a corner. King Agrippa, believest thou the prophets? 27 I know that thou believest. And Agrippa *said* unto 28 Paul, With but* little persuasion thou wouldest fain make me a Christian. And Paul *said*, I would to 29 God, that whether with little† or with much, not thou only, but also all that hear me this day, might become such as I am, except these bonds.

And the king rose up, and the governor, and Ber- 30 nice, and they that sat with them: and when they 31 had withdrawn, they spake one to another, saying, This man doeth nothing worthy of death or of bonds. And Agrippa said unto Festus, This man 32 might have been set at liberty, if he had not appealed unto Cæsar.

And when it was determined that we should sail **27** for Italy, they delivered Paul and certain other prisoners to a centurion named Julius, of the Augustan ¹band. And embarking in a ship of Adramyt- 2 tium, which was about to sail unto the places on the coast of Asia, we put to sea, Aristarchus, a Macedonian of Thessalonica, being with us. And the next 3 day we touched at Sidon: and Julius treated Paul kindly, and gave him leave to go unto his friends and ²refresh himself. And putting to sea from 4 thence, we sailed under the lee of Cyprus, because the winds were contrary. And when we had sailed 5 across the sea which is off Cilicia and Pamphylia, we came to Myra, *a city* of Lycia. And there the 6 centurion found a ship of Alexandria sailing for Italy; and he put us therein. And when we had 7 sailed slowly many days, and were come with difficulty over against Cnidus, the wind not ³further suffering us, we sailed under the lee of Crete, over against Salmone; and with difficulty coasting along 8 it we came unto a certain place called Fair Havens; nigh whereunto was the city of Lasea.

And when much time was spent, and the voyage 9

¹ Or, *cohort.*

² Gr. *receive attention.*

³ Or, *suffering us to get there.*

---

* "With but" etc. add marg. Or, *In a little time*—*Am. Com.*
† "whether with little" etc. add marg. Or, *both in little and in great,* i.e. in all respects—*Am. Com.*

was now dangerous, because the Fast was now already gone by, Paul admonished them, and said unto them, Sirs, I perceive that the voyage will be with injury and much loss, not only of the lading and the ship, but also of our lives. But the centurion gave more heed to the master and to the owner of the ship, than to those things which were spoken by Paul. And because the haven was not commodious to winter in, the more part advised to put to sea from thence, if by any means they could reach Phœnix, and winter *there;* which is a haven of Crete, looking [1] north-east and south-east. And when the south wind blew softly, supposing that they had obtained their purpose, they weighed anchor and sailed along Crete, close in shore. But after no long time there beat down from it a tempestuous wind, which is called Euraquilo: and when the ship was caught, and could not face the wind, we gave way *to it,* and were driven. And running under the lee of a small island called [2]Cauda, we were able, with difficulty, to secure the boat: and when they had hoisted it up, they used helps, under-girding the ship; and, fearing lest they should be cast upon the Syrtis, they lowered the gear, and so were driven. And as we laboured exceedingly with the storm, the next day they began to throw *the freight* overboard; and the third day they cast out with their own hands the [3]tackling of the ship. And when neither sun nor stars shone upon *us* for many days, and no small tempest lay on *us,* all hope that we should be saved was now taken away. And when they had been long without food, then Paul stood forth in the midst of them, and said, Sirs, ye should have hearkened unto me, and not have set sail from Crete, and have gotten this injury and loss. And now I exhort you to be of good cheer: for there shall be no loss of life among you, but *only* of the ship. For there stood by me this night an angel of the God whose I am, whom also I serve, saying, Fear not, Paul; thou must stand before Cæsar: and lo, God hath granted thee all them that sail with thee. Wherefore, sirs, be of good cheer: for I believe God, that it shall be even so as it hath been spoken unto me. Howbeit we must be cast upon a certain island.

But when the fourteenth night was come, as we were driven to and fro in the *sea of* Adria, about midnight the sailors surmised that they were drawing near to some country; and they sounded, and

[1] Gr. *down the south-west wind and down the north-west wind.*

[2] Many ancient authorities read *Clauda.*

[3] Or, *furniture*

found twenty fathoms: and after a little space, they sounded again, and found fifteen fathoms. And 29 fearing lest haply we should be cast ashore on rocky ground, they let go four anchors from the stern, and ¹wished for the day. And as the sailors were seek- 30 ing to flee out of the ship, and had lowered the boat into the sea, under colour as though they would lay out anchors from the foreship, Paul said to the cen- 31 turion and to the soldiers, Except these abide in the ship, ye cannot be saved. Then the soldiers cut 32 away the ropes of the boat, and let her fall off. And while the day was coming on, Paul besought 33 them all to take some food, saying, This day is the fourteenth day that ye wait and continue fasting, having taken nothing. Wherefore I beseech you to 34 take some food: for this is for your safety: for there shall not a hair perish from the head of any of you. And when he had said this, and had taken 35 bread, he gave thanks to God in the presence of all: and he brake it, and began to eat. Then were they 36 all of good cheer, and themselves also took food. And we were in all in the ship ²two hundred three- 37 score and sixteen souls. And when they had eaten 38 enough, they lightened the ship, throwing out the wheat into the sea. And when it was day, they 39 knew not the land: but they perceived a certain bay with a beach, and they took counsel whether they could ³drive the ship upon it. And casting off 40 the anchors, they left them in the sea, at the same time loosing the bands of the rudders; and hoisting up the foresail to the wind, they made for the beach. But lighting upon a place where two seas met, they 41 ran the vessel aground; and the foreship struck and remained unmoveable, but the stern began to break up by the violence *of the waves*. And the soldiers' 42 counsel was to kill the prisoners, lest any *of them* should swim out, and escape. But the centurion, 43 desiring to save Paul, stayed them from their pur- pose; and commanded that they which could swim should cast themselves overboard, and get first to the land: and the rest, some on planks, and some 44 on *other* things from the ship. And so it came to pass, that they all escaped safe to the land.

And when we were escaped, then we knew that **28** the island was called ⁴Melita. And the barbarians 2 shewed us no common kindness: for they kindled a

1 Or, *prayed*

2 Some ancient authorities read *about threescore and sixteen souls.**

3 Some ancient authorities read *bring the ship safe to shore.*

4 Some ancient authorities read *Melitene.*

---

* Omit marg. ². — *Am. Com.*

fire, and received us all, because of the present rain, 3 and because of the cold. But when Paul had gathered a bundle of sticks, and laid them on the fire, a viper came out ¹by reason of the heat, and fastened 4 on his hand. And when the barbarians saw the beast hanging from his hand, they said one to another, No doubt this man is a murderer, whom, though he hath escaped from the sea, yet Justice 5 hath not suffered to live. Howbeit he shook off the 6 beast into the fire, and took no harm. But they expected that he would have swollen, or fallen down dead suddenly: but when they were long in expectation, and beheld nothing amiss come to him, they changed their minds, and said that he was a god.

7 Now in the neighbourhood of that place were lands belonging to the chief man of the island, named Publius; who received us, and entertained us three days 8 courteously. And it was so, that the father of Publius lay sick of fever and dysentery: unto whom Paul entered in, and prayed, and laying his hands 9 on him healed him. And when this was done, the rest also which had diseases in the island came, and 10 were cured: who also honoured us with many honours; and when we sailed, they put on board such things as we needed.

11 And after three months we set sail in a ship of Alexandria, which had wintered in the island, whose 12 sign was ²The Twin Brothers. And touching at 13 Syracuse, we tarried there three days. And from thence we ³made a circuit, and arrived at Rhegium: and after one day a south wind sprang up, and on 14 the second day we came to Puteoli; where we found brethren, and were intreated to tarry with them 15 seven days: and so we came to Rome. And from thence the brethren, when they heard of us, came to meet us as far as The Market of Appius, and The Three Taverns: whom when Paul saw, he thanked God, and took courage.

16 And when we entered into Rome. ⁴Paul was suffered to abide by himself with the soldier that guarded him.

17 And it came to pass, that after three days he called together ⁵those that were the chief of the Jews: and when they were come together, he said unto them, I, brethren, though I had done nothing against the people, or the customs of our fathers, yet was delivered prisoner from Jerusalem into the hands of 18 the Romans: who, when they had examined me,

1 Or, *from the heat*

2 Gr. *Dioscuri.*

3 Some ancient authorities read *cast loose.*

4 Some ancient authorities insert *the centurion delivered the prisoners to the captain of the prætorian guard: but*

5 Or, *those that were of the Jews first*

desired to set me at liberty, because there was no cause of death in me. But when the Jews spake 19 against it, I was constrained to appeal unto Cæsar; not that I had aught to accuse my nation of. For 20 this cause therefore did I ¹intreat you to see and to speak with *me*: for because of the hope of Israel I am bound with this chain. And they said unto him, 21 We neither received letters from Judæa concerning thee, nor did any of the brethren come hither and report or speak any harm of thee. But we desire to 22 hear of thee what thou thinkest: for as concerning this sect, it is known to us that everywhere it is spoken against.

And when they had appointed him a day, they 23 came to him into his lodging in great number; to whom he expounded *the matter*, testifying the kingdom of God, and persuading them concerning Jesus, both from the law of Moses and from the prophets, from morning till evening. And some believed the 24 things which were spoken, and some disbelieved. And when they agreed not among themselves, they 25 departed, after that Paul had spoken one word, Well spake the Holy Ghost ²by Isaiah the prophet unto your fathers, saying, 26

> Go thou unto this people, and say,
> By hearing ye shall hear, and shall in no wise understand;
> And seeing ye shall see, and shall in no wise perceive:
> For this people's heart is waxed gross, 27
> And their ears are dull of hearing,
> And their eyes they have closed;
> Lest haply they should perceive with their eyes,
> And hear with their ears,
> And understand with their heart,
> And should turn again,
> And I should heal them.

Be it known therefore unto you, that this salvation 28 of God is sent unto the Gentiles: they will also hear.³

And he abode two whole years in his own hired 30 dwelling, and received all that went in unto him, preaching the kingdom of God, and teaching the 31 things concerning the Lord Jesus Christ with all boldness, none forbidding him.

---

¹ Or, *call for you, to see and to speak with* you

² Or, *through*

³ Some ancient authorities insert ver. 29 *And when he had said these words, the Jews departed, having much disputing among themselves.*

THE EPISTLE OF PAUL THE APOSTLE

TO THE

ROMANS.

1 Paul, a ¹servant of Jesus Christ, called *to be* an
2 apostle, separated unto the gospel of God, which he
promised afore ²by his prophets in the holy script-
3 ures, concerning his Son, who was born of the seed
4 of David according to the flesh, who was ³declared
to be the Son of God ⁴with power, according to the
spirit of holiness, by the resurrection of the dead;
5 *even* Jesus Christ our Lord, through whom we received grace and apostleship, unto obedience ⁵of
faith among all the nations, for his name's sake:
6 among whom are ye also, called *to be* Jesus Christ's:
7 to all that are in Rome, beloved of God, called *to be*
saints: Grace to you and peace from God our Father and the Lord Jesus Christ.
8 First, I thank my God through Jesus Christ for
you all, ⁶that your faith is proclaimed throughout
9 the whole world. For God is my witness, whom I
serve in my spirit in the gospel of his Son, how unceasingly I make mention of you, always in my
10 prayers making request, if by any means now at
length I may be prospered ⁷by the will of God to
11 come unto you. For I long to see you, that I may
impart unto you some spiritual gift, to the end ye
12 may be established; that is, that I with you may be
comforted in you, each of us by the other's faith,
13 both yours and mine. And I would not have you
ignorant, brethren, that oftentimes I purposed to
come unto you (and was hindered hitherto), that I
might have some fruit in you also, even as in the
14 rest of the Gentiles. I am debtor both to Greeks
and to Barbarians, both to the wise and to the fool-
15 ish. So, as much as in me is, I am ready to preach

1 Gr. *bondservant*.

2 Or, *through*

3 Gr. *determined*.

4 Or, *in*

5 Or, *to the faith*

6 Or, *because*

7 Gr. *in*.

the gospel to you also that are in Rome. For I am 16
not ashamed of the gospel: for it is the power of
God unto salvation to every one that believeth; to
the Jew first, and also to the Greek. For therein is 17
revealed a righteousness of God ¹by faith* unto
faith: as it is written, But the righteous shall live
¹by faith*.

For ²the wrath of God is revealed from heaven 18
against all ungodliness and unrighteousness of men,
who ³hold down† the truth in unrighteousness; be- 19
cause that which may be known of God is manifest
in them; for God manifested it unto them. For 20
the invisible things of him since the creation of the
world are clearly seen, being perceived through the
things that are made, *even* his everlasting power
and divinity; ⁴that they may be without excuse:
because that, knowing God, they glorified him not 21
as God, neither gave thanks; but became vain in
their reasonings, and their senseless heart was darkened. Professing themselves to be wise, they be- 22
came fools, and changed the glory of the incorrup- 23
tible God for the likeness of an image of corruptible
man, and of birds, and fourfooted beasts, and creeping things.

Wherefore God gave them up in the lusts of their 24
hearts unto uncleanness, that their bodies should be
dishonoured among themselves: for that they ex- 25
changed the truth of God for a lie, and worshipped
and served the creature rather than the Creator, who
is blessed ⁵for ever. Amen.

For this cause God gave them up unto ⁶vile pas- 26
sions: for their women changed the natural use
into that which is against nature: and likewise also 27
the men, leaving the natural use of the woman, burned in their lust one toward another, men with men
working unseemliness, and receiving in themselves
that recompense of their error which was due.

And even as they ⁷refused to have God in *their* 28
knowledge, God gave them up unto a reprobate
mind, to do those things which are not fitting; being 29
filled with all unrighteousness, wickedness, covetousness, maliciousness; full of envy, murder, strife,
deceit, malignity; whisperers, backbiters, ⁸hateful to 30
God, insolent, haughty, boastful, inventors of evil

---

1 Gr. *from*.

2 Or, *a wrath*

3 Or, *hold the truth*

4 Or, *so that they are*

5 Gr. *unto the ages*.
6 Gr. *passions of dishonour*.

7 Gr. *did not approve*.

8 Or, *haters of God*

---

* For "by faith" read "from faith" and omit the marg.—*Am. Com.*

† For "hold down" read "hinder"—*Am. Com.*

31 things, disobedient to parents, without understanding, covenant-breakers, without natural affection,
32 unmerciful: who, knowing the ordinance of God, that they which practise such things are worthy of death, not only do the same, but also consent with them that practise them.

2 Wherefore thou art without excuse, O man, whosoever thou art that judgest: for wherein thou judgest ¹another, thou condemnest thyself; for thou that
2 judgest dost practise the same things. ²And we know that the judgement of God is according to truth
3 against them that practise such things. And reckonest thou this, O man, who judgest them that practise such things, and doest the same, that thou shalt es-
4 cape the judgement of God? Or despisest thou the riches of his goodness and forbearance and longsuffering, not knowing that the goodness of God leadeth
5 thee to repentance? but after thy hardness and impenitent heart treasurest up for thyself wrath in the day of wrath and revelation of the righteous judge-
6 ment of God; who will render to every man accord-
7 ing to his works: to them that by patience in welldoing seek for glory and honour and incorruption,
8 eternal life: but unto them that are factious, and obey not the truth, but obey unrighteousness, *shall be*
9 wrath and indignation, tribulation and anguish, upon every soul of man that worketh evil, of the Jew first,
10 and also of the Greek; but glory and honour and peace to every man that worketh good, to the Jew
11 first, and also to the Greek: for there is no respect of
12 persons with God. For as many as have sinned* without law shall also perish without law: and as many as have sinned under law shall be judged by
13 law; for not the hearers of a law† are ³just before
14 God, but the doers of a law shall be ⁴justified: |for when Gentiles which have not‡ law do by nature the things of the law, these, having no§ law, are a law
15 unto themselves; in that they shew the work of the law written in their hearts, their conscience bearing witness therewith, and their ⁵thoughts one with an-
16 other accusing or else excusing *them*¶; in the day

1 Gr. *the other.*
2 Many ancient authorities read *For.*
3 Or, *righteous*
4 Or, *accounted righteous*
5 Or, *reasonings*

---

* "have sinned" add marg. Gr. *sinned.—Am. Com.*
† For "a law" read "the law"—*Am. Com.*
‡ For "which have no" read "that have not the"—*Am. Com.*
§ For "having no" read "not having the"—*Am. Com.*
| Enclose ver. 14 and 15 in a parenthesis.—*Am. Com.*
¶ "their thoughts" etc. add marg. Or, *their thoughts accusing or else excusing* them *one with another*—*Am. Com.*

¹ Or, *judgeth*
² Or, *a law*
³ Or, *the Will*
⁴ Or, *provest* the things that differ*
⁵ Or, *an instructor*
⁶ Or, *commit sacrilege*
⁷ Gr. *Be it not so: and so elsewhere.*

when God ¹shall judge the secrets of men, according to my gospel, by Jesus Christ. But if thou bearest the name of a Jew, and restest upon ²the law, and gloriest in God, and knowest ³his will, and ⁴approvest the things that are excellent, being instructed out of the law, and art confident that thou thyself art a guide of the blind, a light of them that are in darkness, ⁵a corrector of the foolish, a teacher of babes, having in the law the form of knowledge and of the truth; thou therefore that teachest another, teachest thou not thyself? thou that preachest a man should not steal, dost thou steal? thou that sayest a man should not commit adultery, dost thou commit adultery? thou that abhorrest idols, dost thou ⁶rob temples†? thou who gloriest in ²the law, through thy transgression of the law dishonourest thou God? For the name of God is blasphemed among the Gentiles because of you, even as it is written. For circumcision indeed profiteth, if thou be a doer of the law: but if thou be a transgressor of the law, thy circumcision is become uncircumcision. If therefore the uncircumcision keep the ordinances of the law, shall not his uncircumcision be reckoned for circumcision? and shall not the uncircumcision which is by nature, if it fulfil the law, judge thee, who with the letter and circumcision art a transgressor of the law? For he is not a Jew, which is one outwardly; neither is that circumcision, which is outward in the flesh: but he is a Jew, which is one inwardly; and circumcision is that of the heart, in the spirit, not in the letter; whose praise is not of men, but of God.

What advantage then hath the Jew? or what is the profit of circumcision? Much every way: first of all, that they were intrusted with the oracles of God. For what if some were without faith? shall their want of faith make of none effect the faithfulness of God? ⁷God forbid: yea, let God be found true, but every man a liar; as it is written,

That thou mightest be justified in thy words,
And mightest prevail when thou comest into judgement.

But if our unrighteousness commendeth the righteousness of God, what shall we say? Is God un-

---

* In marg. ⁴ for "*provest*" read "*dost distinguish*"—*Am. Com.*
† Omit the marg.—*Am. Com.*

righteous who visiteth with wrath? (I speak after
6 the manner of men.) God forbid: for then how
7 shall God judge the world? ¹But if the truth of
God through my lie abounded unto his glory, why
8 am I also still judged as a sinner? and why not (as
we be slanderously reported, and as some affirm
that we say), Let us do evil, that good may come?
whose condemnation is just.
9 What then? ²are we in worse case* than they?
No, in no wise: for we before laid to the charge
both of Jews and Greeks, that they are all under
10 sin; as it is written,
> There is none righteous, no not one;
11 > There is none that understandeth,
> There is none that seeketh after God;
12 > They have all turned aside, they are together
>   become unprofitable;
> There is none that doeth good, no, not so much
>   as one:
13 > Their throat is an open sepulchre;
> With their tongues they have used deceit:
> The poison of asps is under their lips:
14 > Whose mouth is full of cursing and bitterness:
15 > Their feet are swift to shed blood;
16 > Destruction and misery are in their ways;
17 > And the way of peace have they not known:
18 > There is no fear of God before their eyes.
19 Now we know that what things soever the law
saith, it speaketh to them that are under the law;
that every mouth may be stopped, and all the world
20 may be brought under the judgement of God: because ³by ⁴the works of the law shall no flesh be
⁵justified in his sight: for ⁶through the law *cometh*
21 the knowledge of sin†. But now apart from the
law a righteousness of God hath been manifested,
22 being witnessed by the law and the prophets; even
the righteousness of God through faith ⁷in Jesus
Christ unto all ⁸them that believe; for there is no
23 distinction; for all have sinned‡, and fall short of
24 the glory of God; being justified freely by his grace
through the redemption that is in Christ Jesus:
25 whom God ⁹set forth§ ¹⁰*to be* a propitiation, through

1 Many ancient authorities read *For*.
2 Or, *do we excuse ourselves?*
3 Gr. *out of*.
4 Or, *works of law*
5 Or, *accounted righteous*
6 Or, *through law*
7 Or, *of*
8 Some ancient authorities add *and upon all*.
9 Or, *purposed*
10 Or, *to be propitiatory*

---

* For "in worse case" read "better" and omit the marg.—*Am. Com.*
† Begin a paragraph.—*Am. Com.*
‡ "have sinned" add marg. Gr. *sinned*.—*Am. Com.*
§ "set forth" omit marg. ⁹ ("*purposed*") —*Am. Com.*

TO THE ROMANS.

²⁵ faith, by his blood*, to shew his righteousness, because of the passing over of the sins done aforetime, in the forbearance of God; ²⁶ for the shewing, *I say*, of his righteousness at this present season: that he might himself be ²just, and the ²justifier of him that ³hath faith ⁴in Jesus. ²⁷ Where then is the glorying? It is excluded. By what manner of law? of works? Nay: but by a law of faith. ²⁸ We reckon therefore that a man is justified by faith apart from ⁶the works of the law. ²⁹ Or is God *the God* of Jews only? is he not *the God* of Gentiles also? Yea, of Gentiles also: ³⁰ if so be that God is one, and he shall justify the circumcision ⁷by faith, and the uncircumcision ⁸through faith. ³¹ Do we then make ⁹the law of none effect ⁸through faith? God forbid: nay, we establish ⁹the law†.

⁴ What then shall we say ¹⁰that Abraham, our forefather according to the flesh, hath found‡? ² For if Abraham was justified ⁷by works, he hath whereof to glory; but not toward God. ³ For what saith the scripture? And Abraham believed God, and it was reckoned unto him for righteousness. ⁴ Now to him that worketh, the reward is not reckoned as of grace, but as of debt. ⁵ But to him that worketh not, but believeth on him that justifieth the ungodly, his faith is reckoned for righteousness. ⁶ Even as David also pronounceth blessing upon the man, unto whom God reckoneth righteousness apart from works, *saying*,

⁷ Blessed are they whose iniquities are forgiven,
And whose sins are covered.
⁸ Blessed is the man to whom the Lord will not reckon sin.

⁹ Is this blessing then pronounced upon the circumcision, or upon the uncircumcision also? for we say, To Abraham his faith was reckoned for righteousness. ¹⁰ How then was it reckoned? when he was in circumcision, or in uncircumcision? Not in circumcision, but in uncircumcision: ¹¹ and he received the sign of circumcision, a seal of the righteousness of the faith which he had while he was in uncircumcision: that he might be the father of all them that

---

Marginal notes:
1. Or, *faith in his blood*
2. See ch. ii. 13, margin.
3. Gr. *is of faith*.
4. Or, *of*
5. Many ancient authorities read *For we reckon*.
6. Or, *works of law*
7. Gr. *out of*.
8. Or, *through the faith*
9. Or, *law*
10. Some ancient authorities read *of Abraham, our forefather according to the flesh?*

---

* For "by his blood" read "in his blood" (retaining the comma after "faith") and omit marg. ¹.—*Am. Com.*

† Make a paragraph of verse 31.—*Am. Com.*

‡ For "according to the flesh, hath found" read "hath found according to the flesh" and put the present text into the margin.—*Am. Com.*

TO THE ROMANS.

believe, though they be in uncircumcision, that right-
12 eousness might be reckoned unto them; and the father of circumcision to them who not only are of
the circumcision, but who also walk in the steps of
that faith of our father Abraham which he had in
13 uncircumcision. For not ¹through the law was the
promise to Abraham or to his seed, that he should
be heir of the world, but through the righteousness
14 of faith. For if they which are of the law be heirs,
faith is made void, and the promise is made of none
15 effect: for the law worketh wrath; but where there
16 is no law, neither is there transgression. For this
cause *it is* of faith, that *it may be* according to grace;
to the end that the promise may be sure to all the
seed; not to that only which is of the law, but to
that also which is of the faith of Abraham, who is
17 the father of us all (as it is written, A father of
many nations have I made thee) before him whom
he believed, *even* God, who quickeneth the dead, and
calleth the things that are not, as though they were.
18 Who in hope believed against hope, to the end that
he might become a father of many nations, according to that which had been spoken, So shall thy seed
19 be. And without being weakened in faith he considered his own body ²now as good as dead (he being about a hundred years old), and the deadness of
20 Sarah's womb: yea, looking unto the promise of God,
he wavered not through unbelief, but waxed strong
21 through faith, giving glory to God, and being fully
assured that, what he had promised, he was able also
22 to perform. Wherefore also it was reckoned unto
23 him for righteousness. Now it was not written for
24 his sake alone, that it was reckoned unto him; but
for our sake also, unto whom it shall be reckoned,
who believe on him that raised Jesus our Lord from
25 the dead, who was delivered up for our trespasses,
and was raised for our justification.

5 Being therefore justified ³by faith, ⁴let us have*
peace with God through our Lord Jesus Christ;
2 through whom also we have had our access ⁵by
faith into this grace wherein we stand; and ⁶let
3 us* ⁷rejoice in hope of the glory of God. And not
only so, but ⁸let us* also ⁷rejoice in our tribulations:
4 knowing that tribulation worketh patience; and pa-

¹ Or, *through law*

² Many ancient authorities omit *now*.

³ Gr. *out of*.
⁴ Some authorities read *we have*.
⁵ Some ancient authorities omit *by faith*.
⁶ Or, *we rejoice*
⁷ Gr. *glory*.
⁸ Or, *we also rejoice*.

---

* For "let us have" read "we have" and in marg. ⁴ read Many ancient authorities read *let us have*. So in verses 2, 3 for "let us" read "we" (twice).—Am. Com.

tience, probation; and probation, hope: and hope 5 putteth not to shame; because the love of God hath been shed abroad in our hearts through the ¹Holy Ghost which was given unto us. For while we 6 were yet weak, in due season Christ died for the ungodly. For scarcely for a righteous man will one 7 die: for peradventure for ²the good man some one would even dare to die. But God commendeth his 8 own love toward us, in that, while we were yet sinners, Christ died for us. Much more then, being 9 now justified ³by his blood, shall we be saved from the wrath *of God* through him. For if, while we 10 were enemies, we were reconciled to God through the death of his Son, much more, being reconciled, shall we be saved ³by his life; and not only so, 11 ⁴but we also rejoice in God through our Lord Jesus Christ, through whom we have now received the reconciliation.

Therefore, as through one man sin entered into the 12 world, and death through sin; and so death passed unto all men, for that all sinned:—for until the law 13 sin was in the world: but sin is not imputed when there is no law. Nevertheless death reigned from 14 Adam until Moses, even over them that had not sinned after the likeness of Adam's transgression, who is a figure of him that was to come. But not as the 15 trespass, so also *is* the free gift. For if by the trespass of the one the many died, much more did the grace of God, and the gift by the grace of the one man, Jesus Christ, abound unto the many. And not 16 as through one that sinned, *so* is the gift: for the judgement *came* of one unto condemnation, but the free gift *came* of many trespasses unto ⁵justification. For if, by the trespass of the one, death reigned 17 through the one; much more shall they that receive the abundance of grace and ⁶of the gift of righteousness reign in life through the one, *even* Jesus Christ. So then as through one trespass *the judge-* 18 *ment came* unto all men to condemnation; even so through one act of righteousness *the free gift came* unto all men to justification of life. For as through 19 the one man's disobedience the many were made sinners, even so through the obedience of the one shall the many be made righteous. And ⁷the law came in 20 beside, that the trespass might abound; but where sin abounded, grace did abound more exceedingly:

---

1 Or, *Holy Spirit*: and so throughout this book.

2 Or, *that which is good**

3 Gr. *in.*

4 Gr. *but also glorying.*

5 Gr. *an act of righteousness.*

6 Some ancient authorities omit *of the gift.*

7 Or, *law.*

---

* Omit marg. ² ("*that which is good*") —Am. Com.

21 that, as sin reigned in death, even so might grace reign through righteousness unto eternal life through Jesus Christ our Lord.

6 What shall we say then? Shall we continue in sin, 2 that grace may abound? God forbid. We who died 3 to sin, how shall we any longer live therein? Or are ye ignorant that all we who were baptized into Christ 4 Jesus were baptized into his death? We were buried therefore with him through baptism into death: that like as Christ was raised from the dead through the glory of the Father, so we also might walk in new- 5 ness of life. For if we have become ¹united with *him* by the likeness of his death, we shall be also *by* 6 *the likeness* of his resurrection; knowing this, that our old man was crucified with *him*, that the body of sin might be done away, that so we should no lon- 7 ger be in bondage to sin; for he that hath died is jus- 8 tified* from sin. But if we died with Christ, we be- 9 lieve that we shall also live with him; knowing that Christ being raised from the dead dieth no more; 10 death no more hath dominion over him. For ²the death that he died, he died unto sin ³once: but ²the 11 life that he liveth, he liveth unto God. Even so reckon ye also yourselves to be dead unto sin, but alive unto God in Christ Jesus.

12 Let not sin therefore reign in your mortal body, 13 that ye should obey the lusts thereof: neither present your members unto sin *as* ⁴instruments of unrighteousness; but present yourselves unto God, as alive from the dead, and your members *as* ⁴instru- 14 ments of righteousness unto God. For sin shall not have dominion over you: for ye are not under law, but under grace.

15 What then? shall we sin, because we are not un- 16 der law, but under grace? God forbid. Know ye not, that to whom ye present yourselves *as* ⁵servants unto obedience, his ⁵servants ye are whom ye obey; whether of sin unto death, or of obedience unto 17 righteousness? But thanks be to God, ⁶that, whereas ye were ⁵servants of sin, ye became obedient from the heart to that ⁷form of teaching whereunto ye 18 were delivered; and being made free from sin, ye 19 became ⁵servants of righteousness. I speak after the manner of men because of the infirmity of your flesh: for as ye presented your members *as* servants to uncleanness and to iniquity unto iniquity, even

1 Or, *united with the likeness . . . with the likeness*

2 Or, *in that*
3 Gr. *once for all.*

4 Or, *weapons*

5 Gr. *bondservants.*

6 Or, *that ye were . . . but ye became*

7 Or, *pattern*

---

* "justified" add marg. Or, *released* —*Am. Com.*

so now present your members *as* servants to righteousness unto sanctification. For when ye were ¹servants of sin, ye were free in regard of righteousness. What fruit then had ye at that time in the things whereof ye are now ashamed? for the end of those things is death. But now being made free from sin, and become servants to God, ye have your fruit unto sanctification, and the end eternal life. For the wages of sin is death; but the free gift of God is eternal life in Christ Jesus our Lord.

¹ Gr. *bondservants*.

Or are ye ignorant brethren (for I speak to men that know ²the law), how that the law hath dominion over a man for so long time as he liveth? For the woman that hath a husband is bound by law to the husband while he liveth; but if the husband die, she is discharged from the law of the husband. So then if, while the husband liveth, she be joined to another man, she shall be called an adulteress: but if the husband die, she is free from the law, so that she is no adulteress, though she be joined to another man. Wherefore, my brethren, ye also were made dead to the law through the body of Christ; that ye should be joined to another, *even* to him who was raised from the dead, that we might bring forth fruit unto God. For when we were in the flesh, the ³sinful passions, which were through the law, wrought in our members to bring forth fruit unto death. But now we have been discharged from the law, having died to that wherein we were holden; so that we serve in newness of the spirit, and not in oldness of the letter.

² Or, *law*

³ Gr. *passions of sins*.

What shall we say then? Is the law sin? God forbid. Howbeit, I had not known sin, except through ²the law: for I had not known ⁴coveting, except the law had said, Thou shalt not ⁴covet: but sin, finding occasion, wrought in me through the commandment all manner of ⁴coveting: for apart from ²the law sin *is* dead. And I was alive apart from ²the law once: but when the commandment came, sin revived, and I died; and the commandment, which *was* unto life, this I found *to be* unto death: for sin, finding occasion, through the commandment beguiled me, and through it slew me. So that the law is holy, and the commandment holy, and righteous, and good. Did then that which is good become death unto me? God forbid. But sin, that it might be shewn to be sin, by working death to me through that which is good;—that

⁴ Or, *lust*

—8. 9. TO THE ROMANS.

through the commandment sin might become ex-
14 ceeding sinful. For we know that the law is spirit-
15 ual: but I am carnal, sold under sin. For that
which I ¹do I know not: for not what I would,   1 Gr. *work.*
that do I practise; but what I hate, that I do.
16 But if what I would not, that I do, I consent
17 unto the law that it is good. So now it is no more
18 I that ¹do it, but sin which dwelleth in me. For I
know that in me, that is, in my flesh, dwelleth no
good thing: for to will is present with me, but to
19 ¹do that which is good *is* not. For the good which
I would I do not: but the evil which I would not,
20 that I practise. But if what I would not, that I do,
it is no more I that ¹do it, but sin which dwelleth   2 Or, *in regard of*
21 in me. I find then ²the law, that, to me who would   *the law*
22 do good, evil is present. For I delight ³in the law   3 Gr. *with.*
23 of God after the inward man: but I see a different
law in my members, warring against the law of my   4 Gr. *in.* Many an-
mind, and bringing me into captivity ⁴under the law   cient authorities read *to.*
24 of sin which is in my members. O wretched man   5 Or, *this body of*
that I am! who shall deliver me out of ⁵the body of   *death*
25 this death? ⁶I thank God through Jesus Christ our   6 Many ancient
Lord. So then I myself with the mind serve* the   authorities read *But thanks be to God.*
law of God; but with the flesh the law of sin.

8 There is therefore now no condemnation to them
2 that are in Christ Jesus. For the law of the Spirit
of life in Christ Jesus made me free from the law
3 of sin and of death. For what the law could not
do, ⁷in that it was weak through the flesh, God,   7 Or, *wherein*
sending his own Son in the likeness of ⁸sinful flesh   8 Gr. *flesh of sin.*
⁹and *as an offering* for sin†, condemned sin in the   9 Or, *and for sin*†
4 flesh: that the ¹⁰ordinance of the law might be ful-   10 Or, *requirement*
filled in us, who walk not after the flesh, but after
5 the spirit‡. For they that are after the flesh do
mind the things of the flesh; but they that are after
6 the spirit the things of the spirit‡. For the mind
of the flesh is death; but the mind of the spirit is
7 life and peace: because the mind of the flesh is enmity against God; for it is not subject to the law
8 of God, neither indeed can it be: and they that are
9 in the flesh cannot please God. But ye are not in
the flesh, but in the spirit‡, if so be that the Spirit
of God dwelleth in you. But if any man hath not

---

* For "I myself with the mind serve" read "I of myself with the mind, indeed, serve"—*Am. Com.*

† Let marg. ⁹ ("*and for sin*") and the text exchange places.—*Am. Com.*

‡ For "spirit" read "Spirit"—*Am. Com.*

the Spirit of Christ, he is none of his. And if Christ 10
is in you, the body is dead because of sin; but the
spirit is life because of righteousness. But if the 11
Spirit of him that raised up Jesus from the dead
dwelleth in you, he that raised up Christ Jesus from
the dead shall quicken also your mortal bodies
¹through his Spirit that dwelleth in you.

So then, brethren, we are debtors, not to the flesh, 12
to live after the flesh: for if ye live after the flesh, 13
ye must die; but if by the spirit* ye ²mortify† the
³deeds of the body, ye shall live. For as many as 14
are led by the Spirit of God, these are sons of God.
For ye received not the spirit of bondage again 15
unto fear; but ye received the spirit of adoption,
whereby we cry, Abba, Father. The Spirit himself 16
beareth witness with our spirit, that we are children
of God: and if children, then heirs; heirs of God, 17
and joint-heirs with Christ; if so be that we suffer
with *him*, that we may be also glorified with *him*.

For I reckon that the sufferings of this present 18
time are not worthy to be compared with the glory
which shall be revealed to us-ward. For the ear- 19
nest expectation of the creation waiteth for the re-
vealing of the sons of God. For the creation was 20
subjected to vanity, not of its own will, but by reason of him who subjected it, ⁴in hope that the crea- 21
tion itself also shall be delivered from the bondage
of corruption into the liberty of the glory of the
children of God. For we know that the whole cre- 22
ation groaneth and travaileth in pain ⁵together until
now. And not only so, but ourselves also, which 23
have the firstfruits of the Spirit, even we ourselves
groan within ourselves, waiting for *our* adoption,
to wit, the redemption of our body. For by‡ hope 24
were we saved: but hope that is seen is not hope:
⁶for who ⁷hopeth for that which he seeth? But if 25
we hope for that which we see not, *then* do we with
patience wait for it.

And in like manner the Spirit also helpeth our in- 26
firmity: for we know not how to pray as we ought;
but the Spirit himself§ maketh intercession for *us*
with groanings which cannot be uttered; and he 27
that searcheth the hearts knoweth what is the mind
of the Spirit, ⁸because he maketh intercession for

Marginal notes:
1 Many ancient authorities read *because of*.
2 Gr. *make to die*.
3 Gr. *doings*.
4 Or, *in hope; because the creation &c.*
5 Or, *with us*
6 Many ancient authorities read *for what a man seeth, why doth he yet hope for?*
7 Some ancient authorities read *awaiteth*.
8 Or, *that*

---

* For "spirit" read "Spirit"—*Am. Com.*
† For "mortify" read "put to death" and omit marg. ².—*Am. Com.*
‡ For "by" read "in" (with marg. Or, *by*) —*Am. Com.*
§ For "himself" read "itself"—*Am. Com.*

28 the saints according to *the will of* God. And we
know that to them that love God ¹all things work
together for good, *even* to them that are called ac-
29 cording to *his* purpose. For whom he foreknew,
he also foreordained *to be* conformed to the image
of his Son, that he might be the firstborn among
30 many brethren: and whom he foreordained, them he
also called: and whom he called, them he also justified: and whom he justified, them he also glorified.
31 What then shall we say to these things? If God
32 *is* for us, who *is* against us? He that spared not
his own Son, but delivered him up for us all, how
shall he not also with him freely give us all things?
33 Who shall lay any thing to the charge of God's elect?
34 ²It is God that justifieth; who is he that shall condemn*? ³It is Christ Jesus that died, yea rather, that
was raised from the dead, who is at the right hand
35 of God, who also maketh intercession for us. Who
shall separate us from the love ⁴of Christ? shall
tribulation, or anguish, or persecution, or famine, or
36 nakedness, or peril, or sword? Even as it is written,

> For thy sake we are killed all the day long;
> We were accounted as sheep for the slaughter.

37 Nay, in all these things we are more than conquer-
38 ors through him that loved us. For I am persuaded,
that neither death, nor life, nor angels, nor principalities, nor things present, nor things to come, nor pow-
39 ers, nor height, nor depth, nor any other ⁵creature,
shall be able to separate us from the love of God,
which is in Christ Jesus our Lord.

9 I say the truth in Christ, I lie not, my conscience
2 bearing witness with me in the Holy Ghost, that I
have great sorrow and unceasing pain in my heart.
3 For I could ⁶wish that I myself were anathema from
Christ for my brethren's sake, my kinsmen accord-
4 ing to the flesh: who are Israelites; whose is the
adoption, and the glory, and the covenants, and the
giving of the law, and the service *of God*, and the
5 promises; whose are the fathers, and of whom is
Christ as concerning the flesh, ⁷who is over all,
6 God blessed ⁸for ever. Amen. But *it is* not as
though the word of God hath come to nought.
7 For they are not all Israel, which are of Israel: neither, because they are Abraham's seed, are they all

1 Some ancient authorities read *God worketh all things with them for good.*

2 Or, *Shall God that justifieth?*

3 Or, *Shall Christ Jesus that died, ... us?*

4 Some ancient authorities read *of God.*

5 Or, *creation*

6 Or, *pray*

7 Some modern interpreters place a full stop after *flesh,* and translate, *He who is God over all be (is) blessed for ever:* or, *He who is over all is God, blessed for ever.* Others punctuate, *flesh, who is over all. God be (is) blessed for ever†.*

8 Or, *unto the ages.*

---

* For "shall condemn" read "condemneth"—*Am. Com.*
† For marg. ⁷ read Or, *flesh: he who is over all, God, be blessed for ever* —*Am. Com.*

children: but, In Isaac shall thy seed be called. 8 That is, it is not the children of the flesh that are children of God; but the children of the promise are reckoned for a seed. 9 For this is a word of promise, According to this season will I come, and Sarah shall have a son. 10 And not only so; but Rebecca also having conceived by one, *even* by our father Isaac—11 for *the children* being not yet born, neither having done anything good or bad, that the purpose of God according to election might stand, not of works, but of him that calleth, 12 it was said unto her, The elder shall serve the younger. 13 Even as it is written, Jacob I loved, but Esau I hated.

14 What shall we say then? Is there unrighteousness with God? God forbid. 15 For he saith to Moses, I will have mercy on whom I have mercy, and I will have compassion on whom I have compassion. 16 So then it is not of him that willeth, nor of him that runneth, but of God that hath mercy. 17 For the scripture saith unto Pharaoh, For this very purpose did I raise thee up, that I might shew in thee my power, and that my name might be published abroad in all the earth. 18 So then he hath mercy on whom he will, and whom he will he hardeneth.

19 Thou wilt say then unto me, Why doth he still find fault? For who withstandeth his will? 20 Nay but, O man, who art thou that repliest against God? Shall the thing formed say to him that formed it, Why didst thou make me thus? 21 Or hath not the potter a right over the clay, from the same lump to make one part a vessel unto honour, and another unto dishonour? 22 What if God, willing* to shew his wrath, and to make his power known, endured with much longsuffering vessels of wrath fitted unto destruction: 23 ¹and that he might make known the riches of his glory upon vessels of mercy, which he afore prepared unto glory, 24 *even* us, whom he also called, not from the Jews only, but also from the Gentiles? 25 As he saith also in Hosea,

> I will call that my people, which was not my people;
> And her beloved, which was not beloved.
> 26 And it shall be, *that* in the place where it was said unto them, Ye are not my people,
> There shall they be called sons of the living God.

¹ Some ancient authorities omit *and*.

---

* "willing" add marg. Or, *although willing* —*Am. Com.*

27 And Isaiah crieth concerning Israel, If the number of the children of Israel be as the sand of the sea, it is
28 the remnant that shall be saved: for the Lord will execute *his* word upon the earth, finishing it and cut-
29 ting it short. And, as Isaiah hath said before,
> Except the Lord of Sabaoth had left us a seed,
> We had become as Sodom, and had been made like unto Gomorrah.
30 What shall we say then? That the Gentiles, which followed not after righteousness, attained to righteousness, even the righteousness which is of faith:
31 but Israel, following after a law of righteousness,
32 did not arrive at *that* law. Wherefore? ¹Because *they sought it* not by faith, but as it were by works.
33 They stumbled at the stone of stumbling; even as it is written,
> Behold, I lay in Zion a stone of stumbling and a rock of offence:
> And he that believeth on ²him shall not be put to shame.

10 Brethren, my heart's ³desire and my supplication
2 to God is for them, that they may be saved. For I bear them witness that they have a zeal for God, but
3 not according to knowledge. For being ignorant of God's righteousness, and seeking to establish their own, they did not subject themselves to the right-
4 eousness of God. For Christ is the end of the law
5 unto righteousness to every one that believeth. For Moses writeth that the man that doeth the righteous-
6 ness which is of the law shall live thereby. But the righteousness which is of faith saith thus, Say not in thy heart, Who shall ascend into heaven? (that is, to
7 bring Christ down:) or, Who shall descend into the abyss? (that is, to bring Christ up from the dead.)
8 But what saith it? The word is nigh thee, in thy mouth, and in thy heart: that is, the word of faith,
9 which we preach: ⁴because if thou shalt ⁵confess with thy mouth Jesus *as* Lord, and shalt believe in thy heart that God raised him from the dead, thou
10 shalt be saved: for with the heart man believeth unto righteousness; and with the mouth confession
11 is made unto salvation. For the scripture saith,
> Whosoever believeth on him shall not be put to
12 shame. For there is no distinction between Jew and Greek: for the same *Lord* is Lord of all, and is
13 rich unto all that call upon him: for, Whosoever shall call upon the name of the Lord shall be saved.
14 How then shall they call on him in whom they have

---

¹ Or, *Because, doing it not by faith, but as it were by works, they stumbled*

² Or, *it*

³ Gr. *good pleasure.*

⁴ Or, *that*

⁵ Some ancient authorities read *confess the word with thy mouth, that Jesus is Lord.*

not believed? and how shall they believe in him whom they have not heard? and how shall they hear without a preacher? and how shall they preach, except they be sent? even as it is written, How beautiful are the feet of them that bring ¹glad tidings of good things!

But they did not all hearken to the ²glad tidings. For Isaiah saith, Lord, who hath believed our report? So belief *cometh* of hearing, and hearing by the word of Christ. But I say, Did they not hear? Yea, verily,

Their sound went out into all the earth,
And their words unto the ends of ³the world.

But I say, Did Israel not know? First Moses saith,
I will provoke you to jealousy with that which is no nation,
With a nation void of understanding will I anger you.

And Isaiah is very bold, and saith,
I was found of them that sought me not;
I became manifest unto them that asked not of me.

But as to Israel he saith, All the day long did I spread out my hands unto a disobedient and gainsaying people.

I say then, Did God cast off his people? God forbid. For I also am an Israelite, of the seed of Abraham, of the tribe of Benjamin. God did not cast off his people which he foreknew. Or wot ye not what the scripture saith ⁴of Elijah? how he pleadeth with God against Israel, Lord, they have killed thy prophets, they have digged down thine altars: and I am left alone, and they seek my life. But what saith the answer of God unto him? I have left for myself seven thousand men, who have not bowed the knee to Baal. Even so then at this present time also there is a remnant according to the election of grace. But if it is by grace, it is no more of works: otherwise grace is no more grace. What then? That which Israel seeketh for, that he obtained not; but the election obtained it, and the rest were hardened: according as it is written, God gave them a spirit of stupor, eyes that they should not see, and ears that they should not hear, unto this very day. And David saith,

Let their table be made a snare, and a trap,
And a stumblingblock, and a recompense unto them:

---

¹ Or, *a gospel*
² Or, *gospel*
³ Gr. *the inhabited earth*.
⁴ Or, *in*

10 Let their eyes be darkened, that they may not see,
And bow thou down their back alway.
11 *I say then, Did they stumble that they might fall? God forbid: but by their ¹fall salvation *is come* unto
12 the Gentiles, for to provoke them to jealousy. Now if their fall is the riches of the world, and their loss the riches of the Gentiles; how much more their fulness?
13 But I speak to you that are Gentiles. Inasmuch then as I am an apostle of Gentiles, I glorify my
14 ministry: if by any means I may provoke to jealousy *them that are* my flesh, and may save some of
15 them. For if the casting away of them *is* the reconciling of the world, what *shall* the receiving *of them*
16 *be*, but life from the dead? And if the firstfruit is holy, so is the lump: and if the root is holy, so are
17 the branches. But if some of the branches were broken off, and thou, being a wild olive, was grafted in among them, and didst become partaker with them ²of the root of the fatness of the olive tree;
18 glory not over the branches: but if thou gloriest, it is not thou that bearest the root, but the root thee.
19 Thou wilt say then, Branches were broken off, that
20 I might be grafted in. Well; by their unbelief they were broken off, and thou standest by thy faith.
21 Be not highminded, but fear: for if God spared not
22 the natural branches, neither will he spare thee. Behold then the goodness and severity of God: toward them that fell, severity; but toward thee, God's goodness, if thou continue in his goodness: otherwise thou
23 also shalt be cut off. And they also, if they continue not in their unbelief, shall be grafted in: for
24 God is able to graft them in again. For if thou wast cut out of that which is by nature a wild olive tree, and wast grafted contrary to nature into a good olive tree: how much more shall these, which are the natural *branches*, be grafted into their own olive tree?
25 For I would not, brethren, have you ignorant of this mystery, lest ye be wise in your own conceits, that a hardening in part hath befallen Israel, until
26 the fulness of the Gentiles be come in; and so all Israel shall be saved: even as it is written,
There shall come out of Zion the Deliverer;
He shall turn away ³ungodliness from Jacob:
27 And this is ⁴my covenant unto them,
When I shall take away their sins.

1 Or, *trespass*

2 Many ancient authorities read *of the root and of the fatness.*

3 Gr. *ungodlinesses.*
4 Gr. *the covenant from me.*

* Begin the paragraph here instead of at ver. 13.—*Am. Com.*

As touching the gospel, they are enemies for your 28
sake: but as touching the election, they are beloved
for the fathers' sake. For the gifts and the calling 29
of God are ¹without repentance. For as ye in time 30
past were disobedient to God, but now have obtained mercy by their disobedience, even so have these 31
also now been disobedient, that by the mercy shewn
to you they also may now obtain mercy. For God 32
hath shut up all unto disobedience, that he might
have mercy upon all.

O the depth ²of the riches ³both of the wisdom 33
and the knowledge of God! how unsearchable are
his judgements, and his ways past tracing out!
For who hath known the mind of the Lord? or 34
who hath been his counsellor? or who hath first 35
given to him, and it shall be recompensed unto
him again? For of him, and through him, and unto 36
him, are all things. To him be the glory ⁴for ever.
Amen.

I beseech you therefore, brethren, by the mercies **12**
of God, to present your bodies a living sacrifice,
holy, ⁵acceptable to God, *which is* your ⁶reasonable*
⁷service. And be not fashioned according to this 2
⁸world: but be ye transformed by the renewing of
your mind, that ye may prove what is ⁹the good and
⁵acceptable and perfect will of God.

For I say, through the grace that was given me, 3
to every man that is among you, not to think of
himself more highly than he ought to think; but so
to think as to think soberly, according as God hath
dealt to each man a measure of faith. For even as 4
we have many members in one body, and all the
members have not the same office: so we, who are 5
many, are one body in Christ, and severally members one of another. And having gifts differing according to the grace that was given to us, whether 6
prophecy, *let us prophesy* according to the proportion of ¹⁰our faith; or ministry, *let us give ourselves* 7
to our ministry; or he that teacheth, to his teaching; or he that exhorteth, to his exhorting: he that 8
giveth, *let him do it* with ¹¹liberality; he that ruleth,
with diligence; he that sheweth mercy, with cheerfulness. Let love be without hypocrisy. Abhor 9
that which is evil; cleave to that which is good. In 10

Marginal notes:
1 Gr. *not repented of*.
2 Or, *of the riches and the wisdom &c.*
3 Or, *both of wisdom &c.*
4 Gr. *unto the ages*.
5 Gr. *well-pleasing*.
6 Or, *spiritual*
7 Or, *worship*
8 Or, *age*
9 Or, *the will of God, even the thing which is good and acceptable and perfect*
10 Or, *the faith*†
11 Gr. *singleness*.

* For "reasonable" read "spiritual" with marg. Gr. *belonging to the reason.*—*Am. Com.*
† Omit marg. ¹⁰ ("*the faith*") —*Am. Com.*

love of the brethren be tenderly affectioned one to
11 another; in honour preferring one another; in diligence not slothful; fervent in spirit; serving ¹the
12 Lord; rejoicing in hope; patient in tribulation; con-
13 tinuing stedfastly in prayer; communicating to the necessities of the saints; ²given to hospitalit..
14 Bless them that persecute you; bless, and curse not.
15 Rejoice with them that rejoice; weep with them that
16 weep. Be of the same mind one toward another. Set not your mind on high things, but ³condescend to ⁴things that are lowly. Be not wise in your own
17 conceits. Render to no man evil for evil. Take thought for things honourable in the sight of all men.
18 If it be possible, as much as in you lieth, be at peace
19 with all men. Avenge not yourselves, beloved, but give place unto ⁵wrath: for it is written, Vengeance belongeth unto me; I will recompense, saith the
20 Lord. But if thine enemy hunger, feed him; if he thirst, give him to drink: for in so doing thou shalt
21 heap coals of fire upon his head. Be not overcome of evil, but overcome evil with good. *

13 Let every soul be in subjection to the higher powers: for there is no power but of God; and the *powers*
2 that be are ordained of God. Therefore he that resisteth the power, withstandeth the ordinance of God: and they that withstand shall receive to themselves
3 judgement. For rulers are not a terror to the good work, but to the evil. And wouldest thou have no fear of the power? do that which is good, and thou
4 shalt have praise from the same: for ⁶he is a minister of God to thee for good. But if thou do that which is evil, be afraid; for ⁶he beareth not the sword in vain: for ⁶he is a minister of God, an avenger for
5 wrath to him that doeth evil. Wherefore *ye* must needs be in subjection, not only because of the wrath,
6 but also for conscience sake. For for this cause ye pay tribute also; for they are ministers of God's service, attending continually upon this very thing.
7 Render to all their dues: tribute to whom tribute *is due*; custom to whom custom; fear to whom fear; honour to whom honour.
8 Owe no man any thing, save to love one another: for he that loveth ⁷his neighbour hath fulfilled ⁸the
9 law. For this, Thou shalt not commit adultery, Thou shalt not kill, Thou shalt not steal, Thou shalt

1 Some ancient authorities read *the opportunity.*

2 Gr. *pursuing.*

3 Gr. *be carried away with.*
4 Or, *them*

5 Or, *the wrath of God**

6 Or, *it*

7 Gr. *the other.*
8 Or, *law*

---

* Let marg. ⁵ ("*the wrath* of God") and the text exchange places.—
1 m. *Com.*

not covet, and if there be any other commandment, it is summed up in this word, namely, Thou shalt love thy neighbour as thyself. Love worketh no ill 10 to his neighbour: love therefore is the fulfilment of ¹the law.

And this, knowing the season, that now it is high 11 time for you to awake out of sleep: for now is ²salvation nearer to us than when we *first* believed. The 12 night is far spent, and the day is at hand: let us therefore cast off the works of darkness, and let us put on the armour of light. Let us walk honestly, 13 as in the day; not in revelling and drunkenness, not in chambering and wantonness, not in strife and jealousy. But put ye on the Lord Jesus Christ, 14 and make not provision for the flesh, to *fulfil* the lusts *thereof*.

But him that is weak in faith receive ye, *yet* not **14** ³to doubtful disputations. One man hath faith to 2 eat all things: but he that is weak eateth herbs. Let 3 not him that eateth set at nought him that eateth not; and let not him that eateth not judge him that eateth: for God hath received him. Who art thou that 4 judgest the ⁴servant of another? to his own lord he standeth or falleth. Yea, he shall be made to stand; for the Lord hath power to make him stand. One 5 man esteemeth one day above another: another esteemeth every day *alike*. Let each man be fully assured in his own mind. He that regardeth the day, 6 regardeth it unto the Lord: and he that eateth, eateth unto the Lord, for he giveth God thanks; and he that eateth not, unto the Lord he eateth not, and giveth God thanks. For none of us liveth to himself, and 7 none dieth to himself. For whether we live, we 8 live unto the Lord; or whether we die, we die unto the Lord: whether we live therefore, or die, we are the Lord's. For to this end Christ died, and lived 9 *again*, that he might be Lord of both the dead and the living. But thou, why dost thou judge thy 10 brother? or thou again, why dost thou set at nought thy brother? for we shall all stand before the judgement-seat of God. For it is written, 11

    As I live, saith the Lord, to me every knee shall bow,
    And every tongue shall ⁵confess to God.

So then each one of us shall give account of himself 12 to God.

Let us not therefore judge one another any more: 13 but judge ye this rather, that no man put a stumbling-

---

1 Or, *law*
2 Or, *our salvation nearer than when, &c.*
3 Or, *for decisions of doubts*
4 Gr. *household-servant.*
5 Or, *give praise*

block in his brother's way, or an occasion of falling.
14 I know, and am persuaded in the Lord Jesus, that nothing is unclean of itself: save that to him who accounteth any thing to be unclean, to him it is un-
15 clean. For if because of meat thy brother is grieved, thou walkest no longer in love. Destroy not with
16 thy meat him for whom Christ died. Let not then
17 your good be evil spoken of: for the kingdom of God is not eating and drinking, but righteousness and
18 peace and joy in the Holy Ghost. For he that herein serveth Christ is well-pleasing to God, and approved
19 of men. So then [1]let us follow after things which make for peace, and things whereby we may edify
20 one another. Overthrow not for meat's sake the work of God. All things indeed are clean; howbeit
21 it is evil for that man who eateth with offence. It is good not to eat flesh, nor to drink wine, nor *to do*
22 *any thing* whereby thy brother stumbleth[2]. The faith which thou hast, have thou to thyself before God. Happy is he that judgeth not himself in that which
23 he [3]approveth. But he that doubteth is condemned if he eat, because *he eateth* not of faith; and whatsoever is not of faith is sin[4].

15 Now we that are strong ought to bear the infirmi-
2 ties of the weak, and not to please ourselves. Let each one of us please his neighbour for that which
3 is good, unto edifying. For Christ also pleased not himself; but, as it is written, The reproaches of them
4 that reproached thee fell upon me. For whatsoever things were written aforetime were written for our learning, that through patience and through comfort
5 of the scriptures we might have hope. Now the God of patience and of comfort grant you to be of the same mind one with another according to Christ
6 Jesus: that with one accord ye may with one mouth glorify the God and Father of our Lord Jesus Christ.
7 Wherefore receive ye one another, even as Christ
8 also received [5]you, to the glory of God. For I say that Christ hath been made a minister of the circumcision for the truth of God, that he might confirm
9 the promises *given* unto the fathers, and that the Gentiles might glorify God for his mercy; as it is written,
 Therefore will I [6]give praise unto thee among the Gentiles,
 And sing unto thy name.
10 And again he saith,
 Rejoice, ye Gentiles, with his people.

---

1 Many ancient authorities read *we follow*.

2 Many ancient authorities add *or is offended, or is weak*.

3 Or, *putteth to the test*

4 Many authorities, some ancient, insert here ch. xvi. 25-27.

5 Some ancient authorities read *us*.

6 Or, *confess*

And again, 11
> Praise the Lord, all ye Gentiles;
> And let all the peoples praise him.

And again, Isaiah saith, 12
> There shall be the root of Jesse,
> And he that ariseth to rule over the Gentiles;
> On him shall the Gentiles hope.

Now the God of hope fill you with all joy and peace 13 in believing, that ye may abound in hope, in the power of the Holy Ghost.

And I myself also am persuaded of you, my breth- 14 ren, that ye yourselves are full of goodness, filled with all knowledge, able also to admonish one another. But I write the more boldly unto you in 15 some measure, as putting you again in remembrance, because of the grace that was given me of God, that I should be a minister of Christ Jesus 16 unto the Gentiles, [1]ministering the gospel of God, that the offering up of the Gentiles might be made acceptable, being sanctified by the Holy Ghost. I 17 have therefore my glorying in Christ Jesus in things pertaining to God. For I will not dare to speak 18 of any [2]things save those which Christ wrought through me, for the obedience of the Gentiles, by word and deed, in the power of signs and wonders, 19 in the power of [3]the Holy Ghost; so that from Jerusalem, and round about even unto Illyricum, I have [4]fully preached the gospel of Christ; yea, [5]making 20 it my aim so to preach the gospel, not where Christ was *already* named, that I might not build upon another man's foundation; but, as it is written, 21
> They shall see, to whom no tidings of him came,
> And they who have not heard shall understand.

Wherefore also I was hindered these many times 22 from coming to you: but now, having no more any 23 place in these regions, and having these many years a longing to come unto you, whensoever I go unto 24 Spain (for I hope to see you in my journey, and to be brought on my way thitherward by you, if first in some measure I shall have been satisfied with your company)—but now, *I say*, I go unto Jerusa- 25 lem, ministering unto the saints. For ℵ hath been 26 the good pleasure of Macedonia and Achaia to make a certain contribution for the poor among the saints that are at Jerusalem. Yea, it hath been their good 27 pleasure; and their debtors they are. For if the

---

[1] Gr. *ministering in sacrifice.*
[2] Gr. *of those things which Christ wrought not through me.*
[3] Many ancient authorities read *the Spirit of God.* One reads *the Spirit.*
[4] Gr. *fulfilled.*
[5] Gr. *being ambitious.*

Gentiles have been made partakers of their spiritual things, they owe it *to them* also to minister unto
28 them in carnal things. When therefore I have accomplished this, and have sealed to them this fruit,
29 I will go on by you unto Spain. And I know that, when I come unto you, I shall come in the fulness of the blessing of Christ.
30 Now I beseech you, brethren, by our Lord Jesus Christ, and by the love of the Spirit, that ye strive together with me in your prayers to God for me;
31 that I may be delivered from them that are disobedient in Judæa, and *that* my ministration which *I have* for Jerusalem may be acceptable to the saints;
32 that I may come unto you in joy through the will
33 of God, and together with you find rest. Now the God of peace be with you all. Amen.

16 I commend unto you Phœbe our sister, who is a
2 ¹servant of the church that is at Cenchreæ: that ye receive her in the Lord, worthily of the saints, and that ye assist her in whatsoever matter she may have need of you: for she herself also hath been a succourer of many, and of mine own self.   1 Or, *deaconess*
3 Salute Prisca and Aquila my fellow-workers in
4 Christ Jesus, who for my life laid down their own necks; unto whom not only I give thanks, but also all
5 the churches of the Gentiles: and *salute* the church that is in their house. Salute Epænetus my beloved,
6 who is the firstfruits of Asia unto Christ. Salute
7 Mary, who bestowed much labour on you. Salute Andronicus and ²Junias, my kinsmen, and my fellow-prisoners, who are of note among the apostles,   2 Or, *Junia*
8 who also have been in Christ before me. Salute
9 Ampliatus my beloved in the Lord. Salute Urbanus our fellow-worker in Christ, and Stachys my
10 beloved. Salute Apelles the approved in Christ. Salute them which are of the *household* of Aristo-
11 bulus. Salute Herodion my kinsman. Salute them of the *household* of Narcissus, which are in the Lord.
12 Salute Tryphæna and Tryphosa, who labour in the Lord. Salute Persis the beloved, which laboured
13 much in the Lord. Salute Rufus the chosen in the
14 Lord, and his mother and mine. Salute Asyncritus, Phlegon, Hermes, Patrobas, Hermas, and the breth-
15 ren that are with them. Salute Philologus and Julia, Nereus and his sister, and Olympas, and all the
16 saints that are with them. Salute one another with a holy kiss. All the churches of Christ salute you.

Now I beseech you, brethren, mark them which 17 are causing the divisions and occasions of stumbling, contrary to the ¹doctrine which ye learned: and turn away from them. For they that are such 18 serve not our Lord Christ, but their own belly; and by their smooth and fair speech they beguile the hearts of the innocent. For your obedience is come 19 abroad unto all men. I rejoice therefore over you: but I would have you wise unto that which is good, and simple unto that which is evil. And the God 20 of peace shall bruise Satan under your feet shortly. The grace of our Lord Jesus Christ be with you. Timothy my fellow-worker saluteth you; and Lu- 21 cius and Jason and Sosipater, my kinsmen. I Ter- 22 tius, ²who write the epistle, salute you in the Lord. Gaius my host, and of the whole church, saluteth 23 you. Erastus the treasurer of the city saluteth you, and Quartus the brother.³

⁴Now to him that is able to stablish you accord- 25 ing to my gospel and the preaching of Jesus Christ, according to the revelation of the mystery which hath been kept in silence through times eternal, but 26 now is manifested, and ⁵by the scriptures of the prophets, according to the commandment of the eternal God, is made known unto all the nations unto obedience ⁶of faith; to the only wise God, through Je- 27 sus Christ, ⁷to whom be the glory ⁸for ever. Amen.

1 Or, *teaching*
2 Or, *who write the epistle in the Lord, salute you.*
3 Some ancient authorities insert here ver. 24 *The grace of our Lord Jesus Christ be with you all. Amen,* and omit the like words in ver. 20.
4 Some ancient authorities omit ver. 25-27. Compare the end of ch. xiv.
5 Gr. *through.*
6 Or, *to the faith*
7 Some ancient authorities omit *to whom.*
8 Gr. *unto the ages.*

THE FIRST EPISTLE OF PAUL THE APOSTLE TO THE CORINTHIANS.

1 Paul, called *to be* an apostle of Jesus Christ through the will of God, and Sosthenes [1]our brother, 2 unto the church of God which is at Corinth, *even* them that are sanctified in Christ Jesus, called *to be* saints, with all that call upon the name of our Lord Jesus Christ in every place, their *Lord* and ours: 3 Grace to you and peace from God our Father and the Lord Jesus Christ. 4 I thank [2]my God always concerning you, for the grace of God which was given you in Christ Jesus; 5 that in every thing ye were enriched in him, in all 6 [3]utterance and all knowledge; even as the testimony 7 of Christ was confirmed in you: so that ye come behind in no gift; waiting for the revelation of our 8 Lord Jesus Christ; who shall also confirm you unto the end, *that ye be* unreproveable in the day of our 9 Lord Jesus Christ. God is faithful, through whom ye were called into the fellowship of his Son Jesus Christ our Lord. 10 Now I beseech you, brethren, through the name of our Lord Jesus Christ, that ye all speak the same thing, and *that* there be no divisions among you; but *that* ye be perfected together in the same 11 mind and in the same judgement. For it hath been signified unto me concerning you, my brethren, by them *which are of the household* of Chloe, 12 that there are contentions among you. Now this I mean, that each one of you saith, I am of Paul; and I of Apollos; and I of Cephas; and I of Christ. 13 [4]Is Christ divided? was Paul crucified for you? or 14 were ye baptized into the name of Paul? [5]I thank

[1] Gr. *the brother.*
[2] Some ancient authorities omit *my.*
[3] Gr. *word.*
[4] Or, *Christ is divided. Was Paul crucified for you?*
[5] Some ancient authorities read *I give thanks that.*

God that I baptized none of you, save Crispus and Gaius; lest any man should say that ye were baptized into my name. And I baptized also the household of Stephanas: besides, I know not whether I baptized any other. For Christ sent me not to baptize, but to preach the gospel: not in wisdom of words, lest the cross of Christ should be made void.

For the word of the cross is to them that are perishing foolishness; but unto us which are being saved* it is the power of God. For it is written,

 I will destroy the wisdom of the wise,
 And the prudence of the prudent will I reject†.

Where is the wise? where is the scribe? where is the disputer of this ¹world? hath not God made foolish the wisdom of the world? For seeing that in the wisdom of God the world through its wisdom knew not God, it was God's good pleasure through the foolishness of the ²preaching to save them that believe. Seeing that Jews ask for signs, and Greeks seek after wisdom: but we preach ³Christ crucified, unto Jews a stumblingblock, and unto Gentiles foolishness; but unto ⁴them that are called, both Jews and Greeks, Christ the power of God, and the wisdom of God. Because the foolishness of God is wiser than men; and the weakness of God is stronger than men.

For ⁵behold your calling, brethren, how that not many wise after the flesh, not many mighty, not many noble, ⁶*are called*: but God chose the foolish things of the world, that he might put to shame them that are wise; and God chose the weak things of the world, that he might put to shame the things that are strong; and the base things of the world, and the things that are despised, did God choose, *yea* ⁷and the things that are not, that he might bring to nought the things that are: that no flesh should glory before God. But of him are ye in Christ Jesus, who was made unto us wisdom from God, ⁸and righteousness and sanctification, and redemption: that, according as it is written, He that glorieth, let him glory in the Lord.

And I, brethren, when I came unto you, came not with excellency of ⁹speech or of wisdom, pro-

---

1 Or, *age*
2 Gr. *thing preached.*
3 Or, *a Messiah*
4 Gr. *the called themselves.*
5 Or, *ye behold*
6 Or, *have part therein‡*
7 Many ancient authorities omit *and.*
8 Or, *both righteousness and sanctification and redemption*
9 Or, *word*

---

* For "are perishing ... are being saved" read "perish ... are saved" and put the present text into the marg.—*Am. Com.*
† For "And ... reject" read "And the discernment of the discerning will I bring to nought"—*Am. Com.*
‡ Omit marg. ⁶ (Or, "have part therein")—*Am. Com.*

2 claiming to you the ¹mystery of God. For I determined not to know any thing among you, save
3 Jesus Christ, and him crucified. And I was with you in weakness, and in fear, and in much trembling.
4 And my ²speech and my ³preaching were not in persuasive words of wisdom, but in demonstration
5 of the Spirit and of power: that your faith should not ⁴stand in the wisdom of men, but in the power of God.
6 Howbeit we speak wisdom among the ⁵perfect*: yet a wisdom not of this ⁶world, nor of the rulers
7 of this ⁶world, which are coming to nought: but we speak God's wisdom in a mystery, *even* the *wisdom* that hath been hidden, which God foreordained be-
8 fore the worlds unto our glory: which none of the rulers of this world knoweth†: for had they known it, they would not have crucified the Lord of glory:
9 but as it is written,

> Things which eye saw not, and ear heard not,
> And *which* entered not into the heart of man,
> Whatsoever things God prepared for them that love him.

10 ⁷But unto us God revealed ⁸*them* through the Spirit: for the Spirit searcheth all things, yea, the deep
11 things of God. For who among men knoweth the things of a man, save the spirit of the man, which is in him? even so the things of God none knoweth,
12 save the Spirit of God. But we received, not the spirit of the world, but the spirit which is of God‡; that we might know the things that are freely
13 given to us by God§. Which things also we speak, not in words which man's wisdom teacheth, but which the Spirit teacheth; ⁹ ¹⁰comparing spiritual
14 things with spiritual‖. Now the natural¶ man receiveth not the things of the Spirit of God: for they are foolishness unto him; and he cannot know
15 them, because they are spiritually ¹¹judged. But he that is spiritual ¹²judgeth all things, and he himself
16 is ¹¹judged of no man. For who hath known the mind of the Lord, that he should instruct him? But we have the mind of Christ.

1 Many ancient authorities read *testimony*.
2 Or, *word*
3 Gr. *thing preached*.
4 Gr. *be*.
5 Or, *fullgrown*
6 Or, *age*: and so in ver. 7, 8; but not in ver. 12.
7 Some ancient authorities read *For*.
8 Or, *it*
9 Or, *combining*
10 Or, *interpreting spiritual things to spiritual men*
11 Or, *examined*
12 Or, *examineth*

---

* For "the perfect" read "them that are fullgrown"—*Am. Com.*
† For "knoweth" read "hath known"—*Am. Com.*
‡ For "is of God" read "is from God"—*Am. Com.*
§ For "are freely given to us by God" read "were freely given to us of God"—*Am. Com.*
‖ For "comparing spiritual things with spiritual" read "combining spiritual things with spiritual *words*" and omit marg. ⁹.—*Am. Com.*
¶ "natural" add marg. Or, *unspiritual* Gr. *psychical*.—*Am. Com.*

And I, brethren, could not speak unto you as unto spiritual, but as unto carnal, as unto babes in Christ. I fed you with milk, not with meat; for ye were not yet able *to bear it*: nay, not even now are ye able; for ye are yet carnal: for whereas there is among you jealousy and strife, are ye not carnal, and walk after the manner of men? For when one saith, I am of Paul; and another, I am of Apollos; are ye not men? What then is Apollos? and what is Paul? Ministers through whom ye believed; and each as the Lord gave to him. I planted, Apollos watered; but God gave the increase. So then neither is he that planteth any thing, neither he that watereth; but God that giveth the increase. Now he that planteth and he that watereth are one: but each shall receive his own reward according to his own labour. For we are God's fellow-workers: ye are God's ¹husbandry, God's building.

According to the grace of God which was given unto me, as a wise masterbuilder I laid a foundation; and another buildeth thereon. But let each man take heed how he buildeth thereon. For other foundation can no man lay than that which is laid, which is Jesus Christ. But if any man buildeth on the foundation gold, silver, costly stones, wood, hay, stubble; each man's work shall be made manifest: for the day shall declare it, because it is revealed in fire; ²and the fire itself shall prove each man's work of what sort it is. If any man's work shall abide which he built thereon, he shall receive a reward. If any man's work shall be burned, he shall suffer loss: but he himself shall be saved; yet so as through fire.

Know ye not that ye are a ³temple of God, and *that* the Spirit of God dwelleth in you? If any man destroyeth the ³temple of God, him shall God destroy; for the ³temple of God is holy, ⁴which *temple* ye are.

Let no man deceive himself. If any man thinketh that he is wise among you in this ⁵world, let him become a fool, that he may become wise. For the wisdom of this world is foolishness with God. For it is written, He that taketh the wise in their craftiness: and again, The Lord knoweth the reasonings of the wise, that they are vain. Wherefore let no one glory in men. For all things are yours; whether Paul, or Apollos, or Cephas, or the world, or life, or death, or things present, or things to come; all are yours; and ye are Christ's; and Christ is God's.

---

¹ Gr. *tilled land.*

² Or, *and each man's work, of what sort it is, the fire shall prove it.*

³ Or, *sanctuary*

⁴ Or, *and such are ye*

⁵ Or, *age*

4 Let a man so account of us, as of ministers of
2 Christ, and stewards of the mysteries of God. Here, moreover, it is required in stewards, that a man be
3 found faithful. But with me it is a very small thing that I should be ¹judged of you, or of man's ²judge-
4 ment: yea, I ³judge not mine own self. For I know nothing against myself; yet am I not hereby justi-
5 fied: but he that ⁴judgeth me is the Lord. Wherefore judge nothing before the time, until the Lord come, who will both bring to light the hidden things of darkness, and make manifest the counsels of the hearts; and then shall each man have his praise from God.

6 Now these things, brethren, I have in a figure transferred to myself and Apollos for your sakes; that in us ye might learn not *to go* beyond the things which are written; that no one of you be puffed up
7 for the one against the other. For who maketh thee to differ? and what hast thou that thou didst not receive? but if thou didst receive it, why dost
8 thou glory, as if thou hadst not received it? Already are ye filled, already ye are become rich, ye have reigned* without us: yea and I would that ye did reign, that we also might reign with you.
9 For, I think, God hath set forth us the apostles last of all, as men doomed to death: for we are made a spectacle unto the world, ⁵and to angels†, and to
10 men. We are fools for Christ's sake, but ye are wise in Christ; we are weak, but ye are strong; ye
11 have glory, but we have dishonour. Even unto this present hour we both hunger, and thirst, and are naked, and are buffeted, and have no certain dwell-
12 ingplace; and we toil, working with our own hands: being reviled, we bless; being persecuted, we en-
13 dure; being defamed, we intreat: we are made as the ⁶filth of the world, the offscouring of all things, even until now.

14 I write not these things to shame you, but to ad-
15 monish you as my beloved children. For though ye should have ten thousand tutors in Christ, yet *have ye* not many fathers: for in Christ Jesus I be-
16 gat you through the gospel. I beseech you there-
17 fore, be ye imitators of me. For this cause have I sent unto you Timothy, who is my beloved and faithful child in the Lord, who shall put you in re-

¹ Or, *examined*
² Gr. *day*.
³ Or, *examine*
⁴ Or, *examineth*

⁵ Or, *both to angels and men*

⁶ Or, *refuse*

---

* For "have reigned" read "have come to reign"—*Am. Com.*
† For "and to angels" read "both to angels" and substitute the present text for the marg.—*Am. Com.*

membrance of my ways which be in Christ, even as I teach everywhere in every church. Now some 18 are puffed up, as though I were not coming to you. But I will come to you shortly, if the Lord will; and 19 I will know, not the word of them which are puffed up, but the power. For the kingdom of God is not 20 in word, but in power. What will ye? shall I come 21 unto you with a rod, or in love and a spirit of meekness*?

It is actually reported that there is fornication 5 among you, and such fornication as is not even among the Gentiles, that one *of you* hath his father's wife. And ¹ye are puffed up, and ²did not rather 2 mourn, that he that had done this deed might be taken away from among you. For I verily, being 3 absent in body but present in spirit, have already, as though I were present, judged him that hath so wrought this thing, in the name of our Lord Jesus, 4 ye being gathered together, and my spirit, with the power of our Lord Jesus, to deliver such a one unto 5 Satan for the destruction of the flesh, that the spirit may be saved in the day of the Lord ³Jesus. Your 6 glorying is not good. Know ye not that a little leaven leaveneth the whole lump? Purge out the 7 old leaven, that ye may be a new lump, even as ye are unleavened. For our passover also hath been sacrificed, *even* Christ: wherefore let us ⁴keep the 8 feast, not with old leaven, neither with the leaven of malice and wickedness, but with the unleavened bread of sincerity and truth.

I wrote unto you in my epistle to have no com- 9 pany with fornicators; ⁵not altogether with the for- 10 nicators of this world, or with the covetous and extortioners, or with idolaters; for then must ye needs go out of the world: but⁶ now I write unto you not 11 to keep company, if any man that is named a brother be a fornicator, or covetous, or an idolater, or a reviler, or a drunkard, or an extortioner; with such a one no, not to eat. For what have I to do with 12 judging them that are without? Do not ye judge them that are within, whereas them that are without 13 God judgeth? Put away the wicked man from among yourselves.

Dare any of you, having a matter against ⁷his 6 neighbour, go to law before the unrighteous, and not

1 Or, *are ye puffed up?*
2 Or, *did ye not rather mourn, ... you?*
3 Some ancient authorities omit *Jesus.*
4 Gr. *keep festival.*
5 Or, *not at all meaning the fornicators†, &c.*
6 Or, *as it is, I wrote†.*
7 Gr. *the other.*

---

* For "meekness" read "gentleness"—*Am. Com.*
† Let marg. ⁵ and ⁶ and the text exchange places.—*Am. Com.*

I. CORINTHIANS.

2 before the saints? Or know ye not that the saints shall judge the world? and if the world is judged by you, are ye unworthy ¹to judge the smallest mat-
3 ters? Know ye not that we shall judge angels? How much more, things that pertain to this life?
4 If then ye have ²to judge things pertaining to this life, ³do ye set them to judge who are of no account
5 in the church? I say *this* to move you to shame. Is it so, that there cannot be *found* among you one wise man, who shall be able to decide between his
6 brethren, but brother goeth to law with brother, and
7 that before unbelievers? Nay, already it is altogether ⁴a defect in you, that ye have lawsuits one with another. Why not rather take wrong? why
8 not rather be defrauded? Nay, but ye yourselves
9 do wrong, and defraud, and that *your* brethren. Or know ye not that the unrighteous shall not inherit the kingdom of God? Be not deceived: neither fornicators, nor idolaters, nor adulterers, nor effemi-
10 nate, nor abusers of themselves with men, nor thieves, nor covetous, nor drunkards, nor revilers, nor extor-
11 tioners, shall inherit the kingdom of God. And such were some of you: but ye ⁵were washed, but ye were sanctified, but ye were justified in the name of the Lord Jesus Christ, and in the Spirit of our God.
12 All things are lawful for me; but not all things are expedient. All things are lawful for me; but I
13 will not be brought under the power of any. Meats for the belly, and the belly for meats: but God shall bring to nought both it and them. But the body is not for fornication, but for the Lord; and the Lord
14 for the body: and God both raised the Lord, and
15 will raise up us through his power. Know ye not that your bodies are members of Christ? shall I then take away the members of Christ, and make
16 them members of a harlot? God forbid. Or know ye not that he that is joined to a harlot is one body?
17 for, The twain, saith he, shall become one flesh. But
18 he that is joined unto the Lord is one spirit. Flee fornication. Every sin that a man doeth is without the body; but he that committeth fornication sinneth
19 against his own body. Or know ye not that your body is a ⁶temple of the ⁷Holy Ghost which is in you, which ye have from God? and ye are not your own;
20 for ye were bought with a price: glorify God therefore in your body.

7 Now concerning the things whereof ye wrote: It
2 is good for a man not to touch a woman. But, be-

---

1 Gr. *of the smallest tribunals.*
2 Gr. *tribunals pertaining to.*
3 Or, *set them ... church.*
4 Or, *a loss to you*
5 Gr. *washed yourselves.*
6 Or, *sanctuary*
7 Or, *Holy Spirit*

cause of fornications, let each man have his own wife, and let each woman have her own husband. Let the husband render unto the wife her due: and 3 likewise also the wife unto the husband. The wife 4 hath not power over her own body, but the husband: and likewise also the husband hath not power over his own body, but the wife. Defraud ye not one 5 the other, except it be by consent for a season, that ye may give yourselves unto prayer, and may be together again, that Satan tempt you not because of your incontinency. But this I say by way of per- 6 mission*, not of commandment. [1] Yet I would that 7 all men were even as I myself. Howbeit each man hath his own gift from God, one after this manner, and another after that.

[1] Many ancient authorities read *For*.

But I say to the unmarried and to widows, It is 8 good for them if they abide even as I. But if they 9 have not continency, let them marry: for it is better to marry than to burn. But unto the married I 10 give charge, *yea* not I, but the Lord, That the wife depart not from her husband (but and if she depart, 11 let her remain unmarried, or else be reconciled to her husband); and that the husband leave not his wife. But to the rest say I, not the Lord: If any 12 brother hath an unbelieving wife, and she is content to dwell with him, let him not leave her. And the 13 woman which hath an unbelieving husband, and he is content to dwell with her, let her not leave her husband. For the unbelieving husband is sancti- 14 fied in the wife, and the unbelieving wife is sanctified in the brother: else were your children unclean; but now are they holy. Yet if the unbelieving de- 15 parteth, let him depart: the brother or the sister is not under bondage in such *cases*: but God hath called [2] us in peace. For how knowest thou, O wife, 16 whether thou shalt save thy husband? or how knowest thou, O husband, whether thou shalt save thy wife? Only, as the Lord hath distributed to each 17 man, as God hath called each, so let him walk. And so ordain I in all the churches. Was any man called 18 being circumcised? let him not become uncircumcised. Hath any been called in uncircumcision? let him not be circumcised. Circumcision is nothing, 19 and uncircumcision is nothing; but the keeping of the commandments of God. Let each man abide 20 in that calling wherein he was called. Wast thou 21

[2] Many ancient authorities read *you*.

---

* For "permission" read "concession"—*Am. Com.*

called being a bondservant? care not for it: ¹but if* 22 thou canst become free, use *it* rather. For he that was called in the Lord, being a bondservant, is the 23 Lord's freedman: likewise he that was called, being 24 free, is Christ's bondservant. Ye were bought with a price; become not bondservants of men. Brethren, let each man, wherein he was called, therein abide with God.

25 Now concerning virgins I have no commandment of the Lord: but I give my judgement, as one that 26 hath obtained mercy of the Lord to be faithful†. I think therefore that this is good by reason of the present distress‡, *namely*, that it is good for a man 27 ²to be as he is. Art thou bound unto a wife? seek not to be loosed. Art thou loosed from a wife? 28 seek not a wife. But and if thou marry, thou hast not sinned; and if a virgin marry, she hath not sinned. Yet such shall have tribulation in the flesh: 29 and I would spare you. But this I say, brethren, the time ³is shortened, that henceforth both those that have wives may be as though they had none; 30 and those that weep, as though they wept not; and those that rejoice, as though they rejoiced not; and 31 those that buy, as though they possessed not; and those that use the world, as not ⁴abusing it§: for the 32 fashion of this world passeth away. But I would have you to be free from cares. He that is unmarried is careful for the things of the Lord, how he 33 may please the Lord: but he that is married is careful for the things of the world, how he may please 34 his ⁵wife. And there is a difference also between the wife and the virgin. She that is unmarried is careful for the things of the Lord, that she may be holy both in body and in spirit: but she that is married is careful for the things of the world, how 35 she may please her husband. And this I say for your own profit; not that I may cast a ⁶snare upon you, but for that which is seemly, and that ye may 36 attend upon the Lord without distraction. But if any man thinketh that he behaveth himself unseemly toward his virgin⁷ *daughter*, if she be past the

---

1 Or, *nay, even if*

2 Gr. *so to be*.

3 Or, *is shortened henceforth, that both those, &c.*

4 Or, *using it to the full*

5 Or, *wife, and is divided.* So also the wife and the virgin: she that is unmarried is careful, &c. Many ancient authorities read wife, and is divided. So also the woman that is unmarried and the virgin is careful, &c.

6 Or, *constraint* Gr. *noose*.

7 Or, *virgin* (omitting *daughter*)

---

* Let marg.¹ ("*nay, even if*") and the text exchange places.—*Am. Com.*

† For "faithful" read "trustworthy"—*Am. Com.*

‡ For "the present distress" read "the distress that is upon us"—*Am. Com.*

§ For "abusing it" read "using it to the full" and omit the margin.—*Am. Com.*

flower of her age, and if need so requireth, let him do what he will; he sinneth not; let them marry. But he that standeth stedfast in his heart, hav- 37 ing no necessity, but hath power as touching his own will, and hath determined this in his own heart, to keep his own ¹virgin *daughter*, shall do well. So then both he that giveth his own ¹virgin 38 *daughter* in marriage doeth well; and he that giveth her not in marriage shall do better. A wife is 39 bound for so long time as her husband liveth; but if the husband be ²dead, she is free to be married to whom she will; only in the Lord. But she is hap- 40 pier if she abide as she is, after my judgement: and I think that I also have the Spirit of God.

Now concerning things sacrificed to idols: We 8 know that we all have knowledge. Knowledge puffeth up, but love ³edifieth. If any man think- 2 eth that he knoweth any thing, he knoweth not yet as he ought to know; but if any man loveth God, 3 the same is known of him*. Concerning therefore 4 the eating of things sacrificed to idols, we know that no idol is *anything* in the world, and that there is no God but one. For though there be that are called 5 gods, whether in heaven or on earth; as there are gods many, and lords many; yet to us there is one 6 God, the Father, of whom are all things, and we unto him; and one Lord, Jesus Christ, through whom are all things, and we through him. How- 7 beit in all men there is not that knowledge: but some, being used until now to the idol, eat as *of* a thing sacrificed to an idol; and their conscience being weak is defiled. But meat will not commend† 8 us to God: neither, if we eat not, ⁴are we the worse; nor, if we eat, ⁵are we the better. But take heed 9 lest by any means this ⁶liberty of yours become a stumblingblock to the weak. For if a man see thee 10 which hast knowledge sitting at meat in an idol's temple, will not his conscience, if he is weak, ⁷be emboldened to eat things sacrificed to idols? For 11 ⁸through thy knowledge he that is weak perisheth, the brother for whose sake Christ died. And thus, 12 sinning against the brethren, and wounding their conscience when it is weak, ye sin against Christ. Wherefore, if meat maketh my brother to stumble, 13 I will eat no flesh for evermore, that I make not my brother to stumble.

1 Or, *virgin* (omitting *daughter*)
2 Gr. *fallen asleep.*
3 Gr. *buildeth up.*
4 Gr. *do we lack.*
5 Gr. *do we abound.*
6 Or, *power*
7 Gr. *be builded up.*
8 Gr. *in.*

---

* For "of him" read "by him"—*Am. Com.*
† "commend" add marg. Gr. *present.*—*Am. Com.*

9 Am I not free? am I not an apostle? have I not seen Jesus our Lord? are not ye my work in the 2 Lord? If to others I am not an apostle, yet at least I am to you: for the seal of mine apostleship are 3 ye in the Lord. My defence to them that examine 4 me is this. Have we no right to eat and to drink? 5 Have we no right to lead about a wife that is a ¹believer, even as the rest of the apostles, and the 6 brethren of the Lord, and Cephas? Or I only and Barnabas, have we not a right to forbear working? 7 What soldier ever serveth at his own charges? who planteth a vineyard, and eateth not the fruit thereof? or who feedeth a flock, and eateth not of the 8 milk of the flock? Do I speak these things after the manner of men? or saith not the law also the 9 same? For it is written in the law of Moses, Thou shalt not muzzle the ox when he treadeth out the 10 corn. Is it for the oxen that God careth, or ²saith he it altogether* for our sake? Yea, for our sake it was written: because he that ploweth ought to plow in hope, and he that thresheth, *to thresh* in hope of 11 partaking. If we sowed unto you spiritual things, is it a great matter if we shall reap your carnal 12 things? If others partake of *this* right over you, do not we yet more? Nevertheless we did not use this right; but we bear all things, that we may cause no 13 hindrance to the gospel of Christ. Know ye not that they which minister about sacred things eat *of* the things of the temple, *and* they which wait upon 14 the altar have their portion with the altar? Even so did the Lord ordain that they which proclaim 15 the gospel should live of the gospel. But I have used none of these things: and I write not these things that it may be so done in my case: for *it were* good for me rather to die, than that any man 16 should make my glorying void. For if I preach the gospel, I have nothing to glory of; for necessity is laid upon me; for woe is unto me, if I preach not 17 the gospel. For if I do this of mine own will, I have a reward: but if not of mine own will, I have 18 a stewardship intrusted to me. What then is my reward? That, when I preach the gospel, I may make the gospel without charge, so as not to use to the 19 full my right in the gospel. For though I was free from all *men*, I brought myself under bondage to all,

1 Gr. *sister*.

2 Or, *saith he it, as he doubtless doth, for our sake?*

---

* "altogether" let "assuredly" be the rendering in the text, and substitute "*altogether*" for the marg.—*Am. Com.*

that I might gain the more. And to the Jews I be- 20
came as a Jew, that I might gain Jews; to them
that are under the law, as under the law, not being
myself under the law, that I might gain them that
are under the law; to them that are without law, 21
as without law, not being without law to God, but
under law to Christ, that I might gain them that
are without law. To the weak I became weak, 22
that I might gain the weak: I am become all things
to all men, that I may by all means save some. And 23
I do all things for the gospel's sake, that I may be
a joint partaker thereof. Know ye not that they 24
which run in a ¹race run all, but one receiveth the
prize? Even so run, that ye may attain. And ev- 25
ery man that striveth in the games is temperate in
all things. Now they *do it* to receive a corruptible
crown; but we an incorruptible. I therefore so 26
run, as not uncertainly; so ²fight I, as not beating
the air: but I ³buffet my body, and bring it into 27
bondage: lest by any means, after that I have
preached* to others, I myself should be rejected.

For I would not, brethren, have you ignorant, how **10**
that our fathers were all under the cloud, and all
passed through the sea; and were all baptized ⁴unto 2
Moses in the cloud and in the sea; and did all eat 3
the same spiritual meat; and did all drink the same 4
spiritual drink: for they drank of a spiritual rock
that followed them: and the rock was Christ. How- 5
beit with most of them God was not well pleased:
for they were overthrown in the wilderness. Now 6
⁵these things were our examples, to the intent we
should not lust after evil things, as they also lusted.
Neither be ye idolaters, as were some of them; as it 7
is written, The people sat down to eat and drink,
and rose up to play. Neither let us commit forni- 8
cation, as some of them committed, and fell in one
day three and twenty thousand. Neither let us 9
tempt the ⁶Lord, as some of them tempted, and perished by the serpents. Neither murmur ye, as some 10
of them murmured, and perished by the destroyer.
Now these things happened unto them ⁷by way of 11
example; and they were written for our admonition,
upon whom the ends of the ages are come. Where- 12
fore let him that thinketh he standeth take heed
lest he fall. There hath no temptation taken you 13
but such as man can bear: but God is faithful, who

---

1 Gr. *racecourse*.

2 Gr. *box*.
3 Gr. *bruise*.

4 Gr. *into*.

5 Or, *in these things they became figures of us*

6 Some ancient authorities read *Christ*.

7 Gr. *by way of figure*.

* "have preached" add marg. Or, *have been a herald* —*Am. Com.*

will not suffer you to be tempted above that ye are able; but will with the temptation make also the way of escape, that ye may be able to endure it.

14 Wherefore, my beloved, flee from idolatry. I speak
15 as to wise men; judge ye what I say. The cup of
16 blessing which we bless, is it not a ¹communion of the blood of Christ? The ²bread which we break, is
17 it not a ¹communion of the body of Christ? ³seeing that we, who are many, are one ²bread, one body:
18 for we all partake ⁴of the one ²bread. Behold Israel after the flesh: have not they which eat the
19 sacrifices communion with the altar? What say I then? that a thing sacrificed to idols is any thing,
20 or that an idol is any thing? But *I say*, that the things which the Gentiles sacrifice, they sacrifice to ⁵devils, and not to God: and I would not that ye
21 should have communion with ⁵devils. Ye cannot drink the cup of the Lord, and the cup of ⁵devils:
22 ye cannot partake of the table of the Lord, and of the table of ⁵devils. Or do we provoke the Lord to jealousy? are we stronger than he?
23 All things are lawful; but all things are not expedient. All things are lawful; but all things ⁶edify
24 not. Let no man seek his own, but *each* his neigh-
25 bour's *good*. Whatsoever is sold in the shambles,
26 eat, asking no question for conscience sake; for the
27 earth is the Lord's, and the fulness thereof. If one of them that believe not biddeth you *to a feast*, and ye are disposed to go; whatsoever is set before you,
28 eat, asking no question for conscience sake. But if any man say unto you, This hath been offered in sacrifice, eat not, for his sake that shewed it, and for
29 conscience sake: conscience, I say, not thine own, but the other's; for why is my liberty judged by
30 another conscience? ⁷If I by grace partake, why am I evil spoken of for that for which I give thanks?
31 Whether therefore ye eat, or drink, or whatsoever
32 ye do, do all to the glory of God. Give no occasion of stumbling, either to Jews, or to Greeks, or
33 to the church of God: even as I also please all men in all things, not seeking mine own profit, but the
11 *profit* of the many, that they may be saved. Be ye imitators of me, even as I also am of Christ.
2 Now I praise you that ye remember me in all things, and hold fast the traditions, even as I deliv-
3 ered them to you. But I would have you know, that the head of every man is Christ; and the head of the woman is the man; and the head of Christ is

¹ Or, *participation in*
² Or, *loaf*
³ Or, *seeing that there is one bread, we, who are many, are one body*
⁴ Gr. *from*.
⁵ Gr. *demons*.
⁶ Gr. *build not up*.
⁷ Or, *If I partake with thankfulness*

God. Every man praying or prophesying, having ⁴ his head covered, dishonoureth his head. But every ⁵ woman praying or prophesying with her head unveiled dishonoureth her head: for it is one and the same thing as if she were shaven. For if a ⁶ woman is not veiled, let her also be shorn: but if it is a shame to a woman to be shorn or shaven, let her be veiled. For a man indeed ought not to ⁷ have his head veiled, forasmuch as he is the image and glory of God: but the woman is the glory of the man. For the man is not of the woman; but ⁸ the woman of the man: for neither was the man ⁹ created for the woman; but the woman for the man: for this cause ought the woman to ¹have *a sign of* ¹⁰ authority* on her head, because of the angels. Howbeit neither is the woman without the man, nor the ¹¹ man without the woman, in the Lord. For as the ¹² woman is of the man, so is the man also by the woman; but all things are of God. Judge ye ²in ¹³ yourselves: is it seemly that a woman pray unto God unveiled? Doth not even nature itself teach ¹⁴ you, that, if a man have long hair, it is a dishonour to him? But if a woman have long hair, it is a ¹⁵ glory to her: for her hair is given her for a covering. But if any man seemeth to be contentious, we ¹⁶ have no such custom, neither the churches of God.

But in giving you this charge, I praise you not, ¹⁷ that ye come together not for the better but for the worse. For first of all, when ye come together ³in ¹⁸ the church, I hear that ⁴divisions exist among you; and I partly believe it. For there must be also ¹⁹ ⁵heresies† among you, that they which are approved may be made manifest among you. When there- ²⁰ fore ye assemble yourselves together, it is not possible to eat the Lord's supper: for in your eating each ²¹ one taketh before *other* his own supper; and one is hungry, and another is drunken. What? have ye ²² not houses to eat and to drink in? or despise ye the ⁶church of God, and put them to shame that ⁷have not? What shall I say to you? ⁸shall I praise you in this? I praise you not. For I received of the ²³ Lord that which also I delivered unto you, how that the Lord Jesus in the night in which he was betrayed took bread; and when he had given thanks, he ²⁴ brake it, and said, This is my body, which ⁹is for

---

1 Or, *have authority over*
2 Or, *among*
3 Or, *in congregation*
4 Gr. *schisms.*
5 Or, *factions*
6 Or, *congregation*
7 Or, *have nothing*
8 Or, *shall I praise you? In this I praise you not.*
9 Many ancient authorities read *is broken for you.*

---

* Omit marg. ¹ ("*have authority over*") —*Am. Com.*

† For "heresies" read "factions" (with marg. Gr. *heresies*).—*Am. Com.*

25 you: this do in remembrance of me. In like manner also the cup, after supper, saying, This cup is the new ¹covenant in my blood: this do, as oft as ye
26 drink *it*, in remembrance of me. For as often as ye eat this bread, and drink the cup, ye proclaim the
27 Lord's death till he come. Wherefore whosoever shall eat the bread or drink the cup of the Lord unworthily*, shall be guilty of the body and the blood
28 of the Lord. But let a man prove himself, and so
29 let him eat of the bread, and drink of the cup. For he that eateth and drinketh, eateth and drinketh judgement unto himself, if he ²discern not the body.
30 For this cause many among you are weak and sick-
31 ly, and not a few sleep. But if we ³discerned our-
32 selves, we should not be judged. But ⁴when we are judged, we are chastened of the Lord, that we may
33 not be condemned with the world. Wherefore, my brethren, when ye come together to eat, wait one for
34 another. If any man is hungry, let him eat at home; that your coming together be not unto judgement. And the rest will I set in order whensoever I come.

12 Now concerning spiritual *gifts*, brethren, I would
2 not have you ignorant. Ye know that when ye were Gentiles *ye were* led away unto those dumb
3 idols, howsoever ye might be led. Wherefore I give you to understand, that no man speaking in the Spirit of God saith, Jesus is anathema; and no man can say, Jesus is Lord, but in the Holy Spirit.
4 Now there are diversities of gifts, but the same
5 Spirit. And there are diversities of ministrations,
6 and the same Lord. And there are diversities of workings, but the same God, who worketh all things
7 in all. But to each one is given the manifestation
8 of the Spirit to profit withal. For to one is given through the Spirit the word of wisdom; and to another the word of knowledge, according to the same
9 Spirit: to another faith, in the same Spirit; and to
10 another gifts of healings, in the one Spirit; and to another workings of ⁵miracles; and to another prophecy; and to another discernings of spirits: to another *divers* kinds of tongues; and to another the inter-
11 pretation of tongues: but all these worketh the one and the same Spirit, dividing to each one severally even as he will.
12 For as the body is one, and hath many members, and all the members of the body, being many, are

1 Or, *testament*
2 Gr. *discriminate.*
3 Gr. *discriminated.*
4 Or, *when we are judged of the Lord, we are chastened*
5 Gr. *powers.*

---

* For "unworthily" read "in an unworthy manner"—*Am. Com.*

one body; so also is Christ. For in one Spirit were 13
we all baptized into one body, whether Jews or
Greeks, whether bond or free; and were all made to
drink of one Spirit. For the body is not one mem- 14
ber, but many. If the foot shall say, Because I am 15
not the hand, I am not of the body; it is not therefore
not of the body. And if the ear shall say, Because 16
I am not the eye, I am not of the body; it is not
therefore not of the body. If the whole body were 17
an eye, where were the hearing? If the whole were
hearing, where were the smelling? But now hath 18
God set the members each one of them in the body,
even as it pleased him. And if they were all one 19
member, where were the body? But now they are 20
many members, but one body. And the eye cannot 21
say to the hand, I have no need of thee: or again
the head to the feet, I have no need of you. Nay, 22
much rather, those members of the body which
seem to be more feeble are necessary: and those 23
parts of the body, which we think to be less honour-
¹ Or, *put on*   able, upon these we ¹bestow more abundant honour;
and our uncomely *parts* have more abundant comeli-
ness; whereas our comely *parts* have no need: but 24
God tempered the body together, giving more abundant honour to that *part* which lacked; that there 25
should be no schism in the body; but *that* the members should have the same care one for another.
And whether one member suffereth, all the members 26
² Or, *glorified*   suffer with it; or *one* member is ²honoured, all the
members rejoice with it. Now ye are the body of 27
³ Or, *members each in his part* Christ, and ³severally members thereof. And God 28
hath set some in the church, first apostles, secondly
⁴ Gr. *powers.*   prophets, thirdly teachers, then ⁴miracles, then gifts
⁵ Or, *wise counsels* of healings, helps, ⁵governments, *divers* kinds of
tongues. Are all apostles? are all prophets? are all 29
teachers? are all *workers of* ⁴miracles? have all gifts 30
of healings? do all speak with tongues? do all interpret? But desire earnestly the greater gifts. 31
And a still more excellent way* shew I unto you.

If I speak with the tongues of men and of angels, **13**
but have not love, I am become sounding brass, or a
clanging cymbal. And if I have *the gift of* proph- 2
ecy, and know all mysteries and all knowledge; and
if I have all faith, so as to remove mountains, but
have not love, I am nothing. And if I bestow all 3
⁶ Many ancient authorities read *that I may glory.*   my goods to feed *the poor*, and if I give my body ⁶to

---

* Read "And moreover a most excellent way" etc.—*Am. Com.*

be burned, but have not love, it profiteth me noth-
4 ing. Love suffereth long, *and* is kind; love envieth
5 not; love vaunteth not itself, is not puffed up, doth
not behave itself unseemly, seeketh not its own, is
6 not provoked, taketh not account of evil; rejoiceth
not in unrighteousness, but rejoiceth with the truth;
7 ¹beareth all things, believeth all things, hopeth all
8 things, endureth all things. Love never faileth: but
whether *there be* prophecies, they shall be done away;
whether *there be* tongues, they shall cease; whether
9 *there be* knowledge, it shall be done away. For we
10 know in part, and we prophesy in part: but when
that which is perfect is come, that which is in part
11 shall be done away. When I was a child, I spake
as a child, I felt as a child, I thought as a child:
now that I am become a man, I have put away
12 childish things. For now we see in a mirror, ²dark-
ly; but then face to face: now I know in part; but
then shall I ³know even as also I have been ⁴known*.
13 But now abideth faith, hope, love, these three; ⁵and
the ⁶greatest of these is love.

1 Or, *covereth*

2 Gr. *in a riddle.*
3 Gr. *know fully.*
4 Gr. *known fully.*
5 Or, *but greater than these*†
6 Gr. *greater.*

14 Follow after love; yet desire earnestly spiritual
2 *gifts*, but rather that ye may prophesy. For he that
speaketh in a tongue speaketh not unto men, but
unto God; for no man ⁷understandeth; but in the
3 spirit he speaketh mysteries. But he that prophesieth speaketh unto men edification, and comfort‡,
4 and consolation. He that speaketh in a tongue ⁸edifieth himself; but he that prophesieth ⁸edifieth the
5 church. Now I would have you all speak with
tongues, but rather that ye should prophesy: and
greater is he that prophesieth than he that speaketh
with tongues, except he interpret, that the church
6 may receive edifying. But now, brethren, if I come
unto you speaking with tongues, what shall I profit
you, unless I speak to you either by way of revelation, or of knowledge, or of prophesying, or of
7 teaching? Even things without life, giving a voice,
whether pipe or harp, if they give not a distinction
in the sounds, how shall it be known what is piped
8 or harped? For if the trumpet give an uncertain
9 voice, who shall prepare himself for war? So also
ye, unless ye utter by the tongue speech easy to be
understood, how shall it be known what is spoken?

7 Gr. *heareth.*

8 Gr. *buildeth up.*

---

* Read "then shall I know fully even as also I was fully known"
and omit marg. ³ and ⁴.—*Am. Com.*
† Omit marg. ⁵ ("*but greater than these*")—*Am. Com.*
‡ For "comfort" read "exhortation"—*Am. Com.*

for ye will be speaking into the air. There are, it 10 may be, so many kinds of voices in the world, and ¹no *kind* is without signification. If then I know 11 not the meaning of the voice, I shall be to him that speaketh a barbarian, and he that speaketh will be a barbarian ²unto me. So also ye, since ye are zeal- 12 ous of ³spiritual *gifts*, seek that ye may abound unto the edifying of the church. Wherefore let him that 13 speaketh in a tongue pray that he may interpret. For if I pray in a tongue, my spirit prayeth, but 14 my understanding is unfruitful. What is it then? 15 I will pray with the spirit, and I will pray with the understanding also: I will sing with the spirit, and I will sing with the understanding also. Else if 16 thou bless with the spirit, how shall he that filleth the place of ⁴the unlearned say the Amen at thy giving of thanks, seeing he knoweth not what thou sayest? For thou verily givest thanks well, but the 17 other is not ⁵edified. I thank God, I speak with 18 tongues more than you all: howbeit in the church 19 I had rather speak five words with my understanding, that I might instruct others also, than ten thousand words in a tongue.

Brethren, be not children in mind: howbeit in 20 malice be ye babes, but in mind be ⁶men. In the 21 law it is written, By men of strange tongues and by the lips of strangers will I speak unto this people; and not even thus will they hear me, saith the Lord. Wherefore tongues are for a sign, not 22 to them that believe, but to the unbelieving: but prophesying *is for a sign*, not to the unbelieving, but to them that believe. If therefore the whole 23 church be assembled together, and all speak with tongues, and there come in men unlearned or unbelieving, will they not say that ye are mad? But if 24 all prophesy, and there come in one unbelieving or unlearned, he is ⁷reproved by all, he is judged by all; the secrets of his heart are made manifest; and 25 so he will fall down on his face and worship God, declaring that God is ⁸among you indeed.

What is it then, brethren? When ye come to- 26 gether, each one hath a psalm, hath a teaching, hath a revelation, hath a tongue, hath an interpretation. Let all things be done unto edifying. If 27 any man speaketh in a tongue, *let it be* by two, or at the most three, and *that* in turn; and let one interpret: but if there be no interpreter, let him keep si- 28 lence in the church; and let him speak to himself,

---

1 Or, *nothing is without voice*
2 Or, *in my case*
3 Gr. *spirits*.
4 Or, *him that is without gifts*: and so in ver. 23, 24.
5 Gr. *builded up*.
6 Gr. *of full age*.
7 Or, *convicted*
8 Or, *in*

29 and to God. And let the prophets speak *by* two or
30 three, and let the others ¹discern. But if a revelation be made to another sitting by, let the first keep
31 silence. For ye all can prophesy one by one, that
32 all may learn, and all may be ²comforted; and the
spirits of the prophets are subject to the prophets;
33 for God is not *a God* of confusion, but of peace; as*
in all the churches of the saints.
34 Let the women keep silence in the churches: for
it is not permitted unto them to speak; but let them
35 be in subjection, as also saith the law. And if they
would learn any thing, let them ask their own husbands at home: for it is shameful for a woman to
36 speak in the church. What? was it from you that the
word of God went forth? or came it unto you alone?
37 If any man thinketh himself to be a prophet, or
spiritual, let him take knowledge of the things which
I write unto you, that they are the commandment of
38 the Lord. ³But if any man is ignorant, let him be
ignorant.
39 Wherefore, my brethren, desire earnestly to proph-
40 esy, and forbid not to speak with tongues. But let
all things be done decently and in order.

15 Now I make known unto you, brethren, the gospel
which I preached unto you, which also ye received,
2 wherein also ye stand, by which also ye are ⁴saved†;
I make known, I say, ⁵in what words I preached it
unto you, if ye hold it fast, except ye believed ⁶in
3 vain. For I delivered unto you first of all that which
also I received, how that Christ died for our sins
4 according to the scriptures; and that he was buried;
and that he hath been raised on the third day accord-
5 ing to the scriptures; and that he appeared to Cephas;
6 then to the twelve; then he appeared to above five
hundred brethren at once, of whom the greater part
7 remain until now, but some are fallen asleep; then
8 he appeared to James; then to all the apostles; and
last of all, as unto one born out of due time‡, he ap-
9 peared to me also. For I am the least of the apostles,
that am not meet to be called an apostle, because I
10 persecuted the church of God. But by the grace of
God I am what I am: and his grace which was be-

1 Gr. *discriminate.*

2 Or, *exhorted*

3 Many ancient authorities read *But if any man knoweth not, he is not known.*

4 Or, *saved, if ye hold fast what I preached unto you, except, &c.*

5 Gr. *with what word.*

6 Or, *without cause*

---

* For "of peace; as" etc. read "of peace. As in all the churches of the saints, let" etc. [and begin the paragraph with "As" etc.] — *Am. Com.*

† Adopt marg. ⁴ for the text (substituting "*the word which*" for "*what*"). — *Am. Com.*

‡ For "as unto ... time" read "as to the *child* untimely born"— *Am. Com.*

stowed upon me was not found ¹vain; but I laboured more abundantly than they all: yet not I, but the
grace of God which was with me. Whether then *it* 11
be I or they, so we preach, and so ye believed.

Now if Christ is preached that he hath been raised 12
from the dead, how say some among you that there
is no resurrection of the dead? But if there is no 13
resurrection of the dead, neither hath Christ been
raised: and if Christ hath not been raised, then is 14
our preaching ¹vain, ²your faith also is ¹vain. Yea, 15
and we are found false witnesses of God; because
we witnessed of God that he raised up ³Christ:
whom he raised not up, if so be that the dead are
not raised. For if the dead are not raised, neither 16
hath Christ been raised: and if Christ hath not been 17
raised, your faith is vain; ye are yet in your sins.
Then they also which are fallen asleep in Christ 18
have perished. ⁴If in this life only we have hoped 19
in Christ*, we are of all men most pitiable.

But now hath Christ been raised from the dead, 20
the firstfruits of them that are asleep. For since by 21
man *came* death, by man *came* also the resurrection
of the dead. For as in Adam all die, so also in 22
³Christ shall all be made alive. But each in his own 23
order: Christ the firstfruits; then they that are
Christ's, at his ⁵coming. Then *cometh* the end, 24
when he shall deliver up the kingdom to ⁶God, even
the Father; when he shall have abolished all rule
and all authority and power. For he must reign, 25
till he hath put all his enemies under his feet. The 26
last enemy that shall be abolished is death. For, He 27
put all things in subjection under his feet. ⁷But
when he saith, All things are put in subjection, it is
evident that he is excepted who did subject all things
unto him. And when all things have been subject- 28
ed unto him, then shall the Son also himself be subjected to him that did subject all things unto him,
that God may be all in all.

Else what shall they do which are baptized for the 29
dead? If the dead are not raised at all, why then
are they baptized for them? why do we also stand in 30
jeopardy every hour? I protest by ⁸that glorying in 31
you, brethren, which I have in Christ Jesus our Lord,
I die daily. If after the manner of men I fought 32
with beasts at Ephesus, ⁹what doth it profit me? If
the dead are not raised, let us eat and drink, for to-

1 Or, *void*

2 Some ancient authorities read *our*.

3 Gr. *the Christ*.

4 Or, *If we have only hoped in Christ in this life*

5 Gr. *presence*.

6 Gr. *the God and Father*.

7 Or, *But when he shall have said, All things are put in subjection (evidently excepting him that did subject all things unto him), when, I say, all things, &c.*

8 Or, *your glorying*

9 Or, *what doth it profit me, if the dead are not raised? Let us eat, &c.*

---

* Let marg. ³ and the text exchange places. —*Am. Com.*

I. CORINTHIANS. —15. 52.

33 morrow we die. Be not deceived: Evil company
34 doth corrupt good manners*. ¹Awake up† righteously, and sin not; for some have no knowledge of God: I speak *this* to move you to shame.
35 But some one will say, How are the dead raised? and with what manner of body do they come?
36 Thou foolish one, that which thou thyself sowest is
37 not quickened, except it die: and that which thou sowest, thou sowest not the body that shall be, but a bare grain, it may chance of wheat, or of some other
38 kind; but God giveth it a body even as it pleased
39 him, and to each seed a body of its own. All flesh is not the same flesh: but there is one *flesh* of men, and another flesh of beasts, and another flesh of
40 birds, and another of fishes. There are also celestial bodies, and bodies terrestrial: but the glory of the celestial is one, and the *glory* of the terrestrial is an-
41 other. There is one glory of the sun, and another glory of the moon, and another glory of the stars; for one star differeth from another star in glory.
42 So also is the resurrection of the dead. It is sown
43 in corruption; it is raised in incorruption: it is sown in dishonour; it is raised in glory: it is sown in
44 weakness; it is raised in power: it is sown a natural‡ body; it is raised a spiritual body. If there is
45 a natural body, there is also a spiritual *body*. So also it is written, The first man Adam became a living soul. The last Adam *became* a life-giving spirit.
46 Howbeit that is not first which is spiritual, but that
47 which is natural‡; then that which is spiritual. The first man is of the earth, earthy: the second man is of
48 heaven. As is the earthy, such are they also that are earthy: and as is the heavenly, such are they also that
49 are heavenly. And as we have borne the image of the earthy, ²we shall also bear the image of the heavenly.
50 Now this I say, brethren, that flesh and blood cannot inherit the kingdom of God; neither doth
51 corruption inherit incorruption. Behold, I tell you a mystery: We shall not all§ sleep, but we shall all
52 be changed, in a moment, in the twinkling of an eye, at the last trump: for the trumpet shall sound, and the dead shall be raised incorruptible, and we

1 Gr. *Awake out of drunkenness righteously.*

2 Many ancient authorities read *let us also bear.*

---

* For "Evil company doth corrupt good manners" read "Evil companionships corrupt good morals"—*Am. Com.*
† For "Awake up" read "Awake to soberness" and omit marg. ¹.—*Am. Com.*
‡ "natural" add marg. Gr. *psychical.*—*Am. Com.*
§ For "We shall not all" read "We all shall not" and put the present text into the marg.—*Am. Com.*

shall be changed. For this corruptible must put 53
on incorruption, and this mortal must put on immortality. But when ¹this corruptible shall have 54
put on incorruption, and this mortal shall have put
on immortality, then shall come to pass the saying
that is written, Death is swallowed up ²in victory.
O death, where is thy victory? O death, where is 55
thy sting? The sting of death is sin; and the pow- 56
er of sin is the law: but thanks be to God, which 57
giveth us the victory through our Lord Jesus Christ.
Wherefore, my beloved brethren, be ye stedfast, un- 58
moveable, always abounding in the work of the
Lord, forasmuch as ye know that your labour is
not ³vain in the Lord.

Now concerning the collection for the saints, as **16**
I gave order to the churches of Galatia, so also do
ye. Upon the first day of the week let each one of 2
you lay by him in store, as he may prosper, that no
collections be made when I come. And when I ar- 3
rive, ⁴whomsoever ye shall approve by letters, them
will I send to carry your bounty unto Jerusalem:
and if it be meet for me to go also, they shall go 4
with me. But I will come unto you, when I shall 5
have passed through Macedonia; for I do pass
through Macedonia; but with you it may be that 6
I shall abide, or even winter, that ye may set me
forward on my journey whithersoever I go. For I 7
do not wish to see you now by the way; for I hope
to tarry a while with you, if the Lord permit. But 8
I will tarry at Ephesus until Pentecost; for a great 9
door and effectual is opened unto me, and there are
many adversaries.

Now if Timothy come, see that he be with you 10
without fear; for he worketh the work of the Lord,
as I also do: let no man therefore despise him. But 11
set him forward on his journey in peace, that he
may come unto me: for I expect him with the brethren. But as touching Apollos the brother, I be- 12
sought him much to come unto you with the brethren: and it was not at all ⁵his will to come now;
but he will come when he shall have opportunity.

Watch ye, stand fast in the faith, quit you like 13
men, be strong. Let all that ye do be done in love. 14

Now I beseech you, brethren (ye know the house 15
of Stephanas, that it is the firstfruits of Achaia, and
that they have set themselves to minister unto the
saints), that ye also be in subjection unto such, and 16
to every one that helpeth in the work and labour-

---

1 Many ancient authorities omit *this corruptible shall have put on incorruption, and.*

2 Or, *victoriously.*

3 Or, *void*

4 Or, *whomsoever ye shall approve, them will I send with letters*

5 Or, God's will that he should come now

17 eth. And I rejoice at the ¹coming of Stephanas and
18 Fortunatus and Achaicus: for that which was lacking on your part they supplied. For they refreshed my spirit and yours: acknowledge ye therefore them that are such.
19 The churches of Asia salute you. Aquila and Prisca salute you much in the Lord, with the church
20 that is in their house. All the brethren salute you. Salute one another with a holy kiss.
21 The salutation of me Paul with mine own hand.
22 If any man loveth not the Lord, let him be ana-
23 thema. ²Maran atha. The grace of the Lord Jesus
24 Christ be with you. My love be with you all in Christ Jesus. Amen.

1 Gr. *presence*.

2 That is, *Our Lord cometh*.

THE SECOND EPISTLE OF PAUL THE APOSTLE TO THE CORINTHIANS.

Paul, an apostle of Christ Jesus through the will of God, and Timothy ¹our brother, unto the church of God which is at Corinth, with all the saints which are in the whole of Achaia: Grace to you and peace from God our Father and the Lord Jesus Christ. Blessed *be* the God and Father of our Lord Jesus Christ, the Father of mercies and God of all comfort; who comforteth us in all our affliction, that we may be able to comfort them that are in any affliction, through the comfort wherewith we ourselves are comforted of God. For as the sufferings of Christ abound unto us, even so our comfort also aboundeth through Christ. But whether we be afflicted, it is for your comfort and salvation; or whether we be comforted, it is for your comfort, which worketh in the patient enduring of the same sufferings which we also suffer: and our hope for you is stedfast; knowing that, as ye are partakers of the sufferings, so also are ye of the comfort. For we would not have you ignorant, brethren, concerning our affliction which befell *us* in Asia, that we were weighed down exceedingly, beyond our power, insomuch that we despaired even of life: ²yea, we ourselves have had the ³answer* of death within ourselves, that we should not trust in ourselves, but in God which raiseth the dead: who delivered us out of so great a death, and will deliver: on whom we have ⁴set our hope that he will also still deliver us; ye also helping together on our be-

¹ Gr. *the brother.*

² Or, *but we ourselves*
³ Or, *sentence*

⁴ Some ancient authorities read *set our hope; and still will he deliver us.*

---

* For "answer" read "sentence" (with marg. Gr. *answer*).—*Am. Com.*

half by your supplication; that, for the gift bestowed upon us by means of many, thanks may be given by many persons on our behalf.

12 For our glorying is this, the testimony of our conscience, that in holiness and sincerity of God, not in fleshly wisdom but in the grace of God, we behaved ourselves in the world, and more abundantly to you-
13 ward. For we write none other things unto you, than what ye read or even acknowledge, and I hope
14 ye will acknowledge unto the end: as also ye did acknowledge us in part, that we are your glorying, even as ye also are ours, in the day of our Lord Jesus.
15 And in this confidence I was minded to come before* unto you, that ye might have a second ¹benefit;
16 and by you to pass into Macedonia, and again from Macedonia to come unto you, and of you to be set
17 forward on my journey unto Judæa. When I therefore was thus minded, did I shew fickleness? or the things that I purpose, do I purpose according to the flesh, that with me there should be the yea yea and
18 the nay nay? But as God is faithful, our word to-
19 ward you is not yea and nay. For the Son of God, Jesus Christ, who was preached among you ²by us, even ²by me and Silvanus and Timothy, was not yea
20 and nay, but in him is yea. For how many soever be the promises of God, in him is the yea: wherefore also through him is the Amen, unto the glory of God
21 through us. Now he that stablisheth us with you
22 ³in Christ, and anointed us, is God; ⁴who also sealed us, and gave *us* the earnest of the Spirit in our hearts.
23 But I call God for a witness upon my soul, that to
24 spare you I forbare to come unto Corinth. Not that we have lordship over your faith, but are helpers of
2 your joy: for by ⁵faith ye stand†. ⁶But I determined this for myself, that I would not come again to you
2 with sorrow. For if I make you sorry, who then is he that maketh me glad, but he that is made sorry
3 by me? And I wrote this very thing, lest, when I came, I should have sorrow from them of whom I ought to rejoice; having confidence in you all, that
4 my joy is *the joy* of you all. For out of much affliction and anguish of heart I wrote unto you with many tears; not that ye should be made sorry, but that ye might know the love which I have more abundantly unto you.

1 Or, *grace* Some ancient authorities read *joy*.

2 Gr. *through*.

3 Gr. *into*.
4 Or, *seeing that he both sealed us*

5 Or, *your faith*
6 Some ancient authorities read *For*.

---

* For "before" read "first"—*Am. Com.*
† Read in the text "for in faith ye stand fast"—*Am. Com.*

But if any hath caused sorrow, he hath caused 5
sorrow, not to me, but in part (that I press not too
heavily) to you all. Sufficient to such a one is this 6
punishment which was *inflicted* by [1]the many; so 7
that contrariwise ye should [2]rather forgive him and
comfort him, lest by any means such a one should
be swallowed up with his overmuch sorrow. Where- 8
fore I beseech you to confirm *your* love toward him.
For to this end also did I write, that I might know 9
the proof of you, [3]whether ye are obedient in all
things. But to whom ye forgive any thing, I *for-* 10
give also: for what I also have forgiven, if I have
forgiven any thing, for your sakes *have I forgiven it*
in the [4]person of Christ; that no advantage may be 11
gained over us by Satan: for we are not ignorant
of his devices.

Now when I came to Troas for the gospel of 12
Christ, and when a door was opened unto me in the
Lord, I had no relief for my spirit, because I found 13
not Titus my brother: but taking my leave of them,
I went forth into Macedonia. *But thanks be unto 14
God, which always leadeth us in triumph in Christ,
and maketh manifest through us the savour of his
knowledge in every place. For we are a sweet 15
savour of Christ unto God, in them that are being
saved, and in them that are perishing†; to the one a 16
savour from death unto death; to the other a savour
from life unto life. And who is sufficient for these
things? For we are not as the many, [5]corrupting 17
the word of God: but as of sincerity, but as of God,
in the sight of God, speak we in Christ.

Are we beginning again to commend ourselves? 3
or need we, as do some, epistles of commendation to
you or from you? Ye are our epistle, written in 2
our hearts, known and read of all men; being made 3
manifest that ye are an epistle of Christ, ministered
by us, written not with ink, but with the Spirit of the
living God; not in tables of stone, but in tables *that
are* hearts of flesh. And such confidence have we 4
through Christ to God-ward: not that we are suffi- 5
cient of ourselves, to account any thing as from ourselves; but our sufficiency is from God; who also 6
made us sufficient as ministers of a new [6]covenant;
not of the letter, but of the spirit: for the letter killeth, but the spirit giveth life. But if the ministra- 7

---

[1] Gr. *the more.*
[2] Some ancient authorities omit *rather.*
[3] Some ancient authorities read *whereby.*
[4] Or, *presence*
[5] Or, *making merchandise of the word of God*
[6] Or, *testament*

* Begin a new paragraph with this verse.—*Am. Com.*
† For "are being saved ... are perishing" read "are saved ... perish" and put the present text into the marg.—*Am. Com.*

tion of death, ¹written, *and* engraven on stones, came
²with glory, so that the children of Israel could not
look stedfastly upon the face of Moses for the glory
8 of his face; which *glory* ³was passing away: how
9 shall not rather the ministration of the spirit be
with glory? ⁴For if the ministration of condemnation is glory*, much rather doth the ministration
10 of righteousness exceed in glory. For verily that
which hath been made glorious hath not been made
glorious in this respect, by reason of the glory that
11 surpasseth. For if that which ⁵passeth away *was*
⁶with glory, much more that which remaineth *is* in
glory.
12 Having therefore such a hope, we use great boldness
13 of speech, and *are* not as Moses, *who* put a veil
upon his face, that the children of Israel should not
look stedfastly ⁷on the end of that which ³was passing
14 away: but their ⁸minds were hardened: for until
this very day at the reading of the old ⁹covenant
the same veil ¹⁰remaineth unlifted; which *veil* is
15 done away in Christ. But unto this day, whensoever
Moses is read, a veil lieth upon their heart.
16 But whensoever ¹¹it shall turn to the Lord, the veil
17 is taken away. Now the Lord is the Spirit: and
18 where the Spirit of the Lord is, *there* is liberty. But
we all, with unveiled face ¹²reflecting as a mirror†
the glory of the Lord, are transformed into the same
image from glory to glory, even as from ¹³the Lord
the Spirit.

4 Therefore seeing we have this ministry, even as
2 we obtained mercy, we faint not: but we have renounced the hidden things of shame, not walking
in craftiness, nor handling the word of God deceitfully; but by the manifestation of the truth commending ourselves to every man's conscience in the
3 sight of God. But and if our gospel is veiled, it is
4 veiled in them that are perishing§: in whom the
god of this ¹⁴world hath blinded the ⁸minds of the
unbelieving, ¹⁵that the ¹⁶light of the gospel of the
glory of Christ, who is the image of God, should
5 not dawn *upon them*. For we preach not ourselves,
but Christ Jesus as Lord, and ourselves as your

1 Gr. *in letters*.
2 Gr. *in*.
3 Or, *was being done away*
4 Many ancient authorities read *For if to the ministration of condemnation there is glory*.
5 Or, *is being done away*
6 Gr. *through*.
7 Or, *unto*
8 Gr. *thoughts*.
9 Or, *testament*
10 Or, *remaineth, it not being revealed that it is done away*
11 Or, *a man shall turn*
12 Or, *beholding as in a mirror*
13 Or, *the Spirit which is the Lord*‡
14 Or, *age*
15 Or, *that they should not see the light . . . image of God*
16 Gr. *illumination*.

---

* For "is glory" read "hath glory" and let marg. ⁴ run Many etc. *For if the ministration of condemnation is glory.*—*Am. Com.*
† Let marg. ¹² and the text exchange places—*Am. Com.*
‡ Omit marg. ¹³ ("*the Spirit* which is *the Lord*")—*Am. Com.*
§ For "are perishing" read "perish" and put the present text into the marg.—*Am. Com.*

servants ²for Jesus' sake. Seeing it is God, that said, Light shall shine out of darkness, who shined in our hearts, to give the ³light of the knowledge of the glory of God in the face of Jesus Christ.

But we have this treasure in earthen vessels, that the exceeding greatness of the power may be of God, and not from ourselves; *we are* pressed on every side, yet not straitened; perplexed, yet not unto despair; pursued, yet not ⁴forsaken; smitten down, yet not destroyed; always bearing about in the body the ⁵dying of Jesus, that the life also of Jesus may be manifested in our body. For we which live are alway delivered unto death for Jesus' sake, that the life also of Jesus may be manifested in our mortal flesh. So then death worketh in us, but life in you. But having the same spirit of faith, according to that which is written, I believed, and therefore did I speak; we also believe, and therefore also we speak; knowing that he which raised up ⁶the Lord Jesus shall raise up us also with Jesus, and shall present us with you. For all things *are* for your sakes, that the grace, being multiplied through ⁷the many, may cause the thanksgiving to abound unto the glory of God.

Wherefore we faint not; but though our outward man is decaying, yet our inward man is renewed day by day. For our light affliction, which is for the moment, worketh for us more and more exceedingly an eternal weight of glory; while we look not at the things which are seen, but at the things which are not seen: for the things which are seen are temporal; but the things which are not seen are eternal.

For we know that if the earthly house of our ⁸tabernacle be dissolved, we have a building from God, a house not made with hands, eternal, in the heavens. For verily in this we groan, longing to be clothed upon with our habitation which is from heaven: if so be that being clothed we shall not be found naked. For indeed we that are in this ⁸tabernacle do groan, ⁹being burdened; not for that we would be unclothed, but that we would be clothed upon, that what is mortal may be swallowed up of life. Now he that wrought us for this very thing is God, who gave unto us the earnest of the Spirit. Being therefore always of good courage, and knowing that, whilst we are at home in the body, we are absent from the Lord (for we walk by faith, not by ¹⁰sight); we are of good courage, I say, and are will-

---

1 Gr. *bondservants.*
2 Some ancient authorities read *through Jesus.*
3 Gr. *illumination.*
4 Or, *left behind*
5 Gr. *putting to death.*
6 Some ancient authorities omit *the Lord.*
7 Gr. *the more.*
8 Or, *bodily frame*
9 Or, *being burdened, in that we would not be unclothed, but would be clothed upon*
10 Gr. *appearance.*

ing rather to be absent from the body, and to be at
9 home with the Lord. Wherefore also we ¹make it   1 Gr. *are ambitious.*
our aim, whether at home or absent, to be well-
10 pleasing unto him. For we must all be made manifest before the judgement-seat of Christ; that each
one may receive the things *done* ²in the body, according to what he hath done, whether *it be* good   2 Gr. *through.*
or bad.
11 Knowing therefore the fear of the Lord, we persuade men, but we are made manifest unto God;
and I hope that we are made manifest also in your
12 consciences. We are not again commending ourselves unto you, but *speak* as giving you occasion
of glorying on our behalf, that ye may have wherewith to answer them that glory in appearance, and
13 not in heart. For whether we ³are beside ourselves,   3 Or, *were*
it is unto God; or whether we are of sober mind,
14 it is unto you. For the love of Christ constraineth
us; because we thus judge, that one died for all,
15 therefore all died; and he died for all, that they
which live should no longer live unto themselves,
but unto him who for their sakes died and rose
16 again. Wherefore we henceforth know no man
after the flesh: even though we have known Christ
after the flesh, yet now we know *him so* no more.
17 Wherefore if any man is in Christ, ⁴*he is* a new   4 Or, *there is a new creation*
creature: the old things are passed away; behold,
18 they are become new. But all things are of God,
who reconciled us to himself through Christ, and
19 gave unto us the ministry of reconciliation; to wit,
that God was in Christ reconciling the world unto
himself, not reckoning unto them their trespasses,
and having ⁵committed unto us the word of recon-   5 Or, *placed in us*
ciliation.
20 We are ambassadors therefore on behalf of Christ,
as though God were intreating by us: we beseech
you on behalf of Christ, be ye reconciled to God.
21 Him who knew no sin he made *to be* sin on our
behalf; that we might become the righteousness of
6 God in him. And working together *with him* we
intreat also that ye receive not the grace of God in
2 vain (for he saith,

At an acceptable time I hearkened unto thee,
And in a day of salvation did I succour thee:
behold, now is the acceptable time; behold, now is
3 the day of salvation): giving no occasion of stumbling in any thing, that our ministration be not
4 blamed; but in every thing commending ourselves,

as ministers of God, in much patience, in afflictions, in necessities, in distresses, in stripes, in imprisonments, in tumults, in labours, in watchings, in fastings; in pureness, in knowledge, in longsuffering, in kindness, in the ¹Holy Ghost, in love unfeigned, in the word of truth, in the power of God; ²by the armour of righteousness on the right hand and on the left, by glory and dishonour, by evil report and good report; as deceivers, and *yet* true; as unknown, and *yet* well known; as dying, and behold, we live; as chastened, and not killed; as sorrowful, yet alway rejoicing; as poor, yet making many rich; as having nothing, and *yet* possessing all things.

Our mouth is open unto you, O Corinthians, our heart is enlarged. Ye are not straitened in us, but ye are straitened in your own affections. Now for a recompense in like kind (I speak as unto *my* children), be ye also enlarged.

Be not unequally yoked with unbelievers: for what fellowship have righteousness and iniquity? or what communion hath light with darkness? And what concord hath Christ with ³Belial? or what portion hath a believer with an unbeliever? And what agreement hath a ⁴temple of God with idols? for we are a ⁴temple of the living God; even as God said, I will dwell in them, and walk in them; and I will be their God, and they shall be my people. Wherefore

    Come ye out from among them, and be ye separate,
saith the Lord,
    And touch no unclean thing;
    And I will receive you,
    And will be to you a Father,
    And ye shall be to me sons and daughters,
saith the Lord Almighty. Having therefore these promises, beloved, let us cleanse ourselves from all defilement of flesh and spirit, perfecting holiness in the fear of God.

⁵Open your hearts to us: we wronged no man, we corrupted no man, we took advantage of no man. I say it not to condemn *you*: for I have said before, that ye are in our hearts to die together and live together. Great is my boldness of speech toward you, great is my glorying on your behalf: I am filled with comfort, I overflow with joy in all our affliction.

For even when we were come into Macedonia, our flesh had no relief, but *we were* afflicted on every

---

1 Or, *Holy Spirit*: and so throughout this book.
2 Gr. *through*.
3 Gr. *Beliar*.
4 Or, *sanctuary*.
5 Gr. *Make room for us*.

6 side; without *were* fightings, within *were* fears. Nevertheless he that comforteth the lowly, *even* God,
7 comforted us by the ¹coming of Titus; and not by his ¹coming only, but also by the comfort wherewith he was comforted in you, while he told us your longing, your mourning, your zeal for me; so that I re-
8 joiced yet more. For though I made you sorry with my epistle, I do not regret it, though* I did regret; ²for I see that that epistle made you sorry, though
9 but for a season. Now I rejoice, not that ye were made sorry, but that ye were made sorry unto repentance: for ye were made sorry after a godly
10 sort, that ye might suffer loss by us in nothing. For godly sorrow worketh repentance ³unto salvation, *a repentance* which bringeth no regret: but the sor-
11 row of the world worketh death. For behold, this selfsame thing, that ye were made sorry after a godly sort, what earnest care it wrought in you, yea, what clearing of yourselves, yea, what indignation, yea, what fear, yea, what longing, yea, what zeal, yea, what avenging! In every thing ye approved your-
12 selves to be pure in the matter. So although I wrote unto you, *I wrote* not for his cause that did the wrong, nor for his cause that suffered the wrong, but that your earnest care for us might be made manifest
13 unto you in the sight of God. Therefore we have been comforted: and in our comfort we joyed the more exceedingly for the joy of Titus, because his
14 spirit hath been refreshed by you all. For if in any thing I have gloried to him on your behalf, I was not put to shame; but as we spake all things to you in truth, so our glorying also, which I made before
15 Titus, was found to be truth. And his inward affection is more abundantly toward you, whilst he remembereth the obedience of you all, how with fear
16 and trembling ye received him. I rejoice that in every thing I am of good courage concerning you.

8 Moreover, brethren, we make known to you the grace of God which hath been given in the churches
2 of Macedonia; how that in much proof of affliction the abundance of their joy and their deep poverty
3 abounded unto the riches of their ⁴liberality. For according to their power, I bear witness, yea and beyond their power, *they gave* of their own accord, be-
4 seeching us with much intreaty in regard of this

1 Gr. *presence.*

2 Some ancient authorities omit *for.*

3 Or, *unto a salvation which bringeth no regret*

4 Gr. *singleness.*

---

* For "I do not regret it, though" etc. read "I do not regret it: though I did regret *it* (for I see that that epistle made you sorry, though but for a season), I now rejoice" etc.—*Am. Com.*

grace and the fellowship in the ministering to the saints: and *this*, not as we had hoped, but first they 5 gave their own selves to the Lord, and to us by the will of God. Insomuch that we exhorted Titus, that 6 as he had made a beginning before, so he would also complete in you this grace also. But as ye abound 7 in every thing, *in* faith, and utterance, and knowledge, and *in* all earnestness, and *in* ¹your love to us, see that ye abound in this grace also. I speak not by 8 way of commandment, but as proving through the earnestness of others the sincerity also of your love. For ye know the grace of our Lord Jesus Christ, 9 that, though he was rich, yet for your sakes he became poor, that ye through his poverty might become rich. And herein I give *my* judgement: for 10 this is expedient for you, who were the first to make a beginning a year ago, not only to do, but also to will. But now complete the doing also; that as 11 *there was* the readiness to will, so *there may be* the completion also out of your ability. For if the read- 12 iness is there, *it is* acceptable according as *a man* hath, not according as *he* hath not. For *I say* not 13 *this*, that others may be eased, *and* ye distressed: but 14 by equality; your abundance *being a supply* at this present time for their want, that their abundance also may become *a supply* for your want; that there may be equality: as it is written, He that *gathered* 15 much had nothing over; and he that *gathered* little had no lack.

But thanks be to God, which putteth the same 16 earnest care for you into the heart of Titus. For in- 17 deed he accepted our exhortation; but being himself very earnest, he went forth unto you of his own accord. And we have sent together with him the 18 brother whose praise in the gospel *is spread* through all the churches; and not only so, but who was also 19 appointed by the churches to travel with us in *the matter of* this grace, which is ministered by us to the glory of the Lord, and *to shew* our readiness: avoid- 20 ing this, that any man should blame us in *the matter of* this bounty which is ministered by us: for we 21 take thought for things honourable, not only in the sight of the Lord, but also in the sight of men. And 22 we have sent with them our brother, whom we have many times proved earnest in many things, but now much more earnest, by reason of the great confidence which *he hath* in you. Whether *any inquire* about 23 Titus, *he is* my partner and *my* fellow-worker to you-

¹ Some ancient authorities read *our love to you.*

ward; or our brethren, *they are* the ¹messengers of
24 the churches, *they are* the glory of Christ. ²Shew
ye therefore unto them in the face of the churches
the proof of your love, and of our glorying on your
behalf.

9 For as touching the ministering to the saints, it is
2 superfluous for me to write to you: for I know your
readiness, of which I glory on your behalf to them of
Macedonia, that Achaia hath been prepared for a
year past; and ³your zeal hath stirred up ⁴very many
3 of them. But I have sent the brethren, that our
glorying on your behalf may not be made void in
this respect; that, even as I said, ye may be prepared:
4 lest by any means, if there come with me any of
Macedonia, and find you unprepared, we (that we
say not, ye) should be put to shame in this confidence.
5 I thought it necessary therefore to intreat the brethren, that they would go before unto you, and make
up beforehand your afore-promised ⁵bounty, that the
same might be ready, as a matter of bounty, and not
of ⁶extortion.
6 But this *I say*, He that soweth sparingly shall reap
also sparingly; and he that soweth ⁷bountifully shall
7 reap also ⁷bountifully. *Let* each man *do* according
as he hath purposed in his heart; not ⁸grudgingly,
or of necessity: for God loveth a cheerful giver.
8 And God is able to make all grace abound unto you;
that ye, having always all sufficiency in everything,
9 may abound unto every good work: as it is written,
> He hath scattered abroad, he hath given to the poor;
> His righteousness abideth for ever.
10 And he that supplieth seed to the sower and bread
for food, shall supply and multiply your seed for
sowing, and increase the fruits of your righteous-
11 ness: ye being enriched in everything unto all ⁹liberality, which worketh through us thanksgiving to
12 God. For the ministration of this service not only
filleth up the measure of the wants of the saints,
but aboundeth also through many thanksgivings
13 unto God; seeing that through the proving *of you*
by this ministration they glorify God for the obedience of your confession unto the gospel of Christ,
and for the ⁹liberality of *your* contribution unto them
14 and unto all; while they themselves also, with supplication on your behalf, long after you by reason of
15 the exceeding grace of God in you. Thanks be to
God for his unspeakable gift.

1 Gr. *apostles.*
2 Or, *Shew ye therefore in the face ... on your behalf unto them.*
3 Or, *emulation of you*
4 Gr. *the more part.*
5 Gr. *blessing.*
6 Or, *covetousness*
7 Gr. *with blessings.*
8 Gr. *of sorrow.*
9 Gr. *singleness.*

Now I Paul myself intreat you by the meekness **10** and gentleness of Christ, I who in your presence am lowly among you, but being absent am of good courage toward you: yea, I beseech you, that I may 2 not when present shew courage with the confidence wherewith I count to be bold against some, which count of us as if we walked according to the flesh. For though we walk in the flesh, we do not war ac- 3 cording to the flesh (for the weapons of our warfare 4 are not of the flesh, but mighty before God to the casting down of strong holds); casting down ¹imag- 5 inations, and every high thing that is exalted against the knowledge of God, and bringing every thought into captivity to the obedience of Christ; and being 6 in readiness to avenge all disobedience, when your obedience shall be fulfilled. ²Ye look at the things 7 that are before your face. If any man trusteth in himself that he is Christ's, let him consider this again with himself, that, even as he is Christ's, so also are we. For though I should glory somewhat 8 abundantly concerning our authority (which the Lord gave for building you up, and not for casting you down), I shall not be put to shame: that I may 9 not seem as if I would terrify you by my letters. For, His letters, they say, are weighty and strong; 10 but his bodily presence is weak, and his speech of no account. Let such a one reckon this, that, what 11 we are in word by letters when we are absent, such *are we* also in deed when we are present. For we 12 are not bold ³to number or compare ourselves with certain of them that commend themselves: but they themselves, measuring themselves by themselves, and comparing themselves with themselves, are without understanding. But we will not glory beyond *our* 13 measure, but according to the measure of the ⁴prov- ince which God apportioned to us as a measure, to reach even unto you. For we stretch not ourselves 14 overmuch, as though we reached not unto you: for we ⁵came even as far as unto you in the gospel of Christ: not glorying beyond *our* measure, *that is*, in 15 other men's labours; but having hope that, as your faith groweth, we shall be magnified in you accord- ing to our ⁴province unto *further* abundance, so as 16 to preach the gospel even unto the parts beyond you, *and* not to glory in another's ⁴province in re- gard of things ready to our hand. But he that 17 glorieth, let him glory in the Lord. For not he that 18 commendeth himself is approved, but whom the Lord commendeth.

---

1 Or, *reasonings*

2 Or, *Do ye look ... face?*

3 Gr. *to judge our-selves among, or to judge ourselves with.*

4 Or, *limit* Gr. *measuring-rod.*

5 Or, *were the first to come*

11 Would that ye could bear with me in a little foolishness: ¹nay indeed bear with me. For I am jealous over you with ²a godly jealousy: for I espoused you to one husband, that I might present you *as* a pure virgin to Christ. But I fear, lest by any means, as the serpent beguiled Eve in his craftiness, your ³minds should be corrupted from the simplicity and the purity that is toward Christ. For if he that cometh preacheth another Jesus, whom we did not preach, or *if* ye receive a different spirit, which ye did not receive, or a different gospel, which ye did not accept, ye do well to bear with *him*. For I reckon that I am not a whit behind ⁴the very chiefest apostles. But though *I be* rude in speech, yet *am I* not in knowledge; nay, in every thing we have made *it* manifest among all men to you-ward. Or did I commit a sin in abasing myself that ye might be exalted, because I preached to you the gospel of God for nought? I robbed other churches, taking wages *of them* that I might minister unto you; and when I was present with you and was in want, I was not a burden on any man; for the brethren, when they came from Macedonia, supplied the measure of my want; and in every thing I kept myself from being burdensome unto you, and *so* will I keep *myself*. As the truth of Christ is in me, no man shall stop me of this glorying in the regions of Achaia. Wherefore? because I love you not? God knoweth. But what I do, that I will do, that I may cut off ⁵occasion from them which desire an occasion; that wherein they glory, they may be found even as we. For such men are false apostles, deceitful workers, fashioning themselves into apostles of Christ. And no marvel; for even Satan fashioneth himself into an angel of light. It is no great thing therefore if his ministers also fashion themselves as ministers of righteousness; whose end shall be according to their works.

16 I say again, Let no man think me foolish; but if *ye do*, yet as foolish receive me, that I also may glory a little. That which I speak, I speak not after the Lord, but as in foolishness, in this confidence of glorying. Seeing that many glory after the flesh, I will glory also. For ye bear with the foolish gladly, being wise *yourselves*. For ye bear with a man, if he bringeth you into bondage, if he devoureth you, if he taketh you *captive*, if he exalteth himself, if he smiteth you on the face. I speak by way of disparagement, as though we had been weak. Yet whereinso-

---

¹ Or, *but indeed ye do bear with me.*
² Gr. *a jealousy of God.*
³ Gr. *thoughts.*
⁴ Or, *those preeminent apostles*
⁵ Gr. *the occasion of them.*

ever any is bold (I speak in foolishness), I am bold also. Are they Hebrews? so am I. Are they Israelites? so am I. Are they the seed of Abraham? so am I. Are they ministers of Christ? (I speak as one beside himself) I more; in labours more abundantly, in prisons more abundantly, in stripes above measure, in deaths oft. Of the Jews five times received I forty *stripes* save one. Thrice was I beaten with rods, once was I stoned, thrice I suffered shipwreck, a night and a day have I been in the deep; *in* journeyings often, *in* perils of rivers, *in* perils of robbers, *in* perils from *my* ¹countrymen, *in* perils from the Gentiles, *in* perils in the city, *in* perils in the wilderness, *in* perils in the sea, *in* perils among false brethren; *in* labour and travail, in watchings often, in hunger and thirst, in fastings often, in cold and nakedness. ²Beside those things that are without, there is that which presseth upon me daily, anxiety for all the churches. Who is weak, and I am not weak? who is made to stumble, and I burn not? If I must needs glory, I will glory of the things that concern my weakness. The God and Father of the Lord Jesus, he who is blessed ³for evermore, knoweth that I lie not. In Damascus the governor under Aretas the king guarded the city of the Damascenes, in order to take me: and through a window was I let down in a basket by the wall, and escaped his hands.

⁴I must needs glory, though it is not expedient; but I will come to visions and revelations of the Lord. I know a man in Christ, fourteen years ago (whether in the body, I know not; or whether out of the body, I know not; God knoweth), such a one caught up even to the third heaven. And I know such a man (whether in the body, or apart from the body, I know not; God knoweth), how that he was caught up into Paradise, and heard unspeakable words, which it is not lawful for a man to utter. On behalf of such a one will I glory: but on mine own behalf I will not glory, save in *my* weaknesses. For if I should desire to glory, I shall not be foolish; for I shall speak the truth: but I forbear, lest any man should account of me above that which he seeth me *to be*, or heareth from me. And by reason of the exceeding greatness of the revelations—wherefore*, that I should not be

---

1 Gr. *race.*

2 Or, *Beside the things which I omit* Or, *Beside the things that come out of course*

3 Gr. *unto the ages.*

4 Some ancient authorities read *Now to glory is not expedient, but I will come &c.*

* Strike out "—wherefore" and add marg. Some ancient authorities read —*wherefore.*—*Am. Com.*

exalted overmuch, there was given to me a ¹thorn in
the flesh, a messenger of Satan to buffet me, that I
8 should not be exalted overmuch. Concerning this
thing I besought the Lord thrice, that it might de-
9 part from me. And he hath said unto me, My grace
is sufficient for thee: for *my* power is made perfect
in weakness. Most gladly therefore will I rather
glory in my weaknesses, that the strength of Christ
10 may ²rest upon me. Wherefore I take pleasure in
weaknesses, in injuries, in necessities, in persecutions, in distresses, for Christ's sake: for when I am
weak, then am I strong.
11 I am become foolish: ye compelled me; for I
ought to have been commended of you: for in
nothing was I behind ³the very chiefest apostles,
12 though I am nothing. Truly the signs of an apostle were wrought among you in all patience, by
13 signs and wonders and ⁴mighty works. For what
is there wherein ye were made inferior to the rest
of the churches, except *it be* that I myself was not
a burden to you? forgive me this wrong.
14 Behold, this is the third time I am ready to come
to you; and I will not be a burden to you: for I seek
not yours, but you: for the children ought not to lay
up for the parents, but the parents for the children.
15 And I will most gladly spend and be ⁵spent for your
souls. If I love you more abundantly, am I loved
16 the less? But be it so, I did not myself burden you;
17 but, being crafty, I caught you with guile. Did I
take advantage of you by any one of them whom I
18 have sent unto you? I exhorted Titus, and I sent
the brother with him. Did Titus take any advantage
of you? walked we not by the same Spirit? *walked
we* not in the same steps?
19 ⁶Ye think all this time that we are excusing ourselves unto you. In the sight of God speak we in
Christ. But all things, beloved, *are* for your edify-
20 ing. For I fear, lest by any means, when I come,
I should find you not such as I would, and should
myself be found of you such as ye would not; lest
by any means *there should be* strife, jealousy, wraths,
factions, backbitings, whisperings, swellings, ⁷tu-
21 mults; lest, when I come again, my God should
humble me before you, and I should mourn for
many of them that have sinned heretofore, and repented not of the uncleanness and fornication and
lasciviousness which they committed.

1 Or, *stake*

2 Or, *cover me* Gr. *spread a tabernacle over me.*

3 Or, *those preeminent apostles*

4 Gr. *powers.*

5 Gr. *spent out.*

6 Or, *Think ye . . . you?*

7 Or, *disorders*

II. CORINTHIANS. 13. 1.

13 This is the third time I am coming to you. At the mouth of two witnesses or three shall every word be established. 2 I have said ¹beforehand, and I do say ¹beforehand, ²as when I was present the second time, so now, being absent, to them that have sinned heretofore, and to all the rest, that, if I come again, I will not spare; 3 seeing that ye seek a proof of Christ that speaketh in me; who to you-ward is not weak, but is powerful in you: 4 for he was crucified through weakness, yet he liveth through the power of God. For we also are weak ³in him, but we shall live with him through the power of God toward you. 5 Try your own selves, whether ye be in the faith; prove your own selves. Or know ye not as to your own selves, that Jesus Christ is in you? unless indeed ye be reprobate. 6 But I hope that ye shall know that we are not reprobate. 7 Now we pray to God that ye do no evil; not that we may appear approved, but that ye may do that which is honourable, ⁴though we be as reprobate. 8 For we can do nothing against the truth, but for the truth. 9 For we rejoice, when we are weak, and ye are strong: this we also pray for, even your perfecting. 10 For this cause I write these things while absent, that I may not when present deal sharply, according to the authority which the Lord gave me for building up, and not for casting down.

11 Finally, brethren, ⁵farewell. Be perfected; be comforted; be of the same mind; live in peace: and the God of love and peace shall be with you. 12 Salute one another with a holy kiss.

13 All the saints salute you.

14 The grace of the Lord Jesus Christ, and the love of God, and the communion of the Holy Ghost, be with you all.

---

1 Or, *plainly*
2 Or, *as if I were present the second time, even though I am now absent*
3 Many ancient authorities read *with*.
4 Gr. *and that*.
5 Or, *rejoice: be perfected*

THE EPISTLE OF PAUL

TO THE

GALATIANS.

1 Paul, an apostle (not from men, neither through ¹man, but through Jesus Christ, and God the Father, 2 who raised him from the dead), and all the brethren which are with me, unto the churches of Galatia: 3 Grace to you and peace ²from God the Father, and 4 our Lord Jesus Christ, who gave himself for our sins, that he might deliver us out of this present evil ³world, according to the will of our God and Father: 5 to whom *be* the glory ⁴for ever and ever. Amen. 6 I marvel that ye are so quickly removing from him that called you in the grace of Christ unto a different 7 gospel; which is not another *gospel*: only* there are some that trouble you, and would pervert the gospel 8 of Christ. But though we, or an angel from heaven, should preach ⁵unto you any gospel ⁶other than that which we preached unto you, let him be anathema. 9 As we have said before, so say I now again, If any man preacheth unto you any gospel other than that 10 which ye received, let him be anathema. For am I now persuading men, or God†? or am I seeking to please† men? if I were still pleasing men, I should not be a ⁷servant of Christ. 11 For I make known to you, brethren, as touching the gospel which was preached by me, that it is not after 12 man. For neither did I receive it from ¹man, nor was I taught it, but *it came to me* through revelation of 13 Jesus Christ. For ye have heard of my manner of life in time past in the Jews' religion, how that beyond

1 Or, *a man*

2 Some ancient authorities read *from God our Father, and the Lord Jesus Christ.*

3 Or, *age*

4 Gr. *unto the ages of the ages.*

5 Some ancient authorities omit *unto you.*

6 Or, *contrary to that*

7 Gr. *bondservant.*

---

* "which is not another *gospel*: only" etc. add the marg. Or, *which is nothing else save that* etc.—*Am. Com.*
† Read "For am I now seeking the favour of men or of God" and for "seeking to please" read "striving to please."—*Am. Com.*

measure I persecuted the church of God, and made havock of it: and I advanced in the Jews' religion 14 beyond many of mine own age ¹among my countrymen, being more exceedingly zealous for the traditions of my fathers. But when it was the good pleasure 15 of God, who separated me, *even* from my mother's womb, and called me through his grace, to reveal 16 his Son in me, that I might preach him among the Gentiles; immediately I conferred not with flesh and blood: neither went I up to Jerusalem to them 17 which were apostles before me: but I went away into Arabia; and again I returned unto Damascus.

Then after three years I went up to Jerusalem 18 to ²visit Cephas, and tarried with him fifteen days. But other of the apostles saw I none, ³save James 19 the Lord's brother. Now touching the things which 20 I write unto you, behold, before God, I lie not. Then 21 I came into the regions of Syria and Cilicia. And 22 I was still unknown by face unto the churches of Judæa which were in Christ: but they only heard 23 say, He that once persecuted us now preacheth the faith of which he once made havock; and they glorified 24 God in me.

Then ⁴after the space of fourteen years I went up 2 again to Jerusalem with Barnabas, taking Titus also with me. And I went up by revelation; and I laid 2 before them the gospel which I preach among the Gentiles, but privately before them who ⁵were of repute, lest by any means I should be running, or had run, in vain. But not even Titus who was 3 with me, being a Greek, was compelled to be circumcised: ⁶and that because of the false brethren 4 privily brought in, who came in privily to spy out our liberty which we have in Christ Jesus, that they might bring us into bondage: to whom we gave 5 place in the way of subjection, no, not for an hour; that the truth of the gospel might continue with you. But from those who ⁵were reputed to be 6 somewhat (⁷whatsoever they were, it maketh no matter to me: God accepteth not man's person)— they, I say, who were of repute imparted nothing to me: but contrariwise, when they saw that I had 7 been intrusted with the gospel of the uncircumcision, even as Peter with *the gospel* of the circumcision (for he that wrought for Peter unto the apostleship 8 of the circumcision wrought for me also unto

---

¹ Gr. *in my race.*
² Or, *become acquainted with*
³ Or, *but only*
⁴ Or, *in the course of* *
⁵ Or, *are*
⁶ Or, *but it was because of*
⁷ Or, *what they once were*

* Strike out marg. ⁴ ("*in the course of*")—*Am. Com.*

9 the Gentiles); and when they perceived the grace that was given unto me, James and Cephas and John, they who ¹were reputed to be pillars, gave to me and Barnabas the right hands of fellowship, that we should go unto the Gentiles, and they unto
10 the circumcision; only *they would* that we should remember the poor; which very thing I was also zealous to do.
11 But when Cephas came to Antioch, I resisted him
12 to the face, because he stood condemned. For before that certain came from James, he did eat with the Gentiles: but when they came, he drew back and separated himself, fearing them that were of
13 the circumcision. And the rest of the Jews dissembled likewise with him; insomuch that even Barnabas was carried away with their dissimula-
14 tion. But when I saw that they walked not uprightly according to the truth of the gospel, I said unto Cephas before *them* all, If thou, being a Jew, livest as do the Gentiles, and not as do the Jews, how compellest thou the Gentiles to live as do the
15 Jews? We being Jews by nature, and not sinners
16 of the Gentiles, yet knowing that a man is not justified by ²the works of the law, ³save* through faith in Jesus Christ, even we believed on Christ Jesus, that we might be justified by faith in Christ, and not by the works of the law: because by the works
17 of the law shall no flesh be justified. But if, while we sought to be justified in Christ, we ourselves also were found sinners, is Christ a minister of sin?
18 God forbid. For if I build up again those things which I destroyed, I prove myself a transgressor.
19 For I through ⁴the law died unto ⁴the law, that I
20 might live unto God. I have been crucified with Christ; ⁵yet I live; *and yet* no longer I†, but Christ liveth in me: and that *life* which I now live in the flesh I live in faith, *the faith* which is in the Son of God, who loved me, and gave himself up for me.
21 I do not make void the grace of God: for if righteousness is through ⁴the law, then Christ died for nought.
3 O foolish Galatians, who did bewitch you, before whose eyes Jesus Christ was openly set forth cruci-
2 fied? This only would I learn from you, Received ye the Spirit by ²the works of the law, or by the

1 Or, *are*
2 Or, *works of law*
3 Or, *but only*
4 Or, *law*
5 Or, *and it is no longer I that live, but Christ &c.*

---

* For "save" read "but" and omit marg. ³—*Am. Com.*
† For "yet I live; *and yet* no longer I" read "and it is no longer I that live" and omit marg. ⁵—*Am. Com.*

hearing of faith? Are ye so foolish? having begun in the Spirit, ²are ye now perfected in the flesh? Did ye suffer so many things in vain? if it be indeed in vain. He therefore that supplieth to you the Spirit, and worketh ³miracles ⁴among you, *doeth he it* by ⁵the works of the law, or by the ¹hearing of faith? Even as Abraham believed God, and it was reckoned unto him for righteousness. ⁶Know therefore that they which be of faith, the same are sons of Abraham. And the scripture, foreseeing that God ⁷would justify the ⁸Gentiles by faith, preached the gospel beforehand unto Abraham, *saying*, In thee shall all the nations be blessed. So then they which be of faith are blessed with the faithful Abraham. For as many as are of ⁵the works of the law are under a curse: for it is written, Cursed is every one which continueth not in all things that are written in the book of the law, to do them. Now that no man is justified ⁹by the law in the sight of God, is evident: for, The righteous shall live by faith; and the law is not of faith; but, He that doeth them shall live in them. Christ redeemed us from the curse of the law, having become a curse for us: for it is written, Cursed is every one that hangeth on a tree: that upon the Gentiles might come the blessing of Abraham in Christ Jesus; that we might receive the promise of the Spirit through faith.

Brethren, I speak after the manner of men: Though it be but a man's ¹⁰covenant, yet when it hath been confirmed, no one maketh it void, or addeth thereto. Now to Abraham were the promises spoken, and to his seed. He saith not, And to seeds, as of many; but as of one, And to thy seed, which is Christ. Now this I say; A ¹⁰covenant confirmed beforehand by God, the law, which came four hundred and thirty years after, doth not disannul, so as to make the promise of none effect. For if the inheritance is of the law, it is no more of promise: but God hath granted it to Abraham by promise. What then is the law? It was added because of transgressions, till the seed should come to whom the promise hath been made; *and it was* ordained through angels by the hand of a mediator. Now a mediator is not *a mediator* of one; but God is one. Is the law then against the promises of God? God forbid: for if there had been a law given which could make alive, verily righteousness would

---

¹ Or, *message*
² Or, *do ye now make an end in the flesh?*
³ Gr. *powers*.
⁴ Or, *in*
⁵ Or, *works of law*
⁶ Or, *Ye perceive*
⁷ Gr. *justifieth*.
⁸ Gr. *nations*.
⁹ Gr. *in*.
¹⁰ Or, *testament*

22 have been of the law. Howbeit the scripture hath shut up* all things under sin, that the promise by faith in Jesus Christ might be given to them that believe.
23 But before ¹faith came, we were kept in ward under the law, shut up unto the faith which should
24 afterwards be revealed. So that the law hath been‡ our tutor *to bring us* unto Christ, that we might
25 be justified by faith. But now that faith is come,
26 we are no longer under a tutor. For ye are all
27 sons of God, through faith, in Christ Jesus. For as many of you as were baptized into Christ did put
28 on Christ. There can be neither Jew nor Greek, there can be neither bond nor free, there can be no male and female: for ye all are one *man* in Christ
29 Jesus. And if ye are Christ's, then are ye Abraham's seed, heirs according to promise.

4 But I say that so long as the heir is a child, he differeth nothing from a bondservant, though he is
2 lord of all; but is under guardians and stewards
3 until the term appointed of the father. So we also, when we were children, were held in bondage under
4 the ²rudiments of the world: but when the fulness of the time came, God sent forth his Son, born of a
5 woman, born under the law, that he might redeem them which were under the law, that we might re-
6 ceive the adoption of sons. And because ye are sons, God sent forth the Spirit of his Son into our
7 hearts, crying, Abba, Father. So that thou art no longer a bondservant, but a son; and if a son, then an heir through God.
8 Howbeit at that time, not knowing God, ye were in bondage to them which by nature are no gods:
9 but now that ye have come to know God, or rather to be known of God, how turn ye back again to the weak and beggarly ²rudiments, whereunto ye desire
10 to be in bondage over again? Ye observe days,
11 and months, and seasons, and years. I am afraid of you, lest by any means I have bestowed labour upon you in vain.
12 I beseech you, brethren, be§ as I *am*, for I *am* as‖
13 ye *are*. Ye did me no wrong: but ye know that because of an infirmity of the flesh I preached the

1 Or, *the faith*
2 Or, *elements*

---

* For "hath shut up" read "shut up"—*Am. Com.*
† Omit marg. ¹ ("*the faith*")—*Am. Com.*
‡ For "hath been" read "is become"—*Am. Com.*
§ For "be" read "become"—*Am. Com.*
‖ For "I *am* as" read "I also *am become* as"—*Am. Com.*

gospel unto you the ¹first time: and that which was a temptation to you in my flesh ye despised not, nor ²rejected; but ye received me as an angel of God, *even* as Christ Jesus. Where then is that gratulation ³of yourselves? for I bear you witness, that, if possible, ye would have plucked out your eyes and given them to me. So then am I become your enemy, because I ⁴tell you* the truth? They zealously seek you in no good way; nay, they desire to shut you out, that ye may seek them. But it is good to be zealously sought in a good matter at all times, and not only when I am present with you. My little children, of whom I am again in travail until Christ be formed in you†, yea, I could wish to be present with you now, and to change my voice; for I am perplexed about you.

Tell me, ye that desire to be under the law, do ye not hear the law? For it is written, that Abraham had two sons, one by the handmaid, and one by the freewoman. Howbeit the *son* by the handmaid is born after the flesh; but the *son* by the freewoman *is born* through promise. Which things contain an allegory: for these *women* are two covenants; one from mount Sinai, bearing children unto bondage, which is Hagar. ⁵Now this Hagar is mount Sinai in Arabia, and answereth to the Jerusalem that now is: for she is in bondage with her children. But the Jerusalem that is above is free, which is our mother. For it is written,

Rejoice, thou barren that bearest not;
Break forth and cry, thou that travailest not:
For more are the children of the desolate than
of her which hath the husband.

Now ⁶we, brethren, as Isaac was, are children of promise. But as then he that was born after the flesh persecuted him *that was born* after the Spirit, even so it is now. Howbeit what saith the scripture? Cast out the handmaid and her son: for the son of the handmaid shall not inherit with the son of the freewoman. Wherefore, brethren, we are not children of a handmaid, but of the freewoman. ⁷With freedom‡ did Christ set us free: stand fast therefore, and be not entangled again in a yoke of bondage.

Behold, I Paul say unto you, that, if ye receive circumcision, Christ will profit you nothing. Yea,

---

1 Gr. *former.*
2 Gr. *spat out.*
3 Or, *of yours*
4 Or, *deal truly with you*
5 Many ancient authorities read *For Sinai is a mountain in Arabia.*
6 Many ancient authorities read *ye.*
7 Or, *For freedom*

---

* For "because I tell you" read "by telling you"—*Am. Com.*
† Substitute a dash for the comma after "you"—*Am. Com.*
‡ Substitute marg. ⁷ ("*For freedom*") for the text.—*Am. Com.*

TO THE GALATIANS.

I testify again to every man that receiveth circumcision, that he is a debtor to do the whole law. Ye
are ¹severed from Christ, ye who would be justified
by the law; ye are fallen away from grace. For we
through the Spirit by faith wait for the hope of
righteousness. For in Christ Jesus neither circumcision availeth any thing, nor uncircumcision; but
faith ²working through love. Ye were running well;
who did hinder you that ye should not obey the truth?
This persuasion *came* not of him that calleth you.
A little leaven leaveneth the whole lump. I have
confidence to you-ward in the Lord, that ye will be
none otherwise minded: but he that troubleth you
shall bear his judgement, whosoever he be. But I,
brethren, if I still preach circumcision, why am I
still persecuted? then hath the stumblingblock of
the cross been done away. I would that they which
unsettle you would even ³cut themselves off*.

For ye, brethren, were called for freedom; only
use not your freedom for an occasion to the flesh,
but through love be servants one to another. For
the whole law is fulfilled in one word, *even* in this;
Thou shalt love thy neighbour as thyself. But if ye
bite and devour one another, take heed that ye be
not consumed one of another.

But I say, Walk by the Spirit, and ye shall not
fulfil the lust of the flesh. For the flesh lusteth
against the Spirit, and the Spirit against the flesh;
for these are contrary the one to the other; that ye
may not do the things that ye would. But if ye are
led by the Spirit, ye are not under the law. Now
the works of the flesh are manifest, which are *these*,
fornication, uncleanness, lasciviousness, idolatry,
sorcery, enmities, strife, jealousies, wraths, factions,
divisions, ⁴heresies†, envyings, drunkenness, revellings, and such like: of the which I ⁵forewarn you,
even as I did ⁵forewarn you, that they which practise such things shall not inherit the kingdom of
God. But the fruit of the Spirit is love, joy, peace,
longsuffering, kindness, goodness, faithfulness, meekness, ⁶temperance: against such there is no law.
And they that are of Christ Jesus have crucified
the flesh with the passions and the lusts thereof.
If we live by the Spirit, by the Spirit let us also

¹ Gr. *brought to nought*.
² Or, *wrought*
³ Or, *mutilate themselves*
⁴ Or, *parties*
⁵ Or, *tell you plainly*
⁶ Or, *self-control*

---

* For "cut themselves off" read "go beyond circumcision"—*Am. Com.*
† Substitute marg. ⁴ ("*parties*") for the text.—*Am. Com.*

walk. Let us not be vainglorious, provoking one 26
another, envying one another.

Brethren, even if a man be overtaken in any tres- 6
pass*, ye which are spiritual, restore such a one in a
spirit of meekness; looking to thyself, lest thou also
be tempted. Bear ye one another's burdens, and so 2
fulfil the law of Christ. For if a man thinketh him- 3
self to be something, when he is nothing, he deceiveth
himself. But let each man prove his own work, and 4
then shall he have his glorying in regard of himself
alone, and not of ¹his neighbour. For each man shall 5
bear his own ²burden.

¹ Gr. *the other.*
² Or, *load*

But let him that is taught in the word communi- 6
cate unto him that teacheth in all good things. Be not 7
deceived; God is not mocked: for whatsoever a man
soweth, that shall he also reap. For he that soweth 8
unto his own flesh shall of the flesh reap corruption;
but he that soweth unto the Spirit shall of the Spirit
reap eternal life. And let us not be weary in well- 9
doing: for in due season we shall reap, if we faint not.
So then, as† we have opportunity, let us work that 10
which is good toward all men, and especially toward
them that are of the household of the faith.

See with how large letters I ³have written‡ unto 11
you with mine own hand. As many as desire to 12
make a fair show in the flesh, they compel you to be
circumcised; only that they may not be persecuted
⁴for the cross of Christ. For not even they who 13
⁵receive circumcision do themselves keep ⁶the law;
but they desire to have you circumcised, that they
may glory in your flesh. But far be it from me to 14
glory, save in the cross of our Lord Jesus Christ,
through ⁷which the world hath been crucified unto
me, and I unto the world. For neither is circum- 15
cision any thing, nor uncircumcision, but a new
⁸creature. And as many as shall walk by this rule, 16
peace *be* upon them, and mercy, and upon the Israel of God.

³ Or, *write*

⁴ Or, *by reason of*
⁵ Some ancient authorities read *have been circumcised.*
⁶ Or, *a law*

⁷ Or, *whom*

⁸ Or, *creation*

From henceforth let no man trouble me: for I bear 17
branded on my body the marks of Jesus.

The grace of our Lord Jesus Christ be with your 18
spirit, brethren. Amen.

---

* "in any trespass" add marg. Or, *by*—*Am. Com.*
† "as" add marg. Or, *since*—*Am. Com.*
‡ Let the marg. ("*write*") and the text exchange places.—*Am. Com.*

THE EPISTLE OF PAUL THE APOSTLE

TO THE

EPHESIANS.

1 Paul, an apostle of Christ Jesus through the will of God, to the saints which are [1]at Ephesus, and the
2 faithful in Christ Jesus: Grace to you and peace from God our Father and the Lord Jesus Christ.
3 Blessed *be* the God and Father of our Lord Jesus Christ, who hath blessed us with every spiritual
4 blessing in the heavenly *places* in Christ: even as he chose us in him before the foundation of the world, that we should be holy and without blemish before
5 [2]him in love: having foreordained us unto adoption as sons through Jesus Christ unto himself, accord-
6 ing to the good pleasure of his will, to the praise of the glory of his grace, [3]which he freely bestowed on
7 us in the Beloved: in whom we have our redemption through his blood, the forgiveness of our tres-
8 passes, according to the riches of his grace, [4]which he made to abound toward us in all wisdom and
9 prudence, having made known unto us the mystery of his will, according to his good pleasure which he
10 purposed in him unto a dispensation of the fulness of the [5]times, to sum up all things in Christ, the things [6]in the heavens, and the things upon the
11 earth; in him, *I say*, in whom also we were made a heritage, having been foreordained according to the purpose of him who worketh all things after the
12 counsel of his will; to the end that we should be unto the praise of his glory, we who [7]had before
13 hoped in Christ: in whom ye also, having heard the word of the truth, the gospel of your salvation,—in whom, having also believed, ye were sealed with the
14 Holy Spirit of promise, which is an earnest of our

[1] Some very ancient authorities omit *at Ephesus*.

[2] Or, *him: having in love foreordained us*

[3] Or, *wherewith he endued us*

[4] Or, *wherewith he abounded*

[5] Gr. *seasons*.
[6] Gr. *upon*.

[7] Or, *have*

inheritance, unto the redemption of *God's* own possession, unto the praise of his glory.

For this cause I also, having heard of the faith in the Lord Jesus which is ¹among you, and ²which *ye shew** toward all the saints, cease not to give thanks for you, making mention *of you* in my prayers; that the God of our Lord Jesus Christ, the Father of glory, may give unto you a spirit of wisdom and revelation in the knowledge of him; having the eyes of your heart enlightened, that ye may know what is the hope of his calling, what the riches of the glory of his inheritance in the saints, and what the exceeding greatness of his power to us-ward who believe, according to that working of the strength of his might which he wrought in Christ, when he raised him from the dead, and made him to sit at his right hand in the heavenly *places*, far above all rule, and authority, and power, and dominion, and every name that is named, not only in this ³world, but also in that which is to come: and he put all things in subjection under his feet, and gave him to be head over all things to the church, which is his body, the fulness of him that filleth all in all.

And you *did he quicken*, when ye were dead through your trespasses and sins, wherein aforetime ye walked according to the ⁴course of this world, according to the prince of the power† of the air, of the spirit that now worketh in the sons of disobedience; among whom we also all once lived in the lusts of our flesh, doing the desires of the flesh and of the ⁵mind, and were by nature children of wrath, even as the rest:—but God, being rich in mercy, for his great love wherewith he loved us, even when we were dead through our trespasses, quickened us together ⁶with Christ (by grace have ye been saved), and raised us up with him, and made us to sit with him in the heavenly *places*, in Christ Jesus: that in the ages to come he might shew the exceeding riches of his grace in kindness toward us in Christ Jesus: for by grace have ye been saved through faith; and that not of yourselves: *it is* the gift of God: not of works, that no man should glory. For we are his workmanship,

15
16
17
18
19
20
21
22
23

2
2
3
4
5
6
7
8
9
10

1 Or, *in*
2 Many ancient authorities insert *the love.*

3 Or, *age*

4 Gr. *age.*

5 Gr. *thoughts.*

6 Some ancient authorities read *in Christ.*

---

* For "and which *ye shew*" read "and the love which *ye shew*" and in marg.² for "insert" read "omit".—*Am. Com.*

† For "power" read "powers" (with marg. Gr. *power*.)—*Am. Com.*

TO THE EPHESIANS.

created in Christ Jesus for good works, which God afore prepared that we should walk in them.

11 Wherefore remember, that aforetime ye, the Gentiles in the flesh, who are called Uncircumcision by that which is called Circumcision, in the flesh, made
12 by hands; that ye were at that time separate from Christ, alienated from the commonwealth of Israel, and strangers from the covenants of the promise,
13 having no hope and without God in the world. But now in Christ Jesus ye that once were far off are
14 made nigh in the blood of Christ. For he is our peace, who made both one, and brake down the mid-
15 dle wall of partition, having abolished in his flesh the enmity, *even* the law of commandments *contained* in ordinances; that he might create in himself of
16 the twain one new man, *so* making peace; and might reconcile them both in one body unto God through
17 the cross, having slain the enmity thereby: and he came and ¹preached peace to you that were far off,
18 and peace to them that were nigh: for through him we both have our access in one Spirit unto the Fa-
19 ther. So then ye are no more strangers and sojourners, but ye are fellow-citizens with the saints, and of
20 the household of God, being built upon the foundation of the apostles and prophets, Christ Jesus him-
21 self being the chief corner stone; in whom ²each several building, fitly framed together, groweth into
22 a holy ³temple in the Lord; in whom ye also are builded together ⁴for a habitation of God in the Spirit.

3 For this cause I Paul, the prisoner of Christ Jesus
2 in behalf of you Gentiles,—if so be that ye have heard of the ⁵dispensation of that grace of God which
3 was given me to you-ward; how that by revelation was made known unto me the mystery, as I wrote
4 afore in few words, whereby, when ye read, ye can perceive my understanding in the mystery of Christ;
5 which in other generations was not made known unto the sons of men, as it hath now been revealed unto
6 his holy apostles and prophets in the Spirit; *to wit*, that the Gentiles are fellow-heirs, and fellow-members of the body, and fellow-partakers of the prom-
7 ise in Christ Jesus through the gospel, whereof I was made a minister, according to the gift of that grace of God which was given me according to the work-
8 ing of his power. Unto me, who am less than the least of all saints, was this grace given, to preach unto
9 the Gentiles the unsearchable riches of Christ; and

1 Gr. *preached good tidings of peace.*

2 Gr. *every building.*

3 Or, *sanctuary.*

4 Gr. *into.*

5 Or, *stewardship.*

to ¹make all men see what is the ²dispensation of the
mystery which from all ages hath been hid in God
who created all things; to the intent that now unto
the principalities and the powers in the heavenly
places might be made known through the church
the manifold wisdom of God, according to the ³eternal purpose which he purposed in Christ Jesus our
Lord: in whom we have boldness and access in confidence through ⁴our faith in him. Wherefore I ask
that ye ⁵faint not* at my tribulations for you, which
⁶are your glory.

For this cause I bow my knees unto the Father, from whom every ⁷family in heaven and on earth is named, that he would grant you, according to the riches of his glory, that ye may be strengthened with power through his Spirit in the inward man; that Christ may dwell in your hearts through faith; to the end that ye, being rooted and grounded in love, may be strong to apprehend with all the saints what is the breadth and length and height and depth, and to know the love of Christ which passeth knowledge, that ye may be filled unto all the fulness of God.

Now unto him that is able to do exceeding abundantly above all that we ask or think, according to the power that worketh in us, unto him *be* the glory in the church and in Christ Jesus unto ⁸all generations for ever and ever. Amen.

I therefore, the prisoner in the Lord, beseech you to walk worthily of the calling wherewith ye were called, with all lowliness and meekness, with longsuffering, forbearing one another in love; giving diligence to keep the unity of the Spirit in the bond of peace. *There is* one body, and one Spirit, even as also ye were called in one hope of your calling; one Lord, one faith, one baptism, one God and Father of all, who is over all, and through all, and in all. But unto each one of us was the grace given according to the measure of the gift of Christ. Wherefore he saith,

    When he ascended on high, he led captivity
        captive,
    And gave gifts unto men.

(Now this, He ascended, what is it but that he also descended ⁹into the lower parts of the earth? He that descended is the same also that ascended far

---

¹ Some ancient authorities read *bring to light what is.*
² Or, *stewardship*
³ Gr. *purpose of the ages.*
⁴ Or, *the faith of him*
⁵ Or, *I*
⁶ Or, *is*
⁷ Gr. *fatherhood.*
⁸ Gr. *all the generations of the age of the ages.*
⁹ Some ancient authorities insert *first.*

* For "ye faint not" read "I may not faint" (with marg. Or, *ye*)
—Am. Com.

above all the heavens, that he might fill all things.)
11 And he gave some *to be* apostles; and some, prophets; and some, evangelists; and some, pastors and
12 teachers; for the perfecting of the saints, unto the work of ministering, unto the building up of the
13 body of Christ: till we all attain unto the unity of the faith, and of the knowledge of the Son of God, unto a full-grown man, unto the measure of the
14 stature of the fulness of Christ: that we may be no longer children, tossed to and fro and carried about with every wind of doctrine, by the sleight of men,
15 in craftiness, after the wiles of error; but ¹speaking truth in love, may grow up in all things into him,
16 which is the head, *even* Christ; from whom all the body fitly framed and knit together ²through that which every joint supplieth, according to the working in *due* measure of each several part, maketh the increase of the body unto the building up of itself in love.
17 This I say therefore, and testify in the Lord, that ye no longer walk as the Gentiles also walk, in the
18 vanity of their mind, being darkened in their understanding, alienated from the life of God because of the ignorance that is in them, because of the harden-
19 ing of their heart; who being past feeling gave themselves up to lasciviousness, ³to work all un-
20 cleanness with ⁴greediness. But ye did not so learn
21 Christ; if so be that ye heard him, and were taught
22 in him, even as truth is in Jesus: that ye put away, as concerning your former manner of life, the old man, which waxeth corrupt after the lusts of deceit;
23 and that ye be renewed in the spirit of your mind,
24 and put on the new man, ⁵which after God hath been created in righteousness and holiness of truth.
25 Wherefore, putting away falsehood, speak ye truth each one with his neighbour: for we are members
26 one of another. Be ye angry, and sin not: let not
27 the sun go down upon your ⁶wrath: neither give
28 place to the devil. Let him that stole steal no more: but rather let him labour, working with his hands the thing that is good, that he may have whereof to
29 give to him that hath need. Let no corrupt speech proceed out of your mouth, but such as is good for ⁷edifying as the need may be, that it may give grace
30 to them that hear. And grieve not the Holy Spirit of God, in whom ye were sealed unto the day of re-
31 demption. Let all bitterness, and wrath, and anger, and clamour, and railing, be put away from you,

1 Or, *dealing truly*

2 Gr. *through every joint of the supply.*

3 Or, *to make a trade of*

4 Or, *covetousness*

5 Or, *which is after God, created &c.*

6 Gr. *provocation.*

7 Gr. *the building up of the need.*

with all malice: and be ye kind one to another, ten- 32
derhearted, forgiving each other, even as God also
in Christ forgave ¹you.

Be ye therefore imitators of God, as beloved chil- 5
dren; and walk in love, even as Christ also loved 2
you, and gave himself up for ²us, an offering and a
sacrifice to God for an odour of a sweet smell. But 3
fornication, and all uncleanness, or covetousness,
let it not even be named among you, as becometh
saints; nor filthiness, nor foolish talking, or jesting, 4
which are not befitting: but rather giving of thanks.
For this ye know of a surety, that no fornicator, 5
nor unclean person, nor covetous man, which is an
idolater, hath any inheritance in the kingdom of
Christ and God. Let no man deceive you with 6
empty words: for because of these things cometh
the wrath of God upon the sons of disobedience.
Be not ye therefore partakers with them; for ye 7
were once darkness, but are now light in the Lord: 8
walk as children of light (for the fruit of the light 9
is in all goodness and righteousness and truth), prov- 10
ing what is well-pleasing unto the Lord; and have 11
no fellowship with the unfruitful works of darkness, but rather even ³reprove them; for the things 12
which are done by them in secret it is a shame
even to speak of. But all things when they are 13
⁴reproved are made manifest by the light: for every
thing that is made manifest is light. Wherefore 14
he saith, Awake, thou that sleepest, and arise from
the dead, and Christ shall shine upon thee.

Look therefore carefully how ye walk, not as un- 15
wise, but as wise; ⁵redeeming the time, because the 16
days are evil. Wherefore be ye not foolish, but 17
understand what the will of the Lord is. And be 18
not drunken with wine, wherein is riot, but be filled
⁶with the Spirit; speaking ⁷one to another in psalms 19
and hymns and spiritual songs, singing and making
melody with your heart to the Lord; giving thanks 20
always for all things in the name of our Lord Jesus
Christ to ⁸God, even the Father; subjecting your- 21
selves one to another in the fear of Christ.

Wives, *be in subjection* unto your own husbands, 22
as unto the Lord. For the husband is the head of 23
the wife, as Christ also is the head of the church, *being* himself the saviour of the body. But as the 24
church is subject to Christ, ⁹so *let* the wives also *be*
to their husbands in every thing. Husbands, love 25
your wives, even as Christ also loved the church,

---

1 Many ancient authorities read *us*.

2 Some ancient authorities read *you*.

3 Or, *convict*

4 Or, *convicted*

5 Gr. *buying up the opportunity.*

6 Or, *in spirit*

7 Or, *to yourselves*

8 Gr. *the God and Father.*

9 Or, *so are the wives also*

26 and gave himself up for it; that he might sanctify it, having cleansed it by the ¹washing of water with
27 the word, that he might present the church to himself a glorious *church*, not having spot or wrinkle or any such thing; but that it should be holy and with-
28 out blemish. Even so ought husbands also to love their own wives as their own bodies. He that lov-
29 eth his own wife loveth himself: for no man ever hated his own flesh; but nourisheth and cherisheth
30 it, even as Christ also the church; because we are
31 members of his body. For this cause shall a man leave his father and mother, and shall cleave to his
32 wife; and the twain shall become one flesh. This mystery is great: but I speak in regard of Christ
33 and of the church. Nevertheless do ye also severally love each one his own wife even as himself; and *let* the wife *see* that she fear her husband.

1 Gr. *laver.*

6 Children, obey your parents in the Lord: for this is
2 right. Honour thy father and mother (which is the
3 first commandment with promise), that it may be well with thee, and thou ²mayest live long on the
4 ³earth. And, ye fathers, provoke not your children to wrath: but nurture them in the chastening and admonition of the Lord.

2 Or, *shalt*
3 Or, *land*

5 ⁴Servants, be obedient unto them that according to the flesh are your ⁵masters, with fear and trembling, in singleness of your heart, as unto Christ;
6 not in the way of eyeservice, as men-pleasers; but as ⁴servants of Christ, doing the will of God from
7 the ⁶heart; with good will doing service, as unto the
8 Lord, and not unto men; knowing that whatsoever good thing each one doeth, the same shall he receive again from the Lord, whether *he be* bond or
9 free. And, ye ⁵masters, do the same things unto them, and forbear threatening: knowing that both* their Master and yours is in heaven, and there is no respect of persons with him.

4 Gr. *Bondservants.*
5 Gr. *lords.*
6 Gr. *soul.*

10 ⁷Finally, ⁸be strong in the Lord, and in the strength
11 of his might. Put on the whole armour of God, that ye may be able to stand against the wiles of
12 the devil. For our wrestling is not against flesh and blood, but against the principalities, against the powers, against the world-rulers of this darkness, against the spiritual *hosts* of wickedness in the hea-
13 venly *places*. Wherefore take up the whole armour of God, that ye may be able to withstand in the evil

7 Or, *From henceforth*
8 Gr. *be made powerful.*

---

* For "both" read "he who is both"—*Am. Com.*

day, and, having done all, to stand. Stand therefore, having girded your loins with truth, and having put on the breastplate of righteousness, and having shod your feet with the preparation of the gospel of peace; withal taking up the shield of faith, wherewith ye shall be able to quench all the fiery darts of the evil *one*. And take the helmet of salvation, and the sword of the Spirit, which is the word of God: with all prayer and supplication praying at all seasons in the Spirit, and watching thereunto in all perseverance and supplication for all the saints, and on my behalf, that utterance may be given unto me ¹in opening my mouth, to make known with boldness the mystery of the gospel, for which I am an ambassador in ²chains; that in it I may speak boldly, as I ought to speak.

But that ye also may know my affairs, how I do, Tychicus, the beloved brother and faithful minister in the Lord, shall make known to you all things: whom I have sent unto you for this very purpose, that ye may know our state, and that he may comfort your hearts.

Peace be to the brethren, and love with faith, from God the Father and the Lord Jesus Christ. Grace be with all them that love our Lord Jesus Christ in uncorruptness.

---

¹ Or, *in opening my mouth with boldness, to make known*

² Gr. *a chain*.

THE EPISTLE OF PAUL THE APOSTLE

TO THE

PHILIPPIANS.

---

1 Paul and Timothy, [1]servants of Christ Jesus, to all the saints in Christ Jesus which are at Philippi,
2 with the [2]bishops and deacons: Grace to you and peace from God our Father and the Lord Jesus Christ.
3 I thank my God upon all my remembrance of you,
4 always in every supplication of mine on behalf of
5 you all making my supplication with joy, for your fellowship in furtherance of the gospel from the first
6 day until now; being confident of this very thing, that he which began a good work in you will perfect
7 it until the day of Jesus Christ: even as it is right for me to be thus minded on behalf of you all, because [3]I have you in my heart, inasmuch as, both in my bonds and in the defence and confirmation of the gospel, ye all are partakers with me of grace.
8 For God is my witness, how I long after you all in
9 the tender mercies of Christ Jesus. And this I pray, that your love may abound yet more and more in
10 knowledge and all discernment; so that ye may [4]approve the things that are excellent; that ye may be sincere and void of offence unto the day of Christ;
11 being filled with the [5]fruits of righteousness, which are through Jesus Christ, unto the glory and praise of God.
12 Now I would have you know, brethren, that the things *which happened* unto me have fallen out rather
13 unto the progress of the gospel; so that my bonds became manifest in Christ [6]throughout the whole
14 prætorian guard, and to all the rest; and that most of the brethren in the Lord, [7]being confident through my bonds, are more abundantly bold to speak the

[1] Gr. *bondservants.*
[2] Or, *overseers*
[3] Or, *ye have me in your heart*
[4] Or, *prove the things that differ*
[5] Gr. *fruit.*
[6] Gr. *in the whole Prætorium.*
[7] Gr. *trusting in my bonds.*

word of God without fear. Some indeed preach 15
Christ even of envy and strife; and some also of good
will: the one* *do it* of love, knowing that I am set for 16
the defence of the gospel: but the other† proclaim 17
Christ of faction, not sincerely, thinking to raise up
affliction for me in my bonds. What then? only 18
that in every way, whether in pretence or in truth,
Christ is proclaimed; and therein I rejoice, yea, and
will rejoice. For I know that this shall turn to my 19
salvation, through your supplication and the supply
of the Spirit of Jesus Christ, according to my ear- 20
nest expectation and hope, that in nothing shall I
be put to shame, but *that* with all boldness, as always, *so* now also Christ shall be magnified in my
body, whether by life, or by death. For to me to 21
live is Christ, and to die is gain. ¹But if to live in 22
the flesh,—*if* this is the fruit of my work‡, then
²what I shall choose ³I wot not. But I am in a 23
strait betwixt the two, having the desire to depart
and be with Christ; for it is very far better: yet to 24
abide in the flesh is more needful for your sake.
And having this confidence, I know that I shall 25
abide, yea, and abide with you all, for your progress
and joy ⁴in the faith; that your glorying may abound 26
in Christ Jesus in me through my presence with you
again. Only ⁵let your manner of life be worthy of 27
the gospel of Christ: that, whether I come and see
you or be absent, I may hear of your state, that ye
stand fast in one spirit, with one soul striving ⁶for
the faith of the gospel; and in nothing affrighted 28
by the adversaries: which is for them an evident
token of perdition, but of your salvation, and that
from God; because to you it hath been granted in 29
the behalf of Christ, not only to believe on him, but
also to suffer in his behalf: having the same con- 30
flict which ye saw in me, and now hear to be in me.

If there is therefore any comfort‖ in Christ, if **2**
any consolation of love, if any fellowship of the
Spirit, if any tender mercies and compassions, ful- 2
fil ye my joy, that ye be of the same mind, having
the same love, being of one accord, ⁷of one mind;

---

¹ Or, *But if to live in the flesh be my lot, this is the fruit of my work: and what I shall choose I wot not.*
² Or, *what shall I choose?*
³ Or, *I do not make known*§
⁴ Or, *of faith*
⁵ Gr. *behave as citizens worthily.*
⁶ Gr. *with.*
⁷ Some ancient authorities read *of the same mind.*

* To "the one" etc. add marg. Or, *they that are moved by love* do it—*Am. Com.*
† To "but the other" etc. add the marg. Or, *but they that are factious proclaim Christ*—*Am. Com.*
‡ Read in the text "*if* this shall bring fruit from my work" with marg. Gr. *this is for me fruit of work.*—*Am. Com.*
§ Omit marg. ³ ("*I do not make known*")—*Am. Com.*
‖ For "comfort" read "exhortation"—*Am. Com.*

3 *doing* nothing through faction or through vainglory, but in lowliness of mind each counting other
4 better than himself; not looking each of you to his own things, but each of you also to the things of
5 others. Have this mind in you, which was also in
6 Christ Jesus: who, ¹being* in the form of God, counted it not ²a prize to be on an equality with
7 God†, but emptied himself, taking the form of a
8 ³servant, ⁴being made in the likeness of men; and being found in fashion as a man, he humbled himself, becoming obedient *even* unto death, yea, the
9 death of the cross. Wherefore also God highly exalted him, and gave unto him the name which is
10 above every name; that in the name of Jesus every knee should bow, of *things* in heaven and *things* on
11 earth and ⁵*things* under the earth, and that every tongue should confess that Jesus Christ is Lord, to the glory of God the Father.
12 So then, my beloved, even as ye have always obeyed, not ⁶as in my presence only, but now much more in my absence, work out your own salvation
13 with fear and trembling; for it is God which worketh in you both to will and to work, for his good
14 pleasure. Do all things without murmurings and
15 disputings‡; that ye may be§ blameless and harmless, children of God without blemish in the midst of a crooked and perverse generation, among whom
16 ye are seen as ⁷lights in the world, holding forth the word of life; that I may have whereof to glory in the day of Christ, that I did not run in vain neither
17 labour in vain. Yea, and if I am ⁸offered upon the sacrifice and service of your faith, I joy, and rejoice
18 with you all: and in the same manner do ye also joy, and rejoice with me.
19 But I hope in the Lord Jesus to send Timothy shortly unto you, that I also may be of good com-
20 fort, when I know your state. For I have no man like-minded, who will care ⁹truly for your state.
21 For they all seek their own, not the things of Jesus
22 Christ. But ye know the proof of him, that, as a child *serveth* a father, *so* he served with me in fur-
23 therance of the gospel. Him therefore I hope to

1 Gr. *being originally.*
2 Gr. *a thing to be grasped.*
3 Gr. *bondservant.*
4 Gr. *becoming in.*

5 Or, *things of the world below*

6 Some ancient authorities omit *as.*

7 Gr. *luminaries.*

8 Gr. *poured out as a drink-offering.*

9 Gr. *genuinely.*

---

* For "being" read "existing" and omit marg. ¹—*Am. Com.*
† Let the text run "counted not the being on an equality with God a thing to be grasped" and omit marg. ²—*Am. Com.*
‡ For "disputings" read "questionings"—*Am. Com.*
§ For "may be" read "may become"—*Am. Com.*

send forthwith, so soon as I shall see how it will go with me: but I trust in the Lord that I myself also 24 shall come shortly. But I counted it necessary to 25 send to you Epaphroditus, my brother and fellow-worker and fellow-soldier, and your ¹messenger and minister to my need; since he longed ²after you all, 26 and was sore troubled, because ye had heard that he was sick: for indeed he was sick nigh unto death: 27 but God had mercy on him; and not on him only, but on me also, that I might not have sorrow upon sorrow. I have sent him therefore the more dili- 28 gently, that, when ye see him again, ye may rejoice, and that I may be the less sorrowful. Receive him 29 therefore in the Lord with all joy; and hold such in honour: because for the work of ³Christ he came 30 nigh unto death, hazarding his life to supply that which was lacking in your service toward me.

Finally, my brethren, ⁴rejoice in the Lord. To **3** write the same things to you, to me indeed is not irksome, but for you it is safe. Beware of the dogs, 2 beware of the evil workers, beware of the concision: for we are the circumcision, who worship by the 3 Spirit of God, and glory in Christ Jesus, and have no confidence in the flesh: though I myself might 4 have confidence even in the flesh: if any other man ⁵thinketh to have confidence in the flesh, I yet more: circumcised the eighth day, of the stock of Israel, 5 of the tribe of Benjamin, a Hebrew of Hebrews; as touching the law, a Pharisee; as touching zeal, per- 6 secuting the church; as touching the righteousness which is in the law, found blameless. Howbeit 7 what things were ⁶gain to me, these have I counted loss for Christ. Yea verily, and I count all things 8 to be loss for the excellency of the knowledge of Christ Jesus my Lord: for whom I suffered the loss of all things, and do count them but ⁷dung, that I may gain Christ, and be found in him, ⁸not having 9 a righteousness of mine own, *even* that which is of the law, but that which is through faith in Christ, the righteousness which is of God† ⁹by faith: that 10 I may know him, and the power of his resurrection, and the fellowship of his sufferings, becoming con-formed unto his death; if by any means I may at- 11 tain unto the resurrection from the dead. Not that 12 I have already obtained, or am already made per-

---

1 Gr. *apostle.*
2 Many ancient authorities read *to see you all.*
3 Many ancient authorities read *the Lord.*
4 Or, *farewell*
5 Or, *seemeth*
6 Gr. *gains.*
7 Or, *refuse**
8 Or, *not having as my righteousness that which is of the law*
9 Gr. *upon*

* Substitute marg. ⁷ ("*refuse*") for the text.—*Am. Com.*
† For "of God" read "from God"—*Am. Com.*

TO THE PHILIPPIANS.

fect: but I press on, if so be that I may ¹apprehend* that for which also I was apprehended by Christ
13 Jesus. Brethren, I count not myself ²yet to have apprehended†: but one thing *I do*, forgetting the things which are behind, and stretching forward to
14 the things which are before, I press on toward the goal unto the prize of the ³high calling of God in
15 Christ Jesus. Let us therefore, as many as be perfect, be thus minded: and if in any thing ye are otherwise minded, even this shall God reveal unto
16 you: only, whereunto we have already attained, by that same *rule* let us walk.
17 Brethren, be ye imitators together of me, and mark them which so walk even as ye have us for an en-
18 sample. For many walk, of whom I told you often, and now tell you even weeping, *that they are* the
19 enemies of the cross of Christ: whose end is perdition, whose god is the belly, and *whose* glory is in
20 their shame, who mind earthly things. For our ⁴citizenship is in heaven; from whence also we wait for
21 a Saviour, the Lord Jesus Christ: who shall fashion anew the body of our humiliation, *that it may be* conformed to the body of his glory, according to the working whereby he is able even to subject all things unto himself.

4 Wherefore, my brethren beloved and longed for, my joy and crown, so stand fast in the Lord, my beloved.
2 I exhort Euodia, and I exhort Syntyche, to be of
3 the same mind in the Lord. Yea, I beseech thee also, true yokefellow, help these women, for they laboured with me in the gospel, with Clement also, and the rest of my fellow-workers, whose names are in the book of life.
4 ⁵Rejoice in the Lord alway: again I will say, ⁵Re-
5 joice‡. Let your ⁶forbearance be known unto all men.
6 The Lord is at hand. In nothing be anxious; but in everything by prayer and supplication with thanksgiving let your requests be made known unto God.
7 And the peace of God, which passeth all understanding, shall guard your hearts and your thoughts in Christ Jesus.
8 Finally, brethren, whatsover things are true, what-

¹ Or, *apprehend, seeing that also I was apprehended*
² Many ancient authorities omit *yet*.
³ Or, *upward*
⁴ Or, *commonwealth*
⁵ Or, *Farewell*
⁶ Or, *gentleness*

---

* For "apprehend ... apprehended" read "lay hold on ... laid hold on", and in marg.¹ for "*apprehend ... apprehended*" read "*lay hold ... laid hold on*"—*Am. Com.*
† For "apprehended" read "laid hold"—*Am. Com.*
‡ Omit marg. ⁵ ("*Farewell*")—*Am. Com.*

soever things are ¹honourable, whatsoever things are just, whatsoever things are pure, whatsoever things are lovely, whatsoever things are ²of good report; if there be any virtue, and if there be any praise, ³think on these things. The things which ye both learned 9 and received and heard and saw in me, these things do: and the God of peace shall be with you.

But I ⁴rejoice in the Lord greatly, that now at 10 length ye have revived your thought for me; ⁵wherein ye did indeed take thought, but ye lacked opportunity. Not that I speak in respect of want: for I 11 have learned, in whatsoever state I am, therein to be content. I know how to be abased, and I know also 12 how to abound: in every thing and in all things have I learned the secret both to be filled and to be hungry, both to abound and to be in want. I can 13 do all things in him that strengtheneth me. How- 14 beit ye did well, that ye had fellowship with my affliction. And ye yourselves also know, ye Philip- 15 pians, that in the beginning of the gospel, when I departed from Macedonia, no church had fellowship with me in the matter of giving and receiving, but ye only; for even in Thessalonica ye sent once and 16 again unto my need. Not that I seek for the gift; 17 but I seek for the fruit that increaseth to your account. But I have all things, and abound: I am 18 filled, having received from Epaphroditus the things *that came* from you, an odour of a sweet smell, a sacrifice acceptable, well-pleasing to God. And my 19 God shall fulfil* every need of yours according to his riches in glory in Christ Jesus. Now unto our 20 God and Father *be* the glory ⁶for ever and ever. Amen.

Salute every saint in Christ Jesus. The brethren 21 which are with me salute you. All the saints salute 22 you, especially they that are of Cæsar's household.

The grace of the Lord Jesus Christ be with your 23 spirit.

---

1 Gr. *reverend*.
2 Or, *gracious*.
3 Gr. *take account of*.
4 Gr. *rejoiced*.
5 Or, *seeing that*.
6 Gr. *unto the ages of the ages*.

* For "fulfil" read "supply" [Comp. "Classes of Passages," xiv.]—*Am. Com.*

THE EPISTLE OF PAUL THE APOSTLE

TO THE

COLOSSIANS.

1 Paul, an apostle of Christ Jesus through the will
2 of God, and Timothy [1]our brother, [2]to the saints
and faithful brethren in Christ *which are* at Colossæ: Grace to you and peace from God our Father.
3 We give thanks to God the Father of our Lord
4 Jesus Christ, praying always for you, having heard
of your faith in Christ Jesus, and of the love which
5 ye have toward all the saints, because of the hope
which is laid up for you in the heavens, whereof ye
heard before in the word of the truth of the gospel,
6 which is come unto you; even as it is also in all
the world bearing fruit and increasing, as *it doth* in
you also, since the day ye heard and knew the grace
7 of God in truth; even as ye learned of Epaphras
our beloved fellow-servant, who is a faithful minis-
8 ter of Christ on [3]our behalf, who also declared unto
us your love in the Spirit.
9 For this cause we also, since the day we heard *it*,
do not cease to pray and make request for you, that
ye may be filled with the knowledge of his will in
10 all spiritual wisdom and understanding, to walk
worthily of the Lord [4]unto all pleasing, bearing
fruit in every good work, and increasing [5]in the
11 knowledge of God; [6]strengthened [7]with all power,
according to the might of his glory, unto all pa-
12 tience and longsuffering with joy; giving thanks
unto the Father, who made [8]us meet to be par-
13 takers of the inheritance of the saints in light; who
delivered us out of the power of darkness, and trans-
14 lated us into the kingdom of the Son of his love; in
whom we have our redemption, the forgiveness of
15 our sins: who is the image of the invisible God, the

[1] Gr. *the brother.*
[2] Or, *to those that are at Colossæ, holy and faithful brethren in Christ*
[3] Many ancient authorities read *your.*
[4] Or, *unto all pleasing, in every good work, bearing fruit and increasing, &c.*
[5] Or, *by*
[6] Gr. *made powerful.*
[7] Or, *in*
[8] Some ancient authorities read *you.*

firstborn of all creation; for in him were all things ¹⁶ created, in the heavens and upon the earth, things visible and things invisible, whether thrones or dominions or principalities or powers; all things have been created through him, and unto him; and he is ¹⁷ before all things, and in him all things ¹consist. And he is the head of the body, the church: who ¹⁸ is the beginning, the firstborn from the dead; ²that in all things he might have the preeminence. ³For ¹⁹ it was the good pleasure *of the Father* that in him should all the fulness dwell; and through him to ²⁰ reconcile all things ⁴unto ⁵himself, having made peace through the blood of his cross; through him, *I say,* whether things upon the earth, or things in the heavens. And you, being in time past alienated ²¹ and enemies in your mind in your evil works, yet now ⁶hath he reconciled in the body of his flesh ²² through death, to present you holy and without blemish and unreproveable before him: if so be that ²³ ye continue in the faith, grounded and stedfast, and not moved away from the hope of the gospel which ye heard, which was preached in all creation under heaven; whereof I Paul was made a minister.

Now I rejoice in my sufferings for your sake, and ²⁴ fill up on my part that which is lacking of the afflictions of Christ in my flesh for his body's sake, which is the church; whereof I was made a minister, according to the ⁷dispensation of God which was ²⁵ given me to you-ward, to fulfil the word of God, *even* the mystery which hath been hid ⁸from all* ²⁶ ages and generations: but now hath it been manifested to his saints, to whom God was pleased to ²⁷ make known what is the riches of the glory of this mystery among the Gentiles, which is Christ in you, the hope of glory: whom we proclaim, admonishing ²⁸ every man and teaching every man in all wisdom, that we may present every man perfect in Christ; whereunto I labour also, striving according to his ²⁹ working, which worketh in me ⁹mightily.

For I would have you know how greatly I strive **2** for you, and for them at Laodicea, and for as many as have not seen my face in the flesh; that their ² hearts may be comforted, they being knit together in love, and unto all riches of the ¹⁰full assurance of understanding, that they may know the mystery of God, ¹¹*even* Christ, in whom are all the treasures of ³

---

¹ That is, *hold together.*
² Or, *that among all he might have*
³ Or, *For the whole fulness of God was pleased to dwell in him*
⁴ Or, *into him*
⁵ Or, *him*
⁶ Some ancient authorities read *ye have been reconciled.*
⁷ Or, *stewardship*
⁸ Gr. *from the ages and from the generations.*
⁹ Or, *in power*
¹⁰ Or, *fulness*
¹¹ The ancient authorities vary much in the text of this passage.

* For "from all" read "for"—*Am. Com.*

TO THE COLOSSIANS.

4 wisdom and knowledge hidden. This I say, that no one may delude you with persuasiveness of
5 speech. For though I am absent in the flesh, yet am I with you in the spirit, joying and beholding your order, and the stedfastness of your faith in Christ.
6 As therefore ye received Christ Jesus the Lord,
7 *so* walk in him, rooted and builded up in him, and stablished [1]in your faith, even as ye were taught, abounding [2]in thanksgiving.
8 [3]Take heed lest there shall be any one that maketh spoil of you through his philosophy and vain deceit, after the tradition of men, after the [4]rudiments
9 of the world, and not after Christ: for in him dwell-
10 eth all the fulness of the Godhead bodily, and in him ye are made full, who is the head of all prin-
11 cipality and power: in whom ye were also circumcised with a circumcision not made with hands, in the putting off of the body of the flesh, in the cir-
12 cumcision of Christ; having been buried with him in baptism, wherein ye were also raised with him through faith in the working of God, who raised
13 him from the dead. And you, being dead through your trespasses and the uncircumcision of your flesh, you, *I say*, did he quicken together with him,
14 having forgiven us all our trespasses; having blotted out [5]the bond written in ordinances that was against us, which was contrary to us: and he hath taken it out of the way, nailing it to the cross;
15 [6]having put off from himself* the principalities and the powers, he made a show of them openly, triumphing over them in it.
16 Let no man therefore judge you in meat, or in drink, or in respect of a feast day or a new moon
17 or a sabbath day: which are a shadow of the things
18 to come; but the body is Christ's. Let no man rob you of your prize [7]by a voluntary humility and worshipping of the angels, [8]dwelling in the things which he hath [9]seen, vainly puffed up by his fleshly mind,
19 and not holding fast the Head, from whom all the body, being supplied and knit together through the joints and bands, increaseth with the increase of God.
20 If ye died with Christ from the [4]rudiments of the world, why, as though living in the world, do ye
21 subject yourselves to ordinances, Handle not, nor
22 taste, nor touch (all which things are to perish with

---

1 Or, *by*
2 Some ancient authorities insert *in it.*
3 Or, *See whether*
4 Or, *elements*
5 Or, *the bond that was against us by its ordinances*
6 Or, *having put off from himself* his *body, he made a show of the principalities, &c.*
7 Or, *of his own mere will, by humility, &c.*
8 Or, *taking his stand upon*
9 Many authorities, some ancient, insert *not.*

---

* For "having put off from himself" read "having despoiled" and substitute the text for marg. [6] —*Am. Com.*

the using), after the precepts and doctrines of men? Which things have indeed a show of wisdom in will-worship, and humility, and severity to the body; but are not of any ¹value against the indulgence of the flesh.

If then ye were raised together with Christ, seek the things that are above, where Christ is, seated on the right hand of God. Set your mind on the things that are above, not on the things that are upon the earth. For ye died, and your life is hid with Christ in God. When Christ, *who is* ²our life, shall be manifested, then shall ye also with him be manifested in glory. ³Mortify* therefore your members which are upon the earth; fornication, uncleanness, passion, evil desire, and covetousness, the which is idolatry; for which things' sake cometh the wrath of God ⁴upon the sons of disobedience; ⁵in the which ye also walked aforetime, when ye lived in these things. But now put ye also away all these; anger, wrath, malice, railing, shameful speaking out of your mouth: lie not one to another; seeing that ye have put off the old man with his doings, and have put on the new man, which is being renewed unto knowledge after the image of him that created him: where there cannot be Greek and Jew, circumcision and uncircumcision, barbarian, Scythian, bondman, freeman: but Christ is all, and in all.

Put on therefore, as God's elect, holy and beloved, a heart of compassion, kindness, humility, meekness, longsuffering; forbearing one another, and forgiving each other, if any man have a complaint against any; even as ⁶the Lord forgave you, so also do ye: and above all these things *put on* love, which is the bond of perfectness. And let the peace of Christ ⁷rule in your hearts, to the which also ye were called in one body; and be ye thankful. Let the word of ⁸Christ dwell in you richly† in all wisdom; teaching and admonishing ⁹one another with psalms *and* hymns *and* spiritual songs, singing with grace in your hearts unto God. And whatsoever ye do, in word or in deed, *do* all in the name of the Lord Jesus, giving thanks to God the Father through him.

Wives, be in subjection to your husbands, as is fitting in the Lord. Husbands, love your wives, and be

---

¹ Or, *honour*
² Many ancient authorities read *your*.
³ Gr. *Make dead*.
⁴ Some ancient authorities omit *upon the sons of disobedience.* See Eph. v. 6.
⁵ Or, *amongst whom*
⁶ Many ancient authorities read *Christ*.
⁷ Gr. *arbitrate*.
⁸ Some ancient authorities read *the Lord*: others, *God*.
⁹ Or, *yourselves*

* For "Mortify" read "Put to death" and omit marg. ³ —*Am. Com.*
† For "richly" read "richly;" and omit the semicolon after "wisdom" putting the present text into the marg.—*Am. Com.*

TO THE COLOSSIANS.

20 not bitter against them. Children, obey your parents
21 in all things, for this is well-pleasing in the Lord. Fathers, provoke not your children, that they be not
22 discouraged. ¹Servants, obey in all things them that are your ²masters according to the flesh; not with eyeservice, as men-pleasers, but in singleness of heart,
23 fearing the Lord: whatsoever ye do, work ³heartily,
24 as unto the Lord, and not unto men; knowing that from the Lord ye shall receive the recompense of the
25 inheritance: ye serve the Lord Christ. For he that doeth wrong shall ⁴receive again for the wrong that he hath done: and there is no respect of persons.

4 ²Masters, render unto your ¹servants that which is just and ⁵equal; knowing that ye also have a Master in heaven.
2 Continue stedfastly in prayer, watching therein
3 with thanksgiving; withal praying for us also, that God may open unto us a door for the word, to speak the mystery of Christ, for which I am also in bonds;
4 that I may make it manifest, as I ought to speak.
5 Walk in wisdom toward them that are without, ⁶re-
6 deeming the time. Let your speech be always with grace, seasoned with salt, that ye may know how ye ought to answer each one.
7 All my affairs shall Tychicus make known unto you, the beloved brother and faithful minister and
8 fellow-servant in the Lord: whom I have sent unto you for this very purpose, that ye may know our
9 estate, and that he may comfort your hearts; together with Onesimus, the faithful and beloved brother, who is one of you. They shall make known unto you all things that *are done* here.
10 Aristarchus my fellow-prisoner saluteth you, and Mark, the cousin of Barnabas (touching whom ye received commandments; if he come unto you, re-
11 ceive him), and Jesus, which is called Justus, who are of the circumcision: these only *are my* fellow-workers unto the kingdom of God, men that have
12 been a comfort unto me. Epaphras, who is one of you, a ⁷servant of Christ Jesus, saluteth you, always striving for you in his prayers, that ye may stand
13 perfect and fully assured in all the will of God. For I bear him witness, that he hath much labour for you, and for them in Laodicea, and for them in Hierapo-
14 lis. Luke, the beloved physician, and Demas salute
15 you. Salute the brethren that are in Laodicea, and ⁸Nymphas, and the church that is in ⁹their house.
16 And when ¹⁰this epistle hath been read among you,

1 Gr. *Bondservants*.
2 Gr. *lords*.
3 Gr. *from the soul*.
4 Gr. *receive again the wrong*.
5 Gr. *equality*.
6 Gr. *buying up the opportunity*.
7 Gr. *bondservant*.
8 The Greek may represent *Nympha*.
9 Some ancient authorities read *her*.
10 Gr. *the*.

cause that it be read also in the church of the Laodiceans; and that ye also read the epistle from Laodicea. And say to Archippus, Take heed to the ministry which thou hast received in the Lord, that thou fulfil it.

The salutation of me Paul with mine own hand. Remember my bonds. Grace be with you.

THE FIRST EPISTLE OF PAUL THE APOSTLE
TO THE
THESSALONIANS.

1 Paul, and Silvanus, and Timothy, unto the church of the Thessalonians in God the Father and the Lord Jesus Christ: Grace to you and peace.
2 We give thanks to God always for you all, mak-
3 ing mention *of you* in our prayers; remembering without ceasing your work of faith and labour of love and patience of hope in our Lord Jesus Christ,
4 before our God and Father; knowing, brethren be-
5 loved of God, your election, [1]how that our gospel came not unto you in word only, but also in power, and in the [2]Holy Ghost, and *in* much [3]assurance; even as ye know what manner of men we shewed
6 ourselves toward you for your sake. And ye became imitators of us, and of the Lord, having received the word in much affliction, with joy of the
7 [2]Holy Ghost; so that ye became an ensample to all
8 that believe in Macedonia and in Achaia. For from you hath sounded forth the word of the Lord, not only in Macedonia and Achaia, but in every place your faith to God-ward is gone forth; so that we
9 need not to speak any thing. For they themselves report concerning us what manner of entering in we had unto you; and how ye turned unto God
10 from idols, to serve a living and true God, and to wait for his Son from heaven, whom he raised from the dead, *even* Jesus, which delivereth us from the wrath to come.

2 For yourselves, brethren, know our entering in
2 unto you, that it hath not been found vain: but having suffered before, and been shamefully entreated, as ye know, at Philippi, we waxed bold in our God to speak unto you the gospel of God in

[1] Or, *because our gospel, &c.*
[2] Or, *Holy Spirit*
[3] Or, *fulness*

much conflict. For our exhortation is not of error, 3
nor of uncleanness, nor in guile: but even as we 4
have been approved of God to be intrusted with the
gospel, so we speak; not as pleasing men, but God
which proveth our hearts. For neither at any time 5
were we found using words of flattery, as ye know,
nor a cloke of covetousness, God is witness; nor 6
seeking glory of men, neither from you, nor from
others, when we might have ¹been burdensome*,
as apostles of Christ. But we were ²gentle in the 7
midst of you, as when a nurse cherisheth her own
children: even so, being affectionately desirous of 8
you, we were well pleased to impart unto you, not
the gospel of God only, but also our own souls, because ye were become very dear to us. For ye remember, brethren, our labour and travail: working 9
night and day, that we might not burden any of you,
we preached unto you the gospel of God. Ye are 10
witnesses, and God also, how holily and righteously
and unblameably we behaved ourselves toward you
that believe: as ye know how we *dealt with* each 11
one of you, as a father with his own children, exhorting you, and encouraging *you*, and testifying,
to the end that ye should walk worthily of God, 12
who ³calleth you into his own kingdom and glory.
And for this cause we also thank God without 13
ceasing, that, when ye received from us ⁴the word
of the message, *even the word* of God, ye accepted *it*
not *as* the word of men, but, as it is in truth, the
word of God, which also worketh in you that believe. For ye, brethren, became imitators of the 14
churches of God which are in Judæa in Christ
Jesus: for ye also suffered the same things of your
own countrymen, even as they did of the Jews;
who both killed the Lord Jesus and the prophets, 15
and drave out us, and please not God, and are contrary to all men; forbidding us to speak to the Gen-16
tiles that they may be saved; to fill up their sins
alway: but the wrath is come upon them to the
uttermost.
But we, brethren, being bereaved of you for ⁵a 17
short season, in presence, not in heart, endeavoured
the more exceedingly to see your face with great
desire: because we would fain have come unto 18
you, I Paul once and again; and Satan hindered us.

---

1 Or, *claimed honour*
2 Most of the ancient authorities read *babes.*
3 Some ancient authorities read *called.*
4 Gr. *the word of hearing.*
5 Gr. *a season of an hour.*

* Let marg.¹ run *claimed authority*, and then let the marg. and the text exchange places.—*Am. Com.*

19 For what is our hope, or joy, or crown of glorying?
Are not even ye, before our Lord Jesus at his ¹com- [1 Gr. *presence*.]
20 ing? For ye are our glory and our joy.

3 Wherefore when we could no longer forbear, we thought it good to be left behind at Athens alone;
2 and sent Timothy, our brother and ²God's minister in the gospel of Christ, to establish you, and to [2 Some ancient authorities read *fellow-worker with God*.]
3 comfort *you* concerning your faith; that no man be moved by these afflictions; for yourselves know
4 that hereunto we are appointed. For verily, when we were with you, we told you ³beforehand that [3 Or, *plainly*] we are to suffer affliction; even as it came to pass,
5 and ye know. For this cause I also, when I could no longer forbear, sent that I might know your faith, lest by any means the tempter had tempted
6 you, and our labour should be in vain. But when Timothy came even now unto us from you, and brought us glad tidings of your faith and love, and that ye have good remembrance of us always,
7 longing to see us, even as we also *to see* you; for this cause, brethren, we were comforted over you in all our distress and affliction through your faith:
8 for now we live, if ye stand fast in the Lord. For
9 what thanksgiving can we render again unto God for you, for all the joy wherewith we joy for your
10 sakes before our God; night and day praying exceedingly that we may see your face, and may perfect that which is lacking in your faith?
11 Now may our God and Father himself, and our
12 Lord Jesus, direct our way unto you: and the Lord make you to increase and abound in love one toward another, and toward all men, even as we also
13 *do* toward you; to the end he may stablish your hearts unblameable in holiness before our God and Father, at the ¹coming of our Lord Jesus with all his saints.⁴ [4 Many ancient authorities add *Amen*.]

4 Finally then, brethren, we beseech and exhort you in the Lord Jesus, that, as ye received of us how ye ought to walk and to please God, even as ye
2 do walk,—that ye abound more and more. For ye know what ⁵charge we gave you through the Lord [5 Gr. *charges*.]
3 Jesus. For this is the will of God, *even* your sanc-
4 tification, that ye abstain from fornication; that each one of you know how to possess himself of
5 his own vessel in sanctification and honour, not in the passion of lust, even as the Gentiles which
6 know not God; that no man ⁶transgress, and wrong [6 Or, *overreach*] his brother in the matter: because the Lord is an

avenger in all these things, as also we ¹forewarned you and testified. For God called us not for uncleanness, but in sanctification. Therefore he that rejecteth, rejecteth not man, but God, who giveth his Holy Spirit unto you.

But concerning love of the brethren ye have no need that one write unto you: for ye yourselves are taught of God to love one another; for indeed ye do it toward all the brethren which are in all Macedonia. But we exhort you, brethren, that ye abound more and more; and that ye ²study to be quiet, and to do your own business, and to work with your hands, even as we charged you; that ye may walk honestly* toward them that are without, and may have need of nothing.

But we would not have you ignorant, brethren, concerning them that fall asleep; that ye sorrow not, even as the rest, which have no hope. For if we believe that Jesus died and rose again, even so them also that are fallen asleep ³in Jesus will God bring with him. For this we say unto you by the word of the Lord, that we that are alive, that are left unto the ⁴coming of the Lord, shall in no wise precede them that are fallen asleep. For the Lord himself shall descend from heaven, with a shout, with the voice of the archangel, and with the trump of God: and the dead in Christ shall rise first: then we that are alive, that are left, shall together with them be caught up in the clouds, to meet the Lord in the air: and so shall we ever be with the Lord. Wherefore ⁵comfort one another with these words.

But concerning the times and the seasons, brethren, ye have no need that aught be written unto you. For yourselves know perfectly that the day of the Lord so cometh as a thief in the night. When they are saying, Peace and safety, then sudden destruction cometh upon them, as travail upon a woman with child; and they shall in no wise escape. But ye, brethren, are not in darkness, that that day should overtake you ⁶as a thief: for ye are all sons of light, and sons of the day: we are not of the night, nor of darkness; so then let us not sleep, as do the rest, but let us watch and be sober. For they that sleep sleep in the night; and they that be drunken are drunken in the night. But let us, since we are of the day, be sober, putting on the breastplate of faith and

---

¹ Or, *told plainly*
² Gr. *be ambitious*.
³ Gr. *through*. Or, *will God through Jesus*
⁴ Gr. *presence*.
⁵ Or, *exhort*
⁶ Some ancient authorities read *as thieves*.

* For "honestly" read "becomingly"—*Am. Com.*

9 love; and for a helmet, the hope of salvation. For God appointed us not unto wrath, but unto the obtaining of salvation through our Lord Jesus Christ,
10 who died for us, that, whether we ¹wake or sleep,
11 we should live together with him. Wherefore ²exhort one another, and build each other up, even as also ye do.
12 But we beseech you, brethren, to know them that labour among you, and are over you in the Lord,
13 and admonish you; and to esteem them exceeding highly in love for their work's sake. Be at peace
14 among yourselves. And we exhort you, brethren, admonish the disorderly, encourage the fainthearted, support the weak, be longsuffering toward all.
15 See that none render unto any one evil for evil; but alway follow after that which is good, one toward
16 another, and toward all. Rejoice alway; pray with-
17
18 out ceasing; in every thing give thanks: for this
19 is the will of God in Christ Jesus to you-ward.
20 Quench not the Spirit; despise not prophesyings;
21 ³prove all things; hold fast that which is good;
22 abstain from every ⁴form* of evil.
23 And the God of peace himself sanctify you wholly; and may your spirit and soul and body be preserved entire, without blame at the ⁵coming of our
24 Lord Jesus Christ. Faithful is he that calleth you, who will also do it.
25 Brethren, pray for us⁶.
26 Salute all the brethren with a holy kiss. I adjure
27 you by the Lord that this epistle be read unto all the ⁷brethren.
28 The grace of our Lord Jesus Christ be with you.

1 Or, *watch*
2 Or, *comfort*
3 Many ancient authorities insert *but*.
4 Or, *appearance*
5 Gr. *presence*.
6 Some ancient authorities add *also*.
7 Many ancient authorities insert *holy*.

* Omit marg.⁴ ("*appearance*")—*Am. Com.*

THE
SECOND EPISTLE OF PAUL THE APOSTLE
TO THE
THESSALONIANS.

1 Paul, and Silvanus, and Timothy, unto the church of the Thessalonians in God our Father and 2 the Lord Jesus Christ; Grace to you and peace from God the Father and the Lord Jesus Christ. 3 We are bound to give thanks to God alway for you, brethren, even as it is meet, for that your faith groweth exceedingly, and the love of each one of 4 you all toward one another aboundeth; so that we ourselves glory in you in the churches of God for your patience and faith in all your persecutions 5 and in the afflictions which ye endure; *which is a* manifest token of the righteous judgement of God; to the end that ye may be counted worthy of the 6 kingdom of God, for which ye also suffer: if so be that it is a righteous thing with God to recompense 7 affliction to them that afflict you, and to you that are afflicted rest with us, at the revelation of the Lord Jesus from heaven with the angels of his pow-8 er in flaming fire, rendering vengeance to them that know not God, and to them that obey not the gospel 9 of our Lord Jesus: who shall suffer punishment, *even* eternal destruction from the face of the Lord 10 and from the glory of his might, when he shall come to be glorified in his saints, and to be marvelled at in all them that believed (because our testimony unto you was believed) in that day. To which end 11 we also pray always for you, that our God may count you worthy of your calling, and fulfil every [1] desire of goodness and *every* work of faith, with 12 power; that the name of our Lord Jesus may be glorified in you, and ye in him, according to the grace of our God and the Lord Jesus Christ.

[1] Gr. *good pleasure of goodness.*

II. THESSALONIANS.

2 Now we beseech you, brethren, ¹touching the ²coming of our Lord Jesus Christ, and our gather-
2 ing together unto him; to the end that ye be not quickly shaken from your mind, nor yet be troubled, either by spirit, or by word, or by epistle as from us, as that the day of the Lord is *now* present*;
3 let no man beguile you in any wise: for *it will not be*, except the falling away come first, and the man
4 of ³sin be revealed, the son of perdition, he that opposeth and exalteth himself against all that is called God or ⁴that is worshipped; so that he sitteth in the
5 ⁵temple of God, setting himself forth as God. Remember ye not, that, when I was yet with you, I
6 told you these things? And now ye know that which restraineth, to the end that he may be reveal-
7 ed in his own season. For the mystery of lawlessness doth already work: ⁶only *there is* one that restraineth now, until he be taken out of the way.
8 And then shall be revealed the lawless one, whom the Lord ⁷Jesus shall ⁸slay with the breath of his mouth, and bring to nought by the manifestation of
9 his ²coming; *even he*, whose ²coming is according to the working of Satan with all ⁹power and signs and
10 lying wonders, and with all deceit of unrighteousness for them that are perishing†; because they received not the love of the truth, that they might
11 be saved. And for this cause God sendeth them a
12 working of error, that they should believe a lie: that they all might be judged who believed not the truth, but had pleasure in unrighteousness.
13 But we are bound to give thanks to God alway for you, brethren beloved of the Lord, for that God chose you ¹⁰from the beginning unto salvation in sanctification of the Spirit and ¹¹belief of the truth:
14 whereunto he called you through our gospel, to the
15 obtaining of the glory of our Lord Jesus Christ. So then, brethren, stand fast, and hold the traditions which ye were taught, whether by word, or by epistle of ours.
16 Now our Lord Jesus Christ himself, and God our Father which loved us and gave us eternal comfort
17 and good hope through grace, comfort your hearts and stablish them in every good work and word.
3 Finally, brethren, pray for us, that the word of the Lord may run and be glorified, even as also *it is* with

1 Gr. *in behalf of.*
2 Gr. *presence.*
3 Many ancient authorities read *lawlessness.*
4 Gr. *an object of worship.*
5 Or, *sanctuary*
6 Or, *only until he that now restraineth be taken &c.*
7 Some ancient authorities omit *Jesus.*
8 Some ancient authorities read *consume.*
9 Gr. *power and signs and wonders of falsehood.*
10 Many ancient authorities read *as firstfruits.*
11 Or, *faith*

---

* For "is *now* present" read "is just at hand"—*Am. Com.*
† For "are perishing" read "perish" with the text in the marg.—*Am. Com.*

you; and that we may be delivered from unreason- 2
able and evil men; for all have not ¹faith*. But the 3
Lord is faithful, who shall stablish you, and guard
you from ²the evil *one*. And we have confidence in 4
the Lord touching you, that ye both do and will do
the things which we command. And the Lord direct 5
your hearts into the love of God, and into the patience
of Christ.

Now we command you, brethren, in the name of 6
our Lord Jesus Christ, that ye withdraw yourselves
from every brother that walketh disorderly, and not
after the tradition which ³they received of us. For 7
yourselves know how ye ought to imitate us: for we
behaved not ourselves disorderly among you; neither 8
did we eat bread for nought at any man's hand, but
in labour and travail, working night and day, that
we might not burden any of you: not because we 9
have not the right, but to make ourselves an ensample unto you, that ye should imitate us. For even 10
when we were with you, this we commanded you, If
any will not work, neither let him eat. For we hear of 11
some that walk among you disorderly, that work not
at all, but are busybodies. Now them that are such 12
we command and exhort in the Lord Jesus Christ, that
with quietness they work, and eat their own bread.
But ye, brethren, be not weary in well-doing. And 13
if any man obeyeth not our word by this epistle, note 14
that man, that ye have no company with him, to the
end that he may be ashamed. And *yet* count him not 15
as an enemy, but admonish him as a brother.

Now the Lord of peace himself give you peace at 16
all times in all ways. The Lord be with you all.

The salutation of me Paul with mine own hand, 17
which is the token in every epistle: so I write. The 18
grace of our Lord Jesus Christ be with you all.

---

¹ Or, *the faith*
² Or, *evil*
³ Some ancient authorities read *ye*.

* Omit marg. ¹ ("*the faith*")—*Am. Com.*

THE FIRST EPISTLE OF PAUL THE APOSTLE TO TIMOTHY.

1 Paul, an apostle of Christ Jesus according to the commandment of God our Saviour, and Christ Jesus
2 our hope; unto Timothy, my true child in faith: Grace, mercy, peace, from God the Father and Christ Jesus our Lord.
3 As I exhorted thee to tarry at Ephesus, when I was going into Macedonia, that thou mightest charge cer-
4 tain men not to teach a different doctrine, neither to give heed to fables and endless genealogies, the which minister questionings, rather than a ¹dispensation of
5 God which is in faith; *so do I now*. But the end of the charge is love out of a pure heart and a good
6 conscience and faith unfeigned: from which things some having ²swerved have turned aside unto vain
7 talking; desiring to be teachers of the law, though they understand neither what they say, nor whereof
8 they confidently affirm. But we know that the law
9 is good, if a man use it lawfully, as knowing this, that law is not made for a righteous man, but for the lawless and unruly, for the ungodly and sinners, for the unholy and profane, for ³murderers of fa-
10 thers and ³murderers of mothers, for manslayers, for fornicators, for abusers of themselves with men, for men-stealers, for liars, for false swearers, and if there be any other thing contrary to the ⁴sound ⁵doctrine;
11 according to the gospel of the glory of the blessed God, which was committed to my trust.
12 I thank him that ⁶enabled me, *even* Christ Jesus our Lord, for that he counted me faithful, appoint-
13 ing me to *his* service; though I was before a blasphemer, and a persecutor, and injurious: howbeit I obtained mercy, because I did it ignorantly in unbe-

1 Or, *stewardship*
2 Gr. *missed the mark*.
3 Or, *smiters*
4 Gr. *healthful*.
5 Or, *teaching*
6 Some ancient authorities read *enableth*.

lief; and the grace of our Lord abounded exceed-14
ingly with faith and love which is in Christ Jesus.
Faithful is the saying, and worthy of all acceptation, 15
that Christ Jesus came into the world to save sinners; of whom I am chief: howbeit for this cause 16
I obtained mercy, that in me as chief might Jesus
Christ shew forth all his longsuffering, for an ensample of them which should hereafter* believe on
him unto eternal life. Now unto the King [1]eternal, 17
incorruptible, invisible, the only God, *be* honour and
glory [2]for ever and ever. Amen.

This charge I commit unto thee, my child Timo-18
thy, according to the prophecies which [3]went before on thee†, that by them thou mayest war the good
warfare; holding faith and a good conscience; which 19
some having thrust from them made shipwreck
concerning the faith: of whom is Hymenæus and 20
Alexander; whom I delivered unto Satan, that they
might be taught not to blaspheme.

I exhort therefore, first of all, [4]that supplications, **2**
prayers, intercessions, thanksgivings, be made for
all men; for kings and all that are in high place; 2
that we may lead a tranquil and quiet life in all godliness and gravity. This is good and acceptable in 3
the sight of God our Saviour; who willeth that all 4
men should be saved‡, and come to the knowledge of
the truth. For there is one God, one mediator also 5
between God and men, *himself* man, Christ Jesus,
who gave himself a ransom for all; the testimony 6
to be borne in its own times; whereunto I was ap- 7
pointed a [5]preacher and an apostle (I speak the truth,
I lie not), a teacher of the Gentiles in faith and truth.

I desire therefore that the men pray in every place, 8
lifting up holy hands, without wrath and [6]disputing.
In like manner, that women adorn themselves in 9
modest apparel, with shamefastness and sobriety;
not with braided hair, and gold or pearls or costly
raiment; but (which becometh women professing 10
godliness) through good works. Let a woman learn 11
in quietness with all subjection. But I permit not 12
a woman to teach, nor to have dominion over a man,
but to be in quietness. For Adam was first formed, 13
then Eve; and Adam was not beguiled, but the wom-14

---

[1] Gr. *of the ages.*
[2] Gr. *unto the ages of the ages.*
[3] Or, *led the way to thee*
[4] Gr. *to make supplications;* &c.
[5] Gr. *herald.*
[6] Or, *doubting*

* For "hereafter" read "thereafter"—*Am. Com.*
† Substitute marg. [3] ("*led the way to thee*") for the text.—*Am. Com.*
‡ Read "who would have all men to be saved"—*Am. Com.*

I. TIMOTHY.

15 an being beguiled hath fallen into transgression: but she shall be saved through ¹the childbearing,* if they continue in faith and love and sanctification with sobriety.

3 ²Faithful is the saying, If a man seeketh the office
2 of a ³bishop, he desireth a good work. The ³bishop therefore must be without reproach, the husband of one wife, temperate, soberminded, orderly, given to
3 hospitality, apt to teach; ⁴no brawler, no striker; but
4 gentle, not contentious, no lover of money; one that ruleth well his own house, having *his* children in
5 subjection with all gravity; (but if a man knoweth not how to rule his own house, how shall he take
6 care of the church of God?) not a novice, lest being puffed up he fall into the ⁵condemnation of the devil.
7 Moreover he must have good testimony from them that are without; lest he fall into reproach and the
8 snare of the devil. Deacons in like manner *must be* grave, not doubletongued, not given to much wine,
9 not greedy of filthy lucre; holding the mystery of
10 the faith in a pure conscience. And let these also first be proved; then let them serve as deacons, if
11 they be blameless. Women in like manner *must be* grave, not slanderers, temperate, faithful in all
12 things. Let deacons be husbands of one wife, rul-
13 ing *their* children and their own houses well. For they that have served well as deacons gain to themselves a good standing, and great boldness in the faith which is in Christ Jesus.
14 These things write I unto thee, hoping to come
15 unto thee shortly; but if I tarry long, that thou mayest know ⁶how men ought to behave themselves in the house of God, which is the church of the liv-
16 ing God, the pillar and ⁷ground of the truth. And without controversy great is the mystery of godliness; ⁸He who was manifested in the flesh, justified in the spirit, seen of angels, preached among the nations, believed on in the world, received up in glory.

4 But the Spirit saith expressly, that in later times some shall fall away from the faith, giving heed to
2 seducing spirits and doctrines of ⁹devils, through the hypocrisy of men that speak lies, ¹⁰branded in their
3 own conscience as with a hot iron; forbidding to marry, *and commanding* to abstain from meats, which God created to be received with thanksgiv-
4 ing by them that believe and know the truth. For

1 Or, *her childbearing*
2 Some connect the words *Faithful is the saying* with the preceding paragraph.
3 Or, *overseer*
4 Or, *not quarrelsome over wine*
5 Gr. *judgement.*
6 Or, *how thou oughtest to behave thyself*
7 Or, *stay*
8 The word *God*, in place of *He who*, rests on no sufficient ancient evidence. Some ancient authorities read *which*.
9 Gr. *demons.*
10 Or, *seared*

---

* Let marg.¹ and the text exchange places.—*Am. Com.*

every creature of God is good, and nothing is to be rejected, if it be received with thanksgiving: for it 5 is sanctified through the word of God and prayer.

If thou put the brethren in mind of these things, 6 thou shalt be a good minister of Christ Jesus, nourished in the words of the faith, and of the good doctrine which thou hast followed *until now*: but re- 7 fuse profane and old wives' fables. And exercise thyself unto godliness: for bodily exercise is profit- 8 able ¹for a little; but godliness is profitable for all things, having promise of the life which now is, and of that which is to come. Faithful is the saying, 9 and worthy of all acceptation. For to this end we 10 labour and strive, because we have our hope set on the living God, who is the Saviour of all men, specially of them that believe. These things command 11 and teach. Let no man despise thy youth; but be 12 thou an ensample to them that believe, in word, in manner of life, in love, in faith, in purity. Till I 13 come, give heed to reading, to exhortation, to teaching. Neglect not the gift that is in thee, which was 14 given thee by prophecy, with the laying on of the hands of the presbytery. Be diligent in these 15 things; give thyself wholly to them; that thy progress may be manifest unto all. Take heed to thy- 16 self, and to thy teaching. Continue in these things; for in doing this thou shalt save both thyself and them that hear thee.

Rebuke not an elder, but exhort him as a father; 5 the younger men as brethren: the elder women as 2 mothers; the younger as sisters, in all purity. Honour widows that are widows indeed. But if any 4 widow hath children or grandchildren, let them learn first to shew piety towards their own family, and to requite their parents: for this is acceptable in the sight of God. Now she that is a widow indeed, and 5 desolate, hath her hope set on God, and continueth in supplications and prayers night and day. But 6 she that giveth herself to pleasure is dead while she liveth. These things also command, that they may 7 be without reproach. But if any provideth not for 8 his own, and specially his own household, he hath denied the faith, and is worse than an unbeliever. Let none be enrolled as a widow under threescore 9 years old, *having been* the wife of one man, well reported of for good works; if she hath brought up 10 children, if she hath used hospitality to strangers, if she hath washed the saints' feet, if she hath relieved

¹ Or, *for little*

the afflicted, if she hath diligently followed every
11 good work. But younger widows refuse: for when
they have waxed wanton against Christ, they desire
12 to marry; having condemnation, because they have
13 rejected their first faith*. And withal they learn
also *to be* idle, going about from house to house; and
not only idle, but tattlers also and busybodies, speak-
14 ing things which they ought not. I desire therefore
that the younger ¹*widows* marry, bear children, rule   1 Or, women
the household, give none occasion to the adversary
15 for reviling: for already some are turned aside after
16 Satan. If any woman that believeth hath widows,
let her relieve them, and let not the church be burdened; that it may relieve them that are widows
indeed.
17 Let the elders that rule well be counted worthy of
double honour, especially those who labour in the
18 word and in teaching. For the scripture saith,
Thou shalt not muzzle the ox when he treadeth out
the corn. And, The labourer is worthy of his hire.
19 Against an elder receive not an accusation, except at
20 *the mouth of* two or three witnesses. Them that sin
reprove in the sight of all, that the rest also may be
21 in fear. I charge *thee* in the sight of God, and Christ
Jesus, and the elect angels, that thou observe these
things without ²prejudice, doing nothing by partial-   2 Or, *preference*
22 ity. Lay hands hastily on no man, neither be par-
23 taker of other men's sins: keep thyself pure. Be no
longer a drinker of water, but use a little wine for
thy stomach's sake and thine often infirmities.
24 Some men's sins are evident, going before unto
judgement; and some men also they follow after.   3 Gr. *the works*
25 In like manner also ³there are good works that are   *that are good are evident.*
evident; and such as are otherwise cannot be hid.

6 Let as many as are ⁴servants under the yoke   4 Gr. *bondservants.*
count their own masters worthy of all honour, that
the name of God and the doctrine be not blasphemed.
2 And they that have believing masters, let them not
despise them, because they are brethren; but let
them serve them the rather, because they that ⁵par-   5 Or, *lay hold of*
take of the benefit are believing and beloved. These
things teach and exhort.
3 If any man teacheth a different doctrine, and con-
senteth not to ⁶sound words, *even* the words of our   6 Gr. *healthful.*
Lord Jesus Christ, and to the doctrine which is
4 according to godliness; he is puffed up, knowing

---

* For "faith" read "pledge" (with marg. Gr. *faith.*)—*Am. Com.*

nothing, but ¹doting about questionings and disputes of words, whereof cometh envy, strife, railings, evil surmisings, wranglings of men corrupted in mind 5 and bereft of the truth, supposing that godliness is a way of gain. But godliness with contentment is 6 great gain: for we brought nothing into the world, 7 for neither can we carry anything out; but having 8 food and covering ²we shall be therewith content. But they that desire* to be rich fall into a tempta- 9 tion and a snare and many foolish and hurtful lusts, such as drown men in destruction and perdition. For the love of money is a root of all ³kinds of evil: 10 which some reaching after have been led astray from the faith, and have pierced themselves through with many sorrows.

But thou, O man of God, flee these things; and 11 follow after righteousness, godliness, faith, love, patience, meekness. Fight the good fight of the faith, 12 lay hold on the life eternal, whereunto thou wast called, and didst confess the good confession in the sight of many witnesses. I charge thee in the sight 13 of God, who ⁴quickeneth all things, and of Christ Jesus, who before Pontius Pilate witnessed the good confession; that thou keep the commandment, with- 14 out spot, without reproach, until the appearing of our Lord Jesus Christ: which in ⁵its own times 15 he shall shew, who is the blessed and only Potentate, the King of ⁶kings, and Lord of ⁷lords; who 16 only hath immortality, dwelling in light unapproachable; whom no man hath seen, nor can see: to whom *be* honour and power eternal. Amen.

Charge them that are rich in this present ⁸world, 17 that they be not highminded, nor have their hope set on the uncertainty of riches, but on God, who giveth us richly all things to enjoy; that they do 18 good, that they be rich in good works, that they be ready to distribute, ⁹willing to communicate; lay- 19 ing up in store for themselves a good foundation against the time to come, that they may lay hold on the life which is *life* indeed.

O Timothy, guard ¹⁰that which is committed unto 20 *thee,* turning away from the profane babblings and oppositions of the knowledge which is falsely so called; which some professing have ¹¹erred concern- 21 ing the faith.

Grace be with you.

---

1 Gr. *sick.*
2 Or, *in these we shall have enough*
3 Gr. *evils.*
4 Or, *preserveth all things alive*
5 Or, *his*
6 Gr. *them that reign as kings.*
7 Gr. *them that rule as lords.*
8 Or, *age*
9 Or, *ready to sympathise*
10 Gr. *the deposit.*
11 Gr. *missed the mark.*

* For "desire" read "are minded"—*Am. Com.*

THE SECOND EPISTLE OF PAUL THE APOSTLE TO TIMOTHY.

1 Paul, an apostle of Christ Jesus [1]by the will of God, according to the promise of the life which is 2 in Christ Jesus, to Timothy, my beloved child: Grace, mercy, peace, from God the Father and Christ Jesus our Lord. 3 I thank God, whom I serve from my forefathers in a pure conscience, how unceasing is my remem- 4 brance of thee in my supplications, night and day longing to see thee, remembering thy tears, that I 5 may be filled with [2]joy; having been reminded of the unfeigned faith that is in thee; which dwelt first in thy grandmother Lois, and thy mother Eu- 6 nice; and, I am persuaded, in thee also. For the which cause I put thee in remembrance that thou [3]stir up the gift of God, which is in thee through 7 the laying on of my hands. For God gave us not a spirit of fearfulness; but of power and love and 8 [4]discipline. Be not ashamed therefore of the testimony of our Lord, nor of me his prisoner: but suffer hardship with the gospel according to the power 9 of God; who saved us, and called us with a holy calling, not according to our works, but according to his own purpose and grace, which was given us 10 in Christ Jesus before times eternal, but hath now been manifested by the appearing of our Saviour Christ Jesus, who abolished death, and brought life and incorruption* to light through the gospel, 11 whereunto I was appointed a [5]preacher, and an 12 apostle, and a teacher. For the which cause I suffer

[1] Gr. *through.*

[2] Or, *joy in being reminded*

[3] Gr. *stir into flame.*

[4] Gr. *sobering.*

[5] Gr. *herald.*

---

* For "incorruption" read "immortality" with marg. Gr. *incorruption.*—Am. Com.

also these things: yet I am not ashamed; for I know him whom I have believed, and I am persuaded that he is able to guard ¹that which I have committed unto him against that day. Hold the pattern of ²sound words which thou hast heard from me, in faith and love which is in Christ Jesus. ³That good thing which was committed unto *thee* guard through the ⁴Holy Ghost which dwelleth in us.

This thou knowest, that all that are in Asia turned away from me; of whom are Phygelus and Hermogenes. The Lord grant mercy unto the house of Onesiphorus: for he oft refreshed me, and was not ashamed of my chain; but, when he was in Rome, he sought me diligently, and found me (the Lord grant unto him to find mercy of the Lord in that day); and in how many things he ministered at Ephesus, thou knowest very well.

Thou therefore, my child, be strengthened in the grace that is in Christ Jesus. And the things which thou hast heard from me among many witnesses, the same commit thou to faithful men, who shall be able to teach others also. ⁵Suffer hardship with *me*, as a good soldier of Christ Jesus. No soldier on service entangleth himself in the affairs of *this* life; that he may please him who enrolled him as a soldier. And if also a man contend in the games, he is not crowned, except he have contended lawfully. The husbandman that laboureth must be the first to partake of the fruits. Consider what I say; for the Lord shall give thee understanding in all things. Remember Jesus Christ, risen from the dead, of the seed of David, according to my gospel: wherein I suffer hardship unto bonds, as a malefactor; but the word of God is not bound. Therefore I endure all things for the elect's sake, that they also may obtain the salvation which is in Christ Jesus with eternal glory. Faithful is the ⁶saying: For if we died with him, we shall also live with him: if we endure, we shall also reign with him: if we shall deny him, he also will deny us: if we are faithless, he abideth faithful; for he cannot deny himself.

Of these things put them in remembrance, charging *them* in the sight of ⁷the Lord, that they strive not about words, to no profit, to the subverting of them that hear. Give diligence to present thyself approved unto God, a workman that needeth not to be ashamed, ⁸handling aright the word of truth. But shun profane babblings: for they will proceed fur-

---

1 Or, *that which he hath committed unto me* Gr. *my deposit.*
2 Gr. *healthful.*
3 Gr. *The good deposit.*
4 Or, *Holy Spirit*
5 Or, *Take thy part in suffering hardship, as &c.*
6 Or, *saying; for if &c.*
7 Many ancient authorities read *God.*
8 Or, *holding a straight course in the word of truth* Or, *rightly dividing the word of truth*

17 ther in ungodliness, and their word will ¹eat as doth
a gangrene: of whom is Hymenæus and Philetus;
18 men who concerning the truth have ²erred, saying
that ³the resurrection is past already, and overthrow
19 the faith of some. Howbeit the firm foundation of
God standeth, having this seal, The Lord knoweth
them that are his: and, Let every one that nameth
the name of the Lord depart from unrighteousness.
20 Now in a great house there are not only vessels of
gold and of silver, but also of wood and of earth;
and some unto honour, and some unto dishonour.
21 If a man therefore purge himself from these, he
shall be a vessel unto honour, sanctified, meet for
the master's use, prepared unto every good work.
22 But flee youthful lusts, and follow after righteousness, faith, love, peace, with them that call on the
23 Lord out of a pure heart. But foolish and ignorant questionings refuse, knowing that they gender
24 strifes. And the Lord's ⁴servant must not strive,
but be gentle towards all, apt to teach, forbearing,
25 in meekness ⁵correcting them that oppose themselves; if peradventure God may give them repent-
26 ance unto the knowledge of the truth, and they may
⁶recover themselves out of the snare of the devil,
having been ⁷taken captive ⁸by the Lord's servant
unto the will of God*.

3 But know this, that in the last days grievous times
2 shall come. For men shall be lovers of self, lovers
of money, boastful, haughty, railers, disobedient to
3 parents, unthankful, unholy, without natural affection, implacable, slanderers, without self-control,
4 fierce, no lovers of good, traitors, headstrong, puffed
up, lovers of pleasure rather than lovers of God;
5 holding a form of godliness, but having denied the
6 power thereof: from these also turn away. For of
these are they that creep into houses, and take captive silly women laden with sins, led away by di-
7 vers lusts, ever learning, and never able to come to
8 the knowledge of the truth. And like as Jannes
and Jambres withstood Moses, so do these also withstand the truth; men corrupted in mind, reprobate
9 concerning the faith. But they shall proceed no further: for their folly shall be evident unto all men,
10 as theirs also came to be. But thou didst follow
my teaching, conduct, purpose, faith, longsuffering,

---

¹ Or, *spread*
² Gr. *missed the mark.*
³ Some ancient authorities read *a resurrection.*
⁴ Gr. *bondservant.*
⁵ Or, *instructing*
⁶ Gr. *return to soberness.*
⁷ Gr. *taken alive.*
⁸ Or, *by the devil, unto the will of God* Gr. *by him, unto the will of him.* In the Greek the two pronouns are different.

* Read "having been taken captive by him unto his will"; and let marg. ⁸ run Or, *by him, unto the will of God* Gr. *by him* etc.—*Am. Com.*

love, patience, persecutions, sufferings; what things 11 befell me at Antioch, at Iconium, at Lystra; what persecutions I endured: and out of them all the Lord delivered me. Yea, and all that would live 12 godly in Christ Jesus shall suffer persecution. But 13 evil men and impostors shall wax worse and worse, deceiving and being deceived. But abide thou in 14 the things which thou hast learned and hast been assured of, knowing of ¹whom thou hast learned them; and that from a babe thou hast known the 15 sacred writings which are able to make thee wise unto salvation through faith which is in Christ Jesus. ²Every scripture inspired of God *is* also prof-16 itable for teaching, for reproof, for correction, for ³instruction which is in righteousness: that the man 17 of God may be complete, furnished completely unto every good work.

⁴I charge *thee* in the sight of God, and of Christ 4 Jesus, who shall judge the quick and the dead, and by his appearing and his kingdom; preach the word; 2 be instant in season, out of season; ⁵reprove, rebuke, exhort, with all longsuffering and teaching. For 3 the time will come when they will not endure the ⁶sound ⁷doctrine; but, having itching ears, will heap to themselves teachers after their own lusts; and 4 will turn away their ears from the truth, and turn 5 aside unto fables. But be thou sober in all things, suffer hardship, do the work of an evangelist, fulfil thy ministry. For I am already being ⁸offered, and 6 the time of my departure is come. I have fought 7 the good fight, I have finished the course, I have kept the faith: henceforth there is laid up for me 8 the crown of righteousness, which the Lord, the righteous judge, shall give to me at that day: and not only to me, but also to all them that have loved his appearing.

Do thy diligence to come shortly unto me: for 9
Demas forsook me, having loved this present ⁹world, 10
and went to Thessalonica; Crescens to ¹⁰Galatia, Titus to Dalmatia. Only Luke is with me. Take 11 Mark, and bring him with thee: for he is useful to me for ministering. But Tychicus I sent to Ephe-12 sus. The cloke that I left at Troas with Carpus, 13 bring when thou comest, and the books, especially the parchments. Alexander the coppersmith ¹¹did 14 me much evil: the Lord will render to him according to his works: of whom be thou ware also; for 15 he greatly withstood our words. At my first de-16

---

1 Gr. *what persons.*
2 Gr. *Every scripture is inspired of God, and profitable.*
3 Or, *discipline.*
4 Or, *I testify in the sight . . . dead, both of his appearing &c.*
5 Or, *bring to the proof.*
6 Gr. *healthful.*
7 Or, *teaching.*
8 Gr. *poured out as a drink-offering.*
9 Or, *age.*
10 Or, *Gaul.*
11 Gr. *shewed.*

fence no one took my part, but all forsook me: may
17 it not be laid to their account. But the Lord stood
by me, and ¹strengthened me; that through me the
²message might be fully proclaimed, and that all the
Gentiles might hear: and I was delivered out of the
18 mouth of the lion. The Lord will deliver me from
every evil work, and will save me unto his heavenly kingdom: to whom *be* the glory ³for ever and
ever. Amen.
19 Salute Prisca and Aquila, and the house of One-
20 siphorus. Erastus abode at Corinth: but Trophimus
21 I left at Miletus sick. Do thy diligence to come before winter. Eubulus saluteth thee, and Pudens, and Linus, and Claudia, and all the brethren.
22 The Lord be with thy spirit. Grace be with you.

1 Or, *gave me power*
2 Or, *proclamation*
3 Gr. *unto the ages of the ages.*

THE EPISTLE OF PAUL
TO
TITUS.

¹ Gr. *bondservant.*

² Or, *its*

³ Or, *proclamation*

PAUL, a ¹servant of God, and an apostle of Jesus Christ, according to the faith of God's elect, and the knowledge of the truth which is according to godliness, in hope of eternal life, which God, who cannot lie, promised before times eternal*; but in ²his own seasons manifested his word in the ³message, wherewith I was intrusted according to the commandment of God our Saviour; to Titus, my true child after a common faith: Grace and peace from God the Father and Christ Jesus our Saviour.

⁴ Or, *overseer*

⁵ Or, *not quarrelsome over wine*

For this cause left I thee in Crete, that thou shouldest set in order the things that were wanting, and appoint elders in every city, as I gave thee charge; if any man is blameless, the husband of one wife, having children that believe, who are not accused of riot or unruly. For the ⁴bishop must be blameless, as God's steward; not selfwilled, not soon angry, ⁵no brawler, no striker, not greedy of filthy lucre; but given to hospitality, a lover of good, soberminded, just, holy, temperate; holding to the faithful word which is according to the teaching, that he may be able both to exhort in the ⁶sound ⁷doctrine, and to convict the gainsayers.

⁶ Gr. *healthful.*
⁷ Or, *teaching*

⁸ Gr. *bellies.*

For there are many unruly men, vain talkers and deceivers, specially they of the circumcision, whose mouths must be stopped; men who overthrow whole houses, teaching things which they ought not, for filthy lucre's sake. One of themselves, a prophet of their own, said, Cretans are alway liars, evil beasts, idle ⁸gluttons. This testimony is true. For which

1
2
3

4

5

6
7

8
9

10
11

12
13

---

* "before times eternal" add marg. Or, *long ages ago—Am. Com.*

TO TITUS.

cause reprove them sharply, that they may be ¹sound
14 in the faith, not giving heed to Jewish fables, and
commandments of men who turn away from the
15 truth. To the pure all things are pure: but to them
that are defiled and unbelieving nothing is pure;
but both their mind and their conscience are de-
16 filed. They profess that they know God; but by
their works they deny him, being abominable, and
disobedient, and unto every good work reprobate.

2 But speak thou the things which befit the ²sound
2 ³doctrine: that aged men be temperate, grave, sober-
3 minded, ¹sound in faith, in love, in patience: that
aged women likewise be reverent in demeanour, not
slanderers nor enslaved to much wine, teachers of
4 that which is good; that they may train the young
women to love their husbands, to love their children,
5 *to be* soberminded, chaste, workers at home, kind,
being in subjection to their own husbands, that the
6 word of God be not blasphemed: the younger men
7 likewise exhort to be soberminded: in all things
shewing thyself an ensample of good works; in
8 thy doctrine *shewing* uncorruptness, gravity, sound
speech, that cannot be condemned; that he that is
of the contrary part may be ashamed, having no evil
9 thing to say of us. *Exhort* ⁴servants to be in subjection to their own masters, *and* to be well-pleasing *to*
10 *them* in all things; not gainsaying; not purloining,
but shewing all good fidelity; that they may adorn
11 the doctrine of God our Saviour in all things. For
the grace of God ⁵hath appeared, bringing salvation
12 to all men, instructing us, to the intent that, denying ungodliness and worldly lusts, we should live
soberly and righteously and godly in this present
13 ⁶world; looking for the blessed hope and appearing of the glory ⁷of our great God and Saviour Je-
14 sus Christ*; who gave himself for us, that he might
redeem us from all iniquity, and purify unto himself a people for his own possession, zealous of good
works.
15 These things speak and exhort and reprove with
all ⁸authority. Let no man despise thee.

3 Put them in mind to be in subjection to rulers,
to authorities, to be obedient, to be ready unto ev-
2 ery good work, to speak evil of no man, not to be
contentious, to be gentle, shewing all meekness to-
3 ward all men. For we also were aforetime foolish,

1 Gr. *healthy*.

2 Gr. *healthful*.
3 Or, *teaching*

4 Gr. *bondservants*.

5 Or, *hath appeared to all men, bringing salvation*

6 Or, *age*
7 Or, *of the great God and our Saviour*

8 Gr. *commandment*.

---

* Let the text and marg. ⁷ exchange places.—*Am. Com.*

disobedient, deceived, serving divers lusts and pleasures, living in malice and envy, hateful, hating one another. But when the kindness of God our Saviour, and his love toward man, appeared, not by works *done* in righteousness, which we did ourselves, but according to his mercy he saved us, through the ¹washing of regeneration ²and renewing of the ³Holy Ghost, which he poured out upon us richly, through Jesus Christ our Saviour; that, being justified by his grace, we might be made ⁴heirs according to the hope of eternal life. Faithful is the saying, and concerning these things I will that thou affirm confidently, to the end that they which have believed God may be careful to ⁵maintain good works. These things are good and profitable unto men: but shun foolish questionings, and genealogies, and strifes, and fightings about the law; for they are unprofitable and vain. A man that is ⁶heretical* after a first and second admonition ⁷refuse; knowing that such a one is perverted, and sinneth, being self-condemned.

When I shall send Artemas unto thee, or Tychicus, give diligence to come unto me to Nicopolis: for there I have determined to winter. Set forward Zenas the lawyer and Apollos on their journey diligently, that nothing be wanting unto them. And let our *people* also learn to ⁵maintain good works for necessary ⁸uses, that they be not unfruitful.

All that are with me salute thee. Salute them that love us in faith.

Grace be with you all.

---

1 Or, *laver*
2 Or, *and through renewing*
3 Or, *Holy Spirit*
4 Or, *heirs, according to hope, of eternal life*
5 Or, *profess honest occupations*
6 Or, *factious*
7 Or, *avoid*
8 Or, *wants*

* For "A man ... heretical" read "a factious man"—*Am. Com.*

THE EPISTLE OF PAUL

TO

PHILEMON.

1 Paul, a prisoner of Christ Jesus, and Timothy
  ¹our brother, to Philemon our beloved and fellow-
2 worker, and to Apphia ²our sister, and to Archippus
  our fellow-soldier, and to the church in thy house:
3 Grace to you and peace from God our Father and
  the Lord Jesus Christ.
4 I thank my God always, making mention of thee
5 in my prayers, hearing of ³thy love, and of the faith
  which thou hast toward the Lord Jesus, and toward
6 all the saints; that the fellowship of thy faith may
  become effectual, in the knowledge of every good
7 thing which is in ⁴you, unto Christ. For I had much
  joy and comfort in thy love, because the hearts of
  the saints have been refreshed through thee, brother.
8 Wherefore, though I have all boldness in Christ
9 to enjoin thee that which is befitting, yet for love's
  sake I rather beseech, being such a one as Paul ⁵the
10 aged, and now a prisoner also of Christ Jesus: I beseech thee for my child, whom I have begotten in
11 my bonds, ⁶Onesimus, who was aforetime unprofitable to thee, but now is profitable to thee and to me:
12 whom I have sent back to thee in his own person,
13 that is, my very heart: whom I would fain have
  kept with me, that in thy behalf he might minister
14 unto me in the bonds of the gospel: but without
  thy mind I would do nothing; that thy goodness
15 should not be as of necessity, but of free will. For
  perhaps he was therefore parted *from thee* for a sea-
16 son, that thou shouldest have him for ever; no longer as a ⁷servant, but more than a ⁷servant, a brother
  beloved, specially to me, but how much rather to
17 thee, both in the flesh and in the Lord. If then thou

1 Gr. *the brother*.
2 Gr. *the sister*.
3 Or, *thy love and faith*
4 Many ancient authorities read *us*.
5 Or, *an ambassador, and now &c.*
6 The Greek word means *Helpful*.
7 Gr. *bondservant*.

countest me a partner, receive him as myself. But if he hath wronged thee at all, or oweth *thee* aught, put that to mine account; I Paul write it with mine own hand, I will repay it: that I say not unto thee how that thou owest to me even thine own self besides. Yea, brother, let me have ¹joy of thee in the Lord: refresh my heart in Christ. Having confidence in thine obedience I write unto thee, knowing that thou wilt do even beyond what I say. But withal prepare me also a lodging: for I hope that through your prayers I shall be granted unto you.

Epaphras, my fellow-prisoner in Christ Jesus, saluteth thee; *and so do* Mark, Aristarchus, Demas, Luke, my fellow-workers.

The grace of ²our Lord Jesus Christ be with your spirit. ³Amen.

---

1 Or, *help*

2 Some ancient authorities read *the*.

3 Many ancient authorities omit *Amen*.

THE EPISTLE OF PAUL THE APOSTLE

TO THE

HEBREWS.

1 God, having of old time spoken unto the fathers in the prophets by divers portions and in divers
2 manners, hath at the end of these days spoken unto us in ¹his Son, whom he appointed heir of all things,
3 through whom also he made the ²worlds; who being the effulgence of his glory, and ³the very image of his substance, and upholding all things by the word of his power, when he had made purification of sins, sat down on the right hand of the Majesty
4 on high; having become by so much better than the angels, as he hath inherited a more excellent
5 name than they. For unto which of the angels said he at any time,

> Thou art my Son,
> This day have I begotten thee?

and again,

> I will be to him a Father,
> And he shall be to me a Son?

6 ⁴And when he again ⁵bringeth in the firstborn into ⁶the world he saith, And let all the angels of God
7 worship him. And of the angels he saith,

> Who maketh his angels ⁷winds*,
> And his ministers a flame of fire:

8 but of the Son *he saith*,

> Thy throne, O God, is for ever and ever;
> And the sceptre of uprightness is the sceptre of ⁸thy kingdom.

9   Thou hast loved righteousness, and hated iniquity;

1 Gr. *a Son*.
2 Gr. *ages*.
3 Or, *the impress of his substance*
4 Or, *And again, when he bringeth in*
5 Or, *shall have brought in*
6 Gr. *the inhabited earth.*
7 Or, *spirits*
8 The two oldest Greek manuscripts read *his*.

---

* Omit marg. ⁷ ("*spirits*")—*Am. Com.*

Therefore God*, thy God, hath anointed thee
With the oil of gladness above thy fellows.
And, 10
Thou, Lord, in the beginning hast laid the foundation of the earth,
And the heavens are the works of thy hands:
They shall perish; but thou continuest: 11
And they all shall wax old as doth a garment;
And as a mantle shalt thou roll them up, 12
As a garment, and they shall be changed:
But thou art the same,
And thy years shall not fail.
But of which of the angels hath he said at any time, 13
Sit thou on my right hand,
Till I make thine enemies the footstool of thy feet?
Are they not all ministering spirits, sent forth to do 14 service for the sake of them that shall inherit salvation?

Therefore we ought to give the more earnest heed **2** to the things that were heard, lest haply we drift away *from them*. For if the word spoken through 2 angels proved stedfast, and every transgression and disobedience received a just recompense of reward; how shall we escape, if we neglect so great salva- 3 tion? which having at the first been spoken through the Lord, was confirmed unto us by them that heard; God also bearing witness with them, both by 4 signs and wonders, and by manifold powers, and by [1]gifts of the [2]Holy Ghost, according to his own will. For not unto angels did he subject [3]the world to 5 come, whereof we speak. But one hath somewhere 6 testified, saying,

What is man, that thou art mindful of him?
Or the son of man, that thou visitest him?
Thou madest him [4]a little lower than the angels; 7
Thou crownedst him with glory and honour,
[5]And didst set him over the works of thy hands:
Thou didst put all things in subjection under 8 his feet.

For in that he subjected all things unto him, he left nothing that is not subject to him. But now we see not yet all things subjected to him. But we behold 9 him who hath been made [4]a little lower than the angels, *even* Jesus, because of the suffering of death crowned with glory and honour, that by the grace

---

1 Gr. *distributions*.
2 Or, *Holy Spirit*: and so throughout this book.
3 Gr. *the inhabited earth*.
4 Or, *for a little while lower*
5 Many authorities omit *And didst … hands*.

---

* To the first "God" add marg. Or, *O God—Am. Com.*

10 of God he should taste death for every *man.* For it became him, for whom are all things, and through whom are all things, ¹in bringing many sons unto
11 glory, to make the ²author of their salvation perfect through sufferings. For both he that sanctifieth and they that are sanctified are all of one: for which cause he is not ashamed to call them breth-
12 ren, saying,

> I will declare thy name unto my brethren,
> In the midst of the ³congregation will I sing thy praise.

13 And again, I will put my trust in him. And again, Behold, I and the children which God hath given
14 me. Since then the children are sharers in ⁴flesh and blood, he also himself in like manner partook of the same; that through death he ⁵might bring to nought him that ⁶had the power of death, that is,
15 the devil; and ⁵might deliver all them who through fear of death were all their lifetime subject to bond-
16 age. For verily not of angels doth he take hold,*
17 but he taketh hold of the seed of Abraham. Wherefore it behoved him in all things to be made like unto his brethren, that he might be† a merciful and faithful high priest in things pertaining to God, to
18 make propitiation for the sins of the people. ⁷For ⁸in that he himself hath suffered being tempted, he is able to succour them that are tempted.

1 Or, *having brought*
2 Or, *captain*

3 Or, *church*

4 Gr. *blood and flesh.*

5 Or, *may*
6 Or, *hath*

7 Or, For having been himself tempted in that wherein he hath suffered
8 Or, *wherein*

3 Wherefore, holy brethren, partakers of a heavenly calling, consider the Apostle and High Priest of
2 our confession, *even* Jesus; who was faithful to him that ⁹appointed him, as also was Moses in all ¹⁰his
3 house. For he hath been counted worthy of more glory than Moses, by so much as he that ¹¹built the
4 house hath more honour than the house. For every house is ¹¹builded by some one; but he that ¹¹built
5 all things is God. And Moses indeed was faithful in all ¹⁰his house as a servant, for a testimony of those things which were afterward to be spoken;
6 but Christ as a son, over ¹⁰his house; whose house are we, if we hold fast our boldness and the glory-
7 ing of our hope firm unto the end. Wherefore, even as the Holy Ghost saith,

> To-day if ye shall hear his voice,
8 > Harden not your hearts, as in the provocation,

9 Gr. *made.*
10 That is, God's house. See Num. xii. 7.

11 Or, *established*

---

* Let the text run "For verily not to angels doth he give help but he giveth help to" etc. (with marg. Gr. *For verily not of angels doth he take hold, but he taketh hold of* etc.)—*Am. Com.*
† For "might be" read "might become"—*Am. Com.*

Like as in the day of the temptation in the wilderness,
¹Wherewith* your fathers tempted *me* by proving *me*, 9
And saw my works forty years.
Wherefore I was displeased with this generation, 10
And said, They do alway err in their heart:
But they did not know my ways;
As† I sware in my wrath, 11
²They shall not enter into my rest.
Take heed, brethren, lest haply there shall be in 12
any one of you an evil heart of unbelief, in falling
away from the living God: but exhort one another 13
day by day, so long as it is called To-day; lest any
one of you be hardened by the deceitfulness of sin:
for we are become partakers ³of Christ, if we hold 14
fast the beginning of our confidence firm unto the
end: while it is said, 15
To-day if ye shall hear his voice,
Harden not your hearts, as in the provocation.
For who, when they heard, did provoke? nay, did 16
not all they that came out of Egypt by Moses?
And with whom was he displeased forty years? was 17
it not with them that sinned, whose ⁴carcases fell in
the wilderness? And to whom sware he that they 18
should not enter into his rest, but to them that were
disobedient? And we see that they were not able 19
to enter in because of unbelief.

Let us fear therefore, lest haply, a promise being **4**
left of entering into his rest, any one of you should
seem to have come short of it. For indeed we 2
have had ⁵good tidings‡ preached unto us, even as
also they: but the word of hearing did not profit
them, because ⁶they were not united by faith with
them that heard. ⁷For we which have believed do 3
enter into that rest; even as he hath said,
As I sware in my wrath,
⁸They shall not enter into my rest:
although the works were finished from the foundation of the world. For he hath said somewhere of 4
the seventh *day* on this wise, And God rested on the
seventh day from all his works; and in this *place* 5
again,

---

1 Or, *Where*

2 Gr. *If they shall enter.*

3 Or, *with*

4 Gr. *limbs.*

5 Or, *a gospel*

6 Some ancient authorities read *it was.*

7 Some ancient authorities read *We therefore.*

8 Gr. *If they shall enter.*

* Let marg. ¹ ("*Where*") and the text exchange places.—*Am. Com.*
† "As" add marg. Or, *So*   So in iv. 3.—*Am. Com.*
‡ Let the text and marg. ⁵ exchange places, reading in marg.
"Many ancient authorities" etc.—*Am. Com.*

¹They shall not enter into my rest. ^{1 Gr. *If they shall enter.*}

6 Seeing therefore it remaineth that some should enter thereinto, and they to whom ²the good tidings were before preached failed to enter in because of 7 disobedience, he again defineth a certain day*, ³saying in David, after so long a time, To-day, as it hath been before said, ^{2 Or, *the gospel was*} ^{3 Or, *To-day, saying in David, after so long a time, as it hath been &c.*}

> To-day if ye shall hear his voice,
> Harden not your hearts.

8 For if ⁴Joshua had given them rest, he would not 9 have spoken afterward of another day. There remaineth therefore a sabbath rest for the people of 10 God. For he that is entered into his rest hath himself also rested from his works, as God did from 11 his. Let us therefore give diligence to enter into that rest, that no man fall ⁵after the same example 12 of disobedience. For the word of God is living, and active, and sharper than any two-edged sword, and piercing even to the dividing of soul and spirit, of both joints and marrow, and quick to discern the 13 thoughts and intents of the heart. And there is no creature that is not manifest in his sight: but all things are naked and laid open before the eyes of him with whom we have to do. ^{4 Gr. *Jesus.*} ^{5 Or, *into* Gr. *in.*}

14 Having then a great high priest, who hath passed through the heavens, Jesus the Son of God, let us 15 hold fast our confession. For we have not a high priest that cannot be touched with the feeling of our infirmities; but one that hath been in all points 16 tempted like as *we are, yet* without sin. Let us therefore draw near with boldness unto the throne of grace, that we may receive mercy, and may find grace to help *us* in time of need.

5 For every high priest, being taken from among men, is appointed for men in things pertaining to God, that he may offer both gifts and sacrifices for 2 sins: who can bear gently with the ignorant and erring, for that he himself also is compassed with in3 firmity; and by reason thereof is bound, as for the 4 people, so also for himself, to offer for sins. And no man taketh the honour unto himself, but when 5 he is called of God, even as was Aaron. So Christ also glorified not himself to be made a high priest, but he that spake unto him,

---

* Read "a certain day, To-day, saying in David, so long a time afterward (even as hath been said before), To-day if ye" etc.—*Am. Com.*

> Thou art my Son,
> This day have I begotten thee:

as he saith also in another *place*,

> Thou art a priest for ever
> After the order of Melchizedek.

Who in the days of his flesh, having offered up prayers and supplications with strong crying and tears unto him that was able to save him ¹from death, and having been heard for his godly fear, though he was a Son, yet learned obedience by the things which he suffered; and having been made perfect, he became unto all them that obey him the ²author of eternal salvation; named of God a high priest after the order of Melchizedek.

Of ³whom we have many things to say, and hard of interpretation, seeing ye are become dull of hearing. For when by reason of the time ye ought to be teachers, ye have need again ⁴that some one teach you the rudiments of the ⁵first principles of the oracles of God; and are become such as have need of milk, and not of solid food. For every one that partaketh of milk is without experience of the word of righteousness; for he is a babe. But solid food is for ⁶full-grown men, *even* those who by reason of use have their senses exercised to discern good and evil.

Wherefore let us ⁷cease* to speak of the first principles of Christ, and press on unto ⁸perfection; not laying again a foundation of repentance from dead works, and of faith toward God, ⁹of the teaching of ¹⁰baptisms, and of laying on of hands, and of resurrection of the dead, and of eternal judgement. And this will we do, if God permit. For as touching those who were once enlightened ¹¹and tasted of the heavenly gift, and were made partakers of the Holy Ghost, and ¹²tasted the good word of God, and the powers of the age to come, and *then* fell away, it is impossible to renew them again unto repentance; ¹³seeing they crucify to themselves the Son of God afresh, and put him to an open shame. For the land which hath drunk the rain that cometh oft upon it, and bringeth forth herbs meet for them for whose sake it is also tilled, receiveth blessing from God: but if it beareth thorns and thistles, it is re-

---

1 Or, *out of*
2 Gr. *cause.*
3 Or, *which*
4 Or, *that one teach you which be the rudiments*
5 Gr. *beginning.*
6 Or, *perfect*
7 Gr. *leave the word of the beginning of Christ.*
8 Or, *full growth*
9 Some ancient authorities read, *even the teaching of.*
10 Or, *washings*
11 Or, *having both tasted of . . . and being made . . . and having tasted &c.*
12 Or, *tasted the word of God that it is good*
13 Or, *the while*

* For "let us cease" etc. read "leaving ¹³ the doctrine of the first principles of Christ, let us" with marg. ¹³ Gr. *the word of the beginning of Christ.—Am. Com.*

9 But, beloved, we are persuaded better things of you, and things that ¹accompany salvation, though [1 Or, *are near to**]
10 we thus speak: for God is not unrighteous to forget your work and the love which ye shewed toward his name, in that ye ministered unto the saints, and
11 still do minister. And we desire that each one of you may shew the same diligence unto the ²fulness [2 Or, *full assurance*]
12 of hope even to the end: that ye be not sluggish, but imitators of them who through faith and patience inherit the promises.
13 For when God made promise to Abraham, since he could swear by none greater, he sware by himself,
14 saying, Surely blessing I will bless thee, and multi-
15 plying I will multiply thee. And thus, having pa-
16 tiently endured, he obtained the promise. For men swear by the greater: and in every dispute of theirs
17 the oath is final for confirmation. Wherein God, being minded to shew more abundantly unto the heirs of the promise the immutability of his coun-
18 sel, ³interposed with an oath: that by two immuta- [3 Gr. *mediated.*] ble things, in which it is impossible for God to lie, we may have a strong encouragement, who have fled for refuge to lay hold of the hope set before
19 us; which we have as an anchor of the soul, *a hope* both sure and stedfast and entering into that which
20 is within the veil; whither as a forerunner Jesus entered for us, having become a high priest for ever after the order of Melchizedek.

7 For this Melchizedek, king of Salem, priest of God Most High, who met Abraham returning from the
2 slaughter of the kings, and blessed him, to whom also Abraham divided a tenth part of all (being first, by interpretation, King of righteousness, and then also King of Salem, which is, King of peace;
3 without father, without mother, without genealogy, having neither beginning of days nor end of life, but made like unto the Son of God), abideth a priest continually.
4 Now consider how great this man was, unto whom Abraham, the patriarch, gave a tenth out of the chief
5 spoils. And they indeed of the sons of Levi that receive the priest's office have commandment to take tithes of the people according to the law, that is, of their brethren, though these have come out of the

---

* In marg. ¹ for "*are near to*" read "*belong to*"—Am. Com.

loins of Abraham: but he whose genealogy is not counted from them hath taken tithes of Abraham, and hath blessed him that hath the promises. But without any dispute the less is blessed of the better. And here men that die receive tithes; but there one, of whom it is witnessed that he liveth. And, so to say, through Abraham even Levi, who receiveth tithes, hath paid tithes; for he was yet in the loins of his father, when Melchizedek met him.

Now if there was perfection through the Levitical priesthood (for under it hath the people received the law), what further need *was there* that another priest should arise after the order of Melchizedek, and not be reckoned after the order of Aaron? For the priesthood being changed, there is made of necessity a change also ¹of the law. For he of whom these things are said ²belongeth to another tribe, from which no man hath given attendance at the altar. For it is evident that our Lord hath sprung out of Judah; as to which tribe Moses spake nothing concerning priests. And *what we say* is yet more abundantly evident, if after the likeness of Melchizedek there ariseth another priest, who hath been made, not after the law of a carnal commandment, but after the power of an ³endless life: for it is witnessed of him,

    Thou art a priest for ever
    After the order of Melchizedek.

For there is a disannulling of a foregoing commandment because of its weakness and unprofitableness (for the law made nothing perfect), and a bringing in thereupon of a better hope, through which we draw nigh unto God. And inasmuch as *it is* not without the taking of an oath (for they indeed have been made priests without an oath; but he with an oath ⁴by him that saith ⁵of him,

    The Lord sware and will not repent himself,
    Thou art a priest for ever);

by so much also hath Jesus become the surety of a better ⁶covenant. And they indeed have been made priests many in number, because that by death they are hindered from continuing: but he, because he abideth for ever, ⁷hath his priesthood ⁸unchangeable. Wherefore also he is able to save ⁹to the uttermost them that draw near unto God through him, seeing he ever liveth to make intercession for them.

For such a high priest became us, holy, guileless, undefiled, separated from sinners, and made higher

---

1 Or, *of law*
2 Gr. *hath partaken of.* See ch. ii. 14.
3 Gr. *indissoluble.*
4 Or, *through*
5 Or, *unto*
6 Or, *testament*
7 Or, *hath a priesthood that doth not pass to another*
8 Or, *inviolable*
9 Gr. *completely.*

27 than the heavens; who needeth not daily, like those high priests, to offer up sacrifices, first for his own sins, and then for the *sins* of the people: for this he
28 did once for all, when he offered up himself. For the law appointeth men high priests, having infirmity; but the word of the oath, which was after the law, *appointeth* a Son, perfected for evermore.

8 ¹Now ²in the things which we are saying the chief point *is this*: We have such a high priest, who sat down on the right hand of the throne of the Majesty
2 in the heavens, a minister of ³the sanctuary, and of the true tabernacle, which the Lord pitched, not man.
3 For every high priest is appointed to offer both gifts and sacrifices: wherefore it is necessary that this *high*
4 *priest* also have somewhat to offer. Now if he were on earth, he would not be a priest at all, seeing there are those who offer the gifts according to the law;
5 who serve *that which is* a copy and shadow of the heavenly things, even as Moses is warned *of God* when he is about to ⁴make the tabernacle: for, See, saith he, that thou make all things according to the
6 pattern that was shewed thee in the mount. But now hath he obtained a ministry the more excellent, by how much also he is the mediator of a better ⁵covenant, which hath been enacted upon better promises.
7 For if that first *covenant* had been faultless, then
8 would no place have been sought for a second. For finding fault* with them, he saith,

    Behold, the days come, saith the Lord,
    That I will ⁶make a new ⁵covenant with the house of Israel and with the house of Judah;
9   Not according to the ⁵covenant that I made with their fathers
    In the day that I took them by the hand to lead them forth out of the land of Egypt;
    For they continued not in my ⁵covenant,
    And I regarded them not, saith the Lord.
10   For this is the ⁵covenant that ⁷I will make with the house of Israel
    After those days, saith the Lord;
    I will put my laws into their mind,
    And on their heart also will I write them:
    And I will be to them a God,
    And they shall be to me a people:
11   And they shall not teach every man his fellow-citizen,

1 Or, *Now to su up what we a saying: We ha &c.*
2 Gr. *upon.*
3 Or, *holy things*
4 Or, *complete*
5 Or, *testament*
6 Gr. *accomplish.*
7 Gr. *I will co nant.*

---

* "finding fault" etc. add marg. Some ancient authorities read *finding fault* with it *he saith unto them.—Am. Com.*

And every man his brother, saying, Know the Lord:
For all shall know me,
From the least to the greatest of them.
For I will be merciful to their iniquities, 12
And their sins will I remember no more.

In that he saith, A new *covenant*, he hath made the first old. But that which is becoming old and waxeth aged is nigh unto vanishing away. 13

Now even the first *covenant* had ordinances of divine service, and its sanctuary, *a sanctuary* of this world. 9 For there was a tabernacle prepared, the first, wherein ¹were the candlestick, and the table, and ²the shewbread; which is called the Holy place. And after the second veil, the tabernacle which is called the Holy of holies; having a golden ³censer*, and the ark of the covenant overlaid round about with gold, wherein ⁴was a golden pot holding the manna, and Aaron's rod that budded, and the tables of the covenant; and above it cherubim of glory overshadowing ⁵the mercy-seat; of which things we cannot now speak severally. Now these things having been thus prepared, the priests go in continually into the first tabernacle, accomplishing the services; but into the second the high priest alone, once in the year, not without blood, which he offereth for himself, and for the ⁶errors of the people: the Holy Ghost this signifying, that the way into the holy place hath not yet been made manifest, while as the first tabernacle is yet standing; which *is* a parable† for the time *now*‡ present; according to which are offered both gifts and sacrifices that cannot, as touching the conscience, make the worshipper perfect, *being* only (with meats and drinks and divers washings) carnal ordinances, imposed until a time of reformation. 2 3 4 5 6 7 8 9 10

But Christ having come a high priest of ⁷the good things to come, through the greater and more perfect tabernacle, not made with hands, that is to say, not of this creation, nor yet through the blood of goats and calves, but through his own blood, entered in once for all into the holy place, having obtained eternal redemption. For if the blood of goats and bulls, and the ashes of a heifer sprinkling 11 12 13

1 Or, are
2 Gr. *the setting forth of the loaves.*
3 Or, *altar of incense*
4 Or, is
5 Gr. *the propitiatory.*
6 Gr. *ignorances.*
7 Some ancient authorities read *the good things that are come.*

---

* Let marg. ³ and the text exchange places.—*Am. Com.*
† For "parable" read "figure" So in xi. 19.—*Am. Com.*
‡ Omit "*now.*"—*Am. Com.*

them that have been defiled, sanctify unto the clean-
14 ness of the flesh: how much more shall the blood of Christ, who through the eternal Spirit* offered himself without blemish unto God, cleanse ¹your conscience from dead works to serve the living
15 God? And for this cause he is the mediator of a new ²covenant, that a death having taken place for the redemption of the transgressions that were under the first ²covenant, they that have been called may receive the promise of the eternal inheritance.
16 For where a ²testament is, there must of necessity
17 ³be the death of him that made it. For a ²testament† is of force ⁴where there hath been death: ⁵for doth it ever avail while he that made it liveth?
18 Wherefore even the first *covenant* hath not been ded-
19 icated without blood. For when every commandment had been spoken by Moses unto all the people according to the law, he took the blood of the calves and the goats, with water and scarlet wool and hyssop, and sprinkled both the book itself, and all the
20 people, saying, This is the blood of the ²covenant
21 which God commanded to you-ward. Moreover the tabernacle and all the vessels of the ministry he
22 sprinkled in like manner with the blood. And according to the law, I may almost say, all things are cleansed with blood, and apart from shedding of blood there is no remission.
23 It was necessary therefore that the copies of the things in the heavens should be cleansed with these; but the heavenly things themselves with better sacri-
24 fices than these. For Christ entered not into a holy place made with hands, like in pattern to the true; but into heaven itself, now to appear before the face
25 of God for us: nor yet that he should offer himself often; as the high priest entereth into the holy place
26 year by year with blood not his own; else must he often have suffered since the foundation of the world: but now once at the ⁶end of the ages hath he been manifested to put away sin ⁷by the sacri-
27 fice of himself. And inasmuch as it is ⁸appointed unto men once to die, and after this *cometh*
28 judgement; so Christ also, having been once offered to bear the sins of many, shall appear a second time, apart from sin, to them that wait for him, unto salvation.

1 Many ancient authorities read *our*.
2 The Greek word here used signifies both *covenant* and *testament*.
3 Gr. *be brought*.
4 Gr. *over the dead*.
5 Or, *for it doth never ... liveth*.
6 Or, *consummation*
7 Or, *by his sacrifice*.
8 Gr. *laid up for*.

---

* "the eternal Spirit" add marg. Or, his *eternal spirit—Am. Com.*
† Let marg. ⁴ and the text exchange places.—*Am. Com.*

For the law having a shadow of the good *things* to 10
come, not the very image of the things, ¹they can*
never with the same sacrifices year by year, which
they offer continually, make perfect them that draw
nigh. Else would they not have ceased to be offered, 2
because the worshippers, having been once cleansed,
would have had no more conscience of sins? But in 3
those *sacrifices* there is a remembrance made of sins
year by year. For it is impossible that the blood of 4
bulls and goats should take away sins. Wherefore 5
when he cometh into the world, he saith,

> Sacrifice and offering thou wouldest not,
> But a body didst thou prepare for me;
> In whole burnt offerings and *sacrifices* for sin 6
>   thou hadst no pleasure:
> Then said I, Lo, I am come 7
> (In the roll of the book it is written of me)
> To do thy will, O God.

Saying above, Sacrifices and offerings and whole 8
burnt offerings and *sacrifices* for sin thou wouldest
not, neither hadst pleasure therein (the which are
offered according to the law), then hath he said, Lo, 9
I am come to do thy will. He taketh away the
first, that he may establish the second. ²By which 10
will we have been sanctified through the offering of
the body of Jesus Christ once for all. And every 11
³priest indeed standeth day by day ministering and
offering oftentimes the same sacrifices, the which
can never take away sins: but he, when he had of- 12
fered one sacrifice for ⁴sins for ever, sat down on
the right hand of God; from henceforth expecting 13
till his enemies be made the footstool of his feet.
For by one offering he hath perfected for ever them 14
that are sanctified. And the Holy Ghost also bear- 15
eth witness to us: for after he hath said,

> This is the ⁵covenant that ⁶I will make with 16
>   them
> After those days, saith the Lord;
> I will put my laws on their heart,
> And upon their mind also will I write them;

then saith he,

> And their sins and their iniquities will I re- 17
>   member no more.

Now where remission of these is, there is no more 18
offering for sin.

Margin notes:
1 Some ancient authorities read *it can*.
2 Or, *In*
3 Some ancient authorities read *high priest*.
4 Or, *sins, for ever sat down &c.*
5 Or, *testament*
6 Gr. *I will covenant*.

* For "they can" read "can" (and for marg. ¹ read Many ancient authorities read *they can*.)—*Am. Com.*

TO THE HEBREWS.

19 Having therefore, brethren, boldness to enter into
20 the holy place by the blood of Jesus, by the way
which he dedicated for us, a new and living way,
21 through the veil, that is to say, his flesh; and *having* [1 Or, *full assurance*]
22 a great priest over the house of God; let us draw
near with a true heart in ¹fulness* of faith, having [2 Or, *conscience: and having our body washed with pure water, let us hold fast*]
our hearts sprinkled from an evil ⁷conscience, and
23 our body washed with pure water: let us hold fast
the confession of our hope* that it waver not; for he
24 is faithful that promised: and let us consider one
25 another to provoke unto love and good works; not
forsaking the assembling of ourselves together†, as
the custom of some is, but exhorting *one another*;
and so much the more, as ye see the day drawing
nigh.
26 For if we sin wilfully after that we have received
the knowledge of the truth, there remaineth no more
27 a sacrifice for sins, but a certain fearful expectation
of judgement, and a ³fierceness of fire which shall [3 Or, *jealousy*]
28 devour the adversaries. A man that hath set at
nought Moses' law dieth without compassion on *the*
29 *word of* two or three witnesses: of how much sorer
punishment, think ye, shall he be judged worthy,
who hath trodden under foot the Son of God, and
hath counted the blood of the covenant, wherewith
he was sanctified, ⁴an unholy thing, and hath done [4 Gr. *a common thing.*]
30 despite unto the Spirit of grace? For we know him
that said, Vengeance belongeth unto me, I will recompense. And again, The Lord shall judge his
31 people. It is a fearful thing to fall into the hands
of the living God.
32 But call to remembrance the former days, in
which, after ye were enlightened, ye endured a great
33 conflict of sufferings; partly, being made a gazingstock both by reproaches and afflictions; and partly,
becoming partakers with them that were so used.
34 For ye both had compassion on them that were in [5 Or, *that ye have your own selves for a better possession*]
bonds, and took joyfully the spoiling of your possessions, knowing ⁵that ⁶ye yourselves have‡ a bet- [6 Some ancient authorities read ye have for yourselves a better possession.]
35 ter possession and an abiding one. Cast not away
therefore your boldness, which hath great recom-
36 pense of reward. For ye have need of patience,

---

* Let the text and marg. ¹ exchange places.—*Am. Com.*
† For " the assembling of ourselves together " read " our own assembling together "—*Am. Com.*
‡ For " ⁶ ye yourselves have " read " ⁵ ye have for yourselves "
(and omit marg. ⁶ letting marg. ⁵ read Many ancient authorities read *that ye have your own selves for a* etc.)—*Am. Com.*

that, having done the will of God, ye may receive the promise. For yet a very little while, He that cometh shall come, and shall not tarry. But ¹my righteous one shall live by faith: And if he shrink back, my soul hath no pleasure in him. But we are not ²of them that shrink back unto perdition; but of them that have faith unto the ³saving of the soul.

Now faith is ⁴the assurance of *things* hoped for*, the ⁵proving of things not seen. For therein the elders had witness borne to them. By faith we understand that the ⁶worlds have been framed by the word of God, so that what is seen hath not been made out of things which do appear. By faith Abel offered unto God a more excellent sacrifice than Cain, through which he had witness borne to him that he was righteous, ⁷God bearing witness ⁸in respect of his gifts: and through it he being dead yet speaketh. By faith Enoch was translated that he should not see death; and he was not found, because God translated him: for before his translation he hath had witness borne to him that he had been† well-pleasing unto God: and without faith it is impossible to be well-pleasing *unto him*: for he that cometh to God must believe that he is, and *that* he is a rewarder of them that seek after him. By faith Noah, being warned *of God* concerning things not seen as yet, moved with godly fear, prepared an ark to the saving of his house; through which he condemned the world, and became heir of the righteousness which is according to faith. By faith Abraham, when he was called, obeyed to go out unto a place which he was to receive for an inheritance; and he went out, not knowing whither he went. By faith he became a sojourner in the land of promise, as in a *land* not his own, ⁹dwelling in tents, with Isaac and Jacob, the heirs with him of the same promise: for he looked for the city which hath the foundations, whose ¹⁰builder and maker is God. By faith even Sarah herself received power to conceive seed when she was past age, since she counted him faithful who

---

1 Some ancient authorities read *the righteous one.*
2 Gr. *of shrinking back . . . but of faith.*
3 Or, *gaining*
4 Or, *the giving substance to*
5 Or, *test*
6 Gr. *ages.*
7 The Greek text in this clause is somewhat uncertain.
8 Or, *over his gifts*
9 Or, *having taken up his abode in tents*
10 Or, *architect*

---

* Read "faith is assurance of things hoped for, a conviction" etc. —*Am. Com.*
† Read in the text "for he hath had witness borne to him that before his translation he had been" etc. with the present text in the marg.—*Am. Com.*

12 had promised: wherefore also there sprang of one, and him as good as dead, *so many* as the stars of heaven in multitude, and as the sand, which is by the sea shore, innumerable.

13 These all died ¹in faith, not having received the promises, but having seen them and greeted them from afar, and having confessed that they were 14 strangers and pilgrims on the earth. For they that say such things make it manifest that they are seek-15 ing after a country of their own. And if indeed they had been mindful of that *country* from which they went out, they would have had opportunity to 16 return. But now they desire a better *country*, that is, a heavenly: wherefore God is not ashamed of them, to be called their God: for he hath prepared for them a city.

17 By faith Abraham, being tried, ²offered up Isaac: yea, he that had gladly received the promises was 18 offering up his only begotten *son*; *even he* ³to whom 19 it was said, In Isaac shall thy seed be called: accounting that God *is* able to raise up, even from the dead; from whence he did also in a parable receive 20 him back. By faith Isaac blessed Jacob and Esau, 21 even concerning things to come. By faith Jacob, when he was a dying, blessed each of the sons of Joseph; and worshipped, *leaning* upon the top of his 22 staff. By faith Joseph, when his end was nigh, made mention of the departure of the children of Israel; 23 and gave commandment concerning his bones. By faith Moses, when he was born, was hid three months by his parents, because they saw he was a goodly child; and they were not afraid of the king's com-24 mandment. By faith Moses, when he was grown up, refused to be called the son of Pharaoh's daughter; 25 choosing rather to be evil entreated with the people of God, than to enjoy the pleasures of sin for a sea-26 son; accounting the reproach of ⁴Christ greater riches than the treasures of Egypt: for he looked unto 27 the recompense of reward. By faith he forsook Egypt, not fearing the wrath of the king: for he en-28 dured, as seeing him who is invisible. By faith he ⁵kept the passover, and the sprinkling of the blood, that the destroyer of the firstborn should not touch 29 them. By faith they passed through the Red sea as by dry land: which the Egyptians assaying to do 30 were swallowed up. By faith the walls of Jericho fell down, after they had been compassed about for 31 seven days. By faith Rahab the harlot perished

1 Gr. *according to.*

2 Gr. *hath offered up.*

3 Or, *of*

4 Or, *the Christ*

5 Or, *instituted* Gr. *hath made.*

not with them that were disobedient, having received the spies with peace. And what shall I 32 more say? for the time will fail me if I tell of Gideon, Barak, Samson, Jephthah; of David and Samuel and the prophets: who through faith sub- 33 dued kingdoms, wrought righteousness, obtained promises, stopped the mouths of lions, quenched the 34 power of fire, escaped the edge of the sword, from weakness were made strong, waxed mighty in war, turned to flight armies of aliens. Women received 35 their dead by a resurrection: and others were ¹tortured, not accepting ²their deliverance; that they might obtain a better resurrection: and others had 36 trial of mockings and scourgings, yea, moreover of bonds and imprisonment: they were stoned, they 37 were sawn asunder, they were tempted, they were slain with the sword: they went about in sheepskins, in goatskins; being destitute, afflicted, evil entreated (of whom the world was not worthy), 38 wandering in deserts and mountains and caves, and the holes of the earth. And these all, having had 39 witness borne to them through their faith, received not the promise, God having ³provided some better 40 thing concerning us, that apart from us they should not be made perfect.

Therefore let us also, seeing we are compassed 12 about with so great a cloud of witnesses, lay aside ⁴every weight, and the sin which ⁵doth so easily beset us, and let us run with patience the race that is set before us, looking unto Jesus the ⁶author and 2 perfecter of *our* faith, who for the joy that was set before him endured the cross, despising shame, and hath sat down at the right hand of the throne of God. For consider him that hath endured such 3 gainsaying of sinners against ⁷themselves*, that ye wax not weary, fainting in your souls. Ye have 4 not yet resisted unto blood, striving against sin: and 5 ye have forgotten the exhortation, which reasoneth with you as with sons,

My son, regard not lightly the chastening of the Lord,
Nor faint when thou art reproved of him;
For whom the Lord loveth he chasteneth, 6
And scourgeth every son whom he receiveth.

⁸It is for chastening that ye endure; God dealeth 7

1 Or, *beaten to death*
2 Gr. *the redemption.*
3 Or, *foreseen*
4 Or, *all cumbrance*
5 Or, *doth closely cling to us* Or, *is admired of many*
6 Or, *captain*
7 Many authorities, some ancient, read *himself.*
Or, *Endure unto chastening*

---

* For "themselves" read "himself" (and let marg. ⁷ run Many ancient authorities read *themselves.*) — *Am. Com.*

—12. 24. TO THE HEBREWS. 383

with you as with sons; for what son is there whom
8 *his* father chasteneth not? But if ye are without
chastening, whereof all have been made partakers,
9 then are ye bastards, and not sons. Furthermore,
we had the fathers of our flesh to chasten us, and
we gave them reverence: shall we not much rather
be in subjection unto the Father of ¹spirits, and live?   1 Or, *our spirits*
10 For they verily for a few days chastened *us* as seem-
ed good to them; but he for *our* profit, that *we* may
11 be partakers of his holiness. All chastening seemeth for the present to be not joyous, but grievous:
yet afterward it yieldeth peaceable fruit unto them
that have been exercised thereby, *even the fruit* of
12 righteousness. Wherefore ²lift up the hands that   2 Gr. *make straight.*
13 hang down, and the palsied knees; and make straight
paths for your feet, that that which is lame be not   3 Or, *put out of joint*
³turned out of the way, but rather be healed.
14   Follow after peace with all men, and the sanctification without which no man shall see the Lord: 4 Or, *whether*
15 looking carefully ⁴lest *there be* any man that ⁵falleth   5 Or, *falleth back from*
short of the grace of God; lest any root of bitterness
springing up trouble *you*, and thereby the many be
16 defiled; ⁴lest *there be* any fornicator, or profane person, as Esau, who for one mess of meat sold his own
17 birthright. For ye know that even when he afterward desired to inherit the blessing, he was rejected
(for he found no place of repentance*), though he
sought it diligently with tears.
18   For ye are not come unto ⁶*a mount* that might be   6 Or, *a palpable and kindled fire*
touched, and that burned with fire, and unto black-
19 ness, and darkness, and tempest, and the sound of a
trumpet, and the voice of words; which *voice* they
that heard intreated that no word more should be
20 spoken unto them: for they could not endure that
which was enjoined, If even a beast touch the
21 mountain, it shall be stoned; and so fearful was the
appearance, *that* Moses said, I exceedingly fear and
22 quake: but ye are come unto mount Zion, and unto
the city of the living God, the heavenly Jerusalem,   7 Or, *and to innumerable hosts, the general assembly of angels, and the church, &c.*
23 ⁷and to ⁸innumerable hosts of angels, to the general
assembly and church of the firstborn who are en-
rolled in heaven, and to God the Judge of all, and   8 Gr. *myriads of angels.*
24 to the spirits of just men made perfect, and to Jesus
the mediator of a new ⁹covenant, and to the blood   9 Or, *testament*

---

* For "rejected (for . . . of repentance)" read "rejected; for he
found no place for a change of mind *in his father*" with marg. Or,
rejected (for he found no place of repentance), etc. Or, *rejected; for . . .
of repentance* etc.—Am. Com.

of sprinkling that speaketh better ¹than *that of* Abel. See that ye refuse not him that speaketh. 25 For if they escaped not, when they refused him that warned *them* on earth, much more *shall not* we *escape*, who turn away from him ²that *warneth* from heaven: whose voice then shook the earth: 26 but now he hath promised, saying, Yet once more will I make to tremble not the earth only, but also the heaven. And this *word*, Yet once more, signifieth 27 the removing of those things that are shaken, as of things that have been made, that those things which are not shaken may remain. Wherefore, receiving 28 a kingdom that cannot be shaken, let us have ³grace, whereby we may offer service well-pleasing to God with ⁴reverence and awe: for our God is a consum- 29 ing fire.

13

Let love of the brethren continue. Forget not to shew love unto strangers: for thereby some have en- 2 tertained angels unawares. Remember them that 3 are in bonds, as bound with them; them that are evil entreated, as being yourselves also in the body. *Let* marriage *be* had in honour among all, and *let* the 4 bed *be* undefiled: for fornicators and adulterers God will judge. ⁵Be ye free from the love of money; 5 content with such things as ye have: for himself hath said, I will in no wise fail thee, neither will I in any wise forsake thee. So that with good cour- 6 age we say,

The Lord is my helper; I will not fear:
What shall man do unto me?

Remember them that had the rule over you, which 7 spake unto you the word of God; and considering the issue of their ⁶life, imitate their faith. Jesus 8 Christ *is* the same yesterday and to-day, *yea* and ⁷for ever. Be not carried away by divers and strange 9 teachings: for it is good that the heart be stablished by grace; not by meats, wherein they that ⁸occupied themselves were not profited. We have an altar, 10 whereof they have no right to eat which serve the tabernacle. For the bodies of those beasts, whose 11 blood is brought into the holy place ⁹by the high priest *as an offering* for sin, are burned without the camp. Wherefore Jesus also, that he might 12 sanctify the people through his own blood, suffered without the gate. Let us therefore go forth unto 13 him without the camp, bearing his reproach. For 14 we have not here an abiding city, but we seek after *the city* which is to come. Through him ¹⁰then let us 15

---

1 Or, *than Abel*
2 Or, *that is from heaven*
3 Or, *thankfulness*
4 Or, *godly fear*
5 Gr. Let *your turn of mind be free.*
6 Gr. *manner of life.*
7 Gr. *unto the ages.*
8 Gr. *walked.*
9 Gr. *through.*
10 Some ancient authorities omit *then.*

offer up a sacrifice of praise to God continually, that is, the fruit of lips which make confession to his
16 name. But to do good and to communicate forget not: for with such sacrifices God is well pleased.
17 Obey them that have the rule over you, and submit *to them*: for they watch in behalf of your souls, as they that shall give account; that they may do this with joy, and not with ¹grief: for this *were* unprofitable for you.

<small>1 Gr. *groaning*.</small>

18 Pray for us: for we are persuaded that we have a good conscience, desiring to live honestly* in all
19 things. And I exhort *you* the more exceedingly to do this, that I may be restored to you the sooner.
20 Now the God of peace, who brought again from the dead the great shepherd of the sheep ²with the blood of the eternal† covenant, *even* our Lord Jesus,
21 make you perfect in every good ³thing to do his will, working in ⁴us that which is well-pleasing in his sight, through Jesus Christ; to whom *be* the glory ⁵for ever and ever. Amen.

<small>2 Or, *by* Gr. *in*.
3 Many ancient authorities read *work*.
4 Many ancient authorities read *you*.
5 Gr. *unto the ages of the ages*.</small>

22 But I exhort you, brethren, bear with the word of exhortation: for I have written unto you in few
23 words. Know ye that our brother Timothy hath been set at liberty; with whom, if he come shortly, I will see you.
24 Salute all them that have the rule over you, and all the saints. They of‡ Italy salute you.
25 Grace be with you all. Amen.

---

* For "honestly" read "honourably"—*Am. Com.*
† For "the eternal" read "an eternal"—*Am. Com.*
‡ "They of" add marg. Or, *The* brethren *from*—*Am. Com.*

THE GENERAL EPISTLE OF
JAMES.

---

¹ Gr. *bondservant.*

² Gr. *wisheth joy.*

³ Or, *trials*

⁴ Or, *that a doubleminded man, unstable in all his ways, shall receive any thing of the Lord.*

⁵ Gr. *from.*

⁶ Or, *is untried in evil*

⁷ Gr. *evil things.*

⁸ Or, *tempted by his own lust, being drawn away by it, and enticed*

1 JAMES, a ¹servant of God and of the Lord Jesus Christ, to the twelve tribes which are of the Dispersion, ²greeting.
2 Count it all joy, my brethren, when ye fall into manifold ³temptations; 3 knowing that the proof* of your faith worketh patience. 4 And let patience have *its* perfect work, that ye may be perfect and entire, lacking in nothing.
5 But if any of you lacketh wisdom, let him ask of God, who giveth to all liberally and upbraideth not; and it shall be given him. 6 But let him ask in faith, nothing doubting: for he that doubteth is like the surge of the sea driven by the wind and tossed. 7 For let not that man think ⁴that he shall receive any thing of the Lord; 8 a doubleminded man, unstable in all his ways.
9 But let the brother of low degree glory in his high estate: 10 and the rich, in that he is made low: because as the flower of the grass he shall pass away. 11 For the sun ariseth with the scorching wind, and withereth the grass; and the flower thereof falleth, and the grace of the fashion of it perisheth: so also shall the rich man fade away in his goings.
12 Blessed is the man that endureth temptation: for when he hath been approved, he shall receive the crown of life, which *the Lord* promised to them that love him. 13 Let no man say when he is tempted, I am tempted ⁵of God: for God ⁶cannot be tempted with ⁷evil, and he himself tempteth no man: 14 but each man is ⁸tempted, when he is drawn away by his own lust, and enticed. 15 Then the lust, when it

---

* For "proof" read "proving"—*Am. Com.*

hath conceived, beareth sin: and the sin, when it is
16 fullgrown, bringeth forth death. Be not deceived,
17 my beloved brethren. Every good ¹gift and every
perfect boon* is from above, coming down from the
Father of lights, with whom can be no variation,
18 neither shadow that is cast by turning. Of his own
will he brought us forth by the word of truth, that
we should be a kind of firstfruits of his creatures.
19 ²Ye know *this*, my beloved brethren. But let every
man be swift to hear, slow to speak, slow to wrath:
20 for the wrath of man worketh not the righteousness
21 of God. Wherefore putting away all filthiness and
overflowing of ³wickedness, receive with meekness
the ⁴implanted word, which is able to save your
22 souls. But be ye doers of the word, and not hear-
23 ers only, deluding your own selves. For if any one
is a hearer of the word, and not a doer, he is like
unto a man beholding ⁵his natural face in a mir-
24 ror: for he beholdeth himself, and goeth away, and
straightway forgetteth what manner of man he was.
25 But he that looketh into the perfect law, the *law* of
liberty, and *so* continueth, being not a hearer that
forgetteth, but a doer that worketh, this man shall
26 be blessed in his doing. If any man ⁶thinketh himself to be religious, while he bridleth not his tongue
but deceiveth his heart, this man's religion is vain.
27 Pure religion and undefiled before our God and Father is this, to visit the fatherless and widows in
their affliction, *and* to keep himself unspotted from
the world.

2 My brethren,⁷hold not the faith of our Lord Jesus
Christ, *the Lord* of glory, with respect of persons.
2 For if there come into your ⁸synagogue a man with
a gold ring, in fine clothing, and there come in also
3 a poor man in vile clothing; and ye have regard to
him that weareth the fine clothing, and say, Sit thou
here in a good place; and ye say to the poor man,
4 Stand thou there, or sit under my footstool; ⁹are ye
not divided ¹⁰in your own mind, and become judges
5 with evil thoughts? Hearken, my beloved brethren;
did not God choose them that are poor as to the
world *to be* rich in faith, and heirs of the kingdom
6 which he promised to them that love him? But ye
have dishonoured the poor man. Do not the rich
oppress you, and themselves drag you before the
7 judgement-seats? Do not they blaspheme the hon-

1 Or, *giving*

2 Or, *Know ye*

3 Or, *malice*
4 Or, *inborn*

5 Gr. *the face of his birth.*

6 Or, *seemeth to be*

7 Or, *do ye, in accepting persons, hold the faith ... glory?*
8 Or, *assembly*

9 Or, *do ye not make distinctions*
10 Or, *among yourselves*

---

* For "boon" read "gift"—*Am. Com.*

ourable name ¹by the which ye are called? Howbeit if ye fulfil the royal law, according to the scripture, Thou shalt love thy neighbour as thyself, ye do well: but if ye have respect of persons, ye commit sin, being convicted by the law as transgressors. For whosoever shall keep the whole law, and yet stumble in one *point*, he is become guilty of all. For he that said, Do not commit adultery, said also, Do not kill. Now if thou dost not commit adultery, but killest, thou art become a transgressor of the law. So speak ye, and so do, as men that are to be judged by a law of liberty. For judgement *is* without mercy to him that hath shewed no mercy: mercy glorieth against judgement.

What doth it profit, my brethren, if a man say he hath faith, but have not works? can that faith save him? If a brother or sister be naked, and in lack of daily food, and one of you say unto them, Go in peace, be ye warmed and filled; and yet ye give them not the things needful to the body; what doth it profit? Even so faith, if it have not works, is dead in itself. ²Yea, a man will say, Thou hast faith, and I have works: shew me thy faith apart from *thy* works, and I by my works will shew thee *my* faith. Thou believest that ³God is one; thou doest well: the ⁴devils also believe, and shudder. But wilt thou know, O vain man, that faith apart from works is barren? Was not Abraham our father justified by works, in that he offered up Isaac his son upon the altar? ⁵Thou seest that faith wrought with his works, and by works was faith made perfect; and the scripture was fulfilled which saith, And Abraham believed God, and it was reckoned unto him for righteousness; and he was called the friend of God. Ye see that by works a man is justified, and not only by faith. And in like manner was not also Rahab the harlot justified by works, in that she received the messengers, and sent them out another way? For as the body apart from the spirit is dead, even so faith apart from works is dead.

Be not many* teachers, my brethren, knowing that we shall receive ⁶heavier judgement. For in many things we all stumble. If any stumbleth not in word, the same is a perfect man, able to bridle the whole body also. Now if we put the horses'

---

¹ Gr. *which was called upon you.*
² Or, *But some one will say*
³ Some ancient authorities read *there is one God.*
⁴ Gr. *demons.*
⁵ Or, *Seest thou ... perfect?*
⁶ Gr. *greater.*

* For "many" read "many *of you*"—*Am. Com.*

bridles into their mouths, that they may obey us,
4 we turn about their whole body also. Behold, the ships also, though they are so great, and are driven by rough winds, are yet turned about by a very small rudder, whither the impulse of the steersman
5 willeth. So the tongue also is a little member, and boasteth great things. Behold, ¹how much wood is
6 kindled by how small a fire! And the tongue is ²a fire: ³the world of iniquity among our members is the tongue, which defileth the whole body, and setteth on fire the wheel of ⁴nature, and is set on fire
7 by hell. For every ⁵kind of beasts and birds, of creeping things and things in the sea, is tamed, and
8 hath been tamed ⁶by ⁷mankind: but the tongue can no man tame; *it is* a restless evil, *it is* full of deadly
9 poison. Therewith bless we the Lord and Father; and therewith curse we men, which are made after
10 the likeness of God: out of the same mouth cometh forth blessing and cursing. My brethren, these
11 things ought not so to be. Doth the fountain send forth from the same opening sweet *water* and bitter?
12 can a fig tree, my brethren, yield olives, or a vine figs? neither *can* salt water yield sweet.
13 Who is wise and understanding among you? let him shew by his good life his works in meekness
14 of wisdom. But if ye have bitter jealousy and faction in your heart, glory not and lie not against the
15 truth. This wisdom is not *a wisdom* that cometh down from above, but is earthly, ⁸sensual, ⁹devilish.
16 For where jealousy and faction are, there is confu-
17 sion and every vile deed. But the wisdom that is from above is first pure, then peaceable, gentle, easy to be intreated, full of mercy and good fruits, with-
18 out ¹⁰variance, without hypocrisy. And the fruit of righteousness is sown in peace ¹¹for them that make peace.

4 Whence *come* wars and whence *come* fightings among you? *come they* not hence, *even* of your pleas-
2 ures that war in your members? Ye lust, and have not: ye kill, and ¹²covet, and cannot obtain: ye fight
3 and war; ye have not, because ye ask not. Ye ask, and receive not, because ye ask amiss, that ye may
4 spend *it* in your pleasures. Ye adulteresses*, know ye not that the friendship of the world is enmity with God? Whosoever therefore would be a friend

1 Or, *how great a forest*
2 Or, *a fire, that world of iniquity: the tongue is among our members that which, &c.*
3 Or, *that world of iniquity, the tongue, is among our members that which, &c.*
4 Or, *birth*
5 Gr. *nature.*
6 Or, *unto*
7 Gr. *the human nature.*
8 Or, *natural* Or, *animal*
9 Gr. *demoniacal.*
10 Or, *doubtfulness* Or, *partiality*
11 Or, *by*
12 Gr. *are jealous.*

---

* "Adulteresses" add marg. That is, *who break your marriage vow to God.—Am. Com.*

of the world maketh himself an enemy of God. Or think ye that the scripture ¹speaketh in vain? ²Doth the spirit which ³he made to dwell in us long unto envying? But he giveth ⁴more grace. Wherefore *the scripture* saith, God resisteth the proud, but giveth grace to the humble. Be subject therefore unto God; but resist the devil, and he will flee from you. Draw nigh to God, and he will draw nigh to you. Cleanse your hands, ye sinners; and purify your hearts, ye doubleminded. Be afflicted, and mourn, and weep: let your laughter be turned to mourning, and your joy to heaviness. Humble yourselves in the sight of the Lord, and he shall exalt you.

Speak not one against another, brethren. He that speaketh against a brother, or judgeth his brother, speaketh against the law, and judgeth the law: but if thou judgest the law, thou art not a doer of the law, but a judge. One *only* is the lawgiver and judge, *even* he who is able to save and to destroy: but who art thou that judgest thy neighbour?

Go to now, ye that say, To-day or to-morrow we will go into this city, and spend a year there, and trade, and get gain: whereas ye know not what shall be on the morrow. What is your life? For ye are a vapour, that appeareth for a little time, and then vanisheth away. ⁵For that ye ought to say, If the Lord will, we shall both live, and do this or that. But now ye glory in your vauntings: all such glorying is evil. To him therefore that knoweth to do good, and doeth it not, to him it is sin.

Go to now, ye rich, weep and howl for your miseries that are coming upon you. Your riches are corrupted, and your garments are moth-eaten. Your gold and your silver are rusted; and their rust shall be for a testimony ⁶against you, and shall eat your flesh as fire. Ye have laid up your treasure in the last days. Behold, the hire of the labourers who mowed your fields, which is of you kept back by fraud, crieth out: and the cries of them that reaped have entered into the ears of the Lord of Sabaoth. Ye have lived delicately on the earth, and taken your pleasure; ye have nourished your hearts in a day of slaughter. Ye have condemned, ye have killed the righteous *one*; he doth not resist you.

Be patient therefore, brethren, until the ⁷coming of the Lord. Behold, the husbandman waiteth for the precious fruit of the earth, being patient over it, until ⁸it receive the early and latter rain. Be ye

---

1 Or, *saith in vain,*
2 Or, *The spirit which he made to dwell in us he yearneth for even unto jealous envy.* Or, *That spirit which he made to dwell in us yearneth for us even unto jealous envy.*
3 Some ancient authorities read *dwelleth in us.*
4 Gr. *a greater grace.*
5 Gr. *Instead of your saying.*
6 Or, *unto*
7 Gr. *presence.*
8 Or, *he*

also patient; stablish your hearts: for the ¹coming 9 of the Lord is at hand. Murmur not, brethren, one against another, that ye be not judged: behold, the 10 judge standeth before the doors. Take, brethren, for an example of suffering and of patience, the 11 prophets who spake in the name of the Lord. Behold, we call them blessed which endured: ye have heard of the ²patience of Job, and have seen the end of the Lord, how that the Lord is full of pity, and merciful.

12 But above all things, my brethren, swear not, neither by the heaven, nor by the earth, nor by any other oath: but ³let your yea be yea, and your nay, nay; that ye fall not under judgement.

13 Is any among you suffering? let him pray. Is 14 any cheerful? let him sing praise. Is any among you sick? let him call for the elders of the church; and let them pray over him, ⁴anointing him with oil 15 in the name of the Lord: and the prayer of faith shall save him that is sick, and the Lord shall raise him up; and if he have committed sins, it shall be 16 forgiven him. Confess therefore your sins one to another, and pray one for another, that ye may be healed. The supplication of a righteous man avail-17 eth much in its working. Elijah was a man of like ⁵passions with us, and he prayed ⁶fervently that it might not rain; and it rained not on the earth for 18 three years and six months. And he prayed again; and the heaven gave rain, and the earth brought forth her fruit.

19 My brethren, if any among you do err from the 20 truth, and one convert him; ⁷let him know, that he which converteth a sinner from the error of his way shall save a soul from death, and shall cover a multitude of sins.

1 Gr. *presence.*

2 Or, *endurance*

3 Or, *let yours be the yea, yea, and the nay, nay* Compare Matt. v. 37.

4 Or, *having anointed*

5 Or, *nature*
6 Gr. *with prayer.*

7 Some ancient authorities read *know ye.*

THE FIRST EPISTLE GENERAL OF
PETER.

PETER, an apostle of Jesus Christ, to the elect 1
who are sojourners of the Dispersion in Pontus,
Galatia, Cappadocia, Asia, and Bithynia, according 2
to the foreknowledge of God the Father, in sanctification of the Spirit, unto obedience and sprinkling
of the blood of Jesus Christ: Grace to you and
peace be multiplied.

Blessed *be* the God and Father of our Lord Jesus 3
Christ, who according to his great mercy begat us
again unto a living hope by the resurrection of
Jesus Christ from the dead, unto an inheritance in- 4
corruptible, and undefiled, and that fadeth not
away, reserved in heaven for you, who by the 5
power of God are guarded through faith unto a salvation ready to be revealed in the last time. Where- 6
in ye greatly rejoice, though now for a little while,
if need be, ye have been put to grief in manifold
¹temptations, that the proof of your faith, *being* 7
more precious than gold that perisheth though it is
proved by fire, might be found unto praise and
glory and honour at the revelation of Jesus Christ:
whom not having seen ye love; on whom, though 8
now ye see him not, yet believing, ye rejoice greatly
with joy unspeakable and ²full of glory: receiving 9
the end of your faith, *even* the salvation of *your*
souls. Concerning which salvation the prophets 10
sought and searched diligently, who prophesied of
the grace that *should come* unto you: searching what 11
time or what manner of time the Spirit of Christ
which was in them did point unto, when it testified
beforehand the sufferings ³of Christ, and the glories

1 Or, *trials*

2 Gr. *glorified.*

3 Gr. *unto.*

12 that should follow them. To whom it was revealed, that not unto themselves, but unto you, did they minister these things, which now have been announced unto you through them that preached the gospel unto you ¹by the ²Holy Ghost sent forth from heaven; which things angels desire to look into. 13 Wherefore girding up the loins of your mind, be sober and set your hope perfectly on the grace that ³is to be brought unto you at the revelation of Jesus 14 Christ; as children of obedience, not fashioning yourselves according to your former lusts in the 15 time of your ignorance: but ⁴like as he which called you is holy, be ye yourselves also holy in all man-16 ner of living; because it is written, Ye shall be holy; 17 for I am holy. And if ye call on him as Father, who without respect of persons judgeth according to each man's work, pass the time of your sojourn-18 ing in fear: knowing that ye were redeemed, not with corruptible things, with silver or gold, from your vain manner of life handed down from your 19 fathers; but with precious blood, as of a lamb without blemish and without spot, *even the blood* of Christ: 20 who was foreknown indeed before the foundation of the world, but was manifested at the end of the 21 times for your sake, who through him are believers in God, which raised him from the dead, and gave him glory; so that your faith and hope might be in 22 God. Seeing ye have purified your souls in your obedience to the truth unto unfeigned love of the brethren, love one another ⁵from the heart fervently: 23 having been begotten again, not of corruptible seed, but of incorruptible, through the word of ⁶God, 24 which liveth and abideth. For,

    All flesh is as grass,
    And all the glory thereof as the flower of grass.
    The grass withereth, and the flower falleth:
25   But the ⁷word of the Lord abideth for ever.
And this is the ⁷word of good tidings which was preached unto you.

2 Putting away therefore all ⁸wickedness, and all guile, and hypocrisies, and envies, and all evil speak-2 ings, as newborn babes, long for the ⁹spiritual milk which is without guile, that ye may grow thereby 3 unto salvation; if ye have tasted that the Lord is 4 gracious: unto whom coming, a living stone, rejected indeed of men, but with God elect, ¹⁰precious,

1 Gr. *in*.
2 Or, *Holy Spirit*
3 Gr. *is being brought*.
4 Or, *like the Holy One which called you*
5 Many ancient authorities read *from a clean heart*.
6 Or, *God who liveth*
7 Gr. *saying*.
8 Or, *malice*
9 Gr. *reasonable*.*
10 Or, *honourable*

---
* In marg. ⁹ for "*reasonable*" read "*belonging to the reason.*"—*Am. Com.*

I. PETER. 2. 5—

¹ Or, *a spiritual house for a holy priesthood*

ye also, as living stones, are built up ¹a spiritual house, to be a holy priesthood, to offer up spiritual sacrifices, acceptable to God through Jesus Christ. 5

² Or, *a scripture*

Because it is contained in ²scripture, 6

Behold, I lay in Zion a chief corner stone, elect,

³ Or, *honourable*

³precious:

⁴ Or, *it*

And he that believeth on ⁴him shall not be put to shame.

⁵ Or, *In your sight.*
⁶ Or, *honour*

⁵For you therefore which believe is the ⁶preciousness: but for such as disbelieve, 7

The stone which the builders rejected,

The same was made the head of the corner; and, 8

⁷ Gr. *who.*
⁸ Or, *stumble, being disobedient to the word*

A stone of stumbling, and a rock of offence; ⁷for they ⁸stumble at the word, being disobedient: whereunto also they were appointed. But ye are an elect race, a royal priesthood, a holy nation, a people for *God's* own possession, that ye may shew forth the excellencies of him who called you out of darkness into his marvellous light: which in time past were no people, but now are the people of God: which had not obtained mercy, but now have obtained mercy. 9

10

Beloved, I beseech you as sojourners and pilgrims, to abstain from fleshly lusts, which war against the soul; having your behaviour seemly among the Gentiles; that, wherein they speak against you as evil-doers, they may by your good works, which they behold, glorify God in the day of visitation. 11

12

⁹ Gr. *creation.*

Be subject to every ⁹ordinance of man for the Lord's sake: whether it be to the king, as supreme; 13

¹⁰ Gr. *through.*

or unto governors, as sent ¹⁰by him for vengeance on evil-doers and for praise to them that do well. For so is the will of God, that by well-doing ye should put to silence the ignorance of foolish men: 14

15

¹¹ Gr. *having.*
¹² Or, *malice*

as free, and not ¹¹using your freedom for a cloke of ¹²wickedness, but as bondservants of God. Honour all men. Love the brotherhood. Fear God. Honour the king. 16

17

¹³ Gr. *Householdservants.*

¹³Servants, *be* in subjection to your masters with all fear; not only to the good and gentle, but also to the froward. For this is ¹⁴acceptable, if for conscience ¹⁵toward God a man endureth griefs, suffering wrongfully. For what glory is it, if, when ye sin, and are buffeted *for it,* ye shall take it patiently? but if, when ye do well, and suffer *for it,* ye shall take it patiently, this is ¹⁴acceptable with God. For hereunto were ye called: because Christ 18

19

¹⁴ Gr. *grace.*
¹⁵ Gr. *of.*

20

21

I. PETER.

also suffered for you, leaving you an example, that
22 ye should follow his steps: who did no sin, neither
23 was guile found in his mouth: who, when he was reviled, reviled not again; when he suffered, threatened not; but committed ¹*himself* to him that judg-
24 eth righteously: who his own self ²bare our sins in his body upon the tree, that we, having died unto sins, might live unto righteousness; by whose ³stripes
25 ye were healed. For ye were going astray like sheep; but are now returned unto the Shepherd and ⁴Bishop of your souls.

3 In like manner, ye wives, *be* in subjection to your own husbands; that, even if any obey not the word, they may without the word be gained by the ⁵behav-
2 iour of their wives; beholding your chaste ⁵behav-
3 iour *coupled* with fear. Whose *adorning* let it not be the outward adorning of plaiting the hair, and of wearing jewels of gold, or of putting on apparel;
4 but *let it be* the hidden man of the heart, in the incorruptible *apparel* of a meek and quiet spirit, which
5 is in the sight of God of great price. For after this manner aforetime the holy women also, who hoped in God, adorned themselves, being in subjection to
6 their own ⁶husbands: as Sarah obeyed Abraham, calling him lord: whose children ye now are, if ye do well, and are not ⁷put in fear by any terror.
7 Ye husbands, in like manner, dwell with *your wives* according to knowledge, giving honour ⁸unto the woman, as unto the weaker vessel, as being also joint-heirs of the grace of life; to the end that your prayers be not hindered.
8 Finally, *be* ye all likeminded, ⁹compassionate, lov-
9 ing as brethren, tenderhearted, humbleminded: not rendering evil for evil, or reviling for reviling; but contrariwise blessing; for hereunto were ye called,
10 that ye should inherit a blessing. For,

    He that would love life,
    And see good days,
    Let him refrain his tongue from evil,
    And his lips that they speak no guile:
11   And let him turn away from evil, and do good;
    Let him seek peace, and pursue it.
12   For the eyes of the Lord are upon the righteous,
    And his ears unto their supplication:
    But the face of the Lord is upon them that do evil.
13 And who is he that will harm you, if ye be zealous
14 of that which is good? But and if ye should suffer

---

¹ Or, his cause
² Or, *carried up ... to the tree*
³ Gr. *bruise.*
⁴ Or, *Overseer*
⁵ Or, *manner of life*
⁶ Or, *husbands (as Sarah ... ye are become), doing well, and not being afraid*
⁷ Or, *afraid with*
⁸ Gr. *unto the female vessel, as weaker.*
⁹ Gr. *sympathetic.*

for righteousness' sake, blessed *are ye*: and fear not their fear, neither be troubled; but sanctify in your [15] hearts Christ as Lord: *being* ready always to give answer to every man that asketh you a reason concerning the hope that is in you, yet with meekness and fear: having a good conscience; that, wherein [16] ye are spoken against, they may be put to shame who revile your good manner of life in Christ. For [17] it is better, if the will of God should so will, that ye suffer for well-doing than for evil-doing. Because [18] Christ also [1]suffered for sins once, the righteous for the unrighteous, that he might bring us to God; being put to death in the flesh, but quickened in the spirit; in which also he went and preached unto the [19] spirits in prison, which aforetime were disobedient, [20] when the longsuffering of God waited in the days of Noah, while the ark was a preparing, [2]wherein few, that is, eight souls, were saved through water: which [21] also [3]after a true likeness doth now save you, *even* baptism, not the putting away of the filth of the flesh, but the [4]interrogation of a good conscience toward God, through the resurrection of Jesus Christ; who is on the right hand of God, having gone into [22] heaven; angels and authorities and powers being made subject unto him.

Forasmuch then as Christ suffered in the flesh, [4] arm ye yourselves also with the same [5]mind; for he that hath suffered in the flesh hath ceased [6]from sin; that [7]ye no longer should live the rest of your time [2] in the flesh to the lusts of men, but to the will of God. For the time past may suffice to have wrought [3] the desire of the Gentiles, and to have walked in lasciviousness, lusts, winebibbings, revellings, carousings, and abominable idolatries: wherein they think [4] it strange that ye run not with *them* into the same [8]excess of riot, speaking evil of *you*: who shall give [5] account to him that is ready to judge the quick and the dead. For unto this end [9]was the gospel preached [6] even to the dead, that they might be judged according to men in the flesh, but live according to God in the spirit.

But the end of all things is at hand: be ye therefore [7] of sound mind and be sober unto [10]prayer: above [8] all things being fervent in your love among yourselves; for love covereth a multitude of sins: using [9] hospitality one to another without murmuring: according [10] as each hath received a gift, ministering it among yourselves, as good stewards of the manifold

---

[1] Many ancient authorities read *died*.

[2] Or, *into which few, that is, eight souls, were brought safely through water*

[3] Or, *in the antitype*

[4] Or, *inquiry* Or, *appeal*

[5] Or, *thought*

[6] Some ancient authorities read *unto sins*.

[7] Or, *he no longer ... his time*

[8] Or, *flood*

[9] Or, *were the good tidings preached*

[10] Gr. *prayers*.

11 grace of God; if any man speaketh, *speaking* as it were oracles of God; if any man ministereth, *ministering* as of the strength which God supplieth: that in all things God may be glorified through Jesus Christ, whose is the glory and the dominion ¹for ever and ever. Amen.

¹ Gr. *unto the ages of the ages.*

12 Beloved, think it not strange concerning the fiery trial among you, which cometh upon you to prove you, as though a strange thing happened unto you: 13 but insomuch as ye are partakers of Christ's sufferings, rejoice; that at the revelation of his glory also 14 ye may rejoice with exceeding joy. If ye are reproached ²for the name of Christ, blessed *are ye*; because the *Spirit* of glory and the Spirit of God rest- 15 eth upon you. For let none of you suffer as a murderer, or a thief, or an evil-doer, or as a meddler in 16 other men's matters: but if *a man suffer* as a Christian, let him not be ashamed; but let him glorify 17 God in this name. For the time *is come* for judgement to begin at the house of God: and if *it begin* first at us, what *shall be* the end of them that obey 18 not the gospel of God? And if the righteous is scarcely saved, where shall the ungodly and sinner 19 appear? Wherefore let them also that suffer according to the will of God commit their souls in welldoing unto a faithful Creator.

² Gr. *in.*

5 The elders therefore among you I exhort, who am a fellow-elder, and a witness of the sufferings of Christ, who am also a partaker of the glory that 2 shall be revealed: Tend the flock of God which is among you, ³exercising the oversight, not of constraint, but willingly, ⁴according unto God*; nor yet 3 for filthy lucre, but of a ready mind; neither as lording it over the charge allotted to you, but making 4 yourselves ensamples to the flock. And when the chief Shepherd shall be manifested, ye shall receive 5 the crown of glory that fadeth not away. ⁵Likewise, ye younger, be subject unto the elder. Yea, all of you gird yourselves with humility, to serve one another: for God resisteth the proud, but giveth 6 grace to the humble. Humble yourselves therefore under the mighty hand of God, that he may exalt you 7 in due time; casting all your anxiety upon him, be- 8 cause he careth for you. Be sober, be watchful: your adversary the devil, as a roaring lion, walketh

³ Some ancient authorities omit *exercising the oversight.*

⁴ Some ancient authorities omit *according unto God.*

⁵ Or, *Likewise . . . elder; yea, all of you one to another. Gird yourselves with humility.*

---

* For "according unto God" read "according to *the will of* God" (and so in marg. ⁴). Comp. Rom. viii. 27.—*Am. Com.*

about, seeking whom he may devour: whom withstand stedfast in ¹your faith, knowing that the same sufferings are ²accomplished in your ³brethren who are in the world. And the God of all grace, who called you unto his eternal glory in Christ, after that ye have suffered a little while, shall himself ⁴perfect, stablish, strengthen⁵ you. To him *be* the dominion ⁶for ever and ever. Amen.

By Silvanus, ⁷our faithful brother, as I account him, I have written unto you briefly, exhorting, and testifying that this is the true grace of God: stand ye fast therein. ⁸She that is in Babylon, elect together with *you*, saluteth you; and *so doth* Mark my son. Salute one another with a kiss of love.

Peace be unto you all that are in Christ.

---

1 Or, *the*
2 Gr. *being accomplished.*
3 Gr. *brotherhood.*
4 Or, *restore*
5 Many ancient authorities add *settle.*
6 Gr. *unto the ages of the ages.*
7 Gr. *the.*
8 That is, The church, or, The sister.

THE SECOND EPISTLE GENERAL OF
PETER.

1 ¹Simon Peter, a ²servant and apostle of Jesus Christ, to them that have obtained ³a like precious faith with us in the righteousness of ⁴our God and 2 Saviour Jesus Christ: Grace to you and peace be multiplied in the knowledge of God and of Jesus 3 our Lord; seeing that his divine power hath granted unto us all things that pertain unto life and godliness, through the knowledge of him that called us 4 ⁵by his own glory and virtue; whereby he hath granted unto us his precious and exceeding great promises; that through these ye may become partakers of ⁶the divine nature, having escaped from 5 the corruption that is in the world by lust. Yea, and for this very cause adding on your part all diligence, in your faith supply virtue; and in *your* vir-6 tue knowledge; and in *your* knowledge ⁷temperance; and in *your* ⁷temperance patience; and in *your* 7 patience godliness; and in *your* godliness love of the brethren†; and in *your* love of the brethren love. 8 For if these things are yours and abound, they make you to be not idle nor unfruitful unto the knowl-9 edge of our Lord Jesus Christ. For he that lacketh these things is blind, ⁸seeing only what is near, having forgotten the cleansing from his old sins. 10 Wherefore, brethren, give the more diligence to make your calling and election sure: for if ye do 11 these things, ye shall never stumble: for thus shall be richly supplied unto you the entrance into the eternal kingdom of our Lord and Saviour Jesus Christ.

1 Many ancient authorities read *Symeon.*
2 Gr. *bondservant.*
3 Gr. *an equally precious.*
4 Or, *our God and the Saviour*
5 Some ancient authorities read *through glory and virtue.*
6 Or, *a*
7 Or, *self-control*
8 Or, *closing his eyes*

---

* Let marg. ⁴ and the text exchange places.—*Am. Com.*
† For "love of the brethren" read "brotherly kindness" (twice) with marg. Gr. *love of the brethren.*—*Am. Com.*

II. PETER. 1. 12—

Wherefore I shall be ready always to put you in 12 remembrance of these things, though ye know them, and are established in the truth which is with *you*. And I think it right, as long as I am in this taber- 13 nacle, to stir you up by putting you in remembrance; knowing that the putting off of my taber- 14 nacle cometh swiftly, even as our Lord Jesus Christ signified unto me. Yea, I will give diligence that 15 at every time ye may be able after my ¹decease to call these things to remembrance. For we did not 16 follow cunningly devised fables, when we made known unto you the power and ²coming of our Lord Jesus Christ, but we were eyewitnesses of his majesty. For he ³received from God the Father 17 honour and glory, when there ⁴came such a voice to him from the excellent glory*, This is my beloved Son, in whom I am well pleased: and this voice we 18 *ourselves* heard ⁵come† out of heaven, when we were with him in the holy mount. And we have the 19 word of prophecy *made* more sure; whereunto ye do well that ye take heed, as unto a lamp shining in a ⁶dark place, until the day dawn, and the day-star arise in your hearts: knowing this first, that no 20 prophecy of scripture is of ⁷private interpretation. For no prophecy ever ⁸came by the will of man: 21 but men spake from God, being moved by the ⁹Holy Ghost.

But there arose false prophets also among the peo- **2** ple, as among you also there shall be false teachers, who shall privily bring in ¹⁰destructive heresies, denying even the Master that bought them, bringing upon themselves swift destruction. And many 2 shall follow their lascivious doings; by reason of whom the way of the truth shall be evil spoken of. And in covetousness shall they with feigned words 3 make merchandise of you: whose sentence now from of old lingereth not, and their destruction slumbereth not. For if God spared not angels when 4 they sinned, but ¹¹cast them down to ¹²hell, and committed them to ¹³pits of darkness, to be reserved unto judgement; and spared not the ancient world, 5 but preserved Noah with seven others, ¹⁴a preacher of righteousness, when he brought a flood upon the world of the ungodly; and turning the cities of 6

1 Or, *departure*
2 Gr. *presence*.
3 Gr. *having received*.
4 Gr. *was brought ... by the majestic glory*.
5 Gr. *brought*.
6 Gr. *squalid*.
7 Or, *special*
8 Gr. *was brought*.
9 Or, *Holy Spirit*.
10 Or, *sects of perdition*
11 Or, *cast them into dungeons*
12 Gr. *Tartarus*.
13 Some ancient authorities read *chains*.
14 Gr. *a herald*.

---

* For "came such a voice to him from the excellent glory" read "was borne such a voice to him by the Majestic Glory" and omit marg.⁴.—*Am. Com.*

† For "come" read "borne" and omit marg.⁵.—*Am. Com.*

Sodom and Gomorrah into ashes condemned them with an overthrow, having made them an example
7 unto those that should live ungodly; and delivered righteous Lot, sore distressed by the lascivious life
8 of the wicked (for that righteous man dwelling among them, in seeing and hearing, [1]vexed *his* righteous soul from day to day with *their* lawless deeds):
9 the Lord knoweth how to deliver the godly out of temptation, and to keep the unrighteous under punishment
10 unto the day of judgement; but chiefly them that walk after the flesh in the lust of defilement, and despise dominion. Daring, selfwilled, they
11 tremble not to rail at [2]dignities: whereas angels, though greater in might and power, bring not a railing
12 judgement against them before the Lord. But these, as creatures without reason, born [3]mere animals [4]to be taken and destroyed, railing in matters whereof they are ignorant, shall in their [5]destroying
13 surely be destroyed, suffering wrong as the hire of wrong-doing; *men* that count it pleasure to revel in the day-time, spots and blemishes, revelling in their
14 [6]love-feasts* while they feast with you; having eyes full of [7]adultery, and that cannot cease from sin; enticing unstedfast souls; having a heart exercised
15 in covetousness; children of cursing; forsaking the right way, they went astray, having followed the way of Balaam the *son* of [8]Beor, who loved the hire
16 of wrong-doing; but he was rebuked for his own transgression: a dumb ass spake with man's voice
17 and stayed the madness of the prophet. These are springs without water, and mists driven by a storm; for whom the blackness of darkness hath been reserved.
18 For, uttering great swelling *words* of vanity, they entice in the lusts of the flesh, by lasciviousness, those who are just escaping from them that
19 live in error; promising them liberty, while they themselves are bondservants of corruption; for of [9]whom a man is overcome, of the same is he also
20 brought into bondage. For if, after they have escaped the defilements of the world through the knowledge of [10]the Lord and Saviour Jesus Christ, they are again entangled therein and overcome, the last state is become worse with them than the first.
21 For it were better for them not to have known the way of righteousness, than, after knowing it, to turn

1 Gr. *tormented.*

2 Gr. *glories.*

3 Gr. *natural.*
4 Or, *to take and to destroy*
5 Or, *corruption.*

6 Many ancient authorities read *deceivings.*
7 Gr. *an adulteress.*

8 Many ancient authorities read *Bosor.*

9 Or, *what*

10 Many ancient authorities read *our.*

---

* For "love-feasts" read "deceivings", and in marg. 6 read Some ancient authorities read *love-feasts.*—Am. Com.

back from the holy commandment delivered unto
them. It has happened unto them according to the 22
true proverb, The dog turning to his own vomit
again, and the sow that had washed to wallowing in
the mire.

This is now, beloved, the second epistle that I write **3**
unto you; and in both of them I stir up your sincere
mind by putting you in remembrance; that ye should 2
remember the words which were spoken before by
the holy prophets, and the commandment of the
Lord and Saviour through your apostles: knowing 3
this first, that ¹in the last days mockers shall come
with mockery, walking after their own lusts, and 4
saying, Where is the promise of his ²coming? for,
from the day that the fathers fell asleep, all things
continue as they were from the beginning of the
creation. For this they wilfully forget, that there 5
were heavens from of old, and an earth compacted
out of water and ³amidst water, by the word of God;
by which means the world that then was, being over- 6
flowed with water, perished: but the heavens that 7
now are, and the earth, by the same word have been
⁴stored up for fire, being reserved against the day of
judgement and destruction of ungodly men.

But forget not this one thing, beloved, that one 8
day is with the Lord as a thousand years, and a
thousand years as one day. The Lord is not slack 9
concerning his promise, as some count slackness;
but is longsuffering to you-ward, not wishing that
any should perish, but that all should come to repentance. But the day of the Lord will come as a 10
thief; in the which the heavens shall pass away with
a great noise, and the ⁵elements shall be dissolved
with fervent heat, and the earth and the works that
are therein shall be ⁶burned up. Seeing that these 11
things are thus all to be dissolved, what manner of
persons ought ye to be in *all* holy living and godliness, looking for and ⁷earnestly desiring the ²com- 12
ing of the day of God, by reason of which the heavens being on fire shall be dissolved, and the ⁵elements shall melt with fervent heat? But, according 13
to his promise, we look for new heavens and a new
earth, wherein dwelleth righteousness.

Wherefore, beloved, seeing that ye look for these 14
things, give diligence that ye may be found in peace,
without spot and blameless in his sight. And ac- 15
count that the longsuffering of our Lord is salvation; even as our beloved brother Paul also, ac-

---

1 Gr. *in the last of the days.*

2 Gr. *presence.*

3 Or, *through*

4 Or, *stored with fire*

5 Or, *heavenly bodies*

6 The most ancient manuscripts read *discovered.*

7 Or, *hastening*

cording to the wisdom given to him, wrote unto
16 you; as also in all *his* epistles, speaking in them of
these things; wherein are some things hard to be
understood, which the ignorant and unstedfast wrest,
as *they do* also the other scriptures, unto their own
17 destruction. Ye therefore, beloved, knowing *these
things* beforehand, beware lest, being carried away
with the error of the wicked, ye fall from your own
18 stedfastness. But grow in the grace and knowledge of our Lord and Saviour Jesus Christ. To
him *be* the glory both now and ¹for ever. Amen.

¹ Gr. *unto the day of eternity.*

THE FIRST EPISTLE GENERAL OF
JOHN.

1 That which was from the beginning, that which we have heard, that which we have seen with our eyes, that which we beheld, and our hands handled, 2 concerning the ¹Word of life (and the life was manifested, and we have seen, and bear witness, and declare unto you the life, the eternal *life*, which was with the Father, and was manifested unto us); 3 that which we have seen and heard declare we unto you also, that ye also may have fellowship with us: yea, and our fellowship is with the Father, and with his Son Jesus Christ: 4 and these things we write, that ²our joy may be fulfilled.

5 And this is the message which we have heard from him, and announce unto you, that God is light, and in him is no darkness at all. 6 If we say that we have fellowship with him, and walk in the darkness, we lie, and do not the truth: 7 but if we walk in the light, as he is in the light, we have fellowship one with another, and the blood of Jesus his Son cleanseth us from all sin. 8 If we say that we have no sin, we deceive ourselves, and the truth is not in us. 9 If we confess our sins, he is faithful and righteous to forgive us our sins, and to cleanse us from all unrighteousness. 10 If we say that we have not sinned, we make him a liar, and his word is not in us.

2 My little children, these things write I unto you, that ye may not sin. And if any man sin, we have an ³Advocate with the Father, Jesus Christ the righteous: 2 and he is the propitiation for our sins; and not for ours only, but also for the whole world. 3 And hereby know we that we know him, if we keep his commandments. 4 He that saith, I know him, and keepeth not his commandments, is a liar, and

---

1 Or, *word*

2 Many ancient authorities read ²*your*.

3 Or, *Comforter*
Or, *Helper*
Gr. *Paraclete*.

I. JOHN.

5 the truth is not in him: but whoso keepeth his word, in him verily hath the love of God been perfected.
6 Hereby know we that we are in him: he that saith he abideth in him ought himself also to walk even as he walked.
7 Beloved, no new commandment write I unto you, but an old commandment which ye had from the beginning: the old commandment is the word which
8 ye heard. Again, a new commandment write I unto you, which thing is true in him and in you; because the darkness is passing away, and the true light al-
9 ready shineth. He that saith he is in the light, and hateth his brother, is in the darkness even until now.
10 He that loveth his brother abideth in the light, and
11 there is none occasion of stumbling in him. But he that hateth his brother is in the darkness, and walketh in the darkness, and knoweth not whither he goeth, because the darkness hath blinded his eyes.
12 I write unto you, *my* little children, because your
13 sins are forgiven you for his name's sake. I write unto you, fathers, because ye know him which is from the beginning. I write unto you, young men, because ye have overcome the evil one. [1]I have written unto you, little children, because ye know
14 the Father. [1]I have written unto you, fathers, because ye know him which is from the beginning. [1]I have written unto you, young men, because ye are strong, and the word of God abideth in you,
15 and ye have overcome the evil one. Love not the world, neither the things that are in the world. If any man love the world, the love of the Father is
16 not in him. For all that is in the world, the lust of the flesh, and the lust of the eyes, and the vainglory of life, is not of the Father, but is of the world.
17 And the world passeth away, and the lust thereof: but he that doeth the will of God abideth for ever.
18 Little children, it is the last hour: and as ye heard that antichrist cometh, even now have there arisen many antichrists; whereby we know that it is the
19 last hour. They went out from us, but they were not of us; for if they had been of us, they would have continued with us: but *they went out*, that they might be made manifest [2]how that they all are not of
20 us. And ye have an anointing from the Holy One,
21 [3]and ye know all things. I have not written unto you because ye know not the truth, but because ye
22 know it, and [4]because no lie is of the truth. Who is the liar but he that denieth that Jesus is the Christ?

[1] Or, *I wrote*
[2] Or, *that not all are of us*
[3] Some very ancient authorities read *and ye all know*.
[4] Or, *that*

This is the antichrist, *even* he that denieth the Father and the Son. Whosoever denieth the Son, the same hath not the Father: he that confesseth the Son hath the Father also. As for you, let that abide in you which ye heard from the beginning. If that which ye heard from the beginning abide in you, ye also shall abide in the Son, and in the Father. And this is the promise which he promised ¹us, *even* the life eternal. These things have I written unto you concerning them that would lead you astray. And as for you, the anointing which ye received of him abideth in you, and ye need not that any one teach you; but as his anointing teacheth you concerning all things, ²and is true, and is no lie, and even as it taught you, ³ye abide in him. And now, *my* little children, abide in him; that, if he shall be manifested, we may have boldness, and not be ashamed ⁴before him at his ⁵coming. If ye know that he is righteous, ⁶ye know that every one also that doeth righteousness is begotten of him.

Behold what manner of love the Father hath bestowed upon us, that we should be called children of God: and *such* we are. For this cause the world knoweth us not, because it knew him not. Beloved, now are we children of God, and it is not yet made manifest what we shall be. We know that, if ⁷he shall be manifested, we shall be like him; for we shall see him even as he is. And every one that hath this hope *set* on him purifieth himself, even as he is pure. Every one that doeth sin doeth also lawlessness: and sin is lawlessness. And ye know that he was manifested to ⁸take away sins; and in him is no sin. Whosoever abideth in him sinneth not: whosoever sinneth hath not seen him, neither ⁹knoweth him. *My* little children, let no man lead you astray: he that doeth righteousness is righteous, even as he is righteous: he that doeth sin is of the devil; for the devil sinneth from the beginning. To this end was the son of God manifested, that he might destroy the works of the devil. Whosoever is begotten of God doeth no sin, because his seed abideth in him: and he cannot sin, because he is begotten of God. In this the children of God are manifest, and the children of the devil: whosoever doeth not righteousness is not of God, neither he that loveth not his brother. For this is the message which ye heard from the beginning, that we should love one another: not as Cain was of the evil one, and

---

1 Some ancient authorities read *you*.

2 Or, *so it is true, and is no lie; and even as &c.*
3 Or, *abide ye*

4 Gr. *from him.*
5 Gr. *presence.*
6 Or, *know ye*

7 Or, *it*

8 Or, *bear sins*

9 Or, *hath known*

slew his brother. And wherefore slew he him? Because his works were evil, and his brother's righteous.
13 Marvel not, brethren, if the world hateth you.
14 We know that we have passed out of death into life, because we love the brethren. He that loveth
15 not abideth in death. Whosoever hateth his brother is a murderer: and ye know that no murderer
16 hath eternal life abiding in him. Hereby know we love, because he laid down his life for us: and we
17 ought to lay down our lives for the brethren. But whoso hath the world's goods, and beholdeth his brother in need, and shutteth up his compassion from him, how doth the love of God abide in him?
18 My little children, let us not love in word, neither
19 with the tongue; but in deed and truth. Hereby shall we know that we are of the truth, and shall
20 ¹assure our heart before him, whereinsoever our heart condemn us; because God* is greater than our
21 heart, and knoweth all things. Beloved, if our heart condemn us not, we have boldness toward
22 God; and whatsoever we ask, we receive of him, because we keep his commandments, and do the
23 things that are pleasing in his sight. And this is his commandment, that we should ²believe in the name of his Son Jesus Christ, and love one another,
24 even as he gave us commandment. And he that keepeth his commandments abideth in him, and he in him. And hereby we know that he abideth in us, by the Spirit which he gave us.

4 Beloved, believe not every spirit, but prove the spirits, whether they are of God: because many
2 false prophets are gone out into the world. Hereby know ye the Spirit of God: every spirit which confesseth that Jesus Christ is come in the flesh is
3 of God: and every spirit which ³confesseth not Jesus is not of God: and this is the *spirit* of the antichrist, whereof ye have heard that it cometh;
4 and now it is in the world already. Ye are of God, *my* little children, and have overcome them: because greater is he that is in you than he that is in
5 the world. They are of the world: therefore speak they *as* of the world, and the world heareth them.
6 We are of God: he that knoweth God heareth us; he who is not of God heareth us not. By this we know the spirit of truth, and the spirit of error.

1 Gr. *persuade.*

2 Gr. *believe the name.*

3 Some ancient authorities read *annulleth Jesus.*

---

* For "him, whereinsoever . . . because God" etc. read "him: because if our heart condemn us, God" etc. (with the present text in the marg.).—*Am. Com.*

Beloved, let us love one another: for love is of 7
God; and every one that loveth is begotten of God,
and knoweth God. He that loveth not knoweth 8
not God; for God is love. Herein was the love of 9
God manifested [1]in us, that God hath sent his only
begotten Son into the world, that we might live
through him. Herein is love, not that we loved 10
God, but that he loved us, and sent his Son *to be* the
propitiation for our sins. Beloved, if God so loved 11
us, we also ought to love one another. No man 12
hath beheld God at any time: if we love one another, God abideth in us, and his love is perfected
in us: hereby know we that we abide in him, and 13
he in us, because he hath given us of his Spirit.
And we have beheld and bear witness that the Fa- 14
ther hath sent the Son *to be* the Saviour of the
world. Whosoever shall confess that Jesus is the 15
Son of God, God abideth in him, and he in God.
And we know and have believed the love which 16
God hath [1]in us. God is love; and he that abideth
in love abideth in God, and God abideth in him.
Herein is love made perfect with us, that we may 17
have boldness in the day of judgement; because as
he is, even so are we in this world. There is no 18
fear in love: but perfect love casteth out fear, because fear hath punishment; and he that feareth is
not made perfect in love. We love, because he 19
first loved us. If a man say, I love God, and hateth 20
his brother, he is a liar: for he that loveth not his
brother whom he hath seen, [2]cannot love God whom
he hath not seen. And this commandment have we 21
from him, that he who loveth God love his brother
also.

Whosoever believeth that Jesus is the Christ is 5
begotten of God: and whosoever loveth him that
begat loveth him also that is begotten of him. Here- 2
by we know that we love the children of God, when
we love God, and do his commandments. For this 3
is the love of God, that we keep his commandments:
and his commandments are not grievous. For what- 4
soever is begotten of God overcometh the world:
and this is the victory that hath overcome the world,
even our faith. And who is he that overcometh the 5
world, but he that believeth that Jesus is the Son of
God? This is he that came by water and blood, 6
even Jesus Christ; not [3]with the water only, but
[3]with the water and [3]with the blood. And it is the 7
Spirit that beareth witness, because the Spirit is the

[1] Or, *in our case*

[2] Many ancient authorities read *how can he love God whom he hath not seen?*

[3] Gr. *in*.

8 truth. For there are three who bear witness, the Spirit, and the water, and the blood: and the three
9 agree in one. If we receive the witness of men, the witness of God is greater: for the witness of God is this, that he hath borne witness concerning his Son.
10 He that believeth on the Son of God hath the witness in him: he that believeth not God hath made him a liar; because he hath not believed in the wit-
11 ness that God hath borne concerning his Son. And the witness is this, that God gave unto us eternal
12 life, and this life is in his Son. He that hath the Son hath the life; he that hath not the Son of God hath not the life.
13 These things have I written unto you, that ye may know that ye have eternal life, *even* unto you that
14 believe on the name of the Son of God. And this is the boldness which we have toward him, that, if we ask any thing according to his will, he heareth us:
15 and if we know that he heareth us whatsoever we ask, we know that we have the petitions which we
16 have asked of him. If any man see his brother sinning a sin not unto death, ¹he shall ask, and *God* will give him life for them that sin not unto death. There is ²a sin unto death: not concerning this do I
17 say that he should make request. All unrighteousness is sin: and there is ²a sin not unto death.
18 We know that whosoever is begotten of God sinneth not; but he that was begotten of God keepeth
19 ³him*, and the evil one toucheth him not. We know that we are of God, and the whole world lieth in the
20 evil one. And we know that the Son of God is come, and hath given us an understanding, that we know him that is true, and we are in him that is true, *even* in his Son Jesus Christ. This is the true
21 God, and eternal life. *My* little children, guard yourselves from idols.

1 Or, *he shall ask and shall give him life*, even *to them &c.*

2 Or, *sin*

3 Or, *himself*

---

* Substitute marg. ³ for the text, and add marg. ³ Some ancient manuscripts read *him.—Am. Com.*

THE SECOND EPISTLE OF

JOHN.

1 The elder unto the elect lady* and her children, whom I love in truth; and not I only, but also all 2 they that know the truth; for the truth's sake which 3 abideth in us, and it shall be with us for ever: Grace, mercy, peace shall be with us, from God the Father, and from Jesus Christ, the Son of the Father, in truth and love.

4 I rejoice greatly that I have found *certain* of thy children walking in truth, even as we received com- 5 mandment from the Father. And now I beseech thee, lady*, not as though I wrote to thee a new com- mandment, but that which we had from the begin- 6 ning, that we love one another. And this is love, that we should walk after his commandments. This is the commandment, even as ye heard from the be- 7 ginning, that ye should walk in it. For many de- ceivers are gone forth into the world, *even* they that confess not that Jesus Christ cometh in the flesh. 8 This is the deceiver and the antichrist. Look to yourselves, that ye ¹lose not the things which ²we have wrought, but that ye receive a full reward. 9 Whosoever ³goeth onward and abideth not in the teaching of Christ, hath not God: he that abideth in the teaching, the same hath both the Father and the 10 Son. If any one cometh unto you, and bringeth not this teaching, receive him not into *your* house, 11 and give him no greeting: for he that giveth him greeting partaketh in his evil works.

12 Having many things to write unto you, I would not *write them* with paper and ink: but I hope to come unto you, and to speak face to face that your 13 joy may be fulfilled. The children of thine elect sister salute thee.

1 Or, *destroy*
2 Many ancient authorities read *ye*.
3 Or, *taketh the lead*

---

* "lady" add marg. Or, *Cyria*—Am. Com.

THE THIRD EPISTLE OF
JOHN.

1 THE elder unto Gaius the beloved, whom I love in truth.
2 Beloved, I pray that in all things thou mayest prosper and be in health, even as thy soul prosper-
3 eth. For I [1]rejoiced greatly, when brethren came and bare witness unto thy truth, even as thou walk-
4 est in truth. Greater [2]joy have I none than [3]this, to hear of my children walking in the truth.
5 Beloved, thou doest a faithful work in whatsoever thou doest toward them that are brethren and stran-
6 gers withal; who bare witness to thy love before the church: whom thou wilt do well to set forward on
7 their journey worthily of God: because that for the sake of the Name they went forth, taking nothing
8 of the Gentiles. We therefore ought to welcome such, that we may be fellow-workers with the truth†.
9 I wrote somewhat unto the church: but Diotrephes, who loveth to have the preeminence among
10 them, receiveth us not. Therefore, if I come, I will bring to remembrance his works which he doeth, prating against us with wicked words: and not content therewith, neither doth he himself receive the brethren, and them that would he forbiddeth, and
11 casteth *them* out of the church. Beloved, imitate not that which is evil, but that which is good. He that doeth good is of God: he that doeth evil hath
12 not seen God. Demetrius hath the witness of all *men*, and of the truth itself: yea, we also bear witness; and thou knowest that our witness is true.
13 I had many things to write unto thee, but I am unwilling to write *them* to thee with ink and pen:
14 but I hope shortly to see thee, and we shall speak face to face. Peace *be* unto thee. The friends salute thee. Salute the friends by name.

[1] Or, *rejoice greatly, when brethren come and bear witness*
[2] Some ancient authorities read *grace.**
[3] Or, *these things that I may hear*

---
* Dele marg. 2.—*Am. Com.*
† For "with the truth" read "for the truth."—*Am. Com.*

THE GENERAL EPISTLE OF
JUDE.

¹ Gr. *bondservant.*
² Or, *to them that are beloved in God the Father,*
and kept for Jesus Christ, being *called*

1 JUDAS*, a ¹servant of Jesus Christ, and brother of James, ²to them that are called, beloved in God the Father, and kept for Jesus Christ: Mercy unto you 2 and peace and love be multiplied.

3 Beloved, while I was giving all diligence to write unto you of our common salvation, I was constrained to write unto you exhorting you to contend earnestly for the faith which was once for all delivered unto the saints. 4 For there are certain men crept in privily, *even* they who were of old set forth† unto this condemnation, ungodly men, turning the grace of our God into lasciviousness, and denying ³our only Master and Lord, Jesus Christ.

³ Or, *the only Master, and our Lord Jesus Christ.*

⁴ Many very ancient authorities read *Jesus.*

⁵ Gr. *the second time.*

5 Now I desire to put you in remembrance, though ye know all things once for all, how that ⁴the Lord, having saved a people out of the land of Egypt, ⁵afterward destroyed them that believed not. 6 And angels which kept not their own principality, but left their proper habitation, he hath kept in everlasting bonds under darkness unto the judgement of the great day. 7 Even as Sodom and Gomorrah, and the cities about them, having in like manner with these given themselves over to fornication, and gone after strange flesh, are set forth ⁶as an example, suffering the punishment of eternal fire. 8 Yet in like manner these also in their dreamings defile the flesh, and set at nought dominion, and rail at ⁷dignities. 9 But Michael the archangel, when contending with the devil he disputed about the body of Moses, durst not bring against him a railing judgement,

⁶ Or, *as an example of eternal fire, suffering punishment.*

⁷ Gr. *glories.*

---

* For "Judas" read "Jude" and add marg. Gr. *Judas.*—*Am. Com.*
† For "set forth" read "written of beforehand," putting the present text into the marg.—*Am. Com.*

10 but said, The Lord rebuke thee. But these rail at whatsoever things they know not: and what they understand naturally, like the creatures without rea-
11 son, in these things are they ¹destroyed. Woe unto them! for they went in the way of Cain, and ²ran riotously in the error of Balaam for hire, and per-
12 ished in the gainsaying of Korah. These are they who are ³hidden rocks in your love-feasts when they feast with you, shepherds that without fear feed themselves; clouds without water, carried along by winds; autumn trees without fruit, twice dead,
13 plucked up by the roots; wild waves of the sea, foaming out their own ⁴shame; wandering stars, for whom the blackness of darkness hath been reserved
14 for ever. And to these also Enoch, the seventh from Adam, prophesied, saying, Behold, the Lord
15 came with ⁵ten thousands of his holy ones, to execute judgement upon all, and to convict all the ungodly of all their works of ungodliness which they have ungodly wrought, and of all the hard things which ungodly sinners have spoken against him.
16 These are murmurers, complainers, walking after their lusts (and their mouth speaketh great swelling *words*), shewing respect of persons for the sake of advantage.
17 But ye, beloved, remember ye the words which have been spoken before by the apostles of our Lord
18 Jesus Christ; how that they said to you, In the last time there shall be mockers, walking after ⁶their
19 own ungodly lusts. These are they who make
20 separations, ⁷sensual, having not the Spirit. But ye, beloved, building up yourselves on your most
21 holy faith, praying in the Holy Spirit, keep yourselves in the love of God, looking for the mercy of
22 our Lord Jesus Christ unto eternal life. ⁸And on
23 some* have mercy, ⁹who are in doubt; and some save, snatching them out of the fire; and on some have mercy with fear; hating even the garment spotted by the flesh.
24 Now unto him that is able to guard you from stumbling, and to set you before the presence of his
25 glory without blemish in exceeding joy, to the only God our Saviour, through Jesus Christ our Lord, *be* glory, majesty, dominion and power, before all time, and now, and ¹⁰for evermore. Amen.

1 Or, *corrupted*
2 Or, *cast themselves away through*
3 Or, *spots*
4 Gr. *shames.*
5 Gr. *his holy myriads.*
6 Gr. *their own lusts of ungodlinesses.*
7 Or, *natural* Or, *animal*
8 The Greek text in this passage (*And ... fire*) is somewhat uncertain.
9 Or, *while they dispute with you*
10 Gr. *unto all the ages.*

---

* Against "And on some" etc. add the marg. Some ancient authorities read *And some refute while they dispute with you.*—*Am. Com.*

THE REVELATION

OF

S. JOHN THE DIVINE.

^{1 Or, *gave unto him, to shew unto his servants the things &c.*}
^{2 Gr. *bondservants*: and so throughout this book.}
^{3 Or, *them*}

1 The Revelation of Jesus Christ, which God ¹gave him to shew unto his ²servants, *even* the things which must shortly come to pass: and he sent and signified ³*it* by his angel unto his servant John; 2 who bare witness of the word of God, and of the testimony of Jesus Christ, *even* of all things that he saw. 3 Blessed is he that readeth, and they that hear the words of the prophecy, and keep the things which are written therein: for the time is at hand.

^{4 Or, *which cometh*}
^{5 Many authorities, some ancient, read *washed*.}
^{6 Gr. *in*.}
^{7 Gr. *unto the ages of the ages.* Many ancient authorities omit *of the ages.*}
^{8 Or, *the Lord, the God**}
^{9 Or, *he which*}

4 John to the seven churches which are in Asia: Grace to you and peace, from him which is and which was and ⁴which is to come; and from the seven Spirits which are before his throne; 5 and from Jesus Christ, *who is* the faithful witness, the firstborn of the dead, and the ruler of the kings of the earth. Unto him that loveth us, and ⁵loosed us from our sins ⁶by his blood; 6 and he made us *to be* a kingdom, *to be* priests unto his God and Father; to him *be* the glory and the dominion ⁷for ever and ever. Amen. 7 Behold, he cometh with the clouds; and every eye shall see him, and they which pierced him; and all the tribes of the earth shall mourn over him. Even so, Amen.

8 I am the Alpha and the Omega, saith ⁸the Lord God, ⁹which is and which was and ⁴which is to come, the Almighty.

9 I John, your brother and partaker with you in the tribulation and kingdom and patience *which are* in Jesus, was in the isle that is called Patmos, for

---

* Omit marg. 8 ("*the Lord, the God*").—*Am. Com.*

10 the word of God and the testimony of Jesus. I was
in the Spirit on the Lord's day, and I heard behind
11 me a great voice, as of a trumpet saying, What thou
seest, write in a book, and send *it* to the seven
churches; unto Ephesus, and unto Smyrna, and
unto Pergamum, and unto Thyatira, and unto Sardis, and unto Philadelphia, and unto Laodicea.
12 And I turned to see the voice which spake with me.
And having turned I saw seven golden ¹candlesticks;
13 and in the midst of the ¹candlesticks one like unto
²a son of man, clothed with a garment down to the
foot, and girt about at the breasts with a golden
14 girdle. And his head and his hair were white as
white wool, *white* as snow; and his eyes were as a
15 flame of fire; and his feet like unto burnished brass,
as if it had been refined in a furnace; and his voice
16 as the voice of many waters. And he had in his
right hand seven stars: and out of his mouth proceeded a sharp two-edged sword: and his counte-
17 nance was as the sun shineth in his strength. And
when I saw him, I fell at his feet as one dead. And
he laid his right hand upon me, saying, Fear not;
18 I am the first and the last, and the Living one; and
I ³was dead, and behold, I am alive ⁴for evermore,
19 and I have the keys of death and of Hades. Write
therefore the things which thou sawest, and the
things which are, and the things which shall come
20 to pass hereafter; the mystery of the seven stars
which thou sawest ⁵in my right hand, and the seven
golden ¹candlesticks. The seven stars are the angels of the seven churches: and the seven ¹candlesticks are seven churches.

2 To the angel of the church in Ephesus write;
These things saith he that holdeth the seven stars
in his right hand, he that walketh in the midst of the
2 seven golden ¹candlesticks: I know thy works, and
thy toil and patience, and that thou canst not bear
evil men, and didst try them which call themselves
apostles, and they are not, and didst find them false;
3 and thou hast patience and didst bear for my name's
4 sake, and hast not grown weary. But I have *this*
5 against thee, that thou didst leave thy first love. Remember therefore from whence thou art fallen, and
repent, and do the first works; or else I come to
thee, and will move thy ⁶candlestick out of its place,
6 except thou repent. But this thou hast, that thou

1 Gr. *lampstands.*
2 Or, *the Son of man**
3 Gr. *became.*
4 Gr. *unto the ages of the ages.*
5 Gr. *upon.*
6 Gr. *lampstand.*

---

* Omit marg.² ("*the Son of man*").—*Am. Com.*

hatest the works of the Nicolaitans, which I also hate. He that hath an ear, let him hear what the Spirit saith to the churches. To him that overcometh, to him will I give to eat of the tree of life, which is in the ¹Paradise of God.

And to the angel of the church in Smyrna write; These things saith the first and the last, which ²was dead, and lived *again*: I know thy tribulation, and thy poverty (but thou art rich), and the ³blasphemy of them which say they are Jews, and they are not, but are a synagogue of Satan. Fear not the things which thou art about to suffer: behold, the devil is about to cast some of you into prison, that ye may be tried; ⁴and ye shall have ⁵tribulation ten days. Be thou faithful unto death, and I will give thee the crown of life. He that hath an ear, let him hear what the Spirit saith to the churches. He that overcometh shall not be hurt of the second death.

And to the angel of the church in Pergamum write;

These things saith he that hath the sharp two-edged sword: I know where thou dwellest, *even* where Satan's throne is: and thou holdest fast my name, and didst not deny my faith, even in the days ⁶of Antipas my witness, my faithful one, who was killed among you, where Satan dwelleth. But I have a few things against thee, because thou hast there some that hold the teaching of Balaam, who taught Balak to cast a stumblingblock before the children of Israel, to eat things sacrificed to idols, and to commit fornication. So hast thou also some that hold the teaching of the Nicolaitans in like manner. Repent therefore; or else I come to thee quickly, and I will make war against them with the sword of my mouth. He that hath an ear, let him hear what the Spirit saith to the churches. To him that overcometh, to him will I give of the hidden manna, and I will give him a white stone, and upon the stone a new name written, which no one knoweth but he that receiveth it.

And to the angel of the church in Thyatira write;

These things saith the Son of God, who hath his eyes like a flame of fire, and his feet are like unto burnished brass: I know thy works, and thy love and faith and ministry and patience, and that thy last works are more than the first. But I have *this* against thee, that thou sufferest ⁷the woman Jezebel,

---

1 Or, *garden*: as in Gen. ii. 8.
2 Gr. *became*.
3 Or, *reviling*
4 Some ancient authorities read *and may have*.
5 Gr. *a tribulation of ten days*.
6 The Greek text here is somewhat uncertain.
7 Many authorities, some ancient, read *thy wife*.

which calleth herself a prophetess; and she teacheth and seduceth my servants to commit fornication, 21 and to eat things sacrificed to idols. And I gave her time that she should repent; and she willeth not 22 to repent of her fornication. Behold, I do cast her into a bed, and them that commit adultery with her into great tribulation, except they repent of ¹her 23 works. And I will kill her children with ²death; and all the churches shall know that I am he which searcheth the reins and hearts: and I will give unto 24 each one of you according to your works. But to you I say, to the rest that are in Thyatira, as many as have not this teaching, which know not the deep things of Satan, as they say; I cast upon you none 25 other burden. Howbeit that which ye have, hold 26 fast till I come. And he that overcometh, and he that keepeth my works unto the end, to him will I 27 give authority over the nations: and he shall rule them with a rod of ³iron, as the vessels of the potter 28 are broken to shivers; as I also have received of my 29 Father: and I will give him the morning star. He that hath an ear, let him hear what the Spirit saith to the churches.

¹ Many ancient authorities read *their.*
² Or, *pestilence*
³ Or, *iron; as vessels of the potter, are they broken*

3 And to the angel of the church in Sardis write;

These things saith he that hath the seven Spirits of God, and the seven stars: I know thy works, that thou hast a name that thou livest, and thou art dead. 2 Be thou watchful, and stablish the things that remain, which were ready to die: for I have ⁴found 3 no works of thine fulfilled* before my God. Remember therefore how thou hast received and didst hear; and keep *it*, and repent. If therefore thou shalt not watch, I will come as a thief, and thou shalt not know what hour I will come upon thee. 4 But thou hast a few names in Sardis which did not defile their garments: and they shall walk with me 5 in white; for they are worthy. He that overcometh shall thus be arrayed in white garments; and I will in no wise blot his name out of the book of life, and I will confess his name before my Father, and 6 before his angels. He that hath an ear, let him hear what the Spirit saith to the churches.

⁴ Many ancient authorities read *not found thy works.*

7 And to the angel of the church in Philadelphia write;

These things saith he that is holy, he that is true, he that hath the key of David, he that openeth, and

---

* For "fulfilled" read "perfected"—*Am. Com.*

none shall shut, and that shutteth, and none openeth: I know thy works (behold, I have ¹set before thee a door opened, which none can shut), that thou hast a little power, and didst keep my word, and didst not deny my name. Behold, I give of the synagogue of Satan, of them which say they are Jews, and they are not, but do lie; behold, I will make them to come and worship before thy feet, and to know that I have loved thee. Because thou didst keep the word of my patience, I also will keep thee from the hour of ²trial, that *hour* which is to come upon the whole ³world, to ⁴try them that dwell upon the earth. I come quickly: hold fast that which thou hast, that no one take thy crown. He that overcometh, I will make him a pillar in the ⁵temple of my God, and he shall go out thence no more: and I will write upon him the name of my God, and the name of the city of my God, the new Jerusalem, which cometh down out of heaven from my God, and mine own new name. He that hath an ear, let him hear what the Spirit saith to the churches.

And to the angel of the church in Laodicea write;
These things saith the Amen, the faithful and true witness, the beginning of the creation of God: I know thy works, that thou art neither cold nor hot: I would thou wert cold or hot. So because thou art lukewarm, and neither hot nor cold, I will spew thee out of my mouth. Because thou sayest, I am rich, and have gotten riches, and have need of nothing; and knowest not that thou art the wretched one and miserable and poor and blind and naked: I counsel thee to buy of me gold refined by fire, that thou mayest become rich; and white garments, that thou mayest clothe thyself, and *that* the shame of thy nakedness be not made manifest; and eyesalve to anoint thine eyes, that thou mayest see. As many as I love, I reprove and chasten: be zealous therefore, and repent. Behold, I stand at the door and knock: if any man hear my voice and open the door, I will come in to him, and will sup with him, and he with me. He that overcometh, I will give to him to sit down with me in my throne, as I also overcame, and sat down with my Father in his throne. He that hath an ear, let him hear what the Spirit saith to the churches.

After these things I saw, and behold, a door opened in heaven, and the first voice which I heard, *a voice* as of a trumpet speaking with me, one saying,

---

1 Gr. *given.*
2 Or, *temptation*
3 Gr. *inhabited earth.*
4 Or, *tempt*
5 Or, *sanctuary:* and so throughout this book.

REVELATION.

Come up hither, and I will shew thee the things 2 which must ¹come to pass hereafter. Straightway I was in the Spirit: and behold, there was a throne 3 set in heaven, and one sitting upon the throne; and he that sat *was* to look upon like a jasper stone and a sardius: and *there was* a rainbow round about the 4 throne, like an emerald to look upon. And round about the throne *were* four and twenty thrones: and upon the thrones *I saw* four and twenty elders sitting, arrayed in white garments; and on their heads 5 crowns of gold. And out of the throne proceed lightnings and voices and thunders. And *there were* seven lamps of fire burning before the throne, which 6 are the seven Spirits of God; and before the throne, as it were a glassy sea like unto crystal; and in the midst of the throne*, and round about the throne, four living creatures full of eyes before and behind. 7 And the first creature *was* like a lion, and the second creature like a calf, and the third creature had a face as of a man, and the fourth creature *was* like 8 a flying eagle. And the four living creatures, having each one of them six wings, are full of eyes round about and within: and they have no rest day and night, saying, Holy, holy, holy, *is* the Lord God, the Almighty, which was and which is and ²which 9 is to come. And when the living creatures shall give glory and honour and thanks to him that sitteth on the throne, to him that liveth ³for ever and 10 ever, the four and twenty elders shall fall down before him that sitteth on the throne, and shall worship him that liveth ³for ever and ever, and shall 11 cast their crowns before the throne, saying, Worthy art thou, our Lord and our God, to receive the glory and the honour and the power: for thou didst create all things, and because of thy will they were, and were created.

5 And I saw ⁴in the right hand of him that sat on the throne a book written within and on the back, 2 close sealed with seven seals. And I saw a strong angel proclaiming with a great voice, Who is worthy to open the book, and to loose the seals thereof? 3 And no one in the heaven, or on the earth, or under the earth, was able to open the book, or to look 4 thereon. And I wept much, because no one was found worthy to open the book, or to look thereon:

1 Or, *come to pass*. *After these things straightway &c.*

2 Or, *which cometh.*

3 Gr. *unto the ages of the ages.*

4 Gr. *on.*

---

* "of the throne" add marg. Or, *before* [comp. v. 6; vii. 17]—*Am. Com.*

and one of the elders saith unto me, Weep not: behold, the Lion that is of the tribe of Judah, the Root of David, hath overcome, to open the book and the seven seals thereof. And I saw in the midst of the throne* and of the four living creatures, and in the midst of the elders, a Lamb standing, as though it had been slain, having seven horns, and seven eyes, which are the ¹seven Spirits of God, sent forth into all the earth. And he came, and he ²taketh *it* out of the right hand of him that sat on the throne. And when he had taken the book, the four living creatures and the four and twenty elders fell down before the Lamb, having each one a harp, and golden bowls full of incense, which are the prayers of the saints. And they sing a new song, saying, Worthy art thou to take the book, and to open the seals thereof: for thou wast slain, and didst purchase unto God with thy blood *men* of every tribe, and tongue, and people, and nation, and madest them *to be* unto our God a kingdom and priests; and they reign upon the earth. And I saw, and I heard a voice of many angels round about the throne and the living creatures and the elders; and the number of them was ten thousand times ten thousand, and thousands of thousands; saying with a great voice, Worthy is the Lamb that hath been slain to receive the power, and riches, and wisdom, and might, and honour, and glory, and blessing. And every created thing which is in the heaven, and on the earth, and under the earth, and on the sea, and all things that are in them, heard I saying, Unto him that sitteth on the throne, and unto the Lamb, *be* the blessing, and the honour, and the glory, and the dominion, ³for ever and ever. And the four living creatures said, Amen. And the elders fell down and worshipped.

And I saw when the Lamb opened one of the seven seals, and I heard one of the four living creatures saying as with a voice of thunder, Come⁴. And I saw, and behold, a white horse, and he that sat thereon had a bow; and there was given unto him a crown: and he came forth conquering, and to conquer.

And when he opened the second seal, I heard the second living creature saying, Come⁴. And another *horse* came forth, a red horse: and to him that sat

---

1 Some ancient authorities omit *seven*.
2 Gr. *hath taken*.
3 Gr. *unto the ages of the ages*.
4 Some ancient authorities add *and see*.

---

* "in the midst of the throne" etc. add marg. Or, *between the throne with the four living creatures, and the elders*—*Am. Com.*

thereon it was given to take ¹peace from the earth, and that they should slay one another: and there was given unto him a great sword.

5 And when he opened the third seal, I heard the third living creature saying, Come². And I saw, and behold, a black horse; and he that sat thereon
6 had a balance in his hand. And I heard as it were a voice in the midst of the four living creatures saying, A ³measure* of wheat for a ⁴penny, and three measures of barley for a ⁴penny; and the oil and the wine hurt thou not.
7 And when he opened the fourth seal, I heard the voice of the fourth living creature saying, Come².
8 And I saw, and behold, a pale horse: and he that sat upon him, his name was Death; and Hades followed with him. And there was given unto them authority over the fourth part of the earth, to kill with sword, and with famine, and with ⁵death, and by the wild beasts of the earth.
9 And when he opened the fifth seal, I saw underneath the altar the souls of them that had been slain for the word of God, and for the testimony which
10 they held: and they cried with a great voice, saying, How long, O Master, the holy and true, dost thou not judge and avenge our blood on them that dwell
11 on the earth? And there was given them to each one a white robe; and it was said unto them, that they should rest yet for a little time, until their fellow-servants also and their brethren, which should be killed even as they were, should ⁶be fulfilled†.
12 And I saw when he opened the sixth seal, and there was a great earthquake; and the sun became black as sackcloth of hair, and the whole moon be-
13 came as blood; and the stars of the heaven fell unto the earth, as a fig tree casteth her unripe figs, when
14 she is shaken of a great wind. And the heaven was removed as a scroll when it is rolled up; and every mountain and island were moved out of their
15 places. And the kings of the earth, and the princes, and the ⁷chief captains, and the rich, and the strong, and every bondman and freeman, hid themselves in
16 the caves and in the rocks of the mountains; and they say to the mountains and to the rocks, Fall on

1 Some ancient authorities read *the peace of the earth*.

2 Some ancient authorities add *and see*.

3 Gr. *chœnix*, a small measure.
4 See marginal note on Matt. xviii. 28.

5 Or, *pestilence*

6 Some ancient authorities read *have fulfilled their course*.

7 Or, *military tribunes*
Gr. *chiliarchs*.

---

* "A measure" etc. add marg. [instead of marg.³ and ⁴] Or, *A chœnix* (i. e. about a quart) *of wheat for a shilling*—implying great scarcity.—*Am. Com.*

† For "be fulfilled" read "be fulfilled *in number*" and then let the marg. and the text exchange places.—*Am. Com.*

us, and hide us from the face of him that sitteth on the throne, and from the wrath of the Lamb: for the great day of their wrath is come; and who is able to stand?

After this I saw four angels standing at the four corners of the earth, holding the four winds of the earth, that no wind should blow on the earth, or on the sea, or upon any tree. And I saw another angel ascend from the sunrising, having the seal of the living God: and he cried with a great voice to the four angels, to whom it was given to hurt the earth and the sea, saying, Hurt not the earth, neither the sea, nor the trees, till we shall have sealed the servants of our God on their foreheads. And I heard the number of them which were sealed, a hundred and forty and four thousand, sealed out of every tribe of the children of Israel.

    Of the tribe of Judah *were* sealed twelve thousand:
    Of the tribe of Reuben twelve thousand:
    Of the tribe of Gad twelve thousand:
    Of the tribe of Asher twelve thousand:
    Of the tribe of Naphtali twelve thousand:
    Of the tribe of Manasseh twelve thousand:
    Of the tribe of Simeon twelve thousand:
    Of the tribe of Levi twelve thousand:
    Of the tribe of Issachar twelve thousand:
    Of the tribe of Zebulun twelve thousand:
    Of the tribe of Joseph twelve thousand:
    Of the tribe of Benjamin *were* sealed twelve thousand.

After these things I saw, and behold, a great multitude, which no man could number, out of every nation, and of *all* tribes and peoples and tongues, standing before the throne and before the Lamb, arrayed in white robes, and palms in their hands; and they cry with a great voice, saying, Salvation unto our God which sitteth on the throne, and unto the Lamb. And all the angels were standing round about the throne, and *about* the elders and the four living creatures; and they fell before the throne on their faces, and worshipped God, saying, Amen: [1]Blessing, and glory, and wisdom, and thanksgiving, and honour, and power, and might, *be* unto our God [2]for ever and ever. Amen. And one of the elders answered, saying unto me, These which are arrayed in the white robes, who are they, and whence came they? And I [3]say unto him, My lord, thou knowest.

---

1 Gr. *The blessing, and the glory, &c.*
2 Gr. *unto the ages of the ages.*
3 Gr. *have said.*

And he said to me, These are they which come out of the great tribulation, and they washed their robes, and made them white in the blood of the
15 Lamb. Therefore are they before the throne of God; and they serve him day and night in his temple: and he that sitteth on the throne shall spread
16 his tabernacle over them. They shall hunger no more, neither thirst any more; neither shall the sun
17 strike upon them, nor any heat: for the Lamb which is in the midst of the throne* shall be their shepherd, and shall guide them unto fountains of waters of life: and God shall wipe away every tear from their eyes.

8 And when he opened the seventh seal, there followed a silence in heaven about the space of half an
2 hour. And I saw the seven angels which stand before God; and there were given unto them seven trumpets.
3 And another angel came and stood ¹over the altar, having a golden censer; and there was given unto him much incense, that he should ²add it unto the prayers of all the saints upon the golden altar
4 which was before the throne. And the smoke of the incense, ³with the prayers of the saints, went up
5 before God out of the angel's hand. And the angel ⁴taketh the censer; and he filled it with the fire of the altar, and cast it ⁵upon the earth: and there followed thunders, and voices, and lightnings, and an earthquake.
6 And the seven angels which had the seven trumpets prepared themselves to sound.
7 And the first sounded, and there followed hail and fire, mingled with blood, and they were cast ⁴upon the earth: and the third part of the earth was burnt up, and the third part of the trees was burnt up, and all green grass was burnt up.
8 And the second angel sounded, and as it were a great mountain burning with fire was cast into the sea: and the third part of the sea became blood;
9 and there died the third part of the creatures which were in the sea, *even* they that had life; and the third part of the ships was destroyed.
10 And the third angel sounded, and there fell from heaven a great star, burning as a torch, and it fell upon the third part of the rivers, and upon the foun-
11 tains of the waters; and the name of the star is called

1 Or, *at*
2 Gr. *give*.
3 Or, *for*
4 Gr. *hath taken*.
5 Or, *into*

---

* "of the throne" add marg. Or, *before* (see iv. 6)—*Am. Com.*

Wormwood: and the third part of the waters became wormwood; and many men died of the waters, because they were made bitter.

12 And the fourth angel sounded, and the third part of the sun was smitten, and the third part of the moon, and the third part of the stars; that the third part of them should be darkened, and the day should not shine for the third part of it, and the night in like manner.

13 And I saw, and I heard ¹an eagle, flying in mid heaven, saying with a great voice, Woe, woe, woe, for them that dwell on the earth, by reason of the other voices of the trumpet of the three angels, who are yet to sound.

9 And the fifth angel sounded, and I saw a star from heaven fallen unto the earth: and there was given to 2 him the key of the pit of the abyss. And he opened the pit of the abyss; and there went up a smoke out of the pit, as the smoke of a great furnace; and the sun and the air were darkened by reason of the 3 smoke of the pit. And out of the smoke came forth locusts upon the earth; and power was given them, 4 as the scorpions of the earth have power. And it was said unto them that they should not hurt the grass of the earth, neither any green thing, neither any tree, but only such men as have not the seal of 5 God on their foreheads. And it was given them that they should not kill them, but that they should be tormented five months: and their torment was as 6 the torment of a scorpion, when it striketh a man. And in those days men shall seek death, and shall in no wise find it; and they shall desire to die, and 7 death fleeth from them. And the ²shapes of the locusts were like unto horses prepared for war; and 8 upon their heads as it were crowns like unto gold, and their faces were as men's faces. And they had 9 hair as the hair of women, and their teeth were as *the teeth* of lions. And they had breastplates, as it were breastplates of iron; and the sound of their wings was as the sound of chariots, of many horses 10 rushing to war. And they have tails like unto scorpions, and stings; and in their tails is their power 11 to hurt men five months. They have over them as king the angel of the abyss: his name in Hebrew is Abaddon, and in the Greek *tongue* he hath the name ³Apollyon.

12 The first Woe is past: behold, there come yet two Woes hereafter.

---

1 Gr. *one eagle.*

2 Gr. *likenesses.*

3 That is, *Destroyer.*

13 And the sixth angel sounded, and I heard ¹a voice from the horns of the golden altar which is before
14 God, one saying to the sixth angel, which had the trumpet, Loose the four angels which are bound at
15 the great river Euphrates. And the four angels were loosed, which had been prepared for the hour and day and month and year, that they should kill
16 the third part of men. And the number of the armies of the horsemen was twice ten thousand times ten
17 thousand: I heard the number of them. And thus I saw the horses in the vision, and them that sat on them, having breastplates *as* of fire and of hyacinth and of brimstone: and the heads of the horses are as the heads of lions; and out of their mouths pro-
18 ceedeth fire and smoke and brimstone. By these three plagues was the third part of men killed, by the fire and the smoke and the brimstone, which
19 proceeded out of their mouths. For the power of the horses is in their mouth, and in their tails: for their tails are like unto serpents, and have heads;
20 and with them they do hurt. And the rest of mankind, which were not killed with these plagues, repented not of the works of their hands, that they should not worship ²devils, and the idols of gold, and of silver, and of brass, and of stone, and of wood; which can neither see, nor hear, nor walk:
21 and they repented not of their murders, nor of their sorceries, nor of their fornication, nor of their thefts.

10 And I saw another strong angel coming down out of heaven, arrayed with a cloud; and the rainbow was upon his head, and his face was as the sun, and
2 his feet as pillars of fire; and he had in his hand a little book open: and he set his right foot upon the
3 sea, and his left upon the earth; and he cried with a great voice, as a lion roareth: and when he cried,
4 the seven thunders uttered their voices. And when the seven thunders uttered *their voices*, I was about to write: and I heard a voice from heaven saying, Seal up the things which the seven thunders uttered,
5 and write them not. And the angel which I saw standing upon the sea and upon the earth lifted up
6 his right hand to heaven, and sware by him that liveth ³for ever and ever, who created the heaven and the things that are therein, and the earth and the things that are therein, ⁴and the sea and the things that are therein, that there shall be ⁵time* no

¹ Gr. *one voice.*

² Gr. *demons.*

³ Gr. *unto the ages of the ages.*

⁴ Some ancient authorities omit *and the sea and the things that are therein.*

⁵ Or, *delay*

---

* Substitute marg. ⁵ ("*delay*") for the text.—*Am. Com.*

longer: but in the days of the voice of the seventh 7 angel, when he is about to sound, then is finished the mystery of God, according to the good tidings which he declared to his servants the prophets. And the voice which I heard from heaven, *I heard* 8 *it* again speaking with me, and saying, Go, take the book which is open in the hand of the angel that standeth upon the sea and upon the earth. And I went unto the angel, saying unto him that 9 he should give me the little book. And he saith unto me, Take it, and eat it up; and it shall make thy belly bitter, but in thy mouth it shall be sweet as honey. And I took the little book out of the an- 10 gel's hand, and ate it up; and it was in my mouth sweet as honey: and when I had eaten it, my belly was made bitter. And they say unto me, Thou 11 must prophesy again ¹over many peoples and nations and tongues and kings.

And there was given me a reed like unto a rod: **11** ²and one said, Rise, and measure the temple of God, and the altar, and them that worship therein. And 2 the court which is without the temple ³leave without, and measure it not; for it hath been given unto the nations: and the holy city shall they tread under foot forty and two months. And I will give unto 3 my two witnesses, and they shall prophesy a thousand two hundred and threescore days, clothed in sackcloth. These are the two olive trees and the 4 two ⁴candlesticks, standing before the Lord of the earth. And if any man desireth to hurt them, fire 5 proceedeth out of their mouth, and devoureth their enemies: and if any man shall desire to hurt them, in this manner must he be killed. These have the 6 power to shut the heaven, that it rain not during the days of their prophecy: and they have power over the waters to turn them into blood, and to smite the earth with every plague, as often as they shall desire. And when they shall have finished 7 their testimony, the beast that cometh up out of the abyss shall make war with them, and overcome them, and kill them. And their ⁵dead bodies *lie* in 8 the street of the great city, which spiritually is called Sodom and Egypt, where also their Lord was crucified. And from among the peoples and tribes and 9 tongues and nations do *men* look upon their ⁵dead bodies three days and a half, and suffer not their dead bodies to be laid in a tomb. And they that 10 dwell on the earth rejoice over them, and make

---

1 Or, *concerning*

2 Gr. *saying.*

3 Gr. *cast without.*

4 Gr. *lampstands.*

5 Gr. *carcase.*

merry; and they shall send gifts one to another; because these two prophets tormented them that dwell
11 on the earth. And after the three days and a half the breath of life from God entered into them, and they stood upon their feet; and great fear fell upon
12 them which beheld them. And they heard a great voice from heaven saying unto them, Come up hither. And they went up into heaven in the cloud;
13 and their enemies beheld them. And in that hour there was a great earthquake, and the tenth part of the city fell; and there were killed in the earthquake ¹seven thousand persons: and the rest were affrighted, and gave glory to the God of heaven.

¹ Gr. *names of men, seven thousand.*

14 The second Woe is past: behold, the third Woe cometh quickly.
15 And the seventh angel sounded; and there followed great voices in heaven, and they said, The kingdom of the world is become *the kingdom* of our Lord, and of his Christ: and he shall reign ²for ever
16 and ever. And the four and twenty elders, which sit before God on their thrones, fell upon their faces,
17 and worshipped God, saying, We give thee thanks, O Lord God, the Almighty, which art and which wast; because thou hast taken thy great power, and
18 didst reign. And the nations were wroth, and thy wrath came, and the time of the dead to be judged, and *the time* to give their reward to thy servants the prophets, and to the saints, and to them that fear thy name, the small and the great; and to destroy them that destroy the earth.
19 And there was opened the temple of God that is in heaven; and there was seen in his temple the ark of his ³covenant; and there followed lightnings, and voices, and thunders, and an earthquake, and great hail.

² Gr. *unto the ages of the ages.*

³ Or, *testament.*

12 And a great sign was seen in heaven; a woman arrayed with the sun, and the moon under her feet,
2 and upon her head a crown of twelve stars; and she was with child: and she crieth out, travailing in
3 birth, and in pain to be delivered. And there was seen another sign in heaven; and behold, a great red dragon, having seven heads and ten horns, and
4 upon his heads seven diadems. And his tail draweth the third part of the stars of heaven, and did cast them to the earth: and the dragon stood before the woman which was about to be delivered, that when she was delivered, he might* devour her child.

---

* For "stood ... was ... was ... might" read "standeth ... is ... is ... may"—*Am. Com.*

And she was delivered of a son, a man child, who 5
is to rule all the nations with a rod of iron: and her
child was caught up unto God, and unto his throne.
And the woman fled into the wilderness, where she 6
hath a place prepared of God, that there they may
nourish her a thousand two hundred and threescore
days.

And there was war in heaven: Michael and his 7
angels *going forth* to war with the dragon; and the
dragon warred and his angels; and they prevailed 8
not, neither was their place found any more in
heaven. And the great dragon was cast down, the 9
old serpent, he that is called the Devil and Satan,
the deceiver of the whole [1]world; he was cast down
to the earth, and his angels were cast down with
him. And I heard a great voice in heaven, saying, 10
[2]Now is come the salvation, and the power, and the
kingdom of our God, and the authority of his Christ:
for the accuser of our brethren is cast down, which
accuseth them before our God day and night. And 11
they overcame him because of the blood of the
Lamb, and because of the word of their testimony;
and they loved not their life even unto death.
Therefore rejoice, O heavens, and ye that [3]dwell in 12
them. Woe for the earth and for the sea: because
the devil is gone down unto you, having great
wrath, knowing that he hath but a short time.

And when the dragon saw that he was cast down 13
to the earth, he persecuted the woman which
brought forth the man *child*. And there were giv- 14
en to the woman the two wings of the great eagle,
that she might fly into the wilderness unto her
place, where she is nourished for a time, and times,
and half a time, from the face of the serpent. And 15
the serpent cast out of his mouth after the woman
water as a river, that he might cause her to be carried away by the stream. And the earth helped 16
the woman, and the earth opened her mouth, and
swallowed up the river which the dragon cast out
of his mouth. And the dragon waxed wroth with 17
the woman, and went away to make war with the
rest of her seed, which keep the commandments of
God, and hold the testimony of Jesus: and he **13**
stood* upon the sand of the sea.

And I saw a beast coming up out of the sea, hav-

---

1 Gr. *inhabited earth.*
2 Or, *Now is the salvation, and the power, and the kingdom, become our God's, and the authority is become his Christ's*
3 Gr. *tabernacle.*

* "he stood" add marg. Some ancient authorities read *I stood* etc., connecting the clause with what follows.—*Am. Com.*

ing ten horns and seven heads, and on his horns ten diadems, and upon his heads names of blasphemy. 2 And the beast which I saw was like unto a leopard, and his feet were as *the feet* of a bear, and his mouth as the mouth of a lion: and the dragon gave him his 3 power, and his throne, and great authority. And *I saw* one of his heads as though it had been ¹smitten unto death; and his death-stroke was healed: and 4 the whole earth wondered after the beast; and they worshipped the dragon, because he gave his authority unto the beast; and they worshipped the beast, saying, Who is like unto the beast? and who is able 5 to war with him? and there was given to him a mouth speaking great things and blasphemies; and there was given to him authority ²to continue forty 6 and two months. And he opened his mouth for blasphemies against God, to blaspheme his name, and his tabernacle, *even* them that ³dwell in the 7 heaven. ⁴And it was given unto him to make war with the saints, and to overcome them: and there was given to him authority over every tribe and 8 people and tongue and nation. And all that dwell on the earth shall worship him, *every one* whose name hath not been ⁵written in the book of life of the Lamb that hath been slain from the foundation 9 of the world. If any man hath an ear, let him hear. 10 ⁶If any man ⁷*is* for captivity, into captivity he goeth: if any man shall kill with the sword, with the sword must he be killed. Here is the patience and the faith of the saints.

11 And I saw another beast coming up out of the earth; and he had two horns like unto a lamb, and 12 he spake as a dragon. And he exerciseth all the authority of the first beast in his sight. And he maketh the earth and them that dwell therein to worship the first beast, whose death-stroke was 13 healed. And he doeth great signs, that he should even make fire to come down out of heaven upon 14 the earth in the sight of men. And he deceiveth them that dwell on the earth by reason of the signs which it was given him to do in the sight of the beast; saying to them that dwell on the earth, that they should make an image to the beast, who hath 15 the stroke of the sword, and lived. And it was given *unto him* to give breath to it, *even* to the image

1 Gr. *slain*.

2 Or, *to do his works during* See Dan. xi. 28.

3 Gr. *tabernacle*.

4 Some ancient authorities omit *And it was given . . . overcome them*.

5 Or, *written from the foundation of the world in the book . . . slain**

6 The Greek text in this verse is somewhat uncertain.

7 Or, leadeth *into captivity*

---

* Let marg. ⁵ and the text exchange places. [Comp. xvii. 8.]—Am. Com.

of the beast, ¹that the image of the beast should both
speak, and cause that as many as should not worship
the image of the beast should be killed. And he 16
causeth all, the small and the great, and the rich and
the poor, and the free and the bond, that there be
given them a mark on their right hand, or upon their
forehead; and that no man should be able to buy or 17
to sell, save he that hath the mark, *even* the name of
the beast or the number of his name. Here is wis- 18
dom. He that hath understanding, let him count
the number of the beast; for it is the number of a
man: and his number is ²Six hundred and sixty and
six.

And I saw, and behold, the Lamb standing on the **14**
mount Zion, and with him a hundred and forty and
four thousand, having his name, and the name of
his Father, written on their foreheads. And I heard 2
a voice from heaven, as the voice of many waters,
and as the voice of a great thunder: and the voice
which I heard *was* as *the voice* of harpers harping
with their harps: and they sing as it were a new 3
song before the throne, and before the four living
creatures and the elders: and no man could learn
the song save the hundred and forty and four
thousand, *even* they that had been purchased out of
the earth. These are they which were not defiled 4
with women; for they are virgins. These *are* they
which follow the Lamb whithersoever he goeth.
These were purchased from among men, *to be* the
firstfruits unto God and unto the Lamb. And in 5
their mouth was found no lie: they are without
blemish.

And I saw another angel flying in mid heaven, 6
having an eternal gospel* to proclaim unto them that
³dwell on the earth, and unto every nation and tribe
and tongue and people; and he saith with a great 7
voice, Fear God, and give him glory; for the hour
of his judgement is come: and worship him that
made the heaven and the earth and sea and fountains of waters.

And another, a second angel, followed, saying, 8
Fallen, fallen is Babylon the great, which hath made
all the nations to drink of the wine of the wrath of
her fornication.

And another angel, a third, followed them, saying 9
with a great voice, If any man worshippeth the beast

---

* For "an eternal gospel" read "eternal good tidings."—*Am. Com.*

and his image, and receiveth a mark on his forehead,
10 or upon his hand, he also shall drink of the wine of the wrath of God, which is ¹prepared unmixed in the cup of his anger; and he shall be tormented with fire and brimstone in the presence of the holy angels,
11 and in the presence of the Lamb: and the smoke of their torment goeth up ²for ever and ever; and they have no rest day and night, they that worship the beast and his image, and whoso receiveth the mark
12 of his name. Here is the patience of the saints, they that keep the commandments of God, and the faith of Jesus.
13 And I heard a voice from heaven saying, Write, Blessed are the dead which die ³in the Lord from henceforth: yea, saith the Spirit, that they may rest from their labours; for their works follow with them.
14 And I saw, and behold, a white cloud; and on the cloud *I saw* one sitting like unto ⁴a son of man, having on his head a golden crown, and in his hand
15 a sharp sickle. And another angel came out from the temple, crying with a great voice to him that sat on the cloud, Send forth thy sickle, and reap: for the hour to reap is come; for the harvest of the
16 earth is ⁵over-ripe*. And he that sat on the cloud cast his sickle upon the earth; and the earth was reaped.
17 And another angel came out from the temple which is in heaven, he also having a sharp sickle.
18 And another angel came out from the altar, he that hath power over fire; and he called with a great voice to him that had the sharp sickle, saying, Send forth thy sharp sickle, and gather the clusters of the vine of the earth; for her grapes are fully ripe.
19 And the angel cast his sickle into the earth, and gathered the ⁶vintage of the earth, and cast it into the winepress, the great *winepress*, of the wrath of
20 God. And the winepress was trodden without the city, and there came out blood from the winepress, even unto the bridles of the horses, as far as a thousand and six hundred furlongs.

15 And I saw another sign in heaven, great and marvellous, seven angels having seven plagues, *which are* the last, for in them is finished the wrath of God.

1 Gr. *mingled*.

2 Gr. *unto ages of ages*.

3 Or, *in the Lord. From henceforth, yea, saith the Spirit*

4 Or, *the Son*

5 Gr. *dried up*.

6 Gr. *vine*.

---

* For "over-ripe" read "ripe" with marg. Gr. *become dry.*—*Am. Com.*

And I saw as it were a glassy sea mingled with fire; and them that come* victorious from the beast, and from his image, and from the number of his name, standing ¹by the glassy sea, having harps of God. And they sing the song of Moses the servant of God, and the song of the Lamb, saying, Great and marvellous are thy works, O Lord God, the Almighty; righteous and true are thy ways, thou King of the ²ages. Who shall not fear, O Lord, and glorify thy name? for thou only art holy; for all the nations shall come and worship before thee; for thy righteous acts have been made manifest.

And after these things I saw, and the temple of the tabernacle of the testimony in heaven was opened: and there came out from the temple the seven angels that had the seven plagues, arrayed ³with *precious* stone, pure *and* bright, and girt about their breasts with golden girdles. And one of the four living creatures gave unto the seven angels seven golden bowls full of the wrath of God, who liveth ⁴for ever and ever. And the temple was filled with smoke from the glory of God, and from his power; and none was able to enter into the temple, till the seven plagues of the seven angels should be finished.

And I heard a great voice out of the temple, saying to the seven angels, Go ye, and pour out the seven bowls of the wrath of God into the earth.

And the first went, and poured out his bowl into the earth; and ⁵it became a noisome and grievous sore upon the men which had the mark of the beast, and which worshipped his image.

And the second poured out his bowl into the sea; and ⁵it became blood as of a dead man; and every ⁶living soul died, *even* the things that were in the sea.

And the third poured out his bowl into the rivers and the fountains of the waters; ⁷and ⁵it became blood. And I heard the angel of the waters saying, Righteous art thou, which art and which wast, thou Holy One, because thou didst thus ⁸judge: for they poured out the blood of saints and prophets, and blood hast thou given them to drink: they are worthy. And I heard the altar saying, Yea, O Lord God, the Almighty, true and righteous are thy judgements.

---

1 Or, *upon*
2 Many ancient authorities read *nations*.
3 Many ancient authorities read *in linen*.
4 Gr. *unto the ages of the ages.*
5 Or, *there came*
6 Gr. *soul of life.*
7 Some ancient authorities read *and they became*.
8 Or, *judge. Because they ... prophets, thou hast given them blood also to drink*

* For "that come" read "that come off"—*Am. Com.*

8 And the fourth poured out his bowl upon the sun; and it was given unto ¹it to scorch men with fire. ⁹ And men were scorched with great heat: and they blasphemed the name of the God* which hath the power over these plagues; and they repented not to give him glory. ¹⁰ And the fifth poured out his bowl upon the throne of the beast; and his kingdom was darkened; ¹¹ and they gnawed their tongues for pain, and they blasphemed the God of heaven because of their pains and their sores; and they repented not of their works. ¹² And the sixth poured out his bowl upon the great river, the *river* Euphrates; and the water thereof was dried up, that the way might be made ready ¹³ for the kings that *come* from the sunrising. And I saw *coming* out of the mouth of the dragon, and out of the mouth of the beast, and out of the mouth of the false prophet, three unclean spirits, as it were ¹⁴ frogs: for they are spirits of ²devils, working signs; which go forth ³unto the kings of the whole ⁴world, to gather them together unto the war of the great ¹⁵ day of God, the Almighty. (Behold, I come as a thief. Blessed is he that watcheth, and keepeth his garments, lest he walk naked, and they see his ¹⁶ shame.) And they gathered them together into the place which is called in Hebrew Har-Magedon†. ¹⁷ And the seventh poured out his bowl upon the air; and there came forth a great voice out of the ¹⁸ temple, from the throne, saying, It is done: and there were lightnings, and voices, and thunders; and there was a great earthquake, such as was not since ⁵there were men upon the earth, so great an earth¹⁹ quake, so mighty. And the great city was divided into three parts, and the cities of the nations fell: and Babylon the great was remembered in the sight of God, to give unto her the cup of the wine of the ²⁰ fierceness of his wrath. And every island fled ²¹ away, and the mountains were not found. And great hail, *every stone* about the weight of a talent, cometh down out of heaven upon men: and men blasphemed God because of the plague of the hail; for the plague thereof is exceeding great.

17 And there came one of the seven angels that had the seven bowls, and spake with me, saying, Come

---

¹ Or, *him*
² Gr. *demons.*
³ Or, *upon*
⁴ Gr. *inhabited earth.*
⁵ Some ancient authorities read *there was a man.*

---

* For "the God" read "God"—*Am. Com.*
† "Har-Magedon" add marg. Or, *Ar-Magedon*—*Am. Com.*

hither, I will shew thee the judgement of the great harlot that sitteth upon many waters; with whom the kings of the earth committed fornication, and they that dwell in the earth were made drunken with the wine of her fornication. And he carried me away in the Spirit into a wilderness: and I saw a woman sitting upon a scarlet-coloured beast, [1]full of names of blasphemy, having seven heads and ten horns. And the woman was arrayed in purple and scarlet, and [2]decked with gold and precious stone and pearls, having in her hand a golden cup full of abominations, [3]even the unclean things of her fornication, and upon her forehead a name written, [4]MYSTERY, BABYLON THE GREAT, THE MOTHER OF THE HARLOTS AND OF THE ABOMINATIONS OF THE EARTH. And I saw the woman drunken with the blood of the saints, and with the blood of the [5]martyrs of Jesus. And when I saw her, I wondered with a great wonder. And the angel said unto me, Wherefore didst thou wonder? I will tell thee the mystery of the woman, and of the beast that carrieth her, which hath the seven heads and the ten horns. The beast that thou sawest was, and is not; and is about to come up out of the abyss, [6]and to go into perdition. And they that dwell on the earth shall wonder, *they* whose name hath not been written [7]in the book of life from the foundation of the world, when they behold the beast, how that he was, and is not, and [8]shall come. Here is the [9]mind which hath wisdom. The seven heads are seven mountains, on which the woman sitteth: and [10]they are seven kings; the five are fallen, the one is, the other is not yet come; and when he cometh, he must continue a little while. And the beast that was, and is not, is himself also an eighth, and is of the seven; and he goeth into perdition. And the ten horns that thou sawest are ten kings, which have received no kingdom as yet; but they receive authority as kings, with the beast, for one hour. These have one mind, and they give their power and authority unto the beast. These shall war against the Lamb, and the Lamb shall overcome them, for he is Lord of lords, and King of kings; and they *also shall overcome* that are with him, called and chosen and faithful. And he saith unto me, The waters which thou sawest, where the harlot sitteth, are peoples, and multitudes, and nations, and tongues. And the ten horns which thou sawest, and the beast, these shall hate the har-

---

[1] Or, *names full of blasphemy*
[2] Gr. *gilded*.
[3] Or, *and of the unclean things*
[4] Or, *a mystery*, BABYLON THE GREAT
[5] Or, *witnesses*
[6] Some ancient authorities read *and he goeth*.
[7] Gr. *on*.
[8] Gr. *shall be present*.
[9] Or, *meaning*
[10] Or, *there are*

lot, and shall make her desolate and naked, and shall eat her flesh, and shall burn her utterly with 17 fire. For God did put in their hearts to do his mind, and to come to one mind, and to give their kingdom unto the beast, until the words of God 18 should be accomplished. And the woman whom thou sawest is the great city, which ¹reigneth over the kings of the earth.

¹ Gr. *hath a kingdom.*

18 After these things I saw another angel coming down out of heaven, having great authority; and 2 the earth was lightened with his glory. And he cried with a mighty voice, saying, Fallen, fallen is Babylon the great, and is become a habitation of ²devils, and a ³hold of every unclean spirit, and a 3 ³hold of every unclean and hateful bird. For ⁴by ⁵the wine of the wrath of her fornication all the nations are fallen; and the kings of the earth committed fornication with her, and the merchants of the earth waxed rich by the power of her ⁶wantonness.

² Gr. *demons.*
³ Or, *prison*
⁴ Some authorities read *of the wine ... have drunk.*
⁵ Some ancient authorities omit *the wine of.*
⁶ Or, *luxury*

4 And I heard another voice from heaven, saying, Come forth, my people, out of her, that ye have no fellowship with her sins, and that ye receive not of 5 her plagues: for her sins ⁷have reached even unto heaven, and God hath remembered her iniquities. 6 Render unto her even as she rendered, and double *unto her* the double according to her works: in the cup which she mingled, mingle unto her double. 7 How much soever she glorified herself, and waxed ⁸wanton, so much give her of torment and mourning: for she saith in her heart, I sit a queen, and am no widow, and shall in no wise see mourning. 8 Therefore in one day shall her plagues come, death, and mourning, and famine; and she shall be utterly burned with fire; for strong is ⁹the Lord God which 9 judged her. And the kings of the earth, who committed fornication and lived ¹⁰wantonly with her, shall weep and wail over her, when they look upon 10 the smoke of her burning, standing afar off for the fear of her torment, saying, Woe, woe, the great city, Babylon, the strong city! for in one hour is thy 11 judgement come. And the merchants of the earth weep and mourn over her, for no man buyeth their 12 ¹¹merchandise any more; ¹¹merchandise of gold, and silver, and precious stone, and pearls, and fine linen, and purple, and silk, and scarlet; and all thyine wood, and every vessel of ivory, and every vessel made of most precious wood, and of brass, and iron,

⁷ Or, *clave together*
⁸ Or, *luxurious*
⁹ Some ancient authorities omit *the Lord.*
¹⁰ Or, *luxuriously*
¹¹ Gr. *cargo.*

and marble; and cinnamon, and ¹spice, and incense, 13 and ointment, and frankincense, and wine, and oil, and fine flour, and wheat, and cattle, and sheep; and *merchandise* of horses and chariots and ²slaves; and ³souls of men. And the fruits which thy soul lust- 14 ed after are gone from thee, and all things that were dainty and sumptuous are perished from thee, and *men* shall find them no more at all. The merchants 15 of these things, who were made rich by her, shall stand afar off for the fear of her torment, weeping and mourning; saying, Woe, woe, the great city, she 16 that was arrayed in fine linen and purple and scarlet, and ⁴decked with gold and precious stone and pearl! for in one hour so great riches is made desolate. 17 And every shipmaster, and every one that saileth any whither, and mariners, and as many as ⁵gain their living by sea, stood afar off, and cried out as 18 they looked upon the smoke of her burning, saying, What *city* is like the great city? And they cast dust 19 on their heads, and cried, weeping and mourning, saying, Woe, woe, the great city, wherein were made rich all that had their ships in the sea by reason of her costliness! for in one hour is she made desolate. Rejoice over her, thou heaven, and ye saints, and ye 20 apostles, and ye prophets; for God hath judged your judgement on her.

And ⁶a strong angel took up a stone as it were a 21 great millstone, and cast it into the sea, saying, Thus with a mighty fall shall Babylon, the great city, be cast down, and shall be found no more at all. And 22 the voice of harpers and minstrels and flute-players and trumpeters shall be heard no more at all in thee; and no craftsman, ⁷of whatsoever craft, shall be found any more at all in thee; and the voice of a millstone shall be heard no more at all in thee; and 23 the light of a lamp shall shine no more at all in thee; and the voice of the bridegroom and of the bride shall be heard no more at all in thee: for thy merchants were the princes of the earth; for with thy sorcery were all the nations deceived. And in 24 her was found the blood of prophets and of saints, and of all that have been slain upon the earth.

After these things I heard as it were a great voice **19** of a great multitude in heaven, saying, Hallelujah; Salvation, and glory, and power, belong to our God: for true and righteous are his judgements; for he 2 hath judged the great harlot, which did corrupt the earth with her fornication, and he hath avenged the

---

1 Gr. *amomum*.
2 Gr. *bodies*.
3 Or, *lives*
4 Gr. *gilded*.
5 Gr. *work the sea*.
6 Gr. *one*.
7 Some ancient authorities omit *of whatsoever craft*.

3 blood of his servants at her hand. And a second
time they ¹say, Hallelujah. And her smoke goeth
4 up ²for ever and ever. And the four and twenty
elders and the four living creatures fell down and
worshipped God that sitteth on the throne, saying,
5 Amen; Hallelujah. And a voice came forth from
the throne, saying, Give praise to our God, all ye his
servants, ye that fear him, the small and the great.
6 And I heard as it were the voice of a great multitude, and as the voice of many waters, and as the
voice of mighty thunders, saying, Hallelujah: for
7 the Lord our God, the Almighty, reigneth. Let us
rejoice and be exceeding glad, and let us give the
glory unto him: for the marriage of the Lamb is
8 come, and his wife hath made herself ready. And
it was given unto her that she should array herself
in fine linen, bright *and* pure: for the fine linen is
9 the righteous acts of the saints. And he saith unto
me, Write, Blessed are they which are bidden to the
marriage supper of the Lamb. And he saith unto
10 me, These are true words of God. And I fell down
before his feet to worship him. And he saith unto
me, See thou do it not: I am a fellow-servant with
thee and with thy brethren that hold the testimony
of Jesus: worship God: for the testimony of Jesus
is the spirit of prophecy.

11 And I saw the heaven opened; and behold, a white
horse, and he that sat thereon, ³called Faithful and
True; and in righteousness he doth judge and make
12 war. And his eyes *are* a flame of fire, and upon his
head *are* many diadems; and he hath a name writ-
13 ten, which no one knoweth but he himself. And he
is arrayed in a garment ⁴sprinkled with blood: and
14 his name is called The Word of God. And the armies which are in heaven followed him upon white
15 horses, clothed in fine linen, white *and* pure. And
out of his mouth proceedeth a sharp sword, that
with it he should smite the nations: and he shall
rule them with a rod of iron: and he treadeth the
⁵winepress of the fierceness of the wrath of Almighty
16 God*. And he hath on his garment and on his thigh
a name written, KING OF KINGS, AND LORD OF LORDS.
17 And I saw ⁶an angel standing in the sun; and he
cried with a loud voice, saying to all the birds that
fly in mid heaven, Come *and* be gathered together

1 Gr. *have said.*
2 Gr. *unto the ages of the ages.*
3 Some ancient authorities omit *called.*
4 Some ancient authorities read *dipped in.*
5 Gr. *winepress of the wine of the fierceness.*
6 Gr. *one.*

---

* For "of Almighty God" read "of God, the Almighty"—*Am. Com.*

unto the great supper of God; that ye may eat the flesh of kings, and the flesh of ¹captains, and the flesh of mighty men, and the flesh of horses and of them that sit thereon, and the flesh of all men, both free and bond, and small and great.

And I saw the beast, and the kings of the earth, and their armies, gathered together to make war against him that sat upon the horse, and against his army. And the beast was taken, and with him the false prophet that wrought the signs in his sight, wherewith he deceived them that had received the mark of the beast, and them that worshipped his image: they twain were cast alive into the lake of fire that burneth with brimstone: and the rest were killed with the sword of him that sat upon the horse, *even the sword* which came forth out of his mouth: and all the birds were filled with their flesh.

And I saw an angel coming down out of heaven, having the key of the abyss and a great chain ²in his hand. And he laid hold on the dragon, the old serpent, which is the Devil and Satan, and bound him for a thousand years, and cast him into the abyss, and shut *it*, and sealed *it* over him, that he should deceive the nations no more, until the thousand years should be finished: after this he must be loosed for a little time.

And I saw thrones, and they sat upon them, and judgement was given unto them: and *I saw* the souls of them that had been beheaded for the testimony of Jesus, and for the word of God, and such as worshipped not the beast, neither his image, and received not the mark upon their forehead and upon their hand; and they lived, and reigned with Christ a thousand years. The rest of the dead lived not until the thousand years should be finished. This is the first resurrection. Blessed and holy is he that hath part in the first resurrection: over these the second death hath no ³power; but they shall be priests of God and of Christ, and shall reign with him ⁴a thousand years.

And when the thousand years are finished, Satan shall be loosed out of his prison, and shall come forth to deceive the nations which are in the four corners of the earth, Gog and Magog, to gather them together to the war: the number of whom is as the sand of the sea. And they went up over the breadth of the earth, and compassed the camp of the saints about, and the beloved city: and fire came down⁵

---

1 Or, *military tribunes* Gr. *chiliarchs.*

2 Gr. *upon.*

3 Or, *authority.*

4 Some ancient authorities read *the.*

5 Some ancient authorities insert *from God.*

10 out of heaven, and devoured them. And the devil that deceived them was cast into the lake of fire and brimstone, where are also the beast and the false prophet; and they shall be tormented day and night ¹for ever and ever.

¹ Gr. *unto the ages of the ages.*

11 And I saw a great white throne, and him that sat upon it, from whose face the earth and the heaven fled away; and there was found no place for them.
12 And I saw the dead, the great and the small, standing before the throne; and books were opened: and another book was opened, which is *the book* of life: and the dead were judged out of the things which were written in the books, according to their works.
13 And the sea gave up the dead which were in it; and death and Hades gave up the dead which were in them: and they were judged every man according
14 to their works. And death and Hades were cast into the lake of fire. This is the second death, *even*
15 the lake of fire. And if any was not found written in the book of life, he was cast into the lake of fire.

21 And I saw a new heaven and a new earth: for the first heaven and the first earth are passed away;
2 and the sea is no more. And I saw ²the holy city, new Jerusalem, coming down out of heaven from God, made ready as a bride adorned for her hus-
3 band. And I heard a great voice out of the throne saying, Behold, the tabernacle of God is with men, and he shall ³dwell with them, and they shall be his peoples, and God himself shall be with them, ⁴*and be*
4 their God: and he shall wipe away every tear from their eyes; and death shall be no more; neither shall there be mourning, nor crying, nor pain, any more:
5 the first things are passed away. And he that sitteth on the throne said, Behold, I make all things new. And he saith, ⁵Write: for these words are
6 faithful and true. And he said unto me, They are come to pass. I am the Alpha and the Omega, the beginning and the end. I will give unto him that is athirst of the fountain of the water of life freely.
7 He that overcometh shall inherit these things; and
8 I will be his God, and he shall be my son. But for the fearful, and unbelieving, and abominable, and murderers, and fornicators, and sorcerers, and idolaters, and all liars, their part *shall be* in the lake that burneth with fire and brimstone; which is the second death.
9 And there came one of the seven angels who had

² Or, *the holy city Jerusalem coming down new out of heaven*

³ Gr. *tabernacle.*

⁴ Some ancient authorities omit, and be *their God.*

⁵ Or, *Write, These words are faithful and true.*

the seven bowls, who were laden with the seven last plagues; and he spake with me, saying, Come hither, I will shew thee the bride, the wife of the Lamb. 10 And he carried me away in the Spirit to a mountain great and high, and shewed me the holy city Jerusalem, coming down out of heaven from God, having 11 the glory of God: her ¹light was like unto a stone most precious, as it were a jasper stone, clear as crystal: having a wall great and high; having twelve 12 ²gates, and at the ²gates twelve angels; and names written thereon, which are *the names* of the twelve tribes of the children of Israel: on the east were 13 three ²gates; and on the north three ²gates; and on the south three ²gates; and on the west three ²gates. And the wall of the city had twelve foundations, 14 and on them twelve names of the twelve apostles of the Lamb. And he that spake with me had for a 15 measure a golden reed to measure the city, and the ²gates thereof, and the wall thereof. And the city 16 lieth foursquare, and the length thereof is as great as the breadth: and he measured the city with the reed, twelve thousand furlongs: the length and the breadth and the height thereof are equal. And 17 he measured the wall thereof, a hundred and forty and four cubits, *according to* the measure of a man, that is, of an angel. And the building of the wall 18 thereof was jasper: and the city was pure gold, like unto pure glass. The foundations of the wall of 19 the city were adorned with all manner of precious stones. The first foundation was jasper; the second, ³sapphire; the third, chalcedony; the fourth, emerald; the fifth, sardonyx; the sixth, sardius; the seventh, 20 chrysolite; the eighth, beryl; the ninth, topaz; the tenth, chrysoprase; the eleventh, ⁴jacinth; the twelfth, amethyst. And the twelve ²gates were 21 twelve pearls; each one of the several ²gates was of one pearl: and the street of the city was pure gold, ⁵as it were transparent glass. And I saw no temple 22 therein: for the Lord God the Almighty, and the Lamb, are the temple thereof. And the city hath 23 no need of the sun, neither of the moon, to shine upon it: for the glory of God did lighten it, ⁶and the lamp thereof *is* the Lamb. And the nations shall 24 walk ⁷amidst the light thereof: and the kings of the earth do bring their glory into it. And the ²gates 25 thereof shall in no wise be shut by day (for there shall be no night there): and they shall bring the 26 glory and the honour of the nations into it: and 27

---

1 Gr. *luminary.*

2 Gr. *portals.*

3 Or, *lapis lazuli*

4 Or, *sapphire*

5 Or, *transparent as glass.*

6 Or, *and the Lamb, the lamp thereof.*

7 Or, *by*

there shall in no wise enter into it any thing ¹un- [1 Gr. *common.*]
clean, or he that ²maketh an abomination and a lie: [2 Or, *doeth*]
but only they which are written in the Lamb's book
22 of life. And he shewed me a river of water of life, [3 Or, *the Lamb. In the midst of the street thereof, and on either side of the river, was the tree of life.*]
bright as crystal, proceeding out of the throne of
2 God and of ³the Lamb, in the midst of the street
thereof. And on this side of the river and on that
was ⁴the tree of life, bearing twelve ⁵*manner of* [4 Or, *a tree*]
fruits, yielding its fruit every month: and the leaves [5 Or, *crops of fruit*]
3 of the tree were for the healing of the nations. And
there shall be ⁶no curse any more: and the throne [6 Or, *no more any thing accursed*]
of God and of the Lamb shall be therein: and his
4 servants shall do him service*; and they shall see his
5 face; and his name *shall be* on their foreheads. And
there shall be night no more; and they need no light
of lamp, neither light of sun; for the Lord God shall
give them light: and they shall reign ⁷for ever and [7 Gr. *unto the ages of the ages.*]
ever.
6 And he said unto me, These words are faithful
and true: and the Lord, the God of the spirits of the
prophets, sent his angel to shew unto his servants
7 the things which must shortly come to pass. And
behold, I come quickly. Blessed is he that keepeth
the words of the prophecy of this book.
8 And I John am he that heard and saw these things.
And when I heard and saw, I fell down to worship
before the feet of the angel which shewed me these
9 things. And he saith unto me, See thou do it not:
I am a fellow-servant with thee and with thy brethren the prophets, and with them which keep the
words of this book: worship God.
10 And he saith unto me, Seal not up the words of
the prophecy of this book; for the time is at hand.
11 He that is unrighteous, let him do unrighteousness
⁸still: and he that is filthy, let him be made filthy [8 Or, *yet more*]
⁸still: and he that is righteous, let him do righteousness ⁸still: and he that is holy, let him be made holy
12 ⁸still. Behold, I come quickly; and my ⁹reward is [9 Or, *wages*]
with me, to render to each man according as his work
13 is. I am the Alpha and the Omega, the first and the
14 last, the beginning and the end. Blessed are they that [10 Or, *the authority over*]
wash their robes, that they may have ¹⁰the right *to
come* to the tree of life, and may enter in by the
15 ¹¹gates into the city. Without are the dogs, and the [11 Gr. *portals.*]
sorcerers, and the fornicators, and the murderers,
and the idolaters, and every one that loveth and
¹²maketh a lie. Or, *doeth*

---

* For "do him service" read "serve him"—*Am. Com.*

1 Gr. *over*.	I Jesus have sent mine angel to testify unto you 16 these things ¹for the churches. I am the root and the offspring of David, the bright, the morning star.
2 Or, *Bath*	²And the Spirit and the bride say, Come. And 17 he that heareth, let him say, Come. And he that is athirst, let him come: he that will, let him take the water of life freely.
	I testify unto every man that heareth the words 18 of the prophecy of this book, If any man shall add
3 Gr. *upon*.	³unto them, God shall add ³unto him the plagues which are written in this book: and if any man 19 shall take away from the words of the book of this
4 Or, even from *the things which are written*	prophecy, God shall take away his part from the tree of life, and out of the holy city, ⁴which are written in this book.
5 Some ancient authorities add *Christ*.	He which testifieth these things saith, Yea: I 20 come quickly. Amen: come, Lord Jesus.
6 Two ancient authorities read *with all*.	The grace of the Lord Jesus⁵ be ⁶with the saints. 21 Amen.

www.ingramcontent.com/pod-product-compliance
Lightning Source LLC
Chambersburg PA
CBHW022112300426
44117CB00007B/683